Library of
Davidson College

TAXATION

in Medieval England

BY

SYDNEY KNOX MITCHELL

Edited by Sidney Painter

ARCHON BOOKS
1971

COPYRIGHT, 1951, BY YALE UNIVERSITY PRESS
REPRINTED, 1971, WITH PERMISSION
IN AN UNALTERED AND UNABRIDGED EDITION.

ISBN: 0-208-00956-6
LIBRARY OF CONGRESS CATALOG CARD NUMBER: 77-122407
PRINTED IN THE UNITED STATES OF AMERICA

PREFACE

WHEN Sydney Knox Mitchell died, he left a manuscript on which he had been working for many years. It contained an immense amount of valuable information much of which had been drawn from unpublished sources. Moreover in its pages the balanced judgment, keen historical insight, and burning enthusiasm for research that made Professor Mitchell a great scholar were applied to many subjects of interest to students of medieval England. His family, his colleagues, his former students, and the Yale University Press all felt that this manuscript should be published. A combination of deep affection for Sydney Mitchell and an interest in his subject moved me to assume the task of editing it.

The text has been edited rather less than it would have been had the author been living. When one cannot ask the author's approval of emendations, it is both presumptuous and dangerous to make them. The text is as Professor Mitchell wrote it except for such minor corrections as he would undoubtedly have made himself in a final reading.

Professor Mitchell clearly intended to go over the footnotes completely before he sent the manuscript to the press. A fair number of references were missing and no consistent form was followed. I have found most of the missing references, but in some cases I have been obliged to state that I could not do so. The form for the references is mine.

In conclusion I should like to express my gratitude to Professor Lewis P. Curtis, the editor of the Yale Historical Publications, and to the staff of the Yale University Press for their cordial cooperation and assistance.

SIDNEY PAINTER

CONTENTS

	Preface by Sidney Painter	
I.	The Central Organization	1
II.	The Local Machinery of Taxation	63
III.	The Basis of the Assessment of the Taxes	111
IV.	Consent to Taxation	156
V.	Tallage in the Reign of Henry II	236
VI.	Tallage under Richard I and John	285
VII.	Tallage in the Reign of Henry III	321
VIII.	The End of Royal Tallage	358
	Index	401

I

THE CENTRAL ORGANIZATION

THE years from the accession of Henry II to the death of Henry III, about a century and a quarter (1154–1272), are marked by definite and striking changes in the system of taxation employed by the Angevin princes in England. In part they were the logical development of the existing revenue system due to the changes in economic conditions as influenced by the administrations of Henry II and his successors; the energy of the first three rulers had important results, but no greater than the weak administration of Henry III. Certain practices continued throughout the period unaffected by the character of the monarch or of the reign. In fact, the changes arose out of the employment by the king of two new kinds of aid, the aid on revenues and movables, later on movables alone, and the carucage.

The changes in question affected the administrative organization, the character of taxation, and the structure and power of the government. None of these changes were anticipated or planned; they grew out of the necessity of adjusting the government to new conditions which it faced. Specifically, it was found necessary to create temporarily a central body, a branch of the exchequer, to administer the receipt and sometimes the audit of the new levy. The change was not permanent, but the experience acquired in the handling of unusual sums of money probably led to the expansion of the exchequer under Edward I so that it was able to take over this additional work. It was also discovered that the existing methods of assessing and collecting revenue were inadequate for the new levy, and a new organization was devised which was a modification of the conventional *missi* and a local jury or juries that gradually superseded the customary administrators like the sheriff.

The taxes themselves were incident not merely upon the king's tenants in chief but upon all property holders in the realm except certain clergy, regardless of their status. They retained this character till after the death of Henry III and were always based upon a detailed assessment of the property of every man, save the poorest, and were paid directly to royal officials. To maintain movable property as the real basis of the tax, and with an adequate valuation, was the most arduous task and was not wholly successful, but the attempt led to a great change from the conventionalization that marked all preceding levies.

The earliest authorization of such levies was by the *curia regis* and so it remained all through Henry III's reign. The occasions at first were unusual: for the relief of the Holy Land, for the crusade of 1188, and for the ransom of Richard I. In all these cases the pope and the English clergy gave hearty support. Then began a process of making the aids on property, the carucage and the aid on movables exigible on less extraordinary occasions, for war and finally for the king's debts, always by the consent of the curia regis. Thus it became the normal form of aid and all others practically disappeared. In addition it was levied more frequently. The change in occasion and frequency was coincident with a change in the character of the consent which was always asked for. The consent began to take on a corporate character, the consent of the present binding the absent and the majority binding the minority. Perhaps this developed more readily because of the nature of the tax. As it was based on the movables of everyone, from the first men paid who were not present when the tax was authorized, for they were not members of the great curia regis; practically all those who were subject to this tax were neither present nor summoned. But fear arose among the magnates lest the repeated grants were establishing the king's right to this levy, lest it were becoming a regular aid. From 1237 to 1269 no aid of this kind was granted. Nine refusals are recorded. Nevertheless at the very close of the reign in 1269 one final aid on movables was granted for an extraordinary event, a crusade, in which Edward and Edmund, the king's sons, participated for their aged father.

The reign of Edward I illustrates two features which had been developed in the preceding epoch. First that from time to time an aid was necessary, and second that it should be an aid on movables. This had become a custom. Perhaps it was carried over by the levies on movables of the church for the king from 1250 onward; anyhow, in the period from the accession of Henry III onward two significant modifications were made in the method by which these taxes were granted. As under Henry III the grant on the lands of tenants in chief was made by the great council, but in addition the consent of the shires was given through elected representatives that met with the great council. Furthermore, the king and his council preferred such a tax on the royal demesne to tallage. After considerable experimenting with commissioners who asked for it from the demesne, unit by unit, the council summoned representatives from the towns with power and obtained grants from them of a percentage of movables. Thus the tax on movables became a conventional levy from time to time on all the property of the realm even including that of the beneficed clergy. The consent of each group was corporate. Practically it was a "regular" aid despite the provision in the Confirmation of the Charters.

The changes in economic conditions that made this development possible were the growing accumulation of movable capital and the increase in money in circulation. This is evident from the published pipe rolls of the twelfth and thirteenth centuries and from the published liberate rolls of the reign of Henry III. Modern writers like Tait and Stephenson bear evidence to its truth. The variety and frequency of purchase and sales show the constant use of money. The yield of the three great taxes, the Saladin tithe, the ransom of Richard, and the thirteenth of 1207, all laid up and spent outside the realm, indicate that the supply of silver pence and halfpence was abundant. The growth of capital and the use of money were coincident with increasing expenses of the royal government and of the expenses of each landowner. The number of officials increased; war was more expensive due to the increased length of campaigns, to the more costly equipment of the knight, his armor, and horses; stone castles were replacing wooden ones; articles of utility and luxury were available for a price; a rise in prices reduced the real value of fixed incomes, and a considerable portion of the king's income was, if not immutable, at least very difficult to increase.

The revenues in the twelfth century included the farms of the shires and of the towns, feudal incidents, fines for privileges of various kinds, and amercements. All these were exigible at times and occasions determined by custom. The amounts of some were fixed and of others settled by bargain between the king and the debtor. The shire farms were fixed in amount; the town farms could be increased; the danegeld was a fixed sum, but was shrinking as men secured exemptions from it. The amount of fine for a privilege was variable. An amercement was variable, and the number was increasing. Feudal incidents tended to become fixed but might vary. Along with these revenues was the king's income as a private landholder— the services and payments in kind and in money from royal manors and manors temporarily in hand. Here a process of commutation was in progress. Services and payments in kind, however, were being stabilized and so they remained when commuted into money. Of these sources of revenue, danegeld and the shire and town farms were annual levies while the others fell upon individuals at different times and occasions. From three of these sources it was possible to derive a sudden great increase in revenue to meet a great need: danegeld could be increased; the tallage on the royal demesne levied from time to time might in case of great need be taken; or the scutage used. Scutage originated early in the twelfth century and was the basis for another general levy whereby the payment of a certain number of shillings per fee commuted military service into money.

These revenues, considerable in amount and variety, required an experienced body of administrators if they were to yield their proper amount. This had been created. Out of the curia regis had developed the chamber, the treasury, and finally the exchequer, the last in two parts: the exchequer of receipt where the money was paid in and the exchequer of account where the accounts were audited. There were two rolls: the receipt which was certainly in existence in 1185 and the pipe roll of account that was devised early in the twelfth century. In addition, the use of tallies as receipts was old and was employed in connection with both branches of the exchequer and in the local financial administration. The local financial organization comprised the sheriff and his subordinates, including clerks, the officials of towns and manors, and the king's missi or justices who were adequate to assess, collect, and account for all the varied royal revenues.

Although these sources of revenue were sufficient for the king's ordinary needs, three could be employed for a single unexpected occasion when a great sum of money was required—the feudal incident known as the feudal aid, the scutage, and the tallage. Originally the aid was a lump sum asked of tenants in chief, lay and ecclesiastical, when the king was in great need of money. It was still employed in this way and continued to be used into the thirteenth century. Very early this ancient form was regarded as unsatisfactory. When William II and Henry I wished an aid they employed the danegeld at a higher rate than was customary. Thus they expected to raise a great sum of money which would be paid by a large body of property holders who would not be consulted. But danegeld ceased after 1162. There remained two levies that might conceiv-

THE CENTRAL ORGANIZATION 5

ably be employed to obtain a general levy, the scutage and the tallage. The scutage before Henry II had never been used, so far as is known, as a general aid. It was the commutation for military service and dated from the eleventh century. It may have been originally a lump sum from the tenant who wished to be exempt, but late in Henry I's reign it came to be based upon the knight's fee. Thus it might be used, as had the danegeld, as the basis of a general tax and was so used under Henry II. Tallage was a levy in lump sums upon persons, manors, and towns of the royal demesne. It was taken from time to time, and was available as a financial resource in time of stress. Several of these sources of revenue might be taken at the same time and cover, after a fashion, most of the realm. Thus in 1168 to provide a dowry for his daughter Henry II levied a scutage, a tallage, and aids from the sheriffs and the moneyers. Such a general levy, or a series of levies, was incident upon a considerable number of property holders. The scutage was paid by more than the tenants in chief, for it was passed down from lords to vassals of various degrees, and nonmilitary tenants might be asked for an aid to meet the payment of their lord's scutage. In all these levies, the existing royal administrative system proved adequate. It could also adjust itself without any essential change to a considerable expansion of revenue and accountants.

Thus the iters of the justices were on a grander scale and brought in a host of amercements that would have clogged the pipe roll had the exchequer barons continued their original plan of enrolling them there with the other debts. Instead the sheriff accounted for them in a lump sum and received a dividend tally to be presented in the shape of his own tally to the individuals who had discharged their debts. They had already received a tally from the sheriff. A similar evolution took place in connection with the tallage in Henry II's reign.

Although the council was necessarily greatly interested in expanding the royal income in these ways, it did not envisage the possibility of a grand horizontal regular increase in revenue. Its members thought of increasing the rate of scutage and the number of fees that should pay, and they felt also that additional commutation should be paid by tenants in chief to maintain a larger force in the field for a long period. In this they were partially successful, but the rate could not be raised indefinitely, and the decline in actual service was probably the cause of the decline of the fine for service. Anyhow the dead hand of convention checked adequate development of scutage as a great financial resource, a new land tax. The same was true of tallage. Fortune led the council ultimately to the aid based on movables and revenues. As at first administered it seems not to have been particularly fruitful, but in 1188, on the occasion of the third crusade, the fraction taken—a tenth—exceeded any earlier demand, and the levy was strictly exacted by the use of an adaptation of the missi in collaboration with the local jury. The tax yielded an unusual amount as was indicated by the complaints, and a special group at the central receipt seems to have been set up.

Here was the beginning of a new and extraordinary tax which had a profound influence. It was not for ordinary use, but the impression of its extraordinary utility to the government did not vanish. It affected other taxes, like the revived danegeld, scutage, tallage, and customs, for efforts were made to increase the revenue derived from them.

The taxes on movables and revenues were paid by all property holders in the realm except the lower clergy and certain religious houses. Properly administered they yielded far more than any other levy that we have heard about before, approaching the fabulous sums raised under the Anglo-Saxons. Once this fact had been proved, the council could not fail to devise means to levy them when need should arise. The amount of money and the number of taxpayers with the innumerable rolls of assessment and collection usually made it necessary to create a supernumerary group to act as an exchequer of receipt at least and sometimes an exchequer of account to ease the burden of work thrown upon the regular exchequer. This necessity was not anticipated except perhaps in the case of Richard's ransom, for the special central group was in no other case appointed until the tax was about to be collected. It was an administrative device of the council; although used frequently for about a hundred years, it was finally abandoned when the reorganized exchequer took over. Very likely the experience of this subordinate exchequer with accounts, rolls, and the receiving and handling of big sums taught the officials something about accounting which involved large sums and large numbers of taxpayers. The special exchequer perhaps was employed in the struggle between Henry III and the barons as a device through which the latter could control the extravagant king, but to no avail. No such plan of control could be effective, then or at any other time. These taxes thus made necessary a modification of the central financial organization.

The task of assessment and collection exceeded the capacity of the sheriff's organization and the simple device of dispatching missi to the shires as was done in the cases of *dona* and tallage. Missi were appointed, but they officiated only in one shire, and they were to cooperate with juries from each vill—a new combination of central and local groups on a national scale, repeatedly employed for purposes of national taxation. Thus the property holders continually were taxed by royal officials for the king. A new bond, financial in nature, linked the king and every property holder except the smallest. Assessment and collection rolls were drawn up by the assessors and collectors of the shires. The county commissioners issued tallies to the vills; the collectors of the vills knew who the debtors were in the vills. But to the central officials the vill, not the taxpayer in the vill, became the unit. Hence it would seem that the impossibility of manipulating effectively the rolls of assessment and collection at the central office to control the assessment and collection from individual taxpayers led ultimately to the substitution of a lump sum of tax from the vill with the result that the tax on movables became a land tax. It would not be county commissioners or the village assessors or collectors that would insist on accurate valuation of the movables of individual property holders. Before the death of Henry III the county assessors were mostly local landholders who were appointed by the central government to administer many public functions, taxation being only one of their duties. They were paid by the king and served him, but they also could not be unmindful of local interests. The difficulty of controlling them is evident through the whole period of this study. It is only thinly disguised when we find the prelates allowed to assess and collect the tax on their own lands and those of their tenants by their own men, with a king's clerk as a member of the local shire board, who theoretically would be able to counterbalance the influence of these clergy in the assessment.

In this struggle between the central government and the local taxpayer the king seems to have come off victorious; at the beginning the local baron or his steward was present when the assessment was made and was also allowed to collect the tax, but ultimately the council put the whole work of assessment and collection in the hands of the county commissioners, the village jurors, and the knights of the hundred. Even the sheriff, who had for a generation been the chief collector, was demoted and placed under their orders, to employ distraint in the collection, to summon the men for the assessment, and to supply transportation for the cash and rolls from the shire to the central receivers. Even so it proved impossible to insure a fair valuation; the local property interests were too strong.

In this conflict the government won another temporary victory, for in form a new assessment was made for each tax. The basis of each levy remained the property held by each individual taxpayer in the vill. Moreover the property was not valued as a whole, but each kind of grain was assessed in amount and valued by quarters, hopas, bushels, or a similar unit. Livestock was valued according to the kind of animals—oxen, pigs, and the like. The assessment too was based on the goods and stock held at Michaelmas, at harvest time, for the council was aware of the advantage of an assessment at such a time. That it was difficult is clear when months after Michaelmas they still were assessing property that had been consumed or sold. When the council found themselves forced to send out new missi to correct mistakes of the original assessment, one may doubt their success. When they say the assessors did not spare the poor and let the rich off easily, one may ask who were these poor, for the poor were property holders that were tenants of richer men who would be deprived of revenue by heavy taxation of their tenants. Would this complaint of the unfairness of assessment then mean anything but a failure to assess all goods fairly? Such a situation reflects the influence on the valuations by the local men of importance.

The authorization of the taxes underwent great changes. We have said that all property holders except the lower clergy and certain houses of religious were subject to the taxes on movables. It is true, but how could such a widespread tax be authorized? We must distinguish. The curia regis authorized a tax on the lands of the members of that body, that is, on all the lands held of all tenants of every kind who dwelt on those lands. The king's demesne also usually paid the aid on movables. Shall we therefore conclude that the consent of the great curia regis bound the demesne also? Or that when the tenants in chief had led the way by granting such a tax that the demesne fell in line and agreed to it? The little information as to the method of grant indicates that the demesne was not bound by the decision of the curia regis; that by command or request of the king they themselves granted the aid on movables; perhaps they usually compounded for it.

Thus the authority of the curia regis was not coextensive with the kingdom. In the opinion of its members the consent to taxation

THE CENTRAL ORGANIZATION 9

was individual. So Richard I wrote to the members of his council urging them to make him a generous grant that others might be led to follow their example. Thus in 1225 the bishop of Durham was granted letters patent saying that he had granted the fifteenth "of pure liberality," and in 1235 the king wrote that Richard de Percy had now granted that the fortieth should be collected on his lands. Yet it was difficult to refuse after the great council had given its assent, although the aid was theoretically voluntary. In 1207 the archbishop of York was forced into exile for opposing the thirteenth, and his lands were seized by John. By pressure or persuasion the king usually secured a grant from those opposed.

The character of the aid on movables also affected the concept of consent. Since every property holder on the lands of tenants in chief paid the tax, men were taxed who did not attend the great curia regis and were not even summoned. The tenant in chief could not himself tax these men, yet when the curia regis had assented to the grant, the assessors valued the property and collected a tax for the king directly. Thus in fact if not in theory the curia regis made a corporate grant repeatedly on all the property on their lands regardless of the ownership.

The repetitions of the requests of Henry III for an aid led in 1242 to such unity among the barons that they refused it. This action was followed in the succeeding years by eight refusals. In the face of this attitude the king was unable to secure any aid from the tenants in chief. By union the barons were successful, so finally there developed out of the feudal right of consent the right of united or corporate refusal.

On one occasion, 1254, we seem to presage a change in the situation of the curia regis when diocesan assemblies sent two representatives to report to the council the grant of aid which the local assemblies were prepared to make; also the shire courts were to report similarly through two deputies to the council the aid which the shires were prepared to make. Both of these were in connection with an aid to the king in Gascony. But the arrangement was made under unusual circumstances. The lay and clerical magnates had promised to aid the king either in person with horses and arms or by lump sums of money and refused to grant a general aid. Hence the appeal to the lower clergy and the lesser laity.

But under Edward I, when an aid on movables was asked for, representatives of the shires were also summoned to meet with the great council to give their assent to the aid granted by that body.

The small council also asked an aid on movables from the royal demesne either by commissioners to the towns or by summoning representatives from the towns who granted it on behalf of the towns. Thus the corporate consent to an aid by the great council was supplemented by a corporate grant by representatives of the shires on the same property as the great council, and the demesne, at least the towns, sent representatives who granted an aid on the property of the townsmen.

The consent to the taxes on movables was at first individual and almost purely formal; the repetition of the grants made it practically corporate but still formal; in the last half of the reign of Henry III it became really corporate, from the necessity of unified action, to be strong enough to refuse the aids. Under Edward I the grant of the great council of aids on the movables on the lands held by tenants of all kinds on the lands of tenants in chief was supplemented under the initiative of the king and the small council by the consent of shire deputies. The advantage of aid on movables also led the council to secure it from the royal demesne by an appeal through commissioners sent out as had been customary in the levy of tallages and finally by following the precedent used with the shires of summoning representatives of the towns who were asked and granted an aid on movables on the property of the towns.

The early taxes on movables (1166, 1184) have left no record that the men of the time saw in them anything unusual beyond the scale of other levies with which they were familiar. Only in 1188 did the chroniclers reveal a strong feeling that the Saladin tithe was remarkable for its severity. Thenceforth, the council seems gradually to have realized that several problems of administration were involved. How was an assessment of such magnitude, involving so much detail, to be made—one which concerned the personal property of tens of thousands of property holders? How could the money be speedily and completely collected from such a multitude of taxpayers? On what kinds of movables would it be feasible to assess these taxes? What property and what persons, if any, should be exempt? At what time of year would it be most advantageous to assess the levy? Provision must be made for transporting, counting, weighing, and storing the cash. Would it be possible to devise a method by which the receipts from the realm could actually be brought into the physical possession of the central government and not be dispersed by local officials, especially the sheriff? The

THE CENTRAL ORGANIZATION 11

existing system of audit might need modification in view of the great number of debtors to the crown. The revenue of danegeld in the modified form of the carucage seems to have evoked a sentiment that it was a tax of similar severity to the taxes on movables, perhaps due to a recollection of the crushing burden of danegeld in the past.

The new taxes on personal property were relatively enormous both in total yield and in the number of taxpayers, many of whom had only 2s. or 3s. worth of property.[1] Consequently, because of the number of taxpayers and rolls of assessment and collection, the problem of collection and accounting became extremely complicated.[2] Furthermore, the returns came in when the exchequer was engaged in the ordinary financial business of the kingdom.

We know that in 1200 the exchequer was sitting continually throughout the year. It will be recalled that there were two annual terms of audit: a preliminary one at Easter and the final one for the year at Michaelmas. Two fragmentary memoranda rolls have survived from John's reign.[3] They show that the exchequer was in session from October till nearly the end of March to audit the accounts of sheriffs and other debtors of the crown. Thus in connection with the audit of Michaelmas, 1199, there are continual references to dates for payment and audit from October till March 20 of the following year. The regular sequence of these dates is explicable only on the theory that the exchequer was in constant or almost constant session.[4] There is also a memoranda roll of 10 John, Easter, 1208, to Michaelmas, 1208, and in this the exchequer is seen in session as late as August 2.[5]

Though the council could not have understood at once the difficulties that lay ahead, it seems to have felt that the existing organization was inadequate to perform this additional work. Therefore a branch of the central exchequer at Westminster was formed to administer the receipt of most of the taxes on movables and the

---

1. See for example Subsidies, 242/47, Public Record Office, *passim*.
2. Thus on the manor of Wosresunt 49 tenants were assessed 71s. 2d. of the fifteenth; on the manor of Tilmerch, 55 tenants were assessed 79s. 1d. Subsidies, 242/47, see the returns of a hundred in Suffolk for the thirtieth of 1283 in Dowell, *A Suffolk hundred in 1283;* imagine the difficulty of auditing such returns in the rolls of the thirteenth century.
3. Exchequer L. T. R., 1/4, Public Record Office. *Memoranda roll 1 John*, ed. H. G. Richardson (Pipe Roll Society), LIX.
4. *Ibid.*, pp. 6, 10, 13–16.
5. Exchequer L. T. R., 1/4, m. 12a dorso; see also m. 1, m. 1d, m. 4a, m. 10a dorso, m. 11a, m. 11a dorso.

carucages from 1188 till the death of Henry III. It was abandoned under Edward I when this work was taken over by the reorganized exchequer.

In discussing the evolution of this new central body let us recall the steps in the development of other institutions out of the curia regis. The increasing pressure of business led first to distinct groups, but they were still manned by the whole curia. In time, however, there followed a differentiation of personnel. In the case of taxation we find that a committee of the exchequer was appointed to handle the receipts and accounts of the early levies; this body was sometimes composed of persons who were not members of the exchequer. Very likely this was the method employed from the first, but there always remains the possibility that at the outset the whole exchequer for the time being gave up other business and devoted itself to the receipt of the special levy. The sources are so fragmentary that one cannot decide this question.

There are thus four phases of our subject: the organization of the central office of receipt and account; the local machinery of assessment and collection; the actual property assessed from which the taxes were collected; the method of authorization. For it must be recalled that the idea of carefully evaluating property and basing a contribution to the government upon that valuation was undeveloped. When once someone had seized upon that fruitful conception, a new source of revenue of incalculable richness had been discovered, but it was yet necessary to determine its extent.

The men of the twelfth century had no definite notion regarding the sources of taxation which could be profitably exploited and there was initiated a struggle between the taxpayer and the state over this question. By the close of the reign of Henry III, a solution had been found upon which all the later development was to be based.

A mere suggestion of a new central organization comes from the Saladin tithe of 1188. That tax was levied for a specific religious purpose, and the whole ecclesiastical organization was deeply interested in its success. The local boards of assessment and collection were different in personnel from those hitherto employed in such work. They included the priest, and the dean, a Templar, and a Hospitaler, while the sheriff, the chief local administrative official, was omitted. The assessment was made by ecclesiastical rather than feudal or national areas; for it was by bishoprics and not shires or fiefs. The ecclesiastical purpose of the tax and the exceptional

THE CENTRAL ORGANIZATION 13

local arrangements suggest the conclusion that the receipts would not be paid into the royal exchequer in the usual way, but that special arrangements would be made. A single item on the pipe roll seems to be in harmony with the conclusion that a special central office of receipt for the Saladin tithe was employed. The pipe roll of 1 Richard I (1189) records a payment of 100s. to clerks of the treasurer and chamberlains and to ten tellers who received the money of the tenth at Salisbury.[6] How is this item to be interpreted? The number of tellers was large, four being the ordinary staff.[7] The increase in personnel may be accounted for by the fact that as an unusually large amount of money was being collected, more tellers were deemed necessary. Experience taught that this additional clerical force was unnecessary, for in 1225 only six tellers were needed at the office of receipt of the fifteenth.[8]

The officials in charge of this work were the ordinary clerks at the exchequer of receipt, that is, the clerks of the treasurer and the chamberlains. Strictly speaking, the author of the *Dialogus* refers to these officials at the exchequer of receipt as the clerk of the treasurer and the two knights of the chamberlains,[9] but a little further on he speaks of them in exactly the terms employed here, cited from the pipe roll of 1 Richard I, as the clerks of the treasurer and the chamberlains, those who were in charge of the receipt on behalf of their lords.[10] This little group of experts was not here assembled merely to count the money, for the text, an official document drawn up by men accustomed to exactness in statement, declares precisely that they *received* the money of the tenth at Salisbury.[11] A different expression would probably have been employed had they been merely counting the money, as we may see in the item entered in 1208 when the treasurer, the chamberlains, and their sergeants were at Winchester to count and store 40,000m.[12]

This group was not simply to receive the tenth from Wiltshire; it was either to receive it from a great section of southern England, or perhaps, judging from the number of tellers, from the whole kingdom. What was this office then that was established at Salis-

---

6. *Pipe roll 1 Richard I* (Record Commission), p. 178.
7. R. L. Poole, *The exchequer in the twelfth century* (London, 1912), pp. 73, 82. *Dialogus de scaccario*, ed. Hughes, Crump, and Johnson (Oxford, 1902), p. 22.
8. *Patent rolls, 1225–1232* (Rolls series), p. 93.
9. *Dialogus de scaccario*, p. 62.
10. *Ibid.*, p. 64.
11. *Pipe roll 1 Richard I*, p. 178.
12. *Pipe roll 10 John* (Pipe Roll Society), p. 127.

bury? Either the whole exchequer was moved there, for it was as central a location as Winchester, or a commission was dispatched to Salisbury for this work. In either case, however, the group devoted itself for the time being to the receipt of the Saladin tithe. One may inquire whether these clerks and tellers were the only officials present for this work. No doubt some more important officials were on hand, just as in 1208, when the count of the money at Winchester was attended by the treasurer and chamberlains with minor officials.[13] That some special office of receipt was established at Salisbury is further suggested by payments for carrying considerable sums thence to three different places as if it were a center of deposit: 200m. from Salisbury to Bristol; 2,000m. from Salisbury to Gloucester; and 5,000m. from Salisbury to Southampton.[14] The construction of a great chest for treasure in the castle of Salisbury may point to the same conclusion.[15] Again, the sheriff of Oxford transported treasure to London and also to Salisbury.[16] There is the strong probability therefore that special arrangements were made for the receipt of part or all of the Saladin tithe at Salisbury. No account of the levy appears in the pipe roll, a further indication that the exchequer did not administer the tax as it did the regular revenue.

Part at least of the taxes levied for the ransom of Richard I was paid to a special body of officials. When the exchequer later was summoning men to pay debts on the ransom, the alleged debtors replied that they owed nothing because they had paid it into the "exchequer of the ransom," *scaccarium redemptionis*.[17] This scaccarium was, as Mrs. Stenton has pointed out, not to supersede or supplant the regular exchequer but to help carry on the financial business of the kingdom at a busy time of year.[18]

In 1198 was levied the so-called "great carucage" based upon a new assessment of land: each ploughland of one hundred acres was to pay at first 2s. and later 3s. more. Roger of Howden gives the only detailed account of the levy. He described the method of assessment and collection in great detail, either as a person who took part

13. *Ibid.*
14. *Pipe roll 1 Richard I*, p. 178.
15. *Pipe roll 34 Henry II*, p. 14.
16. *Pipe roll 1 Richard I*, p. 105.
17. *Pipe roll 9 Richard I*, p. 142. *Pipe roll 1 John*, pp. 45, 74, 81, 164, 202, 216, 247–248. *Pipe roll 3 John*, pp. 50, 147, 252.
18. *Pipe roll 7 Richard I*, pp. XV, XVI. Professor Mitchell and Mrs. Stenton arrived at the same conclusion independently (editor).

THE CENTRAL ORGANIZATION

in, or at any rate as one who was deeply interested in and familiar with, the whole procedure. In his description of the collection, he states that the "money was received by the hands of two legal knights in every hundred and by the hand of the bailiff of the hundred, and these men responded for it to the sheriff, and the sheriff by the aforesaid rolls responded for it at the exchequer in the presence of the bishops, abbots, and barons assigned to this work."[19] The designation of certain officials to receive the proceeds of the carucage and the rolls from the sheriffs of all the counties suggests in this case again a committee of the exchequer for this purpose. Another fact which suggests the same conclusion is that no account of the carucage appears in the pipe roll, as we should naturally expect if the sheriff had accounted for it at the regular session of the exchequer.

It is possible that the carucage of 1200 was paid to a special board of receipt. No general account of it appears in the pipe roll, only a few notices find entry there—a circumstance that suggests a special arrangement. Moreover William de Wrotham and his associates were described as *receptores carucagii*—a designation that would fit a central board of receipt. The pipe roll records that the bishop of Exeter had fined in 300*m.* for the confirmation of his charters, to be quit of assessment for the carucage on his demesne, and for confirmation of the chapel of Bosham, and had paid half of it at the exchequer; he should not be summoned by the exchequer for the balance due because William de Wrotham and his companions, receivers of the carucage, testified before the exchequer that they had received that money in their receipt of the carucage.[20] William de Wrotham and J. de Waltham, at the command of Geoffrey Fitz Peter, made a loan to the bishop of Norwich of £60 of the carucage.[21] William de Wrotham was also paid £140 by the abbot of St. Albans of a fine which covered his carucage of 1200.[22] William's connection with this carucage in various ways and in different areas is most easily explained by suggesting that he and his companions formed a central board of receipt. Now it is true that the term receptores carucagii may perhaps mean county or district collectors, but even so they were a local body of assessors and collectors separate from the sheriff, and to whom did they pay

19. Roger of Howden, *Chronica*, ed. William Stubbs (Rolls series), IV, 46.
20. *Pipe roll 2 John*, p. 234. *Rotuli de oblatis et finibus*, ed. T. D. Hardy (Record Commission), p. 53. *Pipe roll 3 John*, p. 222.
21. *Pipe roll 9 John*, p. 165.
22. *Pipe roll 2 John*, p. 47. *Pipe roll 4 John*, p. 265.

the money? Certainly not to the exchequer at its regular session, for that body would certainly have kept an account of it. We are thus forced back upon the inference that there was some special board of receipt, even if we allow William de Wrotham and J. de Waltham to play the parts of county collectors. It may be suggested that William was already an important administrative official, for he was in charge of the stannaries.

A similar case appears in connection with the aid of 1201 for the Holy Land. The local collectors and the sheriff were instructed to appear with the cash and the rolls at the New Temple, London, on January 27, 1202, instead of at Westminster.[23] Probably the money remained in the care of the Templars till the king, by the advice of the bishops and other magnates, had decided how it was to be spent for the Holy Land.[24] In 1203 there is a tantalizing reference to the seventh of movables of that year, levied on the earls and barons for their alleged desertion of the king in Normandy. According to Roger of Wendover, Geoffrey Fitz Peter and Hubert Walter were in charge of its assessment and collection, the one from laymen and the other from the clergy and in the administration they spared no one.[25] Evidence which seems to corroborate the truth of the chronicler's statement comes from the liberate roll which contains two writs, both addressed to Geoffrey Fitz Peter; one orders him to cause the count of Aumale to levy the seventh on his land; the other advises the justice that the king has acquitted Earl William Marshal of the seventh due from his demesne.[26] Both these writs show that Geoffrey was in charge of the levy of the seventh on laymen. He and Hubert therefore may represent a special central organization. The pipe roll of 6 John seems to corroborate the inference. Walter de Pincebec was accounting at the exchequer for the issues of the land of William de Longchamp, which was in hand. He paid nothing *in thesauro*, but among the items of outlay which he balanced off against his debt to the exchequer was a payment of 77s. 2d. from the demesne of William de Longchamp of the seventh given to the king by assize.[27] If this sum had been paid to the exchequer, it would have been entered as in thesauro. It must therefore

23. Roger of Howden, IV, 189.
24. *Rotuli litterarum patentium*, ed. T. D. Hardy (Record Commission), p. 5.
25. Roger of Wendover, *Flores historiarum*, ed. H. G. Hewlett (Rolls series), I, 318–319.
26. *Rotuli de liberate ac de misis et praestitis*, ed. T. D. Hardy (Record Commission), pp. 43, 47.
27. *Pipe roll 6 John*, p. 256.

THE CENTRAL ORGANIZATION 17

have been paid elsewhere, perhaps to the official group in charge of the seventh. Another case is that of William de Berton who was amerced £100 for evading the levy.[28] Thus four cases in four different counties and four rolls, involving great men as well as small, indicate the widespread character of this levy and the likelihood that Roger of Wendover gave a correct report. In 1203 another commission was created to supervise the assessment and collection of a new tax, a fifteenth of certain goods exported and imported by merchants. It was like the tax on movables because it took an aliquot part of their valuation, but fundamentally different because the latter was based upon a single valuation at one specified date. This fifteenth was a continuing valuation over a limited period as merchants exported and imported goods.[29] It was deemed necessary to create special machinery of assessment and collection, and the king appointed a committee to direct the work throughout the kingdom. This was composed of three well-known administrators: Reginald de Cornhill, William de Fornell, and William de Wrotham.[30] In 1204 these officials rendered account of the receipts at the exchequer. None of the members of this body was a baron of the exchequer.[31] The tax had been in effect nearly a year before this committee was appointed.[32]

In 1207 came the great tax of the thirteenth of revenues and movables. It was paid to a special body that is even dignified in the king's writs by the name of exchequer, the exchequer of the thirteenth.[33]

During the remainder of John's reign, no tax on the assessed valuation of property was levied. New financial problems were however created by the interdict and the attendant seizure and retention by the government of great quantities of ecclesiastical property. There were therefore many cases in which a single official or a group, a committee, directed the receipt or expenditure of considerable sums over quite a long period of time, finally rendering an account at the exchequer.

It is clear that the directors of administration favored this method. Out of many the most striking example was that of the

28. *Pipe roll 12 John*, m. 17d, Public Record Office.
29. *Rot. pat.*, p. 42b.
30. *Ibid.*, p. 42.
31. *Pipe roll 6 John*, p. 218.
32. *Ibid.*, p. xliii.
33. *Rotuli litterarum clausarum*, ed. T. D. Hardy (Record Commission), I, 89, 91b. *Pipe roll 9 John*, pp. 63, 71.

bishopric of Durham. In 1211 Aymer, archdeacon of Durham, and Philip de Ulecot rendered their account of receipts and expenditures of the vacant bishopric for the three preceding years. The sum total amounted to over £16,000. About £14,000 had been paid in cash at the exchequer, the chamber, and to local treasuries; the balance had been expended by the custodians.[34] Individual trusted officials had charge not merely of the possessions of a single layman or ecclesiastic or ecclesiastical body but of several. Thus Robert de Braibroc accounted for the abbeys of Peterborough and of Ramsey, a total of £2,241 5s. 7d.[35] John Fitz Hugh accounted for numerous fines, tallages of Jews, contributions from churches, the exchange of London, and the accounts of sundry abbeys, with a grand total of £7,626 2s. 10d.[36] Similarly, Brian de L'Isle accounted for £6,527 and 1m.[37] Another body that had, it would seem, a greater activity than before, as evidenced by the pipe rolls, was the chamber. Never before has the exchequer recorded as large sums paid into the chamber as in the later years of John.[38] Accounts that had ordinarily been rendered at the exchequer were ordered to be made at the chamber, like that of the bishopric of Exeter for two years.[39] We can only infer the reasons for this marked development of financial importance of certain administrative officials alongside the regular local official—the sheriff. Very likely it would have overburdened the sheriff had he been assigned this additional labor. We may note however that the new system seems to have been efficient. The custodians of the bishopric of Durham accounted for all the revenues amounting to £16,787 14s. 10d. ob. in cash or in orders for payments out and were entirely quit by the exchequer.[40] Of the charge of £7,626 2s. 10d. against John Fitz Hugh, £826 7s. 11d. remained as a debt against him after he had rendered his account.[41] Brian de L'Isle had a surplus of 10m. in an account of £6,572 and 50m.[42] Robert de Braibroc paid or accounted for the whole revenue of Ramsey abbey of £1,240 10s. 5d. and had a debt of only £9 3s. 3d.

34. Pipe roll 13 John, m. 4d, Public Record Office.
35. Pipe roll 12 John, m. 19, Public Record Office.
36. Pipe roll 13 John, m. 22, Public Record Office.
37. *Ibid.*, m. 14d.
38. Pipe roll 11 John, m. 3d, Public Record Office. Pipe roll 13 John, m. 14d, m. 22, Public Record Office.
39. Pipe roll 11 John, m. 1, m. 7d, m. 8d, Public Record Office.
40. Pipe roll 13 John, m. 4d, Public Record Office.
41. *Ibid.*, m. 22.
42. *Ibid.*, m. 14d.

out of an account of £1,000 15s. 2d. of the abbey of Peterborough.[43] No wonder the government trusted these administrators. In some way they had solved the problem that confronted every minister of the Angevin monarchy—how to compel debtors to the king to meet their financial obligations. Not theories of political science, but administrative capacity of certain royal officials brought about the change. Bishop Stubbs suggested the reason for the change but accompanied it by an innuendo when he stated that John trusted more and more of his business to his mercenary and foreign captains who heartily backed him in all that he did.

No special central machinery was created for the scutage or aid on knights' fees of 1217. The account of the carucage of that year is not entered in the great roll, a fact that indicates some special arrangements, inasmuch as the sheriffs took part in collecting it. The only notices relative to its payment are to local authorities, to a great baron, to a depository in an abbey, and once when it was ordered to be paid to the king at Winchester, perhaps into the chamber.[44] Reports on the number of hides and carucates in a shire were to be made to the Earl Marshal.[45]

In 1220, when a carucage was levied for the second time under Henry III, a special committee was appointed to receive the tax at the New Temple at London. It was composed of three men: William de Halliwell, a friar, William Fitz Benedict, a citizen of London, and Alexander de Sawbridgeworth, an experienced clerk of the exchequer.[46]

In the summer of 1222 John de Brienne, titular king of Jerusalem, came to England seeking aid for the Holy Land. A great council was called and granted him money assistance. On June 25 writs were issued for its assessment and collection. Each earl was to pay 3m., each baron 1m., each knight 1s., each freeholder 1d., and anyone not possessing land but owning chattels to the value of half a mark was also to pay a penny; "any one of the aforesaid wishing to give more, might give it in the name of the Lord." [47] The receipts were to be brought to London and deposited at the

---

43. Pipe roll 12 John, m. 19, Public Record Office.
44. *Rot. claus.*, I, 306, 318b. *Patent rolls, 1216–1225*, p. 56.
45. *Rot. claus.*, I, 335b.
46. Fine roll 5 Henry III, Part 1, m. 6, Public Record Office. Exchequer L. T. R., Foreign accounts roll, No. 1, m. 1d, Public Record Office. *Patent rolls, 1216–1225*, p. 272. *Book of fees* (Rolls series), I, 292.
47. *Rot. claus.*, I, 516b.

New Temple by November 1 by the view of certain men to be appointed by the magnates.[48]

In 1224 the bishops and the abbots granted a carucage from all their lands but they seem to have retained in their own hands the assessment and collection. No account of this levy appears in the pipe roll, but there are many references to it in the patent and close rolls. In general the ecclesiastics seem to have paid the tax into the wardrobe, most of it at Bedford (where the siege was taking place), the rest at various places, some at the New Temple at London.[49]

In February, 1225, after a long discussion, the great council granted a fifteenth of movables on the laity and clergy. An elaborate plan of assessment and collection was drawn up, probably by the small council after the decision to grant the fifteenth had been made, to insure a comprehensive assessment and a quick and complete collection. For the time being they omitted one part of the organization, apparently after discussion being unable to reach a decision, an indication that some change of the central control was under consideration. Thus after describing in minute detail the method of assessment and collection in the local areas, the writs provided that the receipts were to be deposited under seal in a local cathedral church or religious house "until it shall be provided where they ought to be sent." [50] By May the decision had been made to establish a central board composed of the bishops of Bath and Salisbury to have charge of the receipt and custody of the proceeds of this tax.[51]

Probably no special central organization was created to receive the fortieth of 1232. The county collectors were to store their receipts temporarily in sealed containers in a local castle, church, or house of religious designated in the writ of assessment.[52] Once the record states that the fortieth was to be delivered to the treasurer and chamberlains; [53] perhaps they received it at the exchequer and kept it as a special fund. Certainly they drew up a special roll, for it did not appear on the pipe roll. Later, probably for the most part in 1233 and 1234, the cash was transferred from the local repositories to the wardrobe and the exchequer at Westminster.

48. *Ibid.*, pp. 516b, 567b.
49. *Patent rolls, 1216–1225*, pp. 473, 475, 478, 505–506. *Ibid., 1225–1232*, p. 95.
50. *Ibid., 1216–1225*, pp. 560–561.
51. *Rot. claus.*, II, 73b.
52. *Close rolls, 1231–1234* (Rolls series), pp. 156–160. *Book of fees*, I, 406. *Calendar of patent rolls, 1232–1247* (Rolls series), pp. 15–51, *passim*.
53. This note was left blank by Professor Mitchell and the editor has no idea where to find the reference.

An account drawn up at the exchequer gives the total as £12,924 of which £5,855 were paid in thesauro, and £6,486 into the wardrobe.[54] Thus the plan employed in 1225 was discarded, probably because it hampered the council in its free disposal of the cash. The aid to marry Henry III's beautiful sister to the brilliant Frederick II was at the rate of 2m. per fee on all fees whenever or by whom enfeoffed.[55] Thus it involved an inquest into the feudal holdings of the kingdom as well as the assessment and collection of a tax. The writ of assessment and collection also provided that the county commissioners should store the cash in a secure building, a castle, a church, or an abbey carefully designated. Each of the collectors had a lock and a key to the strong box.[56] At a suitable date these officials were summoned to bring their cash and rolls to Westminster to deliver to the treasurer and chamberlains.[57] The rolls that exist in abundance speak of their paying it in thesauro,[58] the conventional expression for any payment at the exchequer. The enrolled accounts show the most important tenants in each shire rendering their accounts at the exchequer. At the end of the account of each shire it is stated that the collectors have paid a certain sum into the exchequer and owe so much.[59] What happened was that the collectors paid the cash at the exchequer of receipt and received tallies certifying this. The money was set aside in a special deposit under the care of the treasurer and chamberlains. It could now be disbursed if necessary. Later the collectors would appear before the exchequer of account and the audit would be held. Considerable sums were by authorization of the council delivered to the wardrobe even before the money was paid to the exchequer. When the collectors appeared to have their accounts audited, they presented with the tallies from the exchequer of receipt the writs that authorized them to pay sums into the wardrobe.[60]

In 1237 when the thirtieth was levied the kingdom was divided into three parts and a central board was created for each division, one sitting at the Tower of London and the others at the castles of Nottingham and Bristol.[61] The scutage of 1242 presents a little problem. For while the fines levied in connection with the summons

54. Exchequer, L. T. R., Foreign roll, No. 1, m. 6, Public Record Office.
55. *Close rolls, 1234–1237*, p. 189. *Book of fees*, I, 406, 419 and *passim*.
56. *Close rolls, 1234–1237*, pp. 188–191.
57. *Ibid.*, p. 189.
58. *Ibid. Book of fees*, I, 406, 419 and *passim*.
59. *Ibid.*, p. 427.
60. *Ibid.*, pp. 407, 421, 422, 450, 454, 460, 551; II, 1470–1471.
61. *Close rolls, 1237–1242*, p. 116. *Calendar of liberate rolls, 1226–1240*, p. 302.

22 TAXATION IN MEDIEVAL ENGLAND

to the host were entered in the pipe roll, the scutage itself and the aid given by ecclesiastics were not so recorded.[62] The aid of the prelates was entered in a special roll and the scutage probably was entered in the same way, for we have many allusions to its levy and payment though the pipe roll does not contain the account which certainly was rendered on a special roll.[63]

The aids on knights' fees of 1245 and 1253 were paid into the exchequer or the wardrobe like any ordinary scutage. No change took place in this respect with reference to any other normal scutage or tallage. The council however made several experiments with reference to the central receiving body in connection with nearly all of the new and some of the old levies.

In 1269 the twentieth was received by a committee of three, the treasurers of the Templars and the Hospitalers and Giles de Audenarde, long a clerk of the wardrobe.[64]

Committees were by no means always appointed. The aids of 1168, 1193, 1217, 1245, and 1253, that were levied on knights' fees, were assessed and collected by sheriffs and in general paid in at the exchequer, though parts might be ordered to be paid at the wardrobe. The account of the aids on knights' fees were usually entered on the pipe roll like an ordinary scutage.[65]

We need not doubt therefore that special organization at the central government was frequently created in connection with the administration of these special levies. Is it at all possible to go further and discern more of the membership of these bodies and their functions? The problem is not easy because the evidence of their existence is often concealed in orders dealing with their duties or their pay. It was in general a matter of administrative detail. This is especially true of the earlier levies. From 1225 however, perhaps because of the growing frequency of taxation, more notices have survived that enable us to fill in the imperfect outline of the

---

62. *The great roll of the pipe for the twenty-sixth year of the reign of King Henry the third*, ed. H. L. Cannon (New Haven, 1918), *passim*.

63. Pipe roll 29 Henry III, m. 9, Public Record Office. *Book of fees*, II, 1130–1138. Fine roll 26 Henry III, Part II, m. 2, m. 5, Public Record Office.

64. *Calendar of patent rolls, 1266–1272*, p. 439. Thomas Madox, *History and antiquities of the exchequer of the kings of England* (London, 1769), I, 610. Mr. Mitchell used also the edition of 1711. When no volume number appears the reference is to the edition of 1711.

65. 1168, *Pipe roll 14 Henry II, passim*. 1193, *Pipe roll 6 Richard I, passim*. 1217, Pipe roll 2 Henry III, Public Record Office, *passim*. 1245, Pipe roll 29 Henry III, Public Record Office, *passim*. 1253, Pipe roll 37 Henry III, Public Record Office, *passim*.

earlier levies. We must guard against the tempting assumption that all the practices which appeared in 1225 and later were employed in the earliest aids. For it is likely that the council was feeling its way in the administration of these new and abundant sources of revenue.

A customary method of receipt and audit was employed at the exchequer for the ordinary revenue. At conventional dates the debtor (the sheriff or other debtor) delivered the cash at the lower exchequer and received a tally in receipt. He might however pay sums at the chamber or the wardrobe, or to some person by special command of the king; from each he would receive a tally of receipt. At the audit at the upper exchequer the debtor appeared armed with the evidence of his payments. The amount owed from each source of revenue in each county was written in the great roll, then the accounts paid into the exchequer of receipt, into the chamber, or the wardrobe, and the amount paid out to persons, as certified by tallies and writs. If the total of the payments equaled the amount owed, the accountant was declared quit; if the amount was less than the total debt, the accountant was charged in the roll with the balance and it would be demanded of him the following year. Occasionally the accountant paid more than he owed, and the surplus he could deduct from the account next year.[66] This method was adapted to the receipt and account of the new taxes, the carucage, and the levy on movables.

The plan of the council was to have all the revenue from each new tax brought to a common center before it was disbursed since these taxes were always levied for a specific object. But the king's varied needs and desires interfered sometimes with the fulfillment of the plan. Devised by the council as a means of lessening the work of the officials of the exchequer, the work of the central boards varied from one levy to another. They might serve as merely an exchequer of receipt and almost immediately turn over the cash and documents to the exchequer at Westminster. They might retain the cash in their possession and pay it out gradually on the receipt of orders from the council. They might audit the accounts of the shire collectors. In any case the board would finally present a statement of receipts, expenditures, if any, and amounts still due, the rolls and tallies and the cash to the exchequer of account at Westminster and receive writs of quittance. Afterward the direction of the arrears of the special tax and accounts went to the regular exchequer.

66. Poole, *Exchequer in the twelfth century*, chaps. vi, vii.

24 TAXATION IN MEDIEVAL ENGLAND

We now turn to the early levies to discover the members of these special central administrative groups and their activities. In 1166 Gervase of Canterbury reports that the king declared the money "should be collected throughout my lands in the place where I shall decide by [the advice of] the archbishop and bishops who are present with me to determine it." [67] This statement was made in connection with the levy in the French possessions of Henry II; but it may have included England as well, or he may have made similar arrangements in England. We have no specific statement as to England on this point.

The writ for the levy of 1184 says nothing about a central organization. In 1188 the special group that received the tenth at Salisbury issued tallies of receipt to the sheriffs or custodians of honors who brought to them the cash from the bishoprics. Thus Ralph of Worcester accounted to the upper exchequer for the revenues of the honor of Tickhill and presented a tally showing that he had paid £35 13s. 4d. into the treasury; and probably another tally (at least evidence of some kind) showing that he had paid to the receivers of the tenth £4 "of the tenth in aid of the land of Jerusalem." [68]

Some central group audited the accounts of the sheriff who brought the tithe to a central location, perhaps a special body or the regular exchequer of account. Thus the sheriff of Oxfordshire paid out £15 5s. to Robert de Broc and Ralph Frazier [69] from the farm of Great Tew for which he was accounting in obedience to a king's writ to pay out £82. This was the total sum which he was to pay and the balance came from the tenth of Oxfordshire and was in the account of the Saladin tithe for that shire.[70]

We have seen that a special central body was appointed to hold the money of the ransom of Richard I till it was dispatched to Germany. This body was created in accordance with the king's desire. In a letter to his mother and the justices, he ordered that the cash should be delivered to his mother and those whom she desired as colleagues.[71] Roger of Wendover relates that on his arrival in

---

67. Gervase of Canterbury, *Gesta regum*, ed. William Stubbs (Rolls series), I, 199.
68. *Pipe roll 34 Henry II*, pp. 11, 216.
69. Robert del Broc was a royal justice. *Ibid.*, p. 49 and *passim*. *Pipe rolls 1 and 2 Richard I*, *passim*. He and Ralph Frazier were commissioners in 1189-90 to supply the castle of Carmarthen. *Pipe roll 1 Richard I*, p. 163.
70. *Ibid.*, pp. 105-106.
71. Roger of Howden, III, 209.

THE CENTRAL ORGANIZATION 25

England from Germany where he had conferred with the king, the chancellor, William de Longchamp, bishop of Ely, met at St. Albans with the queen mother, the archbishop of Rouen, and other justices. This group, the small council, named the body that was to safeguard the ransom: the queen mother; the archbishop of Rouen; Hubert Walter, just elected archbishop of Canterbury; Richard Fitz Neal, bishop of London; William, earl of Arundel; Hamelin, earl Warenne; and Henry Fitz Alwyn, mayor of London.[72] The money was to be kept under the seals of the queen mother and the archbishop of Rouen until it was delivered to the messengers who were to take it to Germany, and part or all of the proceeds were kept at St. Paul's Cathedral.[73] They may also have acted as the body responsible for the reception and accounting of the ransom, supervising and sharing in the work of a special exchequer of receipt and account (which they established), for most of them were experts in finance. The archbishop of Rouen, Hubert Walter, and Richard Fitz Neal were barons of the exchequer, the last also being treasurer and author of the *Dialogue of the Exchequer*.[74] The mayor of London would be an expert in finance. Both William, earl of Arundel, and Hamelin, earl Warenne, were members of the small council.[75] This inference is fortified by evidence from the pipe roll of 1195 of a payment by the sheriff of London for "two cloths bought for the exchequer of the barons in the king's chamber, in *thalamo regis*, and the other exchequer *in solio* and for putting benches around that exchequer and for rushes for the barons' chambers." [76] There are repeated references in the pipe rolls to purchases of cloth and curtains for the exchequer, but only on one occasion, 1195, to the purchase of cloths for two exchequers. The extra body must have been employed on account of the unusual quantity of revenue.

It seems unnecessary for such a large board of dignitaries to have been designated merely to safeguard the treasure; the actual work of receiving the cash would have been performed by clerks; the most important task would have been auditing the accounts of the various imposts. This is the kind of board that we would

---

72. *Ibid.*, p. 212.
73. *Ibid.*, pp. 210–212. *Pipe roll 5 Richard I*, pp. 14, 37, 73, 158.
74. Madox, *History of the exchequer*, p. 744.
75. Lionel Landon, *The itinerary of King Richard I* (Pipe Roll Society), LI, in index under names of these earls.
76. *Pipe roll 7 Richard I*, p. 113. This evidence was called to my attention by Mrs. Stenton. *Ibid.*, pp. xv, xvi.

expect to be in charge to decide all questions that would arise. It would appear likely therefore that they constituted a special exchequer that received the cash and audited accounts as well.

No special name was needed for the new group because it was merely a branch of the exchequer. Later, however, appear occasional references in the pipe rolls to the "exchequer of the ransom" to distinguish this group from the regular exchequer. The earliest use of this title dates from 1197, four years after the collection of the ransom had begun.[77] All the cases refer to old debts that had been originally incurred after Richard's return from Germany. The term was employed by persons who had been summoned by the regular upper exchequer at Westminster to pay one of these debts with which they were still charged, because no record of payment had been found by that body; in reply the debtor alleged that he had paid the debt into the exchequer of the ransom. Evidently the latter body was no longer in existence. Sometimes it was the sheriff who appeared before the upper chamber of account charged with a debt owed by someone in his bailiwick. For example, that official declared that the 10 m. with which Richard de Dalham in Staffordshire was charged had been paid into the exchequer of the ransom. The debt was due because Richard de Dalham had secured a return into the king's favor.[78] In the same pipe roll in Staffordshire the royal demesne (17 vills) was tallaged in the amount of £16 6s. 8d. In this and the following year the sheriff paid a part in thesauro, leaving a balance due of £13 5s. 4d.[79] The pipe roll of 10 Richard states that this sum was not paid into the exchequer of that year because it was paid into the exchequer of the ransom.[80] Thereafter the sheriff was charged in the roll with 10m. for Richard de Dalham and £13 5s. 4d. for the tallage on the towns with the statement that the sums were not paid because they were paid into the exchequer of the ransom. In 6 John the pipe roll adds the two sums together for a total of £19 18s. 8d. which the sheriff owed "for causes noted in the third year of John which were not paid for the causes stated in that year." [81] A similar statement was made in the pipe roll of 7 John, but in the pipe roll of 8 John the matter was dropped with-

77. *Pipe roll 9 Richard I*, p. 142.
78. *Pipe roll 7 Richard I*, p. 258. *Pipe roll 8 Richard I*, p. 80. *Pipe roll 9 Richard I*, p. 142.
79. I make the payments £2 13s. 4d., leaving a balance of £13 13s. 4d., but the clerks made it £13 5s. 4d.
80. *Pipe roll 10 Richard I*, p. 122.
81. *Pipe roll 6 John*, p. 209.

THE CENTRAL ORGANIZATION 27

out explanation.[82] The history of the hidage of Cumberland is similar. The sheriff owed £20 for the fine which he made with the justices for the hidage of Cumberland which was exacted throughout England for the aid of the king's ransom.[83] This statement was repeated, until in 10 Richard the roll states that it had been paid to master John of Bridport and his associates, "as the sheriff says." [84] In the pipe roll of 3 John this statement was modified: "it was not paid [into the regular exchequer] because it had been paid into the exchequer of the ransom as the sheriff says." [85] Evidently John of Bridport and his associates were the clerks that had received it at the exchequer of the ransom. Still the item remained in successive pipe rolls till 6 John, when it was dropped without explanation. Now these cases continued to appear in the roll after it was known that the sums had been paid, because no proper technical evidence was produced in the shape of a tally or a writ or the personal statement of the clerk who received it. Then apparently each case was dropped after repeated statements by the sheriff.

Some of the debtors however produced proper evidence of having paid their tax. Henry, archdeacon of Stafford, owed £100 of fine for having the king's good will.[86] He paid £49 13s. 6d. in thesauro.[87] The following year (1 John) Master William of Buckingham testified before the barons at the exchequer that Henry had formerly paid £50 at the exchequer of the ransom.[88] Because of this evidence Henry was at once credited with that amount.[89] William Fitz Ernest was charged with 40s. in the pipe roll of 1195 under the heading of *Nova Promissa* levied by Hubert, archbishop of Canterbury.[90] The item appeared in the succeeding pipe rolls till the pipe roll of 1 John added the information that he had paid it into the exchequer of the ransom and so he ought not to be summoned.[91] Since this item was entered in the pipe roll, it is clear that William (or some representative) was accounting for this debt at the regular exchequer of account at Westminster and had claimed that he ought not to be summoned because he had paid at the exchequer of

82. *Pipe roll 7 John*, p. 156. *Pipe roll 8 John*, p. 112.
83. *Pipe roll 6 Richard I*, p. 123.
84. *Pipe roll 10 Richard I*, p. 142.
85. *Pipe roll 3 John*, p. 252.
86. *Pipe roll 7 Richard I*, p. 189.
87. *Pipe roll 10 Richard I*, p. 155.
88. *Pipe roll 1 John*, p. 248.
89. *Pipe roll 2 John*, p. 178.
90. *Pipe roll 7 Richard I*, p. 189.
91. *Pipe roll 1 John*, p. 247.

the ransom. The roll further contains evidence of the truth of his statement, for it adds that William of Buckingham testified he had received the money.[92] This the barons accepted; the pipe roll of the next year contains no reference to the debt.[93] From these two cases it seems that William of Buckingham was a clerk at the exchequer of receipt of the ransom.

William de Duredent owed 30m. for having the benevolence of the king.[94] Of this he paid 10m. in 9 Richard in thesauro and still owed 20m.[95] In the pipe roll of 1 John he was summoned to account for this balance but claimed that he had paid it into the exchequer of the ransom as was proved by a writ of King Richard which was produced by the marshal of the [upper] exchequer.[96] Consequently the charge was dropped from the pipe role.[97] A similar receipt or tally seems to be indicated by the entry concerning Guido de Diva, who the justices of the inquests of 1194 reported had paid 100s. 7d. "at the exchequer [? of the ransom] that has been due from the tax on ten shillings and upwards." They state that he had as evidence of his payment something—the roll here is defective but the logical word would be "tally." [98]

The money from the taxes might be paid in either at the regular exchequer or that of the ransom. The exchequer of the ransom had disappeared when references to it appear; the regular exchequer was collecting old accounts, and the debtors were trying to prove that their debts had been paid. In the production of evidence we see that the organization of the exchequer of the ransom followed the conventional division into the exchequer of receipt and that of account. The members of the exchequer of receipt were clerks like Masters John of Bridport and William of Buckingham. They probably issued tallies to debtors who made payments and later presented them to the exchequer of account as evidence of their payment, whence they received a writ, a duplicate of which the marshal retained. The roll does not state that the payment was made into the special exchequer of the ransom, but it was made for the ransom. Anyhow the procedure in both bodies would be the same.

92. *Ibid.*
93. *Pipe roll 2 John*, pp. 177–178.
94. *Pipe roll 8 Richard I*, p. 271.
95. *Pipe roll 9 Richard I*, p. 149.
96. *Pipe roll 1 John*, p. 202.
97. *Pipe roll 2 John*, p. 10.
98. *Three rolls of the king's court* (Pipe Roll Society), XIV, 109.

THE CENTRAL ORGANIZATION 29

A roll of assessment and collection was drawn up by vills and hundreds, which the sheriff used in collecting these taxes and probably presented at both chambers in rendering his account at the exchequer of the ransom.[99] A receipt roll of 1195 drawn up at the exchequer on Easter, 1195, seems to be a roll of arrears of sundry levies for the ransom.[100] It is likely that the roll of the original levies was drawn up by the exchequer of receipt of the ransom. The hidage of five shires was entered in the pipe roll, that of the other shires was probably entered in another roll drawn up at the exchequer of the ransom.[101]

It is possible that the "exchequer of the ransom" meant only the exchequer of receipt and that accounts were rendered at the regular upper exchequer, but the latter would be as busy as the former and would need the assistance provided by a special exchequer of account. The financial experts on the special board created to safeguard the returns of the ransom were qualified to direct the action of such a special board.[102] The special exchequer probably came to an end after the rush of business was over in 1195, after the reception of the tallage and the carucage, and then the regular exchequer received later payments and issued summonses for unpaid debts.

The cash of the carucage of 1198 was paid by the sheriffs to a body, perhaps a special exchequer of receipt, that was under the orders of a special committee of exchequer barons that acted as an exchequer of account. The duties of the bishops, abbots, and barons mentioned were those of the exchequer of account; with them would be associated clerks of the exchequer to receive the cash.[103] The carucage of 1200 may have been paid to and accounted for at a special board of receipt and account.

But the fifteenth of merchants also involved both a chamber of receipt and one of account. The writ on the patent roll directed the local assessors and collectors to keep all the cash receipts in a secure box with three locks till they were paid to the chief custodians who were to give a receipt (chirograph) for the cash.[104] The labor involved in receiving this money presupposes a body of clerks to assist the three dignitaries who were the chief custodians for the whole

99. *Ibid.*, pp. 84, 87.
100. *Pipe roll 7 Richard I*, pp. 261–263.
101. *Pipe roll 6 Richard I*, pp. 123, 126, 130, 193, 194.
102. Mrs. Stenton has pointed out that in Normandy a "roll of the king's ransom" was drawn up distinct from the regular exchequer roll. *Pipe roll 7 Richard I*, p. xv.
103. Roger of Howden, IV, 46.
104. *Rot. pat.*, p. 42b.

realm. The latter had additional duties. They supervised in general the administration of the tax. They issued permits for the export of wool. They fixed the price of wool which was to be taxed. They judged cases of the violation of the assize of the fifteenth. Moreover they audited the accounts of the local collectors who presented them the cash with the rolls containing the names, the dates of payment, and the amount paid each time, with tallies and rolls showing the names of the taxpayers, the amounts paid by each and the dates of payment.[105] The three receivers rendered to the exchequer an account of the total cash received, arranged by ports, thirty-five in number, the amount paid in thesauro and the outlay authorized by royal writs.[106] The yield given in one account was £4,958 7s. 3d. ob.; the receivers paid into the treasury £2,749 2s. 5d.; they spent £2,159 12s. 4d. ob. and owed £49 12s. 6d.[107] The payments were not made by towns, for the number of tallies received from the exchequer by the committee numbered ten while there were thirty-five towns. There is no indication that the towns accounted later and individually to the upper exchequer.

Thus the chief custodians, *capitales custodes*, had in all seeming a subordinate exchequer of receipt and account for the fifteenth of merchants. Nor were they members of the exchequer of the kingdom. Two of them, however, William de Wrotham and Reginald de Cornhill, were among the most important administrators of the realm. Hence clearly their selection for this important post. The minor details of administration were apparently carried on by clerks under their direction, for at the same time we find William de Wrotham and William de Fornell directing activity about the king's ships;[108] the former was also in charge of the stanneries and in collaboration with Reginald de Cornhill administered the temporalities of the bishopric of Winchester which was vacant.[109]

With the great tax of the thirteenth in 1207 much the same procedure was followed. There seems to have been an exchequer of receipt and of account. Thus there appears an item in the pipe roll that the burgesses of Beverly accounted for 500m. for having the benevolence of the king. This item was underlined for deletion with the comment that by the king's command the burgesses were to

105. *Ibid.*
106. *Pipe roll 6 John*, p. xliii.
107. *Ibid.*, p. 218.
108. *Rot. claus.*, I, 13b.
109. *Ibid.*, pp. 11, 13.

THE CENTRAL ORGANIZATION 31

respond to the custodians of the thirteenth.[110] (This note of course was entered in the upper exchequer as if that body had no care of the account rendered by the burgesses.) A writ on the close roll suggests that this exchequer of the thirteenth was equipped to receive money by weight as well as by tale (the lower exchequer) and that it had clerks to take cognizance of writs of *computate* (the upper exchequer) just as at Westminster.[111] In addition the item shows that the barons of the exchequer of the thirteenth were not merely to receive the money arising out of the tax, but also the collectors (the sheriffs) were to account to them for sums due from their districts.

The writ of assessment and collection states that the sheriffs received every fortnight from justices a copy of the roll of assessment arranged by vills and hundreds and immediately began the collection.[112] This arrangement suggests haste and indicates why a special exchequer was established. The item concerning the sheriff of Nottinghamshire shows that he would appear before the exchequer of the thirteenth to pay the cash collected and render his account for which he had his rolls of assessment and his receipt rolls arranged by vills and hundreds.[113] Otherwise why should the special exchequer be notified about the 100*m.* paid into the chamber?

An item in the fine roll seems to be a preliminary report of the barons of the exchequer of the thirteenth to the exchequer of Westminster. It gives the total amount received from the common thirteenth as well as the fines of the religious and the dona of bishops as £57,421 11*s.* 5*d.*; the amount still owed as £2,615 5*s.* 10*d.*, "besides the debts of the sheriffs of Sussex, and Cumberland who have not yet rendered their accounts and besides certain other debts concerning which we shall speak to you more at length when we come to you." [114] The chiefs of the special exchequer not merely received the cash but also audited the accounts of the sheriffs. This report to the exchequer at Westminster is the final step in the procedure of levying the tax that is recorded. It should be noted however that the justices of assessment took their rolls of assessment to the king, i.e., probably to the exchequer.[115]

110. *Pipe roll 9 John*, p. 71.
111. *Rot. claus.*, I, 91b.
112. *Rot. pat.*, p. 55.
113. *Rot. claus.*, I, 91b.
114. *Rot. oblatis*, p. 459.
115. *Rot. pat.*, p. 55.

32   TAXATION IN MEDIEVAL ENGLAND

The brief report that, as I have suggested, was made to the exchequer at Westminster by the heads of the exchequer of the thirteenth must have been an interim report. It indicates that later a detailed report would be made, probably showing the assessment and the collection by counties, hundreds, and vills, the amount of fines assessed on individuals (chiefly towns, prelates, and religious) and the payments made. Thus the regular exchequer would make use of the rolls of assessment handed in by the justices and those of collection which would accompany the report, as a means of checking the correctness of the work of the special exchequer.

After the exchequer of the thirteenth had made a final report to the exchequer of Westminster, the latter body assumed the work of summoning those taxpayers who were in arrears. Thus the pipe roll contains the account of Thomas de Muleton, sheriff of Lincolnshire, for his deficit of the thirteenth: £44 were paid in thesauro and £14 8s. to the custodians of the thirteenth, from whom Thomas must have received a writ or a tally which he presented at the upper exchequer.[116] The custodians of the thirteenth must have presented this sum in their account.

The barons of the thirteenth whose names we know were William de Wrotham, archdeacon of Taunton, and Aymer, archdeacon of Durham. Neither was a member of the exchequer at Westminster. That these two officials were the custodians or barons of the thirteenth is clear from two references. The first is an order to William, archdeacon of Taunton, and Aymer, archdeacon of Durham, to send Geoffrey Fitz Peter £300 of the money of the thirteenth, and the justiciar would cause this amount to be returned to them from the first money from any source which reached the exchequer at Westminster. The second writ, addressed to the treasurer and the chamberlains of the treasury at Winchester, must have been issued in fulfillment of an earlier promise similar to the one just cited, commanding these officials to pay "from our treasury £100 to our barons of the exchequer of the thirteenth to replace £100 which William de Cornhill paid into our chamber by our command of the money of the thirteenth which had been concealed and which he had received from the county of Lincoln." William and Aymer of the first writ are undoubtedly the barons to whom reference is made in the second.[117] The clerks of the exchequer distinguished between this board, the barons, or custodians, of the thirteenth on the one

116. Pipe roll 13 John, m. 16, Public Record Office.
117. *Rot. claus.*, I, 86, 89.

THE CENTRAL ORGANIZATION 33

hand and the older institutions like the chamber, or the ordinary exchequer, on the other. Thus they record a debt of 700m. of the bishop of Bath, partly for the thirteenth and partly for other things; as to its payment, the roll states: "In the treasury, nothing; and to the king in his chamber four hundred marks by the king's writ; and to the custodians of the exchequer of the thirteenth one hundred marks, by the same writ for which they must respond." [118] Again the clerks correct an entry of the payment of £100 into the treasury with the statement that it was paid to the custodians of the thirteenth.[119] Neither of these officials was a great lord nor a baron of the exchequer, but both were important administrative officers. William in particular was employed in many executive posts, often involving great financial responsibility. He was warden of the stanneries of Devon and Cornwall, was perhaps one of the receivers of the carucage of 1200, with two others he supervised the collection of the fifteenth of merchants in 1204, was the custodian of various lands in the king's hand, acted as warden of the coasts, and so on. He was therefore a man of varied executive experience, well fitted to preside over a complicated financial operation like the receipt of the thirteenth.[120] Aymer, archdeacon of Durham, does not appear in the patent or close rolls before the levy of the thirteenth. As one chosen to be associate of William de Wrotham, he must already have been an official of importance. In 1209 he and Philip de Ulecot were given custody of the great bishopric of Durham. In 1212 William, earl Warenne, Philip de Ulecot, and the archdeacon of Durham were given custody of Northumberland, and as one looks through the close roll of that year it is evident that he was one of the dependable and important officials of King John, along with John Fitz Hugh, Philip Marc, and others.[121] He must have won the confidence of the king's council however in order to have been made in 1209 the custodian of the bishopric of Durham and still earlier even to have been made custodian of the thirteenth.

Of the three receivers of the carucage of 1220, one was Alexander de Sawbridgeworth, an experienced clerk of the wardrobe;[122] another was a certain William Fitz Benedict, a citizen of London,

118. *Pipe roll 9 John*, p. 63.
119. *Ibid.*, p. 71.
120. *Rot. claus.*, I, 10, 48b, 89. See *Dictionary of national biography*, under William de Wrotham.
121. *Rot. pat.*, p. 91. *Rot. claus.*, I, 122b, 124.
122. *Ibid.*, pp. 75, 441b, 449b, 450b, 453. *Patent rolls, 1216–1225*, p. 272.

prominent as a merchant, as a purveyor of supplies to the royal household, and as a creditor of the king. He had been in 1218 in charge of the exchange of London.[123] Before this committee of three appeared the sheriff and county collectors with the cash, the rolls of assessment and collection, and perhaps the countertallies issued by them to the subdivisions of the shire, sealed by the sheriff and the two knights collectors of the shire.[124] The committee received and counted the money, gave the collectors who appeared tallies as receipts, and drew up a roll of the receipts; they paid out part of it on obedience to royal letters patent; placed the balance in forels protected by their seals and locks.[125] They sent £2,000 to the exchequer by November 24, 1220.[126] The total sum which this group received amounted to nearly £3,000, not quite the whole sum realized from the tax.[127] These three commissioners acted only as an office of receipt, but unless their examination of the rolls of collection and the tallies issued by the county collectors to the taxpayers was purely formal, they could decide from these documents whether or not the county collectors had paid in the whole amount that they had collected. There is no indication in the report of Alexander de Sawbridgeworth and his associates that they had compared the receipts with the assessment roll to determine the amounts still due. The exchequer at Westminster also received the rolls of assessment and collection and audited the accounts of the commissioners and of the county assessors and collectors.[128] The chancery rolls record many orders to sheriffs and county assessors to bring the rolls of assessment and collection to exchequer for audit, not to the commissioners at the New Temple.[129] The three receivers rendered the account of their receipts and outlay to the exchequer and were declared quit.[130] Alexander de Sawbridgeworth received £336 16s. 1d. of the carucage to take to the siege of Bytham castle with £320 from other sources. He paid £160 2s. 4d. ob. in

123. *Ibid.*, pp. 104, 138, 151, 160. *Rot. claus.*, I, 344, 346b, 350, 360b, 362, 363, 442, 546.
124. *Ibid.*, p. 437. Fine roll 5 Henry III, Part I, m. 6, Public Record Office. Exchequer L. T. R., Memoranda roll 8 Henry III, m. 5, Public Record Office. Memoranda roll 21 Henry III, m. 1d, m. 22d, Public Record Office.
125. *Book of fees*, II, 1437–1439. Exchequer L. T. R., Memoranda roll 14 Henry III (E 368/11), m. 8, m. 9, Public Record Office.
126. *Patent rolls, 1216–1225*, p. 272. *Rot. claus.*, I, 442.
127. *Book of fees*, II, 1438–1445.
128. *Ibid.*, pp. 1437–1439.
129. Exchequer L. T. R., Memoranda roll 9 Henry III, m. 2. Exchequer K. R., Memoranda roll 12 Henry III, m. 7, Public Record Office.
130. *Book of fees*, II, 1438.

thesauro and laid out the remainder on the expenses of the siege. The work was completed by March 5, 1221. We may therefore conclude that the work of the commissioners drew to a close before that time.

The exchequer also naturally reported to the council the amount of the carucage that remained unpaid, and for years efforts were made to secure the payment of these arrears. Those summoned were the sheriff and the assessors and collectors, not the taxpayers. If an assessor died, his heir was held responsible for the debt.[131] There are numerous instances of the summons of the heir of the collector for the debt of the shire.[132]

The voluntary levy of 1222 to supply money to John de Brienne, king of Jerusalem, was received by Stephen le Gras and Gerard Bat, appointed by the king with the advice of the magnates.[133] They were Londoners and were probably prominent already in financial matters. In 1221 Stephen had been one of two men who had carried £100 of the aid of London to Oxford and delivered it to Hubert de Burgh, and some years later Gerard Bat was associated with Alexander Swereford, dean of St. Paul's Cathedral and an exchequer clerk, with Hugh Giffard, constable of the Tower, and Andrew Bukerel, mayor of London, as a board of inquiry into the accounts of Peter de Rivaux. In 1239 he became sheriff of London.[134]

Stephen and Gerard therefore received the cash at the New Temple. It was at first presented November 1, 1222, by a Templar, or Hospitaler of the house where it was deposited, the sheriff supplying safe conduct.[135] Finally, the sheriffs were ordered to bring all the cash collected including arrears to the New Temple on January 27, 1224, unless some tenants preferred to respond in person for the tax on their lands.[136] The money was to be enclosed in sacks, one for each vill, with the amount recorded inside and outside the sack, which was sealed with the name of the vill. The central committee opened the sacks, counted the cash, and checked it with the amount stated on each sack.[137] Probably they delivered

---

131. Exchequer K. R., Memoranda roll 12 Henry III, m. 7, Public Record Office.
132. Exchequer K. R., Memoranda roll 21 Henry III, m. 21d, Public Record Office.
133. *Patent rolls, 1216–1225*, pp. 512, 527. *Rot. claus.*, I, 516b.
134. *Ibid.*, p. 461. *Close rolls, 1231–1234*, pp. 580–582. *Calendar of liberate rolls, 1226–1240*, pp. 395–396.
135. *Rot. claus.*, I, 516b.
136. *Ibid.*, p. 630.
137. *Ibid.*, pp. 516b, 567.

36 TAXATION IN MEDIEVAL ENGLAND

a tally of receipt to the accountant. They retained the money for some time in their custody, for in 1225 they paid out cash twice by order of the king to a total of 800m. and were granted writs of quittance.[138] They drew up a roll of their receipts, for the writ of assessment stated that the magnates wished to know the amount of the tax paid by each taxpayer and the total yield.[139] The local collectors probably presented their accounts at the regular exchequer. They would have been wise to do so. Long afterward (1230) the council ordered the treasurer to order the sheriffs to inquire at once who were the assessors and collectors of this tax and to summon them all to appear before the barons of the exchequer on January 27, 1230, with their rolls of assessment and collection to render their account and show the arrears still owed.[140] A writ to the sheriffs of London and Middlesex issued in accordance with this order and witnessed by Jocelyn, bishop of Bath, at Westminster December 12, 1230, is found on the memoranda roll.[141]

It is clear that all the sheriffs or the collectors had not presented the accounts of the levy to the exchequer, or at any rate there was no record at the exchequer or with the sheriff of the taxpayers who were in arrears. Only the local collectors could help in this emergency. So the roll reads: "You [the sheriff] distrain all those in your county whom you can ascertain by inquiry through the aforesaid collectors and assessors owe any arrears, distrain them to deliver such arrears to the aforesaid collectors in our own behalf." [142] In this statement appears the conventional method of paying a tax of this kind in 1230. After the tax had been assessed, the assessors sent the rolls of assessment to the exchequer. They then delivered the cash and the rolls of collection to the special exchequer. Then they would appear before the upper exchequer for the final account with transcripts of the rolls of assessment and collection. Would the local collectors (Templar and Hospitaler) not also need to present tallies showing the amount of cash which they had paid to the central receivers and in addition duplicates of the tallies which they had delivered to the collectors in the vills, the chaplain, the two legal men, and the sergeant of the lord? The tellers are not mentioned; was the device of the sealed sack, with

138. *Patent rolls, 1216–1225*, pp. 512, 527.
139. *Rot. claus.*, I, 516b, 567b.
140. Fine roll 14 Henry III, Part I, m. 12d, Public Record Office.
141. Exchequer L. T. R., Memoranda roll 14 Henry III, m. 3d, Public Record Office.
142. *Ibid.*

THE CENTRAL ORGANIZATION 37

the amount stated inside and outside employed to serve the purpose of an unchangeable record made in the vill and intended to reach the central collectors to serve as a check on the sheriff?

The bishops of Bath and Salisbury who were in charge of the receipt and custody of the fifteenth of 1225 were both important tenants in chief, prelates, and barons of the exchequer.[143] For convenience, it was provided that the tax was to be paid at two places, Devizes and Winchester, the collectors of some counties to appear at one place and some at the other. But the plan to have Devizes as one of the offices of receipt was soon abandoned because of the lack of provisions and accommodations at the inns, and the New Temple at London was substituted, an indication of the crowds of animals and men that appeared at these financial centers on the days of accounting.[144] A liberate writ of 1225 furnishes invaluable detail about the receiving office at Winchester. The officers in general charge both at Winchester and at the New Temple were the two bishops. Under the bishop of Salisbury the receiving office at Winchester was in direct charge of William de Chastel, a clerk of the wardrobe. He had as associates two chamberlains, a weigher, three or four tellers, and two ushers—officials like those at the exchequer of receipt at Westminster. The list of payments of these officials recalls the description of the tasks performed in the lower exchequer given in the *Dialogue of the Exchequer*. There were paid 16s. 8d. for 160 canvas sacks to hold the money, 13s. for a new exchequer for calculating, 3s. 4d. for carrying the forels and the scaccarium often from place to place, 10d. ob. for wax and discus, 12d. for a lock on a chest at the Temple, 7s. 7d. for a chest to hold the rolls and the tallies of account, and 3s. 9d. for a black cloth to cover the exchequer for counting the fifteenth, 5s. for carrying the forels of the fifteenth from the room of receipt to the treasury and 12d. for wax to seal the forels and for wood to make tallies. Certainly these are the tasks performed in the lower exchequer, but is this group of officials that body? I suggest that these men were receiving the fifteenth. Certainly this office of receipt was distinct from what we may call the "regular" exchequer at Westminster. It was in session from June 17 till July 13 for the first half of the payment and again from September 29 till November 22 for the second half. These dates are not necessarily the extreme limits of the session, but those for which a certain writ of liberate was is-

143. Madox, *History of the exchequer*, p. 564.
144. *Rot. claus.*, II, 73b, 81.

sued.[145] At both these dates the exchequer was in session. Moreover that they were a separate body is indicated by the instructions to local collectors who were ordered to pay half the cash at each of these dates to the bishops of Bath and Salisbury or their deputies.[146] Nor was this body the wardrobe receiving the money. In none of the instructions or writs was it called the wardrobe. Moreover a record of the wardrobe shows that body receiving money of the fifteenth at the hands of the bishops of Bath and Salisbury, an unnecessary procedure had it already been paid at the wardrobe by the local collectors.[147] This group of men therefore was a committee appointed to receive the fifteenth under the general charge of the two bishops.

This gives a complete picture of the special machinery created at the center to receive the fifteenth. Two men, the bishops of Bath and Salisbury, were in charge. They were important political figures, members of the small council and of the exchequer. Obviously such personages would not weigh the coins that were paid in, cut tallies, and the like. Hence a group of skilled clerks was delegated to perform these mechanical tasks. For this therefore there seems to have been set up a special exchequer, corresponding to the great exchequer of the realm, divided like its prototype into two parts, the exchequer of receipt and the exchequer of account. The former was manned by William de Chastel and his associates, the latter by the bishops of Bath and Salisbury. Let us follow the description and see how it works out. There were two periods of accounting at the exchequer, Easter and Michaelmas. The local collectors were to appear with the first half of the fifteenth at Trinity and the second half at Michaelmas.[148] At the appointed time they appeared with their cash; it was counted or weighed or both, if necessary, for there were a weigher and tellers, i.e., it was tested by weighing, but there seems to have been no assay. There were also two chamberlains; their duties were not described, but there were mentioned sacks of canvas, forels, a chest in which the pence were to be placed, and at the regular exchequer it was the knights of the chamberlains who attended to these duties. Very likely a similar obligation accounts for the presence of the chamberlains at this special exchequer. Thus there was an usher and

145. *Patent rolls, 1216–1225*, p. 541. *Ibid., 1225–1232*, pp. 6, 92.
146. *Rot. claus.*, II, 74, 75b.
147. *Patent rolls, 1225–1232*, p. 15. Chancery miscellanea, Bundle 3, No. 2. Receipt of the wardrobe 10 Henry III, Public Record Office.
148. *Rot. claus.*, II, 81.

wax, and wood for tallies to be sent as receipts for money paid in, also done probably by the chamberlains; the sealing of the forels and chests and bags of money was done not in this case by the clerk of the treasury but by William de Chastel, clerk of the wardrobe, the most important subordinate official.

After the money had been paid in and the tallies issued to the collectors, there remained the business of audit, the work of the upper exchequer. The local collectors had been instructed not only to pay the cash to the bishops of Bath and Salisbury or their deputies but also to render to them the accounts of their receipts, and the account was quite as important as the cash.[149] They perhaps presented the rolls of assessment which they had received from the hundred knights along with the tallies of each vill.[150] There is no indication of any use made of the assessment rolls by the auditors.

The county collectors also presented a roll of the receipts showing the amount collected from each vill. The regular county collectors had already examined the accounts of their subordinates in the shires, the hundred knights, who had received the cash from the men of each vill. Now in their turn they were to have their accounts examined by the bishops of Bath and Salisbury or their deputies.[151]

There was thus an office of receipt and of audit, especially created for the fifteenth, composed of men who were members of the upper and the lower exchequer but detailed for this work. Here then we have again at work the same process which developed the exchequer out of the curia regis. One step is the temporary assignment of certain properly qualified officials to a special task. Later the two bishops in charge rendered an account of their receipts and payments to the exchequer.[152] Each reported the amount received by shires; by the assessors and collectors; by the bishops and certain religious who had assessed and collected their own fifteenth; one liberty, two manors, and two urban areas also paid and accounted for the tax to the special receivers.[153] These last fragmentary entries reflect the casual experimental nature of the new bodies, but their number is small. Some shire collectors divided their account between the two bishops, an indication that this report was of payments only.

149. *Ibid.*, pp. 73b, 81, 146–147, 148b, 152.
150. William Stubbs, *Select charters* (Oxford, 1895), pp. 355–357.
151. *Rot. claus.*, II, 95b, 146, 148b. *Patent rolls, 1225–1232*, p. 18.
152. Exchequer L. T. R., Foreign roll, 1m., m. 5, Public Record Office.
153. *Ibid.*

This account covered the period from June, 1225, to January 11, 1227. It included all the shires and all arrears as well as the early payments. There is no statement of the amount still due from the shire collectors, except in the case of King's Lynn, apparently an entry made just before the account was rendered.[154] It indicates that in general this roll was an account of the collection of the fifteenth, and shows what the council probably had in mind when they set up this special organization or at any rate the purpose it served. It aimed at a complete and supervised collection of the levy. In addition we have a complete statement of the disbursements. The sum of £1,292 13s. 4d. was paid in thesauro, and the balance was expended almost wholly for the expedition to Gascony, each item being authorized by letters patent. The two heads had no authority to spend anything except by the command of the council. There is no hint of the total amount assessed in these accounts. The purpose of the audit was to ascertain whether all the money collected in each shire reached the special exchequer and to see that it was spent by due authorization. The items of expenditure also appear for the most part in the patent rolls.[155]

A few items that appear later in the chancery rolls indicate that further arrears were administered by the regular exchequer of account.[156] This body probably possessed copies of the rolls of assessment as well as the rolls of collection. The former contained the sum assessed on each vill, and since the special exchequer had already checked the accuracy of the rolls of collection, it would be only necessary to compare the amount assessed in each vill with the amount collected to ascertain the amount still due from each area. There would be no useful purpose served by having the county assessors appear before the exchequer of account for they had no means of verifying the correctness of the assessment roll. Hence probably the only audit made was that of the hundred knights by the county assessors and of the county assessors by the special exchequer.

We have seen that the fortieth was paid at the exchequer and was perhaps held as a special fund by the treasurer and chamberlains. The audit was made by the barons of the exchequer who had already received copies of the rolls of assessment and of collec-

---

154. *Ibid. Patent rolls, 1225–1232*, p. 107.
155. The total amount levied is reported as £57,838 13s. 6d. Sydney Knox Mitchell, *Studies in taxation under John and Henry III* (New Haven, 1914), p. 169.
156. *Rot. claus.*, II, 147b. Exchequer K. R., Memoranda roll 12 Henry III, m. 7, Public Record Office.

THE CENTRAL ORGANIZATION 41

tion.[157] On an appointed day, the sheriff and one or more of the collectors of a given shire appeared before the barons with their rolls of assessment and collection, and with the tallies which certified what they had collected.[158] For the assessors had struck a tally of the sum total collected in each vill with the baron of the vill or the steward of the lord of the liberty and presented this when they rendered their account.[159] This provision of the writ concerning tallies was probably conventional. Eight years later Baldwin de Bethune claimed that he should not be taxed for the fortieth on the property on some lands which he had acquired from Earl Richard of Cornwall after the tax had been levied. The council instructed the barons of the exchequer to advise Baldwin that if he could show them the tallies which Richard had received from the shire collectors for his fortieth, Baldwin could be acquitted of the charge, even though one of those who received the fortieth was dead.[160] Does it not seem likely that these were the tallies that the assessors struck with the lord of each vill and that the local royal officials preserved the duplicates as evidence of the amount of cash which they had received?

In addition the assessors produced the tallies which showed what they had paid at the exchequer of receipt, along with writs and tallies that showed the payments which they had made to the officials of the wardrobe, or to anyone else.[161] One writ ordered the constable of the Tower to pay to the treasurer and chamberlains the fortieth from several shires that he was guarding under lock and seal.[162] It may be that the treasurer and chamberlains received the tax from a special group of clerks and then audited the accounts and had the special roll of the account drawn up that has survived on the Foreign Roll.[163]

Although the exchequer possessed the complete rolls of assessment and collection, the enormous number of rolls of vills with the accompanying swarms of taxpayers and the record of their assessments and payments seems to have overwhelmed the exchequer at a time when it was also receiving the regular income. Those officials

157. *Close rolls, 1231–1234,* pp. 295, 299.
158. Exchequer L. T. R., Memoranda roll 21 Henry III, m. 14d, Public Record Office.
159. *Close rolls, 1231–1234,* p. 155.
160. *Ibid., 1237–1242,* p. 183.
161. Exchequer L. T. R., Foreign roll, No. 1, m. 6, Public Record Office.
162. *Calendar of patent rolls, 1232–1247,* p. 15. *Close rolls, 1234–1237,* p. 189.
163. Exchequer L. T. R., Foreign roll, No. 1, m. 6, Public Record Office.

certainly began to take account only of the total return from each vill. Thus the council wrote to the sheriff of Middlesex that since the assessors had reported certain vills were in arrears and they were unable to distrain the debtors he should aid them with distraint.[164] The council did not name the debtors in the vills, usually merely commanding the sheriff to distrain all those who owed anything to the fortieth to pay it to the county collectors.[165] Sometimes the writ states that the assessors will supply the sheriff with the names of the delinquents.[166] Certainly the central government regarded their knowledge of the amount of the tax of the vill as adequate to control the collection from individual taxpayers by the local authorities.

The aid to marry Isabella, the king's sister, to Frederick II, the Roman emperor, did not follow conventional usage. It was based on the knight's fee as in 1217 except that it was to be paid on all fees in the kingdom, whenever or by whomsoever they had been enfeoffed.[167] Instead of the sheriff as collector two knights were appointed in each shire to receive the aid from the bailiffs of the king's tenants in chief and deposit it in a designated castle, church, or religious house of the district under their seals and under two locks, each knight having the key to one lock.[168] The writ of collection states that the cash was to be brought to "our exchequer at London and there delivered to our treasurer and chamberlains," half at Michaelmas, 1235, and half at Easter, 1236.[169] This wording perhaps means that these officials held it in a separate deposit, an inference which is fortified by the fact that like the taxes on movables, and unlike other aids on knights' fees, no account of the tax appears in the pipe roll.[170] A receipt was drawn up probably by the lower exchequer, and later the upper exchequer audited the accounts of the county collectors and drew up a roll after the style of the pipe roll.[171]

It will be recalled that the thirtieth of 1237 had been finally granted after a tumultuous session of the great council featured

164. Madox, *History of the exchequer*, II, 193.
165. Exchequer K. R., Memoranda roll 20 Henry III, m. 13, Public Record Office.
166. Exchequer K. R., 17–18 Henry III (E 159/13), m. 7, 7d, Public Record Office. Madox, *History of the exchequer*, II, 193.
167. *Book of fees*, I, 406.
168. *Close rolls, 1234–1237*, pp. 188–191.
169. *Ibid.*, p. 189.
170. *Book of fees*, I, 408.
171. *Ibid.*, pp. 408, 417, 419.

THE CENTRAL ORGANIZATION 43

by such violent criticism of the king's extravagance and mismanagement that Henry III had promised reform. Hence we should expect circumspection on his part when he came to deal with the returns of the tax. The writs had provided that the assessment should begin in September, 1237, and should be paid half on December 1, 1237, and half on May 31, 1238, and had made the conventional provision that the cash should be temporarily stored in safe places in the locality.[172] The subsequent disposal of the receipts was not determined till December 15, 1237, when the tax was being collected. At that time writs were issued to the sheriffs to provide transportation and guards for the assessors and collectors of each county who were to accompany the cash, rolls, and tallies, locked in containers under the seal of the collectors, to one of three designated places convenient to each shire: the Tower of London and the castles of Bristol and Nottingham. A committee of four was appointed at each castle to receive the money and documents. A Templar and a Hospitaler sat in each group of depositaries. The other members belonged to the royal administration.[173]

At London were Richard Renger, the mayor, and a clerk of the exchequer, who was to be appointed by the treasurer, Hugh de Pattishall. At the castle of Nottingham there were John de Lexington and Peter Grimbald.[174] The former was a steward of the royal household, "a man of great holiness and learning," the holder of the king's seal when Henry III went to Gascony in 1242.[175] Peter Grimbald had been long a royal clerk.[176] Though originally appointed to receive the thirtieth, he did not perform that duty but was sent instead to conduct the queen of Scots home. In June, 1238, he was dispatched on a special mission to Ireland to assist in reorganizing the finances there and is described as "our beloved clerk" "in whose fidelity, ability, and sagacity we have the utmost confidence." [177] Concerning William de Peretot who replaced him as receiver of the thirtieth we know little except that he was a royal clerk and in 1237 the warden of Muchelney abbey.[178] At Bristol

172. *Close rolls, 1234–1237*, p. 544.
173. *Ibid., 1237–1242*, p. 119.
174. *Ibid.*, pp. 116, 119.
175. Thomas F. Tout, *Chapters in the administrative history of mediaeval England* (Manchester, 1920–33), I, 288.
176. *Calendar of liberate rolls, 1226–1240*, pp. 6, 71, 128, 157, 170, 200, 216, 256.
177. *Close rolls, 1237–1242*, p. 140.
178. *Ibid., 1231–1234*, pp. 434, 497. *Ibid., 1234–1237*, p. 35. *Ibid., 1237–1242*, p. 6. *Calendar of patent rolls, 1232–1247*, p. 51.

John de Plessey and John Mansel were the lay receivers. The former was warden of the castle of Devizes, and the latter was a royal clerk who had been in charge of the king's wines, a tallager of the Jews in 1234, custodian of the vacant bishopric of Worcester in 1236, and a baron of the exchequer. He received the king's seal in 1242.[179] He had begun his remarkable career in the king's service.

The first half of the levy was to be delivered to the new depositaries on January 20 or 27, 1238,[180] and the second half presumably soon after the date of payment to the county collectors, viz., May 31, but it proved impossible to enforce this date. By the advice of his council, because of the alleged poverty of the taxpayers, the king on May 19 ordered a fourth of the levy to be collected on May 31, together with arrears, and the final fourth postponed till September 29.[181] Even this concession proved inadequate, for on October 31 all the sheriffs were ordered to distrain those in arrears of the thirtieth and provide safe conduct "for the carrying of the fourth part of the thirtieth which they ought to have received at Michaelmas last" to the receivers at London, Bristol, and Nottingham respectively.[182] At some time in 1239 the whole thirtieth was moved to London and the other two places of deposit were abandoned. On November 6, 1239, a writ was issued directing the transmission of the thirtieth of Buckingham to the New Temple at London to Hugh de Stocton, a Templar, and his fellows, who were called the custodians of the whole thirtieth. Deferred payments were henceforth sent direct to London from all shires.[183]

The task of these three committees of receipt is nowhere described. Perhaps their duties were detailed to them by word of mouth as in the case of the receivers in 1269.[184] From various orders we are able to form a fairly definite picture of their duties. Before them appeared the sheriff and the collectors of each county, or the prelate or baron who had been allowed to assess and collect the tax on his lands. They came with cash, rolls, and tallies sealed in containers with the seals of the assessors, showing the total amount

179. *Calendar of liberate rolls, 1226–1240*, pp. 244, 246, 252, 259, 266, 279, 282, 312. *Close rolls, 1237–1242*, pp. 4, 7, 15, 16, 18, 30, 32, 33, 34. *Calendar of patent rolls, 1232–1247*, pp. 75, 82, 313, 508.
180. *Close rolls, 1237–1242*, pp. 116–117. *Calendar of liberate rolls, 1226–1240*, pp. 302–303.
181. *Close rolls, 1237–1242*, p. 130.
182. *Calendar of liberate rolls, 1226–1240*, p. 349.
183. *Close rolls, 1237–1242*, pp. 116, 117, 153, 171, 172, 187.
184. *Calendar of patent rolls, 1266–1272*, p. 439.

THE CENTRAL ORGANIZATION 45

of the thirtieth collected from the whole area as well as the amount collected in each hundred and vill.[185] The tallies brought by the collectors under seal with the cash and rolls were probably duplicates of those issued to each vill or lord, not to each taxpayer in the vill. This was the method provided in 1232. The seals were broken, the coins counted and weighed, and the number compared with the accompanying tallies and rolls, that is, an audit was made of the amount collected.

This procedure is clear from the equipment which the receivers required, viz., a chequer board and balances, and the presence of tellers. Probably they also cut tallies of receipt for the local collectors.[186] Probably too there were present subordinate officials in addition to the tellers (*numeratoribus*), the weigher and the chamberlains, to complete this special exchequer of receipt, for such it evidently was. These receivers also sorted the coins (hence the *scutellis* or dishes) placing halfpence (*oboli*) by themselves, so that it was a simple matter for the king to bestow on a friend a gift of £36 of the halfpence of the thirtieth in the custody of the receivers at Nottingham.[187] They stored the cash, the rolls, and tallies in sacks and chests locked and sealed with the seals of the Templar and Hospitaler in each center to await further orders from the king.[188] Very likely after they had issued tallies to the county collectors for the cash which they had delivered they drew up a roll of receipts. Thus on June 26, 1240, William de Haverhill, the treasurer, received by the hand of Brother Ralph a roll of the thirtieth received at Nottingham. This recorded the total amount received from the collectors of the thirtieth in three counties and certain associates, the receivers at Nottingham, of the term of the octave of St. Hilary 1238 (this was one date set for payment).[189]

The county assessors had drawn up a roll of receipts of the shire giving the amounts paid by each vill and the sum of the hundred. Such was the roll of Essex that has been preserved. It corresponds exactly with the description of the rolls that the county collectors were to deliver to one of the three central offices of receipt, "by rolls and tallies showing the sum and the items of the thirtieth." That roll contains the total tax paid in the hundred and the shire and

185. *Calendar of liberate rolls, 1226–1240*, p. 326. *Close rolls, 1237–1242*, pp. 116–118.
186. *Ibid.*, p. 23. *Calendar of liberate rolls, 1226–1240*, pp. 314, 333.
187. *Ibid.*, p. 331. *Calendar of patent rolls, 1232–1247*, pp. 220, 230.
188. *Close rolls, 1237–1242*, p. 119.
189. *Ibid.*, p. 119. E 179/270/30, Public Record Office.

the items which were the amount paid by each vill. We have no specific statement this year as to the character of the tally issued by the shire collectors; if they followed the procedure employed in 1225 and 1232, they issued a tally to each vill; this would be a check on the amount of the receipts of the vill given in the roll.[190]

The three groups of depositaries at the Tower, at Bristol, and at Nottingham were thus concerned with receipt, that is, with the amount and the correctness of the roll of receipt delivered by the shire collectors. They might also pay out moneys by the command of the council as indeed might the county collectors.[191] Robert Fitz William and Henry de Bodrigan, collectors of the thirtieth in Cornwall, paid by order 500m. of the thirtieth into the wardrobe December 26, 1238.[192] In 1241 the king ordered the barons of the exchequer to credit the collectors with that amount against the time when they were to render their account of the thirtieth.[193]

The final audit was to be made by the regular exchequer. In November, 1238, the council wrote the assessors and collectors to bring all arrears of the thirtieth to London and added, "They [the assessors] shall also provide that they shall be ready to render a full account of the thirtieth shortly, *in proximo*, at the king's order and to acquit themselves thereof against him." [194] As to arrears, the barons of the exchequer received the cash, audited the accounts of local collectors, and drew up the roll thereof.[195] For this operation they had the rolls of assessment containing the name and assessment of each person in each vill, the tallies given by the county collectors to the men of the vill, one tally for each vill, the tally showing the amount paid at the exchequer by the depositaries, and finally the writs showing the amount paid out by order of the king and the tally or some evidence showing that this had actually been done.

The summons to pay arrears of the thirtieth was issued to the assessors and collectors, not to the individual taxpayer. The sheriff was ordered to distrain those taxpayers whose names the assessors

190. E 179/81/1 and E 179/130/1, 2, Public Record Office. R. C. Fowler, "An early Essex subsidy," *Transactions of the Essex archaeological society*, XIX, 27–37.
191. Madox, *History of the exchequer*, II, 201. Memoranda roll 25 Henry III, m. 6d, Public Record Office. *Calendar of liberate rolls, 1226–1240*, pp. 209, 212, 459, 468.
192. *Ibid.*, p. 357.
193. Madox, *History of the exchequer*, II, 201.
194. *Calendar of liberate rolls, 1226–1240*, p. 350.
195. *Close rolls, 1237–1242*, pp. 187, 263, 295.

THE CENTRAL ORGANIZATION 47

and collectors would give him.[196] If a collector was dead, his heir was summoned in his stead.[197]

The twentieth on the laity and the baronies of the prelates was granted in the summer and autumn of 1269; on the demesnes of the prelates and on other clergy in the spring of 1270.[198] While the machinery of assessment had been set in motion in 1269, the earliest orders for the collection that have survived in the rolls are dated April 2, 1270.[199] On May 5 the assessment in Yorkshire had not been completed.[200] On July 10, 1270, the king ordered all the money of the twentieth sent to the New Temple at London and on the same date the treasurers of the Templars and the Hospitalers, and Giles de Audenarde, an experienced clerk of the exchequer of the wardrobe, were authorized by letters patent to receive and hold the money of the twentieth at the Temple and acquit those who had paid the cash. These three had already been appointed orally. At this time notices of payment of the twentieth begin to appear in the rolls. Ludlow paid £20 at some date between June 8 and July 10; Newcastle on Tyne £100 on July 19; the bishop of Lincoln £50 of the fine on his demesne, July 25.[201] The employment of a central committee to receive the tax was therefore the device of the small council. The three members were men of great financial experience. Such a conclusion is obvious concerning the members of the two orders. Giles had long been a trusted financial official. He had been a clerk of the wardrobe for years; he was underkeeper when Peter of Winchester was keeper.[202] With his associates he supervised the assessment of the twentieth in London,[203] with Hugh Fitz Otto he had audited the accounts of the great fine of 20,000 m. on London, and with Peter of Winchester and the treasurer of the bishopric of Salisbury he audited the accounts of the tenth on the bishopric of Bath and Wells.[204] While these appointees were experienced ad-

196. Exchequer L. T. R., Memoranda roll 27 Henry III, m. 2. Exchequer K. R., Memoranda roll 27 Henry III, m. 1, Public Record Office. Madox, *History of the exchequer*, II, 193.
197. Pipe roll 46 Henry III, m. 4, Public Record Office. Exchequer K. R., Memoranda roll 37–38 Henry III, m. 18d, Public Record Office.
198. Mitchell, *Studies in taxation*, p. 295 et seq. William Edward Lunt, *Financial relations of the papacy with England to 1327* (Cambridge, 1939), p. 230.
199. *Calendar of patent rolls, 1266–1272*, p. 418.
200. *Ibid.*, p. 424.
201. *Ibid.*, pp. 439, 445, 448. *Royal and other historical letters illustrative of the reign of Henry III*, ed. W. W. Shirley (Rolls series), II, 338.
202. Tout, *Chapters in administrative history*, I, 315.
203. *Calendar of patent rolls, 1266–1272*, p. 477.
204. *Ibid.*, pp. 330, 335.

ministrators, none of them approached in political importance the bishops of Bath and Salisbury who constituted the board in 1225. The money and rolls under the seals of the county collectors were conveyed to London by the sheriff with a guard accompanied by the collectors.[205] When the cash had been counted the clerks issued a tally of receipt to the accountant, who then presented it to the higher officials in charge and was given a writ of quittance for the amount which he had paid.[206] The three heads had responsible clerks who could officiate while their chiefs were engaged elsewhere. On December 27, 1270, Giles received £830 18s. of the twentieth of Gloucestershire at Winchester by the hand of Richard Bryan, clerk (of the sheriff).[207] This board of three men held the cash and paid out sums on the order of a second group of three officials acting in behalf of Edward, the archbishop of York, Roger Mortimer, and Robert Burnell, to Prince Edward and Edmund his brother and sundry barons for their expenses on the crusade and for other expenses incident to the levy of the twentieth. The three receivers drew up a roll of their receipts and outlay that exactly balanced at £31,488 17s. 10d. ob.[208] On July 18, 1273, the treasurer and the barons of the exchequer were ordered by Prince Edward's representative to audit the account of the three receivers. This was done; they were acquitted, and this record was entered on the pipe roll. The sum received and paid out, £31,488 17s. 10½d., exactly balanced; it was the amount collected up to October, 1272. From October 20, 1272, William de Middleton and Giles de Audenarde superseded the group of three receivers and auditors and so acted for some time.[209]

This central group not only received and counted the cash and issued receipts but also took account of payments made by the debtors to other collectors. Thus the prior of Bradenstoke paid Giles and his companions on the twentieth 19s. 6d., then presented tallies which showed that he had paid 1m. to the collectors in Wiltshire, 67s. 2d. to the collectors in Dorsetshire, and by order of the

205. Shirley, *Royal letters*, II, 339. Liberate roll 54 Henry III, m. 4, Public Record Office. Pipe roll 56 Henry III, m. 8, Public Record Office. *Cartularium monasterii de Rameseia*, ed. U. H. Hart and A. P. Lyon (Rolls series), II, 293.
206. *Annals of Dunstaple*, ed. H. R. Luard in "Annales monastici," III (Rolls series), p. 257. *Calendar of patent rolls, 1266–1272*, p. 487.
207. *Ibid.*, p. 501.
208. Pipe roll 1 Edward I, m. 6, Public Record Office. *Lancashire lay subsidies*, ed. J. A. C. Vincent (Record Society for Lancashire and Cheshire, London, 1893), I, 100.
209. *Calendar of patent rolls, 1266–1272*, pp. 682–683.

THE CENTRAL ORGANIZATION 49

king he was acquitted for these sums.[210] The committee had definite notions as to what it meant by audit. In 1269 the patent roll states that Giles de Audenarde and Hugh Fitz Otto audited the accounts of the fine for 20,000m. levied on the Londoners, and goes on to define what was meant by the term audit, viz., "how much has been received of the rich and poor of the city and what bailiffs or others received any money on that account and by what warrant and how much each received and if any of it is in arrears, who has it and is answerable for it, and to audit and view how much has been delivered to divers persons and for what purpose." [211]

The work of these three important officials must be inferred from the general statements about them and the references that mention them. A description is important, for it illustrates what the council had in mind at the close of a long period of experiment. As we have said, the body grew out of exchequer practices of the twelfth century, yet the duties of that earlier body differed from those of the exchequer in 1269 because the amounts of money with which they dealt were greater and the individuals that paid them were far more numerous. The tax payers paid varying sums all on a single occasion, the money in theory to be devoted to a single object, and in theory the amount which each man paid was to be based upon an assessment of property each time the tax was levied. What then did this particular committee of experienced administrators and financiers do? We shall see that only part of their spare time was devoted to this work at the New Temple. This is obvious in the case of the heads of the two great orders of Hospitalers and Templars. Giles de Audenarde was engaged in other work while the reception of the twentieth went on. Thus they were the responsible heads of a group of clerks that performed much of the actual work of the office. But it was considered a time-consuming task; in 1276 a writ on the patent roll speaks of the other duties of William de Middleton that leave him no time for the examination of the collection of the twentieth.[212]

Let us survey the committee's duties in connection with the twentieth. It received and held the money at the New Temple, that is, the money assessed and collected by the county collectors.[213] The money was delivered at the New Temple by the sheriff, accompanied

---
210. *Ibid.*, p. 546.
211. *Ibid.*, p. 335.
212. *Calendar of patent rolls, 1272–1281*, p. 154.
213. *Ibid., 1266–1272*, p. 439. Pipe roll 56 Henry III, m. 8, Public Record Office.

50 TAXATION IN MEDIEVAL ENGLAND

by one or more of the collectors; it was in containers that were sealed with the seals of the collectors.[214] The forels also probably contained the roll of collection of the shire and the countertallies, duplicates of the tallies issued by the county collectors to the collectors in the vills. One of the points in the inquests of 1272 was "to inquire concerning the tallies of quittance made by them" (the assessors and collectors of the shire to the collectors in each vill).[215] Otherwise the three and their clerks would have no check on the accuracy of the amount of pence in forels presented to them. The seals were broken and the cash counted and compared with the amounts stated in the rolls by vills and the tallies. We know that they counted the cash for they were to issue acquittances to those who paid over the money.[216] Furthermore they were to make payments out of the twentieth when authorized by the archbishop of York, Roger Mortimer, and Robert Burnell, the representatives of Prince Edward for the expenses of the crusade, since in August, 1270, Henry III had concluded he would be unable to head the crusade and made over to Edward all the moneys collected or to be collected for the twentieth. They might receive the twentieth at a different place, each one acting alone. On December 27, 1270, Giles de Audenarde received at Winchester £830 18s. of the twentieth of Gloucestershire by the hand of Richard Bryan, clerk of the sheriff.[217]

Distinct from these assessed valuations were the lump sums paid by the towns, the prelates on their demesnes, and for the goods on lands held by barony. Many religious houses throughout the realm compounded for the twentieth and generally paid it to the three at the New Temple. The committee of three issued quittances in the shape of writs or tallies either to the assessors and collectors of the shire or to the town or city or to the individual person who had responded personally for the levy. The recipient of the tally then might present it to the chancery and receive letters patent showing that he was quit.[218]

After the tax had been in great part collected, on July 18, 1273, the council ordered the treasurer and barons of the exchequer to audit the accounts of the three, their receipts and disbursements. These accounts exactly balanced at £31,488 17s. 10½d., the

214. Shirley, *Royal letters*, II, 399.
215. *Calendar of patent rolls, 1266–1272*, p. 701.
216. *Ibid.*, p. 439.
217. *Ibid.*, pp. 452, 501. Pipe roll 1 Edward I, m. 6, Public Record Office.
218. *Ibid. Calendar of patent rolls, 1266–1272*, pp. 448, 487, 494, 496, 505, 667.

THE CENTRAL ORGANIZATION 51

amount collected up to October 20, 1272, the account showing that the whole sum collected had been spent.[219] To check this account the exchequer officials had the rolls of collection, by vills and hundreds, of each shire, which had probably been forwarded to them by the county collectors.[220] But no roll of the assessment had been given to the three receivers, Giles and his associates, for they needed none; their audit was to determine that the amount paid in corresponded with the amount stated on the shire rolls of collection and accompanying tallies. A roll of assessment for the shire would however be sent to the exchequer by the county assessors. The barons would use it to check the receipts and the roll of collection to determine which vills still owed part of the twentieth. The audit of arrears would then be made before the barons of the exchequer. Thus in 1275 Ralph de Trihampton, son and heir of Ralph, the assessor and collector of the twentieth in Lincolnshire, was summoned by the exchequer to pay £23 7s. 3d., of this tax still owed by his deceased father.[221] In the account of the twentieth audited and passed by the barons of the exchequer in 1273, amounting to £2,208 2s. 8d. as collected at that time, no unpaid balance is mentioned. So the account produced by Giles and his companions and passed by the exchequer comprised the moneys that had been collected.

The rolls of assessment in the hands of the exchequer were probably the original rolls of assessment showing the amount and value of each kind of property held by the taxpayer. In dealing with arrears of the twentieth however the local officials record payments only by vills or manors, with no mention of persons, as though the vill was the essential taxable unit. Local collectors would know who in the vill was in arrears.[222] The collectors in Gloucestershire paid to Giles de Audenarde £830 18s. of the twentieth of the country on December 27, 1270, and were given acquittances of that amount. This was the sum that the committee of three accounted for to the exchequer nearly two years later (October 20, 1272). It was therefore only an account of the money collected.

The three took no account of the total amount owed by the tax-

219. Pipe roll 1 Edward I, m. 6, Public Record Office. Vincent, *Lancashire lay subsidies*, I, 100.
220. *Ibid.*
221. *Calendar of fine rolls, 1272-1307*, p. 59. *Calendar of close rolls, 1272-1279*, p. 298.
222. Lay subsidies, E 179/155/1, Public Record Office. Minister's accour`, 1118/17, m. 1, 2, Public Record Office.

payer, only of the amounts paid. The patent roll records that the prior and convent of Bradenstoke fined in ten pounds for the twentieth. Giles and his associates issued a tally or a writ certifying that the prior had paid 100s. at the New Temple on January 20, 1271. On June 28, 1271, the prior paid 19s. 6d. in cash at the New Temple and presented tallies showing that he had paid 1m. to the collectors in Wiltshire and 67s. 2d. to the collectors in Dorsetshire. Giles de Audenarde acquitted him of these sums by writ or tally, and the council acquitted the prior by letters patent.[223] This discharged the prior's debt, but the roll makes no record of this fact. Thus the audit of the three receivers noticed only the payments made by the taxpayer; it took no account of his total tax owed.

The utility of the committee of three was that it relieved the exchequer of the labor of receiving the cash, of checking the amounts paid with the roll of collection of each shire, of disbursing the receipts and keeping an account of the disbursements. Such labors would require the assistance of a body of skilled clerks. The calculation of arrears, which would involve the comparison of the payments from each vill with the roll of assessment, would be made by the exchequer of account.

These two bodies of officials therefore were engaged in the work of receiving the tax: the clerks, weighers, tally-cutters, and the like who performed the actual labor, and the body of dignitaries who supervised the receipt in person or by deputy and were responsible for its accuracy. The former correspond in some respects to the exchequer of receipt and the latter to the upper exchequer, or the exchequer of account. There is no mention of a special oath of office taken by any of these men for the reason in all probability that they were already royal officials and were merely temporarily assigned to this work. The lesser clerks were paid and their chiefs sometimes, perhaps always, received special remuneration.[224]

The aim of the council was to bring together quickly the yield of the new taxes to a central locality to meet an insistent need for an unusual sum of money such as was demanded by the crusades of Henry II and Henry III, the ransom of Richard I, the recovery of John's lands in France after the French conquest of Normandy (the thirteenth of 1207), the protection of Aquitaine against the steady advance of the French (the fifteenth of 1225), long-con-

223. *Calendar patent rolls, 1266–1272*, pp. 508, 546.
224. *Rot. pat.*, p. 72b. *Pipe roll 1 Richard I*, p. 178. *Patent rolls, 1216–1225*, p. 541. *Ibid., 1225–1232*, pp. 6, 92. *Calendar of liberate rolls, 1226–1240*, pp. 311, 312, 334.

THE CENTRAL ORGANIZATION 53

tinued campaigns as under Richard I in 1198, the expenses of relief as in 1200, unprecedented debts as in 1232, royal marriages as in 1235 and 1237. There was no thought of increasing royal revenue for the ordinary expenses of the government. Each levy stood by itself as a nonrecurring tax. Yet such a statement of these occasions shows how easily a tax for unusual needs became so frequent a levy that it resulted in a new custom. Hence the central government must devise means to bring the whole yield into the possession of the central authority. Moreover, since the taxes on movables and the carucages were new levies, no one had a definite notion as to the amount that could be expected and accordingly the interest was intense to learn the total yield that would be available. Broadly speaking, the government was successful in assembling without much waste the yield of these taxes, as we shall see more in detail in the next chapter. The establishment of the special central groups to receive the taxes may have been a factor in the success.

In general, members of the special central boards were always expert administrators, loyal to the king and usually skilled in finance. They would always reduce the possibility of error and corruption. They were also important political figures. Sometimes, as in the case of the levy for Richard's ransom, they might be strong enough to prevent the diversion of the proceeds of the taxes to other uses, but in this case members were unique in their political importance and the occasion was unique. However, after the king's return, he diverted part of the scutage raised for the ransom to the war against Philip Augustus. The bishops of Bath and Salisbury, both distinguished political figures, probably played a significant role in devoting all but a small part of the fifteenth of 1225 to the campaign for the recovery of Gascony, but their success may have been due to their importance on the council and to the further fact that Henry III was a minor.

Hubert Walter and Geoffrey Fitz Peter were in charge of the seventh of 1203; they would not hesitate to oppose the king. No one could be more influential than they, but we know little about this tax. No other members of any of these bodies could oppose the council effectively. The royal treasurer, the treasurers of the Hospitalers and Templars, the clerks of the exchequer or the wardrobe, administrators like William de Wrotham or John Mansel, would be in no position to determine government policy as to expenditures. Henry III had a free hand in disposing of the fortieth, the aid of

1235, and the thirtieth. He had a partial justification for this because both in 1232 and 1237 the taxes were requested partly on the plea of his debts. Thus the new central organization really was unable to check the king. Yet the bulk of the taxes was spent on the purpose for which they were asked, not because the central boards could prevent the king from diverting the money to other uses but because the government usually aimed to spend the money for the purpose stated.

The scanty evidence concerning the early special exchequer indicates that through the thirteenth of 1207 this body received the cash, acted as an exchequer of receipt, counting the cash, issuing tallies to the county collectors, and probably drawing up a roll of receipts. There is some evidence that the special body also audited the accounts of the local collectors, not merely comparing the amount collected with the rolls of collection, but also with the rolls of assessment to ascertain the amount still due. Except in connection with the fifteenth of 1203, little evidence appears that the special body retained possession of the money and paid it out on the receipt of orders from the council. At some time afterward the special board delivered the cash and rolls to the exchequer at Westminster and their accounts were audited. The regular exchequer received arrears and later accounts from all collectors.

Under Henry III our information is more complete and we can state definitely the functions of the new exchequer though it was no longer given that name. This body or bodies had two functions: that of the exchequer of receipt to receive, count, and weigh the cash and draw up a roll of receipts; and to audit in part the accounts of the county collectors, comparing the amount of cash received with the county roll of collection and also with the countertallies struck by county collectors with the collectors of the vill or any other local collectors.

The final audit of the county collectors was made with the upper exchequer at Westminster; that body had the rolls of assessment containing the name of each taxpayer and the amount and value of each kind of property that he held, the total value of each man's property and the amount of his tax, the total value of the property and the total tax in the vill. It also had the county or diocesan rolls of collection received either from the special exchequer or the county collectors. With this information the upper exchequer could calculate the arrears of the tax, and then the council summoned the county collectors to appear before the regular exchequer with

THE CENTRAL ORGANIZATION

the cash and rolls. Special collectors were sometimes sent out to receive the cash from the shire collectors; they drew up a roll and presented cash and rolls to the exchequer. This procedure indicates that it was difficult to secure the attendance of the county assessors at the exchequer. Very likely, too, the existence of the special exchequer with its review of the receipts with the rolls and tallies of collection made it less essential for the collectors to appear at the exchequer of account for the comparison of the rolls of assessment with the rolls of collection and payments out. The exchequer barons could secure no additional information regarding the assessment than they already had. They were not concerned with the assessment or the collection from the persons within the vill. When the council issued a call for arrears they demanded the total arrears from the county collectors, or more specifically they noted the vills and the amount each vill still owed.

This development grew naturally out of the custom in assessing levies of grouping all the taxpayers by vills. The method goes back to the aid of 1166, and was steadily continued. The assessment remained an assessment on individual property holders and that never changed in our period. But the notion of the vill as the unit that was followed up for arrears soon arose. It appears in the inquests of 1194. In some cases in Wiltshire the jurors reported or at least the royal commissioners took down the amounts paid by vills.[225] The levy of the fortieth of 1201 was by vills as was the thirteenth of 1207. The rolls of collection that were delivered to the special exchequer and passed to the regular exchequer do not seem to have contained anything lower than the total sum paid by the vill. In this characteristic we see the similarity to the tallage except when there was a levy per capita.

The exchequer was concerned merely with the amount due from an area; as far as these officials were concerned, the first step had been taken that was to transform the tax on movables into a fixed levy upon certain areas of land, a process that took definite shape in the decade 1330–40. The special receivers often took over another task which grew naturally out of the conventional acts of any collector and of the regular exchequer: the disbursement of the cash which they had received. Sometimes they spent very little and turned practically the whole sum over to the exchequer. At other times the special exchequer held the cash and paid it out on receipt of orders from the council. Its functions were apparently always

225. *Three rolls of the king's court,* pp. 87, 93, 99.

determined by the council. Finally it rendered an account of its receipts and expenditures to the exchequer at Westminster.

In cases when no special exchequer was created, as in 1232 and 1235, the money was received in the conventional fashion at the exchequer of receipt or at the wardrobe by special order. The audit of receipt and disbursement was made by the exchequer of account. Perhaps special arrangements were made in these cases for the receipts to be held as a special fund to be spent only by a special order by the king. At this period in his career Henry III was beginning to feel sensitive to the outspoken criticism of his extravagance which he realized was a vice, for the record says once in 1232 and many times in 1235 that the money collected was to be paid in thesauro to the treasurer and chamberlains. The mention of these officials was unusual, though any money paid in thesauro was paid to them. Like many weak men, the king sought to curb a bad habit by some arrangement which superficially would make it difficult for him to yield to temptation, in this case, to spend money, although in reality he knew that the device was only a sham control. Thus once in this decade he declared that he would only spend money by the assent of the legate Otto. At another time he ordered the treasurer and chamberlains to place certain moneys in the Tower of London, in the custody of the constable of the Tower, a Templar, and a Hospitaler "in such wise that the said Treasurer and Chamberlain have on the said money a lock and key and each of the latter have a lock and a key and that nothing of the said money shall be taken for any order which the king may make to the treasurer and chamberlains." [226] At another time he ordered the treasurer to place certain moneys in the Tower "in such wise that nothing shall be taken from it by the king or any one else except by the special command of the king in person." [227] Another order to the treasurer commanded him to place the money in the Tower under his seal till the king commanded him otherwise, "so that the money shall be there as though buried." [228] All such arrangements were merely devices of a weak man to keep himself from fault, for none of these officials could resist his command.

The development of these supplementary bodies was the work of the council, the small group of experts of the curia regis, probably without intervention by the king or the great barons, except those

226. *Calendar patent rolls, 1232–1247*, p. 249.
227. *Close rolls, 1237–1242*, p. 268.
228. *Ibid.*, p. 252.

intimately connected with the administration like Hubert Walter or Geoffrey Fitz Peter. By this device the royal government could more effectively administer the sudden influx of unusual sums of cash and keep the accounts involving large numbers of taxpayers. There is no indication of any interest in the management of the cash on the part of the magnates till 1222, when a writ on the close roll records that the money of the aid of that year was to be deposited in the New Temple by the view of those whom the magnates might depute; these appointees were to ascertain the amount of the tax paid by each taxpayer and the total yield, probably because the magnates, as well as the council, desired to know these facts. The appeal for a great tax in 1225 resulted in the grant of a fifteenth of movables which evoked discussion and opposition. More than one meeting of the great curia regis seems to have been held, and it proved necessary for the king in return for a grant to confirm the charters. One other result may have been the abandonment of revenues as part of the basis of the levy and of confining it to movables. A later reference indicates that the magnates had endeavored to limit the control of the council over the returns of this impost. At the trial of Hubert de Burgh in 1239 it was charged against him that the great council had provided that the fifteenth was to be held in deposit till the king came of age, and that during this period none of it should be spent except by the assent of six bishops and six earls specially delegated for this purpose, and, in any case, only for the defense of the realm.[229] Though this account is not contemporary and though it is one of the charges in a judicial process which might be exaggerated or even falsified, many magnates were living who could remember the events described. In the animated discussion over the fifteenth this proposal may have been advanced and the council may have assented to it. But the execution of the plan rested in their hands and they carried it out to suit themselves and yet to conform in a measure to the desires of the magnates that the money should be properly kept and expended. So they appointed the bishops of Bath and of Salisbury receivers and custodians and left them with a wide control for a long time. In person or by their deputies these officials apparently gave a final audit to the accounts of all local collectors. These receivers, both of whom were members of the exchequer and great prelates, kept a sharp eye upon attempts to draw off money for purposes alien to the desires of the magnates. Most of the fifteenth was spent by the

229. Matthew Paris, *Chronica maiora*, ed. H. R. Luard (Rolls series), VI, 65–66.

custodians for expenses in Gascony in accordance with the original request of the council. The existence of so large a sum of ready money was a terrible temptation to a needy government to divert it to general purposes. Hence the council succeeded in obtaining part of the money for the exchequer and the wardrobe to spend for necessities.[230] Thus the two bishops were ordered to make payments to the legate Otto and to repay merchants for loans made to further the king's affairs at Rome.[231] Once the money was in hand, Henry III made sundry loans and gifts from the receipts. At times the government borrowed from the custodians but had to promise to repay the debt later from the normal income, and sometimes we have a record that the promise was kept. If the king was unable to repay, the custodians were not to be held responsible.[232] As far as our rolls go, the bishops exercised quite a strict control; so much so that only a small proportion of the tax was laid out on purposes alien to the original request. The power exercised by the two bishops apparently made a deep impression on the council for the councilors lost a free control over this lucrative source of revenue. Never again was such a powerful committee constituted by Henry III. In 1232 the king and his council preferred not to create such a central group for the care of the fortieth. In the writ of collection no statement was made about the destination of the cash after collection save that it was to be deposited in a castle, a church, or a house of religious in the shire under the seals of the collectors. Orders were issued later that it was to be delivered sealed to the treasurer and chamberlains of the king. Perhaps this expression meant payment into the exchequer of receipt like any debt. The special mention of the treasurer and chamberlains who did not receive cash directly but through their deputies in the exchequer of receipt suggests that these important officials received the money and held it in a special deposit. Evidently, if this was true, the king had greater control than in 1225, for much of it was soon transferred directly to the wardrobe before it was paid in at Westminster or spent on new obligations of the king, such as the war in the west. Again, the aid on knights' fees of 1235 was stored in similar secure places in the locality, thence transferred to the exchequer into the hands of the treasurer and chamberlains, the suggestion being that

230. *Patent rolls, 1216–1225*, pp. 272, 282. *Rot. claus.*, I, 442. *Calendar of liberate rolls, 1226–1240*, p. 317. Tout, *Chapters in administrative history*, I, 235, 237.
231. *Patent rolls, 1216–1225*, p. 535. *Ibid., 1225–1232*, p. 88.
232. *Ibid.*, pp. 42, 46, 48, 90. *Ibid., 1216–1225*, pp. 547–548. *Calendar of patent rolls, 1232–1247*, pp. 209, 212, 217, 218, 220, 222. *Rot. claus.*, I, 64b, 66.

THE CENTRAL ORGANIZATION 59

they were to keep it on deposit, but that the control exercised over the cash by the king was more complete than in 1225, because they were the regular officials and not high enough in dignity to resist the king.[233] At the same time, perhaps, the king felt he needed some supervision and that he was doing it in this way to demonstrate to the magnates his intention to spend his money carefully. Most of the cash was paid into the exchequer, as would be expected since the writ to all collectors gave this instruction, though some was paid into the wardrobe.[234]

In 1237 Matthew Paris reveals the strong opposition to the tax and the sharp criticism of the king's extravagant administration. The money was to be stored in castles; if the king did not keep his word about the proper enforcement of the charters, it might be returned to the taxpayer. The king's council was to be reinforced by three barons, William de Ferrers, earl of Derby, Earl William de Warenne, and John Fitz Geoffrey.[235] The king solemnly confirmed the charters and promised that he would never again ask for an aid of this kind. After the money had been collected the council issued orders to assemble it in three castles—Nottingham, Bristol, and the Tower of London—where it was received and held by a committee of four until in 1238 it was brought to London. These provisions insured careful collection, accounting, and assembling at London, but none of them assured any control over the king in his expenditure. Now the tone of the criticism of the barons indicated that they desired the king to heed the advice of his barons. This was felt by Henry III, for he declared that he would spend nothing without the approval of the legate Otto—in appearance intended as a concession to the barons. Moreover, the provision that the three committees of four officials should receive the cash and rolls in the three castles looks like a pretense at imitation of the control exercised by the bishops of Bath and Salisbury, a substitute for baronial advisers promised or at least suggested in the council that granted the thirtieth. The measures however did not restrain Henry's outlay, although he had in hand still at least £800 of the thirtieth.[236] But his request for an additional aid in 1242 brought forth the complaint that in 1237 he had promised of his own free will and by the advice of all the baronage that the thirtieth should

233. *Close rolls, 1234–1237*, p. 189.
234. *Book of fees*, I, 407, 418, 421, 424, 427; II, 1470.
235. Paris, *Chronica maiora*, III, 382.
236. *Calendar of patent rolls, 1232–1247*, p. 281.

be stored in castles under the care of four magnates, William de Warenne and three others, and that it should be spent by their view and counsel to the advantage of the king and kingdom when necessary.[237] Whether or not the king had definitely made such a promise, the barons felt in 1242 that he had done so and that only in this way could expenditure be judicious. Thus the device originally employed by royal officials to supplement the work of the exchequer now was regarded as a means by which the magnates could control expenditure. The period from 1225 to 1242 therefore laid the ground for a dispute between the king and his barons over two interrelated points: the right to refuse an aid and the right to exercise some control over revenue by the supervision of expenditures by a baronial committee. After Henry III's return from Gascony the barons advanced to new ground; the demand for the appointment of magnates to the offices of chancellor, justiciar, and treasurer. This demand was connected with the hostility to Henry's Poitevin advisers and led up to the Provisions of Oxford and later to the final triumph of the king.

The central committee of 1269 partook of the nature of the committees of 1237 and of 1225. In composition it was like that of 1237, for it was composed of an experienced clerk of the wardrobe and the treasurers of the Hospitalers and the Templars—men who could not adopt an independent attitude toward the king as could the committee of 1225. It was a body of administrative officials and financiers. It was like the committee of 1225 in that it retained control of the proceeds of the twentieth for a long time and paid them out on the receipt of orders from the council. The effort of the barons to turn the composition of the central committee to their own advantage had failed. Nevertheless, Henry III administered the receipts in accordance with the general desire. As far as we know it was nearly all spent on the crusade, and although Henry III did not go, his two sons, Edward and Edmund, were the leaders. Hence, no complaint was made about the diversion of the tax from its original purpose.

There were acts which the custodians could not perform. They could not of their own authority spend any of the money of which they were wardens but paid it out only on the receipts of writs from the king or the council.[238] When in 1225 we find that the bishops

237. Paris, *Chronica maiora*, IV, 186.
238. *Rot. claus.*, I, 89b. *Calendar of close rolls, 1272-1279*, p. 220. Vincent, *Lancashire lay subsidies*, I, 102.

THE CENTRAL ORGANIZATION 61

of Bath and Salisbury ordered payments to be made out of the fifteenth, we must recall that they were barons of the exchequer and members of the council as well as custodians of the fifteenth. Even such petty obligations as wages to the tellers and other minor officials or any expenses connected with the administration of the tax could not be discharged without a writ from the council.[239] The custodians had no control over the local collectors. All the orders to the latter to render their accounts, to collect from some property holders, or to exempt others, issued from the council, the chancery, or the exchequer. They had no authority to allow a taxpayer to substitute a fine for an assessed valuation of his property or to assess and collect the tax on his own lands in any way different from that provided in the general regulations.[240] All this sort of executive work was retained by the exchequer or the council. The powers of these boards were thus restricted to certain financial duties.

The question may be immediately raised whether these men were not after all only keepers of the king's treasure of whom he had many in the various strong places throughout the kingdom. No one has ever described the duties of keepers, but it is certain that the central boards did not receive sealed bags containing treasure and merely guard them till the orders were received to turn them over to the exchequer or the wardrobe. The difference between their duties and those of a warden of a castle with reference to these receipts may be seen in the command issued to the warden of the Tower of London in 1232 when no such central board was created. He was directed to pay the treasury the money of the fortieth as it had been delivered to him under the seals of the collectors.[241] All of the fifteenth, the fortieth, and the thirtieth were to be stored temporarily under the seals of the county collectors and the sheriff till it should be sent to the central treasury. If these had been the only duties of the central body, there would have been no need of rolls, scales, and other paraphernalia of the treasury such as were mentioned above. In these boards we see the modification of the methods of accounting by which the work of the exchequer was reduced. The special boards received the cash, certified the accuracy of the rolls of collection, and discharged the county collectors. The latter no longer had to appear at the exchequer of account except for arrears. This body compared the rolls of collection of each vill with

239. *Patent rolls, 1225–1232*, p. 92. *Calendar of liberate rolls, 1226–1240*, p. 314.
240. *Calendar of patent rolls, 1266–1272*, pp. 369, 543.
241. Madox, *History of the exchequer*, I, 269.

62   TAXATION IN MEDIEVAL ENGLAND

the rolls of assessment and summoned collectors to collect the arrears and present such sums to the regular exchequer of receipt and account.

Let us pursue briefly the course of this development into the reign of Edward I. In 1275 much of the fifteenth was received by Giles de Audenarde and by Italian merchants who were royal creditors.[242] The thirtieth of 1283 was in part paid into the wardrobe and in part to Luccan bankers, and the later taxes on movables were all paid directly into the exchequer or the wardrobe that had developed to such a degree that they could handle the receipt efficiently.[243] The special boards therefore disappeared. Although they had handled immense sums of money, they did not become a permanent part of the financial organization. The cause for their disappearance lay in the fact that they had been called into existence for a single tax; after its collection and disbursement these officials resumed their ordinary duties. The exchequer and the wardrobe were in continuous session and finally expanded so that they became able to administer the receipt of the new taxes. The significance of these boards lies in the experience gained by royal officials and their adaptability to more complex financial conditions. Their history affords evidence of the flexibility of the Anglo-Norman state.

242. Vincent, *Lancashire lay subsidies*, I, 159.
243. *Ibid.*, pp. 169, 170, 179, 180. Tout, *Chapters in administrative history*, II, 114.

II

THE LOCAL MACHINERY OF TAXATION

ALTHOUGH the government gained experience in dealing with financial problems, no new permanent branch of the central organization was created. The local devices which it employed had more specific and more important results. A novel and permanent plan was evolved for assessing property: a new method was discovered to draw property holders into the ranks of governmental officials; and a new and unintended but nevertheless powerful attack was delivered against the political power which each lord exercised over his tenants. The jury was constantly used in connection with many of these taxes. Its close connection with taxation may also have played a part in the introduction of the representative principle into government. We are here however concerned with administration and shall pay no attention to the history of representative assemblies.

In 1272 at the close of the reign of Henry III the government, which a century earlier had been groping for a method of assessing and collecting a tax on personal property, now understood how it could be done and had devised a rather effective organization.

This local machinery had been employed so often before by the Anglo-Norman kings in both financial and judicial business that one hardly realizes that any problem of adjustment existed. As early as the *Domesday Book*, it had been employed on a grand scale. The king appointed commissioners to represent him in various localities before whom appeared groups or individual persons that swore to certain facts. This was one of the governmental devices brought by the Normans to England. In the form the organization finally assumed in the thirteenth century it consisted of two parts: first, a body of appointed commissioners who had general charge of the assessment and collection of the tax throughout the whole country; and second, a body of men elected or appointed in each vill to assess and collect the tax there. For nearly a century experimenting went on in the levy of about a dozen taxes before this form was finally adopted with modifications of the general outline. The reasons for the experiments were that the levies were believed to be inaccurate, incomplete, and dilatory and perhaps that the subordinate officials and barons lined their own purses with profits.

One feature of the new system was employed almost from the start and was never changed: the appointment of a body of county commissioners or taxers (usually appointed by the central government) to supervise the levy in each shire.

If we start with the papal levy of 1184 we find that two men were appointed to direct the levy in each bishopric, a Templar and a Hospitaler.[1] The Angevin government had nothing to do with its assessment and collection. Ecclesiastical as well as English governmental precedent therefore favored the appointment of a general committee to have charge of the levy of a tax within each large subdivision of the realm. If such a tax was really levied in 1184, the procedure may have affected later methods; the English government may well have been partly guided in its choice of means by the example of the church. That influence may possibly be seen in the fact that each local committee to levy the Saladin tithe in 1188 included a Templar and a Hospitaler. The choice of the members of these orders would, however, be natural inasmuch as the Saladin tithe was a tax for the relief of the Holy Land to whose service those orders were especially dedicated. Notice that part of the fortieth of 1201 for the aid of the Holy Land was to be carried by these orders to Palestine.[2] Ecclesiastical as well as English precedent therefore favored the appointment of a group to have charge of the levy of a tax within each subdivision of the realm.

The use of such commissioners is clearly seen in the levy of the Saladin tithe. Benedict of Peterborough has preserved the ordinance regulating the plan of assessment.[3] He states that in each parish the assessment was to be made by the following men: the priest of the parish, and the dean, a Templar, a Hospitaler, a sergeant and a clerk of the baron, and a clerk of the bishop. The last member of this list of officials and the statement that the tax was to be collected by parishes [4] suggests that the bishopric and not the shire formed the local district of assessment. Bearing these points in mind, the list of assessors thus will fall naturally into two categories. The Templar, the Hospitaler, the sergeant and the clerk of the king, and the clerk of the bishop form one group. They would

1. *Munimenta gildhallae Londoniensis,* ed. H. T. Riley (Rolls series), II, 654.
2. *Rot. pat.,* p. 5.
3. William Stubbs, *Select charters,* p. 160.
4. *Ibid.*

THE LOCAL MACHINERY OF TAXATION   65

constitute the royal commissioners to the bishopric, who would act throughout the whole area. The priest, the dean, and the sergeant and clerk of the baron would form a group that would act within a much smaller area, a parish or a small group of parishes. The composition of the body of royal commissioners in this case differs from that employed in the later taxes on personal property, but the principle of composition is the same.

The writs for the assessment of the ransom of King Richard I are not extant, but some information concerning the assessors can be gleaned from the curia regis rolls of 1194. These preserve the results of an inquest into the aids in Wiltshire. The jurors of Longbridge told the justices that the aid of the fourth on personal property and revenue in their hundred had been paid to four knights of the county, Robert Gild, Roger Fitz Everard, and two others. From the reports of other hundreds one can find the names of two or more other knights.[5] The phrase, "knights of the county" (*milites comitatus*) suggests the body of commissioners delegated to work throughout the whole shire. The hidage levied for the ransom was also assessed by a group in each county.[6]

The carucage of 1198 was also assessed in each county by a centrally appointed group consisting of a knight and a clerk who were reinforced by knights elected in the county court.[7] Concerning the carucage of 1200 and the seventh of 1203 our information is scanty, and nothing for or against such machinery has been preserved. The employment of a local committee representing the government is also seen in the fifteenth on merchants. In this case it is not a county committee, for the tax was just collected in the ports, so that each port had such a committee.[8]

But when we arrive at the thirteenth of 1207, the committee to assess the tax in each shire again appears.[9] Under Henry III it was uniformly employed. In 1217 such a device was used, though perhaps the unsettled conditions of that year threw most of the business into the hands of political and military leaders like the sheriffs.[10] In 1220 the carucage and in 1225, 1232, and 1237 the taxes on movables all employed it.[11] In 1235 the aid on fees held by military tenure to marry the king's sister was curiously enough to

5. *Three rolls of the king's court*, pp. 88, 90, 95, 98, 106.
6. Thomas Madox, *History of the exchequer*, p. 412.
7. Roger of Howden, IV, 46.
8. *Rot. pat.*, p. 42.
9. *Ibid.*, p. 72b.
10. *Rot. claus.*, I, 306, 307.
11. Stubbs, *Select charters*, pp. 352, 355, 360, 366.

be collected by a committee of two in each county—curiously because such a levy was conventionally collected by the sheriff or paid directly by the debtors to the exchequer or one of its branches.[12] The change in procedure certainly reflects growth of administrative organization. But it was only an indication of change for later aids on knights' fees of the same kind were collected in the customary way.[13] Finally in 1269 the twentieth of that year was assessed and collected by two knights elected in each county.[14]

These county commissioners must be viewed as part of the administrative organization that was taking shape. In the twelfth century we find that the sheriffs were coming more and more from the class of "curial officials," [15] from among small tenants in chief, or from rear vassals whose power as administrators depended more and more upon the royal authority and less upon their own wealth and personal influence within their own shire.[16] They have become the heads of a local administrative body; there was also a sheriff's roll.[17] Besides such officials there appeared in the twelfth century special commissioners, or missi, occasionally employed by the king to investigate some matter in which he was interested; a little later he allowed them to investigate a case in which a subject was concerned. Under Henry II the sporadic missi became the itinerant justices with the whole realm divided into circuits. They were in full swing in 1164, at the time of the assize of Clarendon, with both judicial and administrative functions, their powers being only limited by the necessities of the moment. The expansion of royal business is reflected by a further development under Richard I and John. Groups of special commissioners were appointed, no longer to execute a variety of tasks, executive, financial, and judicial, throughout the counties, but to discharge a single commission such as to levy a tallage in a single county, to hold a single case of the petty assizes, to perambulate a specific forest, and so on. To be sure this is the way in which the missi began to function in England at some time after the Norman Conquest; perhaps they had always continued to officiate thus. Nevertheless it remains true that we have from now on two kinds of missi, the itinerant justices who covered

12. *Ibid.*, p. 364.
13. Pipe rolls 29 and 37 Henry III, Public Record Office.
14. D. Wilkins, *Concilia Magnae Britanniae et Hiberniae* (London, 1737), II, 21.
15. W. A. Morris, *The mediaeval English sheriff* (Manchester, 1927), p. 114.
16. *Ibid.*, p. 143.
17. *Ibid.*, p. 115. George E. Woodbine, "County court rolls and county court records," *Harvard law review*, XLVIII (1929–30), 1095.

THE LOCAL MACHINERY OF TAXATION 67

an area handling a variety of business and the group sent out for a single task. So the employment of the missi to direct a specific task continued. The introduction of the taxes on personal property and those on land like the carucage stimulated the development. In order to levy the carucage the number of carucates had to be ascertained; in order to assess movables it was necessary to discover their amount or value, or both. Nothing would be more "natural" than to appoint in each county a group of commissioners representing the king as had often been done in connection with other matters. Such officials were delegated at one time and acted throughout the realm at the same time in the same way. They therefore impressed the chroniclers in striking and dramatic manner as did the barons of the Domesday survey.[18] Hence almost all the taxes of this kind are noted by some of the chroniclers. These commissioners represent the evolution of the administration in the twelfth and thirteenth centuries; such indeed is their primary significance. They grew naturally and logically out of the necessities of administration and out of groups and devices already habitual. Let us put it another way: they represent the adjustment of society to a new condition—taxation. They were employed in two taxes in the reign of Henry II (1184, 1188); in two in the reign of Richard I (the ransom and the carucage of 1198); in two of John's reign (the fifteenth of merchants and the thirteenth of 1207); and in seven of the reign of Henry III (the carucages of 1217 and 1220, the taxes on movables of 1225, 1232, 1237, 1269, and the aid on knights' fees of 1235), thirteen taxes in all. In four taxes we have no means of knowing whether or not they were employed (the carucage of 1200, the seventh of 1203, the aid for the titular king of Jerusalem in 1222, and the aid on the clergy in 1224, called a carucage). That is, the employment of the county commissioners was a convention by the close of the reign of Henry III in case of taxation.

We should also remember the tallagers as examples of commissioners appointed to assess and collect taxes. They were special commissioners who covered several counties, appointed from among men that were regularly engaged upon administrative tasks of the royal government, in fact forming part of the professional personnel of the central administration. Hence they were more like itinerant justices than were the missi discussed above in that they were all the time engaged upon the king's business. The county knights were not so professional a group, but from time to time,

18. Stubbs, *Select charters*, pp. 134, 160, 256, 272, 273.

as need arose, they were drawn into the ranks of administrative officials, to act as justices in a suit, to perambulate a forest, to supervise the sale of fallen wood, and other similar tasks. Their primary business in life was not that of administrative officials.

Although nine (if we include the aid of 1184) taxes of the new sort were levied in the period ending with the death of John, we have not much specific information concerning the composition of the county boards apart from the general descriptions in the writs. We would like to consider the names of those employed before 1215 to discover if possible whether the composition of the county boards differed before and after that date and whether the government of Richard and John, increasingly absolutist, differed in its choice of commissioners from that of the period of the supremacy of Hubert de Burgh and the barons and also from that of the period when Henry III himself ruled. While abundant material has survived on this point from Henry III's reign, chance has preserved the names of only a few members of these county boards from the period prior to 1215. Under Richard I the names of the members of four or five commissions have survived and three from the reign of John. But we are further handicapped before 1201, for the chancery rolls begin with John, and consequently evidence concerning the parts played by these officials under Richard is peculiarly scanty. We may find that they were knights or clerks, and if laymen, not all tenants in chief. We should like to know in addition to their position in the landed hierarchy whether they were often called upon to act as royal officials. The four knights of the county in Wilts that seem to have received the aid for Richard's ransom in 1194 were Robert Gild, Roger Fitz Everard and "*alii duo*," who seem to have been Walter Giffard and Robert Gynet.[19] We can find little concerning any of these officials under Richard. John le Poer was one of the two assessors of the hidage of 1193 in Worcestershire and held two fees of the bishop of Worcester in that county.[20] Nicholas de Meriet was assessor and collector of the same levy in the counties of Dorset and Somerset. He held 1½ fees in Somersetshire.[21] Robert Gerebut, one of the receivers of the aid in Wilts, was one of the tallagers in that same county in 1197 and one who bore this name was an itinerant justice in Dorsetshire that same year.[22]

19. *Three rolls of the king's court*, pp. 83, 88, 90, 95, 98, 106.
20. *Book of fees*, I, 36; II, 1208–1209.
21. *Pipe roll 9 Richard I*, p. 138. *Book of fees*, I, 86, 96.
22. *Pipe roll 9 Richard I*, pp. 136, 215.

THE LOCAL MACHINERY OF TAXATION 69

Ralph Fitz Stephen, who received part of the aid in the hundred of Malmesbury, was constable of Malmesbury castle.[23] Alexander, dean of Wells, and Adam de Grenvill, two of the five assessors of the hidage of 1194 in Dorsetshire and Somersetshire also belonged to the group that tallaged those shires in 1196.[24] Nicholas de Meriet, who held 2½ fees in those shires, was also one of the group that assessed that hidage.[25] Master John of Bridport and his associates received the hidage of Cumberland.[26]

From John's reign more abundant information comes concerning the commissioners of the thirteenth of 1207. From the chancery rolls we can discern more clearly the positions and careers of the county assessors in the three shires of Lincoln, Gloucester, and Warwick. All, or nearly all, of these justices, as they are called, were landholders or churchmen in the county to which they were assigned in connection with the thirteenth and hence had personal knowledge of men and conditions there.

In Gloucestershire there were six justices—Robert de Berkeley, William de Falaise, Adam Fitz Nigel, Walter de Aura, Master Robert of Gloucester, and Richard de Mucegros.[27] Robert de Berkeley held the barony of Berkeley for 5 fees.[28] William de Falaise held ¾ fee of the honor of Gloucester.[29] Adam Fitz Nigel held ⅕ of a fee of the same honor.[30] Walter de Aura was a landowner of some position in Gloucestershire.[31] Master Robert of Gloucester was one of King John's favorite clerks.[32] Richard de Mucegros was a landholder in the shire.[33]

In Lincolnshire there were fourteen justices. Robert de Percy was the head of a cadet branch of that great house and held lands from the senior line. Simon de Kyme held a small fief *in capite* and some 30 mesnie fees of which 15 were held of the earl of Chester.[34] William de Cornhill was a member of the great London merchant family of that name and one of King John's most trusted clerks.

23. *Three rolls of the king's court*, p. 78.
24. *Pipe roll 8 Richard I*, p. 220.
25. *Ibid.*, p. 222. *Pipe roll 6 Richard I*, p. 193.
26. *Pipe roll 10 Richard I*, p. 142.
27. *Rot. pat.*, p. 72b.
28. *Pipe roll 3 John*, p. 43. *Book of fees*, I, 50.
29. *Pipe roll 3 John*, p. 56.
30. *Ibid.*
31. *Rot. oblatis*, p. 342.
32. *Rot. claus.*, I, 93. He was a protégé of John de Gray, bishop of Norwich.
33. *Rot. oblatis*, p. 294.
34. William Farrer, *Honors and knights' fees* (London, 1924), II, 122-125.

Alexander de Pointon was a tenant of the honor of Richmond. Fulk de Oiri held small fiefs of the Aincourt barony and of the count of Aumale and was the latter's seneschal.[35] Jollan de Nevill had been given a small but valuable fief by King Richard.[36] Simon de Driby held $1\frac{1}{3}$ fees of Gilbert de Ghent and $1\frac{1}{6}$ fees of Robert de Tateshall.[37] Eustace de Leadenham held $\frac{1}{4}$ fee of the honor of Richmond.[38] Walter de Pincebec had 2 fees of the honor of Craon.[39] Peter de Beckerings, Roger de Stikeswald, and Andrew de Witton were also landholders.[40] The other two justices are unidentifiable.

In Warwickshire and Leicestershire Robert de Roppeley and John de Witing were appointed to correct the mistakes of the first assessment. Robert had married one of the heiresses of the barony of Limesi and was a vassal of William de Albini of Belvoir.[41]

Only three of the members of these three commissions were tenants in chief and only two of them of any consequence; even these were not among the chief barons of the county, except perhaps Robert de Berkeley. Yet almost without exception the commissioners were landholders in the shire to which they were appointed justices and in general their chief lands lay in that county. This cannot be chance; it must have been deliberate. Thus the direction of the levy of these taxes lay in the hands of the lesser landholders and primarily of the rear vassals of each shire. But there is another characteristic of these commissioners that must be noted: many, perhaps all, of these county commissioners had held other office under John in the county to which they were now appointed as assessors of the thirteenth. They had acted as wardens of castles, custodians of lands in hand, tallagers, and the like. The justices were therefore chosen from among the ranks of the king's local administrative officials. They had already a certain experience as executives; they had demonstrated their loyalty to the king; they had broadened their knowledge of local conditions—all these things gave them qualities essential to their success in the new office.

Of the justices appointed in Gloucestershire, Richard de Mucegros was made custodian of Gloucester castle and sheriff of the county in 1207 after the assessment of the thirteenth; in 1208 he

---

35. *Book of fees*, pp. 178, 193. *Rot. pat.*, p. 41.
36. *Rotuli chartarum*, ed. T. D. Hardy (Record Commission), p. 12b.
37. *Book of fees*, I, 163, 166, 182.
38. *Ibid.*, I, 186.
39. *Ibid.*, I, 193, 195.
40. *Ibid.*, I, 179, 189. *Curia regis rolls* (Rolls series), I, 259, 322, 430; III, 225. *Rot. oblatis*, p. 589.
41. *Book of fees*, I, 102, 123, 184, 194. *Curia regis rolls*, VI, 168.

THE LOCAL MACHINERY OF TAXATION 71

was made constable of Chichester castle.[42] Appointment to such an important position surely shows that before 1207 he was known for a tried and true man. Robert de Berkeley was justice to hold an assize of novel disseizin in Gloucestershire and was a justice and a tallager in Worcestershire in 1204 and 1205.[43] William de Falaise was custodian of the honor of Gloucester from 1201 to 1208.[44] Walter de Aura was a landholder of some importance connected with the administration of the forests about this time, for in 10 John the pipe roll records that he and Walter de Huntil' owed £76 13s. 1d. of arrears of their collection of forest debts.[45] In Lincolnshire Simon de Kyme had been sheriff of that county under Richard I; in 1207 he had been sent there in company with Simon de Pattishall and the archdeacon of Stafford to deliver the gaol, hear an appeal of robbery, and all the assizes of novel disseizin; in 1201 he and Jollan de Nevill were sent to Lincoln to assess a fine of 400m. and 7 palfreys levied upon the city for having its liberties and for a breach of the peace.[46] Robert de Percy, another commissioner, was the royal official who was ordered to distrain a group of clergy in Yorkshire for debts which they owed to the king; in 1213 he was sheriff of that county; in 1208 he was one of the officials who were commanded to arrest ships in the harbors of Yorkshire. His importance may be seen from the fact that in other counties this duty was confided to men like Earl Aubrey de Vere, William de Wrotham, Gerard de Athies, and Fulk de Cantilupe.[47] Simon de Driby, another commissioner, was one of three bailiffs in charge of Lincolnshire in 1204, had been a tallager in that county in 1205, and rendered its *proficuum* in 1208.[48] Alexander de Pointon was one of two custodians of the honor of Richmond in 1204, and in 1205 one of two custodians of the lands of the archbishopric of Canterbury which lay within Lincolnshire.[49] William de Cornhill was a very active royal official; among other positions which he held was, in 1206, that of custodian of the bishopric of Lincoln.[50] Robert de Roppeley was one of two justices sent to Warwickshire to correct

---

42. *Rot. pat.*, pp. 71, 78b.
43. *Rot. oblatis*, p. 228. *Pipe roll 7 John*, p. 267.
44. *Pipe roll 3 John*, p. 54.
45. *Pipe roll 10 John*, p. 22. *Pipe roll 12 John*, m. 13, Public Record Office.
46. *Rot. claus.*, I, 83b. *Rot. oblatis*, pp. 113. Farrer, *Honors and knights' fees*, II, 122–125
47. *Rot. claus.*, I, 115. *Rot. pat.*, pp. 84, 97.
48. *Ibid.*, p. 47. *Rot. claus.*, I, 41b. *Rot. oblatis*, pp. 113, 338, 419.
49. *Rot. pat.*, p. 47. *Rot. claus.*, I, 46b.
50. *Rot. pat.*, p. 65.

the mistakes of the first assessment. He was in charge of the king's crown and jewels, held the custody of the honor of Leicester, Kenilworth castle, and of the counties of Warwick and Leicester.[51] Such were some of the men upon whom John relied for the assessment of the thirteenth. As these names have been preserved by chance, they are likely to be fairly representative of the county assessors throughout the realm. Along with such men who acted often as officials of the government appear the names of men that are hardly ever found again in the rolls, possibly men of little importance and who hence rarely served. The latter, however, would be useful perhaps in supplying an even more intimate knowledge of certain parts of the county and under the direction of the more important assessors would carry on the work of assessment quite efficiently.

If we pass to the reign of Henry III, we find abundant information concerning the county commissioners. As far as we are able to judge, there seems to be no difference between the character of the commissioners under Henry III and those employed under his father. In both reigns knights from each county formed the majority of the boards of assessors in that district. Some assessors seem to have been unimportant men for they appear only once in the patent or close rolls; others were more considerable landholders and prominent in the local administrative system of the monarchy, acting as wardens of lands in hand, as tallagers, as itinerant justices, justices of assize, forest justices, and the like. These were the men whom the Angevin monarchy employed to carry on the work of government. They had gained practical knowledge of men and of conditions in the county to which they were now sent as tax commissioners in various branches of executive and judicial work. Hence they were the very men to choose to represent the king. This knowledge was now to be of service in the evolution of a new system of taxation. This piece of taxing machinery originated therefore during the most absolutist period of the Angevin monarchy and was not at all changed by the uprising of 1215 which resulted in the Magna Carta.

Let us test our hypothesis by considering the cases of the assessors of some county chosen at random, e.g., Lincolnshire. The assessors there in 1220 for the carucage of that year were Henry de Langton and Alexander de Pointon.[52] Henry de Langton appears only once in any of the official records when he was in 1220 ap-

51. *Ibid.*, pp. 65, 68b, 72, 74, 77b.
52. Exchequer L. T. R., Memoranda roll 7 Henry III. Public Record Office.

THE LOCAL MACHINERY OF TAXATION

pointed a justice to hold an assize of novel disseizin in Lincolnshire. He was associated in this work with William de Welles, William de Willoughby, and Hervey de Arcy; as these were all landholders in Lincolnshire it seems probable that Henry was one too, especially as he was a justice in a land case there.[53] Henry de Langton was a Lincolnshire landholder, not of grand status, for he can be found only one time apart from this tax, but one who was drafted into the local administrative organization of the state for judicial as well as fiscal purposes. Alexander de Pointon was a small rear vassal in Lincolnshire who held a quarter of a knight's fee there; he may also be the tenant in the honor of Boulogne in Essex and Hertfordshire listed as holding ¼ fee in Chesterhunt. His career as a public official began under John, who gave him many tasks, especially in Lincolnshire. He may have been rewarded with these lands which he held in that shire and in Essex and Hertfordshire, and also in the counties of Warwick and Leicester, Oxford, and Hereford.[54] Thus his lands, apparently small in amount, were scattered over several shires, not as tenant in chief but as rear vassal. He was listed in 1212 as holding ¼ of a fee of Oliver de Vallibus of the honor of Craon and again in 1242 ¼ of a fee of Petronilla de Craon. His position as official however was much more important than his place in the landholding hierarchy. Indeed probably he received part of his lands as pay for his work as official and to that let us now turn. In 1200 he was already accounting for the lands of the honor of Richmond in Lincolnshire and it was in that county that his official life was pursued. In 1204 he and Peter de Lyons were appointed custodians of the honor. In 1205 he and Alexander de Reepham were appointed custodians of the lands and properties of the archbishop of Canterbury in Lincolnshire. Later in the reign we find that he has been custodian of the bishopric of Lincoln and of the barony of Gilbert Peche. In 1213 he had the custody of Lincolnshire. In 1212 he and John de Birkin had held inquests of forests of the north of England. In 1213 he, Ralph de Normanville, and Thomas de Muleton formed the group that inquired into the losses to the church and the clergy caused during the interdict in the bishopric of Lincoln.[55] In the rebellion of 1215 Alexander sided with the barons, was deprived of his lands and naturally of his

53. *Patent rolls, 1216–1225*, p. 306. *Rot. claus.*, I, 327. *Book of fees*, I, 161.
54. *Book of fees*, pp. 123, 195; II, 1002, 1010, 1089. *Rot. claus.*, I, 234b, 250b, 308b, 374.
55. *Pipe roll 2 John*, p. 87. *Rot. pat.*, pp. 48b, 65, 97. *Rot. claus.*, I, 46, 120, 123, 125, 164b.

offices too, but after the death of John he was restored to the king's allegiance.⁵⁶ After some time a career of local judicial and administrative activity began anew for this experienced executive trained in the Angevin school. In 1221 he was one of a group of five appointed by the council to take in hand the royal demesne and the escheats; the others were the sheriff of Lincolnshire, William de Welles, Thomas de Middleton, and William de Willoughby.⁵⁷ The other members were men frequently engaged in local administrative tasks. From this time on his name appears often in the rolls, acting in Lincolnshire as a local justice, holding petty assizes.⁵⁸ Thus when the council desired a man of proven administrative capacity and one familiar with conditions and men in Lincolnshire, they appointed Alexander de Pointon. So he serves in that county as assessor and collector of the fifteenth in 1225 and of the fortieth in 1232.⁵⁹

Let us now pass to the fifteenth in Lincolnshire. There were five assessors and collectors, as follows: Alexander de Pointon, Simon de Roppeley, John Coleman, Thomas de Muleton, and William de Ralegh.⁶⁰ Bear in mind that this levy represented a lot of thinking on the part of the government which before it summoned the Great Council that granted the tax had determined to try this kind of a levy. If the council had gone as far as this, we may be sure that it had discussed how the tax was to be assessed and collected. Unquestionably there was opposition to the grant, indicated especially by the reissue of the Charters with a few modifications. Although we have no detailed record of the discussion, it does not seem to have concerned the question of the county commissioners, for they include the same sort of men as before.

Thus Alexander de Pointon, whom we have already discussed, an experienced and trusted local official, formed one member of the board. Simon de Roppeley was small tenant in Lincolnshire. In 1242 he is reported to have held 1¼ fees of the old enfeoffment of the heirs of William de Albini in Lincolnshire, and one fee of Roesia de Verdun and she of Earl William de Ferrers and he of the king. The *Red Book* gives a Simon de Roppeley as holding three knights in Leicestershire of William de Albini Brito in 1166.⁶¹ He therefore

56. *Ibid.*, pp. 234b, 241b, 250b, 308b, 374b.
57. *Ibid.*, p. 471b.
58. *Patent rolls, 1216-1225*, pp. 391, 398, 409. *Ibid., 1225-1232, passim.*
59. *Rot. claus.*, II, 146b. *Close rolls, 1231-1234*, p. 158.
60. *Patent rolls, 1216-1225*, p. 561.
61. *Book of fees*, I, 518, 522, 594; II, 954, 1027, 1037, 1091. *The red book of the exchequer*, ed. Hubert Hall (Rolls series), I, 328.

THE LOCAL MACHINERY OF TAXATION   75

had land in at least two shires as a rear vassal. As a landholder he was not important. But in 1223 he begins to appear as a local official or justice, when he was appointed to hear an assize of novel disseizin in Lincolnshire with Alexander de Pointon, Osbert de Bobi, and Ralph de Diva.[62] In the autumn of 1225 we find him hearing and determining pleas in that shire with Jordan de Esseby, Ralph Fitz Reginald, and John Gubaud, and in 1227 he was appointed one of three tallagers (the others being Henry de Walpole and the sheriff) in Lincolnshire.[63] During the period 1227-29 he and William de Welles with others were appointed to such jobs.[64] Thus he was a dependable local judicial and administrative official who comes into view a little before 1225 and continues for twenty years.

The third assessor and collector was Thomas de Muleton. Thomas had married the widow of Richard de Lucy of Egremont in Cumberland and had married his two sons to Richard's two daughters. He was thus the chief baron of Cumberland. Otherwise he was a minor mesnie tenant with a fee of the honor of Lancaster in Suffolk and one of the honor of Richmond in Lincolnshire.[65] He was also a tried servant of the crown. He began his career in 1205 as sheriff of Lincolnshire.[66] In 1212 he, with Simon de Kyme, was the confidential messenger conveying 1,000m. from the Temple to the king.[67] The following year he with Ralph de Normanville and Alexander de Pointon was designated to appraise the losses suffered by the bishopric of Lincoln during the interdict.[68] In 1214 he went over to France on the campaign.[69] He sided with the barons against John and returned to allegiance in 1217.[70] His career as a public official continued under Henry III. He was an itinerant justice in Cumberland, Westmoreland, and Lancashire in 1218, justice to hold inquests into the forests in Cumberland, custodian of the forest in that county in 1219, inquisitor into the forests in Yorkshire, Cumberland, and Northumberland in 1219 with John Marshal, Philip de Ulecot, Adam de Newmarket, and Ely Brito,

62. *Patent rolls, 1216-1225*, p. 409.
63. *Patent rolls, 1225-1232*, pp. 71, 72. *Rot. claus.*, II, 209.
64. *Patent rolls, 1225-1232*, pp. 156, 159, 166, 208, 209, 212, 213, 293, 301, 303.
65. *Red book of the exchequer*, II, 519, 590. *Book of fees*, I, 193, 195, 266, 597; II, 1236.
66. *Rot. pat.*, p. 57.
67. *Rot. claus.*, I, 124b.
68. *Ibid.*, p. 164b.
69. *Ibid.*, p. 201.
70. *Ibid.*, pp. 313b, 317b, 374.

clerk. This was a general inquiry throughout the realm.[71] His activities were not confined to Lincolnshire; he was one of the general officials of the administration who might go anywhere, as may be seen above. With others he was appointed to hold various of the petty assizes: in Lincolnshire in 1222, also in 1223; in Westmoreland in 1223; in Lincolnshire in 1229; in Yorkshire in 1232.[72] He was also custodian of the Boston fair in 1226.[73] In 1226 he joined with the sheriff of Gloucester and Ralph Fitz Nicholas to determine the division of lands between Reginald de Braose and John de Braose. He and Robert de Lexington were appointed justices of gaol delivery at Wallingford in 1228. These two with their associates were to examine the weirs in the Severn in Shropshire in 1227. He and William de London were appointed to hear and determine all pleas remaining untried in the liberty of Gilbert, earl of Gloucester and Hertford, since the preceding eyre of justices in Kent. In 1230 he was given custody of the castle of Miserden. That same year he and John Gubaud were wardens of the coasts of Lincolnshire. He was justice of gaol delivery at York in 1232 with William de Cunstable, Gilbert de Aton, and William Buscel.[74] In 1232 he was appointed sheriff of Cumberland.[75] Moreover he seems to have been a member of the king's council. In 1224 the letters patent issued to the clergy show that their grant of a carucage toward the expenses of the campaign against the castle of Bedford was witnessed by Hubert de Burgh, William, earl of Salisbury, and, among others, by Thomas de Muleton.[76] An exchange of words between the bishop of Durham and the king was also witnessed by Thomas de Muleton in 1225. He was custodian of the honor of Richmond in Lincolnshire in 1224, an itinerant justice in Northumberland with the abbot of Whitby, Martin de Pattishall, Peter de Bruce, and William de Tameton in 1226.[77] He was itinerant justice in Lancashire the same year with John de Lacy, constable of Chester, Martin de Pattishall, Ranulf Fitz Robert, and Brian Fitz Alan, and in Yorkshire in the same year with Robert de Vieuxpont, Martin de Pattishall, John Fitz Robert, Brian de L'Isle, and Henry

---

71. *Patent rolls, 1216–1225*, pp. 208, 218, 325. *Rot. claus.*, I, 434b, 513.
72. *Patent rolls, 1216–1225*, pp. 347, 391, 410. *Ibid., 1225–1232*, pp. 290, 516, 517.
73. *Ibid.*, p. 40.
74. *Ibid.*, pp. 90, 163, 223, 292, 349, 364, 518.
75. *Ibid., 1232–1247*, p. 8.
76. *Ibid., 1216–1225*, p. 465.
77. *Ibid., 1225–1232*, pp. 70, 173. *Rot. claus.*, II, 4, 151b.

THE LOCAL MACHINERY OF TAXATION 77

de Braibroc.[78] In 1226 he was a tallager in Norfolk with three others, and in 1227 again a tallager in the county of Somerset with Robert de Lexington and the sheriff. He was itinerant justice to entertain complaints in Hereford, Shropshire, Staffordshire, Devon, Hants, and Berks in 1227 with Robert de Lexington, Maurice de Ghent, and Ralph Musard.[79] This list of the activities of this official is not exhaustive, but it is obvious that in him we see an experienced official in whom the government had confidence both under John and Henry III. Such a one was assessor and collector of the fifteenth in Lincolnshire in 1225.

The fourth commissioner was William de Ralegh. He was frequently appointed for various official tasks. He was at one time a member of the king's council, not of course before 1225. He was treasurer of the bishopric of Exeter.[80] He was appointed sheriff of Devonshire in October, 1225, was assessor of the tallage of 1227 in Cumberland with Richard Duket and William de L'Isle, and in Northumberland with these two and William de Bayeux added, and was justice of various assizes in different counties.[81] In 1229 he was appointed with Stephen de Segrave and William de London as justice *ad omnia placita* in Essex. His increased importance is shown by the fact that in 1231 he was appointed justice of assize of novel disseizin in Gloucestershire with those "whom he will associate with him." [82] He was therefore a justice and an administrative official and a councilor from the time of his appointment as assessor of the fifteenth. I conclude that this distinction was merely coincident with his work as tax assessor and collector, that he must have to a certain degree trained before, or he would not have been deemed worthy to be made sheriff of Devon in October, 1225.

The last member of the board of assessors and collectors for this county was John Coleman, the least distinguished of the group. He was a rear vassal in Lincolnshire, holding 1½ fees of William de Vescy.[83] He appears for the first time as a justice to hold an assize of novel disseizin in Lincoln in 1223 with three other justices. Dur-

78. *Ibid.*, p. 151b.
79. *Ibid.*, pp. 158, 204, 208b, 213.
80. *Calendar of charter rolls, 1226–1257*, pp. 192, 193, 217, 220, 237, 243. *Calendar of liberate rolls, 1226–1240*, pp. 332, 363.
81. *Patent rolls, 1216–1225*, p. 554. *Ibid., 1225–1232*, pp. 71, 74, 293, 294, 297, 355, 367, 446. *Rot. claus.*, II, 208b.
82. *Patent rolls, 1225–1232*, pp. 302, 447, 508, 509.
83. *Book of fees*, II, 1026, 1040, 1086. He was an agent of Eustace de Vesci in 1213. *Rot. claus.*, I, 146 (editor).

ing the period from 1223 to 1231 he occasionally acted as justice of special cases of the petty assizes in Lincolnshire. He was associated in this work with Simon de Roppeley, Jordan de Esseby, Alexander de Pointon, Baldwin de Paunton, Gerard de Huwell, Theobald de Hautein, Hugo de Humby, Ralph de Trihampton, William de Land, Hugh le Breton, and William Fitz Robert.[84]

These commissioners were rear vassals and some were very important royal officials. All from time to time served as royal officials in Lincolnshire. Two clerks accompanied this body of county commissioners: John de Colemerand and Martin de Cybecay. John had long been a clerk in the royal service, and he retained an important position and a trusted one, for in 1230 he was custodian of wines which he had sold to the value of over £70.[85] Thus, though trusted, dependable and capable, he seems to have been in a subordinate position as far as the assessment and collection were concerned.

We now pass to the fortieth of 1232 and the following men served as assessors and collectors in Lincolnshire: Simon de Roppeley, Alexander de Pointon, William de Welles, Walter Bec, John de Bractoft, and Henry le Moine. Alexander and Simon we have already shown to have been experienced and dependable officials. William de Welles held in 1219 ¾ of a fee of the honor of Richmond in Lincolnshire. He had often been designated for official business within Lincolnshire as justice of various assizes beginning in 1220. In 1230 he was delegated with the sheriff of Lincolnshire to seize all ships in that county fit for the king's service for the expedition to France in the spring of that year.[86]

Walter Bec was a vassal of the bishop of Durham in Lincolnshire and also a vassal of the earl of Chester. He appears once in our rolls as a justice of assize of novel disseizin in Lincolnshire with Warner Engayne, Robert de Driby, and Alexander de Pointon in 1230.[87]

The two assessors and collectors in Holland in Lincolnshire are most difficult to find in the rolls. John de Bractoft does not appear in either the *Book of Fees* or the *Red Book*. He was a special justice of assize twice, was commissioned as a special justice to inquire into various levies (*prisis et toltis*) in the land of the abbot of Peter-

84. *Patent rolls, 1216–1225,* p. 397. *Ibid., 1225–1232,* pp. 206, 220, 281, 297, 352, 444.
85. *Ibid.,* pp. 415–417. *Rot. pat.,* p. 197b.
86. *Rot. claus.,* I, 385b, 404b, II, 77. *Patent rolls, 1216–1225,* pp. 306, 307, 347, 391. *Patent rolls, 1225–1232,* pp. 5, 155, 156, 159, 166, 201, 209, 212, 213, 288, 290, 293, 296, 301, 303, 306, 349, 356, 515, 523. *Close rolls, 1227–1231,* p. 387.
87. *Ibid., 1231–1234,* p. 264. *Patent rolls, 1225–1232,* p. 357. *Book of fees,* II, 1023, 1053, 1026, 1080.

THE LOCAL MACHINERY OF TAXATION 79

borough in Lincolnshire with Hugh de Harington and Alexander de Sleaford. In 1227 he was one of the knights who witnessed a chirograph by which the bishop of Lincoln rented land from a lord for a period of years, and in 1237 he was one of the assessors and collectors of the thirtieth in Lincolnshire in Holland.[88] He was thus a knight who was a rear vassal. Henry le Moine, also an assessor in Holland, was also assessor and collector of the thirtieth in 1237, but beyond this I have found no other mention of him in the rolls.

Let us now pass to the aid on knights' fees in 1235, assessed and collected in Lincolnshire by Jollan de Nevill and William de Bayeux. Jollan held two fees of the honor of Richmond, one in Lincolnshire and the other in Nottinghamshire, and some other small portions of fees as a rear vassal.[89] He was appointed an itinerant justice with Robert de Ros, William de Eboraco, Roger Bertram, and Adam de Newmarket in Yorkshire and Northumberland in 1234. In 1241 he was a justice to inquire into royal castles in Lincolnshire with Simon de Roppeley, William de Welles, old hands, and Guy Wake. In 1244 he was a justice to hold assizes of novel disseizin in Lincolnshire, and in 1245 he was appointed to hold common pleas in Norfolk and Suffolk with three other justices.[90] These references to his position after 1235 merely show the general official capacity of the man. He however was appointed in 1235 undoubtedly because he was a knight and because he had enjoyed some administrative experience. He continued to deserve the confidence of the government.

William de Bayeux had one fee in Bucks in 1235.[91] Although he does not appear as a local administrative official in the decade of the thirties, it is not an indication that he was insignificant, for he had been a coroner in 1230 and had therefore been exempted from assizes, juries, and suits of counties. He stands thus for a knight experienced in local administration. He held ½ of a fee in Lincolnshire in the wapentake of Walscroft and with John de Cotesm a whole fee in the wapentake of Ludhesk.[92]

We may now pass to the aid of 1237. The assessors and collectors in Lincolnshire were Norman de Arcy, William de Rowell, Hugh de Harington, William de Welles, Warner Engayne, and the clerk was

88. *Patent rolls, 1225–1232*, pp. 351, 515. *Calendar of charter rolls, 1226–1257*, p. 63. *Close rolls, 1234–1237*, p. 550.
89. *Book of fees*, I, 548; II, 1020, 1074, 1087. *Close rolls, 1227–1231*, p. 342.
90. *Calendar of patent rolls, 1232–1247*, pp. 78, 462. *Close rolls, 1237–1242*, p. 346.
91. *Book of fees*, I, 465; II, 892.
92. *Close rolls, 1227–1231*, p. 357. *Book of fees*, II, 1017, 1080, 1083, 1087.

Thomas de Askeby.[93] William de Welles we have already discussed in connection with the aid of 1232, where we showed that he had been an experienced official. Norman de Arcy was a great baron in the county with 20 fees.[94] He had been appointed itinerant justice in Lincolnshire in 1234 with the earl of Lincoln, William de Eboraco, Robert de Ros, and the abbot of Bardny, but he did not serve as county commissioner, for the name was changed to William de Rowell. William de Rowell held, in 1212, 1 fee, ⅔ fee, and 2 fees in Lincolnshire as a rear vassal. He was employed in local royal administration, being keeper of the escheats in Lincolnshire in 1232 with Simon de Roppeley.[95]

Hugh de Harington held two fees in Lincolnshire of the bishop of Durham and other scattered small pieces as a rear vassal in that county. He was a coroner in Lincolnshire in 1235 and in 1242 was appointed to swear arms in Lincolnshire and keep the peace with Robert de Tateshall and Hugh Fitz Ralph.[96]

Warner Engayne held various pieces of land of the honor of Richmond in Lincolnshire. He was thus a rear vassal, but he held many administrative positions under Henry III, not in Lincolnshire alone but throughout England. He was the bailiff of Peter, count of Brittany, custodian of part of the coast of the realm, custodian with Walter de Burgh in 1236 and 1237 of the royal demesnes. In 1241 he was tallager of the royal demesne in Nottingham and Derbyshire.[97] He was thus a man of experience well fitted to supervise the levy of the thirtieth in Lincolnshire.

In Kesteven, the assessors and collectors of the thirtieth were Simon de Roppeley, Richard Duket, Gerard de Huwell, who upon his death was succeeded by William de Beningworth. Simon we have already shown was an experienced official. Richard Duket held land as a rear vassal in small patches in Lincolnshire and in Kent. He was one of the king's envoys to Ireland in 1233, a witness to Henry III's agreement with Hubert de Burgh in 1232, a tallager with John Gubaud in the counties of Northampton, Bucks and

---

93. *Close rolls, 1234–1237*, p. 549.
94. *Book of fees*, I, 548.
95. *Calendar of patent rolls, 1232–1247*, pp. 76, 77. *Close rolls, 1231–1234*, p. 130. *Ibid., 1234–1237*, p. 549. *Book of fees*, I, 158, 166, 183; II, 1081.
96. *Ibid.*, II, 1020, 1044, 1057, 1064. *Close rolls, 1234–1237*, p. 208. *Ibid., 1237–1242*, p. 484.
97. *Book of fees*, II, 925, 930, 1011, 1039, 1071. *Close rolls, 1231–1234*, pp. 163, 476. *Ibid., 1234–1237*, pp. 297, 298, 306, 445, 579. *Ibid., 1237–1242*, p. 296. *Calendar of patent rolls, 1232–1247*, p. 146.

THE LOCAL MACHINERY OF TAXATION 81

Bedford, Cambridge and Huntingdon, and Norfolk and Suffolk in 1241.[98] William de Beningworth held land in Lincolnshire and of Ranulf, earl of Chester, and was a small rear vassal. He was a justice of assize in Lincolnshire in 1230 and in 1232.[99] His associates were men of experience.

The assessors of Holland in 1237 included John de Bractoft and Henry le Moine, who were assessors of the fortieth of 1232 and have already been discussed. The two others were Alexander de Wybetoft and John de Oiri concerning whom I have found nothing more.

With the levy of 1237, the employment of commissioners for purposes of extraordinary taxation ceases for a long time because such taxes are discontinued. The tallages continued with their trained taxers. The aids on knights' fees of 1245 and 1253 and the scutages of 1242 and 1257 were levied and paid in conventional style as far as local collection was concerned, the tenant in person or the sheriff appearing at the exchequer or before some committee. If we pass into the ecclesiastical sphere of financial activity where the king certainly had financial interests, we find that the central power was represented by committees chosen in each archdeaconry to supervise the assessment and collection in each area of that sort. They were often changed, but the principle remained the same, viz., to have missi appointed by the central authority who functioned throughout some subdivision and who were ordinarily connected with that area so that they were familiar with conditions and the population there.

It should be recalled however that the use of circuit justices and special commissioners of all sorts was constantly extending in England during this epoch. So when we come to the twentieth of 1269, the first tax on the assessed valuation of movable property of laymen since 1237, let us not be surprised if we find the county commissioners again employed. Such a procedure has become a custom.

We wish to know whether they retain the same characteristics of the age of expansion which closed in 1237. Are they still rear vassals in the county to which they are assigned? Are they men experienced in administration in other ways? Are they practically (like the tallagers) members of the local royal administration to such an extent that they devote all their time to the service of the royal

98. *Book of fees*, I, 616; II, 668, 1037, 1044, 1075. *Calendar of patent rolls, 1232–1247*, pp. 11, 30, 263.
99. *Book of fees*, II, 1474. *Close rolls, 1227–1231*, p. 289. *Ibid., 1231–1234*, pp. 60, 263.

82 TAXATION IN MEDIEVAL ENGLAND

government and receive their living from the royal exchequer? Let us continue in Lincolnshire. The assessors and collectors were Richard de Harington, John Pikot, Roger de Trihampton, and Simon de Driby, all knights.[100] In 1271 appeared an order empowering five men among whom were the above Richard, John, and Simon, to seize all malefactors and plunderers in Lincolnshire and send them to Newgate and to inquire who had harbored them. These assessors therefore seem to be like those of a generation earlier, landholders in this county of respect and importance who were from time to time called upon to aid the king in government.[101]

Is it fair to say that along with these assessors and collectors who were rear vassals and occasional loyal local officials of the king, there were officials who should be designated as professional royal administrative officials? Certainly. There are men who, though landholders, circulate everywhere, but it is too much to say that we can find them on the board appointed in every county.

Is it fair to say that among these missi are to be found barons of the first rank who thus lend their personal prestige to the assessment, even though not in every county? It is true of the fifteenth of 1225, but not to any great extent in any other levy. How about 1269? How about the stewards or the rear vassals of the barons of the first rank? Isn't that really the same thing?

Thus in 1225 the following men appeared as assessors and collectors (with the number of their fees annexed):

Name	County	Number of Fees
Ralph Musard	Nottingham and Derby	15
William Fitz Warin	Hereford	30
William de Avranches	Kent	21½
William de Beauchamp	Buckingham and Bedford	45+
Henry de Braibroc	"	13½
Alured de Lincoln	Dorset	25
Oliver de Vallibus	Norfolk and Suffolk	22½
Roger de Merlay	Northumberland	4
Roger Bertram	"	5
William Pantulf	Shropshire	5
Thomas Mauduit	"	5½

This is the largest list that we have.

The carucage of 1220 contains some important names as financial missi, as follows:

100. *Calendar patent rolls, 1266–1272*, p. 406.
101. *Ibid.*, pp. 150, 177, 543.

THE LOCAL MACHINERY OF TAXATION   83

Name	County	Number of Fees
Adam de Port	Buckingham and Bedford	55
Fulk Baynard	Norfolk	8½

From the fortieth of 1232 we choose the following:

Name	County	Number of Fees
Henry de Tracy	Devon	28
William Basset	Leicester	7
Ralph de Bloiho	Cornwall	7
William Blundell	Lancashire	7
Fulk Baynard	Norfolk	8½

It should be noted however that such barons were also employed in the local government by the king. They were not simply called upon in connection with taxes to give their support; they were coroners, justices of assize, verderers, sellers of the king's wood, etc. That evidently is why they were appointed to assess the taxes. Much of the success of each tax depended upon the experience of these commissioners, their executive ability, their knowledge of local conditions, and their devotion to the service of the king. Who were the men who filled such important positions? How were they selected? How were the commissioners appointed? Were they elected? Did they take an oath? How were they paid, or were they paid? The early notices of these officials speak of their duties rather than of the method of their appointment. In the assize of arms in 1181 the commissioners in charge were called justices and hence seem to be members of the council of the king and so would be designated for this work by the curia regis, i.e., the small curia regis.[102] The commissioners of the Saladin tithe seem to have been appointed by the king, that is to say, by the council.[103] In 1198 a knight and a clerk were sent to each county by "the king," and they were to be assisted by a group elected in the county court.[104] In this case we have the combination of appointment by the council and election by a local body. The carucage of 1200 may also have been levied in the same way for a chronicler states that the "order went throughout all England by the justices [or from the justices] or the king," [105] which seems to mean that the justices were appointed by the king to collect it.

102. Stubbs, *Select charters*, p. 155.
103. Benedict of Peterborough, *Gesta regis Henrici secundi*, ed. William Stubbs (Rolls series), II, 33.
104. Roger of Howden, IV, 46.
105. Ralph de Coggeshall, *Chronicon Anglicanum*, ed. Joseph Stevenson (Rolls series), p. 101.

84   TAXATION IN MEDIEVAL ENGLAND

In 1201 the fortieth was to be collected in each shire by "discreet and legal men" who were to cooperate with the sheriff under his direction. They were to be such as were competent to undertake this business. No indication is given as to whether they were to be elected or appointed, but their authority for this work was the command of the king.[106] The assessors of the fifteenth on exports and imports in 1204 were to be "elected" in each port but how is not stated, perhaps by the merchants of the port.[107] In 1207 the commissioners were appointed by the council because the king refers to them in his letters patent as "our justices" (*justiciae nostri*), as if they were judges, and declares that "we send in our place Robert de Berkeley and the others and that every one is to be intending to them as to ourselves."[108] All the orders concerning these justices are on the patent roll and are addressed to the people as a whole and not to the individual justice. In 1217 the commissioners to assess the carucage of that year were appointed by the king.[109]

With the exception of one occasion, that of the carucage of 1220, the commissioners were appointed presumably by the king's council, for the writs appointing them were issued by the chancery.[110] In 1220 the assessors and collectors were elected in the county court. This work was done under the supervision of the sheriff, and it was he who was instructed to summon the county court, have these collectors chosen, and have them cooperate with him. It was to him that the orders which have survived were issued containing the directions for the assessment and collection of the carucage of that year.[111]

The county commissioners of the twentieth of 1269 were evidently also appointed by the king's council, for we have letters patent appointing Richard de Harington to assess the twentieth. The king in person might appoint collectors, and later the formal document of appointment would be issued. "Appointment of William de Grantcourt and William de Ripariis, late taxors of the twentieth in the county of Essex, with the abbot of Waltham, to collect the said twentieth in the said county as the king had enjoined on them by word of mouth."[112]

106. Roger of Howden, IV, 188–189.
107. *Rot. pat.*, p. 42b.
108. *Ibid.*, p. 72.
109. *Rot. claus.*, I, 306.
110. *Patent rolls, 1216–1225*, p. 560. *Close rolls, 1231–1234*, p. 157. *Ibid., 1234–1237*, pp. 188, 553.
111. *Rot. claus.*, I, 437.
112. *Calendar of patent rolls, 1266–1272*, pp. 406, 418.

THE LOCAL MACHINERY OF TAXATION 85

In 1207 we have only the writ on the patent roll directing everyone to cooperate with the commissioners who represented the king. In 1198 they were partly appointed (a knight and a clerk) and partly elected in the county court.[113] From the beginning they took a special oath to perform their duties faithfully, probably in the presence of and under the direction of the sheriff.[114] Their duties were at first merely to assess but later, beginning in 1220, to assess and collect also.[115] What inducement had the commissioners to undertake this difficult and responsible task? No indication of any direct remuneration appears till we reach the fifteenth of 1225. Then appear certain items regarding pay which begin to have the semblance of an honorarium. Robert Amauri owed 40s. to the treasury for a certain "*angulo vestito tenui q ' rto.*" He was pardoned that sum for the good and faithful service which he had rendered in collecting the fifteenth.[116] Robert Munsorel was one of the justices of the fifteenth in Gloucestershire; he received 2m. for his "expenses" in collecting the fifteenth and bringing it to Winchester at Michaelmas and 1m. for the carriage of the fifteenth at Trinity Term to Winchester.[117] Peter de Abingdon received 40s. for his "expenses" in assessing and collecting the fifteenth in Berks, and Robert, chaplain of the earl, the same amount for the same work in Sussex.[118]

As in all the cases the amount of the "expenses" came to 40s., perhaps this was the regular fee for such work. In 1232 and later all of these justices received a regular fee, *pro expensis suis*, a phrase which I interpret to mean their honorarium for this work. It varies from 5m. to 10m. for each tax. Did they receive nothing earlier? It is inconceivable to me that they received nothing. It was apparently inconceivable to them that they should receive nothing, for they began soon to get a regular wage. If the king would not pay them, someone else would do so, for in investigations into the aid of 1269 the justices were to inquire "of the behaviour of the taxors and the collectors of the twentieth in their office, if they received anything by reason of the said office, how much they received from the commonalty for their expenses and if anything was concealed there so that the taxation and collection had not yet been

---

113. *Rot. pat.*, p. 72. Roger of Howden, IV, 46.
114. *Ibid. Rot. pat.*, p. 72. *Close rolls, 1234–1237*, p. 545.
115. Wilkins, *Concilia*, II, 21.
116. Pipe roll 10 Henry III, m. 12d, Public Record Office.
117. *Patent rolls, 1225–1232*, p. 3.
118. *Ibid.*, p. 10.

fully made, as it is charged against them before the king, and to enquire concerning the tallies of quittances made by them." [119] Certainly if the king was not paying these officials, someone else might take the job in hand.

In 1269 the sum received by the commissioners from the royal revenue was usually £5.[120] Occasionally the sums paid varied. William Hay and Eustace de Waterford were given £15 for services in Northamptonshire. Four taxers and collectors were given £10, apparently 50s. each, though even in this case it may be a first installment of half of their salary. The same taxers and collectors that levied the twentieth in Cumberland above were the commissioners in Westmoreland, and they received there 50s. each, so that their real pay for assessing the tax was in this case £5.[121] Four assessors and collectors in Lancashire were paid 5m. each.[122] In Wiltshire there were four commissioners paid as follows: the prior of Farley, 100s.; John de Cormailles, 100s.; Peter de Scudmore, 7m.; Richard de Worcester, 4m.; and William de Caune 4m.[123]

Probably this variation in the salary represents the difference in the social and economic importance of the commissioners, for we find that Giles de Audenarde, who was one of the taxers in London, was paid £10 for his expenses.[124] Now Giles was one of the most important officials of the wardrobe, and his salary was probably commensurate with his official prominence. These men's salaries are variously described. Sometimes they are said to be *pro expensis suis circa taxacionem et collectionem vicesime;* [125] sometimes for their expenses and those of their clerks; sometimes for their *misae* and expenses and those of their clerks. Once the chancery clerk states that this allowance was by the special favor of the king.[126] Shall we conclude therefore that these sums were allotted them merely to reimburse them for their outlay or do they really represent salaries for work done?

The earlier justices performed other work for the government just as the later ones did; they were commissioners of various kinds, tallagers and the like. It is not likely that they did such work for

119. *Calendar of patent rolls, 1266–1272*, p. 701.
120. Liberate roll 54 Henry III, m. 2, m. 3, m. 9, m. 11, Public Record Office.
121. *Ibid.*, m. 3. Liberate roll 55 Henry III, m. 1, m. 10, m. 11, Public Record Office.
122. Liberate roll 54 Henry III, m. 2, Public Record Office.
123. Liberate roll 56 Henry III, m. 9, Public Record Office.
124. Pipe roll 54 Henry III, m. 12d, Public Record Office.
125. Liberate roll 54 Henry III, Public Record Office.
126. *Ibid.*, m. 2. Liberate roll 55 Henry III, m. 10, Public Record Office.

THE LOCAL MACHINERY OF TAXATION

nothing. They were probably paid as many feudal servants were paid, not by a salary for a special task but by being pardoned debts or by being assigned lands the income of which they enjoyed. This I suggest is the way in which these early justices were paid.

When the commissioners entered upon their work, how did they get in touch with the taxpayer to assess his property and collect the tax? The small council of the king grappled with this problem in a series of experiments which aimed to secure an adequate assessment of the property and a quick and complete collection of the tax. Difficulties faced them. The new taxes were not sanctioned by local custom and so evasion, false swearing, and concealment of goods probably were considered justifiable. This feeling affected all classes. Thus they were spoken of as "unheard of." [127] Gerald of Barri declared that the blessing of the people departed from the king because of the levy of the Saladin tithe.[128] All and sundry grieved because of such a great oppression and all cursed the archbishop although he was absent.[129] It was too heavy a tax which terrified clergy and laity by its violence and which under the form of alms concealed rapacity.[130] These expressions of the chroniclers find confirmation in various acts given in the records. Richard Fitz Osbern was "appealed" during Richard's reign for saying in his stone house, in connection with the aids for the ransom to which he had contributed, that he wished the chancellor had been hanged; a certain Jordan had been present when Richard said that he hoped the lord king might always be where he now was, and Robert Brand declared that whoever came or went the Londoners had no other king but the mayor.[131] Any tax was too heavy.[132] The early chronicle speaks of the severity of punishment on those who failed to pay.[133]

The government had to pay attention to the feelings of the taxpayer. Either the taxpayer made oath personally or was present when a jury assessed him. In 1198 each baron was to distrain his men and if he failed to do so, then the king would levy the sum due

127. Benedict of Peterborough, II, 59.
128. Giraldus Cambrensis, *Opera*, ed. J. S. Brewer, J. F. Dimock, and G. F. Warner (Rolls series), VIII, 253.
129. Gervase of Canterbury, I, 422.
130. William de Newburgh, *Historia rerum Anglicanum*, ed. Richard Howlett in "Chronicles of the reigns of Stephen, Henry II, and Richard I" (Rolls series), I, 280. Ralph de Diceto, *Opera historica*, ed. William Stubbs (Rolls series), II, 73.
131. *Rotuli curiae regis*, ed. F. Palgrave (Record Commission), I, 69.
132. Ralph de Coggeshall, p. 101.
133. Benedict of Peterborough, II, 33.

88 TAXATION IN MEDIEVAL ENGLAND

from the baron's demesne but not from the baron's men. Lords apparently resented outside interference between themselves and their men.[134] Men refused to pay.[135] They concealed their property on the lands of monasteries.[136] This feeling only gradually disappeared. It was not the sentiment felt toward scutage or tallage. Those levies seem to have been regarded as legitimate, if properly assessed. Scutage has received great advertisement as the type of illegal exaction by its mention in the Great Charter. We should recall however that the provision was directed against the illegal levies; in 1217 the barons, after further deliberation, said that scutage should be taken as it had been taken under Henry II. Tallage never was mentioned as an unjust tax. But the carucage and the tax on personal property never received universal acceptance as legitimate till the very end of the reign of Henry III. Even then a special form of consent was required for their legitimate assessment. Small and great for a long time opposed these taxes. Sometimes they absolutely refused to pay. Such an attitude may be implied in the harsh statement in the chronicle concerning the treatment of those who would not pay the Saladin tithe. "If they found any rebellious, immediately the king had them imprisoned and put in irons till they had paid the uttermost farthing." [137] This is biblical language, but no such expressions emerge in connection with scutages and tallages. Roald Fitz Alan was fined 200m. and four palfreys "because he refused to swear for the thirteenth and for recovering the castle of Richmond whence he had been disseized on that account." The abbot of Selby refused to pay the thirteenth, and the king ordered him to be amerced as much as possible.[138] Everyone knows the famous case of the Yorkshire barons who declined at first to agree to the carucage of 1220 but whose resistance was finally overcome.[139] The question of the method of obtaining the consent is not in this case the primary problem—it is the feeling of opposition to such financial exactions. In speaking of the grant in aid of the titular king of Jerusalem, the Waverly chronicler said: "This grant amounted to little or nothing because it was afterward opposed and produced little." [140] The fifteenth in 1225

134. Stubbs, *Select charters*, p. 257.
135. Pipe roll 12 John, m. 17d, Public Record Office.
136. *Rot. pat.*, p. 71.
137. Benedict of Peterborough, II, 33.
138. *Pipe roll 9 John*, p. 71.
139. W. W. Shirley, *Royal letters*, I, 157.
140. *Annals of Waverley*, ed. H. R. Luard, in "Annales monastici," II (Rolls series), p. 296.

THE LOCAL MACHINERY OF TAXATION 89

was only granted on condition of the reissue of the Great Charter.[141] In 1232 the assessors and collectors of the fortieth were unable to assess and collect the tax on the lands of Richard de Percy as long as he was unwilling; he finally in 1236 allowed it to be collected.[142] Indeed it was only after long debate and postponement that the grant was made.[143] In 1238 the thirtieth was not granted till the king promised to issue letters patent that it should not constitute a precedent for future levies.[144] As a result of the grant of the thirtieth, three barons were added to the king's council: the earl Warenne; William de Ferrers, earl of Derby; and John Fitz Geoffrey. There was long and animated discussion over the tax in the great council of the king, and much opposition developed which was finally overcome.[145]

A gracious aid levied like that of 1217 to raise money for the debt owed by the little king Henry III to Prince Louis of France might be opposed in the same way.[146] In 1242 the king attempted to raise another aid to supply him with money for a campaign in Gascony, but the great council refused the grant, and without this assent he was unable to raise any sums not sanctioned by custom.[147] We may emphasize the point justly that a grant was necessary if the king desired to raise one of the new kind of levies. But another significant comment is that there was general opposition to the new kind of taxes, particularly because people felt that they were beginning to be customary. In 1237 we find too clear evidence of untrustworthy assessment by jurors.

As a result of general opposition taxes of the new sort ceased for over a generation except for levies upon the clergy. Lords of manors resented outside interference between themselves and their tenants, even though a great council of the kingdom had assented to the levy of a tax. Now of course this opposition may have come in part from tenants in chief that had been absent when the tax was granted and did not feel bound by the consent of others. Corporate consent had not yet been established. In addition let us recall the magnitude of the task—to assess the property of all men in the kingdom numbering tens of thousands, to collect the tax from each, to have some

---

141. Sydney Knox Mitchell, *Studies in taxation*, p. 160.
142. *Calendar of patent rolls, 1232–1247*, p. 159.
143. Mitchell, *Studies in taxation*, pp. 204–205.
144. *Ibid.*, p. 219.
145. Matthew Paris, *Chronica maiora*, III, 382.
146. Pipe roll 5 Henry III, m. 2a, Public Record Office.
147. Mitchell, *Studies in taxation*, p. 224.

system of accounts by which it could be known who had failed to pay in order that without delay appropriate action could be taken against the delinquent; and to do all this within a few months.

The government experimented with two methods already often employed in other connections. By the one each taxpayer appeared before the commissioners and took oath to the amount and value of his property. This was the tale, the *conte*, to which a plaintiff swore in court in a suit now carried over into another sphere. It was the conte of his property. Such in effect was the scheme employed by Henry II in his great inquest of service in 1166 but no oath was employed. By the other plan a jury of the locality assessed the property of each man in the district except their own in the presence of the commissioners. The property of the jurors was then assessed by another jury. Such was the machinery of the Domesday survey; ever since that date this method had been more and more widely used to determine royal rights of all sorts. It had just recently been employed in the Assize of Arms in 1181.[148] The attitude of the barons toward these methods seems to have been at first against any assessment at all; and then, after they had been forced from that position, in favor of the personal oath; while the king's council came more and more to favor assessment and collection by a local jury under the supervision of the county commissioners. The result of a long struggle finally gave the victory to the government.

The stages in the conflict may be imperfectly detailed. In levying the Saladin tithe each taxpayer apart from the townspeople swore to the amount and value of his property. He risked the safety of his soul if he swore falsely, but the commissioners were not solely dependent on this deterrent as an encouragement to honesty. The oath was sworn in the presence of the men of the vill who knew very well the amount of land, stock, goods, and revenues belonging to each inhabitant. The justices were evidently in some way to ascertain this public opinion, for the regulations of assessment provided that in case it was suspected anyone had sworn falsely a jury of his neighbors was to make this assessment. At the outset, therefore, the government seems to have understood the advantages of the jury system. Additional evidence of this knowledge is found in the fact that the tithe was assessed in the towns by a jury.[149] A disadvantage of the personal oath may have lain in the difficulty of ensuring a full attendance of the property holders to meet the jus-

148. Stubbs, *Select charters*, pp. 154–156.
149. William de Newburgh, I, 273. Benedict of Peterborough, II, 31, 33.

THE LOCAL MACHINERY OF TAXATION 91

tices. What was done about absentees is not stated, but in any case they would delay completing the assessment of the tax.

We know nothing as to the method employed to evaluate the amount to be contributed by each to ransom Richard I, but the plan which was adopted to assess the carucage of 1198 shows that the king's council had been pondering on the subject. The proposal to make a new assessment of the arable land and levy a tax on each carucate of 100 acres apparently led the government to adopt a new method by which something other than the personal oath of the taxpayer would be employed. Two commissioners were sent to each county; to them were joined knights elected by the county court; the jurisdiction of this combined elected and appointed body extended over the whole shire. In each hundred the commission was assisted by two knights elected from that administrative division. Before this commission a jury from each vill appeared, consisting of four men and the reeve, and they swore to the number and value of the carucates in the vill and the sort of tenure by which all the land was held. The lords of the vill or their stewards were present to correct or verify the assessment. When the knights of the hundred were satisfied that the appraisal was correct they approved it; and the commissioners for the county, if in their turn they were satisfied, ordered it to be enrolled as official.[150] That the assessment was made by jurors instead of by the oaths of individual property holders is indicated also by the reports on sergeanties contained in the *Book of Fees*, for the method employed in assessing the sergeanties was the same as in other land. The commissioners only wanted additional information about the former.[151]

The jury was used again in the levy of a special customs tax in the seaport towns in 1204. This tax was assessed and collected in each port by a commission of six or seven townsmen, a knight, and a clerk.[152] In the thirteenth of 1207 however each property holder took oath personally. In this latter year no provision was made in the official order for assessment to check the valuation made by each property holder by informal inquiry among his neighbors. This must have been done however for men were punished for false swearing and for storing their property on the lands of others in the

150. Roger of Howden, IV, 46, 47. Compare Howden's description of the information to be supplied with the reports concerning serjeanties in the *Book of fees*. Book of fees, I, 8, 10.
151. *Ibid.*, pp. 4, 7, 8, 10.
152. *Rot. pat.*, p. 42b.

92 TAXATION IN MEDIEVAL ENGLAND

hope of escaping assessment.[153] The assessment of the carucage of 1217 was made by the personal oath of each landholder;[154] the thoroughly voluntary nature of the carucage of 1224 is shown by the fact that the royal government had nothing to do with its assessment and collection.[155] In 1225 though, when it was necessary to raise as large a sum of money as possible with little delay, the provisions suggest that the government aimed at having an unusually large number of assessors under the direct control of the more responsible and important county commissioners to eliminate the influence of friendly or hostile assessors, to avoid delay caused by absentees from meeting of assessors and taxpayers and the loss which would arise from the pessimistic valuation placed by each man on his own property. Thus county commissioners, usually four in number, were to be assisted by four knights elected in each hundred, the commissioners assessing part of the county in cooperation with the hundred knights, but in other parts of the county the knights of the hundred worked alone. The commissioners in this way had a check on the valuations submitted by the knights, and the larger number of assessors could complete the work more quickly. The hundred knights were not to assess any property in their own hundred—an attempt to eliminate the element of fear and favor. Before these commissioners appeared the stewards of the earls, barons, and knights from each vill and swore to the value of their lords' property in that vill; there seems to have been no further check on the valuations submitted by this class. A sort of combination of the jury and the personal oath was devised for the classes below the knights. All serfs and freemen should swear to the value of their property in the vill and to that of two of their neighbors. In case of dispute a jury of twelve should decide the matter. If, moreover, one attempted to escape assessment by absenting himself, his property would be assessed by his neighbors, a stimulus to be present. Here we see that the government was moving in the direction of assessment of all property by the jury, a method which met the opposition of the great men.[156]

In 1232 this method actually was adopted and henceforth was never again abandoned. Four men and the reeve of each vill were chosen, met the county commissioners on a date and at a place fixed

153. *Rot. oblatis*, p. 374. *Rot. pat.*, p. 71.
154. *Rot. claus.*, I, 306, 335b.
155. *Patent rolls, 1216–1225, passim.*
156. Stubbs, *Select charters*, pp. 355–357.

THE LOCAL MACHINERY OF TAXATION 93

by the latter, and there drew up a roll of assessment of the property belonging to all within the vill except that of the clergy.[157] The property of the jury was in turn assessed by two other men of the vill. The baron of the vill, if he desired, was allowed to collect the tax on his own land.

In 1237 the same method was followed with some slight modification. The lay lord of the vill could no longer collect the tax except by a special dispensation; the priors were collectors as well as assessors. But stewards might be present, if they desired, when the assessment was made to check the accuracy. The great clerical tenants in chief were granted the right to collect the levy on their lands by their knights or freemen in this way and then turn it over to the county knights.[158]

Then such taxes ceased for a generation, until 1269. We may cast a glance at the taxes upon the clergy in the period 1253–58 and find that they too make use of a jury in assessing the valuation of Norwich. Shall we say that this represents English rather than continental ecclesiastical experience? Who can doubt that it was indigenous to England to employ the central committee at the outset as well as the local committee to assess valuations?[159]

In 1269, after a lapse of thirty-two years—more than a generation—a twentieth was granted for the crusade. But the method of assessment followed the precedent with one variation. In 1232 and in 1237 the sheriff had supervised the election of the jurors of the vill. In 1269 this power was taken from him. The county commissioners met the men of each hundred and caused twelve legal and discreet men to be elected who in turn chose six men from each vill to act as assessors of the vill.[160] After 1269 in the reign of Edward I this jury becomes the normal device.

When we say that a jury assesses the property, do we mean that it views the property of each man and then from memory estimates its value? Or rather that it does not view the property at all after being chosen as a jury but wholly from memory assesses the property of each man in the vill? When before 1232 a dispute arose over an assessment and it was referred to a jury of the neighbors, did the jurors return to the vill, view the property, return to the justices and make their sworn statement or did they speak from memory?

157. *Ibid.*, p. 361.
158. *Close rolls, 1234–1237*, pp. 544, 555–556.
159. William Edward Lunt, *The valuation of Norwich* (Oxford, 1926).
160. J. A. C. Vincent, *Lancashire lay subsidies*, p. 93.

94 TAXATION IN MEDIEVAL ENGLAND

As to this, we are left wholly in the dark at the outset. We may conjecture that the latter method was pursued.[161] Such a method was feasible because the vill was a small community and communal farming was practiced. Such knowledge is taken for granted when in 1225 each man in the vill was to swear to the property of two of his neighbors.[162] The difficulty was to check the accuracy of the assessment. Everyone knew that jurors had to be supervised. The sheriff and the county commissioners could exercise some control over the valuations by their knowledge of local prices of stock and goods. Sometimes the stewards were present when the jurors made the assessment and could therefore at once protest against an overvaluation of their lords' property.[163] Once at least there were elected knights for the whole county and knights from each hundred to reinforce the body of county commissioners before whom the jurors made oath.[164] If complaint were made, a new assessment might be ordered.[165] If this showed inaccuracy in the first assessment, the first jurors might be punished. Even poor peasants might raise such a complaint that the government would intervene in their behalf.[166] With all this the feeling grew in the king's council that the assessments were partial to the taxpayer, that the jurors were not acting without fear or favor as they had been instructed. The first open proof of this conviction that has survived comes from the thirtieth of 1237. News, probably reported by the county commissioners, came to the exchequer from Kent as soon as the assessment had begun that the jurors were violating their oaths by assessing

161. This conclusion is based wholly on inference. It should be noticed first, that the county commissioners did not view the property at all in cases where no dispute arose; that jurors summoned to decide civil and criminal cases judge of their own knowledge; the provision of 1225 that each man swear to the value of his own goods and those of two of his neighbors indicates common knowledge of the property in the vill; the language of the writs in 1232 and 1237 suggests that the jurors spoke of their own previous knowledge. The writs do not state that the commissioners go from vill to vill in the hundred, but that on a certain day the jurors of the vill shall appear before the commissioners, take the oath to make the assessment without fear and favor and that afterward the roll was drawn up and approved by the commissioners. Thus the jurors of several vills seem to appear at one and the same place and make the assessment there without returning home. Stubbs, *Select charters*, p. 367.

162. *Ibid.*, p. 356.

163. In 1198 and 1237.

164. In 1198. Notice that in 1198 the jurors of the hundred are to serve in their own hundred while in 1225 they must serve in a different hundred.

165. As in 1207, 1209, 1225, and 1237.

166. *Close rolls, 1231–1234*, p. 297. *Ibid., 1234–1237*, p. 539. *Patent rolls, 1216–1225*, p. 572. *Calendar of patent rolls, 1266–1272*, p. 585. Roger of Howden, IV, 47.

THE LOCAL MACHINERY OF TAXATION 95

property at too low a figure. "They value," says the writ on the close rolls, "an ox at five shillings when it is ordinarily worth ten or even more, a pig which is worth two or three shillings, they value at sixpence, a sheep worth sixteen pence or more, they value at sixpence. If they go on as they have begun, they and all other such assessors will certainly be guilty of perjury, and we shall not have half the tax so generously granted to us by our magnates." Quite so, but what was the remedy? "You are hereby ordered that in any such case you shall in company with knights of the county go personally and view the property and make a fair assessment and punish for perjury those aforesaid four men and thus make an example which will induce others to act honestly." This order was sent to all commissioners and sheriffs.[167] This instruction was not in the original writ to the commissioners. It was issued after the assessment had begun. The jurors of the vill had still quite a free hand. The justices would only take action if they suspected perjury. It was thought that the fear of reassessment by the commissioners would keep the jurors in line. Now here is a curious fact. The next tax of this sort was not levied on laymen till 1269, thirty-two years later. It seems incredible that in the thirteenth century men would look back thirty years and consult the records of a preceding tax for information to guide them in making an assessment. Yet such seems to have been the case. In 1269 there was a new method of choosing the jurors of the vill, new that is in taxation. The commissioners summoned the county court and had twelve loyal and discreet men chosen in every hundred; the twelve then chose six men in each vill as assessors. The original writ of assessment further provides that these six should assess the goods of all in the vill but if there is any failure on their part then the county commissioners in company with the six jurors shall make the assessment.[168] Thus the method for controlling the jurors in 1269 was apparently built directly on the experience of 1237. Still the system did not work to complete satisfaction. In 1290 we have the last stage in this development in the thirteenth century in a provision by which the government made use of the intimate knowledge possessed by the jurors of the vill and sought to compel them by a double supervision to make an honest use of their information. Elected in the way just described the village jurors, five in number, walked from house to house in company with twelve men of the

167. *Close rolls, 1234–1237*, p. 569.
168. Vincent, *Lancashire lay subsidies*, p. 93. Wilkins, *Concilia*, II, 20.

hundred and assessed the goods on the spot. The county commissioners with their clerk followed them from vill to vill checking in person the result of the first assessment.[169] It was a long, tedious process and for the first time two years were assigned as the period within which the assessment and collection were to be completed. It was clearly necessary however. We might say that there was a triple check on the jurors of the vill. They no longer made their declaration from their previous knowledge but in the presence of the property, of the owner, and of their supervisors.

The government had already employed the jury on innumerable occasions. It was a quicker method than the personal oath. Not every man from a vill would be able to appear on an appointed day before the justices to make oath individually. The sheriff could more easily secure the presence of four or five representative men of the vill. From the first, disputes over the correctness of an assessment were settled by a jury. Why then did the government hesitate to adopt this method? Was it because possibly the great landed proprietors opposed the assessment of their property by their villeins and free tenants? The Saladin tithe was assessed in the country districts by the personal oath, in the towns by a jury of the citizens. Nothing in the character of the work made this difference in method necessary. The special customs tax of the fifteenth in 1204 was assessed and collected in the towns by a commission of six or seven townsmen, a knight, and a clerk. When the jury came to be generally employed in assessment, the government at first took pains to consider the interests of the great landholders. Now they were permitted to collect the tax due from their lands after it had been assessed; now it was provided that the lord or his steward should be present when the men of the vill made the assessment in order to safeguard his interests.[170] It may be of course that the government was in doubt as to which method would be most effective.

After the assessment, the collection. The existing methods of collecting dues seem to have been manifold. Within the same vill or hundred some might be collected by the sheriff, some by lords who had lands there, some by itinerant justices, some by wardens of land in the king's hand, some, like tallage, by special commissioners. How it was in practice done at the outset with the new levies may be seen in the picture presented by the report of the jurors of the

169. Vincent, *Lancashire lay subsidies*, p. 177.
170. Roger of Howden, IV, 47. Stubbs, *Select charters*, pp. 361, 367.

THE LOCAL MACHINERY OF TAXATION 97

hundreds in Wiltshire. They declared that the following persons received the aids for Richard's ransom: the bailiffs of the bishop of Salisbury, the sheriff and his clerks, certain knights who were the royal commissioners to the county, the bailiffs of Count John, of the abbess of St. Edwards', of John Marshal, of Ralph Fitz Stephen (the constable of Malmesbury castle), *plures*, the abbot of Malmesbury, the sergeant of the hundred, and the reeve and the burgesses of Wilton.[171] If the council was to have any satisfactory collection and accounting of the aids, it must have provided for a more systematic method than is suggested by this chaotic list of names, even though this list falls naturally into three groups: the lords, the county commissioners, and the sheriff with his clerks.

The writs providing the method of assessment of Richard's ransom have not come to light, but some of the testimony of the jurors and a couple of extracts from the pipe rolls given by Madox indicate that the sheriff was the official responsible for the collection of all the aids in the county and that he rendered the account at the central office of receipt. The county commissioners who assessed the taxes were associated with him as collectors for the county.[172] In the actual work they might receive some of the money directly, which they delivered to the sheriff. Much of the money was collected by the various lords within the hundred from their men and they in turn paid it to the sheriff, who thus became responsible for the whole sum assessed within the county. A baron might, however, pay directly to the central office.[173]

For the carucage of 1198, Roger of Howden describes the plan of collection which was devised by the council. In each vill every baron was to collect the tax from all men on his land, pay it to two elected knights and the bailiff of the hundred; they in turn delivered the money to the sheriff who brought it with the rolls of assessment to the exchequer where he rendered the account of the carucage of the shire. If a baron failed to collect from his men he was to be distrained in the whole sum due from his land only on his demesne. Later he could collect from his men.[174]

Now the sources of our information concerning the collection of these last two taxes are quite different. For the ransom we have two entries on the pipe roll and the testimony of jurors as to who

---

171. *Three rolls of the king's court*, pp. 84, 86, 87, 88, 90, 91, 95, 98, 99, 100, 108, 109.
172. *Ibid.*, pp. 85, 88, 93, 108. Madox, *History of the exchequer*, p. 412.
173. *Three rolls of the king's court*, pp. 87, 100.
174. Roger of Howden, IV, 47.

received the money. For the carucage of 1198 we have a chronicler's description, evidently taken from the writ of assessment. A comparison seems to show that the methods of collection were quite similar, if not the same. In the description of the ransom no mention was made of the bailiff of the hundred as one of the collectors. Possibly however he played the same part as in 1198, for in two cases mention is made that the tax was paid to the sergeant of the hundred.[175]

Thus at the close of the twelfth century a definite system of collection seems to have been formulated by which debtors could be quickly identified and compelled to pay. That it was not wholly satisfactory in bringing the money into the treasury may be inferred from the necessity of the inquests of 1194 and 1198. The strength of the feudal baron is shown by the fact that he was to be the collector even when a jury made the assessment. It is thus a combination of the old feudal idea and the new national idea of national machinery. The plan to distrain the baron's demesne and not his men for the carucage due from his men shows the strength of the feudal idea that the baron and not his men owed the tax to the king. Practically it must have proved difficult to enforce.

When, as in the fifteenth on merchants in 1204, we get a tax where feudal lords are not primarily concerned, a jury was easily and naturally adopted as not only the best way to assess the tax but also the best way to collect it.[176]

The writ of assessment for the thirteenth of 1207 merely states that the sheriff was to receive the assessment rolls from the county commissioners and make the collection. Very likely much the same method was followed as in the taxes before 1200.

Up to 1220 therefore the sheriff has been the dominant figure in the collection. In that year we seem to see the beginning of his decline. The two knights elected in the county court were to collaborate with him not only in assessing but also in collecting the carucage of that year. A further restriction appears in the regulation that the money when collected was to be placed under the seals of the sheriff and the knights and brought in the sealed chests or barrels to the New Temple at London.[177] Do we not have here an attempt by the council to secure the delivery of the whole tax at

175. *Three rolls of the king's court,* pp. 86–87.
176. *Rot. pat.,* p. 42b.
177. *Rot. claus.,* I, 437.

THE LOCAL MACHINERY OF TAXATION 99

the central office of receipt and prevent its being frittered away by demands of the all-powerful sheriff and an attempt to supervise his control of this additional income? Although the council sought to make the knights coordinate in responsibility with the sheriff, they were unsuccessful. They indeed summoned both, but if the sheriff did not come, nothing really could be done, and finally the memoranda roll notes that the sheriffs had a day for accounting for the carucage.[178] They still were the officials responsible for the collection of the tax. Moreover, they continued to be able to use part of the receipts for local outlay, and the council still found it difficult to secure the return of the money. On occasion, too, the sheriff would decline to allow the elected knights any share in the work of collection. Alexander de Pointon and Henry de Langton had no roll to collect the tax in Lincolnshire and they collected none of it, they say, but the sheriff received it all.[179] Roger of Stanford took part in the collection and testified that the sheriff's clerk received all the carucage recorded in the roll which he himself delivered to the treasurer; Stanford knew that on one occasion they sent money to the New Temple at London, but he did not know the amount. At another time, he said, they sent money to London, but he does not know whether or not they paid it into the exchequer.[180]

The great levy of 1225 introduced a striking change. The sheriff retired as director of collection in favor of the county commissioners. The reeve and four men of each vill collected the tax in that area (as they had probably always done), but now were instructed to deliver it to the county commissioners or their deputies, not to the sheriff, and were given tallies as receipts. The commissioners were directed to store the money in a secure building, a castle, a church, or an abbey till they delivered it at the central office of receipt for the account.[181] The sheriff still had his part to play: he would distrain debtors; he would provide safe conduct for the receipts when they were moved; in 1232 he held one of the keys to the locks which contained the money, and he sealed one of the seals of the coffers while they were temporarily held within the

178. Exchequer L. T. R., Memoranda roll 9 Henry III, m. 2d, m. 3d. Memoranda roll 7 Henry III, m. 11, Public Record Office.
179. Exchequer L. T. R., Memoranda roll 9 Henry III, m. 2, m. 3d. Memoranda roll 7 Henry III, m. 11, Public Record Office.
180. Exchequer L. T. R., Memoranda roll 9 Henry III, m. 2, m. 14.
181. Stubbs, *Select charters*, pp. 356, 361, 367. *Rot. claus.*, II, 152. *Calendar of patent rolls, 1266–1272*, pp. 543, 585.

100   TAXATION IN MEDIEVAL ENGLAND

county. But his former place of primacy in the assessment and collection was gone.[182] It remained possible for a baron to collect the tax due from the men on his lands, but it was by special permission, and he paid the money and rendered his account to the county commissioners or the central office.[183] The one great exception to uniformity was the clergy. Their anomalous arrangements ranged from the payment of a lump sum by an individual and evasion of assessment to a special permit to assess and collect the thirtieth on all their lands in the method prescribed in general and evasion of assessment by the county committee, or a special permit to an individual to assess and collect (or just collect) a tax on his own lands by employing his own tenants, or a permit for all the clergy to assess and collect the tax on their own lands by their own local tenants after the fashion prescribed in the general order of assessment and collection.[184] Such was the arrangement in the carucage of 1224 of Bedford and the thirtieth of 1237.[185] In case the tenant was permitted to assess and collect the tax by the use of the royal system but employing his own men, the government might insist on having a royal representative as a member of the board, or might appoint the assessors and collectors themselves, perhaps from among the men of the tenant.[186]

So customary was this system becoming that in 1235 when the aid on knights' fees was authorized the assessment and collection was in charge of county committees.[187] Such a course was unusual, as can be seen by the practice of 1217, 1245, and 1253. The resort to this method is significant of its appeal to the council. Thus by 1237 a new system of collection had been evolved in connection with the new taxes on land and movables; it was more orderly and better controlled by the council.

When the collector had collected the tax, he presented it with the rolls to the central office. As has been shown elsewhere, there was, except in 1232, a special group of receivers who received the

182. Madox, *History of the exchequer*, II, 193. *Rot. claus.*, II, 81. Pipe roll 10 Henry III, m. 11, Public Record Office. Stubbs, *Select charters*, p. 361.
183. *Rot. claus.*, II, 81, 40b. *Close rolls, 1231–1234*, p. 301. *Ibid., 1237–1242*, p. 45.
184. *Rot. claus.*, I, 84, 477, 595b, II, 21b. *Rot. oblatis*, p. 45. Fine roll 17 Henry III, m. 6, m. 8, m. 9, Public Record Office. *Close rolls, 1231–1234*, pp. 292, 293, 301, 302. *Patent rolls, 1216–1225*, pp. 571–572.
185. Mitchell, *Studies in taxation*, p. 217.
186. *Patent rolls, 1216–1225*, pp. 571–572. *Close rolls, 1231–1234*, p. 291. Exchequer L. T. R., Memoranda roll 22 Henry III, m. 5d. Exchequer K. R. Memoranda roll 21 Henry III, m. 22, Public Record Office.
187. *Book of fees*, I, 407, 417 et seq.

THE LOCAL MACHINERY OF TAXATION 101

money and sometimes audited the accounts. The local collectors could not compel complete payment at once. The question is, what measures did the government employ to force recalcitrant or dilatory debtors to pay? It seems at first sight curious that the individual debtor should not have been summoned by the sheriff before the exchequer, and indeed this may have been done.[188] Yet the practice was for the exchequer to summon the county commissioners before it to report the amounts still due.[189] The sheriff accordingly was ordered to distrain the taxpayers to pay to the assessors and collectors. They, the taxpayers, were practically never ordered to appear and account to the exchequer or the special exchequer.[190] If the collector died, his heir was responsible for the debt.[191] While the sheriff early in the assessment stepped aside, later he might receive the tax from the collector and so become responsible. But the danger was that whatever came into the sheriff's hands might remain there.[192]

Thus a new system of collection was evolved which was more orderly and systematic and could be seemingly more easily and directly controlled by the king's council, but also which threw the responsibility upon the assessors and collectors, and rarely if ever brought the individual taxpayer into the exchequer or other central financial office. When the great baron or churchman collected, the same thing was true in effect, for the property holder paid the money to his lord who in turn paid it and was responsible for it to the central government. Such a change may not have been accidental. It represents the growth in efficiency of the royal administrative system. Debtors could be more easily followed up; the sum total of receipts was easily obtained. Consider that we have nowhere a calculation by the finance officers of the amount yielded by a scutage or a tallage, while during this time we have numerous contemporary statements of the yield of the new taxes. The exchequer therefore possessed definite information concerning the exact amount not only of the amount of the assessment but also of the collection. Now this was due to the new machinery which was created.

188. *Calendar of patent rolls, 1232-1247*, p. 19.
189. Exchequer K. R., Memoranda roll 17-18 Henry III, m. 6d, m. 13d. *Ibid.*, 21 Henry III, m. 14d, Public Record Office.
190. Exchequer K. R., Memoranda roll 20 Henry III, m. 9, m. 11d, m. 13d, m. 14. Memoranda roll 21 Henry III, m. 16, m. 23d, m. 24, Public Record Office.
191. Exchequer K. R., Memoranda roll 37-38 Henry III, m. 18d. Pipe roll 46 Henry III, m. 5. Pipe roll 49 Henry III, m. 8d, Public Record Office.
192. Exchequer K. R., Memoranda roll 40 Henry III, m. 14d, Public Record Office.

All this had been done by the time of the levy of the thirtieth in 1237. Now came a revolutionary change. The barons on the great council refused to grant any further gracious aids that took the form of a tax on personal property; the king in the face of such refusal was unable to levy them. The refusal was repeated many times. From 1237 to 1269 no such levy was taken though both scutage and tallage were levied in the customary way. Two aids on knights' fees (both allowed by the law) were assessed and collected, not employing the special machinery of 1235 but taken in the older conventional fashion. Yet when we come to 1269 the method of assessment and collection was essentially that followed in the taxes taken a generation earlier. Some ecclesiastics, indeed many of them, fined in lump sums for the twentieth and paid it themselves to the central office of receipt.[193] Perhaps there was more of this method than earlier, but it was not because they were ignorant of the other general system, for the county assessors were collectors also.[194] The sheriff might transport the treasure, but it was in sealed receptacles; it was the assessors that were to render the account, and it was they who were later summoned to collect the balance of the levy, though sometimes a new appointee supplanted the original commissioners.[195] A new commissioner might be appointed to review the work of the original assessors and collectors,[196] but in all these cases the special commissioner had charge of the assessment and collection. Many, perhaps all, of the cities and boroughs fined for the twentieth, thus turning it into the likeness of a tallage.[197] The question of the record of the levy was regarded as important at the outset. An organization that possessed pipe rolls and receipt rolls that over a century before had felt it necessary to enroll and abstract the records of the Domesday inquiry would (we would expect) deliberate on the record of the new taxes which should be kept. We shall find that very early the record of assessment was in duplicate or triplicate, that a record of collections was also made, and that additional rolls were drawn up to record the tax of

193. *Cartularium monasterii de Rameseia*, II, 293. *Calendar of patent rolls, 1266–1272*, pp. 448, 466, 495, 496, 639, 667, 682.
194. *Ibid.*, p. 701. Liberate roll 55 Henry III, m. 9, Public Record Office. Wilkins, *Concilia*, II, 21.
195. Liberate roll 54 Henry III, m. 3, Public Record Office. Shirley, *Royal letters*, II, 338. Vincent, *Lancashire lay subsidies*, p. 100. Lay subsidy roll, E 179/155, I. *Calendar of patent rolls, 1266–1272*, p. 520.
196. *Ibid.*, pp. 543, 585.
197. *Ibid.*, pp. 525, 540, 542, 643. Vincent, *Lancashire lay subsidies*, p. 97. Mitchell, *Studies in taxation*, p. 297.

THE LOCAL MACHINERY OF TAXATION   103

the vill, hundred, and county as well as valuations of property and amount of taxes charged against individual persons. Most of these records have disappeared. The accounts were not systematically entered upon the pipe roll and after a time the practical value of preserving them for reference passed away. But enough allusions and fragments of rolls have survived to enable us to view the elaborate system of account evolved by the clerks of the council and of the exchequer.

With the county commissioners went one or more clerks to draw up a roll of the assessment.[198] This roll contained the names of the property holders, the amount of each kind of taxable property and its value, and the amount of the tax.[199] From the first this roll was drawn up by vills.[200] Very early we have evidence of duplicates. In 1198 there were to be four copies drawn up, one each for the knight, the clerk, the sheriff, and one for each baron, containing the details of the tax on his men. In 1207 the roll of each vill was made out and from it either a duplicate was made, or a roll containing the names of the men, the total assessed value of their property, and the amount of the tax.[201] Besides the roll of assessment, a roll of the collection was drawn up.[202] In later taxes we have evidence that from the first roll another roll of the vill was prepared containing the names of the men, the total assessed value of their property, and the amount of their tax.[203] Then there was a roll of each hundred with the amount due from each vill, of the county with amount due from each hundred, and finally one for the whole kingdom by counties.[204] We cannot say where the line should be drawn between the rolls which were drawn up in the county and those drawn up at the central office of receipt or the exchequer. There is a duplicate roll of assessment, one retained by the assessors and one sent to the exchequer. There is a roll of collection drawn up which is presented with the money.[205]

198. Stubbs, *Select charters*, pp. 160, 257, 284. *Pipe roll 1 Richard I*, pp. 105–106.
199. *Book of fees*, I, 4 *et seq.*, 289 *et seq.* Vincent, *Lancashire lay subsidies*, p. 134. Stubbs, *Select charters*, p. 257. Miss N. Niemeyer, "An assessment for the fortieth of 1232," *English historical review*, XXIV (1909), 733.
200. Stubbs, *Select charters*, pp. 160, 257, 356, 361, 367. *Rot. pat.*, p. 72. *Rot. claus.*, I, 428b. *Book of fees*, I, 302–306.
201. *Rot. pat.*, p. 72. Lay subsidy roll, 242/47, m. 7, m. 12, Public Record Office.
202. *Close rolls, 1231–1234*, p. 295.
203. Lay subsidy rolls, E 179/276/76 and E 179/71/1, Public Record Office.
204. *Ibid.*, 123/2/4.
205. *Ibid.*, E 179/81/1. Exchequer L. T. R., Foreign roll, 1 m., Public Record Office.

One or two other matters of improvement in detail may be noted. When the tax on personal property was levied first, the assessment was made as soon as the decision to levy the tax had been taken. Sometimes this grant was made in early summer, or in March or April. At such times most of the stock had been butchered, and the farther the date was from the preceding autumn the larger the proportion of grain that had been consumed and sold.[206] In 1232 it happened that the tax was granted in September and the assessment began at once.[207] A great light seems to have dawned on the government. Autumn was the season when the amount of grain and stock in the country was at its maximum and hence was the most advantageous time to levy a tax. Accordingly while the thirtieth was granted in January, 1237, the assessment was not to begin till the following September and thereafter in the thirteenth century the goods taxed were those on hand in that month of the year, no matter when the tax was granted.[208] The regulation aroused complaint. In 1269, says Thomas Wykes, the assessment could not be completed till the following year, and while the taxers would have been willing to tax and to assess at a reasonable valuation those goods which they found, inasmuch as barns had been emptied and animals had died or been killed, royal greed, not content with such a taxation or appraisal, compelled them to tax all kinds of property which they had in hand at the Michaelmas just preceding; so it was that despite complaint what at first was granted of grace was paid by a necessity which could not be gainsaid, not without the greatest murmurs by the people.[209] Notwithstanding the opposition and the difficulties of assessing property which had disappeared, the government succeeded in carrying its policy into effect.[210]

It had long been the practice of the exchequer to have sheriffs account for the income of the realm twice a year, the final reckoning being at Michaelmas. It was also the custom for debtors to the crown to pay their obligations in installments. But this last was done always as a result of a special bargain between the debtor and the proper royal official. All special levies, scutages, tallages, and

206. Gervase of Canterbury, I, 409. Benedict of Peterborough, II, 33. Stubbs, *Select charters*, p. 283. *Rot. claus.*, II, 62.
207. *Close rolls, 1231–1234*, p. 155.
208. *Close rolls, 1234–1237*, p. 544. Vincent, *Lancashire lay subsidies*, p. 93.
209. *Chronicon Thomae Wykes*, ed. H. R. Luard, in "Annales monastici," IV (Rolls series), pp. 227–228.
210. Vincent, *Lancashire lay subsidies*, p. 167.

THE LOCAL MACHINERY OF TAXATION   105

the like were considered due as soon as they had been decided upon, though they were not all paid at once. When any of these taxes were paid in installments, as often happened, it was done as the result of a special agreement. The farm of the county was payable in two installments of fixed amount. Nothing illustrates better the fiscal ignorance of these experimenters than their failure to consider that it might be difficult if not impossible for the taxpayer to supply at once in cash the whole sum owed by him to the government. This is exactly the attitude taken toward the taxes on movables. When once the grant had been made, the government considered the whole sum due and the officials were instructed to demand it as soon as the assessment had been completed. Moreover, inasmuch as the carucages and the early taxes on personal property were all levied to meet some urgent necessity, it was apparently thought necessary as well as possible to collect the whole sum at once, without spreading the payment over any considerable space of time unless some special arrangement were made with the individual taxpayer. The orders given in 1207 illustrate this attitude beautifully. In that year the county commissioners were to deliver the rolls of assessment to the sheriff every two weeks and the collection was to be made with all possible haste.[211] That is, the collection was to be begun before the assessment was finished.

From the beginning of the reign of Henry III a change was made. The exchequer adopted the policy of having the aids on knights' fees paid in two equal installments and they experimented with the plan in the other general levies, not at first making it a matter of principle.[212] In 1220 the orders for the assessment of the carucage of that year were sent out early in August and the assessment was to be completed and the tax collected by Michaelmas.[213] The original instructions for the levy of the fifteenth in 1225 and the thirtieth in 1237 provided that they were to be paid in two installments,[214] changed in the case of the latter to four installments.[215] The fortieth of 1232 and the twentieth of 1269 were to be assessed and collected as quickly as possible.[216] In Edward I's

211. *Rot. pat.*, p. 72.
212. *Rot. claus.*, I, 371. *Close rolls, 1234–1237*, p. 189. Mitchell, *Studies in taxation*, pp. 242, 254.
213. *Rot. pat.*, p. 437.
214. Stubbs, *Select charters*, pp. 356, 364, 367. *Patent rolls, 1216–1225*, p. 541. *Ibid., 1225–1232*, p. 6.
215. *Calendar of liberate rolls, 1226–1240*, p. 350.
216. *Close rolls, 1231–1234*, p. 156. Vincent, *Lancashire lay subsidies*, pp. 94–97.

reign however the plan was finally permanently adopted of having the collectors account in two or four equal parts for the sum due from their counties.[217]

An important problem of a medieval government was the safeguarding and the transportation of treasure. The pipe rolls are full of references to movements of the king with his treasure and rolls packed in casks and loaded in wagons. Treasure was deposited in castles and when it had to be moved, the sheriff provided the wagons, the casks, and the guard. He was credited with an amount to cover this outlay.[218] Such was probably the method by which the receipts from the new taxes of Richard and John were transported to the place of receipt packed in boxes with the rolls of collection. During these reigns the king's council apparently contented itself with fixing the date when the sheriff should appear before the central office of receipt with the money of the tax. At the appointed time that official would arrive with his precious freight, pay in the money, and render his account. The arrangement of the details of the storing and the transportation of the money and rolls were left to his discretion. Surely these officers had experience enough to guide them. With the accession of Henry III, however, the council began to lay down more specific rules. The sheriff ceased to be the dominant figure that he had been in assessment and collection. The specially appointed assessors and collectors, the justices of the tax, replaced him. They were henceforth to be responsible for the assessment, the collection, the delivery of the money, and the accounts. For the successful fulfillment of these duties, they must have the cooperation of the local governments who must, it was felt, be informed in detail concerning their relations with new officials. The first evidence of the desire of the central government to get quick and effective control over the receipts is in the provision made in 1220 that the receipts from each county were to be placed under the seals of the sheriff and the collectors till they were brought to the New Temple at London. In 1225 the government went further. The writ of collection provided that the receipts in each county should be temporarily stored in a castle, a church, or an abbey, chosen by the local authorities, under the seals of the county commissioners and of the hundred knights. The central places of receipt were fixed at Winchester and at London; the

217. *Ibid.*, pp. 168, 177, 180.
218. *Pipe roll 1 Richard I*, p. 178.

THE LOCAL MACHINERY OF TAXATION 107

second was originally the castle of Devizes, but on account of the lack of accommodation there, it was changed to the New Temple at London. In May, 1225, detailed instructions were issued to transport the money and rolls from the local centers where it had been temporarily deposited. To Winchester were to be brought the receipts from the neighboring shires; those from more distant counties were assembled at a local center—Northampton, Gloucester, York, St. Albans, Oxford, Nottingham, Sherborne, Southwark—under the care of the sheriff, a guard, and the county collectors. From these intermediate centers the money and rolls were to be finally carried, at dates set by the council, to Winchester or the New Temple in charge of representatives of the clergy, who had special permission to collect the fifteenth on part of their lands, and of two county collectors with one clerk; each sheriff through whose bailiwick the train went was to provide wagons and guards.

In these details, insignificant and irritating though they may seem, we see the remarkable care taken by the king's council to insure the creation of a machine which would quickly bring the whole of the receipts into the hands of the central government. In 1232 some change was made. The council designated the place within each county where the tax was to be deposited with rolls under the seals of the collectors. Later the sheriffs of all counties were to carry the sealed barrels and boxes to a half dozen central points where they were to be placed also under the seal of the sheriff delivering them. Later still some of this money was paid into the exchequer, but a great proportion of it was not disposed of in this way: it was paid directly into the wardrobe by the county collectors. In 1237 a detail was changed: transportation to three central places was provided by the sheriff for the money and rolls under lock and seal, but the assessors and collectors accompanied it and paid it to the receivers. All deliveries were to be at a fixed date.

In 1235 the aid on knights' fees, if precedent had been followed, would have been paid and the account rendered by the tenant in chief or the sheriff. The new organization led to the designation by the council of the places within each county where the receipts were to be deposited, and instructions were given that they were to be placed under the seals of the two knights (assessors and collectors) and with two locks, each assessor possessing the key to one of them. Thus no money could be withdrawn by one without the help of the other. This was of course a conventional regulation of the exchequer in connection with the "regular" revenue. The places named for deposit were castles, churches, abbeys, priories. In 1232 and 1237 similar places were chosen for local deposit.

It has been observed that the council found difficulty in insisting that an assessment of property should actually be made. Let us recall the novelty of the scheme. How far they succeeded at the outset in enforcing the provision that the property should actually be assessed we have no means of knowing, but it is clear that there was opposition to the assessment and that the opposition was so strong that the government was willing to allow taxpayers to compound in lump sums, and thus avoid assessment of their property and paying the old-fashioned donum, as had often been done during the reign of Henry II. Thus the first pipe roll of John contains the record of lump sums charged against twenty-three counties for the carucage of 1198. The sums were levied either as the sum total charged against the county or as a fine to escape an inquest into the number of carucates which should have been taxed; in either case however this record shows the opposition to the newfangled system of property assessment.[219] The citizens of London paid a lump sum which included their aid for the ransom of Richard.[220] But the greatest opposition arose, as we should naturally expect, among the clergy, and throughout the whole period many of them, particularly religious houses, were allowed to compound. At first it is possible that in general the great ecclesiastical barons were allowed to compound. We might expect that the government would be willing to accept a lump sum in place of levying a fixed proportion on sacred gold and silver vessels, as happened in the case of the abbot of St. Albans, who paid 200m. to redeem all the gold and silver vessels of his church for the ransom of Richard, or the York church which redeemed the gold cross taken for the ransom.[221] At the outset the government aimed to assess all property whether held by a church or on any kind of tenure. Thus the carucage of 1200 gives us an assessment of the land of a parish church, land held in free alms, land on the demesne of an abbot and his men, on a prebend as well as on land held by military tenure or in free and common socage.[222]

219. *Pipe roll 1 John*, p. 36. Mitchell, *Studies in taxation*, p. 8.
220. Madox, *History of the exchequer*, p. 412.
221. Thomas Walsingham, *Gesta abbatum monasterii Sancti Albani*, ed. Henry Thomas Riley (Rolls series), I, 214. *The fabric rolls of York minster*, ed. James Raine, Jr. (Surtees Society), XXXV, p. 152.
222. Lay subsidy rolls, 242/113, Public Record Office.

THE LOCAL MACHINERY OF TAXATION 109

This opposition to assessment by royal officials was so widespread that in 1207 the thirteenth is classified as the common thirteenth, the fines of religious, and the dona of bishops; and in 1217 the clergy paid dona instead of the carucage levied in that year.[223] In 1224 the clergy granted the king a carucage, but kept the assessment and collection entirely in their own hands. With the levy of the great taxes on personal property which began in Henry III's reign in 1225, the issue of assessment and collection was sharply drawn between government and clergy. In 1225 the ecclesiastical barons in general assessed and collected it on their demesne lands and by special arrangement were also allowed to collect it on the lands held by them on military tenure. It should be observed however that what they paid was not dona but a tax based on the assessed valuation of their goods. In 1237 they were allowed to assess and collect the tax on all their lands. In 1269 the prelates fined in lump sums for their demesnes; they declined to grant the twentieth in 1269, as had the great curia regis. In their grant they stated that the proceeds were to be held on deposit until the king or his son departed on the crusade. We see here their mistrust of the king's motives.

It is difficult for us to appreciate the causes of this opposition, for taxes are so much a matter of habit today. Two elements enter into the feeling of opposition; first, the fact that these taxes were not owed, they were aids of grace; second, even if not owed, repetition would make them a new obligatory due. Hence the necessity of careful examination of the grounds for the tax.

One result of the taxation of the period from 1188 to 1272 was thus the elaboration of a branch of the administrative system. This grew directly out of the institutions of the twelfth century. It was the outcome of constant study and experiment. Experience gained in one levy was applied to the next. Methods were modified; slight changes were made in detail. Yet the final result was great and significant; the taxation of later years would have been impossible without this machinery. Who was responsible for this development? Surely not kings like Richard, John, or Henry III, or the magnates assembled in the great council. They would not be interested, indeed they would hardly understand, the importance of such dry and minute details of administration.

Men like Hubert Walter, Hubert de Burgh, and Peter des Roches were interested in managing the great governmental machine; they were interested in finance, in calculating how taxes could

223. Mitchell, *Studies in taxation*, pp. 87–89, 123–124.

be collected, and so on. They must have had much influence. The very character of the changes which we have discussed at such length suggests another source of influence. There was a great body of men, skilled in administrative detail, always in action, a body which carried on the precedents and traditions of the past, a group who loved detail, who knew both how things had worked in the past and how to refresh their memory by the records. This was the curia regis, the small curia regis, and its offspring, the exchequer, the chamber, and the wardrobe. The men on these bodies must be those who were largely responsible for the growth of this system.

The new machinery was entirely controlled by the king, and its growth meant therefore the growth of the royal power even under a weak king like Henry III. A new tie, financial in nature, had been created which bound every man but the poorest to the king. As the system finally developed, royal representatives entered the land of almost everyone, assessed his property, and collected a tax from him. This obligation was quite as strictly enforced as the rent which was owed to a lord. If a man refused to pay, his goods were seized and held. He was compelled by judicial process to discharge the debt. The baron at first had collected the tax; then he was pushed aside from this position and allowed to watch the assessment; but he was finally dropped entirely. The small peasant or freeholder was left to deal as best he could with the royal representatives. This lessened the local political power of the barons; their control over their men was diminished, because it was now shared with the strongest lord in England. They did not clearly see the danger. In finance therefore as in the administration of justice the local political power of the baron was retiring before the expanding power of the royal government.

III

THE BASIS OF THE ASSESSMENT OF THE TAXES

THE taxes we have been discussing originated in the twelfth century and were levied from time to time. By the reign of Henry III they had taken definite shape and possessed three well-marked characteristics. First, they had to be authorized in some new, special manner, for they did not simply grow out of existing dues through extension by the mere authority of the lord or king. When the records become full we find that the authorization was made by the king, after a discussion and agreement in the council of tenants in chief. The discussion and grant was the application of feudal custom; it was essential because the levy of an unusual due based on property was so novel that its assessment and collection from men who held nothing of the king would have been usually difficult and often impossible. Second, they were paid to the king by a large proportion of the property holders, regardless of their status in feudal or manorial organization. Third, the amount of the tax was intended to be proportionate to the value or amount of property which each tenant held. In the case of carucage, it was calculated according to the number of carucates that he held; in scutage, according to the number of knights' fees in his holding; in the tax on personal property, according to the amount and value of his personal property and at first of his revenue also.

This basis of assessment was gradually developed. Originally the tenant made his lord a gift, a donum, the amount of which should be commensurate with his importance. Later probably the amount was fixed by a bargain with the king, and the tenant raised the money in any way he chose. Such was one method employed in the tallage in the royal demesne. The lord, or the inhabitants of an area tallaged, attended to the assessment. The amount agreed upon was affected by the size of previous payments, by any recent strain on the resources of the area, or by the fact that the king had recently taken a tallage. Another form of contribution, probably of later origin, was the donation based upon a valuation of land or other property and calculated at a fixed rate per unit of land or property. Such was the danegeld based on a valuation of land, movables, and revenues; the assessment seems to have been employed to determine the relative capacity to pay among the hundreds of each shire and was represented by the number of hides or carucates or sulungs allotted to each hundred. This number was therefore a measure of the valuation of taxable property in the hundred, not the actual number of hides or carucates therein—fiscal units rather than real units. The amount of the tax was reckoned at a certain number of shillings per unit. The total number of units of land or property was then subdivided among the property holders of the district (the vill or hundred). After 1086 no new assessment was made; like the commutation of services or payments in kind into money, the valuation remained fixed unless by special arrangement the tenant received a reduction or even was totally exempted; on special occasions the tenants in chief might agree to pay a higher rate, but the valuation, i.e., the number of units with which each district was charged, remained unchanged.

Opposition to the danegeld led to its abandonment, at first under Stephen, then again after 1162, following a brief revival, under Henry II. It was again revived to help raise the ransom of Richard in 1194, on the basis of the assessment of 1084. There followed experiments to establish a new basis of the hidage or carucage on the real hide or carucate, first by counting the hides or carucates, second, by counting the number of teams. Another donation by special bargain was the composition for military service. It may have been at first in a lump sum, but as early as Henry I's reign the composition was reckoned at so much per fee.[1] Unlike the danegeld, the assessment was on each tenant in chief, not on the vill or hundred. Under Henry II the problem arose as to the number of fees for which each tenant should pay—the *servitium debitum* or the total number of fees enfeoffed by tenants in chief on their holdings. There is no evidence that the king had hitherto paid attention to the enfeoffments made by his vassals. Henry II, however, began to take a great interest in this question either because his attention was directed to it from his collection of scutage or because of his interest in the amount of military service which he could exact from his vassals, or perhaps for both reasons. In 1166 he held a great inquest to determine the amount of military service that had been

1. F. M. Stenton, *The first century of English feudalism* (Oxford, 1932), p. 180.

BASIS OF THE ASSESSMENT OF TAXES   113

enfeoffed by his tenants in chief to that date. In 1168, to marry his daughter Matilda, he levied an aid based either on all the fees held of a tenant in chief or on the servitium debitum if a vassal had enfeoffed less than his service. Henceforth the knight's fee was one of the bases for the levy of aids as well as of scutages. Efforts were made to base them on all lands held by military service at a fixed rate per fee. The feeling continued to exist that all fees were not registered and were escaping service or taxation. An indication of the cessation of military enfeoffment was the command of the council to compel all tenants by military service to take up knighthood, and later that each free man holding land by free tenure of an annual value of £20 and later £15 should be enfeoffed by military tenure. Thus the basis of the scutage or aid was the knight's fee and the number of fees did not materially increase after 1166.

The most fruitful of all the levies was the tax on movables and revenues, later on movables alone. The tax was based upon valuation of personal property and a certain proportion, such as a tenth, or a fifteenth, was levied upon this valuation. The government aimed, as in the case of the scutage and the carucage, to base the levy upon the amount of property in the possession of each property holder when the tax was levied. An additional problem was to decide the kinds of property which should be taxed. It took a long time, until after the close of Henry III's reign, to reach a decision on this point. Revenues were exempted after 1207, but some doubt existed as to where the line should be drawn between taxable and exempt personal property. As a result of this indecision down to the close of our period each tax was based on a fresh assessment.

In tallage the question as to the increase in the basis of the levy did not arise till after the death of Henry III, for up to 1272 there was no definite property basis for this levy. Thus the tax on movables remained for a long time a fluid levy based upon a new assessment each time, not on the district but on each property holder. In this respect it did not differ from carucage or scutage. In all three levies the government aimed to base the levy upon the number of taxable units in hand at the date of the levy.

After the aid on knights' fees was based upon the fief, there is no record of any composition. In the aid on movables the aim of the government was to base the levy upon a definite valuation of property; in the carucage the aim was to base it on each carucate, that is, each real unit of land; yet all through the period composition had to be allowed, especially among the clergy, on account of the opposition of property holders to assessment of their property. A curious variation occurred in the case of the scutage taken in lieu of service. Composition in a lump sum, called a fine, was sometimes exacted by the king in lieu of military service instead of scutage at a certain rate per fee.

The taxes on revenues and movables appear to have had their origin in a series of levies made in the twelfth century to support crusades. In 1146 King Louis VII of France imposed a tax to raise money for his expedition to Palestine. While we have no information about the precise nature of this impost, it seems clear from contemporary accounts that it was a general levy on all the people of the realm.[2] As such it may well have been the prototype for the levies made in both France and England in 1166.

At Le Mans in 1166 Henry II by the counsel and assent of the archbishops, bishops, and barons of his French possession levied an aid for the Holy Land. He was influenced, he said, to take this action by the example and request of his lord, Louis VII. Thus according to the English chronicler Gervase of Canterbury the initiative in the levy was taken by the French king.[3] The levy was unprecedented in its scope. It was paid by archbishops, bishops, mitered abbots and clerks, earls, barons, vavasors, knights, citizens, burgesses, and peasants. It was based on all revenues and movables, including gold and silver plate and ornaments, animals, money, and debts that were certain to be recovered, but excepting precious stones and clothes. Deduction was to be made for the expenses of cultivation of arable land and vineyards. For each pound of revenue or movables twopence should be given for the current year, and a penny for each of the four following years or a fortieth in all. Anyone not having property or revenue of this value but possessing a house or a trade should give a penny. The estates of those who died before the date of payment should, after debts had been paid, give a tenth of the balance.[4]

2. William Edward Lunt, *Valuation of Norwich*, p. 1. Ralph de Diceto, *Opera historica*, I, 256–257. Achille Luchaire, *Manuel des institutions françaises* (Paris, 1892), pp. 578–579; and Luchaire, *Histoire des institutions monarchiques de la France* (Paris, 1891), I, 120–123. Alexander Cartellieri, *Philipp II August, König von Frankreich* (Leipzig, 1899–1921), II, 5. Robert de Torigni, *Chronica*, ed. Richard Howlett, in "Chronicles of the reigns of Stephen, Henry II, and Richard I," IV (Rolls series), p. 154.
3. Gervase of Canterbury, I, 198.
4. *Ibid.*, pp. 198–199. Robert de Torigni, p. 227. William Edward Lunt, "The consent of the English lower clergy to taxation, 1166–1216," *Facts and factors in*

BASIS OF THE ASSESSMENT OF TAXES 115

The decision at Le Mans did not apply to England, but the tax was levied in the island kingdom too. Under the date 1166 the Peterborough chronicle records that the men of the realm were forced to swear that they would pay of their cattle, movables, and real property an undesignated number of pence in each pound.[5] Ralph de Diceto stated that a locked chest was placed in each church in England to receive the donations destined for Jerusalem in amounts determined by oath taken publicly throughout the kingdom, and that fourpence in each mark was paid. That would be sixpence in the pound—the same rate as that adopted for Henry II's French possessions.[6] Since this method of collection was the same as that provided in France, and the sum taken was the same, it is obvious that the reference is to the levy of the same tax in England.[7]

When we consider that this was almost the first general levy we are surprised at its comprehensive nature and wonder out of what it arose. The influence of the church was marked. The tax on revenues and movables may have been suggested by the tithe. In France at the middle of the twelfth century the tithe was levied on agricultural products and by the consent of the donor on seigneurial revenues.[8] In England probably the same was true, for the abbot of Abingdon received grants of goods and revenue as tithe.[9]

The house tax was in familiar use in the cens and the champart. The tax on those that had a trade was a form of capitation tax that was familiar.[10] The donation of a tenth of property of the deceased after their debts had been paid illustrates the ecclesiastical influence. The deduction of expenses of cultivation before calculating the basis on which the tax was estimated may come from a manorial custom. The innovation lay not in the invention of any detail but in the combination of these provisions in a tax levied throughout the French possessions of Henry II and the kingdom of England. The comprehensiveness of this levy both as to the persons who were

---

economic history (Cambridge, 1932), pp. 64–66. Cartellieri, *Philipp II August*, II, 7–8.

5. *Chronicon Petroburgense*, ed. Thomas Stapleton (Camden Society), XLVIII, p. 3.

6. Ralph de Diceto, I, 329.

7. Lunt, "Consent of lower clergy," p. 65.

8. P. Viard, *Histoire de la dîme ecclésiastique dans le royaume de France aux XII et XIII siècles* (Paris, 1912), p. 260.

9. *Chronicon monasterii de Abingdon*, ed. J. Stevenson (Rolls series), II, 159.

10. Henri Sée, *Les classes rurales et le régime domanial en France au moyen age* (Paris, 1901), pp. 78, 79, 356, 358–359.

liable and the property that was taxed arouses surprise since it is the first levy we know of. But as it was levied for the Holy Land, a purpose that would appeal to the feelings of all Christians, it would be proper to include all people and property. Hence the tithe would be a natural model. Hence too the provision that estates of those deceased before the date of payment should contribute after their debts had been paid. The notion that even the poorest should contribute would arise naturally out of the concept of alms.

Cartellieri emphasized the high degree of taxing skill displayed in this levy of 1166.[11] This is shown by the fact that everyone had to contribute, that the tax was based on wealth, that it was intended to be proportionate to the capacity of everyone to pay, and that the levy would be uniform throughout King Henry's dominions in France. But we should also notice the inexperience displayed. There is the provision that debts certain to be repaid should be included in the list of taxable property. There is the stipulation that gold, silver, and coins should be taxed—impossible to enforce and later abandoned. There was the item that revenues should be taxed. This was abandoned in taxes on English laymen after 1207 though it continued to be used in France and in levies on the English clergy.

The fact that hardly any property was to be exempt illustrates the novelty of the assessment. As soon as careful assessment began to be made, the government discovered that it was impracticable to include every kind of property. In 1166 only gems and cut clothes were to be exempt. This insignificant list does not indicate a most exacting valuation or an established tax; on the contrary, it suggests little or no assessment, a first attempt. How much did the king hope to raise? Evidently a large sum in all. The language of the chronicler implies that he felt that a great effort was being made. Although the rate of two pennies in a pound was only $\frac{1}{120}$ of the total value of the proposed assessment, the additional payment of a penny in the pound for four years would mean in all a fortieth, a considerable quota.

This tax was an important precedent. It was uniform; it was based on property and revenues; it was all paid to the king; it was proportioned to wealth; all members of all classes were liable. The king and his council, however, did not realize in 1166 that in movable property and revenue they had something from which they could raise additional revenue in considerable quantity. They were

11. Cartellieri, *Philipp II August*, II, 9.

BASIS OF THE ASSESSMENT OF TAXES 117

only aiming to secure alms in as large an amount as possible from everyone. Suppose that one failed to pay or valued his property at too small a figure. No adequate machinery had been devised to guard against such a contingency.

Despite the fact that the king had never levied a tax of this sort before, no complaint is recorded. Ralph de Diceto who described the discontent of the French in 1146 gave a brief unemotional summary of the levy. The Peterborough chronicle registered no local excitement, and Gervase of Canterbury, who gave an elaborate but calm statement of the levy in Henry II's continental possessions, did not even mention the levy in England. It would seem fair to conclude that the lack of complaint about a tax which in form was unprecedented in its severity indicates that in reality it was not heavy, that it was taken in conventional amounts, perhaps freewill donations for the Holy Land that were deposited at the parish churches. That is, while the kind of a tax had been discovered that would bring in a great yield, the method of its assessment and collection was not efficient enough to enforce an exact and complete assessment and collection.

The next case of a levy of this kind was in 1183 in Palestine and is noted here because of the close connection between East and West and because it seems to have been copied in France and England in 1184. It was levied to raise money to protect the kingdom of Jerusalem against the increasing attacks of the Moslems. This tax was based on revenues and movables belonging to both clergy and laity, in both city and country, adjusting the assessment to the wealth of each, not taxing the rich lightly and not overburdening the poor.[12] For each 100 bezants of movable goods, including debts owed to the taxpayer, 1 bezant was to be paid; 2 bezants for each 100 bezants of revenue. If the movables were worth less than 100 bezants, a hearth tax of 1 bezant was paid; if the property holder was unable to pay this amount, he might be taxed ½ bezant or less. Lords of rural areas were charged 1 bezant for each hearth, and could pass the tax on to their peasants, "So that if a village had a hundred hearths, the lord compelled the peasants to pay a hundred bezants." Those holding money fiefs had to pay 1 bezant for each 100 bezants of salary. This tax was thus based on revenues and movables, the former being taxed at double the rate of the

12. William, archbishop of Tyre, *A history of deeds done beyond the sea*, Book XXII, chap. xiii. In the translation by E. A. Babcock and A. C. Krey (New York, 1943), II, 486–489.

latter. No exemptions were listed and no list of taxable property was given.[13]

The levy of 1184 in both French and English possessions seems to have been influenced by the Palestinian tax, as is indicated by the consistent employment of the unit of 100 in calculating the impost.[14] It was to be paid by both clergy and laity annually for three years. Every one who had 100s. of movables or less should pay 2d. for each occupied house. Residents of the French king's domains who had movables worth more than 100s. should pay for each 20s. worth 2d. in the coin of Provins. Men of the same wealth in the French lands of Henry II would pay 2d. Angevin and those of similar status in England 1d. sterling. Those who had lands or other sources of revenues of £100 or more should pay annually at the rate of £1 for each £100 of revenue.[15] Thus it was a graduated tax: 2d., the kind of money not stated, for each house on the property of the taxpayer who had movables worth less than 100s.; those with movables valued at more than 100s. paid in England $\frac{1}{240}$; those with revenues of £100 paid $\frac{1}{100}$ and also $\frac{1}{120}$ of their movables. Moreover, for those who died within ten years after June 24, 1184, and who could and ought to make alms for the good of their souls a tenth was to be given for the Holy Land, saving the rights of their lords and churches.[16] The term tenth, *decima*, thus applies only to this item concerning the alms for deceased persons and not to the tax as a whole; and the period, ten years, applies only to this provision.

A much greater variety of goods was exempted in 1184 than in 1166: for clerks, the treasures and church decorations, books, horses, plate, vestments, gems, and necessary articles in daily use in the church service; for knights, horses, arms, military equipment of any kind, and clothing. Yet the exemptions applied only to clerks and knights; they exhibit no reflection by the authorities on the practicability of taxing all movables of the peasant or burgess. Lunt is skeptical whether the tax actually was levied or even was authorized, chiefly because of the lack of corroborative evi-

13. Cartellieri, *Philipp II August*, II, 14–16. Lunt, *Valuation of Norwich*, pp. 3–4. G. Dodu, *Histoire des institutions monarchiques dans le royaume latin de Jérusalem* (Paris, 1894), pp. 256–258.
14. Cartellieri, *Philipp II August*, II, 16.
15. William Edward Lunt, "The text of the ordinance of 1184 concerning an aid for the Holy Land," *English historical review*, XXXVII (1922), 240–242.
16. *Ibid.*

BASIS OF THE ASSESSMENT OF TAXES   119

dence in other sources. But how account for the great number of manuscripts of the writ?[17]

No one knows how much was realized from either the levies of 1166 or 1184, or even how generally they were paid. In 1188, however, though no rolls of assessment or receipt have survived, enough notices of the tax have been preserved to show that it was generally collected. Thus there is a record of the payment of wages to clerks of the treasurer and chamberlains and to ten tellers who received the money of the tenth at Salisbury. This was probably a central office of receipt. The pipe roll also refers to an account of the tenths.[18] Gervase of Canterbury declares that the Christians in England gave £70,000 and even more and the Jews £60,000.[19] Benedict of Peterborough relates in detail the method by which the tithe was assessed in cities.[20]

The tax was based upon movables and revenues, with an elaborate list of exempted property: books, clerical vestments, precious stones, clothes—all these belonging to both laity and clergy; for knights in addition there were exempted war (or riding) horses, arms, clothes, and jewels—practically the list of 1184. All clergy and laity except crusaders were to pay and they were to have the tithe arising from their lands.[21] These areas paid the tax although it did not go into the royal treasury.

This tax showed notable innovations. It was a uniform tax. The gradation according to the wealth of the taxpayer was abandoned. The whole revenue and movables of each person were valued and the same fraction of the amount was paid. This plan endured for centuries. An aliquot part of significance was paid once and for all; in 1188 it was a tenth, with no thought of payments running over a period of years. This is the sort of levy later used constantly. The list of exemptions changed with the years. Among others, the house tax was abandoned. The council or the exchequer decided that it was not feasible to tax everything. Let us put it another way. With added experience in assessment, the problem as to goods to be exempted became acute.

The Saladin tithe was therefore an elaborate and comprehensive

17. Lunt, *Valuation of Norwich*, pp. 4–6. Lunt, "Consent of lower clergy," p. 70. Lunt, "Text of the ordinance of 1184," p. 240.
18. *Pipe roll 1 Richard I*, pp. 105–106, 178.
19. Gervase of Canterbury, I, 422.
20. Benedict of Peterborough, II, 33.
21. *Ibid.*, p. 30. William de Newburgh, I, 273.

levy, covering all revenues and movables. One provision demonstrates how the government had pondered on certain features of taxation and aimed to appraise the full value of goods and revenues. This levy was authorized at a meeting of the great council which was held on February 11, 1188, at Geddington.[22] The assessment would begin in the middle of winter when a considerable proportion of the grain would have been consumed or sold. The commissioners were authorized not to assess the grain of the preceding autumn, but the next crop. "Each one should give a tenth of all revenues of one year and of all the movables that he now possesses except the grain of this year . . . and of the grain of the coming year a tenth will be given." [23] This provision would result in an increase in the yield of the tax. In default of a roll we cannot definitely say how searching an assessment was actually made. The chroniclers speak of the great sums of money which Richard found in his father's treasure. Benedict of Peterborough says that in number and in weight more than £900,000 in gold and silver was there.[24] Roger of Howden states that the amount found exceeded 100,000m.[25] The pipe roll of Richard speaks in one place of sending 25,000m. to the king.[26] The provision that both revenues and movables should be taxed was enforced. Among other references we find the allusion to the "tenths of certain revenues and chattels" of the abbey of St. Mary of Leicester.[27] Two items from the pipe roll of Richard I seem to tell us that grain was assessed as a whole, a rough approximation, without definite measurement by bushels or by varieties. The bishoprics of London and Winchester were in hand. The custodian of Winchester accounted among other items of expense for moneys paid out for the "tenth of the grain of five manors," for the crusade; and the custodian of London accounted for the tenth of the grain given in aid of Jerusalem.[28] But as this is not the original entry, the clerks may have lumped various kinds of grain under the heading of *bladum*. The item shows that grain was in some way assessed distinct from other chattels. Taken in connection with the other items above, the entry indicates that the

22. Gervase of Canterbury, I, 409.
23. William de Newburgh, I, 273.
24. Benedict of Peterborough, II, 76.
25. Roger of Howden, III, 8.
26. *Pipe roll 1 Richard I*, p. 5.
27. *Pipe roll 34 Henry II*, p. 216.
28. *Pipe roll 1 Richard I*, pp. 5, 12.

BASIS OF THE ASSESSMENT OF TAXES 121

tax was based on some kind of a valuation of revenues and movables.

A modification of this plan was employed in towns. A group of the wealthier men of each town was summoned, two hundred from London, one hundred from York, and from other cities in proportion to the number of the citizens. These met with the king on certain days, and in his presence their revenues and movables were assessed by a jury of the locality. If any opposed the assessment or collection, they were imprisoned until they had paid to the uttermost farthing.[29] The statement indicates the merciless character of the assessment, the unprecedented attempt to assess all property and collect a tax on this basis.

This system recalls the description of the method of levying tallage given in the *Dialogus* when representatives of the king met with the chief men of a town to negotiate about the amount of tallage. The presence of the king himself indicates an unusual demand. Does it mean that the group was to agree to a valuation of their property and revenues under threat of punishment if they refused? At any rate the presence of the king suggests the fear by the government of local opposition. For the first time there is recorded great complaint and opposition to taxation in England. In 1187 a tallage was levied in the royal demesne. The pipe roll of that year contains the accounts of the tallage in twenty-five shires.

The obvious explanation of these facts is the opposition of the demesne to the new levy. Geoffrey of Coldingham said that this assessment which had been promised for the honor of God and the salvation of souls, exceeded the measure of piety and tortured the Lord in the hearts of many by excessive exactions, that it arose from the root of cupidity, that it shone not from the authority of piety.[30] Ralph de Coggeshall declared that the government tithed the possessions of clergy and laity "by violence."[31] Ralph de Diceto said that the "general tithe terrified both clergy and laity by its violent exaction and under the cloak of alms included the vice of rapacity."[32] The account of Benedict of Peterborough suggests the violence of opposition when it states that if anyone in the towns rebelled against the levy, the king imprisoned him and put him in

29. Benedict of Peterborough, II, 33.
30. *Historiae Dunelmensis scriptores tres,* ed. James Raine (Surtees Society), IX, p. 13.
31. Ralph de Coggeshall, p. 25.
32. Ralph de Diceto, II, 73.

chains till he had paid the uttermost farthing.[33] Gervase of Canterbury stated that all grieved at so great a grievance and many were terrified at future calamity; all poured out fearful imprecations against the archbishop although he was absent, for they had heard that the tithes of this kind had been adopted by his advice.[34] In his reflections on Henry II's death William de Newburgh declared that the king had never imposed a heavy financial burden upon England or his possessions overseas till that final tithe for the Holy Land which was too great in all his possessions.[35] Gerald of Barri records the bitter criticism of Henry II by Margaret de Bohun. She "feared for his state because the blessing of the people departed from him, due to the exaction of the tenths." In anger Henry II said: "These wicked people curse without reason, but if I live and return, they shall not curse me without cause." "The Lord," remarks Gerald judicially, "punished this enormous exaction soon afterward by an unexpected death." [36] The opposition herein described did not arise from the comprehensive list of property taxed but from the definite effort for the first time to base the levy upon a careful assessment of property, depending not on a man's conscience or an anathema but on the judgment of neighbors under the direction of royal representatives. Hence we find the renewed emphasis on exempt property which was necessary if the government was to enforce a *versus valor* as the basis of the tax. Here began the struggle between the taxpayers on the one hand and the government on the other over the question of the basis of the tax, between a real valuation of property or a lump sum as a donum by the taxpayer.

Thus the Saladin tithe marked both in the machinery of assessment and the basis of the tax the beginning of a new epoch in financial history. The reason for the new basis was the necessity of raising an unusual sum of money for the crusade in which Henry II himself was to participate, not from a theory that economic change made necessary an increase in the revenues of the state, or an unperceived economic change that forced the king to levy heavier taxes to defray the ordinary expenses of government. Curiously enough this tax initiated a period of unusual demands for money on a larger scale than hitherto; first for the ransom of Richard,

33. Benedict of Peterborough, II, 33.
34. Gervase of Canterbury, I, 422.
35. William de Newburgh, I, 282.
36. Giraldus Cambrensis, *Opera*, VIII, 253.

BASIS OF THE ASSESSMENT OF TAXES 123

and then in the later years of Richard's reign and the early years of John for the costly struggle with France, a conflict that resulted not in a mere defeat but in the "loss of Normandy." The ransom was so huge that every conceivable source of taxation was resorted to, beginning with a tax on personal property and revenue. Yet to base a general levy on revenues and movables was so extraordinary an act that except for this levy no other general tax of this character was taken from 1188 to 1207. The fruitfulness of this type of levy is shown by John's effort to calculate the fines on his barons "for desertion" in 1203 by taking a seventh of movables and by the fifteenth of merchants. Yet the crying need for money for the war is shown by the frequency of tallage, of scutage with the accompanying development of fines, and the emergence of hidage on a new basis with a new name, carucage.

The ransom of Richard I was the most important levy of the twelfth century, for it brought under contribution a wider range of property holders than even the Saladin tithe. It probably was more fruitful, for the amount raised in England probably exceeded that collected in 1188. Yet it is difficult to say much that is definite regarding the basis of this tax. Unlike the tithe of 1188 or the aid of 1166, no writs of assessment have been preserved. We are mainly dependent on the chroniclers who devoted little attention to the subject of the assessment. They have emphasized the demands for the treasures of the churches and the abbeys and the extortionate nature of the levies. The taxes on property were recorded on special rolls of which one fragment has come to light. A few fines and the amount of the hidage in three or four counties are enrolled in the pipe rolls. The returns of the inquest into the levy which was made in the autumn of 1194 have survived in summary for Wiltshire.

The taxation for the ransom was a series of levies on different bases: movables, revenues, knights' fees, the hide of danegeld, the commutation of the assessment of property into lump sums or fines, and the treasures of the churches, often commuted into lump sums. The scutage and the danegeld were based on a definite assessment at a rate per unit, but the notices that have survived of the other levies show that there were many cases of fines and commutation into lump sums instead of an actual valuation.

The amount of the ransom was finally fixed by the emperor on June 29, 1193, at £100,000, two thirds (100,000m.) to be paid before the king's release; the payment of the balance of 50,000m.

was guaranteed by sixty-seven hostages.[37] The amount that England would have to raise, even though the other possessions of Richard I paid a share, meant that every kind of levy had to be employed.

Of these levies all were taken or begun in 1193 except the hidage which was granted to the king in April, 1194, after his return and the tenth and twentieth on the churches, the date of which is not stated.[38] The most fruitful tax was the fourth. The great yield of the Saladin tithe must have impressed officials, so that when they were called on to raise an enormous sum for the ransom they turned to this tax but at a greatly increased rate, a fourth instead of a tenth. The first question to be discussed is whether it was a fourth of revenues or of both revenues and movables. It had long been thought that the levy was based on both. For example, Bishop Stubbs stated that the aid was "a fourth part of all revenues, clerical and lay, with an equal sum to be levied on personal property."[39] That the fourth was levied on both revenues and movables is indicated by the careful statement of Roger of Howden, viz., that the queen mother and the royal justices, i.e., the council, determined that clergy and laity would all give a fourth of their revenues of this year (1193) and that they should add the same proportion of their movables, so that the king would be grateful to them.[40]

This is the only clear statement among the choniclers that both revenues and movables were taxed, but it is so carefully phrased that it can hardly be disregarded. In the fragment of a receipt roll containing tardy payments on the ransom are two items of grain sold from two areas (vills or manors) for the ransom and paid into the exchequer by Geoffrey Fitz Peter.[41] This entry indicates that the fourth was levied on grain, i.e., on movables. William de Newburgh states in a rhetorical passage that "there was no distinction between clergy and laity, secular and religious, townspeople and country people, but all equally either according to their wealth or according to the amount of their revenues were forced to pay a fair amount of money for the ransom."[42] It seems a fair interpretation that the chronicler had in mind the fourth on revenues and movables.

37. Roger of Howden, III, 209, 215–216.
38. *Ibid.*, p. 242.
39. *Ibid.*, p. xciv.
40. *Ibid.*, p. 210.
41. *Pipe roll 7 Richard I*, p. 262.
42. William de Newburgh, I, 399–400.

BASIS OF THE ASSESSMENT OF TAXES 125

It is true that other choniclers state that the fourth was levied on revenues only. Ralph de Diceto makes this statement; he is an excellent authority, but Bishop Stubbs, not referring to this point, concludes that while Diceto's historical grasp is excellent, he is weak on detail.[43] Gervase of Canterbury and Ralph de Coggeshall refer to the fourth of revenues. None [44] of these authors individually ranks with Roger of Howden for accuracy in the period from 1192 to the close of his life.

Roger of Howden gave the most complete account of the aids for the ransom. Both he and Ralph de Diceto mention the fourth on laity and clergy, the gold and silver of the churches, the wool of the Cistercian order and that of Sempringham, and the tenth of certain clergy. But in addition, Roger alone of all the chroniclers mentioned a fourth of the revenues of certain clergy—the fruitless effort of the archbishop of York to obtain a fourth from his canons, the levy of a scutage, and the carucage. He alone mentions that the Cistercians compounded for their wool. He gives the most complete and definite account of the arrangements concerning the ransom. This is why it seems to me best to follow his account as to the incidence of the fourth.

The fourth was not always based on an assessed valuation of property. Even in this critical period the council had to accept lump sums in composition, probably on account of the unwillingness of the great men to submit to such control. No assessment by royal officers was made on the demesne of the abbot of Malmesbury for he paid £40 for all his demesne.[45] Geoffrey of St. Martin in Wiltshire fined for his fourth.[46] The abbess of Wilton fined for all her lands for £80; Robert Gerebert also fined. The prior of Farley fined for all his lands in Wiltshire.[47] The bishop of Durham sent £2,000 for the ransom, and it was apparently not raised by an assessment of property, at least by royal officers. I conclude this from the round sum that is given. These sums probably cover the fourth, perhaps the other levies in addition.[48] The abbot of Peterborough gave 1,000m. for the ransom and for his liberties.[49] Even when the taxpayer's property was assessed by the king's officers, a

---

43. Ralph de Diceto, II, lvii–lviii.
44. Gervase of Canterbury, I, 516. Ralph de Coggeshall, p. 60.
45. *Three rolls of the king's court*, p. 87.
46. *Ibid.*, p. 104.
47. *Ibid.*, pp. 81–82.
48. *Historiae Dunelmensis scriptores tres*, p. 14.
49. Pipe roll 8 Richard I, p. 35. Pipe roll 9 Richard I, p. 84.

general estimate was made rather than a precise assessment. This is shown by the round sums entered on the rolls. The fourth was also levied on the royal demesne. Thus Calne paid 4m. of the fourth, the manor of Melkesham £4 20d., the borough of Bedewinde 40s., Malmesbury 68s. 6d., and the borough of Cricklade £3 10s.[50]

Another tax was the levy on "ten shillings and upwards." Maitland has pointed out that this levy could not be a levy "of ten shillings on the hide for the returns bear no constant relation to the amount." He suggests that perhaps the statement refers to an additional impost on either movables or revenues. It was certainly on some property that was widely held, for many cases were reported in the inquests of 1194 in Wiltshire and several entries appear in the fragment of the receipt roll that has been discovered.[51] More definite information is wanting. Certainly the early efforts to raise the ransom had to be supplemented by further levies. William de Newburgh states definitely though rhetorically that the council was disappointed in the results of the first levy and had to resort to a second and a third tax; then they were forced to ask the gold and silver plate of the churches.[52]

In a more sober strain, Roger of Howden states that 100,000m. were to be paid before Richard's release and hostages were to be left as security for the balance.[53] It is likely that the gold and silver of the churches was asked at the outset. The general accuracy of William de Newburgh's account as to the necessity of additional levies is confirmed by official documents. The returns of the inquests of 1194 speak of the first levy (the fourth), the second levy (the aid on 10s. and upward), and the third levy (the hidage) which was not authorized until April, 1194.[54] The pipe roll also recorded two collections in 1193.[55]

The gold and silver and the treasure of the churches would naturally receive dramatic mention in monastic records. Frequently, perhaps generally, the council allowed the clergy to compound, though Ralph de Diceto says that the greater churches promised to give their treasures collected from ancient times and the parish churches their silver chalices. Richard I himself had written earlier

50. *Three rolls of the king's court*, pp. 80, 86, 93, 95, 99.
51. *Ibid.*, pp. xxiii, 91, 95, 107. *Pipe roll 7 Richard I*, pp. 261–263.
52. William de Newburgh, I, 399–400.
53. Roger of Howden, III, 215–216.
54. *Ibid.*, p. 242. *Three rolls of the king's court*, pp. 78 *et seq.*
55. *Pipe roll 5 Richard I*, pp. 14, 69, 73.

BASIS OF THE ASSESSMENT OF TAXES 127

to his mother to give a written receipt for the gold and silver and to declare by oath that the treasures should be restored.[56] The abbot of St. Albans redeemed all his chalices by paying 200m.[57] The church of Durham paid the same amount.[58] York Minster gave a golden cross for its contribution, and it was later redeemed for a sum of money.[59] The monastery of Bury St. Edmunds paid 100m. and a gold chalice, a present from Henry II; it was later returned by Queen Eleanor.[60] The abbot of Meaux paid 300m. for his year's wool crop and for his gold and silver plate, etc.[61] When Richard found that country churches had been despoiled, he ordered chalices to be made for them.[62] It is likely that there was no general spoliation of all the treasures of the churches. What occurred was a token payment, either in some appropriately valuable article or in a suitable representative sum, as is indicated in the cases cited above.

The scutage was the second aid in history based on the knight's fee. An imperfect record of the returns appears in the pipe roll. An interesting arrangement was made in connection with this aid. As soon as the king returned, he found himself at war with France and summoned the host for a campaign. He asked each tenant to supply a third of his service.[63] Many of those who failed to serve were subject to a fine for exemption.[64] The fine was not a substitute for the scutage for the ransom; the two payments were not legally connected. But those tenants who had performed their military service naturally did not pay a fine; in addition they were excused from paying the ransom.[65]

After the king's return, when he found himself confronted with war at home and abroad in addition to the expenses of the ransom, he turned to the ancient due of hidage.[66] Maitland has shown that this levy at 2s. per hide was based on the ancient assessment of 1084 antedating that of *Domesday Book* without the exemptions

56. Ralph de Diceto, II, 110. Roger of Howden, III, 208–209.
57. Thomas Walsingham, *Gesta abbatum Sancti Albani*, I, 214.
58. *Historiae Dunelmensis scriptores tres*, p. 14.
59. *Fabric rolls of York minster*, p. 152.
60. *Memorials of St. Edmund's abbey*, ed. Thomas Arnold (Rolls series), I, 251.
61. Thomas Burton, *Chronica monasterii de Melsa*, ed. Edward A. Bond (London, 1866), p. 273.
62. Roger of Howden, III, 290.
63. *Ibid.*, p. 242.
64. *Pipe roll 6 Richard I*, pp. 36, 94, 117, 119, 120, 134, 135, 139, 162. *Pipe roll 7 Richard I*, pp. 109, 160, 222, 233.
65. *Pipe roll 6 Richard I*, pp. 17–18, 75, 85, 94, 119, 125, 143, 210, 219, 230.
66. Roger of Howden, III, 242.

that had been allowed at that time.[67] Thus in Lincolnshire the men of Kesteven and Holland paid 100m. that they might be held to such service of carucates and hides as in the time of the king's ancestors, viz., to defend five carucates of Kesteven and Holland against two carucates of Lindsey.[68] The fine shows that the government of Richard I aimed to increase the yield of the hidage.

In the autumn of 1194 a tallage was levied on the royal demesne although it had paid the fourth the preceding year. The government also demanded a year's wool from the Cistercians, the Gilbertines, and the Premonstratensians. In 1194 the king commuted the demand for the wool into a fine of 1,000m.[69] The parish clergy paid various fractional parts of their revenues. Some report a fourth part of their tithes; others a fourth of their revenues; a tenth of their revenues; or a twentieth; or a tenth of their prebends.[70] Thus the beneficed clergy paid various fractional parts of their revenues; their familiarity with the levies on revenues may account for the chroniclers emphasizing the fourth of revenues on the lands of tenants in chief and their omission of the fourth of movables.

Thus every conceivable basis for a levy was employed, an indication of the enormous effort which the government put forth. Yet despite the need and the desire to meet it, it proved impossible to abandon wholly conventional methods of calculating the amounts that individuals should pay, and the substitution of lump sums seems to have been regularly employed instead of an assessment of property and revenue.

Four years later came a new experiment in taxation, the carucage of 1198, apparently suggested by the hidage or danegeld of 1194. Instead of using the conventional basis of that levy they proposed to establish it upon a careful enumeration of the carucates in England, and at the same time establish a uniform carucate of 100 acres, at least for taxing purposes.[71] While the suggestion for

67. F. W. Maitland in *Three rolls of the king's court*, p. xxiv. Doris Stenton in *Pipe roll 6 Richard I*, p. xxiv.
68. *Pipe roll 6 Richard I*, p. 118.
69. Roger of Howden, III, 210, 242. *Annals of Waverley*, p. 248. Ralph de Diceto, II, 110. William de Newburgh, I, 399; II, 416–617. *Chronica de Melsa*, p. 273.
70. *Ibid.* Roger of Howden, III, 222. Ralph de Diceto, II, 110. *Pipe roll 7 Richard I*, p. 263.
71. Round believes this was a long hundred of 120 acres, but Vinogradoff takes it to be 100 acres. John Horace Round, *Feudal England* (London, 1895), p. 70. Paul Vinogradoff, *English society in the eleventh century* (Oxford, 1908), p. 156. Roger of Howden, IV, 46.

BASIS OF THE ASSESSMENT OF TAXES 129

this tax came from the danegeld, it was a totally different levy based on real rather than fiscal carucates. The rate also was increased; the plan was originally to levy the tax at 2s. per carucate and was later increased by 3s., a total of 5s. per carucate.[72] Our knowledge of this tax derives from two sources that form a harmonious picture. There are no contradictory statements to embarrass us. They show first that the assessment and perhaps the collection took place in the first half of 1198. Roger of Howden stated that the levy was put in charge in 1198 but then included a second source, the articles of the inquest of the great eyre that operated in the fall and winter of 1198, two chapters of which order an inquiry into the assessment and the collection of the carucage.[73] The *Book of Fees* contains a report from the justices who were assessing the carucage in Yorkshire that the sergeants whose lands they had noted and valued would not be able to appear in London before the barons of the exchequer until June 7, 1198. This fixed the date of the completion of the assessment in that county at the close of May. Thus it is likely that the assessment in all shires was finished before the eyre of the autumn began.

Strict regulations were established to insure an exact assessment of the amount of taxable land: a local jury should swear to the number of carucates held in each vill, the number held in free alms which the donors or their heirs were held to acquit or for which the religious performed service. Freeholds of parish churches were exempt. Escheats of lords were subject to the tax.[74] Land held of the king in sergeanty was to be exempt, but the commissioners were to report the names of the sergeants and the amount and value of lands held by each in each vill. The sergeants themselves were to appear at the exchequer in May "to hear and to do what the king should command." [75] Religious orders that refused to pay the tax were deprived of the protection of the courts. This quickly persuaded them to offer composition.[76]

No detailed accounts of the carucage have survived, but a considerable number of the assessments on sergeants with valuations have been preserved in the *Book of Fees*.[77] They give the impression of having been drawn up with care. Nevertheless the councilors

72. *Pipe roll 1 John*, pp. xix, xx.
73. Roger of Howden, IV, 62.
74. *Ibid.*, pp. 46–47.
75. *Ibid.*, p. 47. *Book of fees*, I, 4 *et seq.*
76. Roger of Howden, IV, 66.
77. *Book of fees*, I, 4–10.

believed that the assessment was inadequate and that the amount of tax did not correspond to the amount of taxable land. Hence the justices that went on eyre in the autumn and winter of 1198–99 were instructed to inquire into the assessment. The criticism applied both to the returns about the sergeants and also to the carucage proper. What the councilors felt is clearly expressed in the instructions to the justices. They believed that the list of sergeants was incomplete, for the justices were to report the names of those who held sergeanties; the valuations, they felt, were too low, for the justices were to ask by whom they were valued and how much they were worth; that some sergeants had not made a fine, so the justices were to arrange the fines.

As to the hidage or carucage, they suspected that the assessors had not made a fair assessment, for they asked the new justices to ascertain how the assessors and collectors had conducted themselves. Had they collected from everyone who ought to pay? Had they concealed any money or anything? Had everyone answered the summons of the justices? What were the names of those taxpayers who had failed to appear before the assessors?[78] In these two articles appears the whole problem of making a new accurate valuation, despite the experience and the local knowledge of the assessors.

The orders to the new justices were undoubtedly justified, but it proved infeasible to enforce them against the laity as well as against the religious. The property holders opposed a new assessment. In at least twenty counties, as probably in all, the new justices had to be content with a fine, not from delinquent taxpayers, but from the county as a whole. Such is the meaning of the notations annexed to the fines in the pipe roll. They were designated as levied "for the carucage," "for quittance of the carucage," "for quittance that no inquest should be made of the carucage levied in the period of King Richard," and the like.[79] The total amount of the fines reported in the pipe roll from twenty-two counties was about £1,000. As these shires that fined were in all parts of the kingdom, it is likely that the fines were generally levied in all shires.

These fines were not levied in lieu of the original assessment of the carucage. They were to escape an inquest into the assessment, as is occasionally stated, to be exempt from an examination into the accuracy of the assessment. Thus the assessment was clearly

78. Roger of Howden, IV, 62.
79. *Pipe roll 1 John*, pp. 16, 19, 36, 58, 84, 98.

BASIS OF THE ASSESSMENT OF TAXES   131

imperfect. Despite the experience and local knowledge possessed by the county assessors and men of the vill, and despite sharp penalties threatened against perjured jurors, the government was unable to obtain a satisfactory assessment. Nor was it more successful in the investigation later by the itinerant justices. The opposition was so strong that the justices compromised for fines. The attempt therefore to revive the danegeld and place it upon a new basis of a real agricultural unit of measurement, the carucate, was a failure.

The possibility of using this sort of a levy was not however forgotten. In 1200 another change in the basis of the carucage was made for the next levy of that tax. The rate was 3s. per unit.[80] Instead of the carucate, the unit was the plow team. Thus the heading of a schedule of assessment of the tax on the abbot of Abingdon runs, "This is the number of plows of the abbot of Abingdon on his lands in Berkshire." Two items in the list give in order "eight car' and five oxen" and "four car' and two oxen," meaningless expressions unless *car'* means team, or plow. This roll belongs to the aid of 1200 for the total levy on the abbey of Abingdon was £101 15s. 6d. and the number of teams 678½ which gives the rate as 3s. —the rate of the levy of 1200.[81] Various property holders avoided the assessment of their teams by paying a lump sum. They might combine other privileges with the fine for the carucage. The bishop of Exeter fined in 300m. for the confirmation of his charters to have his chapel of Bosham, and to be quit of the tallage of the carucae of his demesnes and of his serfs.[82] The men of Kesteven and Holland again fined, this time in £100 (instead of 100m. as in 1194), to have their ancient assessment, clearly an indication of opposition to a new assessment.[83] In both 1198 and 1200 the government was stressing an exact assessment and searching for the most advantageous unit of assessment. They succeeded to some extent in having the local assessors carry out their instructions prescribed in the writs.

A different experiment was made in 1201 with the levy of a fortieth on revenues for a year. Innocent III who had ordered in 1199 the levy of this percentage on clerical revenues asked John

---

80. Roger of Howden, IV, 107. *Annals of Dunstaple*, p. 27. *Pipe roll 2 John*, pp. 102, 128, 185, 239. Ralph de Coggeshall, p. 101.
81. Lay subsidy roll, 73/1a, Public Record Office.
82. *Pipe roll 2 John*, p. 234. *Rot. oblatis*, p. 53. Mitchell, *Studies in taxation*, pp. 33–34.
83. *Pipe roll 2 John*, p. 86.

and Philip II for an aid for the Holy Land.[84] In 1201 the kings acceded to the pope's request and followed his example by granting a fortieth of their own revenues for a year. John included in his grant a fortieth of his demesne revenues in England, his wards and escheats, and at the suggestion of the magnates with him in France he sent letters patent to the English barons urging them to grant some proportion of the revenues of their lands for a year as an act of charity.[85]

In this connection for the first time we have an explanation in a writ of what the council meant in this case by a tax on revenues. In 1166, 1184, 1188, and 1194, they ordered revenues to be taxed, but had never explained to the assessors what the tax covered.

The term *redditus* however must have meant some kind of income clearly understood by both assessors and taxpayers, perhaps money rents, perhaps *redditus assisae*, fixed rents regulated by the character of the agreement between lord and tenant, not by the custom of the manor.[86] Thus in 1207 the thirteenth of revenues was levied upon the redditus assisae.[87] But in 1201 an attempt was made to expand the tax on redditus so that it would mean the equivalent in cash of all kinds of revenues from land, perhaps also including services if commuted into money. Accordingly Geoffrey Fitz Peter issued writs to all the sheriffs explaining how the revenues on which the fortieth was to be paid should be estimated. The earls and barons of his bailiwick should be urged by the sheriff to collect the aid on all their revenues and on the revenues of all the lands held of them in the following way. Each earl and baron should reckon the amount for which he could farm the lands of each of his demesne vills and collect a fortieth of that sum for the aid.[88] That is, their demesne lands were actually held of them by a variety of obligations, services, payments in kind, and money rents, but they were to assess the fortieth on the basis of the cash value for which they could farm their whole demesne. If there were tenants by military service in the vill, each of them should reckon the amount for which they could place their demesne lands at farm and pay a fortieth of that sum. Free tenants in the vill should calculate the amount of cash rent which they might pay their lords for

84. Lunt, *Valuation of Norwich*, p. 240.
85. Roger of Howden, IV, 188.
86. Miss N. Neilson, "Customary rents," *Oxford studies in social and legal history*, ed. Paul Vinogradoff (Oxford, 1910), II, 6–7.
87. *Pipe roll 9 John*, p. 13.
88. Roger of Howden, IV, 188.

BASIS OF THE ASSESSMENT OF TAXES

all their lands. Lands held in frankalmoign were exempt. We have no records that indicate to what extent these provisions were executed. They seem to aim at an increase of the taxable revenue. Since, however, they were a voluntary grant, probably conventional donations were made. The returns from the royal demesne do not indicate an expanded basis of the levy. But the provisions indicate the disappointment on the part of the council with the yield of taxes on revenues. The following returns are given in the pipe roll of 1202 of the fortieth from the king's demesne:

	£	s.	d.
Worcestershire	3	5	0
Herefordshire	2	5	6
The bishopric of Lincoln (in hand)	6	14	1
Staffordshire	2	5	6
Nottingham (borough)	1	6	4
Notts and Derby	9	4	6
Gloucestershire	4	3	3
Shropshire	2	7	5
Abbey of Ramsey (in hand)	6	15	0
Northamptonshire	1	8	0

It is impossible to ascertain the part of the county farms whence in these cases the fortieth was derived. It may be concluded however, from the unevenness of the sums paid in each shire for the fortieth, that the levy was not capriciously determined but was based in each shire on certain royal revenues that we cannot now distinguish. The amount of the fortieth on the borough of Nottingham was £1 6s. 4d., almost exactly a fortieth of the farm of the borough (£52).[89] In general the fortieth was calculated upon some basis less than the county farms.

The notion of the great return from a tax on movables is shown by two levies in 1203. In that year John fined the barons who, he alleged, had deserted him in France, by taking a seventh of the value of their movables. Such was the aim of the government, although we cannot tell how complete an assessment was made.[90] In the same year he requested of all laity and clergy in the islands of Jersey and Guernsey a fifth of revenues for one year, whether held in fief or in alms, to provide for the defense of the islands.[91]

---

89. *Pipe roll 4 John*, p. 187.
90. *Memorials of St. Edmund's abbey*, II, 12. Roger of Wendover, I, 318. *Rot. liberate*, pp. 43, 47. *Pipe roll 6 John*, p. 256.
91. *Rot. pat.*, p. 33b.

In 1203 a levy of a similar nature, the fifteenth on exports and imports, also shows that the exchequer officials were well aware of the variety and volume of the movement of goods in trade, and of the accumulation of such goods in the country. The existence of wealth of this sort and its large volume lay at the basis of the development of new taxation. Certain goods were exempted from the fifteenth: grain, wines, salt, wax, vair, miniver, *werellum*, and tin; other goods, viz., any kind of grain, pork or any other meat, cheese, butter, honey, salt, herring, or salmon,[92] could not be exported without a permit from the committee of three who were in general charge of the fifteenth, or of Geoffrey Fitz Peter, or of the king.

The detailed accounts of the thirteenth of 1207 have disappeared, but the writs state that it was to be based on revenues and movables of every sort on the lands that were held by lay tenure, on the property of certain religious who did not hold by military service, and on the king's demesne. The lower secular clergy were asked for an aid, but after some negotiation do not seem to have made a grant.[93] The only surviving specific notices of revenues taxed were the rents of assize. Ralph de Trubleville in his account of the lands of Baldwin Wac accounted for £8 4s. 3d. of the thirteenth of the assized rents of those lands in Lincolnshire.[94] The only movables that have received mention were livestock.

The omission in the writs of definite lists of goods and revenues which were to be assessed and exempted may mean that the levy was to be based on certain goods and revenues well understood as customary. It is more likely that the king and his council had instructed the justices to base the tax on as comprehensive a list of both goods and revenues as possible. This is indicated by the statement in the writ that for each layman of whomsoever he may hold with a tenement yielding a mark of revenue annually 12d. should be paid; and also for any mark's worth of any kind of movable chattel whatever 12d. should be paid, and so on in proportion.[95]

No further carucages or taxes on movables were levied in John's reign. The late scutages of John were levied on the conventional

92. *Ibid.*, p. 72. *Rot. claus.*, I, 84. *Rot. oblatis*, p. 413. Gervase of Canterbury, II, LVIII. N. S. B. Gras, *The early English customs system* (Cambridge, 1918), pp. 218, 220, 221.
93. *Rot. claus.*, I, 81, 85. *Pipe roll 9 John*, p. 71. *Annals of Dunstaple*, p. 29. *Rot. pat.*, p. 72. Mitchell, *Studies in taxation*, pp. 86–87.
94. *Pipe roll 9 John*, p. 13. *Pipe roll 10 John*, p. 89.
95. *Rot. pat.*, p. 71.

BASIS OF THE ASSESSMENT OF TAXES

number of fees that had been taxed, usually the servitium debitum. It is clear that the council or the exchequer had formed the definite concept that it was risky to attempt to increase the revenue by the continual use of fines for military service, since out of the last four scutages only one was accompanied by fines, a definite change of policy. It is also evident that the authorities believed that a carucage should be based upon the actual number of carucates or plow teams and the tax on movables on an actual assessment of property. The control of church lands during the interdict must have impressed the guiding spirits of the royal administration with the enormous sums of cash in the hands of the clergy that might be tapped if favorable opportunity should present itself. But no necessity for the effort arose in John's reign.

In the reign of Henry III, we can see more clearly how the taxes were levied. The aid on knights' fees (scutage), carucage, tallage, and the taxes on personal property were all employed. Once also a poll tax was resorted to, but as it yielded little it was not used again. Scutage was used in the conventional way; it formed one of the regular sources as a general levy, but little expansion of revenue could be derived from it as the custom of collecting it in a fixed fashion was too strong. It had no future, we know, though this fact was concealed from the men of the time. Carucage was taken three times: in 1217 (during the civil war); in 1220; and in 1224 from the clergy only.

The government continued its efforts to base a levy upon an exact assessment of units of land in the case of the carucage and a careful valuation of property in the case of the taxes on movables. There are indications of opposition not only to the frequency of aids and to the occasions for which they were requested but also to basing them each time on a new valuation. The causes of opposition lay in the growing use of money in private transactions, of the consequent desire to increase private revenues, and the unwillingness to increase financial obligations.

At the beginning of the reign two aids were taken, the carucage to raise money for the war against Prince Louis, and the scutage on all fees to pay him the 10,000m. when he retired to France at the close of the war. The carucage was levied at 3s. on each carucate or hide.[96] We should not expect a careful assessment in such a time of disorder, yet the aim was to ascertain the number of hides or carucates in each bailiwick. Thus when the sheriff of Gloucester-

96. Exchequer L. T. R., Memoranda roll 2 Henry III, m. 8d, Public Record Office.

shire was ordered to respite the demand for the carucage on the Hospitalers, he was to report the number of hides or carucates which they held in his bailiwick.[97]

The aid of 1217 on knights' fees at 2m. was based on the conventional number of fees and collected as in the past by the sheriff, or paid by the tenant in chief direct to the exchequer. Since the barons were in control, a levy on fees would be moderate in rate and conventional in character.[98]

In the carucage of 1220, the council insisted on a definite assessment of property, and based it on the plow team instead of the carucate, or hide, a change that was for the first time clearly demonstrated by the editors of the *Book of Fees*.[99] The writ of assessment indicates this interpretation by the statement that it was to be assessed on the plows as yoked on June 21, 1220.[100] The conclusive proof lies in the records of the assessment in Hertfordshire which contain items each listing a number of car' and one or more *teste*, or heads, i.e., heads of oxen, a fraction of a team. So car' must mean *caruca*, or plow, for plow team.[101] Two kinds of rolls of the carucage have survived: assessment rolls and receipt rolls. To the assessment rolls belong those of the bailiwicks of Windsor, Gloucestershire, Oxfordshire, Norfolk and Suffolk, Huntingdonshire, and Northamptonshire.[102] In all these districts, the units assessed were integral units or aliquot fractional parts of the ox team; usually a team of eight oxen, but thirds, sixths, or twelfths may refer to teams of six, nine, or twelve oxen, for teams varied in their composition.[103] The rest are receipt rolls: Berkshire, Hertfordshire, and the honor of Wallingford. These receipt rolls furnish a variety of aliquot fractions of teams, halves, quarters, sixths, thirds, and in addition sums that cannot be related to any aliquot fraction, e.g., 5d., 7d., 7d. ob., 17d., 3d. ob., and so seem to contradict the theory that the tax was based on the team or a part of it.[104]

The fact that these curious fractions occur only in the receipt rolls suggests (as the editors of the *Book of Fees* first pointed out)

97. *Rot. claus.*, I, 307, 335b.
98. Mitchell, *Studies in taxation*, pp. 125–126.
99. *Book of fees*, I, 289–290.
100. *Rot. claus.*, I, 437b.
101. *Book of fees*, I, 331–333.
102. *Ibid.*, pp. 308, 311, 312, 315, 319, 326, 333.
103. *Pipe roll 7 Richard I*, p. xxiii. Exchequer L. T. R., Memoranda roll 9 Henry III, m. 3, Public Record Office.
104. *Book of fees*, I, 290, 292, 293, 294, 296, 302, 312, 331, 333.

BASIS OF THE ASSESSMENT OF TAXES 137

that they are due to partial payments of a man's debt and not to some unusual team or a part of it.[105] In Berkshire, the vill of Winterborne paid for 16 plow teams and a half and a part of a team, 33s. 5d.; in the rolls of arrears of laymen, it still owed 3s. 1d. on 1½ car' and parte, so that its total assessment was 36s. 6d. or 18¼ carucae.[106] The vill of Aldermaston paid for 21 carucae and a half and a part 43s. 7d. ob., in the arrears it owed or paid "pro parte caruce 4d. ob.," so the total assessment was 44s. on 22 carucae.[107] A complete account therefore of the assessments of Wallingford, Berkshire, and Oxfordshire might resolve these difficult items and show that no divergence existed from the custom that appears in the assessment rolls of the other shires. It is impossible to decide whether the levy on plow teams or on carucates would be more searching. The assessment proved impossible to carry through at once, for in some counties the roll records that the levy was not made. That the failure may have been due to the opposition of the baronage to Pandulph's government is indicated by the rebellion centered around the castle of Bytham. A considerable number of barons refused at first to pay the tax. Such acts must have affected the character of the assessment. In the account furnished the exchequer early in 1221 by the three special commissioners only 28 shires were reported.[108] Yet in areas where the assessment was carried out the enumeration of fractional teams indicates that the council aimed to base the tax upon the amount of land actually in cultivation instead of a conventional assessment.

The carucage of 1224 was taken in connection with the siege of Bedford and illustrates again the desire to base the levy on actual property. Though there are many references to the levy, we know little about it because the clergy assessed and collected the tax themselves and no detailed accounts, even fragmentary ones, have survived. The statements by the chroniclers and in the official accounts as to the way in which the tax was assessed suggest that it was based upon an actual counting of plows or teams rather than being an arbitrary assessment of lump sums. Thus the prelates promised to give the king for the expenses of the siege of Bedford half a mark from each caruca of the lands of their demesnes which

105. *Ibid.*, p. 290.
106. *Ibid.*, pp. 293, 297–298.
107. *Ibid.*, pp. 294, 298.
108. *Ibid.*, III, 1437–1439. W. W. Shirley, *Royal letters*, I, 151.

were separate from their churches and 2s. from the carucae of their knights and free tenants. The regular clergy gave 2s. for each caruca on all their lands.[109]

In 1222 appeared a poll tax, i.e., a head tax levied generally throughout the kingdom for the benefit of the kingdom of Jerusalem. There was some attention paid to property. After fixing the rates at 3m. for each earl, 1m. for each baron, 1s. for each knight, 1d. for each freeholder, the original writ of assessment issued June 25 continued: "and he who has no land, but has chattels, to the value of half a mark, shall pay a penny." [110] Such taxpayers included citizens and burgesses who we know from another clause in the writ were taxed. The yield of the tax was not great because it was a voluntary grant.[111] On November 24, 1222, other writs were issued anew rehearsing the grant as before with two modifications: instead of the item about the free tenant who was to pay a penny there was introduced the statement that "any one who cultivated the soil should pay a penny," thus adding the serf. In the earlier writ no provision was made for exemptions, but the November document provided that tenants who held only of religious houses or ecclesiastical persons should be exempt. There was no provision for distraint in the June writ, but the sheriffs were distraining and were directed to refrain from it, since the magnates had made this an aid without distraint. This command was issued on November 3, but on November 24 the new writs of assessment made a cautious provision for distraint "if it should be necessary for assessing and collecting these pennies, the sheriff was directed to distrain as it would seem useful to him to fulfill this command of the king." [112]

The reissue of the writ of assessment and collection five months after its original issue with the statement that the grant was made by the assent of the archbishop of Canterbury, the bishops, earls, barons, and magnates, that these payments should be made by the common desire of all, viz., an earl 3m. and so on with only one significant change, viz., the cautious threat of distress, indicates opposition, inadequate returns, or a real failure of the voluntary levy. It seems to confirm one chronicler's judgment that the "grant yielded little or nothing," because soon after it was opposed and led

109. *Patent rolls, 1216-1225*, pp. 464-465. *Annals of Dunstaple*, p. 86. Walter of Coventry, *Memoriale*, ed. William Stubbs (Rolls series), II, 254-255.
110. *Rot. claus.*, I, 516b.
111. *Ibid.*, p. 518b.
112. *Ibid.*, p. 567b.

BASIS OF THE ASSESSMENT OF TAXES 139

to little result.[113] The two notices of the total received from this levy that have survived amount to 800m.—evidence that this was not the levy that would solve financial stringency of the government.[114]

It seems to be clear that the council which had tried several experiments with taxation under Henry III now directed its attention to movable property as the basis of a tax. We turn to the great taxes on personal property which were so important in the reign of this king and later. They were four in number: a fifteenth in 1225, a fortieth in 1232, a thirtieth in 1237, and a twentieth in 1269. They display clearly the emphasis on personal property as the basis of taxation, but also the critical attitude of the great barons toward taxation of this kind. They struck out the tax on revenues and they limited the taxable goods to products that might be a source of private revenue. The free hand enjoyed by the assessors in 1207 was therefore struck away; a check was put to the fiscal encroachments of the crown precisely because the assessment was no longer a rough estimate but a definite valuation.

There was in 1225 no statement of the goods to be taxed, but the writs contain the longest, most detailed, and careful statement of goods to be exempted. For all ecclesiastics and freemen who were not merchants the following property was exempt: books, ornaments of churches and chapels, riding, cart, and sumpter horses, arms of all sorts, jewels, vases, utensils, the contents of larders and cellars, hay and grain purchased for the supply of castles; for merchants, their arms, riding horses, and furniture, the contents of their larders and cellars for their own use; for villeins, arms, furniture, tools, flesh, food, drink, hay and forage that were not for sale.[115] These elaborate provisions reflect the development of the council's knowledge of taxation and no doubt also the baronial opposition to the fiscal encroachments of the royal power. There was long debate over this tax before it was granted. The point of the exemptions seems to have been not to tax certain articles of luxury and defense and also not to weaken the manorial economic organization. It looks in part like a detailed statement of the goods referred to in Article XX of the Magna Carta which aimed to protect the barons from excessive mulcting by the courts. The protection accorded to the merchants and villeins was probably not

113. *Annals of Waverley*, p. 296.
114. *Patent rolls, 1216–1225*, pp. 512, 527.
115. *Ibid.*, p. 560.

because they made representations to the council but because in so doing the feudal lord was protecting his own interest. The detailed list of exemptions implies that the remaining property was to be carefully valued and taxed. This indeed seems to have been true. Disputes arose. In Sussex and Hampshire the assessors claimed that boats, nets, and ropes should be taxed; they were not specified in the writs as exempt. The question was referred back to the council which, in accordance with the principle of exempting a villein's necessary equipment, declared that such property was not subject to taxation. After a similar discussion, wine was taxed. The instructions were carefully obeyed as is evident from the three fragmentary rolls that have survived.[116]

The rolls indicate an effort to make an exact valuation: they contain many items like a sow with two little pigs, a cow with a calf, two heifers, four little pigs that have been weaned, six breeding ewes, a yearling colt, one blind mare and one lame mare, two yearling calves; they distinguish mature and young cattle of different ages; they note animals that were "*debiles.*" [117] Goods omitted in these rolls were: butter, cheese, apples, wax, wool, nuts, doves, hay, chickens, geese, and ducks, such as would be found in a manorial account, but omissions should not be stressed for we have only a few rolls.[118]

These rolls show that the government aimed to make a searching and exact valuation of movables. They indicate that each person was assessed individually, that each kind of property was assessed, showing the amount or number of items and the value of each. On the total valuation of the goods of each owner the tax was calculated.[119] Broadly speaking, the valuations of all animals varied sufficiently for us to conclude that a definite attempt was made to fix a fair value in the assessment. Work horses varied from 2*s.* 6*d.* to 4*s.*; cows from 2*s.* to 4*s.*, though most valuations were 2*s.* 6*d.* and 3*s.*; oxen from 2*s.* to 5*s.*; mares 1*s.* to 5*s.*, usually 3*s.* and 4*s.*; young cattle, such as bullocks and heifers range from 1*s.* to 3*s.*; colts (pullus) from 6*d.* to 3*s.* 6*d.*, and vituli from 5*d.* to 18*d.* Small animals like pigs and sheep varied in value, though distinctions in size among them probably would be less marked; grown pigs from 3*s.* to 18*d.*; little pigs

116. Lay subsidy rolls, 242/47, 242/127, 242/2, Public Record Office.
117. *Ibid.*, 242/127, m. 7–m. 19.
118. *The pipe roll of the bishopric of Winchester for the fourth year of the pontificate of Peter des Roches, 1208–1209,* ed. under the supervision of Hubert Hall (London, 1903), p. xxvii.
119. Lay subsidy roll, 242/47, m. 1, Public Record Office.

2d., 3d.; sheep and lambs practically always at 4d., but sheep alone at 4d. or even as little as 8d.[120]

A definite effort was also made to make an exact assessment of the amount and value of grain and other merchandise. Variations in valuations placed upon grain appear: oats at 8d. and 1s. a quarter; wheat at 2s., 2s. 4d., 2s. 8d., 3s., 3s. 4d. a quarter; corn at 2s., 2s. 4d., 2s. 8d. a quarter; mixed grain at 15d., 2s., 2s. 4d., or 2s. 8d. a quarter; barley at 3s., 20d.; peas at 15d., 16d., 12d., and 2s. a quarter; beans at 16d., 18d. or 2s. a quarter; malt at 12d. 2s. 6d. a summa.[121] Grain was not in general assessed in a lump sum but each property owner reported the amount on hand, in quarters, summas, bushels, strikas, or hopas. Henry Brazur was assessed for one bushel of wheat valued at 3s. (and more), two summas of oats valued at 2s. and half a summa of beans, 8d.; Turold Lagus, one bushel of wheat, 9d.; one summa of oats, 1s.[122] Most of the measures were in quarters or summas. In case the grain had not been threshed, the amount and value were estimated.[123] The writ of assessment states that goods produced on the manor and not sold or for sale were not subject to the assessment for the fifteenth.[124]

These articles however would be consumed in the course of the year unless sold. Suppose grain, for example, were used for seed and not consumed. The assessors followed a convention, for no notice of referring this problem to the council appears. Grain used for seed was taxed. Thus oats sowed before mid-Lent (March 9 in 1225) when the assessors had not arrived were taxed as well as those remaining in the barn.[125] Money occasionally was included among movables to be taxed.[126] Other movables besides grain and livestock were assessed, an indication of the searching nature of the assessment.[127] Or, putting it another way, looking at the assessments on individual owners, notice the variations in assessment. William Brun' had two oxen each worth 3s. and two other oxen each worth 7d. William Fitz Arkel had five oxen, the price of two oxen being 4s. 6d. each; of two others, 3s. 6d. each, and of the fifth, 2s. 6d. He had three mares, two valued at 2s. 6d. each and the third at

120. *Ibid.*, 242/127, m. 8.
121. *Ibid.*, m. 2. *Ibid.*, 242/47, m. 6 and *passim*.
122. *Ibid.*, m. 1, m. 9, m. 32. *Ibid.*, 242/127, m. 2, m. 9.
123. *Ibid.*, m. 6, m. 18, m. 19.
124. William Stubbs, *Select charters*, pp. 355–357.
125. Lay subsidy roll, 242/47, m. 27, m. 28, m. 29, m. 30, m. 31, m. 33, Public Record Office.
126. *Ibid.*, 242/127, m. 2, m. 3, m. 6, m. 15.
127. *Ibid.*, m. 7, m. 8, m. 8d, m. 9, m. 11, m. 13, m. 15. *Ibid.*, 242/47, m. 6, m. 7, m. 11.

4s.; and four colts, two valued at 15d. each and the other two at 6d. each; six cows, two valued at 3s. 6d. each, two at 3s. each, and two at 2s. 6d. each; five oxen, three valued at 15d. each and two at 10d. each.[128]

Or let us take a different approach and look for the minimum amount of property which one had to possess in order to be taxed. Perhaps owners of only a few goods would slip through the untrained fingers of the new taxers. Not at all. Cristina had one mare worth 2s. Her tax was 1½d.[129] Walter Sucore had one cow valued at 2s. 6d. and one bullock worth 15d. His fifteenth was 3d.[130] Eustace had one cow valued at 2s. 6d. His fifteenth was 2d.[131] Sometimes the assessors did not bother to list the property if there was a single item, only entering the amount of the tax.[132]

The assessors did not stop with such small property holders. They went so far that complaints against their exactions reached the council and orders were issued in consequence not to press too hard on the poor.

And since we have heard that you do not spare poor women, exacting the fifteenth from them, even if they have only a trifling string of beads or something cheap like that, or a silver brooch worth a penny, two pence, or three pence, wherefore many curses of the poor will rise up to heaven which we do not desire to fall upon our head, we command you not to exact the fifteenth from trifling objects of this sort, particularly on brooches and other trinkets of this kind, inasmuch anyway as jewels are exempted from the fifteenth.[133]

The royal demesne also paid the fifteenth of movables. Broadly speaking, the fifteenth was based upon a comprehensive valuation of movables.[134] A great advance was made in basing the fifteenth on an assessed valuation of movables in the case of the prelates. In 1207 they had often compounded for the thirteenth. But in 1220 and 1224 they paid according to an assessment of their teams made by their own men. Now they yielded a little more ground to the king, for although they made the assessment by their own men,

---

128. *Ibid.*, 242/127, m. 2, m. 4.
129. *Ibid.*, 242/47, m. 29.
130. *Ibid.*, m. 18.
131. *Ibid.*
132. *Ibid.*, m. 5, m. 9, m. 16, m. 18, m. 20.
133. *Patent rolls, 1216–1225*, p. 572.
134. *Ibid.*, p. 562. Roger of Wendover, II, 318.

BASIS OF THE ASSESSMENT OF TAXES 143

a royal clerk collaborated. None are recorded as compounding except the Templars and the Cistercians.[135]

The sixteenth on the property of the beneficed clergy was based on revenues, not movables, on property that had not paid the fifteenth, specifically prebends and revenues from the common property of each church or chapter. This levy was not so heavy as a tax on movables would have been, for the latter was refused. The tax might include the revenue from lands held by military or other free tenants, or from grain grown on land belonging to churches.[136]

The writ for the fortieth of 1232 was based directly on the experience gained in 1225. Persons holding less than 40d. worth of property were not to be taxed, a provision which in principle became a rule in later levies. The objection may have come from lords, not small men. That settled the grievance of one class of taxpayers, i.e., the barons who objected to such crippling levies. As to goods to be taxed, a change in statement was employed in the writ. Instead of listing the goods exempted, it contained a list of the goods which were to be assessed, viz., a fortieth of all movables belonging to each property holder as he held them on the morrow of St. Matthew (September 22), 1232, that is, grain of all kinds, plow teams, sheep, cows, pigs, stud horses, cart horses, and work horses. No exempt goods were listed.[137] This is a striking change, for always in the recent past the writs listed those goods that were not to be assessed, or as in 1207 merely stated that all movables held by the laity and revenues were to be taxed. To select certain properties on which alone a tax was to be levied indicates a less comprehensive assessment than to list certain exemptions and tax everything else. It looks like a limitation on the basis of the tax on movables; a further step along the line taken in 1225 when revenues were struck off the list of taxable sources of revenue. Yet the basis of this tax indicates a compromise. While only a limited list of goods was to be assessed, one item was very comprehensive, bladis, grains of all kinds. Moreover since the date of assessment was September 22, the full harvest of the year would

---

135. *Patent rolls, 1216–1225*, pp. 570, 571. *Ibid., 1225–1232. Rot. claus.*, II, 21b, 33b, 40b, 41, 74–75, 177.

136. William Edward Lunt, *Financial relations of the papacy with England*, p. 188. *Patent rolls, 1225–1232*, pp. 64, 249. *Vetus registrum Sarisberiense*, ed. W. Rich-Jones (Rolls series), II, 66. *Rot. claus.*, II, 143, 177.

137. Stubbs, *Select charters*, pp. 360–361. *Close rolls, 1231–1234*, p. 155.

be on hand and certainly the amount of livestock on the manors would be larger than at the middle or close of the winter. While the king's demand did not originally envisage an assessment in September, everyone was aware that a tax levied in that month would yield far more than one in the winter. Recall that the Saladin tithe which was granted in February on grain was to be based on the yield of the following harvest. Hence here was ground laid for a compromise; to reduce the variety of goods taxed and increase the amount of each unit assessed. Another reason for a compromise arose out of the opposition of the magnates to the grant; the laity argued that they owed no aid on this occasion because they had personally served in the campaign in France; the prelates doubted whether they legally owed an aid for they had earlier made an aid for this expedition. We must recall that the fortieth was only granted at the second or the third session where the king's plea for an aid was discussed.[138] With the change in the basis of the tax a new assessment was necessary. Still disputes arose. The commissioners assessed, for example, fish nets, ships, gold, and silver. The council had to intervene and directed that such goods should be exempt, adding a word of reproof to their subordinates, that they should more carefully follow the instructions given in their writ.[139]

In the single short roll that is extant, the intent to base the tax on a new assessment can be seen.[140] Horses, cows, and oxen were listed at various prices; horses at 3s. usually; but also occasionally at 2s., 2s. 6., once at 3s. 6d.; oxen, usually at 3s., but also at other prices, 2s. 6d.; 4 oxen for 13s.; 3 oxen at 10s. Cows and young cattle were listed at varying prices; usually from 2s. to 3s. Yet indications may be seen that valuations might be stereotyped. Sheep in every case were valued at 1s. each; we have seen such a uniformity in assessment in 1225, when on the same manor all sheep were assessed at 5d. each or at 3d. in most cases on a given manor, but Thomas Hauten had 80 sheep valued at 4d. each, while the sheep of other proprietors on the same area were valued at 3d. each.[141]

The most marked indication of conventionalization in the levy was that all grain of a taxpayer was classed together as bladum

138. Mitchell, *Studies in taxation*, p. 200.
139. *Close rolls, 1231–1234*, pp. 288, 290, 291.
140. N. Niemeyer, "Assessment for the fortieth of 1232," pp. 733–735.
141. Lay subsidy roll, 242/127, m. 3, m. 6, Public Record Office.

BASIS OF THE ASSESSMENT OF TAXES

and a lump sum charged against it. The reason may partly be that as the assessment began in September most of the grain was still in the stack and so the assessors estimated the amount of the crop. Such a valuation could be fairly accurate, as is shown by the fact that the proportion of the tax on this roll from grain was generally larger than that from livestock. Yet such a method would not prevent them, if they desired, from listing each kind of grain separately.

In twelve out of twenty-five cases on our roll the value assigned to the grain was 10s., 1m., 1½m., 2m.; in the other thirteen cases there are various numbers of marks or shillings, but the number of pence was always 4 or a multiple. Such regularity was unavoidable if grain was still unthreshed, but it throws an unfavorable light upon the efficiency of the assessment when we compare such figures with those obtained when the amount of grain has been dealt with in a business way, as in sales off a manor. No such regularity emerges. The custodian of the honor of Marlborough in the fourteenth year of Henry III sold off the old grain which he had received from his predecessor and accounted for the following sums received: 9s. 10d., £6 11s. 9d., 49s., 78s. 6d., 119s. 4d. ob.[142]

But the effort that had been made to tax all church property failed; the revenues that had paid a sixteenth in 1226 were exempted this year.[143] Prelates sought and obtained the authority to assess and collect the tax (the fortieth) not only on their demesne but on all their lands by a special group of assessors and collectors, as in the case of the bishop of Ely. In the cases of the bishops of Hereford and Worcester these were vassals of the prelate.[144] The rolls contain a large number of religious that compounded for the fortieth or were exempt, and perhaps this represents a decline in the insistence of assessing property.[145]

The writ of assessment of 1237 reflects the experience gained in the preceding levies. It first states the goods to be taxed practically in the words of the writ of 1232 and in the same order; as though the clerks in 1237 had the earlier writ before them. The new writ ran *"bladis, carucis, ovibus, vaccis, porcis, haraciis, equis, carectariis assignatis ad wainagia,"* and then introduced a

---

142. *Pipe roll 14 Henry III*, ed. Chalfant Robinson (Pipe Roll Society), XLII, p. 1.
143. Stubbs, *Select charters*, p. 361. *Close rolls, 1231–1234*, p. 155.
144. *Ibid.*, pp. 160, 283, 285, 287, 288, 290.
145. *Ibid.*, pp. 290, 291, 292, 295, 303. Pipe roll 17 Henry III, m. 6, m. 8, m. 9. Pipe roll 18 Henry III, m. 7, Public Record Office.

significant closing phrase "*et aliis pecoribus et bonis.*" It was as though the council said, "The preceding property is what you are likely to find, but if you meet with other goods in sufficient quantity, they are liable for taxation." To make the matter still more clear, the instructions continued with a list of exemptions: "*exceptis argento, auro, palefridis, summariis, dextrariis, runcinis, armis, utensilibus, et vasis*"—a considerable list, though not so detailed as in 1225. The statement of taxable and exempt goods formed the most comprehensive yet elastic statement that we have had. The problem was to insure that adequate valuations should be placed upon the taxable property by the local jurors and that property holders should not conceal their goods. This tax had been granted in January, 1237, and the writs of assessment appointing the county assessors had been issued in July.[146] The writ stated that the tax was based on the property in possession on September 15 of that year, and the assessment was to begin in various counties at fixed dates during the subsequent month. It declared that in each vill the actual assessment was to be made by a jury of four legal men of the vill in cooperation with the county assessors. The sheriff was to be aiding the county assessors. Among other duties he was to summon the local jurors who had been designated by the county assessors to meet with the latter. Such was the preparation for the beginning of the assessment on September 15.

The news of the new levy and its method of assessment percolated through the country and prepared the people, reinforced by memories of earlier levies, to meet this new financial burden. The reaction in the localities was to keep the assessment as low as possible and to store goods when feasible on the lands of religious orders that were exempt from the tax, such as Templars, Hospitalers, Gilbertines, Cistercians, and Premonstratensians. Evidence of these activities soon reached Westminster. The council at once struck at both the county assessors and the local juries to secure a higher valuation. On October 6 they wrote to the sheriffs and the assessors in all counties, as follows:

We have lately heard that the four jurors of the vills elected to value chattels for the thirtieth granted to us are violating their oaths by false valuations, namely, they generally value an ox at five shillings, when it is worth ten shillings or even more; a pig which is worth two or

146. *Close rolls, 1234–1237*, p. 545.

BASIS OF THE ASSESSMENT OF TAXES 147

three shillings, they value at 6d.; a sheep which is worth 16d. or even more they value at 6d.; they also falsely value the grain which has been harvested and other chattels in the same way: whence, if they continue as they have begun in their assessment, we are sure that all such assessors will be convicted of perjury and also we shall not receive half of the thirtieth granted to us so generously by the magnates and others of our realm.

In such cases the county assessors were to go in person to the vill, review the assessment, place a just valuation on the goods, and punish the local jurors.[147] They should also make sure that prospective taxpayers were not evading assessment by concealing their property on the lands of religious. These additional measures by the council resulted in a careful assessment although the valuations did not reach the height set in the supplementary instructions. Grain was valued in a lump sum as in 1232, but they returned to the method of 1225 of listing the amount and value of each variety owned by each taxpayer.

We have a single roll of twenty-eight names of the vill of Kennton or Kenniton.[148] Valuations varied: wheat ranged from 3s. to 5s. a quarter though most taxpayers were assessed at 4s.; barley in four cases 1s. a quarter and in one case 1s. 9d.; mestel (10 items) was valued at 2s. or 3s. a quarter with several variants; oats (24 items) were valued at 1s. 3d. in all but two cases; peas (9 items) at 2s. a quarter except in one case; grain (bladum) (12 items) other than wheat (frumentum) ranged from 1s. 3d. a quarter to 3s. 6d. and most rates differed one from another; bere in three out of four cases 2s. a quarter; vetches (4 items) all 18d. a quarter. Broadly speaking therefore there was considerable variety in valuation of grain; in all cases except two (where bushels were used) the measure used was a quarter. We may conclude therefore that various measures were the rule as in 1225. The reasons for the variation in valuations of grain may be that the assessors judged the quality as well as the amount from the grain unthreshed, but it is a difficult problem. The chief varieties of livestock that appeared in this roll were cows, pigs, sheep, wethers, lambs, horses, and oxen, with some young stock. All show considerable variations in the values affixed to them; cows from 3s. 6d. to 6s.; pigs from 6d. to 20d.; sheep from 3d. to 10d. (*oves*

---

147. *Ibid.*, p. 569.
148. Lay subsidy roll, 242/74, Public Record Office.

matries) ; lambs from a penny to over 8*d.* each (9 lambs for 60*d.*), 20 lambs almost mature, 14*s.* 4*d.*; horses (caballus) 4*s.* to 8*s.*; stots (stotici) from 10*d.* to half a mark; oxen from 3*s.* to 6*s.* 8*d.* A few comments also indicate attempts to graduate the assessment to the quality of the animal. The variations in valuations occur in the property of the same taxpayer, not merely higher on one person and lower on another. For example,

At the house of Alice Church (Alicia de Ecclesia), 1 quarter of bladum, price 3 shillings; and 1 old cow with a broken foot, price 3 shillings; and 1 pig, 19 pence; and three pigs, 18 pence; and 2 wethers (cestriz) 21 pence; and 10 ewes (ovis) 6 shillings; and 11 ewes, 5 shillings; and 8 lambs (angni) 20 pence; 3 lambs, 3 pence; 1 bullock, 21 pence; 1 caballus debilis, 3 shillings; 2 quarters of oats, 30 pence.[149]

These valuations are not so high as those mentioned in the king's writ, but the variations and the fact that they fall within the limits stated in the writ suggest that the assessors were placing values which were defensible. The most striking feature of the assessment however was the omission of hay, butter, cheese, hides, wool, and the small amount of young stock, except lambs. The valuations which the exchequer suggested as normal were higher than any found earlier in the rolls and higher than valuations reported by custodians for the property on their manors.

Thus by 1237 considerable progress had been made in establishing a method of taxing movable property. Each time a new assessment was made, the valuations varied according to conditions. The goods taxed comprised some though not all of the important agricultural products; wood, hay, young stock, honey, wax, hides seem to have been generally omitted. After 1237 no tax of this kind was levied till 1269 when with the levy of a twentieth for the crusade, taxation on personal property was resumed on the foundation prepared a generation earlier. As in 1237, both goods taxed and those exempt were listed though not in as much detail as earlier; the orders specify grain, livestock, and other products of the land and all other movable goods, both of magnates and of knights, as well as of other laity, except war horses, saddle horses, and other riding horses of freemen, and except treasure, like gold, silver, gold and silver plate, and precious stones.[150]

149. *Ibid.*, m. 1, m. 2.
150. D. Wilkins, *Concilia*, II, 21. J. A. C. Vincent, *Lancashire lay subsidies*, I, 93

BASIS OF THE ASSESSMENT OF TAXES

This tax was granted apparently in August, 1269, but it was to be based upon the goods in hand the following Michaelmas. Thomas Wykes emphasizes the pressure exerted upon the assessors by the council to effect such a valuation. It aroused great complaint among the people because the assessment and collection lasted into the spring and summer of 1270, and the goods on which the tax was based had been in part sold or consumed before the assessors arrived. These officials, according to the chronicler, were willing to assess the property which they found in hand when, long after Michaelmas, they arrived at a given vill, but the council insisted on their valuing the property as it had existed at Michaelmas, 1269.[151] There may be rhetoric in the complaint of the chronicler, as when he says that the assessment on the laity was delayed till the following summer. The valuations made in the summer of 1270 were chiefly of the clergy, for they had not granted the twentieth till Easter; or when he says the tax was based on both movables and immovables—taxation on immobilia might mean land values or revenues, neither of which apparently was taxed. These phrases seem to reveal the struggle between the taxpayers and the local assessors on the one hand and the royal government on the other, which was seeking to establish a verus valor as of the date when most goods were on hand. A single membrane of the tax seems to indicate that "royal cupidity" was not so successful in enforcing its will as Thomas represented.[152] It contains the names of 24 taxpayers and reveals how the assessors interpreted their oath. With each name is given the number of animals that each had and the value and the amount and value per unit in quarters and bushels of each kind of grain. This plan followed the precedent of earlier taxes. The only kinds of grain mentioned were wheat, barley, and oats; less than half (9 out of 24) reported barley; as to livestock, 17 tenants reported cows (all, 1 cow each), but only 1 had young cattle (2 bovettas); 7 reported sheep (52 sheep in all); 4 reported pigs (14 in all, 10 of these belonging to Maurice de Berkeley, the great man); 5 reported plow horses (2 having 1 each, and the others 2, 3, and 4 each); only one man reported oxen (2 in number). Certain characteristics of the assessment seem to emerge: the omission of certain of young stock (except 2 bovettas), no colts, young pigs, lambs, young cattle. Does this mean that a convention was in view

---

151. *Chronicon Thomae Wykes*, pp. 227–228.
152. Lay subsidy roll, E 179/242/12.

by the taxpayers and the local assessors to limit the tax to certain livestock and field crops? Some variation occurred still in the valuations of livestock. The total value of the stock was £14 3s.; that of grain £25 6s. 2d.

All valuations of grain were uniform; wheat at 4s. a quarter; oats at 2s. 6d. a quarter; barley at 3s. 4d. a quarter. For livestock there was a fair amount of variation: work horses from 3s. to 6s. 8d.; cows from 5s. to 6s. 6d.; pigs from 1s. to 2s.; sheep (50) were all valued at 1s. each. There was some indication of conventional values, but the fact that grain was subdivided into varieties and assessed at a price per quarter, that the livestock of each taxpayer was numbered and valued per unit indicated that the pressure for a careful assessment was still effective.

We turn to two other groups: the clergy and the royal demesne. Many of the religious that did not hold by military tenure escaped assessment; they fined for the twentieth incident on themselves and their villeins.[153] Prelates that held by military or other lay tenure fined for the levy on their own property and that of their demesnes.[154] Their military tenants paid the county assessors on the assessed valuation of their property. This had now become custom. The demesne, at any rate the royal towns, paid the twentieth, but in lump sums, and the assessors did not enter the towns to levy the tax. A town might fine to be allowed to compound for the twentieth and that it should not be tallaged per capita for the twentieth. Canterbury paid £40 for the twentieth.[155] Thus the towns at least compounded for the twentieth as did many of the bishops, abbots, and the heads of small houses of religious, while the property holders on the lands of the lay tenants in chief and the tenants of the clerical tenants in chief other than those on the demesne had their movables valued and taxed. The parish clergy were taxed on their income.[156]

Probably the yield of the taxes on movables was increased by more careful assessment. The amount of the taxable property was certainly augmented by the simple device of making the assess-

153. *Calendar of patent rolls, 1266–1272*, pp. 467–740, *passim*. Vincent, *Lancashire lay subsidies*, I, 102.
154. *Calendar of patent rolls, 1266–1272*, pp. 469, 487, 495, 509, 511, 514, 518. Pipe roll 1 Edward I, m. 6, Public Record Office.
155. Originalia roll 55 Henry III, m. 1. Fine roll 55 Henry III, m. 14, Public Record Office. *Calendar of patent rolls, 1266–1272*, pp. 416, 423, 439, 445, 466, 487 494, 496, 502, 505, 513, 522, 525, 536, 538, 540, 542, 543, 584, 643, 667.
156. Lunt, "Consent of lower clergy," p. 164.

BASIS OF THE ASSESSMENT OF TAXES 151

ment in the autumn instead of at any other time of year. Curiously enough the council did not apparently think that this was a matter of moment at the opening of Henry III's reign. Yet they knew that the date of assessment would make a difference. The priest took his tithe at harvest time, going into the field and having it carried directly to the tithe barn. As was pointed out above, the Saladin tithe on grain was to be levied in the autumn succeeding the date of the grant, which was made in February. The fifteenth of 1225 was granted in February and the assessment began at once. The goods taxed were those on hand when the tax was granted, that is, about five months after the harvest, when some grain had been sold and some animals slaughtered. The council made no effort to tax property that had been disposed of before the tax was granted. Men were summoned before the commissioners, who proposed to assess their property on the ground that they had possessed it when the tax was granted. On introducing evidence that they had disposed of the goods before the tax was granted, they were exempted from assessment.[157] As a result of assessing the property in February the value of livestock exceeded the value of other property, as can readily be seen from the following lists. In one roll of a single vill containing 36 names the assessment of livestock amounted to £33 15s. 3d., and of grain £12 6s. 8d.; one fourth of the names reported no grain at all.[158] In a second roll containing several vills, of the first 372 names that are legible, the assessment of livestock amounted to £371 8s. 3d., and that of grain £34 17s. 9d.; about two thirds of the taxpayers had no grain at all.[159] In 1232 a short roll of 25 names has survived from the assessment of September after the crops had been harvested. The value of the grain usually exceeded or at least equaled that of the livestock: livestock, £17 13s. 2d.; grain, £19 11s. 4d. In 14 cases the valuation of grain exceeded that of livestock.[160]

The difference in the two years was not of course due to the difference in prices but to the fact that the amount of grain on hand in September was far greater than in February. The change in the date of the assessment was not made however with that point in mind. The great council had been called in March, 1232, and had been asked for a grant to pay the king's debts incurred in

---

157. *Rot. claus.*, II, 62.
158. Lay subsidy roll, 242/2, Public Record Office.
159. *Ibid.*, 247/47.
160. Niemeyer, "Assessment of the fortieth of 1232," pp. 233–235.

152 TAXATION IN MEDIEVAL ENGLAND

the campaign in France which had just terminated. When the king asked for an aid the earl of Chester replied that as the lay tenants had just performed their service in France they legally owed the king nothing. With Henry III's permission the laity then withdrew. The prelates also asked for a delay because of the absence of so large a proportion of their number. The council then was prorogued till after Easter.[161] Following that festival the earls and barons met at London, but no record of their actions has survived.[162] In September a great council met and granted the fortieth. Probably the returns proved the advantage to the government of an assessment in September. At any rate in 1237 the great council which granted the thirtieth met in January, but it decided that the property which should be taxed was that which should be on hand the following September, as the writ of July stated, "when the grain shall have been harvested." [163] In the single roll of the assessment that is on hand the value of the grain exceeded that of the livestock.[164] Thirty names appear in the roll; in sixteen cases the value of livestock exceeded that of grain, but the total assessment of the vill gives grain £56 10s. 5d. and livestock £40 12s. 7d. The single short roll of the assessment of 1269 gives similar results. Twenty-four taxpayers are assessed; grain £25 6s. 2d. and livestock £14 3s.

The returns of the thirtieth of 1283 for the whole hundred of Blackburn in Suffolk indicate that our brief records from Henry III have not been misleading. This tax was made in January, and the assessment of the grain slightly exceeded that of livestock (£1,857 for grain; £1,805 for stock); consequently we should expect that the value of grain on hand in September considerably exceeded that of stock. Yet the results seem to conflict with the valuations in the rolls of the fifteenth of 1225, made in February. In the earlier, a quarter or more of the taxpayers made no return under grain. Such was not the case in 1283; only occasionally did a taxpayer report no grain. If our rolls of 1225 are typical, the high proportion of taxpayers who reported no grain may be due to the leniency of the assessors, or the opposition of the taxpayers, or both.

We come to the close of the reign of Henry III after more than

161. Roger of Wendover, III, 21.
162. Mitchell, *Studies in taxation*, p. 200.
163. *Ibid.*, p. 215. *Close rolls, 1234–1237*, p. 545.
164. Lay subsidy roll, 242/74, Public Record Office.

BASIS OF THE ASSESSMENT OF TAXES 153

a century of experiment with general levies. The aids which they employed at the beginning were probably lump sums, but soon were based upon a definite unit of land, the carucate or the knight's fee, or an assessed valuation of revenues and movables that revolutionized the character of the tax, for it became a contribution that was owed to the king by property owners regardless of whether or not they were his tenants. The problem in each of these levies was to see that each unit throughout the kingdom paid the tax to the king. The simplest case was a scutage on all knights' fees. From very early in the development of scutage as the composition for service the tenants and rear vassals became accustomed to reckon it at a fixed rate per fee. Hence when the king took an aid on knights' fees, it was conventional to reckon the aid on the land of every vassal in this way. A difference of opinion could arise over one point, really a minor point only. Scutage as the composition for military service was the composition on the servitium debitum, not on enfeoffments that exceeded that number. The vassals and rear vassals were conscious of their rights in this connection. In the aid of 1168, the fees above the servitium debitum were charged in the pipe roll but not paid. Nevertheless the council gained along this line. Escheated lands or lands in hand paid on all fees enfeoffed. The aid of 1217 seems to have been based on the same number of fees as in 1168. Certainly this was true of John's reign. But the aids of 1235 aimed to tax all fees whenever enfeoffed. So did the scutage of 1242. Those aids show no marked increase over 1168 in the number of fees taxed. That is, it proved impossible to increase materially the returns from scutage by levying on all land held by military service per fee, for the number of new enfeoffments was not great. Nevertheless the opinion persisted that much land was enfeoffed that was not recorded.[165] So the government tried to insist that men should take out knighthood who held by military service.[166] An extension of this rule was later made to compel all tenants to take out knighthood if they held one fee or even less in urban or rural areas, whether it was held by military or by socage tenure.[167] Additional regulations were added to draw more land into the military group when it was provided that all tenants who held land of the annual value of £20 (later £15) whether of military

165. *Annals of Burton,* ed. H. R. Luard, in "Annales monastici," I (Rolls series), 364.
166. *Rot. claus.,* II, 69b, 172.
167. *Close rolls, 1237-1242,* pp. 239-240.

tenure or socage should take out knighthood.[168] The aim would be to increase both the service and the commutation. To what extent they were successful it is hard to say; a good deal of opposition appeared for there were many orders issued to postpone taking up knighthood, and the returns for scutage in the last half of Henry III's reign show no marked increase.[169] Another way of increasing the returns on composition was by raising the rate and at the same time by exacting a fine. The results of efforts along these lines by John were the limitations imposed by the Great Charter. Under Henry III the rate of scutage rose to $3m.$ per fee and stopped there. Sporadic attempts in this reign to levy fines were not very successful and there were no attempts to employ fines after 1245. Scutage therefore became stereotyped in rate and in number of fees taxed, and the effort to secure larger returns by the use of the fine proved impracticable.

The carucage was derived from the danegeld. Abandoned in 1162 it was thought of in 1194 when the council was pondering ways of raising additional cash to complete Richard's ransom. It was a revival of the assessment of 1084, minus the exemptions that had crept in since that date. The council then determined to revamp the levy by establishing it on a new basis, viz., on the actual unit of land measurement, the carucate or hide, of 120 acres, with only partial success. They then shifted the basis to the plow and team, which, except in 1217, they retained till 1224 when the tax was finally abandoned. They were not always able to secure the assessment and often had to compound for this levy. The effort thus to create a new land tax was partly successful, but the abandonment of scutage and carucage was due to the competition of the levies on personal property that were so much more fruitful.

First employed in connection with the crusades, it then came to be used for general purposes, and as we have seen the government had much success in basing it upon the assessed valuation of movables. The six rolls that have survived, three of the fifteenth of 1225, one each for the levies of 1232, 1237, and 1269, may seem too slight a basis for generalizations concerning levies that embraced thousands of such rolls. But the six rolls have certain advantages: they were all preserved by chance, they represent all the levies, they are all rolls containing the assessment on individual items of property of each property holder. They all show that the

168. *Ibid.*, p. 362. Vincent, *Lancashire lay subsidies*, I, 29.
169. *Close rolls, 1237–1242, passim.* Vincent, *Lancashire lay subsidies*, I, 27.

BASIS OF THE ASSESSMENT OF TAXES

assessments exhibit certain common characteristics. Under the name of each person was listed the number of animals of each kind he possessed and the value of each; and except in one roll, 1232, the amount of each kind of grain and the value of each unit of measure, though in a few cases the amount was estimated "*in tasso*"; there was variety in the values of each kind of stock. It seems fair to conclude that the government succeeded in securing to a moderate degree at least a fair valuation of the goods taxed and a fair list of the goods which each possessed. At the same time, the omission of a considerable number of varieties of animals and grain in 1269, the classification of all varieties of grain under the single head of bladum in 1232, and the complaint in 1237 of low valuations indicates the difficulties under which the government labored to secure a complete and accurate assessment. After 1225 many houses of religious compounded. Since the assessment of certain parts of the movable property on the lands of prelates was always in their hands, we may suspect a less accurate valuation in these cases. Broadly speaking, the taxation of the movables of the laity had established a custom of evaluating the grain, each variety and amount by itself and each unit of livestock, with the ideal of attaining a detailed verus valor. Each tax meant a new valuation. So far they had escaped the conventionalization that had characterized the danegeld and to a lesser extent the scutage.

IV

CONSENT TO TAXATION

THE aspect of the development of taxation that perhaps has attracted most attention is the method of authorization, the question of consent. It has been said that by means of the power of the purse parliament secured control over the king. The connection of parliament with taxation grew out of the procedure by which taxes were authorized by the great curia regis before parliament was created in the last part of the thirteenth century. This practice developed from the principle that governed the relations between lords and vassals and lords and tenants on the manor that obligations were fixed by contract and custom, and that any additional request for services, goods, or money needed the consent of the donor. While it is true that the king at that time did not enjoy the arbitrary authority to levy taxes on property, at the same time no effective control over his policy had been established by the close of the thirteenth century. He had made three great gains in the direction of his own control over taxes on property: first, that taxes should be based upon an assessed valuation of the property in the hands of nearly all property holders in the realm whatever their status in the feudal or manorial system; second, he had succeeded in obtaining grants of taxes with such frequency that they began to assume the character of a *consuetudo*; third, he had multiplied the reasons by which he could legally justify his demand for an aid. War and debt were accepted as proper excuses for such grants. Meanwhile the method of authorization was being imperceptibly transformed from individual into corporate consent.

The revenues of the English kings after the Norman Conquest consisted of customary payments of various kinds of both Saxon and Norman origin:

1. The income from the demesne, the manors held by the king, formed nearly all of the sheriff's farm, the most important single branch of royal revenue. In addition to the occasional levy of tallage, there were payments by urban groups for the right to farm the towns and the town farms themselves. Since all the urban areas

CONSENT TO TAXATION 157

dependent on the king were called part of his demesne, we may include here the revenue that the king derived from them; there were also some judicial fines included in the sheriff's farm.

2. The profits of justice were another important branch of revenue. They included amercements in the royal courts, part of the penalties inflicted in the old communal courts; payments for writs and for favors granted by royal justices.

3. The feudal incidents that accrued to the king from his vassals, including aids.

4. Royal perquisites, such as were derived from tolls, fines for privileges of all kinds, and purveyance.

5. Extraordinary grants, viz., tallage (on the demesne only) and danegeld. While the tallage retained something of its original character as an occasional levy, both it and the danegeld became dues, the tallage varying in amount on each area on which it was levied according to the bargain made with the assessors; the danegeld soon becoming a fixed annual due at 2s. the hide, like a rent.

Many of these sources of revenue proved to be susceptible of increase. Although they were customary as far as the obligation was concerned, the amount rendered to the king could be legally augmented. As we have seen the county farms could be increased in addition to the fine paid by the successful appointee to the office of sheriff. The feudal incidents were capable of great increase. With the growth of the royal administrative system the income from fines for privileges and amercements enormously increased. The commutation of services and payments in kind into money may not have resulted in economic advantage to the king, but the change greatly enlarged his cash revenues. For example, the scutage with the accompanying fines for military service formed in the year it was levied a very significant proportion of the income of the year, although it may not have profited the king as much as full military service from all his vassals. From 1066 the Norman kings employed the rights they enjoyed under Anglo-Saxon and Norman law as a means of increasing their revenues.[1] Their efforts were not unnoticed, for the temper of the age was based on contract and on custom. All tenants both free and servile sought successfully to delimit their services and payments. The same charters that illustrate the king's efforts to increase his revenue show the opposition and criticism by the barons. The *Black Book of Peterborough*

1. F. M. Stenton, *English feudalism*, pp. 218–220.

illustrates the great extent to which the obligations of serfs to their lords had become fixed by 1125.²

None of these sources of revenue was susceptible of a sudden marked expansion to meet an extraordinary demand for money, for they all applied to individual persons or areas, except two, the gracious aid, one of the feudal incidents, and the tallage on the demesne.

The development of consent to taxation involves various factors. One of these was the extent to which consent involved a right to refuse as well as to assent to a levy on the part of tenants who were not powerful. Theoretically the gracious aid could not be taken except by the consent of the tenant; practically it was difficult to refuse the king. Thus in 1093 when Anselm's promise to William Rufus of £500 as an aid for the conquest of Normandy was rejected by the king as inadequate and the archbishop refused to increase it, his refusal led to troubles with William Rufus. The bishops advised him to pay the £500 and to promise the king an additional sum which he would collect from his men "and we believe that the king will restore you to his friendship and give peace to you and yours." ³ In 1096 when William Rufus was raising 10,000m. to loan Robert of Normandy, Anselm by the advice of his bishops contributed 200m. which the king accepted.⁴ Another factor was the extent to which a grant bound absentees or property holders who were not consulted at all—such as rear vassals, and freemen and serfs on the demesnes of vassals and rear vassals—that is, the extent to which the transformation of individual into corporate consent had progressed by the evolution of groups that were distinct from the great curia regis which had to be consulted about their taxes, such as the freemen and rear vassals. The frequency of levies was a very important consideration, for a levy that occurred once in a generation would not exert as much influence on the age as one that was taken every four or five years.

The strength of the nobles and of custom in Anglo-Saxon society established the principle that all contributions were fixed by custom and the will of the individual. Custom also ruled Norman society: the free tenants held their lands on definite conditions; any service beyond these conditions had to be by bargain between lord and

2. "Liber niger monasterii S. Petri de Burgo" in appendix to *Chronicon Petroburgense*, pp. 157 *et seq.*
3. Eadmer, *Historium novorum in Anglia*, ed. Martin Rule (Rolls series), pp. 49–51.
4. *Ibid.*, p. 75.

vassal. What any lord, the king included, might do on his demesne as to services, payments in kind, and money payments might be less restrained, but there too custom bound the lord as well as his servile or socage tenants.

We must first determine the source and character of the notion of consent and then follow the changes in the notion with reference to taxation down into the last quarter of the thirteenth century. The origin of consent is to be found in the feudal notion that in case of great need the lord had the right to ask his vassal for aid over and above the established dues and services. This in the feudal language was the gracious aid.

The aid was a voluntary contribution by the vassals. It was probably derived from the general obligation that in time of great need the vassal would come to the assistance of his lord in every possible way. Some needs were so recurrent that the aid had become no longer voluntary but customary. Such were the three regular aids in England. Glanvill speaks only of two aids that the lord could exact from his men, to knight his eldest son, and to marry his first-born daughter. He states however that after a lord and the heir of his tenant had agreed on a reasonable relief, the heir could demand a reasonable aid from his men. This must be moderate, according to the number of the tenant's fees and his wealth.[5] If a lord were at war, Glanvill doubted whether he could demand an aid from his men, since he could not legally distrain them to pay it. Such an aid would be voluntary, or a gracious aid. No principle differentiated the regular from the gracious aid; the difference lay in the fact that some were older and had become customary; all were in origin gracious aids. The most fruitful feudal incident because it involved an assessment on all tenants in chief at one time was the feudal aid. It was the most flexible part of the revenue. It was the germ out of which grew the extraordinary levies of the twelfth century and later.

One problem presented to the council in connection with the aid was how the amount to be paid by each tenant should be determined. A conventional method was to bargain with each tenant for a lump sum. In preparing for an invasion of Normandy in 1094 William II secured an aid of this kind from the prelates, the occasion when Anselm offered £500 as his donation. The gift was refused on the ground that it was too small.[6] Later, when the king

5. Glanvill, *De legibus*, ed. George E. Woodbine (New Haven, 1932), p. 130.
6. Eadmer, p. 43.

was raising an aid of 10,000*m*. as a loan to Duke Robert, the prelates made dona to him individually, and Anselm offered 200*m*.[7] In 1159, for the campaign of Toulouse, Henry II asked and was given large lump sums in aid by the prelates.[8]

Another method was to levy a round sum on each shire. Examples appear in the reigns of Henry I and Henry II.[9] Some conventional method of allocating these aids among landholders was followed similar to allocation of the *murdrum* and other amercements.[10] Danegeld was a lump sum assigned to hundreds and vills and allocated among the landholders in each vill.

Very early the beginning of a radical transformation of the gracious aid was made by the union of two dissimilar elements: first, the feudal notion that in case of great necessity an aid should be given to a lord by his vassals; and second, by the employment, when such a levy was made by the king, of some unit of property or revenue to calculate the amount of the tax owed by each debtor to the king. In form this arrangement was merely a regularization of the process by which vassals who paid an aid to their lord in his time of need obtained the money by demanding in turn an aid from their own tenants. Once this combination had been formed, the levy was incident upon all persons who possessed such units on the lands held of tenants in chief, and they became responsible for the aid to the king whether they were his vassals or not. Thus a general tax on land or other property was levied when an aid was granted to the king.

The question of consent to such an impost involved far more than a private arrangement between each vassal and his lord; notice also that a description of such a grant suggests that it was made not by individual but by corporate consent, while dona clearly were by individual consent.

The question of consent to such an impost involved all the factors in an aid made by private arrangement between the king and each of his vassals and additional factors as well. We begin with the simple question of an aid rarely asked and arranged by a series of bargains at some meeting of the great council. That each tenant was expected to agree is indicated by the attitude of the bishops

7. *Ibid.*, p. 75.
8. John Horace Round, *Feudal England*, pp. 277-279.
9. *Pipe roll 31 Henry I* (Record Commission), *passim*. *Pipe roll 2 Henry II* (Record Commission), p. 23 and *passim*. *Pipe roll 6 Henry II* (Pipe Roll Society), p. 51 and *passim*.
10. *Pipe roll 31 Henry I*, p. 13.

CONSENT TO TAXATION

when Anselm refused to accede to William II's desires. They regarded the archbishop's attitude as naïve and lacking in understanding of the realities of the case. Thus the king must ask his vassals for the aid, but they were not free to refuse. The consent was individual; the consent of the present did not bind the absent, nor did the majority bind the minority. The grantors could appeal to their tenants for an aid to meet their sudden heavy obligation, and so the royal levy would be passed on down from one grade of tenants to another. Nevertheless each tenant made an aid to his lord in his necessity, not to the king. Since consent of the members of the curia regis was individual, the decision could not affect property holders on the king's demesne or any tenant who was not bound to aid his lord in a material way in case of necessity like tenants in frankalmoign, the beneficed clergy whose lands were to support the Christian religion.

The combination of the aid which, though of grace yet was difficult to refuse, with its levy on certain units of property, thus transforming it into a property tax, exigible by royal officials from all property holders on the lands of tenants in chief, set in motion forces to transform this levy. Combine with this action the increase in frequency from 1189 on.

The increased frequency with which the king asked and obtained such grants however began to raise apprehension in the minds of the tenants in chief that the gracious aid for war or debt was becoming a "regular" aid, and that a new custom was being established. Finally, the discontent with repeated taxes on grounds that would make them exigible very frequently led to such strong opposition that, beginning with 1242, the magnates refused to grant aids, a refusal which was repeated nine times. In the face of this united opposition the king was unable to secure any aid from property on the lands of his tenants in chief. The right to consent was interpreted as the right to refuse taxes. By the close of this reign the competence of the great council expanded to include corporate consent and the refusal of aids, not on all property in the realm but on all the property on the lands of the tenants in chief. Its authority was not expanded to cover the royal demesne, or the property of the clergy other than that on the lands held by barony.

This authority of the great council continued in the reign of Edward I, with one modification, at first in appearance slight but in time of profound significance. The great council granted the aid as under Henry III, but the king summoned representatives of the shires who gave a supplementary assent to the levy, that is, to the levy on the property on the lands of the tenants in chief. The tax on movables was also definitely extended to the king's demesne, at first by the employment of clerks who went out to the demesne as had been customary in tallage and then by the summons of representatives from the towns with power to grant a tax. When this method was adopted the rural demesne may have had no special representatives, but it may have been assessed by the county assessors. The clergy gave assent to a tax through their representatives. In this way the aids on movables were extended to cover all property in the realm. The only problem that is cloudy is the relation between the grant by the representatives of the shires and that by the great council. That body had always granted the aid on the property on the lands of all tenants in chief. So they did under Edward I, but the representatives of the shires made the same grant. Since the shire court contained all classes of tenants, great and small, tenants in chief and subtenants of all grades, even villeins, their representatives, if granted full authority, could logically have granted a tax on all the property on the lands held by tenants in chief. And the most important influence in the choice of representatives would be that of the great men. Why then did the king's council add this consent of representatives of the shires? Was a division made between the demesnes of the tenants in chief and the lands of their vassals of various degrees? In that case, how shall we explain why the two groups always voted the same aliquot fraction of the assessed valuation of their movables, the sudden abandonment of a long continued practice of grant by the great council, and the full powers to be granted to the representatives of the shires to agree to what the magnates had already provided? And how shall we explain the grant by the knights of the shire, when the barons were unavoidably absent on the campaign in Wales, of a thirtieth, provided the barons granted as much as they did? The shire knights seem here to have supplied a supplementary assent to the grant of the magnates on the movables on the lands held of the tenants in chief. To what this subject led in later times is another matter. The initiative lay in the hands of the king and his council. The corporate action of the great barons that had been developed under Henry III was carried over into the decisions of the representative groups. The repeated grants on movables under Edward I shows that a levy of this sort was coming to be regarded as part of the customary revenue of the king. But the same feeling

CONSENT TO TAXATION 163

that developed under Henry III, that repeated grants of taxes would form a new due, emerged under Edward I.

The feeling about general levies had advanced to new ground. In 1237 Henry III had promised that if he were granted a thirtieth, he would never again ask for a general aid of this kind and would not consider this grant as a precedent for future demands. In 1297 Edward I promised that he would not regard a levy as a precedent for a future tax and would never levy it except by the consent of the commonalty. This concession was immediately followed by the grant of a ninth. Instead of a long period of refusals, as under Henry III, two later taxes on movables were granted to Edward I though there was one refusal before the close of the reign, between 1297 and 1307, indicating the attitude that an occasional levy on movables was part of the custom of the realm.

The increase in frequency meant that the occasions, or the necessity, or cases of great need came more often. The same tenant might pay such an aid several times during his lifetime. Resort to such a levy by the king became conventional. War, a crusade, debt, all common experiences were occasions for aids. Repetition made the gracious aid like a consuetudo. Under these conditions consent began to develop another character, viz., the right to criticize the demand for aid and ultimately to refuse it. Thus what began as consent in form became consent in reality. The king was dependent upon the good will of his vassals for the aid of grace. A method of controlling the king had been evolved. Basing the aid upon property meant that most of the taxpayers were not summoned to the great council of magnates; they were not consulted about the aid at all; they were men who were rear vassals of every grade, freemen, and serfs who were on the demesnes of vassals. With the change from negotiation between the king and his tenants in chief as to the amount which each should give as an aid to a uniform levy based on property and the refusal of aids, arose another characteristic, a corporate grant, or refusal. Either all should pay or be exempt. Thus the consent of the majority would bind the minority and the consent of the present bind the absent. Hence the old individualism of the aid vanished and in its place appeared corporate action. The fruitfulness of the levies on movables and hence the desire to draw all property under contribution and the inability or impracticability of consulting all property holders led to the employment of representatives that might act in behalf of the taxpayers. Thus along with the tenants in chief were summoned representatives of the shire courts composed of tenants in chief and lesser men as well. The representatives were to supplement the action of the magnates regarding a tax on the movables on all their lands. The men on the royal demesne were approached by royal commissioners who were to secure an aid based on an assessed valuation of their movables and after a time representatives were summoned who granted a tax for the demesne. The church too sent its representatives. The principle of corporate decision evolved in the great council was easily applied to these groups. The use of representative groups in collaboration with the great council broadened the basis of the authority of the central assemblies (or assembly) for granting taxes. This final procedure only began under Edward I but easily grew out of the developments of the reign of Henry III.

There were three sorts of levies to which the government resorted in its efforts to secure a uniform tax that would fall upon a larger number of property holders and thus yield an increased revenue. These were taxes on the hide or carucate, on the knight's fee, and on revenues and movables. In every case the council seized upon an existing contribution and modified it to form a new kind of aid.

The aids in this form were not however authorized by the action of the king alone, for in all cases where the question of authorization was mentioned the king did it by the consent of his barons. Thus in 1095 William Rufus raised 10,000m. to loan Duke Robert of Normandy to defray his expenses for the first crusade and as a pledge for payment the king received the duchy. To raise this sum the king received dona from certain prelates and certain treasures of the churches.[11] Such aids were seemingly inadequate, for in addition the king requested and was granted by his barons an aid of 4s. on the hide. This levy was the annual danegeld but higher than the ordinary rate.[12] This statement indicates negotiation as to the rate of the levy rather than consent to it.

In the reign of Henry I, the Abingdon chronicler records a writ of the king by which he acquitted the abbot of the payment due from five hides and "particularly of that aid which my barons gave me."[13] This was probably the aid of 3s. on the hide for the marriage of Matilda to the emperor Henry V, in 1110, a dane-

11. Florence of Worcester, *Chronicon*, ed. Benjamin Thorpe (English Historical Society), II, 40. Eadmer, p. 74.
12. *Chronicon de Abingdon*, II, 38. Florence of Worcester, II, 40. F. Liebermann, *Die Gesetze der Angelsachsen* (Halle, 1903), I, 636. George Burton Adams, *Council and courts in Anglo-Norman England* (New Haven, 1926), p. 41.
13. *Chronicon de Abingdon*, II, 113.

CONSENT TO TAXATION 165

geld at a special rate which was agreed to by the barons.[14] These aids in the form of the danegeld were incident upon the property of everyone, not merely of the king's vassals. As danegeld was levied by the sheriff, the levies were paid to the king by landholders of all grades.[15] Both the basis of the aid and its method of collection would probably insure a larger return and would be collected more readily than a levy in lump sums—hence perhaps the reason for the substitution of danegeld at the increased rate. But danegeld was abandoned by Stephen and although restored by Henry II was not taken after 1163; so for the time being it ceased to serve as a taxing device for levying aids.

For the aid to marry his daughter to Henry the Lion in 1168 Henry II turned to a different unit never yet used for a general levy, the scutage, long since the conventional levy for exemption from military service on each knight's fee. In 1100 "there is mentioned on church lands a payment as scutage when a due quota of knights was not provided." [16] Professor Stenton has shown that it is likely that in 1127 the bishopric of Ely paid a composition of £60 on forty fees or £1 10s. per fee, and that the bishop of Norwich paid at the same rate under Henry I. Scutage was so common under Henry I that mesne tenants were distributing the burden among their men, even granting out land to be held by minute fractions of a knight's fee ($\frac{1}{16}$, $\frac{1}{24}$, $\frac{1}{20}$ of a fee), which can only mean a service by money payment, or scutage.[17] The scutage at a fixed rate per fee was thus established as a conventional money composition in lieu of military service but as far as we know it had never been employed as a general levy.

In 1168 Henry II levied one of the regular feudal aids for the marriage of his eldest daughter, Matilda, to the duke of the Saxons. For the first time a king of England based an aid upon knights' fees at the uniform rate of 1m. per fee. In addition certain prelates who held lands by knight service paid dona, the royal demesne paid a tallage, and certain other groups like sheriffs paid dona. What had been a method of commutation for military service at a uniform rate per fee that had been levied upon those tenants in chief who

14. Henry of Huntingdon, *Historia Anglorum*, ed. Thomas Arnold (Rolls series), p. 237.
15. *Pipe roll 31 Henry I, passim.*
16. William Alfred Morris, *The constitutional history of England to 1216* (New York, 1930), p. 213.
17. Stenton, *English feudalism*, pp. 179, 181, 183, 185. Round, *Feudal England*, pp. 268, 270.

were granted exemption was thus transformed into a general levy on all such tenants. Hence rear vassals (just as in the levy of scutage) were obligated to pay to their lords, or the sheriff, an aid which went directly to the king. Instead of aiding their lords when in great need to pay an obligation to the king, the rear vassals paid directly to the sheriff or to their own lords, but for the king's use. There is no direct evidence how this levy was authorized, by what right the small council decided that the aid should be based upon the knight's fee so that the number of fees determined the amount of aid to be paid by each tenant in chief. This is an extension of the custom followed in the levy of scutage.

The form of statement in the pipe roll indicates that most tenants in chief accounted at the exchequer for the aid.[18] It is clear from the fragment of the receipt roll of 1185 that actually the sheriff had collected the money from debtors and rendered account for it at the exchequer, but the debtor was entered in the pipe roll as rendering the account. Such was the practice though it is concealed by the form of the entries in the pipe roll. In some cases the sheriff rendered the account according to the roll. Thus, for example, when a holding was in hand and not in the possession of a custodian, the sheriff collected the scutage and accounted for it, according to the roll sometimes for the whole holding, as in the case of the honor of Eye; sometimes for each tenant individually, as in the case of the tenants of William Peverel, or of the fee of Wartre.[19] Nevertheless, the vast majority of the holdings appear in the pipe roll as accounted for at the exchequer by the tenant in chief. The explanation is not the importance of such men, for tenants with very small holdings were rendering their accounts of scutage or aid in the roll.[20]

It seems clear that the names entered in the pipe roll are those against whom the clerks made a demand for money, not those who in all cases actually rendered the account at the exchequer. Those who rendered accounts were sheriffs and custodians primarily, though anyone could do so. That those who paid scutage or aid are said to render their account in the pipe roll is no evidence that they actually did so. Hints that this was the procedure in the aid of 1168 appear in the roll of that year. Thus the roll of 1168 states that the bishop of Bath accounts for 20m. of aid (for twenty fees).

18. *Pipe roll 14 Henry II*, p. 20 and *passim*.
19. *Ibid.*, pp. 11, 22, 40, 89.
20. *Ibid.*, pp. 21, 22, 52, 59, 64, 65, 171–172, 180, 194.

CONSENT TO TAXATION 167

He pays into the exchequer 19m. and owes 1m. It appears however in another place that the bishopric was in hand and that the sheriff was accounting for its revenues.[21] Consequently that official rendered the account of the scutage. In Yorkshire most of the important tenants were entered as accounting for their aid, but some who had not sent in a list of their holdings in the inquest of 1166 rendered the account of their aid to marry the king's daughter through the sheriff. This seems to indicate that the sheriff generally collected the aid from the tenants in chief and rendered the account from each. In the case of tenants who had reported their fees in 1166, the charge and the amount still due on the fees that had hitherto never paid a scutage were entered.[22] If, as seems likely, the sheriff collected the aid in each shire and rendered the account at the exchequer, the rear vassals paid to their lord or the sheriff a tax levied for the king, not an aid to their lords to help them discharge their aid to the king. That is, the rear vassals paid a tax that they had not granted and on which they had not been consulted.

This was the first time that an aid was based on the knight's fee. No record has survived as to why the king chose this method. It seems a fair inference that the small council was influenced by the fact that it had received a very detailed report of the great inquest of service of 1166. This inquiry aimed to ascertain the number of fees enfeoffed by the king's vassals (a) before the death of Henry I, the old enfeoffment; (b) since the death of Henry I, the new enfeoffment; (c) the number of knights that they had to supply from their demesnes in order to complete the military service owed to the king from their holdings; and (d) the names of their enfeoffed knights.

The purpose of the inquest is not stated but from the questions and the answers it seems fair to conclude, as Mrs. Stenton has suggested, that the purpose was to inform the king of the status of military service; all the queries relate to that subject. Furthermore, the archbishop of York in his answer stated that the king wished to know the names of the knights so as to have those who had not yet sworn allegiance to him do so by the first Sunday in Lent.[23] With all this detail freshly in hand the council made the knight's fee the basis of the aid to marry the king's daughter. Probably the king

21. *Ibid.*, pp. 143, 168.
22. *Ibid.*, pp. 65, 87–89, 90, 95.
23. Round, *Feudal England,* p. 238. *Red book of the exchequer,* I, 275, 277, 412.

determined this by the grant of the great curia regis. Since a levy of this sort had never been taken, it is likely that Henry II consulted his tenants, but of this decision no trace survives. However one further inference is justifiable—that the small council alone decided to levy it upon all fees enfeoffed by the king's vassals, even though the number exceeded the servitium debitum, without the assent of the great council. For, broadly speaking, the attempt to collect the aid from these additional fees was a failure. As Baldwin remarks, "The accounts for knights *quos non recognoscit* and new enfeoffment fell universally in arrears." [24] Thus practically no one paid on the new enfeoffment; since the record appeared in the pipe roll, it is clear that the sheriffs had been instructed to secure the tax from the new enfeoffment as well as the old. This uniform refusal indicates that in this regular aid the council had demanded something out of the ordinary for which the consent of the great barons would be necessary.

Dona in lump sums, the older method, were also paid by certain religious and secular clergy, the sheriffs, and the moneyers. This marriage was also the occasion for the levy of a tallage on the royal demesne. But the most significant payment was that on knights' fees, a uniform levy which was a kind of land tax on many holders of fees or fractions who paid not because of the need of their lords but because their lords and overlords owed a tax to the king, and they were responsible to the king for paying it although they had not been consulted.

The third and most fruitful form which was employed for the aid was the levy on revenues and movables. This finally superseded all the others. It became the tax which was taken when a gracious aid was asked for and it opened the way for direct taxation on property. The first great case of a tax on movables and revenues in which the English king was involved was the levy of 1166 for the Holy Land—of 2d. in the pound for the first year and 1d. for four successive years, or 6d. in all. Henry II states that he was influenced to levy this tax by the example and request of his lord, the French king. He authorized it first in his French possessions by the counsel of a small group of lay and ecclesiastical barons, and later by a much larger council of the same character.[25]

24. James Fosdick Baldwin, *The scutage and knight service in England* (Chicago, 1897), p. 43.
25. Gervase of Canterbury, I, 198.

CONSENT TO TAXATION 169

This tax was later extended to England.[26] While the grant which resulted in this levy took place in a large assembly of Henry II's vassals, the writ authorizing the impost suggests, though the statement is not so clear as we could wish, that the king swore with each of his vassals to levy the tax. "I first [says the king in the writ] swore with my own hand in the hand of the archbishop of Rouen that I would maintain this decree, and the archbishops, bishops, earls (comites), barons, vavasors, we all declared under oath we would compel all under our rule to swear the same." [27] That is, individual consent was the method employed. It should also be noted that the writ described the procedure in the French provinces, not in England. While the consent was given in the curia regis, Henry II's writ authorizing the levy indicates that each one promised to carry out individually the arrangements made for assessment and collection.

From 1184 appears a document authorizing the assessment and collection of a tax on revenues and movables for a period of three years, payable in France and also in England. As no other notice of this levy appears save the writ in various editions, its genuineness has been questioned. Paid by both clergy and laity, it was initiated by papal command. According to the writ the tax was put in charge by the kings of France and England by the common counsel of the bishops, earls, and barons of their lands at a joint meeting.[28] But fabricated or not, the author of the document believed that the legal method to authorize such a tax was by the king with the common counsel of his vassals.

A third aid for a crusade was levied in 1188 at a very high rate, a tenth of revenues and movables, the Saladin tithe, and was paid generally by lay and ecclesiastical property holders.[29] The authorization of this levy which fell upon masses of people who held nothing of the king was made by bodies that have the traits of the great curia regis.

The news of the defeats of the Christians in Palestine culminating with the capture of Jerusalem by Saladin aroused the West. The pope issued a call for a crusade to recover the Holy Places. Three assemblies were held, in which Henry II took part, which led

26. Ralph de Diceto, I, 329. *Chronicon Petroburgense*, p. 3.
27. Gervase of Canterbury, I, 199.
28. William Edward Lunt, "Text of the ordinance of 1184," pp. 240 *et seq*. *Munimenta gildhallae Londoniensis*, II, 653–654.
29. Benedict of Peterborough, II, 30. Gervase of Canterbury, I, 409.

up to the authorization of the Saladin tithe in England. The first, near Gisors, was attended by the kings of France and England with the "archbishops, bishops, earls, and barons of both kingdoms."[30] The archbishop of Tyre appeared at the conference and preached the crusade with amazing success. Many took the cross, even the two kings, affected probably by the emotions of their barons. By the counsel of their barons the kings decided to levy a tenth of revenues and movables on all who did not participate in the crusade.[31]

On January 30 Henry II landed in England and summoned the curia regis to meet at Geddington on February 11. This council was composed of the usual elements: the archbishop of Canterbury, the bishops and abbots, earls and barons.[32] The meeting was well attended. Roger of Howden noted that many others of the clergy and laity were present.[33] A member of the convent of Canterbury who was present at a council at Northampton that preceded the session at Geddington wrote to his house that the king had a colloquium with all the bishops of England and Wales and the princes and procurators of the land, a description that seems to indicate a large attendance.[34] The statements of both Roger and the monk of Canterbury seem to indicate that the regular members of the council were accompanied by an unusual number of dependent laity and clergy. Before this body the crusade was preached, many took the cross, and the Saladin tithe was put in charge.[35] Thus the decision to take the tax was made by the king in the curia regis. The tax was also paid by the royal demesne in England. But it was not automatically collected from the towns by the local committees established after the meeting at Geddington. Nor was it a tallage, for the part of the tallage of 1187 that had not been collected was delayed and finally almost wholly pardoned on account of the tenths. Evidently the decision in the curia regis did not commit

30. *Ibid.*, p. 406. William de Newburgh, I, 273. Benedict of Peterborough, II, 29. *Oeuvres de Rigord et de Guillaume le Breton*, ed. H. F. Delaborde (Société de l'histoire de France), I, 83.
31. Benedict of Peterborough, II, 31. William de Newburgh, I, 273.
32. *Ibid.*, p. 275. Gervase of Canterbury, I, 409. Benedict of Peterborough, II, 33. Roger of Howden, II, 338.
33. *Ibid.*
34. *Epistolae Cantuarienses*, ed. William Stubbs (Rolls series), p. 167.
35. Benedict of Peterborough, II, 33. Gervase of Canterbury, I, 409. William de Newburgh, I, 275. William Edward Lunt, "Consent of the lower clergy," pp. 71–72. Adams, *Council and courts*, pp. 7–8, 9, 10, 36–39.

CONSENT TO TAXATION 171

the towns. Henry II ordered a group of the wealthier citizens or burgesses from each town to be chosen—from London two hundred, from York one hundred, from other towns a number proportionate to their population and wealth. These representatives were to meet with the king at certain fixed dates and places. From each group he must have secured assent to the tenth, for our sole source states: "From them he took a tenth of their revenues and movables according to the valuation of faithful men who knew." The direct intervention of the king indicates something more than the work of assessment and collection; it must be the agreement of the town with the king to pay the tax.[36] Thus the vassals assembled in the curia regis assented to the tenth at the request of the king, who later in person arranged the levy on the great towns of his demesne. No notice appears as to the method employed on the rural royal demesne.

Five years after the collection of the Saladin tithe a still greater financial problem was presented to the English government in the ransom of Richard I, requiring a total of £100,000, two thirds to be paid before the king was released. The ransom of the king was one of the regular feudal aids due from all his vassals, but the amount required in this case was so enormous that the cooperation and consent of all his tenants was essential if the money was to be raised, even though the king's dominions south of the channel participated. Contemporaries regarded the task as tremendous. William de Newburgh emphasized the searching character of the taxation which spared no one and no kind of wealth. Gervase of Canterbury called the levies *exactiones durissimae*. The chronicle of Thomas Wykes said that the kingdom of England had been so oppressed and exhausted that even the chalices of the churches were sold. Roger of Howden, after saying that the ransom was raised in France also, added "and thus they secured an infinite amount of money." [37] The difficulty of raising the total sum forced the government to resort to every kind of extraordinary levy. Thus, although a ransom called legally for a feudal aid, the demand for a sum like that of 1193 involved cooperation and consent by the vassals.

36. Benedict of Peterborough, II, 33.
37. Stubbs, *Select charters*, pp. 291, 298. Roger of Howden, III, 225. Doris Stenton in *Pipe roll 5 Richard I*, p. xxii. William de Newburgh, I, 399. Gervase of Canterbury, I, 519. *Chronicon Thomae Wykes*, p. 47. *Chronica de Melsa*, p. 273. *Magni rotuli scaccarii Normanniae*, ed. Thomas Stapleton (Record Commission), I, 128, 134, 135, 136, 172, 173.

Richard I wrote two letters from Germany about the ransom in which is revealed his understanding of the character of the aid.[38] Since this concept also reflected the ideas of Hubert Walter, William de Longchamp, bishop of Ely, and William de Sainte Mère Église, all of whom had been in conference with him before he wrote the second letter, it would indicate this was the official view of the character of the aid.

The definite news that the king was a prisoner in Germany had reached England in February and messengers that were sent out by the archbishop of Rouen found Richard shortly before March 21, when he had his first interview with Henry VI to whom he offered a ransom of 100,000m.[39] Hence in his letter of March 26 to the monks of Canterbury the king stated that he could not be released till he had paid that sum. So he begged the monastery as the head of the whole kingdom to give an example to others of affection and loyalty by its generous aid and also to assist him with money "we do not say by giving, but rather by loaning money from the treasures of your church which we will repay twofold." [40] Thus the king appealed for an individual grant and a loan from the Canterbury church. On April 19 the king wrote a second letter addressed to the queen mother, his justices, and all his faithful, the archbishops, bishops, abbots, earls, barons, clerks, and free tenants, stating that an agreement had been made with the emperor by which he must remain in Germany till 70,000m. had been paid.[41] He urged them by the fealty by which they were bound to him to employ all their efforts to raise the money needed. He appealed particularly to the justices who, he said, were above others in the kingdom and besought them to set a good example to others. They should aid him justly and generously from their own property and by loans which they might make from others so that they might set an example to his other faithful of doing the like. "He whom in the moment of our necessity, we shall find prompt to help, will in his necessity find us a friend, ready to reward; and it will be more pleasing to us if, in our absence, any person shall in any way assist us, than if, in our presence, he should give us twice that amount of aid." He asked that the names of the magnates and the contributions made by each in this present emergency should be communicated to him under his

38. *Epistolae Cantuariensis*, p. 362. Roger of Howden, III, 208.
39. *Ibid.*, pp. 196–198.
40. *Epistolae Cantuariensis*, p. 362.
41. *Ibid.*, p. 363. Roger of Howden, III, 209.

CONSENT TO TAXATION

mother's seal so that he might know how much he was bound to render thanks to each and every one. In this second letter, Richard repeated the request made in his letter to the prior of Canterbury that the churches should contribute their gold and silver plate with the additional proviso that an inventory should be drawn up, so that the treasures could later be fully restored.[42]

The concept revealed by these letters was that the aid was a grant by individual tenants in chief of lump sums determined by each, supplemented by loans; and from the churches an aid, or at least the loan of their plate and other treasures. The inquest of 1194 into the aids confirms the conclusion that there was a notion of individual consent. The justices were to inquire concerning all aids for the ransom, how much each had promised and paid, and how much he was in arrears.[43] With this notion of the aid, how were the various levies actually authorized? On receipt of the letter of April 19 the council decided to change the character of the aid from that suggested by the king into a fourth of revenues and movables, accompanied then or later by a definite levy on property, perhaps on revenues, of 10s. and upward, the aid on the knight's fee at 20s., an old customary levy, a demand for a year's yield of a particular product, the wool of the Cistercians and allied orders, or its commutation into money and two other ancient levies—the danegeld and the tallage of the royal demesne.[44] The request for the treasure of the churches was supplemented by a request for a specific fraction of their revenues, fourths, tenths, or twentieths. The fourth of revenues and movables would be paid by all the tenants in chief and by all property holders on their holdings as a levy owed to the king, not to their lords, yet the consent that was given to the king's request was given by the tenants in chief.

Except in connection with the hidage no definite statement has survived of a meeting of the great curia regis to consult about any of the aids for the ransom. At the end of March, 1194, after his return Richard I held a great council at Nottingham and one of the decisions taken there was to levy a carucage or hidage on the basis of the danegeld of 1084. Of earlier meetings on the question of the ransom not much specific information has survived. Yet there is evidence of consultation. Thus the king had made a direct, personal appeal to his tenants. During the assessment this notice

42. *Ibid.*
43. *Ibid.*, p. 263.
44. *Ibid.*, p. 210.

would probably be communicated to all his vassals; after the discovery of the king's whereabouts many of his tenants visited him.[45] In this way by letters and personal interviews Richard influenced his political leaders in the subject of the ransom. There are also vague indications that the council consulted with tenants on this subject. On February 28 a council was held at Oxford that may have discussed the ransom.[46] Ralph de Diceto mentioned four of the levies, the treasures of the churches, the fourth of revenues, the wool, and the tithes of the clergy, adding that it was determined to pay by common assent. Gervase of Canterbury stated that both laity and clergy were summoned to London again and again to ascertain definitely if anything remained to be paid. William de Newburgh related that Richard was wearied of his confinement and reminded his representatives at home and all his faithful by repeated communications to raise the amount of this ransom in every way possible and hasten his liberation.[47]

Taken alone no one of these statements may carry much weight, but all together they create a definite impression of appeals by the king and his council to his lay and clerical tenants in chief, to religious houses and the orders. The gold and silver were requested of the churches by the king and the levy of fractional parts of clerical revenues was taken as a result of grants after the churches had been requested for the grant by their bishops. The council thus retained the appeal to individuals for a grant, as in the case of the gold and silver of the churches, asked for by justices on their rounds.[48] As a result of negotiation, a church might succeed in having its contribution commuted into a fine. Warin, abbot of St. Albans, redeemed all the precious vessels and ornaments of the abbey for 200*m*. The chronicler believed that the abbot's intimacy with the king was responsible for this settlement.[49] The bishop of Durham redeemed all the treasures of the cathedral for a 100 *m*. York Minster gave a gold cross for its contribution, and this was later redeemed.[50]

45. *Ibid.*, pp. 198, 209, 212, 215, 217. William de Newburgh, I, 388. Gervase of Canterbury, I, 516. Doris Stenton in *Pipe roll 5 Richard I*, pp. xx, xxi.
46. *Ibid.*, p. xvi. Roger of Howden, III, 209.
47. *Ibid.*, p. 225. Ralph de Diceto, II, 110. Gervase of Canterbury, I, 519. William de Newburgh, I, 399.
48. *Memorials of St. Edmund's abbey*, I, 297–298.
49. Thomas Walsingham, *Gesta abbatum Sancti Albani*, I, 214.
50. *Historiae Dunelmensis scriptores tres*, p. 17. *The Fabric rolls of York minster*, p. 152.

CONSENT TO TAXATION 175

When the archbishop of York tried to raise a fourth on his church he appealed to the canons individually, particularly those whom he knew best, but they refused, alleging that such a grant would subvert the liberties of their church.[51] On the one hand the fact that so many parts of this levy—the scutage, the hidage, and the taxes of the fourth, the tenth, the twentieth—were levied at a uniform rate gives an air of general consent; if we add to this the custom of putting a levy in charge after consulting with an assembly, this impression of a uniform levy, taken by somebody with authority, is deepened. But on the other hand documents like King Richard's letters, reports concerning the payments in lieu of delivery of church plate, and negotiations with the canons of York by the archbishop indicate that behind this front of uniformity lay individual negotiation and consent which might result in refusal. It is not clear how it was determined that these fractional parts of the revenue of parish clergy (fourths, tenths, twentieths) should be taken. Perhaps the bishops met and agreed to levy them. Anyhow the administration collected the taxes, but they were paid only with the consent of the clergy.[52]

The famous "debate at Oxford on foreign service" deserves comment in connection with the question of consent to taxation. That incident revolved around the consideration of military service indeed but also involved its commutation into a money payment commensurate with the amount of service for which the king was asking. A council of lay and clerical magnates was called by Hubert Walter and met at Oxford, December, 1197.[53] On behalf of the king, who by custom took the initiative in meetings of the curia regis, Hubert revealed the great need for assistance, military and financial, in the war against Philip Augustus. He proposed the formation of a select army of knights to serve in France for a year. In the discussion that followed his demand two proposals are recorded: the first, that the tenants in chief should supply a body of three hundred knights and defray their expenses, or second, that the vassals should provide a sum of money large enough for the king to hire such a force. A third proposal was that the tenants in chief should furnish a tenth of their service; in this case also the group was to serve for a year and each knight was to be paid 3s. a

51. Roger of Howden, III, 222.
52. *Ibid. Pipe roll 7 Richard I*, p. 263.
53. Doris Stenton in *Pipe roll 10 Richard I*, p. xix.

176   TAXATION IN MEDIEVAL ENGLAND

day. This last proposal probably was the arrangement later devised to raise the quota of knights proposed.[54]

Hubert's proposal met with much support in the great council, but the bishop of Lincoln offered stout opposition on the ground that his bishopric owed military service only within England, not beyond the borders of the kingdom, and consequently he could not assent to furnish knights to fight in Normandy. In this opinion the bishop of Salisbury concurred.[55] This refusal was based on custom. As far as the records go, bishop Hugh had never provided any military service, although he had paid four scutages. In the face of his opposition Hubert felt that his attempt would miscarry and abandoned it, despite his supporters in the curia regis.[56] It seems fair to conclude that St. Hugh voiced the attitude of many, else Hubert would not so quickly have shelved the plan. The discussion shows that individual assent was the custom in the great council, since the bishops of Lincoln and Salisbury refused to be bound by the decision of others. St. Hugh clearly expressed this notion when he said that it would be better for him to resign than to lose ancient immunities and subjugate the church committed to him to unaccustomed demands. The bishop of Salisbury declared himself in a similar strain: "It seems to me that apart from the profound disadvantage to my church, I can say or do nothing but what I have heard must be done from the opinion of the lord of Lincoln." [57] That is, each member was bound by his own decision.

Although the great curia regis failed to declare itself in favor of Richard's demand for a long-time force or money composition which would supply it, larger in amount than the conventional scutage, the king's ministers pursued the plan by negotiations and fines levied against individuals. The meeting of the great council therefore seems to have been a conventional method of securing grants from individual tenants by the king. If he failed to obtain them, he pursued his demands further and usually with success. Bishop Hugh was the exception that tested the rule.

54. *Ibid.*, p. xxi. Roger of Howden, IV, 40. *Magna vita sancti Hugonis episcopi Lincolniensis*, ed. James F. Dimock (Rolls series), pp. 248 *et seq.* Jocelin de Brakelond, *Chronica de rebus gestis Samsonis abbatis monasterii Sancti Edmundi*, ed. John L. Rokewode (Camden Society, London, 1840), p. 63.

55. Roger of Howden, IV, 40. *Vita S. Hugonis,* pp. 249–250.

56. *Pipe roll 33 Henry II*, p. 75. *Pipe roll 2 Richard I*, p. 90. *Pipe roll 8 Richard I*, p. 247. *Pipe roll 9 Richard I*, pp. 109–110. Roger of Howden, IV, 40. *Vita S. Hugonis*, p. 249.

57. *Vita S. Hugonis*, pp. 249–250.

CONSENT TO TAXATION

The carucage of 1194 has been shown to have been based upon the old assessment of the danegeld, using the hide as a unit.[58] In 1198 a second carucage was levied of a radically different character: it was to be based on actual carucates each reckoned at 100 or 120 acres, i.e., they counted the carucates and taxed each one 5s.; in 1200 a third carucage was levied and this was assessed by counting the number of plow teams and taxing each 3s. It is obvious that none of these levies was according to custom—the revival of danegeld in 1194 after thirty-two years was startling, for Richard did not venture to levy it except after consultation with the great curia regis; the proposal to base carucage on a carucate of 100 or 120 acres, never before done, was equally startling, and the third proposal to count the teams was also unusual. It seems doubtful that the council in Richard's absence would have ventured on such innovations without consulting the great curia regis, but the fact is that there is no evidence of such consultation. The third of these taxes was stubbornly opposed by Geoffrey, archbishop of York, although the levy had been generally granted throughout England.[59] He was disseized of his holdings. The archbishop finally made a settlement with the king, an illustration of individual opposition and settlement.

A seventh of personal property was levied in 1203 as a penalty for the alleged abandonment of John by his vassals during the wars. The brief notices say nothing as to a consultation with his tenants in chief.

In January, 1207, at a meeting of the great curia regis at Oxford, John asked for an aid on the revenues of the beneficed clergy, but the bishops and abbots present refused and at a deferred meeting of the great council in February the refusal was repeated.[60] The lay tenants in chief however granted John an aid of a thirteenth of revenues and movables on the ground of necessity to recover his lost lands in France. The discussion in the curia regis was marked by hostile criticism, but only one member was singled out as definitely refusing to assent. This was Geoffrey, archbishop of York, who had earlier opposed the levy. He was forced to leave England, excommunicating all who should assess and collect the thirteenth in his bishopric, and as a result his goods and land were

58. F. W. Maitland in *Three rolls of the king's court*, p. xxiv, and Doris Stenton in *Pipe roll 6 Richard I*, p. xxiv.
59. Roger of Howden, IV, 107, 139, 140, 157, 163. Roger of Wendover, I, 301.
60. Sydney Knox Mitchell, *Studies in taxation*, pp. 86–87.

seized by the king.[61] Further indications of the opposition to the thirteenth appear in the language with which the chroniclers almost without exception referred to the levy. Other indications appear in the efforts of taxpayers to elude paying it, and to escape assessment and collection by royal officials.[62] Thus while the grant was made at a meeting of the great curia regis, the levy fell upon property holders who were not summoned and not consulted. When the abbot of Abingdon fined in a lump sum (600m.) for the thirteenth, the king ordered the collectors of the aid and the sheriff to compel the abbot's knights and free tenants to make him an aid.[63] Obviously the archbishop of York did not feel an obligation to pay because of the consent of other tenants in chief. Nevertheless, after the assent obtained from the great curia regis, the government assessed and collected the tax from all property holders on the lands of the tenants in chief. The beneficed clergy were exempt. The royal demesne paid the tax, but we have no information on the method of authorization.

Thus by the close of John's reign four methods of calculating an aid had been employed; the lump sum on the tenant in chief which he secured by an aid from his tenants; the aid on knights' fees, i.e., a general scutage; the carucage, a modification of the ancient danegeld now based on actual property, either by counting the number of plowlands, or plow teams; and finally the assessment of movable property and revenues and the levy of a fractional amount of the value, from a fourth to a thirteenth part. It is seen that what had once been a contribution to the lord's necessities by his vassals was being transformed into a tax on real or personal property paid directly to the king by property holders, most of whom were not his immediate vassals; in the case of the carucage and the tax on movables, the great majority were far removed from any direct legal connection with him. The consent to all these levies was given by the great curia regis and the tenants in chief individually, in so far as we have any information on this topic.

We now turn to the statement about aids in Magna Carta, for the barons after their successful uprising against John, caused in

61. Roger of Wendover, II, 35. Gervase of Canterbury, II, LIX. Walter of Coventry. *Memoriale*, ed. William Stubbs (Rolls series), II, 199. *Annals of Waverley*, p. 259. "Annales Sancti Edmundi" in *Memorials of St. Edmund's abbey*, II, 146.
62. Walter of Coventry, II, 198–199. William de Newburgh, II, 509. *Annales Cambriae*, ed. John Williams ab Ithel (Rolls series), p. 66. *Chronicon Thomae Wykes*, p. 52. Mitchell, *Studies in taxation*, pp. 88–90.
63. *Rot. claus.*, I, 84b.

CONSENT TO TAXATION

part by the financial exactions of the preceding generation, aimed to prevent a recurrence of injustice by making a definite statement of the law in 1215. Magna Carta equated the scutage and the aid. Article XII states that no scutage or aid was to be levied except for the three regular aids save by the *commune consilium regni*. It thus divided the aids into two classes. In one were those to knight the king's son, to marry his first-born daughter, and to ransom the king. Such needed no consent provided they were reasonable. They were customary dues. In the case of any other aid, the gracious aid, the consent of the commune consilium regni was essential. The scutage thus was placed in the same category as the gracious aid. One of the three regular aids, if desired at a higher rate than customary, also required this consent; such is the implication of the statement. But the document went further. As the term commune consilium regni was applicable to sessions of tenants in chief where many were absent, the authors specified in Article XIV that to levy a gracious aid or a scutage the whole body of tenants in chief should be summoned specially for this purpose, the greater barons by individual writs and the lesser tenants by writs addressed to the sheriff, or royal bailiff. The writs should be issued at least forty days in advance of the session, they should state the purpose of the meeting, and on the appointed day the business should be transacted by the decision of those present, whether or not all who had been summoned attended. These provisions were probably not deemed unusual for the levy of a gracious aid, although no such definite statement exists earlier. The descriptions of the bodies by which the Saladin tithe and the thirteenth of 1207 were granted were at least approximations of such a session; they were specially summoned and the decision taken led to the immediate assessment and collection of the aid. We have no specific information as to the use of the great curia regis for the levy of the fourth of movables and revenues of Richard's ransom, merely some general statements. We should expect that the great curia regis would be summoned, because although this was one of the regular feudal aids, a fourth of movable property and revenue, an unprecedented amount, could hardly be denominated a "reasonable aid" although in this case justifiable. Nor have we any information at all about consent to the carucage of 1198, levied for a campaign and based upon a unique assessment on the carucate; nor for the carucage of 1200 for the relief of John's lands in France, unprecedented in another way in being based upon the plow team. Similarly, the seventh

180   TAXATION IN MEDIEVAL ENGLAND

of 1203 justified as an amercement for the desertion by tenants in chief should also have legally been brought before the tenants in chief, and no information on this point is extant. Thus this emphatic statement in Articles XII and XIV regarding aids may reflect discontent among the tenants in chief on some of these occasions. Yet the procedure of 1207 seems to have satisfied custom, and the cases cited were far in the past. But the fever of discontent aroused in the later years of John's reign may have caused vivid recollections of unfair levies and hence this statement. The fact that the second charter of Henry III did not mention aids indicates however that the primary grievances in the articles were not concerned with the gracious aid. But the regulation equating scutage with the gracious aid in its method of grant introduced an unheard-of limitation of the procedure. There are two points to be noticed in this connection: first, the strict regulation that scutage could only be levied at a meeting of the great curia regis to which all tenants in chief had been summoned specifically to consider this subject. As we shall see, scutage seems to have been put in charge by the king, probably after consultation with those tenants who actually had served; not necessarily by all, for the forces might be divided as in 1214, part of the tenants were in Flanders and part in Poitou. John was with the latter group when he proclaimed the scutage at 3m. per fee; second, the new regulation was designed to remedy the abuses from which the barons suffered. If the whole great council were summoned, certain abuses would perhaps be eliminated.

We must first examine scutage, for the barons in 1215 equated aid and scutage in their legal statement. In the twelfth century scutage had been the commutation for military service; the gracious aid had been a free gift by the vassal to his lord to help the latter when he was in great need. In 1159 some tenants had paid lump sums in addition to the scutage; in 1165 many tenants in chief paid sums to defray the wages of sergeants in the campaign of Wales, the sum usually being greater than a scutage. The title of the scutage of Ireland of 1172 suggests that some of the tenants in chief paid the king lump sums in lieu of their service in that campaign. It runs: "Concerning the scutage of barons who neither went with the king to Ireland nor sent knights, or money thither for themselves." [64] No dona however appear in the pipe roll as in 1159. These dona had been fixed in amount by negotiation be-

64. *Pipe roll 19 Henry II*, p. 187 and *passim*.

CONSENT TO TAXATION

tween the tenant and a royal representative. The author of the *Dialogue of the Exchequer* did not mention the fine as a variant of the scutage. From 1172 to 1199 the conventional rate of composition was £1 unless the campaign was short, when it would be less. This does not mean that the commutation of military service had been permanently conventionalized. An expansion of commutation began under Richard I in a curious way, almost by accident. In 1193 one of the levies for the ransom of Richard I was an aid on knights' fees at 20s. per fee. The tax was not accounted for in the pipe roll till 1194 and evidently was not assessed and collected till that year, probably because in 1193 efforts were concentrated on the fourth of revenues and movables.[65] When the king returned early in 1194, he held a great council at Nottingham at the end of March when he asked for a third of the military service from his tenants, who were to assemble at once to accompany him to France. Some tenants were excused from service in this "first army of Normandy" for a lump sum, a fine. Thus these tenants were charged with two contributions in successive years, the aid at 20s. per fee for the ransom and a fine for exemption from military service in France. But those tenants who served paid no fine and in addition their scutage for the ransom was pardoned, although it had no connection with the campaign.[66]

Thus in this case scutage, fine, and service were linked together because a scutage for the campaign of 1194 was not feasible on account of the scutage for the ransom still unpaid; a fine was therefore levied if service was not performed; if service was performed the fine was not levied and the scutage for the ransom was pardoned.

In 1195 and 1196, the years of the second and third campaigns, respectively, of Richard I in France, some tenants in chief fined for their service, a fine which made their composition larger than a scutage at 20s., the amount paid by some tenants and the amount that tenants in chief whether they fined or paid scutage were allowed to collect from their vassals.[67] The new method of composition became customary under John; it was employed in all of the first seven scutages, though not to the exclusion of scutage alone. Some opposition must have developed to it for the last three scutages, those of Scotland, 1209, Wales, 1211, and Poitou, 1214, were unac-

65. *Pipe roll 6 Richard I, passim.*
66. *Ibid.,* p. 139.
67. *Pipe roll 7 Richard I,* p. 98.

companied by fines. Yet the last two were vigorous campaigns, one adjacent to England and one at great distance; consequently some reason other than location of the fighting must have lain behind this change in policy.

The discontent with the fine derived in part from the increase in composition for exemption from service. The principle behind both scutage and fine was composition for military service. At first sight we seem to be dealing with different forms of composition: the scutage was at a uniform rate per fee; the fine was a lump sum either in addition to scutage or including the scutage. In either case the money composition was larger than in scutage alone. Now there is not a single fine that we can discern in the rolls in connection with the Irish scutage (1172), the scutage of Galloway (1187), or the scutage of Wales (1190). The fines began with the army of 1194. The superficial difference between the fine and the scutage may be illustrated by the case of the abbot of Peterborough. In 1195 he was charged with £60 of scutage, the scutage of the "second army of Normandy"; in 1196 he was charged with £60 of the scutage of the "third army of Normandy"; and also with £100 not to cross in the "third army of Normandy" and for having his scutage of sixty knights.[68] Thus his composition was 66⅔ per cent greater the second year. Such variations were not uncommon in fines. The difficulty in distinguishing between the fine and the scutage is that the fine was always stated to be for exemption from service and for having the scutage, while entries of scutage usually said nothing as to an accompanying exemption. Suppose that we find cases where the scutage was referred to in the same language as the fine; it will be obvious that scutage and fine were different expressions of the same thing. For example, the bishop of Coventry accounted for £25 of his fine *ne transfretet* and for having scutage (at 20s.) of twenty-five knights. That is, in this instance, the scutage at 20s. covered the fine ne transfretet and the scutage from the rear vassals. The bishop of Bath paid £20 for twenty knights and ne transfretet.[69]

Such cases indicate that scutage and fine were both forms of commutation for knight service, the fine being a means by which the composition was increased. The difference in principle that existed lay in the fact that the scutage was reckoned at a certain

68. *Pipe roll 8 Richard I*, pp. 39, 40, 45. *Pipe roll 9 Richard I*, pp. 89, 90.
69. *Pipe roll 7 Richard I*, pp. 59, 67, 226. *Pipe roll 9 Richard I*, pp. 31, 73, 74, 91, 92, 154, 159, 214, 215.

rate per fee and the fine at a lump sum and that scutage alone could be collected from the rear vassals. The fine as the composition for service made possible the increase in commutation over the uniform rate per fee at the expense of the tenant in chief, not of his vassals. It further substituted a special bargain between the king and each vassal as to the amount to be paid independent of the rate of scutage which the body of vassals had agreed to or might agree to later when scutage was put in charge. Thus composition for military service that had for at least two generations been at a uniform rate per fee and for forty years at a rate not exceeding £1 per fee was increased at times to $2m.$ and $2\frac{1}{2}m.$, per fee; and in addition by the fine which each individual tenant made composition was greatly increased with no protection from custom, by a special arrangement between tenant and king.

The problem of the relationship of scutage, fine, and service was further complicated by the fact that tenants in chief served with a smaller number of knights than their *servitium debitum*. There are indications of this very early. In the reign of William I *almost all* the knights of the abbot of Abingdon were summoned for a campaign against the Welsh, as if full service were so unusual that it was noteworthy for "almost all" to be summoned.[70] In 1156 one chronicler states that Henry II summoned a third of the military service against the Welsh. In the campaign of Toulouse, 1159, the great barons brought only a few of their tenants.[71] Moreover, a further innovation was attempted: the tenants might indeed serve with reduced contingents, but their period of service should be increased. Moreover, if they wished to be exempted, the commutation in money would be allowed once, but it should be so greatly increased that the king could hire an equal number of knights for a whole year.

On February 22, 1177, Henry II ordered the sheriffs to make an inquest into all the lands held of him in chief by military service, the services owed and who now held them, and what service they actually performed; if any holding had been partitioned, who held each part and by what service. He also summoned all the tenants in chief with their men to appear at London at Easter for an expedition to France. Each tenant in chief was to report at once how many knights he could lead to France for a year without too great hardship. This action on the part of the king was taken after a

70. *Chronicon de Abingdon,* II, 10.
71. Robert de Torigni, pp. 193, 202.

meeting of his small council.[72] In 1194 Richard I summoned a third of the servitium debitum for his proposed campaign in France.[73] In 1196 Richard I summoned the host to be prepared to remain a long time and ordered no one to bring more than seven knights.[74] In 1198 Hubert Walter secured by negotiation and pressure a tenth of military service from some tenants in chief and from others either some service or a fine. Robert Dewias owed the service of nineteen knights; he sent three knights to Normandy for the "third army" and was acquitted of his scutage.[75] There is considerable evidence that in John's reign tenants served with only parts of their contingents and that such quotas were regarded as their full service; no money compensation was exacted in addition. The amount of composition accepted in lieu of service was the result of negotiation between the tenant and a royal official. Thus from 1166 on a series of efforts were initiated by the council or the king designed to secure an increase of service or of composition that would enlarge the fighting forces in number or in length of service, or both, whether they served in England or in France.

We must now examine the procedure by which scutage and fine were authorized before 1215 in order to determine to what extent Magna Carta introduced a change in this respect and here perhaps we shall discover the reason for Articles XII and XIV. This levy was, as we have seen, the commutation of military service. Since military service was one of the obligations of the vassal to his lord, how then did any problem of consent to its commutation arise? The vassal who was summoned was expected to appear; if he failed to perform his service, he might be disseized, though the tenant might by special arrangement substitute a fine.[76] The common use of fines for the campaign of 1194 and later, graduated in amount from a scutage up, the pardoning of the scutage for the ransom of Richard I, if service in the army of 1194 were performed; the employment of service by quota; the levy of fines by negotiation between a special representative of the king and the tenant indicate that the government was initiating an expansion of military service or its commutation.

The contemporary narratives of scutage give little detail on

72. Benedict of Peterborough, I, 138.
73. Roger of Howden, III, 242.
74. Ralph de Diceto, II, LXXX. Doris Stenton in *Pipe roll 8 Richard I*, p. xvii.
75. *Ibid.*, p. 91.
76. Jocelin de Brakelond, p. 63. *Pipe roll 8 Richard I*, p. 186. *Pipe Roll 9 Richard I*, p. 114.

CONSENT TO TAXATION

the method of authorization, an indication that it was granted or authorized in a conventional way. Only incidentally does information appear concerning the method of grant. The *Dialogue of the Exchequer*, almost an official statement, declares that the king determined the purpose of the levy, the occasion, and to a certain extent the rate, for the purpose of paying mercenary soldiers.[77] The influence of the tenants in chief appears even from this biased account. Discarding the benevolent philosophy that Henry II wished to spare the English the dangers of soldiering by employing paid troops, it is a fair inference from the statement that the king was not obtaining full military service from his vassals and supplemented what he secured by mercenaries and probably also by payments to those tenants who actually served. He secured money in lieu of the service owed to him at a certain rate per fee, limited by custom to £1 sterling. In both the reduction of service and the limitation of commutation which the king could exact we see the influence of his vassals. Was scutage levied before or after a campaign? It would be levied at the beginning of a campaign to help provide the funds to wage it. Such was the opinion of the author; clearly although the initiative in the levy lay with the king the opinions of his vassals had to be considered. A discussion in 1198 in the great curia regis is preserved about the question of providing a limited number of knights to serve a year or of compounding for them; but this was an unprecedented proposal, not of a conventional scutage, and so it tells us nothing about ordinary procedure.

In 1204 a scutage at 2½m. was authorized at a session of the great curia regis, the only case recorded of that body being specially summoned for this purpose.[78] This seems unusual, for the king had just returned after the loss of Normandy; he was planning a renewal of the struggle and called the great council to discuss ways and means. This scutage was one of the measures adopted to prepare for a new attack and no expedition of the host was sent or led. In 1205 a great host assembled in response to the summons so that it is likely many of the great barons were present at the discussion. It was decided not to invade France with the host, but to send a picked body of knights and to levy a scutage. Fines were also taken.[79] In these cases therefore a great body of tenants in chief seems to have been present when the scutage was decided on.

77. *Dialogus de scaccario*, p. 98.
78. Roger of Wendover, I, 320. Mitchell, *Studies in taxation*, pp. 63–64.
79. Sidney Smith in *Pipe roll 7 John*, p. xii. Kate Norgate, *John Lackland* (London, 1902), pp. 107–113. Mitchell, *Studies in taxation*, pp. 69–79.

186 TAXATION IN MEDIEVAL ENGLAND

Under Henry II the government sometimes seems to have levied the scutage after the campaign, for the returns did not appear on the pipe roll till the year following. But the scutage of 1156 (enrolled in the pipe roll of that year) seems to have been put in charge during the campaign of that same summer.[80] The scutage of 1159 (enrolled that year) was unquestionably authorized during the spring or early summer of 1159.[81] The scutage of 1165 accompanied by dona for sergeants for the Welsh war of that year appeared in the roll of 1165. Since the campaign did not begin till August, it is clear that the levies must have been put in charge in the summer.[82] The expedition to Ireland set sail in October, 1171, and returned Easter, 1172; the scutage appears in the roll of 1172; consequently we cannot decide from this evidence when the levy was authorized; it could have been during or after the campaign and the account rendered in the roll of 1172.[83]

In July, 1195, hostilities broke out between Philip and Richard, and the English king with an army from both sides of the channel invaded France. This outbreak led to fines and scutages recorded on the pipe roll of 1195, which indicates that the levy was made before hostilities ceased.[84] The following year the host was summoned by Richard on April 15 to come to Normandy without delay.[85] In the pipe roll of 1196 appears a scutage for the third army of Normandy which must be the composition levied for this campaign, thus put in charge before it closed.[86] Under John it became a custom to levy scutage before or during the campaign, and the rate became practically customary at 2m. or more. Further in each scutage many fines were levied for exemption from service. If therefore the scutage was levied early in the campaign or during it, early enough so that the returns could be made at the Michaelmas exchequer of the year, how was it authorized? It must have been by the king and the barons who were present on the expedition.

Thus in 1199, after his coronation, John sailed for Normandy with a great army of English. In a few days a truce was signed with Philip II, and there was no fighting till September; then the

80. Kate Norgate, *England under the Angevin kings* (London, 1887), I, 432.
81. *Ibid.*, p. 461.
82. *Pipe roll 11 Henry II, passim.*
83. *Pipe roll 33 Henry II, passim. Pipe roll 2 Richard I, passim.*
84. Roger of Howden, III, 301. *Pipe roll 7 Richard I*, pp. 22, 203, 204, 234, 235, 449.
85. Doris Stenton in *Pipe roll 8 Richard I*, p. xvii. Ralph de Diceto, II, LXXIX.
86. *Pipe roll 8 Richard I, passim.*

CONSENT TO TAXATION

struggle recommenced and lasted till the end of October when another truce was signed.[87] It is likely that the scutage at 2m. was put in charge during John's brief visit for his coronation, for it was recorded in the pipe roll of Michaelmas, 1199; it would not probably be authorized during the truce, and there would not have been time to levy it and record it, if it had been postponed till hostilities recommenced in September. As war was going on when John left Normandy for England at the end of May, the host was summoned and the accompanying scutage levied to carry on the struggle when he returned to Normandy in June. The fine roll contains fines and aids by tenants in chief that were made for exemption from service before the king sailed. William Fitz Alan fined in 60m. for not crossing with the king. William de Scalariis (15 fees) promised 40m. for quittance from this summons of the army and for having his scutage.[88] It is likely that the rate of scutage was fixed at the meeting of the host and not at a formal meeting of the great council called to discuss the question of scutage.

In 1201 the host was summoned to meet at Portsmouth and there, says Roger of Wendover, many were granted permission to remain at home, giving the king 2m. from each fee.[89] There was no fighting when the host arrived in France. In 1202 and 1203 the scutages of those years must have been authorized by the king by the counsel of those barons with him in France. In 1205 the host was summoned and a great force assembled, but Earl William Marshal and Hubert Walter, who probably represented the opinion of the barons, persuaded John not to invade France with a great force. Instead a selected body of knights was sent to La Rochelle. At the same time scutage was levied by the king before the host was dismissed, for men fined for their service and for having their scutage at 2m. late in May, 1205.[90] Much discussion took place concerning the expedition, and the question of scutage probably was considered. Since the chroniclers report that a great force was assembled, many tenants in chief were probably present.[91] The scutage of 1206 for the campaign that began in June and lasted four months must have been levied at the beginning of the campaign

87. Ralph de Coggeshall, p. 100. Ralph de Diceto, II, 166. Roger of Wendover, I, 288. Roger of Howden, IV, 92, 93, 96, 97. Gervase of Canterbury, II, 92.
88. *Rot. oblatis*, pp. 2, 27.
89. Roger of Wendover, I, 311. Roger of Howden, IV, 163.
90. *Rot. oblatis*, p. 288.
91. Mitchell, *Studies in taxation*, pp. 69–70. Norgate, *John Lackland*, pp. 107–113.

or during it to have the accounts presented at Michaelmas, seemingly by the king taking counsel with those of his barons who were present.[92]

The scutage of Scotland at 20s. was authorized in the summer of 1209, for some counties returned it in that year in the pipe roll. Although an expedition marched against the Scots, no fighting took place.[93] In 1210 the scutage of Ireland appeared in the roll of that year. As the campaign closed at the end of August, it is likely that the scutage was authorized during the campaign, probably early, for the fines were probably levied to raise money for the campaign.[94] The scutage of Wales in 1211 was levied at the close of the campaign (about August 15) and appears in the pipe roll of that year.[95] The order for the scutage of Poitou was issued on May 26 during the campaign so that the authorization was made if at all by the barons with the king, many of whom performed their service.

Thus the conventional method of authorization of scutage was before or during the campaign by the king and probably after consultation with those tenants in chief who had answered the summons to the host. The amount of service considered acceptable and the amount of a fine could only be determined by negotiation between the king's representative and the individual tenant. The king obviously had a great interest in the rate of scutage; the amount of service he could command depended to some extent on the height of the rate of commutation; the revenue from scutage also was conditioned by the rate. The rate of scutage also interested all of the tenants in chief and all the rear vassals of various ranks. Those who had performed their service (or paid a fine) would approve of a high rate of scutage, for in that way they would reduce the amount paid out of their own coffers. Those tenants who paid a scutage to the king and their rear vassals would feel aggrieved on account of the additional cost. For a brief campaign as in 1199, 1209 (Scottish campaign), or no campaign at all as in 1201, 1204, and 1205, it is clear that those who answered the summons and took part in the campaign would favor a high rate of scutage. Those who fined however would have mingled feelings; they would object to a fine for an insignificant campaign; once they had fined, they would want a higher rate of scutage. But tenants in chief who paid

---

92. *Ibid.*, pp. 113–119. Mitchell, *Studies in taxation*, pp. 77–78.
93. *Ibid.*, p. 94.
94. *Ibid.*, p. 96.
95. *Ibid.*, p. 101.

CONSENT TO TAXATION

scutage and all rear vassals would object to scutages for campaigns that were such only in name. A survey of these conditions indicates why the desire arose to check the king's control over scutage and military service. Scutage had changed since the accession of Richard I, in greatly increased frequency (14 times), in increase in rate, in the development of the fine, in a further increase in the commutation of service; in the reduction of service, a reduction which was in practice treated as the servitium debitum; and finally in its levy on occasions merely as an excuse for increasing the king's revenue. All these features show the change that feudal military service was undergoing in an age of increasing money economy.

When however we examine the cases of individual lay tenants in chief, we find that the majority of the great tenants usually did not pay either scutage or fine; they were entered in the pipe rolls under Richard and John as quit by the king's writ. This was probably because they performed their military service. In 1201 about half of the great lay tenants paid scutage or fine and in 1205 perhaps four fifths did so. In no other scutage of John did such a high proportion of the great lay tenants in chief pay; in great part they served. The fines and scutages fell upon the clerical tenants, upon lesser tenants in chief, and upon rear vassals on the lands in hand. Since most of the tenants in chief served with only part of their contingents, the increase in rate struck with greatest force on the rear vassals. Hence when the king took scutage after consultation with his tenants on the campaign, he took it with the advice of the bulk of his military and political advisers—those whom he would expect to take the lead in discussion—except for one group, the prelates. These rarely served and generally compounded. Thus the demand for a statement of the law regarding scutage in 1215 is not easy to explain. There seem to have been two factors that created the demand. The exciting cause was the issue over foreign service or its commutation raised by the Northern barons in 1213 and 1214. When they were summoned to accompany the king to Poitou in July they declared that according to the tenure of their lands they were not bound to perform this service.[96] John marched north to bring them to obedience by force, but was induced by the persuasion and threats of Stephen Langton not to attack them.[97]

The following year, John led the host to Poitou but failed in his great plan of defeating Philip in the north although he had suc-

96. Ralph de Coggeshall, p. 167.
97. Roger of Wendover, II, 83.

cesses in the southwest. In May, during the campaign, he authorized a scutage at 3m. without fines. The "Northerners" refused to pay it on the ground that they did not owe service abroad, although they had paid scutage earlier under Richard and John as well as under Henry II.[98] Thus apparently in 1213 and 1214 John was first refused military service and then its composition and found himself unable to enforce either the service or its commutation. One argument used by archbishop Stephen in 1213 against John's attacking the "Northerners" was that he should not make war against anyone without a judgment of his court. The argument had no effect upon John, but he desisted when Langton threatened to excommunicate all but John who attacked anyone with arms before the interdict was dissolved. Langton refused to let the matter drop until the king appointed a day for the barons to appear at his court to hear the judgment of their peers.[99]

The second factor in the general discontent was the feeling of the prelates, of a few of the great barons, of most of the lesser tenants in chief, and the mass of rear vassals who on account of the growth of service by quota usually paid scutage whether their lords compounded or not. An element of caprice in the administration of the law aggravated discontent among tenants in chief, illustrated by the varying amounts of fines for service, so that one man might pay several times as much as another, though both held by the same amount of knight service. Another source of annoyance was the tremendous fines of the Irish scutage, averaging 10m. per fee. Is this enough cause to explain the curious aberration of 1215 by which the barons equated scutage with aid? We cannot say that it was an article drawn up in haste, for it appears in the articles of the barons as well as in the charter.

It is difficult to understand the emphasis on the provision concerning the aid, that it should be levied only by consent of the great council especially summoned for that purpose. Such had been the method of the Saladin tithe and of the thirteenth of 1207. Our information is imperfect in 1194 but that was one of the regular aids; it is wanting in 1198 and 1200 (carucages), and the great council may not have been used on those occasions. Hence perhaps the demand that it should always be employed in levying gracious aids. As for scutage, the customary method of levying it had led to abuses. The remedy was not to abolish it; that was impossible, for

98. Walter of Coventry, II, 217.
99. Roger of Wendover, II, 83.

CONSENT TO TAXATION 191

it would involve the overthrow of the system of landholding. The solution suggested in Articles XII and XIV was to abandon the conventional method of authorizing scutage by consulting those who were on the campaign, or for the king to advise with those tenants who were in immediate attendance. Instead the great curia regis was to be summoned to a special colloquy. That is, scutage should be put in charge by the king with the advice and consent of all the tenants in chief. This session must therefore be held either before the campaign or after its close. In the former case only could any of the receipts be used for the current expenses of that campaign. The question whether a proper campaign had been waged that would necessitate a scutage would be decided by the whole body of tenants in chief. This procedure might be expected to reduce the frequency of scutage; it would certainly reduce the rate; and it would hamper the levy of fines. Broadly speaking, it might be expected to check the innovations that had so expanded under John. Article XIV was introduced because the phrase per commune consilium regni was ambiguous. It might mean a relatively small group of tenants in chief. And so all scutages of John were authorized legally. Hence the barons now aimed to establish as law that all tenants in chief must be formally summoned. Article XIV described carefully the procedure to be followed in authorizing a scutage or an aid. The greater tenants, both clerical and lay, were to be summoned by individual letters; the lesser tenants by general letters through the king's bailiffs or sheriffs. The writs should state the cause of the summons, the date (at least forty days later), and the place. In this form we seem to see the existing practice when the great curia regis was summoned. The final statement of this article is puzzling. It runs: "And when the summons has been made in this way, the business shall proceed on the appointed day according to the counsel of those present although all who have been summoned may not have come." One interpretation might be that the consent of the present bound the absent of those summoned; that if one were not summoned, he would not be bound by the consent of those present; in effect, this would mean that individual consent had been superseded by corporate consent. Yet it is difficult to believe that the barons would agree to a statement of the law which condemned the action of the Northern barons in 1214 who had been so prominent in the insurrection which had led up to the charter. It would seem a fairer interpretation to say that this clause merely meant that the absence of a few tenants after such a proper summons would not prevent the king and his barons from transacting business. Such was the customary procedure. It would be difficult to secure attendance by everyone. If such was ordinary procedure, why the reference to the action of the council in the absence of a few if new authority of the council was not intended? Because it completed the detailed statement of the procedure to which this article is devoted. The authors have described minutely the measures by which they aimed to secure a full attendance. It almost sounds as though someone suggested "and suppose some are absent." In that case, the article states, the business will go forward in the customary way, as had been done, for example, in 1204. The consent of the present would not bind the absent; the king would negotiate with absentees to secure their consent to the scutage or aid in conventional fashion.

Why then were the articles unsatisfactory and dropped as of doubtful utility (*dubitilia*) in the first reissue of the charter after John's death and the accession of Henry III?[100] Perhaps because they had been introduced to limit John's employment of scutage and aid as a means of exacting money payments on occasions not justified by feudal law, as illustrated on many occasions in scutage and less frequently by aids, as perhaps on the carucage of 1200 for relief of his lands in France, and in 1203 in the seventh of movables as a fine for desertion by his vassals from the campaign in France. Now John was dead, the country was in the turmoil of a civil war; the legal king, Henry III, was a boy in the hands of the barons. Such articles would hamper the levy of an aid or a scutage which they might need to carry on the war. The regency would prefer to return to the customary mode. In this way they were able to levy a carucage in 1217 and an aid on knights' fees for the donation of 10,000*m*. to Prince Louis when peace was made. On neither of these cases could all tenants in chief appear, for many were in arms against Henry III, or had not yet been reconciled with the new king.

The successful uprising against John leading to the grant of Magna Carta followed by a civil war and the death of John, the triumph of his followers and the withdrawal of Prince Louis, the succession of the boy Henry III, and the reissue of the Great Charter with certain modifications as the basis of the law of the realm marks a curious overturn in the political upheaval of the period 1214 to 1217. In place of Articles XII and XIV of the Charter of

100. Stubbs, *Select charters*, p. 342.

1215 appeared a statement of custom: "Scutage shall be levied as it was in the reign of Henry II"—no notice of aid appeared although it would have been simple to have added two words, *vel auxilium*. That scutage should be taken as in the time of Henry II indicates the barons' belief that the abuses of that levy had arisen since the death of that monarch. That aids were omitted in the new charter may mean that they were unable to frame a satisfactory article and it seemed best to leave the subject to the wisdom of the barons if the necessity for an aid should arise. Possibly it means that they believed that with a proper king aid would rarely be necessary. Henry II had levied it only once for a lay purpose, the marriage of his eldest daughter, a regular aid, and once, perhaps twice, for a crusade. No problem would arise for a regular aid, and a crusade in which England would dispatch a force like that in the third crusade was unlikely, at least for some time. The great struggle over Norman and Angevin possessions seemed to have closed, and could be attended to by scutage and tallage as under Henry II. However all this may have been, the regency at first, and later Henry III, found it necessary to resort to the aid to meet the financial needs of the government; the scutage was frequently levied, but not till 1229 did they raise the rate to 3*m*. and levy fines in addition. Thus the government pursued the same road of frequent aids and scutages, and very soon chose the tax on movables as the most fruitful. The reign falls into two well-marked periods; from 1216 to 1237, a period of frequent scutages and of seven aids, three of them on movables, all granted by the great curia regis under the theory of individual consent, yet practically a consent in which the absent were bound by the decision of the present; a period in which the government acted under the theory that all taxpayers on the lands of tenants in chief were constructively present at a meeting of the great curia regis. Although there was much discussion and criticism of the aids, the great barons did not feel free to refuse an aid, a persistence of the original concept of the gracious aid. During this period too the scutage seems to have been decided on during the campaign by the assent of those present, although once it was done at the beginning of the campaign without a formal meeting of the whole body of tenants in chief. It must be said that no criticism of scutage has been recorded; the problem that emerged in connection with the aids was not that they must be granted in a great council as provided in Article XIV of the issue of the Great Charter of 1215, for that method was always employed, but that this method failed to check the king's exactions. Hence a new ground of criticism emerged that a new, regular aid was growing up, a new due or consuetudo; hence too the solemn promises exacted from the king that the levy should not constitute a precedent, and in the last tax of this period, that of the thirtieth of 1237, Henry III's promise that he would never ask again for such an aid.

Thus the ground of criticism had shifted with the new age. The second period from 1237 to 1272 was characterized by repeated refusals by the great council to grant any aids except such as were specifically authorized by feudal law, to marry the king's daughter, to knight the king's son. Of three scutages, only one was accompanied by fines, and only one gracious aid was taken at the close of the reign for a crusade led by Edward and Edmund, the king's two sons.

A sign of another new development appeared. The summons of representatives of shires and of towns to meet with the great council for consultation, though in Henry III's reign not about aids. The genesis of the new order came from the king's use of local groups for all kinds of investigations initiated by the king's council. Particularly noteworthy were the cases of 1261 and 1254, but no question appeared about taxation. We should recall however that representative groups on the initiative of the clergy were employed in taxation. Perhaps this custom affected the great council in its policy toward the laity and taxation, but I think not.

The first period of Henry III's reign, from 1216 to 1237, was marked by frequent scutages (7) and aids (6), so that both the regency first and then Henry III himself followed the same line taken by John.[101] The influence of Magna Carta was certainly felt in scutages each time a genuine campaign was waged; not till 1229 did the rate rise again to $3m.$; only once (1229) were fines levied in addition to scutage; scutage was put in charge as before 1215 by the council and leaders at the beginning or during the campaign, not by a formal meeting of the great curia regis, as provided by Articles XII and XIV of the Magna Carta of 1215.

Broadly speaking, it was the intention to summon the great curia regis to discuss the grant of aid. For the levy of the carucage of 1217 and the aid on knights' fees in 1218, in the disturbed con-

---

101. Scutages: Bytham, 10s., 1221; Montgomery, 2m., 1223; Bedford, 2m., 1224; Kerry, 2m., 1227; Brittany, 3m., 1230; Poitou, 3m., 1230; Elveyn, 2m., 1232. Aids: carucage, 2s., 1220; carucage of Bedford, 1224; fifteenth, 1225; fortieth, 1232; on knights' fees, 2m., 1235; thirtieth, 1237.

CONSENT TO TAXATION 195

ditions it was unlikely that a full attendance was expected, although the writs of collection state that these levies were granted by the commune consilium regni.[102] The writs state that the carucage of 1220 was granted by the great council, but clearly not all of the barons had been summoned, for the tenants in Yorkshire alleged that they had the right to be summoned as had other tenants. The carucage of Bedford was granted by those prelates who were present at the siege.[103]

The three taxes on movables were all granted by the great council. Obviously it was impossible to have a full attendance. The bishop of Durham was absent from the council that granted the fifteenth; at the first meeting when the aid of 1232 was considered, many prelates were absent; and in 1237 Matthew Paris emphasized the very full attendance at the colloquium that granted the thirtieth, as though this meeting of the great council was unusually well attended.[104] One gains the impression that Article XIV of the Great Charter of 1215 was in force under Henry III: "When they meet, the business shall go through on the appointed day although all who have been summoned may not have come." Such seems to have been the established custom.

As in the past there was much discussion and criticism, perhaps more than earlier. In 1225 two sessions were held that resulted in the grant of the fifteenth of movables. In 1232 three sessions were held before the fortieth was granted; in 1235 a single session was sufficient to secure a grant of the 2m. on all knights' fees to provide a dowry for the king's sister, a gracious aid. In 1237 in a tumultuous session bitter criticism was launched at the king's extravagant regime. Henry III promised reform and that no further aids would be demanded,[105] and the grant was made.

With this tax the period of frequent gracious aids in the reign came to a close. Two conflicting theories concerning these aids appear, the one expressed and the other implicit. On the one hand both king and magnates and commentators believed that the aid was an individual grant by each tenant; on the other, the practical effect of the grants by the great curia regis was that the decision was binding on all property holders affected. Thus in the aid of 1217

102. *Rot. claus.*, I, 348b, 371. Mitchell, *Studies in taxation*, pp. 122, 125.
103. Mitchell, *Studies in taxation*, pp. 130, 131, 156. W. W. Shirley, *Royal letters*, I, 151.
104. Mitchell, *Studies in taxation*, pp. 162, 200. Matthew Paris, *Chronica maiora*, III, 380.
105. *Ibid.*, p. 381. Mitchell, *Studies in taxation*, pp. 159, 199, 214.

the bishop of Winchester was charged with 159m. for the aid on knights' fees. He declared before the small council that he had never assented to the aid and the council acquitted him.[106] He had however to appear before the council and prove his case. The writs of assessment declared that the carucage of 1220 had been granted in common by all the magnates and faithful of the realm, but the tenants in Yorkshire refused to assess it because they had not been summoned to the great council and had not granted the tax. If the king should come to York and ask the magnates for the tax, they would assent, said some of the bailiffs [107]—an indication of individual consent. Other barons successfully opposed this levy. Though the reason for their abstention is nowhere given, the levy could not (in face of this attitude) be collected from them. Only in 1227 did Earl Warenne agree that the carucage should be collected on all his lands.

The carucage of the clergy for the expenses of the siege of Bedford (1224) was by individual grant. In various writs the king declared that it was conceded to him by individual prelates.[108]

The importance of individual consent as to the fifteenth appears in the royal letter to the bishop of Durham that declares "the money . . . both within your bishopric and without you have caused to be assessed on your lands and fees in accordance with our prayers," and that the bishop granted the fifteenth by the pure gift of his generosity.[109]

The levy of the sixteenth on the beneficed clergy in 1226 illustrates the difference in the control of the royal government over the taxation of this group. The pope ordered the clergy to make a grant. The archbishop of Canterbury wrote to his bishops saying it was necessary to obey the pope and to make a virtue of necessity, and the king wrote depicting his need and asking for a grant.

If we compare the levy of the sixteenth with that of the fifteenth, we see the different relation of the king to the laity. The laity believed in an occasional aid, even when based on property; the clergy are only brought to pay an aid by the intervention of the pope, followed by the support of the archbishops and bishops and finally the appeal of the king. This attitude was natural for the revenues taxed were established for the support of God's work. No organiza-

106. Pipe roll 5 Henry III, m. 2, Public Record Office. Thomas Madox, *History of the exchequer*, I, 675.
107. *Rot. claus.*, I, 437. Shirley, *Royal letters*, I, 151.
108. *Rot. claus.*, I, 613b, 616. *Patent rolls, 1225–1232*, p. 95.
109. *Rot. claus.*, II, 75b.

CONSENT TO TAXATION

tion similar to the curia regis existed to authorize the tax. The only feasible method was for the king to ask each bishop to take up the matter with his clergy. As Lunt has pointed out, the original proposal of the king was to employ some kind of a diocesan assembly. But finally on the suggestion of the canons of Salisbury a provincial assembly was summoned composed of deans, archdeacons, and other clergy, and this body granted the sixteenth. Some of the clergy preferred a uniform grant lest one cleric pay more than another; they wondered what would happen if some canons refused: they demanded and received a guarantee that the grant would not form a precedent for a future levy. Thus the problem of the method of grant and authorization of a tax on the clergy had a development distinct from that on either the lands of tenants in chief by military tenure or the royal demesne.

In 1226 Henry III was granted a sixteenth on certain clerical revenues that had not been taxed in the fifteenth of 1225. The grant of this tax throws light upon various constitutional questions, such as the absence of a right by the king to tax the lower clergy, the lack of any clerical organization by which a uniform tax could be secured, the feeling among the prelates that their participation in the grant of the fifteenth and earlier taxes had been purely voluntary—their consent had been independent of the action of the lay members of the curia regis, the great authority of the pope in securing the sixteenth for the government and at the same time the power of the lower clergy to determine the form and the amount of their contribution, and the absence of the employment of the curia regis by the king to secure the grant. It should be recalled that the lower clergy had probably contributed to the Saladin tithe and certainly to the ransom of Richard I, that John had attempted and failed to secure a grant from them in 1207. Thus there were precedents for taxing them and also one precedent of refusal by the prelates.

At the time that the great council was granting the fifteenth, Honorius III wrote on February 3, 1225, commanding all the clergy to grant the king an adequate aid according to their wealth. The mandate was addressed to the archbishops, bishops, abbots, priors, and other prelates and rulers (rectores) of the church throughout England.[110] The date of this order, the officials to whom it was addressed, and the language which it employed indicate that it applied to the whole body of ecclesiastics, not merely to the

110. *Patent rolls, 1216-1225*, p. 585.

lower clergy. No statement has survived as to why the pope wrote in behalf of Henry III except the entry in the Dunstaple annals that the secular clergy had refused to pay the fifteenth; [111] but the date of the papal mandate makes such a conclusion impossible, for the letter was being composed in Rome just at the time that the fifteenth was being granted at London. The information which led Honorius to take this action must have reached him earlier; very likely, as has been suggested, it was carried by the royal nuncios sent to Rome, Godfrey de Craucumb and Stephen de Lucy who left England early in November [112] and interviewed the pope December 18. They presented petitions on various questions on English internal affairs and the relations between England and France. It may be that one petition dealt with the finances of the English government for a proposed war with France. It is difficult to understand why no use was made of the papal order till May 27, 1226. Although we do not know when the clergy received the order, it seems certain that they must have received it long before it was used. It seems plausible that when the pope's letter arrived, the fifteenth had already been levied; it had been granted by the prelates, secular and religious, as well as by the laity, and by many orders that compounded. As the beneficed clergy had never paid a tax with such an excuse as was alleged in 1225, the government felt that the purpose of the letter had already been fulfilled. Then apparently some of the council suggested that with a papal mandate they might be able to extend this aid to the lower clergy. The prelates on the council favored it, since all the bishops took part in persuading the clergy to grant it. Thus the plan was formed to extend the aid to the lower clergy. The scheme was carefully worked out. First the king wrote the dean and chapter of Salisbury cathedral, typical of his appeal to lower clergy. He asked for an aid and explained why he was making this request; in so doing he interpreted the papal mandate of February 3, 1225. Some time ago, he said, the pope, filled with pity at our financial condition, wrote to the archbishops, bishops, and all the clergy of the realm, commanding them to make us an adequate aid with which in addition to their loans we might be able to restore peace to church and state. The prelates therefore long ago agreed to grant us a fifteenth of their movables. "Since therefore the completion of this aforesaid business depends on your liberality, we beg your benignity most attentively that you may take

111. *Annals of Dunstaple*, p. 93.
112. *Rot. claus.*, II, 3b.

CONSENT TO TAXATION 199

pity on our necessity and make us such an aid that we should be grateful to both the Roman church and to you." By the counsel of the archbishop of Canterbury and his bishops, the king promised to grant a tenth of the hay and the mills on his demesne to the churches and he would endeavor to persuade the lay magnates to follow his example.[113]

On his part, the archbishop of Canterbury forwarded a copy of the papal brief to the dean and canons of Salisbury and added the comment that since it was necessary to obey the papal mandate, he warned all to turn necessity into a virtue and for all religious of every order and the clergy of the diocese to make a competent aid to the king from those things on which they had not paid a fifteenth. Archbishop Langton also wrote to the bishop of Salisbury reminding him that the pope had written "to us, to you, and to the English church that we should grant a competent aid to the king according to the wealth of our churches." The prelates had granted a fifteenth of their movable goods to the king in this time of need, and the primate felt that the clergy ought to be moved by the same reasons that led the prelates to make the grant. So he commanded the bishop of Salisbury to summon the religious and other clerks of his diocese and induce them to make an aid on those things that had not paid a fifteenth. He urged the bishop to secure a twelfth or a fourteenth and that measures be taken that the same proportion be given throughout the diocese. This grant would not form a precedent; the documents for the bishopric of Salisbury have been preserved, but it is obvious that the same appeals were made in other dioceses. At the suggestion of the canons of Salisbury, the archbishop summoned a provincial assembly composed of the deans and two representatives of the cathedral chapters, the archdeacons and representatives of religious bodies to meet at London a fortnight after Michaelmas, 1226. This representative body granted a sixteenth of revenues of all churches, of prebends, and of common revenues, not to constitute a precedent by grant of the pope and letters patent of Henry III. The sixteenth was based upon the assessment made of the twentieth of 1216.[114]

From this account we observe that the taxation of the lower clergy was initiated and authorized by the pope and that the king requested an aid; but his request was supplemented by the appeals of the archbishop and the bishops on the legal ground that the

113. *Vetus registrum Sarisberiense*, II, 55-56.
114. *Ibid.*, pp. 57-59, 65-67, 69.

clergy must obey the pope's commands, and the statement that the prelates had already done so. The lower clergy thus were not bound either by the grant of the fifteenth by the great curia regis, or by the grant of the prelates. If bound at all, they were bound by the command of the pope.

The employment of a representative body from all England arose from the absence of any assembly that had the authority to make a uniform grant for the lower clergy throughout the kingdom. To secure such a group they adopted the device of employing representatives. The laity already possessed an assembly with the requisite power in the great curia regis. Its authority however did not extend to the lower clergy. Nor did the authority of the king or the bishops extend so far. Their first notion was to summon a diocesan assembly of a representative character, which was an experiment proposed by the council. This was abandoned when the plan was brought to the attention of the council that to insure uniformity a provincial assembly of representatives might be employed, though apparently it did not include representatives of the lower clergy. The language of the king and the archbishop of Canterbury indicates further that while the prelates in the curia regis granted a fifteenth of movables in 1225 they did it on account of the papal mandate and independently of the lay members of the curia regis, though at the same rate. Thus the curia regis did not form an all-inclusive corporate body. This interpretation is borne out by the description of the negotiations over both the fortieth and the thirtieth. The lay barons speaking through the earl of Chester declared that since they had served abroad they did not owe any aid; the clerical members requested a postponement because many were absent. When the fortieth was finally granted in September, 1232, this feeling of division undoubtedly continued. In 1237, although all members of the great council agreed to the aid of the thirtieth, the clergy made special arrangements about assessment and collection, as though a line distinguished clerical and lay tenants one from another.

The opposition by Ranulf, earl of Chester, to the grant of the fortieth in 1232 in the great council indicates individual consent. The chronicler suggests that a united opposition was forming for Ranulf is said to have spoken "for the magnates." [115] The opposition was so strong that only at the third meeting in September was

115. Roger of Wendover, III, 21.

CONSENT TO TAXATION 201

the grant finally made.¹¹⁶ The prelates too asked for an adjournment till after Easter, because many who had been summoned had failed to come. At the new date all might meet to decide what legally ought to be done. Here too the clergy sounded the note of legality in the grant of the aid. After the grant was made in September, 1232, individual opposition remained, in cases, very strong. Richard de Percy, William, count of Aumale, and John, earl of Lincoln, were preventing the assessors from levying the fortieth on their lands three years later in 1235, and in 1236 it is recorded that Richard, who had hitherto prevented the assessment and collection of this tax on his land in the North Riding of Yorkshire, now had granted that it should be collected.¹¹⁷ The government asked the fortieth also of religious that did not hold by military service and who were not summoned to the curia regis but would accept instead a lump sum.¹¹⁸

In the aid to marry the king's sister in 1235 the notion of individual consent appeared. A writ to the barons of the exchequer to grant a respite in the demand for the payment of the aid to the custodian of the heir of Nicholas de Longchamp states that Nicholas had granted this aid to the king.¹¹⁹ Moreover certain prelates received individual letters patent promising that his grant should not constitute a precedent.¹²⁰ Some comments by Matthew Paris concerning the grant of the thirtieth suggest his belief that the consent was individual, e.g., when he remarks that the archbishop of Canterbury first consented to the thirtieth with his bishops and clergy; or that it was often laid down as a condition that the king should abandon his foreign advisers and adhere to his natural councilors.¹²¹

The force of this inference lies primarily in the fact that the general sentiment of the time both on the part of the king and the commentators was for individual consent. Nevertheless, when we recall that the great council up to the present had always granted the levy and despite opposition and criticism the great bulk of it

116. Mitchell, *Studies in taxation*, p. 200.
117. *Calendar of patent rolls, 1232–1247*, pp. 124, 159.
118. Fine roll 17 Henry III, m. 6, m. 8, m. 9, Public Record Office. *Close rolls, 1231–1234*, p. 234. Exchequer K. R., Memoranda roll 20 Henry III, m. 2d.
119. *Excerpta ex rotulis finium in turri Londinensi asservatis Henrico tertio rege*, ed. Charles Roberts (Record Commission), I, 438.
120. *Calendar patent rolls, 1232–1247*, p. 145.
121. Paris, *Chronica maiora*, III, 388.

had been paid, it is apparent that a concept of corporate consent was imperceptibly taking shape, partly because of the frequency of the levy, partly because of its character. A tax rarely asked of the members of a body like the great curia regis could retain its original character of individual consent, but one which recurred at frequent intervals as did aids during this part of Henry III's reign would develop the notion of a corporate consent. Moreover these levies, like the carucage and the tax on movables, fell upon subtenants of all grades and especially on many property holders who did not hold by knight service at all and who were never summoned and never consulted about the tax. These men owed definite dues to their lords; often they were also expected to pay gracious aids on occasions of their lords' need. This tax paid to the king repeatedly would seem to develop the notion that it was owed because of a united grant of the great men rather than an individual offering by a great lord. It is clear that great men and small men opposed these levies. The opposition was stimulated by the growing use of money and its employment in manorial economy. The repetition of requests for taxes by the king testifies to the growth of a money economy and the concomitant criticism. This criticism and opposition seem to have been reflected in the official statements of the authorization of the levies. The changes in the description of the body by which these taxes were authorized reflect deliberation about its competence. In 1207 the writs of collection stated succinctly that the thirteenth (an unprecedented levy at the end of a disastrous war) was granted by the common counsel and assent of our council at Oxford, that is, the great curia regis, but with no special emphasis on the comprehensive nature of the body which authorized the tax.[122] The articles of the barons, as well as Magna Carta, stated merely that scutage or aid should be authorized by the commune consilium regni, but the latter emphasized the comprehensive nature of this body; the latter document describes the mode of summons and states that business would be decided by those who attended. Both provisions were probably conventional but were nevertheless affected by circumstances under which the charter was formulated. The aid of 1217 was authorized by the common council of the realm, that is, of the earls, barons, and other tenants in chief.[123]

The writs for the levy of the carucage of 1220 stated that all the

122. *Rot. claus.*, I, 72.
123. *Ibid.*, p. 371. *Patent rolls, 1216-1225*, p. 125.

CONSENT TO TAXATION 203

magnates and faithful of all of our realm granted in common the carucage for our great necessity and the most pressing urgency of our debts and the preservation of our land of Poitou.[124] This order emphasizes two points, not noted in earlier levies: first, that the aid was granted in common; second, that it was granted by all the magnates and faithful, i.e., unanimity and universality of the grant, the mention of unusual financial necessity perhaps reflecting the discussion in the great council. Out of the discussion concerning an aid to recover Henry III's lands in France in 1225 came a bargain. The king confirmed the charters and in return was granted a fifteenth of movables by the common council and spontaneous desire of "our archbishops, bishops, earls and barons," i.e., by the great council.[125] But the official statement of the grant of the fifteenth which was issued in connection with the charters was much more comprehensive; those who granted the fifteenth were archbishops, bishops, abbots, priors, earls, barons, knights, free holders, and all in our kingdom, far more than were summoned to the great council; according to this statement that body included all free property holders who were taxed.[126] Shall we therefore conclude that the body included members of the middle classes? In all meetings of the great council there were present rear vassals and lesser clergy who accompanied their superiors and in addition curious onlookers might also be present. Such attendants played no part in the decision of the assembly; but their presence in numbers would attract the attention of a chronicler. Their presence did not change the character of the assembly.

In 1232 it appears that the experience of 1225 led to a modification of the statement of the ideal composition and authority of the curia regis. The fortieth was granted by the "archbishops, bishops, abbots, priors, clergy holding land which did not belong to their churches, earls, barons, knights, freemen, and villeins." [127] The change in statement suggests that someone had raised questions about the competence of the great council.

In writs that granted concessions to tenants (especially the clergy) in assessment and collection, it is clear that a line was drawn between the property of the vassal and that of his men. Thus the abbot of Reading was allowed to assess and collect the fortieth on

124. *Rot. claus.*, I, 437.
125. *Rot. claus.*, II, 75.
126. Stubbs, *Select charters*, p. 355.
127. *Ibid.*, p. 360.

his own movables, and on the movables of his men by four knights of his fief.[128] Another illustration of this distinction appears in the close roll. The king was writing to the abbot of Coggeshall urging him to grant an aid. He recalls "how by the common counsel and the unanimous consent of all the magnates of our realm, both bishops and earls, barons, abbots, and priors, an aid was granted to us by them, viz., a fortieth part of all their movables and the movables of others of our kingdom." This statement emphasizes the unanimous consent of the central authorizing body, and the full attendance of the tenants in chief. It also indirectly declares that this body had legal authority to grant an aid on all movable property of their men. The phrase *omnium mobilium suorum et aliorum de regno nostro* has the meaning just given.[129] Taken however in connection with the fact that the fortieth was levied on the property of subvassals and their demesnes, it seems fair to conclude that decision of the great council consciously bound these too to pay the fortieth.

Religious houses that did not hold by military tenure were not bound but made special donations. The grounds for asking a contribution from these nonmilitary organizations are thus explained: "All religious orders, except yours [the Cistercians] have liberally aided us. Your order has never in the past been exempt from an aid nor ought it to be exempt. We, therefore, request that you make us an aid similar to that made by others, although not by the name of a fortieth." [130] The royal demesne paid the fortieth, but probably because of the appeal of their lord, the king, and the moral obligation to contribute in the case of a general aid. That is, in the case of a general aid, groups not in the great council were morally bound to participate.

The grant of the aid in 1235 at 2m. on knights' fees, both of the old and new enfeoffment, was made by the "archbishops, bishops, abbots, priors, earls, barons, and others of our kingdom who held in chief of the king—of their spontaneous desire and without being owed." This is a description of the great curia regis. In 1237 was made a further change in the statement regarding the authority by which the thirtieth was authorized: it was granted by the archbishops, bishops, abbots, priors, clergy having land not belonging

---

128. *Close rolls, 1231–1234*, pp. 160, 283, 285, 288, 290.
129. *Ibid.*, p. 311. *Patent rolls, 1216–1225*, p. 323.
130. *Close rolls, 1231–1234*, p. 311.

to their churches, earls, barons, knights, and freemen, for themselves and their villeins.[131]

That is, the villeins no longer granted but their lords granted for themselves and their villein tenants. In theory therefore the great council represented every taxpayer, except certain religious houses that made special arrangements with the king, and the royal demesne.

The royal demesne does not seem to have paid the thirtieth of 1237, although one chronicler listed citizens as among the members of the great council that granted the tax.[132] The manor of Bridgewater was exempted from the thirtieth "because the King desires it to be tallaged with the royal demesne when the King levies a tallage," and writs were issued not to collect the thirtieth on the demesne in eighteen counties without the special command of the king.[133] In 1238 a tallage was levied.[134] The substitution of a tallage for the thirtieth may indicate opposition of the royal demesne to paying the tax on personal property.

In origin, thus, consent was individual and such it remained in the view of the men of the time. Alongside this concept was emerging a different notion, that of corporate action, where the consent of the present bound the absent, and the consent of the majority bound the minority; such was the practical result of the decisions on the aids during this period of Henry III's reign. First, the grant was always made by the same body, the curia regis. Second, the levies increased in frequency. A rare request might not have effected a change in the concept of the body's action. The repetition to such an extent that the barons feared the establishment of a new custom helped to change the notion of the character of the grant. Third, the character of the aid had a profound effect, since it was based upon a unit of area or property, particularly in the case of the carucage and the tax on movables. As a result the tax was paid directly to the king by thousands of property holders who held nothing of the king, were not summoned to the curia regis, and were never consulted about the tax. With the growth in movable property and its protection by the common law, it became more difficult for a lord to take the goods of men on his land unless he was legally entitled

131. *Ibid., 1234–1237*, pp. 186, 545.
132. *Annals of Tewkesbury*, ed. H. R. Luard, in "Annales monastici," I (Rolls series), p. 102.
133. *Close rolls, 1234–1237*, p. 575. *Ibid., 1237–1242*, pp. 16, 37, 115.
134. *Ibid.*, p. 109.

to them. He must, unless the contribution fell among established dues, secure it by an aid arranged for between lord and tenant. He could not for his own advantage enter the tenant's land, assess the movables, and take a certain percentage of their value. Yet this was what happened. When an aid was granted, royal officials assessed movables and collected a tax based on that assessment. It would seem therefore that a certain authority other than that of an individual lord was inherent in the joint action of the king and the curia regis; a sort of corporate action resulting from the character of the tax.

Another indication of the changed attitude toward the aids was the fear that the king was acquiring the right to levy an aid as a consuetudo, a required due. In 1215 the barons' device to check the king's control over scutages and aids was the formal summons to the great curia regis to make the grant. As we have seen, those articles were dropped, but in practice the king summoned the great curia regis whenever he desired an aid. In 1237 he was obliged to confirm the charters, in the edition of 1225, which referred only to scutage. In addition, he promised that he would not ask another such aid.[135] This guarantee was expressed in letters patent as follows: "We do not desire that from the happening of this aid, a cause henceforth should be formed or drawn into a custom of asking for a similar aid at another time." [136] "The king has made such promises before, but only to the clergy; now the promise was made to the laity as well." [137] In 1244 when Pope Innocent IV asked for a grant from the clergy, they opposed it on the ground that "a thing twice done constitutes a custom," according to the Canon Law, as they alleged.[138] It is obvious that the barons feared that the succession of grants would constitute a custom, especially as, although there had been much criticism and opposition, the discussion had always ended in a grant.

Thus by 1237 a concept had been generated that the curia regis, or the great council, represented the clergy (except certain religious orders not holding by military tenure and except parish and other churches), and all the laity except the royal demesne, and so was qualified to assent to a tax covering them. In theory everyone was present in the great council, and so assented, except villeins

135. Paris, *Chronica maiora*, III, 381.
136. *Close rolls, 1234–1237*, p. 545.
137. Mitchell, *Studies in taxation*, 157, 171, 209, 214, 219.
138. Paris, *Chronica maiora*, IV, 376.

CONSENT TO TAXATION

who were taxed by their lords. Thus the theory of individual consent expanded to cover all free men. Only one group of laity could not fit in exactly to this statement, viz., the tenants on the king's demesne. They had hitherto paid the taxes on personal property, but seemingly were opposed to it, for in 1237 they preferred to pay tallage and did not pay the thirtieth.[139] As tallage was more or less a conventional amount, this shift must have been due to the desire of demesne tenants who thus would escape assessment of their property.

The year 1237 marks the close of an epoch in the history of English taxation. Now the succession of levies on property, hitherto especially frequent in Henry III's reign, the outgrowth of the feudal aid but marking an evolution in it, came to an end for a time. The authorization of all levies was by the curia regis, and though in theory the grant was by individual consent practically those who consented were the tenants in chief of the king, and practically by repetition the king was establishing what in his letters patent to the clergy he denied (probably sincerely) that he was acquiring, viz., the right to levy a tax on property when his debts were great; if he asked the curia regis for such an aid they so far had felt obligated to give it to him. Repetition of the aid, based on property, regardless for the most part of tenure, assessed and collected by royal officials, and legally authorized by the great curia regis, shows that taxation had rapidly changed since the Saladin tithe of 1188.

Although Henry had promised in 1237 never again to ask his baronage for an aid, the lure of opportunity in Gascony pushed this resolution into the background. The revolt of the count of la Marche and certain French barons against Louis IX seemed to offer a favorable opportunity to the English king to regain some of his lost possessions south of the channel. He summoned the great curia regis to meet on January 27, 1242, perhaps with the thought that the appeal of an expedition led by the king himself would induce a generous grant by the nobles, if they were exempted from service, for following the advice of the count of la Marche he proposed to wage the campaign with mercenary forces. The reaction of the lay barons to this unconcealed plan was a surprise to Henry III. When the magnates met many of them swore an oath one with another, under penalty of anathema, that none of them would consent to any grant of money. From this revolutionary decision, Henry III was unable to move them, although he appealed to them

139. *Close rolls, 1234-1237*, p. 575. *Ibid., 1237-1242*, p. 109.

individually by cajolery, by threats, and by claims on friendship. The lay barons stood fast in refusing the grant, and the king found it impossible in the face of this opposition to secure the general aid which he had desired. Nowhere is it stated what kind of a pecuniary aid was wanted, but it is likely that he desired a grant in the nature of a tax on movables. Otherwise he would have summoned the host, put scutage in charge, and levied fines on those who desired exemption. Such had been the procedure at the previous invasion of France in 1230. Though a general aid was not granted, the king as usual appealed to religious houses to make individual grants of dona, the appeal beginning before the council dissolved, and special appeals were made to the Cistercians, Premonstratensians, the Austin monks, and the Black monks.[140]

Henry III was finally compelled to modify his original proposal to wage the campaign with mercenaries and summoned the host on March 24, 1242. All tenants in chief by military service, lay and clerical, all sergeants, and all tenants by military service on lands in hand were directed to appear at Winchester on April 27 ready to cross with horses and arms with the king. Fines were collected and the scutage fixed at $3m.$ per fee before the king's departure on May 5.[141]

The bishops had been summoned with the other tenants in chief to furnish their contingents of knights at Winchester on the appointed day. They opposed this summons and succeeded in establishing an additional precedent that for a campaign in France they were not liable to service or even to a scutage. They granted an aid at $3m.$ per fee on their servitium debitum (the same rate as the scutage) with the proviso that this was not owed and should not be considered as a precedent for future levies. Such had been the arrangement made in 1229 and 1230 (the scutages of Poitou and Brittany) under Hubert de Burgh that the bishops did not owe knight's service across the channel and so did not owe its commutation, scutage, but granted an aid at $5m.$ This had been the plea of St. Hugh, bishop of Lincoln, and Herbert, bishop of Salisbury in 1198. It was however still regarded as a disputed point in the law, for an additional proviso was inserted in the letter patent by the small council to prevent, if possible, this case from establishing a precedent disadvantageous to the king, viz., "that by this action

---

140. *Ibid.*, p. 420. *Calendar of patent rolls, 1232–1247*, pp. 279, 280, 330, 336.
141. *Close rolls, 1237–1242*, p. 435. J. A. C. Vincent, *Lancashire lay subsidies*, I, 116–117.

CONSENT TO TAXATION 209

the rights of the king and his heirs would be neither increased or decreased." It was impossible for the king to check the growth of such a custom since it was the third case, but Henry III was not responsible for the initiation of such a policy. The actions in 1229, 1230, and 1242 formed parts of a common development away from enforcing military service by clerical tenants.

While the refusal of the aid by the magnates was individual, practically it was a corporate act. Thus they swore an oath individually not to make the grant. Practically, on the part of the laity, it was unanimous though some of the religious tenants in chief paid dona. That it was individual action is indicated by statements of Paris that "many others however stood firm and would not in any way swerve from the reply which they had agreed on in common and had sworn to abide by." The king summoned them one by one at different times into his private chamber, like a priest summoning penitents to confession. Paris emphasizes the unanimity of the answer.[142] Unanimity was necessary if they were to succeed in their opposition to the levy. Individual opposition would be vain as had often been shown in the past. By negotiation and pressure the king had overcome them as happened to some in 1242.

Out of the necessities of their position the magnates were imperceptibly forced into united action. The king held several meetings of the great council in 1244–45 in which he asked in person for an aid on various grounds—the debts which he had incurred in Gascony in 1242–43, and afterward the war in Gascony since his return, and the troubles with the Welsh. While the replies of the magnates were unfavorable, the members were not indifferent to the financial position in which Henry III found himself, but they were more concerned over the position in which the repeated taxes by the king would place them. Hence they continued to draw closer together for common action. At first clergy and laity deliberated apart as occasionally in the past, but on the initiative of the clergy they soon made a common front. They formed a committee of twelve to formulate a program on which all could unite in opposition to the king. They demanded that the king should enforce Magna Carta as he had promised in 1237 and that he should appoint a justiciar and a chancellor. Another point raised at some time this year was that he should appoint officials of whom the magnates should approve, and that if an aid were granted it should be expended in accordance with the desires of a committee of twelve.

142. Paris, *Chronica maiora*, IV, 181, 182, 185.

Another proposal was for the magnates to appoint for life by common consent four members of the king's council "of rank and power," at least two of whom should be in constant attendance on the king for counsel. They should supervise the treasury and all expenditures. The four should be present at meetings of the great council. A chancellor, a justiciar, a treasurer, and certain justices should be appointed by the great council. In other words, they had advanced to a new position never before assumed in their disputes with the king, where it was necessary to exercise control over the royal administration, a position which had grown out of the struggle over taxation. The purpose of this control seems to have been not to gain power but to be able to protect themselves from extravagant administration. Henry III's reply to these propositions, if they were actually made to him, is not given. Perhaps these were summaries of discussions rather than actual proposals. Henry III continued to appeal for aid to the council as a whole, to the clergy, and to individuals, but the experience with the king in the past and the organization for discussion held the barons fast to their resolution not to grant a gracious aid without additional concessions in return, and these the king was unwilling to make. Finally, at some time after the Scottish campaign when, as part of the terms of peace, Henry III's daughter Margaret was betrothed to the Scottish heir apparent, in reply to an appeal for an aid the magnates assented to one of 20s. per fee, the feudal aid to marry the king's first-born daughter. The low rate is a further indication of opposition and a feeling that since the girl was only five years of age the grant was really a subterfuge of the king to secure some additional cash.

In 1248 Henry III convoked the great council twice at London "to confer on the affairs of the kingdom which was now greatly disturbed, impoverished, and injured." The first session was attended by nine bishops and nine earls, with many barons, knights, and other nobles, abbots, priors, and clerks. For the first time since 1245 the king asked for an aid in money, a demand "which," says Paris, "was not a secret from the community." The king's excuse for this request was to recover his rights abroad, "which also concerns you." [143] The magnates refused the desired aid, criticizing the king for his extravagant, tyrannical, and inefficient administration and his failure to appoint a chancellor, a justiciar, and a treasurer in accordance with the desires of the magnates "as was cus-

143. *Ibid.,* V, 5, 20.

CONSENT TO TAXATION

tomary." At the second session, as recorded by Paris, the king for the first time refused to appoint the three officials as requested in accordance with the desire of the magnates on the ground that such a demand deprived him of his customary rights.[144] The council broke up in anger without making a grant.

Thus the question at issue between the king and the magnates began to take a new, definite shape; it was not that the king sought to carry on his government without consulting the great council, for he had held many sessions since his return from Gascony, but that, from the king's viewpoint, he should decide policy, appoint his ministers, and administer the government on his own responsibility, provided he called his tenants into consultation. The barons found what they regarded as their just criticisms ignored; they believed that the government was wasteful. Their remedy was that Henry III should adhere to their advice in policy and appointments of officials. Since the king still possessed the initiative in the administration they could criticize only when summoned to the council, but the king's need for money provided them with another weapon, the right of refusing a general aid on movables, for without their assent the king could not assess and collect it. In 1242 it was difficult for them to maintain a united opposition to the king's demand for aid; in 1244–45 it was still an arduous task, but in 1248 the notables held together without much effort, that is, a corporate unity had by this time developed. The positive program of control however that was talked of in 1244 was no longer heard of —that the aid granted should be spent by the advice of a committee of the magnates. Matthew Paris reports only that the three chief administrative officials should be appointed by their advice and that Henry should rule in accordance with the counsel of his natural subjects instead of foreigners. As to aids, the king's excuse for requesting one was as before, the recovery of his rights abroad.

In 1249 the action of Henry III indicates the unity existing throughout the baronage, for he merely sought by writs and by personal appeal to secure dona from individuals, both lay and clerical, with some success, but nothing like the returns of a general aid.[145] The excuse was the end of the truce with St. Louis when the English would reclaim their rights in France by force. But while the nobles could resist the king's demands they hesitated to take the initiative in enforcing their desires concerning the appointment

144. *Ibid.*, p. 21.
145. *Ibid.*, p. 51.

of the chancellor, the justiciar, and treasurer. They had agreed to meet at London after Easter to secure this action from the king and accordingly gathered then, but in the absence of Richard, earl of Cornwall, no action was taken.[146]

In 1250 Henry III decided to take part in the crusade on which Louis IX had met disaster and that same year assumed the cross. This venture promised to add grave expense to a treasury already overburdened by the cost of domestic administration and Gascon troubles. By an unexpected turn of fortune the king became involved in the papal struggle to conquer Sicily from the Hohenstaufen, since his son Edmund had been rewarded with the crown by the pope. Thus to the royal policy of subduing and governing Gascony, questionable in baronial opinion, was added the doubtful question of the crusade on which seemingly Henry had embarked without consulting the great council and the further policy which he had adopted on his own initiative of helping finance the pope's war in Italy. These expensive schemes helped unite the lay barons still more in opposing financial aids to their lord.

But the prelates were in a different position. The pope had already taxed the church for his own advantage, and now employing the excuse that the English prelates had urged him to provide for the expenses of the English crusade out of the revenues of the English clergy and in response to a request of the king, Innocent IV granted him for three years a tenth of the revenues of the English clergy and of the clergy of the other lands subject to Henry III. Although the collectors were appointed in 1250 (later changed in 1253) the actual assessment and collection waited upon the approval of the clerical members of the great council, and this was not secured until May, 1253, after several sessions of the great council.[147] The only specific mention of the lay barons in connection with this period of negotiations about the tenth was in October 1252. When prelates refused to agree to the tenth, Paris reports that after the king had consulted with his barons about Gascony and Simon de Montfort, he asked for money and military aid for the crusade. The barons unanimously replied that their response depended on that of the prelates and so no grant was made.[148]

The king summoned a great parliament (great council) to meet on May 4, 1253, at London where a long session (fifteen days an

146. *Ibid.*, p. 73.
147. Lunt, "Consent of the lower clergy," p. 63. Lunt, *Valuation of Norwich*, p. 6
148. Paris, *Chronica maiora*, V, 335.

CONSENT TO TAXATION 213

more) ensued, "discussing some difficult matters of the kingdom." The difficult matters seem to have been a confirmation of Magna Carta, safeguarding freedom of clerical elections, and the king's urgent need for an aid.[149] Two distinct grants of money were made: the prelates assented to the levy of a tenth for three years to be distributed by the magnates for the expenses of the expedition to the Holy Land, and the whole council granted an aid of 3m. per fee to knight Prince Edward.[150] The discussion was long and troubled, perhaps because the clergy objected to the tenth; perhaps because the laity refused to grant a tax on movables. Anyhow, the levy of an aid on knights' fees when all the preceding efforts had been to obtain a tax on movables indicates that the barons refused a tax of this sort. Perhaps the grant of a tenth of revenues of the clergy for three years led the king to assent to the aid on knights' fees. We should notice that the king asked for an aid from his demesne and also from houses of religious, an indication that he was seeking to obtain as much money as possible. For he immediately summoned the host for a campaign in Gascony whither he sailed in August. Those who desired to be exempt from military service had to pay fines. Thus the money paid by the lay barons was due from them by feudal law, one of the three feudal aids, and in addition fines for military service, and so it would seem that in this way they avoided establishing another precedent of paying a gracious aid. Observe too that the great council granted the aid on knights' fees; the prelates granted the tenth; the king sought an aid from his demesne, and religious houses individually granted sums in aid.

The expense of Henry III's sojourn in France in 1253 led to further demands for aid from the great council; the resultant negotiations early in 1254 led to requests for aid from the lower clergy of each diocese and the laity in shire courts. To insure quick action by these local groups, the council instructed each diocese and each shire to send representatives to the council with power to act. The employment of representatives to meet with the council arose out of the peculiar circumstances created by the replies of the members of the great council to the royal requests for pecuniary aid. The magnates had refused to make a general grant, but as individuals they promised military or pecuniary aid; hence the way was opened for a direct appeal, first, to laity that would normally have been subject to a general aid had it been voted by the great

149. *Ibid.*, p. 373.
150. *Ibid.*, p. 374; VI, 250. *Close rolls, 1251–1253*, p. 353.

council; and second, to the clergy that once before (1226) had been asked for a grant when the great council had granted a fifteenth. As the assessment and collection of taxes on movables and carucates had centered around the county court, it was an obvious precedure to approach the shire courts with a request for a grant of aid, if the great council declined to authorize such a tax.

About December 1, 1253, Henry III wrote to the regents, Queen Eleanor and Richard, earl of Cornwall, directing them to convoke the great council on January 14, 1254, and ask them for aid to meet a threatened attack by the king of Castile. The council was summoned to meet on January 27, and before it was dissolved other messengers arrived from Henry III strongly urging assistance against the king of Castile.[151] Although the magnates were skeptical of the accuracy of the reports of the dangerous situation in which the king found himself, they promised aid.[152] The great lay barons declared that they would appear at Westminster on May 3 with their armed forces ready to go to Henry III's assistance if the king of Castile should attack him. The archbishop of Canterbury, the elect of Winchester, and some of the bishops declared they would go in person with knights. While the other prelates promised to aid in money, they declined to name the amount but said they would have their contributions at Westminster on the same date.[153] Since both clerical and lay magnates had tentatively agreed to furnish either military or pecuniary aid, the way was open to appeal to lesser men for a contribution. So the regents then evidently raised with the magnates the question of some aid from the clergy and laity who would not take part in the expedition or be subject to the individual grants which had been promised. As far as the laity were concerned, they were men who would have been taxed if the great council had granted a general aid on movables.

As the pope had not authorized this tax on the lower clergy, the prelates declined to agree to it. They added that they did not believe that the latter would grant an aid unless Henry III would abandon the tenth of the first year granted for the crusade and postpone the tenths of two additional years till two years before he was to set out for the Holy Land. But the prelates promised to discuss these proposals with their clergy and secure their adhesion to them if

151. Paris, *Chronica maiora*, VI, 282–284; V, 423–424.
152. *Ibid.* Shirley, *Royal letters*, II, 101.
153. *Close rolls, 1253–1254*, p. 111.

CONSENT TO TAXATION   215

possible.[154] So each bishop was to summon his cathedral chapter, the archdeacons, and the representatives of the religious and secular clergy in his diocese to discuss the question, to induce them if possible to give the king a liberal aid, and send representatives to meet with the king's council on April 26 to inform that body of the amount and kind of the subsidy which they would make the king.[155] At this same time the regents issued writs to all greater tenants in chief individually and through the sheriff to lesser men who still performed service to appear on May 3 equipped to accompany the earls and barons to Gascony.[156]

The same writ to the sheriff ordered him to summon the county court, instructing him to point out the promises of the barons to go in person to the king's aid to explain to the members the king's urgent military and financial necessity and to persuade them to make a suitable aid. At the same time two knights were to be chosen from each shire to go before the king's council on April 26 on behalf of the shire and respond definitely about the aforesaid aid for each county. Thus the appeal to the groups of clergy and laity outside the great council followed on the refusal of that body to grant a general aid on movables, although its members had each provisionally promised individually to grant military or pecuniary aid.

The regents probably reported to the king that the magnates insisted that the king must guarantee that their aid in this case must not constitute a precedent, for on March 24 he wrote issuing letters patent to this effect.[157] The regents further stated that there was great complaint in the shires that the Great Charters were not properly enforced by the royal officials and hence that it was unlikely that the lesser laity would grant an aid unless the king ordered the regents to proclaim publicly in the shires the enforcement of the charters. They do not state the source of their knowledge of this complaint, but since the enforcement of the charters was one of the aims of the barons who had secured the preceding year a new confirmation of the charters, it seems likely that the magnates had voiced their complaints in the session with the council and that therefore the appeal to the shire courts was made by their assent. Since the barons or their stewards were members of the

154. Shirley, *Royal letters*, II, 101–102.
155. *Close rolls, 1253–1254*, p. 115.
156. *Ibid.*, pp. 111, 114.
157. *Calendar of patent rolls, 1247–1258*, pp. 280–281.

shire courts, they would be able to influence the decisions of those bodies respecting the aid. There is no indication that limited groups were summoned in the shires to decide on the aid to the exclusion of the barons or other tenants who were to take part in the expedition.

The emphasis in both the local lay and clerical assemblies in informing the members of the king's great need—that the magnates proposed to go in person to his assistance, that a definite answer as to the aid was to be given, the necessity of conciliating the lesser clergy and laity by concessions—indicate that the aid was to be granted by the local groups. The writ addressed to the prelates states that the diocesan groups were to report to the small council on April 23 by certain discreet men concerning the method and amount of the subsidy.[158] The writ to the shires stated that two men were to be elected by the county courts on their behalf, who were to appear before the regents and the small council on April 19, together with the knights of other shires, with whom they should provide the aid which they might desire to grant. The council thus would deal in the same period with both groups of representatives. The writ to the sheriffs is so phrased as to permit the interpretation that the representatives in common would decide the method and amount of the aid, providing that the shire courts gave a general assent. But the measures recommended to conciliate the members of the shire courts regarding the charters, the emphasis to be made by the sheriff concerning the king's great need for money, and the statement that the deputies should be able to respond precisely to the council about the aid on behalf of the shire courts indicate that these bodies were to determine the character and the amount of aid each shire should give.

What purpose then had the small council in the meeting with the deputies? If the decision to grant an aid designating both the kind and the amount was made by the local groups of clergy and laity, then what remained to be done at the meetings of the deputies with the council, other than to report decisions that had already been taken? Certain expressions in the documents indicate that it was expected that supplementary action was to be taken at the sessions of the deputies of clergy and laity with the council. The writ to the sheriffs stated that the representatives of each county, acting in behalf of their shire, would together with the deputies of other shires provide such aid as they might desire in view of such a state

158. *Close rolls, 1253-1254*, p. 115.

CONSENT TO TAXATION

of necessity.[159] Furthermore the regents wrote to Henry III on February 14 reminding him of the colloquy which they were about to hold with the "other clergy and laity" on April 26 about the aid and urging him to express his pleasure about their suggested modifications in the existing plan regarding the triennial tenth and their proposal to proclaim the confirmation of the charters in the shires. The final sentence of their letter suggests that they hoped to secure some financial advantage for the king in these conferences. It ran: "For you will find us prepared and devoted to secure the aforesaid aid for your advantage to the best of our ability and to do everything that will redound to your advantage and the increase of your honor." [160]

In these expressions appears a vague notion that the council might secure some additional financial advantage from this meeting with the deputies. Did the magnates know that the council was making an appeal to the shires for money? The prelates were aware of the request to the lower clergy, for they were in charge of pressing it and of sending the representatives to the council. Probably the magnates knew all about the appeal to the shire courts. The writ to the laity went out on the same date as a letter to the prelates regarding the aid from the lower clergy; the barons were not asked to secure the aid in the shires, for the natural way would be to address the sheriff, just as the simplest way to secure a general grant in the dioceses would be to address the appeal to individual prelates. But the complaints which the regents refer to among the lesser men in the shires relative to defective enforcement of the charters and the local demands for a new proclamation of the charters in the shires and the statement that such an assurance would inspire the lesser laity to give a splendid aid—these complaints and comments from numerous shires would have come from the magnates. Curiously enough the complaints of the lesser men about the charters sound the same note as the barons: in the preceding year the magnates had secured a new formal confirmation of the charters and a new excommunication of violators. It seems likely therefore that after the magnates had given tentative assent to pecuniary or military aid to the king they had discussed with the small council the question of the appeal to the lesser men. Thus this appeal to the lesser men was not a means devised by the council of checkmating the barons, nor did it arise from a feeling that an

159. *Ibid.*
160. Shirley, *Royal letters*, II, 102.

appeal for aid should be properly made to the shire courts instead of to the magnates. It arose from the peculiar situation created by the tentative assent of the magnates to an aid in some form for themselves and their willingness to bind the other laity. The prelates would not assent for the lower clergy. Their presence in the diocesan assemblies where the aid would be discussed assured the prelates of a voice in the decision; the magnates would play the most important part in the decision of each shire court regarding the grant of an aid. When the magnates met after Easter they held a long session, for Earl Richard and others had delayed in attending. Simon de Montfort too appeared from Gascony and informed them that there was no danger from the king of Castile. The magnates declined to go to the king's aid and there is no mention of a grant of money.[161]

In 1255, at Easter, the king asked the great council for pecuniary aid on account of his debts.[162] This was refused and one argument adduced for the refusal was that the magnates had not all been summoned in accordance with the terms of the Great Charter of 1215 (Art. XIV).[163] In 1257 pecuniary aid was again asked and refused.[164] In 1258 the barons refused a grant to the king.[165] There is no record of the king's attempting, in face of the opposition of the barons, to secure an aid from the shire courts. No further aid was asked of the great council after 1258, either by the barons when in control or later when Henry III had recovered his power,[166] until 1269. Then an appeal was made and granted for a crusade to be led by the aged king.[167] The great council granted a twentieth on the lands of all lay tenants in chief and on the lands held of the prelates by knight service.[168] On April 27, 1270, the bishops and the heads of religious houses agreed to pay the twentieth on their demesne lands, though in general each compounded for the levy instead of submitting to an assessed valuation of their goods, and many small houses of religious compounded for the twentieth. The beneficed clergy also granted the twentieth.[169]

161. Paris, *Chronica maiora*, V, 440.
162. *Ibid.*, pp. 493–495.
163. *Ibid.*, p. 520. Mitchell, *Studies in taxation*, p. 275.
164. *Ibid.*, p. 277.
165. *Ibid.*, pp. 271, 276.
166. *Ibid.*, p. 288.
167. D. Wilkins, *Concilia*, II, 20.
168. Mitchell, *Studies in taxation*, p. 296.
169. *Ibid.*, p. 297. *Calendar of patent rolls, 1266–1272*, p. 546. Lunt, "Consent of the lower clergy," 161–164.

CONSENT TO TAXATION

Everyone will remark that the experiment of 1254 was not repeated. The obvious reason one can assign is that the magnates granted the tax for all the men on their lands; they did not make individual grants for themselves alone and thus make possible an appeal to the lesser men by the council. For the first time since 1232 the demesne paid the aid on movables. The grant by the great council probably exerted an influence leading to the payment of the twentieth by the royal demesne; because in the case of a general aid of this sort there was a moral obligation for classes not part of the great council to contribute. But the great council did not authorize the levy of the twentieth on the royal demesne.[170]

The small council sent special representatives to ask for the twentieth from the towns. That is, each town granted the twentieth for itself to the king. For example, on February 27, 1270, five citizens of London were appointed by the council to supervise the assessors.[171] Since the great council had granted the twentieth not later than October, 1269, it seems a fair inference that London was not included in the area covered by the grant, and that sometime before February 27 the citizens had been approached by royal representatives and had granted the twentieth. Other towns fined in lump sums "that they shall be quit of the twentieth," the first case noted in the chancery rolls being Worcester for £100, on March 26, 1270.[172] These fines were made not with the county assessors but with special commissioners, for the former were ordered not to meddle with the taxing of the goods of the towns. William de Holegate, a citizen of Lincoln, probably arranged a fine of 200m. with the council on behalf of Lincoln for the twentieth, perhaps as a deputy of the city; for the council wrote that if citizens were content with the fine, let them pay; otherwise let the mayor and a committee assess the twentieth.[173] The burgesses of Yarmouth fined in £100 for the twentieth, but the sheriff and the assessors of Norfolk "nevertheless proceeded to tax and collect the same in the town"; the burgesses were cautioned to pay no attention to them, for those assessors had been ordered not to meddle. The burgesses should levy the fine of £100 without delay and let the king have it. As this action of the sheriff and the assessors took place on March 21, 1271, it may have been due to the delay of the burgesses in

170. *Liber de antiquis legibus*, ed. Thomas Stapleton (Camden Society), XXXIV, 122.
171. *Calendar of patent rolls, 1266–1272*, p. 477.
172. *Ibid.*, p. 416.
173. *Ibid.*, pp. 417, 422–423.

paying their fine.[174] Thus long after the assessment of the twentieth by the county assessors had begun on the lands of the tenants in chief the council appealed to the towns on the demesne for the twentieth and perhaps threatened to assess the tax if a grant were not made. London granted a twentieth, and other towns perhaps compounded for it instead.

At the close of Henry III's reign, the king levied taxes on movables on his demesne by direct negotiation between the small council and each town without authorization by the great council.[175] Also by the end of his reign certain points relating to the royal revenue were being established in custom. The great council had become the body that had the right not merely to assent to but also to refuse extraordinary taxes on the movable property on lands of its members and of all their tenants, immediate and mediate; this was the greatest single source of extraordinary revenue. Out of the feudal aid to the king by his vassals, based on individual consent and only with the greatest difficulty refused, had been evolved the right of refusal, that is, a right to real consent to taxation. For thirty-two years, in nine cases, the barons stood fast in refusing to grant an aid without a single case of consent (1237–69). Second, in the struggles the magnates were forced to adopt a united front against the king; corporate action was essential else Henry III would succeed in overpowering them by persuasion or pressure of some kind. Individual assent was evolving under the force of necessity and not from any theory of corporate consent to taxation. The barons' success in refusing taxes also, resulting in the inability of the king to secure the levy, repeatedly prevented the establishment of an aid of this kind as an obligatory due. It thus retained the original character of a gracious aid with the added trait that it could be refused. It was also maintained that if an aid should be granted it was to be based upon an assessed valuation of movable property held by everyone except the poorest who dwelt upon the lands that were ultimately held of the king's tenants in chief. Carucage was no longer heard of and the aid on knights' fees was given no consideration by the financiers after 1235, unless by political necessity they were forced in the case of the regular aids to take this kind of aid through want of an alternative.

Despite the failure of the royal government to secure a tax on movables from 1237 to 1269 it seems undeniable that the belief

174. *Ibid.*, p. 525.
175. *Ibid.*, p. 416.

CONSENT TO TAXATION

persisted that the royal government ought to receive an aid on movables from time to time. In part this arose out of the old feudal notion that the vassal should aid his lord in time of need, in part from the fact that the king possessed such a large independent revenue that the refusal of a tax would not hamper him sufficiently to make him conform with the wishes of the barons. Anyhow he could pursue his policy uncontrolled. Many of the things he did had their approval, and their refusals to grant an aid arose out of his treatment of the magnates. Henry III believed that he should call the barons into counsel, but that the final decision always rested with him alone. He felt that he had fulfilled his obligation to them if they had been called together and asked for advice, but had he been a leader of parts and cooperated with them he would have secured an occasional aid. The failure of the barons to manage the government in 1258 and after, and the events of the early years of Edward I, succeeded in restoring the custom of a general levy from time to time. A modification of the method of receiving assent to aids was devised by summoning representatives of the lesser laity for counsel to meet with the great council.

A common practice was to summon representatives of local groups to meet with the council or its representatives to inform the latter of local conditions, and out of such conferences resulted administrative commands. This was a modification of the use of royal commissioners and a jury, the fertile institution of the Norman monarchy. Toward the end of Henry III's reign, in the period of active discord, they began to summon representatives to confer with the council on the business of the realm. In 1261 the magnates summoned three representatives of the shires to treat on the common affairs of the kingdom, but the king instructed the sheriffs to send these deputies to meet with him and his nobles to treat of peace.[176] During the rule of Simon de Montfort in 1264 Henry III summoned "four of the most legal and discreet" knights of each shire to meet on its behalf with the great council to treat of the business of the realm.[177] In December, 1264, he again summoned a great council and also two knights from each shire and two burgesses from each of certain boroughs and two citizens from each of certain cities to meet to discuss the question of peace and certain other business of the kingdom.[178] None of these cases in-

---
176. Stubbs, *Select charters*, pp. 405–406.
177. *Ibid.*, pp. 411–412.
178. *Ibid.*, p. 415.

volved taxation, so far as we know. In the earlier case of 1254 when taxation was involved the representatives of the shires were to report to the small council the action taken by the several shires; the regents however seemed to expect that some common action might be taken by the group when it met with the king's council. However the answer of the shire courts seems to have been in the negative and no tax resulted. The use of representatives of the shires from the whole kingdom for counsel had not been so frequent as to constitute a custom. It was a suggestion which might be followed if the plan appealed to the political leaders of the new reign.

The history of Edward I's reign shows that taxes on movables had become one of the regular sources of revenue. Two new lay bodies were formed to authorize in part the levy on their respective groups: the representatives of the shire courts to consent to a levy on the property already granted by the great council; the representatives of the towns to authorize the tax on the royal demesne, the area that had hitherto paid tallage. These two representative groups had separate development.

The procedure employed under Edward I throws light upon the thinking in Henry III's reign. In 1274 Edward I returned from the crusade deeply in debt. In April, 1275, a parliament was held to which were summoned the great council and the "community of the land." The business included the famous statute of Westminster the First, and the grant of the *antiqua custuma* to the king, and the celebrated customs tax on wool, woolfells, and leather. These and other enactments were said to have been made by the counsel and assent of the archbishops, bishops, abbots, priors, earls, barons, and the commonalty of the land thither summoned. The custom was granted to the king at the request of the merchants by the same groups including the "communities" of the realm.[179]

The summoning of this parliament indicated that the new king intended to follow the precedents of the last years of the previous reign to consult at times with representatives of shires and towns when he summoned the great council. Probably no special significance should be attached to the fact that representatives of shire and towns were summoned to the great council that adopted important new financial regulations. The writ spoke only in general terms of the business of the realm and many subjects were discussed and settled. This was the first meeting of the magnates after Edward's return and the summons to the representatives may have been issued

179. *Ibid.*, pp. 448–451.

on that account, so that the new king might meet with a great assembly of his people. At his accession the regents had convoked a meeting of the great council (the archbishops, bishops, abbots and priors, the earls and barons) and from each county four knights and from each city four citizens, all of whom swore the oath of allegiance to the king.[180] This first parliament after Edward's return may have been planned with this membership so that he could meet a great representative body of his people.

On September 1, 1275, the king summoned a great council and two knights from each shire to Westminster on October 13. The magnates were summoned to treat with the king "both on the state of the realm and on certain business which he would reveal to them there." Since it might be advantageous for knights of the shire to be present, each sheriff was ordered to have two knights elected in full county court to attend at Westminster on behalf of the county to treat with the king and the prelates and the magnates about the "aforesaid business." [181] The county court which elected the deputies was to be a full court, that is, whatever *plenus comitatus* may mean (full meeting without exemptions of a formal meeting), it was one which the sheriff well understood so that he did not have to be informed as to its composition. It was not therefore a session composed of lesser men alone, but contained a conventional personnel of tenants in chief, in person, or their stewards, rear vassals, freemen, and villeins, who by successive arrangements among themselves had become the body acting as the court of the shire. Thus the magnates and the representatives of the shires did not constitute two groups sharply differentiated one from the other. The magnates formed all of one group and probably the most influential part of the body that chose the delegates of the shire, the other group. Assessors (taxers) were appointed in all the shires, including London and Middlesex, and in addition in the Cinque Ports.[182]

It may be therefore that representatives were sent to the parliament by those urban groups. Certain it is however that the towns in general were not commanded to send representatives, for Norwich which would have been included fined for its fifteenth with the taxers (assessors) of Norfolk and Suffolk. Since Norwich, London,

180. *Annals of Winchester,* ed. H. R. Luard, in "Annales monastici," II (Rolls series), p. 113.
181. William Stubbs, *The constitutional history of England* (Oxford, 1880), II, 243 and n. 5.
182. *Calendar of close rolls, 1272–1279,* pp. 250–251.

and the Cinque Ports paid the fifteenth it is clear that the whole of the royal demesne did the same. Leaving the towns for later consideration, let us consider the action of this parliament. The procedure by which the fifteenth was granted is not stated. One writ appointing the assessors says that the fifteenth was granted by the earls, barons, and others of the realm, and another writ says that "the earls, barons, and other magnates and the commonalty of the realm have granted a fifteenth of all their goods."[183]

The expression "the commonalty" was probably inserted to cover the participation of the knights of the shires. Yet in 1269 it had been stated that the twentieth was granted by the *communam* (commonalty) of England to the king and his son in aid of the Holy Land, a levy where we have no mention of the presence of knights of the shire.[184] Since the customary way of granting taxes on movables had always been by the action of the great council, it seems fair to conclude that the fifteenth of 1275 was also granted by that body with the added feature that the knights of the shire were summoned for the counsel and assent. In reaching this assent by the lesser men, the decision of the magnates would be decisive. Individually and collectively they were far more important than the group of knights; in the action of the shire courts they also carried more weight than the lesser men and so they played a significant part in the choice of these representatives. A marked difference is seen as compared with the action of 1254, when the members of the great council had individually already promised military or pecuniary aid before the representatives were summoned when the writs to the sheriffs definitely stated that the reason for the summons was to secure an aid, and they were issued with the knowledge of the great council.

Why then did the king and the small council feel justified in authorizing the fifteenth on the lands of the tenants in chief by the vote of the great council and representatives of the shires, when the mass of property holders had not authorized this action by their deputies and had not even been consulted? On what precedent was this act based? It would have been possible to have laid the question before the shire courts as in 1254, or to have sent royal commissioners to each county court to negotiate the grant after the great council had given its assent to the tax; such a procedure was familiar in the levy of tallage where commissioners went out to the

183. *Ibid. Calendar of patent rolls, 1272-1281*, p. 165.
184. *Ibid., 1266-1272*, p. 508.

CONSENT TO TAXATION

towns and rural demesne. This however had not been the practice in securing aids from property holders on the lands of tenants in chief. The great council alone was accustomed to authorize the levy, and hence such must have been their authority in this case of 1275. The representative knights were introduced as "advantageous" (*expedienis*) "to treat with us and with the magnates concerning the state of the realm and certain other affairs which we shall explain to them." [185] As earlier, these representatives were for decision, support, and assent, but as was conventional, the decision was based on the power and prestige of the magnates and the king.

The thirtieth of 1283 gave rise to special arrangements (which throw light upon the method of granting aids at this time). In March, 1282, war again broke out with the Welsh, and closed only in the autumn of 1283 after a long and expensive campaign, for this time the king had determined to settle accounts with his troublesome neighbors.[186] In June, 1282, John de Kirkby, a clerk of the exchequer, was sent out to negotiate aids or loans with various groups. He enjoyed considerable success. Some towns made generous grants; e.g., London, £4,000; Newcastle on Tyne, 1,750m.; York, 1,040m.; Lincoln, 1,016m.; Yarmouth, 1,000m.; Bristol, 1,000m. Yet the sums would not meet the expenses of the campaign and perhaps his success was not uniform.[187] Perhaps the plan was to secure loans on a grand scale. Anyhow the king decided on a different sort of appeal for aid. With the host in arms at Rhuddlan in the autumn, the king issued writs on November 20, 1282, summoning two assemblies to meet on January 20, 1283, composed of representatives of the shires and towns (also representatives of the clergy), one at Northampton (from 32 shires), the other at York (from five shires). The sheriffs were to summon four knights from each shire and two men from each city, borough, and market town with full power from their communities to hear and to decide on what should be submitted to them by the king.[188] The writ of summons hinted that the purpose was to meet the expenses of the war, as when it said "we have considered that we and the inhabitants of our land should be burdened at present for the common advantage, labors, and expenses to destroy wholly the

---
185. Stubbs, *Constitutional history*, II, 243.
186. Stubbs, *Select charters*, p. 465.
187. John E. Morris, *The Welch wars of Edward I* (Oxford, 1901), p. 186. Dowell, *A Suffolk hundred in 1283*, p. LX.
188. Stubbs, *Select charters*, pp. 465, 467–468.

power for evil of these people (the Welsh) although it may seem a difficult task."[189]

Consequently the members of the shire courts and the sheriffs could divine the purpose of the summons. Since the members of the great council were absent in the army, the representatives met without them. The assembly of the laity at Northampton granted a thirtieth of movables on condition that the nobles should grant as much, which was done.[190] For the first time that we know of the deputies were formally given by the writ full powers "to hear and to do" what would be revealed to them by royal officials. The *plenaria potestas* referred not only to the right to grant a tax by royal authority on behalf of the men of their shires, but also to their ability to assent to a levy in the absence of the barons. Their dependence on the magnates was shown by the statement of the parliament at Northampton that the delegates would grant a thirtieth of movables, if the barons would grant as much.[191]

From this proviso we may conclude that the county representatives in this case had acted prior to the decisions of the magnates because the parliament had been summoned. Thus it is clear that the grant by the representatives was intended to be dependent upon similar action by the barons. The magnates granted the thirtieth as far as in them lay (*quantum in ipsis est*), as they had been asked by the king to do. This statement indicates perhaps that they felt a doubt as to their ability to make a grant alone. We must recall that the great council never assumed to grant for England as a whole; their grants did not cover the royal demesne or the clergy; they covered the property on lands held by the tenants in chief of the king. Consequently this doubt is expressed because they were granting the thirtieth on all movables on such lands. Thus the representatives and the tenants in chief made the grant on the same movables.[192]

While the plan of using representatives originated with the king and his small council, it had the support of the magnates. Just as under Henry III the aids were authorized by the great council, so under Edward I, though with the additional machinery of representatives of the shires, the consent of the magnates was still the determining factor. The position gained by the united action of

189. *Ibid.*, p. 468.
190. *Ibid.*, p. 469.
191. *Ibid.*, p. 465. D. J. Medley, *Original illustrations*, p. 170.
192. *The parliamentary writs and writs of military summons*, ed. Francis Palgrave (Record Commission), I, 12.

CONSENT TO TAXATION

the barons under Henry III over the question of taxation forced by the king's policy of devising additional aids and employing the great council to secure them was maintained under the leadership of Edward I. The relation of the deputies of the shires to the great council comes out clearly in the levy of 1290. On September 22, the writ of assessment states that the "archbishops, bishops, abbots, priors, earls, barons, and all others of our realm have courteously and willingly granted us a fifteenth of all their movable goods." [193]

On June 14, 1290, the king had summoned two or three of the more discreet and capable knights of each shire to be elected not later than July 15. They were to have full power to advise and consent for their community on those matters which the earls, barons, and nobles should be led to agree on. This summons may have arisen out of certain petitions made by some magnates, and the king desired to discuss these matters with the magnates and the men of the counties.[194] No summons to the magnates has survived, nor do we know whether the question of the aid was laid before magnates and knights of the shire at this time. It is likely however that the decision regarding the aid was made around July 15. The assessment would take place in September, when the greatest amount of movables would be on hand. Such a matter was one which concerned the great and the lesser men of the shires, and it seems a fair inference that if the knights of the shire considered the aid, it was after the magnates had agreed to it; that it was a matter on which the barons had reached a decision after which the shire knights were asked to discuss and assent to it.[195]

In 1294, because of trouble abroad, Edward I was forced to adopt extraordinary measures to raise additional revenues. In October he summoned two knights from each shire to Westminster with full powers "in order that matters shall not be undecided for lack of such powers." [196] These elected knights were to meet with the earls, barons, and other nobles with whom the king was to discuss grave affairs affecting the realm; the deputies were to advise and consent for themselves and their communities to those measures which the earls, barons, and magnates might have ordained in common.[197] One of the matters for consideration was an increase

---

193. James Field Willard, *Parliamentary taxes on personal property, 1290-1334* (Cambridge, 1934), p. 14. *Parliamentary writs*, I, 24.
194. Stubbs, *Select charters*, 477-478.
195. *Ibid.*
196. *Ibid.*, pp. 481-482. *Parliamentary writs*, I, 26.
197. *Ibid.* Stubbs, *Select charters*, pp. 481-482.

of revenue, for on November 12, the day the parliament was summoned to meet, a tenth of movables was granted by the earls, barons, and all others to defray the expenses of the war to recover Gascony.[198] This grant thus was one of the matters in which the shire representatives were to agree to what the great men had decided.

In 1295 the writ of collection of the aid declares that it was made by the earls, barons, knights, and others of our kingdom—an eleventh of movables. Thus great men and the representatives of the shires granted the same aliquot part as was conventional. This grant thus was one of the matters in which the shire representatives were to agree to what the great men had decided.

It seems a fair inference therefore that a certain procedure in the grant of taxes on movables continued in the reign of Edward I, viz., that the great council granted the tax on all the lands of tenants in chief, that a new element was introduced by the employment of elected knights of the shire, each representing the shire and binding the shire, but that their assent was supplementary and covered the same movables as did the action of the magnates. This is indicated by the statements in 1290 and 1294 that the representatives were to assent to what the magnates might have agreed on and by the fact that magnates and representatives always voted the same fractional amount, unlike the representatives of the towns and the clergy. It indicates common action by magnates and knights. Thus what was once the decision by the magnates alone became on the initiative of the king the decision of the magnates supplemented by that of the representatives of the shires.

The history of the towns and aids followed an independent line. As we have seen, the cities, boroughs, and rural demesne of the king paid him tallage from time to time. For this levy he did not have to consult the great curia regis with which the royal demesne, urban and rural, was not connected. From time to time the king had the right to levy tallage, a lump sum only roughly corresponding to the wealth of the area, or a levy per capita; in neither form was it a uniform tax based upon an assessed valuation of either property or revenue. Thus the demesne dealt directly with the king, its lord, and had no connection with the great curia regis. It is true that the royal demesne had paid the early taxes on movables down to 1237. But the procedure by which the levies were authorized on the demesne was not often described. In the case of the Saladin tithe,

198. Vincent, *Lancashire lay subsidies*, I, 85–86. *Parliamentary writs*, I, 27.

CONSENT TO TAXATION 229

Benedict of Peterborough states that the king met with groups of the wealthier burgesses from urban areas and levied the tithe upon them, a statement which indicates negotiation for the tax with each urban area.[199]

The statement regarding aids in Magna Carta excluded the demesne from consideration except in the case of London which should grant its aid independently. In stating that London paid the fifteenth of 1225 to the king, Roger of Wendover remarks, "as had been previously granted to him from all England," as though the arrangement with London were especially made after the grant had been made by the great council.[200]

In 1237 the men of the demesne seem to have opposed the thirtieth, for writs were issued exempting the demesne in eighteen shires from paying it on the ground that the king was about to levy a tallage. We may conclude that all the demesne was exempt from the thirtieth. This action by Henry III suggests that the previous payments of the aid on movables by the demesne were made as the result of negotiations between the royal government and the demesne. In 1253, on the occasion of the aid to knight the king's son, Henry III did not levy a tallage on the demesne, perhaps because he had levied a tallage the preceding year. Instead he issued writs asking for a gracious aid from his demesne for this crossing to Gascony.[201]

In 1255, on the occasion of the tallage of that year, the Londoners asserted that they were not liable for tallage and offered to pay an aid instead. In the resultant struggle, the council refused to accept the citizens' contention and proved by citations from the rolls that London had always been subject to tallage, thus forcing the citizens to admit that they were wrong and to pay the tallage. The twentieth of 1269 was paid by the demesne but clearly not by authority of the decision of the great council. Special assessors went out to ask the twentieth of the towns. At the close of Henry III's reign, therefore, the king levied taxes on movables, at least on urban areas, without any authorization by the great council, but by special negotiation.

The fifteenth granted in October, 1275, by the great council and representatives of the shires was also paid by the demesne. No notice has survived that representatives of the towns were sum-

199. Benedict of Peterborough, II, 33.
200. Roger of Wendover, II, 318.
201. Mitchell, *Studies in taxation*, p. 256.

moned to meet with the great council (as were the representatives of the shires). London and the Cinque Ports may have sent representatives to the council, for commissioners were appointed to assess and collect the fifteenth on their goods. This item is evidence that the demesne paid the fifteenth, but Norwich compounded in £100 with the taxers (assessors) of Norfolk and Suffolk, the only town mentioned in the rolls in this connection.[202] Since Norwich was not summoned to send representatives to the great council, probably therefore no other towns were summoned. It may be that the county commissioners were instructed to ask a fifteenth of the towns, urging that they follow the example of London. Thus the towns may have compounded as in 1269. Our information is too scanty to make a definitive decision. It would seem therefore that shires and towns were under royal initiative pursuing an independent development.

In 1282 the council sent out John de Kirkby to secure grants or loans from rural and urban communities and from the religious to meet the heavy expenses of the Welsh war. In the parliaments that were summoned to meet at Northampton and at York the representatives of the towns were for the first time summoned at the same time and places as those of the shires and clergy and were given full powers. They granted a thirtieth with no reference to the action of the magnates. The new plan did not seem to them especially advantageous over the conventional plan of sending representatives of the central government to the towns, so familiar in levying tallage. In 1290, on the king's return from Gascony in debt, he summoned a great council and later representatives of the shires, and a fifteenth was granted. This levy was paid by all the property holders on the lands of the tenants in chief. Moreover London was asked for and consented to a grant of a fifteenth.[203] No notice has been found of a similar appeal to other towns, but since cities, boroughs, and market towns paid the fifteenth, it is likely that such an appeal was made, for such was the case in 1269, in 1283, and later in 1294.[204]

In 1294 a tenth of movables was granted by an assembly of lay barons and representatives of shires, but the royal demesne was taxed by itself. London was asked for and granted a sixth of movables. The example of London was cited in the writs issued by the

202. *Calendar of close rolls, 1272–1279*, p. 285.
203. Vincent, *Lancashire lay subsidies*, I, 182.
204. Willard, *Parliamentary taxes*, pp. 14–15.

council appointing commissioners to "require and induce effectively" the men of the demesne, cities, and vills "to grant and furnish us the aforesaid sixth according to the aforesaid taxation." This order applied to the rural as well as to the urban demesne.[205]

Finally in 1295 the device of summoning representatives of the towns to meet at the same time as the great council and the deputies of the shires was permanently adopted except in the case of the ninth of 1297. That year London granted the ninth of movables. Then the council ordered the assessors and collectors in the counties to assess and collect it in the cities, boroughs, and other demesne of the king.[206]

Thus this procedure was only slowly adopted in the demesne by the initiative of the king and the council independently of the decisions in the great council concerning taxes on movables. The forces impelling this action were the belief that a tax on movables would be more fruitful than a tallage; the example of the payment on movables by the magnates and the shires could be used as an inducement to the demesne to grant such a tax. The experience of the council with the shires probably led the members to conclude that it would be easier and quicker to secure a general grant of a common fraction of movables in an assembly of deputies of the demesne than by special representatives who went from area to area and who might be induced to accept a lump sum in composition, as in the tallage, as illustrated in the taxes on movables in 1269 and 1275. The ancient custom of levying tallage in this way postponed the employment of representatives by the towns. When the new method by representatives was adopted the rural demesne probably paid with the shires and so perhaps had no voice in choosing the shire representatives. The grants of taxes on movables developed corporate action among the magnates by the close of Henry III's reign. The adoption of grants by representatives of shires and towns followed this principle, partly induced by the decisions of the magnates under Edward I and partly due to the character of an aid based on an assessed valuation of property. Thus the reign of Edward I continued a development begun under Henry III. The custom was established that from time to time a tax on movables was necessary and was asked from clergy and laity. The fear also persisted that such an aid might become a custom, as is evidenced by the concession to the archbishop of Canterbury that his grant of

205. *Ibid.* Vincent, *Lancashire lay subsidies*, I, 182-183.
206. *Parliamentary writs*, I, 35-64.

a subsidy should not form a precedent or be drawn into a custom.[207]

As in the past the body consulted for the most important part of this levy on the laity was the great council. Though each member might believe he exercised individual consent, practically the action was corporate; the decision bound not merely the absent but property holders who were not summoned. As soon as the grant was made, the king felt authorized to appoint assessors and collectors.

Alongside the great council, on the initiative of the small council and the king, appeared two new representative bodies, the delegates of the shires and of the towns. The representatives of the shires were summoned for counsel and discussion at first, thus continuing an occasional practice under Henry III. Then the council ordered them to be given full powers by each county court to decide whatever might be brought before them, as in 1290 to agree to what the magnates had decided. That is, their action in taxation seems to have been supplementary to the grant of a tax on movables by the great council on the property held on the lands of tenants in chief. For example, there is no indication that the great council granted the tax on the demesnes of tenants in chief and the knights of the shire on the property of rear vassals and their tenants. Since the tenants in chief were members of the shire courts, no sharp line of division could be drawn between the members of the great council and the shire delegates. In 1254 an effort had been made by the council to draw a line between the laity who would serve in Gascony, the prelates who would serve or contribute lump sums in aid, and the other laity who would grant an aid in each county court. No grant was made by them, but the experiment was not repeated. Was it because of the difficulty of authorizing a tax by the county court on the property of small tenants in chief and great rear vassals who might desire to be associated with the magnates? By the device of a grant by the magnates which might be interpreted to cover all movable property on their fiefs, as in the past, supplemented by the consent of representatives of the shire courts to what the magnates had granted, no necessity existed of making a division in the property between any two groups. This is the significance of the clause *quantum in ipsis est* employed in the king's writ to the knights and freemen of Essex. He thanks them for their grant of the thirtieth which the magnates also granted, "as far as in them lay."

207. *Calendar of patent rolls, 1272-1281*, p. 165.

Both magnates and knights granted the tax which was based upon the undivided goods on the lands held by tenants in chief. This is a logical explanation for the fact that in the thirteenth century magnates and knights always granted the same aliquot part of their movables. In this lies the significance of a statement, as in 1290, that the knights should have full power to assent to what the magnates had already agreed upon. Since the barons before Edward I had always authorized the tax on movables, how would it be possible that the king would suddenly limit their taxing power? The calling of representatives would give the decision of the great barons additional authority. The initiative of the order that the knights should have plenaria potestas lay with the king. Its continued use indicates that the barons did not regard such a body with hostility or jealousy. The part played by the barons in the election of the knights of the shire, the same aliquot part granted by both barons and knights; the fact that the custom was for the barons to consent to (or refuse) a grant of movables; that they acted as a corporate unit in their grant as did seemingly the knights—all suggest that the magnates continued to grant the taxes on all their lands with a supplementary vote of assent by the knights of the shire. As has been shown, the position of the royal demesne was entirely different. The demesne had nothing to do with the curia regis. It had been taxed on movables by direct negotiation with the king; such is the evidence when evidence there is. This era of special negotiation lasted till 1295 when the king forced on the demesne the use of representatives with full power. The case of the ninth in 1297 indicates that the decision of the great council even at that late date would be resented by the king's council. It has been suggested that the demesne had to pay the tax on movables because it was liable to tallage. The implication is that tallage was heavier than a tax on movables; the contrary seems to have been true, for tallage was not a tax on movables. That towns compounded for the tax on movables instead of paying on an assessed valuation indicates that they gained in two ways: by keeping the king's officials out of their area, and by paying a lighter tax. Because a town owed a tallage, a customary due, in a lump sum, does not mean that the king could at will assess their property and take a certain aliquot part of it. It has been suggested that representatives of the shires were summoned and consulted on these taxes as a means of securing local support to facilitate the assessment and collection of the levy. Such a theory would not apply to the towns, for they were always definitely consulted long before the use of representatives by them. The use of delegates in behalf of the shire may have been copied from the church where existed a similar difficulty in differentiating between the rights of the prelates over property and revenues in the hands of subordinate clerics or groups of religious, who were subject in many ways to the jurisdiction of the great churchmen. Thus for over twenty years of Edward I's reign, the king negotiated with his demesne for the taxes on movables, continuing the custom of the preceding reign, but substituting for the tallage a levy on movables which had been recommenced in 1269, a definite extension of his control. For the taxation of the laity Edward I succeeded in making the tax on movables a convention; on the lands of tenants in chief by the assent of the great council and an assembly of knights of the shire; on his demesne by an assembly of representatives of the towns. The consent in all three cases was corporate; refusal as under Henry III again became difficult. The result was a great expansion of royal power. The change in authorization was due to the royal initiative.

Let us review the changes in the notion of consent to taxation that reflect the modification in the social structure of England. We begin with the feudal Anglo-Norman customary organization using an income derived entirely from dues and one special extra source of supply, the feudal gracious aid, an occasional resource. The latter was founded on the principle that in time of great need the vassals ought to come to their lord's assistance, first in services and payments in kind and, by a later interpretation, with money. It was only an occasional levy, taken under extraordinary circumstances. Very soon the council began to base it upon a unit of land or other property, as a result of which the tax was automatically exacted for the king from property holders who were not tenants of the king and hence owed him nothing; such was the use of the danegeld, which was abandoned and then revived as the carucage, of the aid on knights' fees, and the tax on movables and revenues. The authorizing body was the great curia regis. Thus unintentionally and without deliberation the king began to authorize an occasional levy of a general tax on the property belonging to nearly all property holders in the realm regardless of their status in society. The consent of the curia regis to such a levy bound people who were not summoned or consulted. It facilitated later the substitution of corporate for individual consent. As has been said, al-

CONSENT TO TAXATION

though the aid was of grace, an obligation seems to have bound the tenant to grant the aid. The reigns of Richard I and John resulted in a crisis in the relations between king and barons, one subject in dispute being the levy of both aid and scutage. The exciting cause was the increased frequency with which both were taken, particularly scutage. The regulation as given in Articles XII and XIV of Magna Carta declared that neither could be taken as a custom —only by the consent of the great curia regis could they be levied. Thus two facts are to be noted in 1215 in this connection: first, that the barons had the feeling that aids should be regulated, and second, the emphasis on the part to be played in the regulation by the great curia regis, that is, by the barons themselves. The reign of Henry III established the custom that the great council could refuse as well as grant the aid; the notion was established that taxes on movables were essential from time to time, the form that the aid was to take. Though not formally declared, in fact, consent became corporate. Under Edward I we see the truth of these generalizations made for Henry III. In addition, on the initiative of the king, the custom was established that had already been used occasionally in the later years of Henry III, though not in connection with taxation, viz., summoning representatives of the shires to associate themselves with the great council in granting an aid on the property on all the holdings of tenants in chief. Thus the authority of the great council to consent or refuse established under Henry III continued, but for some reason not clearly understood the king decided to associate elected knights of the shire with the great council in the grant. Perhaps they thought to secure better cooperation in the assessment and collection. Perhaps the growing money economy suggested a doubt of the capacity of the council to grant taxes on property not their own. Anyhow the two bodies cooperated in granting taxes on the same property. The demesne continued to negotiate with royal justices who went on iter as in the past (except in 1283) till 1295, when towns and boroughs were summoned by representatives to meet with the council and vote aids. Notice that the reasons for the use of representatives suggested above did not apply to the demesne. The only reason in their case was ease and speed, for at the date they began to use representatives the aid on movables was a convention both in frequency and in amount. Hence its grant could be satisfactorily and easily made by deputies.

V

TALLAGE IN THE REIGN OF HENRY II

ONE of the most important taxes of the early Angevin period was the levy on the royal demesne called *auxilium*, *assisa*, *donum*, and later *tallagium*. The group of fiscal contributions bearing these names fall into two classes. First, the aid usually levied upon the serfs of all demesnes both royal and noble—called the ordinary tallage; second, the aid taken primarily from the freemen on those demesnes, and to this category belongs the aid on the royal demesne. The two levies existed side by side and exhibit certain common traits.[1] The ordinary tallage paid to the lord from his demesne was an annual levy, payable at a certain date in the year, often Michaelmas, fixed in amount by an agreement between the lord and the tenant, not based on an assessed valuation of property, and so commonly limited to villeins that its payment became one of the tests of villeinage. The other tallage was that levied by the king on his demesne, from time to time, paid by freemen usually but occasionally by villeins; it was not based on an assessed valuation of property but was the result of a bargain between royal commissioners and the men of the area.[2] Both levies were sometimes laid upon the individual tenant (per capita), or on a group of the latter, the members of the group or the lord of the vill allocating the amount to be paid by each property holder.[3] Both varieties of tallage were conventionalized in the thirteenth century in amount. Except for the references to the royal tallage in the pipe rolls, little evidence has survived in the twelfth century

1. For comprehensive and scholarly statements regarding the ordinary tallage see N. Neilson, "Customary rents," pp. 90–96; Sir Frederick Pollock and Frederic William Maitland, *History of English law* (Cambridge, 1895), I, 368; Paul Vinogradoff, *Villainage in England* (Oxford, 1892), pp. 83, 92–93, 163; Paul Vinogradoff, *English society in the twelfth century*, p. 143.

2. Stephenson has a scholarly account of royal tallage to which I am greatly indebted. Carl Stephenson, *Borough and town, a study of urban origins in England* (Cambridge, 1933), pp. 160–166. See also his "The seignorial tallage in England," in *Mélanges d'histoire offerts à Henri Pirenne* (Brussels, 1926), pp. 465–474.

3. Neilson, "Customary rents," pp. 90–91.

concerning either; the ordinary tallage antedated *Domesday Book* as a fixed payment.

The striking differences between the levies is that one was often annual and the other occasional; one was paid mainly by villeins and the other by freemen. It seems likely that these two levies went back to a common origin, the aid on the feudal demesne, paid by all on the occasion of some great need.

We are concerned here only with the royal tallage not only because it was an important source of royal revenue, but also because it reflected the deliberate effort of the council to expand the revenue from some existing royal right, and because in assessment, collection, and accounting, the government was extending its administrative experience and unconsciously preparing the way for the administration of a far more complicated levy, the tax on movables.

Broadly speaking, in the twelfth century the obligations of both villeins and freemen were becoming stabilized, as is reflected in the accounts we have given of tallage. Thus both classes of tenants on the demesne had gained at the expense of their lords.

In these chapters we are concerned with the character of the royal tallage which was already conventionalized in the latter half of the twelfth century. The important period was from 1130 to 1272. It was taken rather frequently until the close of Henry III's reign, when it was abandoned until the opening of the fourteenth century. Then it was revived; it was levied once in 1304 by Edward I; once in 1312 by Edward II; and finally a proposal to levy it was made in 1332 under Edward III. On this last occasion parliament protested vigorously and accompanied the remonstrance with the offer of a tax on movables if the king would withdraw the orders for the levy of the tallage. Edward III acceded to the request. He went further. By a statute issued that same year he promised never to levy tallage again "except as it had been done in the time of his other ancestors and as it ought reasonably to be done."[4] This promise was repeated several times in the course of the reign; moreover it was kept, for tallage was never again levied by Edward III or by any of his successors.

Tallage began at the latest early in the twelfth century and its history covers a period of perhaps two hundred years. Its end was unlike that of the carucage which was voluntarily abandoned by the government, probably in view of the richer sources of revenue disclosed by the taxes on personal property. Tallage moreover was

4. *Rotuli parliamentorum* (Record Commission), II, 66.

a due and did not require the consent of the great council as did carucage. It was unlike scutage, too, which was only gradually abandoned in the course of the fourteenth century; it was unlike the feudal incidents that continued into modern times, for tallage declined to an infrequent levy and finally ceased abruptly in response to a protest. Moreover repeated promises were made by the government that it would not be taken except in the conventional way while asserting its right to take tallage. While no one denied its legality tallage was not again taken. It was a curious end to an old and well-established due.

Let us begin our study by examining tallage after it had taken definite shape in the latter part of the reign of Henry II, from 1168 to 1189. The materials for our study will be more abundant than if we attempted a chronological sketch beginning with its origins. At the same time the age of the levy will not be so far removed from the beginnings that its early characteristics will be wholly concealed. After an analysis of the levy in its maturity, we may then turn back to examine its earlier phases.

The chronicles seldom mention the levy. Charters tell something of its incidence and of exemptions. One precious notice comes from the *Dialogue of the Exchequer* revealing its method of assessment and collection and its obligatory character. But for the most part we must depend on the pipe rolls with their elaborate records of assessment and collection. From these alone we ought to be able to form a reasonably accurate picture.

Toward the latter part of the reign of Henry II when tallage had become well established, it was levied on the royal demesne (that is, the cities and boroughs that held of the king and the manors that held of him by menial services, by payments in kind, or their commutation into money), and on the tenants on demesne lands of fiefs that either had escheated to the king, or were temporarily in hand. In our earliest records tallage was assessed by royal justices but was collected and usually accounted for at the exchequer by the sheriff. Occasionally the tallage was paid to some special royal official.

We have referred to this levy as tallage, and such was the name by which it went in general in the thirteenth century. That was not the case in the twelfth century. Only gradually did it assume that name. At first it was called auxilium, donum, and assisa in the pipe roll. It must also have been generally known by the name of tallagium for a royal charter to Nottingham in 1157 declares that every one that dwells (*manserit*) within the borough of whosoever fee he may be ought to share tallages with the burgesses and make good the deficits of the borough.⁵ The council of London states in 1151 that churches and ecclesiastical possessions ought to be free from works and exactions which are commonly called *tenserias*, or *tallagia*.⁶

In the late years of the twelfth century, the word tallagium edged in beside the others in the pipe roll. Sometimes the heading was tallagium and the individual payments under that title were called auxilium, or donum, or assisa. It is, however, impossible to detect any change in the character of the tax corresponding with the change in name. The levies were neither more frequent, more arbitrary, nor were they consistently heavier from 1168.

It was an important occasional tax, for it yielded from £4,000 to £5,000 in the cases of its greatest yield. Most of it was paid quickly, and within a few years the accounts were in great part cleared up. This characteristic remained largely true down to the death of Henry III. Thus the machinery of assessment and collection was effective.

Since tallage was a due from the royal demesne, the question of its authorization did not come before the great council and consequently that body hardly ever registered a protest against excessive levies. Yet something protected the tallage payers, for while there were great variations in the amounts any individual town or rural area might pay, no considerable horizontal increase occurred in the amounts levied throughout the demesne as a whole from 1168 to 1272, the great age of this levy. It never became an annual due. Though efforts that were temporarily successful were made by the council to increase its frequency, in the long run they were unsuccessful. Tallage at the end of Henry III's reign was still taken about as often as at the close of Henry II's reign nearly a hundred years earlier. No doubt custom helped prevent the change, along with the bargaining capacity of the towns and the men who farmed parts of the rural demesne.

If therefore the king had the right to tallage and exercised the right for two hundred years, why did he renounce it even if the tallage yielded less than the tax on personal property? Why moreover did parliament in the fourteenth century request such an ac-

5. Adolphus Ballard, *British borough charters, 1042-1216* (Cambridge, 1913), p. 108.

6. J. H. Round, *Geoffrey de Mandeville* (London, 1892), p. 414.

tion in the case of an old well-established due when other dues, though complained of, were left untouched for generations? The answer to these questions is twofold. With the close of the reign of Henry III began a new era in taxation. It will be recalled that from 1237 to 1269 the great council had refused to grant any tax on the personal property of laymen although during this period churchmen had voted various levies on their property other than that held by barony. Then in 1269 after the civil war and the restoration of peace, Henry III again took up the project of the crusade, sent his son and heir as leader, and secured a grant of a twentieth of personal property from the laity and clergy to defray the expenses of the expedition. It was the first tax of this kind which had been levied on the laity since the thirtieth of 1237. Thus after a generation taxes on personal property of the laity and clergy were resumed. Repeated during the reign of Edward I and thereafter, they became the favorite method for raising extraordinary revenues. Furthermore Edward I developed a new and satisfactory method by which they could be legally authorized. The tax and the method of assessment and collection had all been developed during the first half of the thirteenth century; what had been lacking had been the leadership to satisfy the political chiefs of England that the levies were necessary and a satisfactory method by which the assent could be gained. Under Henry III the consent had been obtained by asking the curia regis. But the controversy that had broken out between the king and the barons had prevented the establishment of a custom that the great council had the authority to grant a tax on all classes of society. Edward I adopted the practice of appealing to the great council and to representative groups and to towns, beginning with London, asking them to grant a uniform levy of a fractional part of their movable property as an aid. For over thirty years he discarded tallage altogether, for the simple reason that it did not yield as much as the levy on movables. Tallage was paid by certain persons in manors and boroughs of the royal demesne. In the course of time some inhabitants had been exempted by custom or by special grant. The new levy on movables was exacted from everyone including those on the royal demesne who possessed property of this new description. But why must the king seek permission to levy a tax on the personal property of the demesne when he already had the right to levy a tallage without special permission of the property holders—an old established due? Because the tallage was a stereotyped form of levy in amounts that were fixed each time by a bargain between the assessors and the taxpayers; the tax on movables was a certain percentage of certain movables held by all owners within the demesne as well as elsewhere. Such a levy required the consent of the owners either individually, by groups, or by qualified representatives. Moreover, the repeated levy of the tax on personal property had led to a change in the character of that tax, which was gradually apparent. Groups began to bargain with the commissioners to accept a lump sum for the tax on their movables. In doing so, they took the first step to assimilate the tallage and the tax on personal property.

Now the danger that had been perceived under Henry III by the barons was that the taxes on movables for which Henry III had always asked the consent of the great council would by repetition become a new and frequent custom which they would be obliged to pay. The problem of refusing a grant became an issue. Hence arose the great political struggle of the reign of Henry III when the great council refused repeatedly to grant a tax and established the principle that it had the right to refuse as well as to grant taxes.

With the repeated taxes on movables under Edward I, the same danger was perceived—that a new customary tax was being established. Out of this feeling arose the opposition movement which led to the Confirmation of the Charters. This document declared merely that the repeated grants of taxes were not creating a new customary tax. This was what the barons wished to prevent and the only way they devised to stop it was by this formal declaration. It will be recalled that Edward I was granted a tax after the Confirmation and he continued from time to time to ask for grants. But the opposition grew to such an extent that in 1304 he was unable to secure the grant of a tax on movables. Consequently, in order to obtain additional money to pay the expenses of the Scottish war, he took a scutage and along with it a tallage, the first of the reign. To levy a tallage it was not necessary to secure the assent of any assembly. Yet it was a landmark in taxation. For although the writs to levy this tallage were couched in the same form as earlier writs, the method of assessment shows a great change. It was in some cases really a tax based upon an assessment of personal property. A similar procedure was followed in the tallage of Edward II in 1312, only this time the government went further and directed the assessors to levy a twelfth of movables in the rural areas and a fourteenth of movables in the towns. Thus though called a tallage this was really a tax on personal property. Again in 1332 the levy, though by name a tallage, was really a tax on movables. Thus as far as the royal demesne (including most boroughs) was concerned, tallage, an obligatory due, was assuming the form of a tax on movables and the tax on movables was in some cases not based on an assessment of personal property at all but a commutation of it into a fixed sum. Tallage and the tax on movables were getting more and more alike, except that the tax on personal property included more areas than the tallage. If this process of assimilation in form became complete, then the king would possess the legal right in levying his tallage to take without consent a tax on movables on the royal demesne.

Now the reigns of Edward I and Edward II had by repeated levies of taxes on personal property made this tax part of the financial system of the state. They had devised the legal method of authorizing these levies by asking representative groups for authority and by sending commissioners to the boroughs and cities, beginning with London, asking them for a grant on movables. Finally the quickest and easiest plan was formed: to have all groups including counties and boroughs send representatives possessing powers to bind their constituents to a central assembly to cooperate with the great council. Hence, in part, arose parliament. No such levy could be taken except through parliament. But to levy a tallage, the old established tax on the demesne, by assessing the movables on the demesne which included cities and boroughs and which was represented in parliament was the negation of the Confirmation of the Charters. It opposed diametrically the constitutional development of the past two reigns. Yet it was impossible for the demesne to refuse the king for he had the ancient right of tallage, since the taxes on movables, levied either in lump sums or by an actual assessment of property, had blotted out the recollection of the original distinction between tallage and the tax on movables. The solution of the difficulty was found in the offer of parliament to grant a tax on movables if the king would rescind his commands to levy a tallage. Thus tallage was abandoned because in the course of time it had become indistinguishable from the tax on movables.

With this preliminary survey of the development of tallage, let us turn back to its characteristics in the late twelfth century. The royal revenues in the twelfth century were primarily customary dues, like the census (rents) of the forest; farms, such as the county farm, town farms, and farms of manors in hand; rents from land in services in kind and in money; fines or oblations for some right or privilege; amercements; feudal incidents; and danegeld. The connotation of these terms often overlapped. These sources of income were always based upon the feudal or other customary law. The king had a legal right to all that he took. The levies were thus not purely arbitrary exactions; yet as the amount taken was variable, there was an element of compulsion and the revenue from these sources was to a certain extent flexible. Thus there was as yet no fixed rate of relief other than that it should be reasonable. Amercement should be reasonable. The customary viewpoint was clearly expressed in the charter issued by Henry I at his accession when it stated that relief shall be "just and legal" (Art. II) and that amercements for crimes would be proportionate to the gravity of the crime and were not to be employed as a means of excessive punishment (Art. VIII). Stephen promised to conserve "just dues [consuetudines] in murder fines and pleas and other causes." [7] Aids should be reasonable (Articles of the Barons, c. 6). Amercements should be proportionate to the gravity of the crime (c. 9). No one should perform more service from a knight's fee than he owed (c. 7). Fines for dowries, marriages, inheritances, and amercements were not to be unjust and against the law of the land (c. 37; Magna Carta of 1215, c. 55).

A borough that desired to assess and collect the farm that was owed to the royal exchequer by the burgesses had only to arrange a satisfactory amount with the royal officials. The sum agreed upon would depend upon the skill of the two sides as negotiators. Some payments were fixed in amount. The murdrum had originally been fixed at 46m., but in the course of the century following the conquest the sums had been greatly reduced, often as low as 10m. or even less.[8]

The danegeld had been fixed at the conventional sum of 2s. a hide, payable annually and attached as a due to definite pieces of land; some areas had been exempted and many landholders had secured exemption. While the king therefore did not have a free hand in levying taxes and dues, he had certain opportunities for expanding his revenue. The royal income seems small to us, yet

7. William Stubbs, *Select charters,* pp. 100–102, 120–121.
8. *Pipe roll 31 Henry I* (Record Commission), pp. 10, 71, 78.

there was constant complaint of the excessive demands of the king.⁹

The borough farms under Henry II were subject to increasing demands by the royal government. Sometimes they were raised so high that payment was greatly delayed and even found too large to be paid, so that the royal government ultimately pardoned part or all of the sum originally demanded.¹⁰ Attempts were also made to increase the county farms with partial success.¹¹ Henry I, says Henry of Huntingdon, "shone resplendent in three particulars: supreme wisdom, victory, and riches. . . . In riches, because in that respect, he far outstripped his predecessors." ¹² Early in Stephen's reign the earl of Gloucester hesitated to revolt because of the king's strength by reason of his great military renown and because of the abundance of money still left from the treasures of the deceased king (Henry I).¹³ William I left his son Henry £5,000 of silver. William II was able to loan 10,000$m.$ in cash to Robert of Normandy. These may be in part exaggerations and rumors, but evidence of a different sort appears with the fact that we have the development of the pipe roll with attendant financial organization to indicate an advanced money economy.

Among the sources of revenue that proved to be capable of expansion was the levy called at first auxilium, donum, assisa, and finally almost exclusively tallagium.¹⁴ It was a levy upon the royal demesne, that is, upon the urban and rural areas which the king had never enfeoffed by knight service. The nucleus was the ancient demesne, the royal lands not enfeoffed at the time of the Conquest. These were considerably reduced at the accession of Henry because many lands had been bestowed on individual barons, monasteries, and the like. The rest of the royal demesne had come into the king's hands by escheat, forfeiture, or during the minority of a tenant, or by a vacancy through the action of feudal or other customary law.¹⁵ The proportion of such lands that were actually tallaged is difficult

9. Stubbs, *Select charters*, pp. 97, 117.
10. James Tait, *The medieval English borough* (Manchester, 1936), pp. 168–176.
11. G. J. Turner, "The sheriff's farm," *Transactions of the royal historical society*, XII (1898).
12. Henry of Huntingdon, p. 255. Robert de Monte, *History of king Henry the first*, trans. by Joseph Stevenson in "Church historians of England," V, Part 1, p. 28.
13. *Ibid.*, p. 230. This reference is an error, and I cannot find the one Professor Mitchell intended. There is a passage that seems suitable in William of Malmesbury, trans. by Joseph Stevenson, "Church historians of England," III, Part 1, pp. 389–390.
14. *Pipe roll 23 Henry II*, pp. 96, 107. *Pipe roll 33 Henry II*, p. 191.
15. *Pipe roll 14 Henry II*, p. 161. *Pipe roll 15 Henry II*, p. 37. *Pipe roll 19 Henry II*, pp. 75, 154, 196.

TALLAGE IN THE REIGN OF HENRY II 245

to state. We are wholly dependent upon the pipe rolls, and their record of tallages varies greatly from one levy to another. Part of this variation is due to the ebb and flow of lands in and out of the royal control, for escheated lands were given out again. Thus in 19 Henry II in Berkshire six areas were tallaged, three of the ancient demesne and three of lands that had fallen into the king's hand; in 20 Henry II four areas of demesne are enrolled and seven areas of tenements that had recently fallen into Henry's hand.[16] Part of the variation is due to the fact that special arrangements were made with custodians to whom demesne lands had been assigned regarding the payment and recording of tallage. How else shall we explain the failure to record a tallage on the roll of manors that appears in the roll as farmed of the king. Thus Richard de Lucy farmed Cookham and Bray each at £60, but no aid or tallage was listed in the roll.[17]

From 1168 to the close of the reign of Henry II it was an irregularly recurring levy, though there had been attempts to take it annually. It was levied in 1168, 1173, 1174, 1177, and 1187. It was levied on some occasion of unusual necessity. In 1168 there was an aid to provide a dowry for Matilda, Henry II's daughter, when she was married to Henry the Lion, duke of the Saxons. On the same occasion an aid was taken on knights' fees at the rate of $1m.$ per fee while other groups, such as the moneyers, and certain great churchmen, sheriffs, and Jews also contributed.

The expedition to Ireland made in 1171 is definitely stated to have been the reason for the aid of $1,000m.$ paid by London in that year.[18] In the pipe roll of 1173, a tallage appears in twenty-nine counties, in 1174, in eighteen counties. Very likely a cause of both levies was the need of meeting the expense of suppressing the great rebellion of 1173 which broke out in April. A suggestion of this is found in the statement in Surrey that the "assize" was levied in part on the lands of the king's enemies.[19] The tallage of 1177 did not accompany a scutage.[20] There were other special sources of expense. The marriage of Joan, Henry II's second daughter, to King William of Sicily occurred in 1176–77; she was dispatched in a style befitting a princess.[21] The summons in February, 1176 or

16. Ibid., p. 66. Pipe roll 20 Henry II, pp. 114, 116.
17. Pipe roll 15 Henry II, pp. 78, 80.
18. Pipe roll 17 Henry II, p. 151.
19. Pipe roll 19 Henry II, p. 94. Pipe roll 21 Henry II, p. 172.
20. Benedict of Peterborough, I, 160.
21. Ibid., p. 120.

1177, to the host to accompany the king to France in May might well have been the cause of the aid of this year on the demesne.[22]

The final tallage of Henry II's reign occurred in 1187 and was seemingly taken in connection with an expedition against the Scots.[23] While the roll does not call it the "tallage of Galloway," the levy follows frequently in the pipe roll the account of the "scutage of Galloway" and so seems to have been levied in connection with the military expedition.[24] Moreover in one case the two levies were directly connected. The honor of the earl of Gloucester was in hand and charged with the scutage.[25] The sum of £6 of scutage on that honor was written off because it was charged against the royal demesne on a manor from which the king had taken tallage.[26] Thus from 1168 to the close of Henry II's reign, tallage was an occasional levy taken to meet some unusual financial need, such as a campaign or one of the feudal aids. It did not become an annual levy, although occasionally areas paid it in two successive years.

No statement appears in chronicle, pipe roll, or charter as to the authority by which tallage was taken. The *Dialogue of the Exchequer*, written late in the reign of Henry II contains an important statement on this point. The document calls the levies *dona vel auxilia civitatum vel burgorum*.[27] Such were the names, as we have seen, given in the pipe roll to this tax. The document is concerned not with the character of the auxilium or donum but with the method of enforcing payment. In discussing this however the author throws light on the authority by which the levy was put in charge. The royal justices bargained with the authorities of the town for the amount of tallage which they should pay. If an agreement was reached, the latter assessed the tallage themselves. If no agreement could be reached, the justices entered the town and assessed the aid on individuals. Thus if the officials of the town refused to pay the tax, the royal officials themselves enforced the assessment and the collection was made by the sheriff.[28] As Adams put it:

The citizens offer the justices a lump sum and, if the offer seems to them worthy of the prince, that is, sufficient for the occasion, they accept it and the citizens themselves become responsible for the pay-

22. *Ibid.*, p. 138.
23. *Pipe roll 33 Henry II*, p. xxiv.
24. *Ibid.*, pp. 80, 81, 147, 155, 156.
25. *Ibid.*, p. 142.
26. *Ibid.*, pp. xxvii, 142.
27. *Dialogus de scaccario*, p. 145.
28. *Ibid.*

ment. . . . What is it that the citizens buy by their offer? . . . It seems to me clear that they buy off the assessment per capita with the resultant method of distraint and that only. *It is not the arbitrary fixing of the tax.* They do not determine the sum to be paid. If the offer does not seem to the justices large enough, the citizens must raise it till the sum is judged to be a fair equivalent of what would be obtained from an assessment per capita. . . . If the citizens refuse to pay a lump sum, will the king receive nothing as would be the case in the auxilium proper? Certainly not. In that case . . . the assessment is made per capita. . . . All that is left to the decision of the citizens is whether they will buy off the assessment per capita or not.[29]

It is clear therefore that the individual cities did not decide whether they should pay tallage, but had a voice in determining the amount to be charged against them. No other authority but the king appears; it would therefore seem just to conclude that tallage was an occasional due levied at the royal will.

The assessment of the aids on the demesne exhibits some variation in method, but was, broadly speaking, delegated to royal commissioners who were specially appointed for this work alone or performed the task as part of their work as itinerant justices. The writs commissioning the justices in 1168 have not survived, but from their acts we can discern a part at least of their duties. They authorized the justices to levy the aid, for in the past justices had not always done so. They were to levy it in common or per capita, for both forms appear in the pipe roll. They were to draw up a roll of the assessment in duplicate, deposit one copy with the exchequer, and deliver the other copy to the collector, usually the sheriff. The pipe rolls contain the names of some of the justices. A group of five was holding pleas in twenty counties, viz., Richard of Ilchester, archdeacon of Poitou, Guy, dean of Waltham, Reginald de Warenne, William Basset, and Henry Fitz Gerald, a chamberlain. Only three of these officials are mentioned by name as assessors of the aid, viz., Richard of Ilchester, Reginald de Warenne and Guy, dean of Waltham, but (as the itinerant justices seem to have formed a group in their other work), it is likely that all shared in the assessment of the aid.[30]

They were described by Madox as "barons of the exchequer, who officiated in any task requiring expert knowledge, in justice, admin-

29. George Burton Adams, *The origin of the English constitution* (New Haven, 1912), pp. 363–364.
30. *Pipe roll 14 Henry II*, pp. 48, 181, 190, 213. *Pipe roll 15 Henry II*, p. 63.

istration, or finance."[31] The use of such officials continued after 1168. The great inquest of sheriffs in 1170 was held by special commissioners who do not seem to have been closely connected with the small curia regis but were important tenants. The kingdom was divided into circuits to each of which was sent a group of commissioners.[32] The aid on the demesne levied in 1173 followed the same procedure. There were six circuits to each of which was assigned a group of assessors as shown in the following table:

Assessors	Counties
Sefrid, archdeacon of Chichester	
Wimar, the chaplain	Essex and Hertfordshire
Adam of Yarmouth	Norfolk and Suffolk
Robert Mantel	Cambridge and Huntingdonshire
Richard Fitz Neal, the Treasurer	Sussex
Nicholas de Sigello	Buckingham and Bedford
Reginald de Warenne	Kent
Gervase de Cornhill	Oxfordshire
	Surrey
William Basset	Northamptonshire
John Mauduit	Lincolnshire (the city only)
John the Clerk	Notts and Derbyshire
John Cumin	
Thurstan Fitz Simon	Herefordshire
Walter Map	Gloucestershire
Guy, dean of Waltham	Hampshire
Richard de Wilton	Berks
Hugh de Bocland	Wilts
William Rufus	Devon
	Dorset and Somerset
John de Dover and "socii sui"	Staffordshire
	Warwick and Leicestershire

These commissioners were both important administrative and judicial officers. Thus Guy, dean of Waltham, Reginald de Warenne, and William Basset had been justices holding pleas in central and southern England in 1168.[33] John Cumin was itinerant justice in 1170 and an assessor of the tallage in 1173 in the circuit embracing Herefordshire and Gloucestershire. Others had been

31. Thomas Madox, *History of the exchequer*, pp. 743, 744.
32. Gervase of Canterbury, I, 216. *Pipe roll 19 Henry II*, p. 182.
33. *Pipe roll 14 Henry II, passim.*

TALLAGE IN THE REIGN OF HENRY II 249

sheriffs and justices, custodians of honors. All were high royal officials, any of whom might be members of the small curia regis.

In the supplementary aid of 1174 (recorded in eighteen counties), the device of circuits was abandoned. A different group of assessors was appointed in each county. In nearly every case the sheriff was in charge, assisted often by one or more small local landholders. Occasionally, a high official cooperated. Richard Fitz Neal (the famous author of the *Dialogus*) was associated with the sheriff of Buckingham and Bedfordshire. Richard de Lucy, the justiciar, assisted the sheriff of Nottinghamshire and Derbyshire. The scheme appears in the following table:

Assessors	*Counties*
Robert Mantel (sheriff) Walter de Hadfield	Essex and Hertfordshire
Randolph de Lench (sheriff) Hugh Poer Osbert de Abetot	Worcestershire
Guido Lestrange (sheriff)	Shropshire
John de Dover and *socii sui*	Warwick and Leicestershire
Richard de Wilton (sheriff) Robert de Lucy	Wiltshire
Alardus Banaster	Oxfordshire
Hugh de Gundevill (sheriff) Hamo Morgan William Bastard Matthew de Excuris John Iukel	Hampshire
William de Braose (sheriff) Milo de Mucegros	Herefordshire
Ralph Fitz Stephen (sheriff) Philip Fitz Ern Alexander Pincerna	Gloucestershire
Alured de Lincoln (sheriff) Walter de St. Quintin	Dorsetshire and Somersetshire
Hugh de Bocland (sheriff) Leonard (knight of Thomas Basset)	Berkshire

250   TAXATION IN MEDIEVAL ENGLAND

Assessors	Counties
Roger Fitz Renfrew William Rufus	Windsor
William Fitz Richard (sheriff) Richard Fitz Neal (treasurer)	Buckingham and Bedfordshire
William Fitz Ralph (sheriff) Richard de Lucy	Nottingham and Derby

In 1176 England was divided into six circuits to each of which were sent three justices to hold pleas, and thenceforth this method became customary. The aid of 1177 was assessed according to this scheme, as the following outline shows.

Assessors	Counties	
Richard de Lucy (justiciar) Roger Fitz Renfrew Gervase de Cornhill	London and Middlesex Bedford and Buckingham Kent Sussex Surrey	
Robert Mantel Ralph Briton	Cambridge and Huntingdon Essex and Hertfordshire Norfolk and Suffolk	
Ralph Fitz Stephen Thurstan Fitz Simon William Rufus	Berkshire Cornwall Devon Gloucester Hampshire	Hereford Oxford Shropshire Worcestershire Wiltshire
William Fitz Ralph William Basset Michael Belet	Yorkshire Lincolnshire Lancashire Nottingham and Derby	Northamptonshire Northumberland Staffordshire Warwick and Leicestershire

These justices were important government officials. Some had served previously as assessors: Gervase de Cornhill, Robert Mantel, Thurstan Fitz Simon, William Rufus, and William Basset. Some had been sheriffs. Richard de Lucy was still justiciar. Practically all had been itinerant justices in the preceding and current years.

There followed, curiously enough, a long period of ten years when the demesne escaped the new form of taxation. Yet it was a time of financial necessity. At length in 1187 the final tallage of Henry II appeared, enrolled in twenty-five counties only. Four groups of assessors appeared in the roll commissioned to go to fifteen counties in circuits; in ten counties the roll does not record the name of the assessors.

Assessors	Counties
Hugh Bardolf	Wiltshire
Thomas de Husseburn	Cornwall
William Brewer	Devon
Godfrey de Lucy	Cumberland
William de Vavasur	Yorkshire
Jocelyn, archdeacon of Chichester	Lincolnshire
	Northumberland
Robert Marmion	Gloucestershire
William Fitz Stephen	Herefordshire
Hugh Pantulf	Staffordshire
Robert de Arden	Worcestershire
Thomas Noel	Oxfordshire
	Shropshire
Ralph, archdeacon of Colchester [34]	Kent
Roger Fitz Renfrew	Essex
Michael Belet	Hertfordshire
Robert de Whitfield	

These groups were itinerant justices who were at work this year in these circuits; some were also sheriffs.[35]

Thus in the five tallages from 1168 to the close of Henry II's reign, except in 1174, the assessment was made by royal commissioners, many of whom were itinerant justices and experienced royal officials. The counties were grouped in circuits, to each of which was assigned a panel of justices as a means of transacting judicial and administrative business more expeditiously. One of their tasks was on occasion the assessment of tallage.

When the justices entered a shire, how did they ascertain the areas on which they were to assess the aid? Perhaps they were given a list of taxable areas, but since the sheriff would be familiar with the royal demesne and the lands in hand, they must have also

34. This group probably also tallaged Essex and Herts. *Pipe roll 33 Henry II*, p. xxxv.
35. *Ibid.*, pp. xxxv, 95, 184.

relied upon his assistance. They passed from county to county, and in each shire they divided into groups for purposes of taxation. Thus Richard of Ilchester and Guy, dean of Waltham, two of the five justices, assessed the aid on Colchester, Lincoln, the hundred of Milton, and Canterbury. Richard is mentioned as taxing Southampton unaided.[36] The *Dialogue of the Exchequer* states that two methods of assessment were employed. Either the justices and the men of the area agreed on a sum that was "worthy of the prince" (in commune) and the latter attended to the assessment themselves, or the justices made the assessment on the individual inhabitants (per capita).[37] This statement is confirmed by the evidence of the pipe rolls. The city of Canterbury promised a donum of £20 in common which they delivered to the sheriff. They evidently made the assessment themselves.[38] The men of Horncastle assessed the aid on their vill by grant of the justices in a different way from that made by the latter. In this case the justices assessed the aid at first per capita, but were persuaded to allow the villagers to make a reassessment.[39] The areas assessed in common would be those that paid a round sum, 1m., 20s., 2m., 5m., and upward.[40] Such sums suggest a bargain between the group as a whole or the lord and the justices, unless there is additional evidence that they were assessed per capita.[41] In assessments per capita the roll reveals the justices levying the aid upon the individuals within the areas that were able to pay. They drew up a roll of assessment of each of these areas and delivered it to the exchequer; often this roll was copied on the pipe roll and reveals something of the character of the assessment per capita.[42] The methods of assessment described as the established form in 1179, the probable date of the *Dialogue*, thus were in common use in 1168.

We have little evidence as to the method employed by the justices to ascertain whether the sum offered by the men of the area was adequate, or how the details of the assessment per capita were established. Probably they consulted with the men of the locality and the sheriff. The *Dialogue of the Exchequer* suggests such a

36. *Pipe roll 14 Henry III*, pp. 28, 76, 190, 213.
37. *Dialogus de scaccario*, p. 145.
38. *Pipe roll 14 Henry II*, p. 105. *Pipe roll 33 Henry II*, p. 209. *Pipe roll 34 Henry II*, p. 205.
39. *Pipe roll 14 Henry II*, p. 65. Ballard, *Borough charters*, p. lxxxi.
40. *Pipe roll 14 Henry II*, pp. 23–26. *Pipe roll 15 Henry II*, pp. 26, 27.
41. *Pipe roll 14 Henry II*, pp. 76, 103–104, 105.
42. *Ibid.*, pp. 40, 47, 48, 76, 129–133, 146–149, 213.

conclusion in its description of the method employed by the sheriff to ascertain whether the assessment "in common" was adequate or not when he was collecting the tax. If some alleged that they were unable to pay the assessment, the sheriff (the collector) was authorized to hold an inquest to determine whether "at the time when the gift or aid was settled upon by the citizens of the area, these persons had appeared incapable of paying the amount charged against them." [43] The result must be certified to the exchequer by the sheriff under oath, *per fidem vicecomitis*.

Now this procedure is incomprehensible if when the assessment was made the justices lacked information in some detail concerning the resources of the area. The details would include some idea of the number and wealth of the contributors. How otherwise would they be able to decide whether to accept the proffered gift or resort to the levy per capita? Hence some kind of discussion—probably not a formal inquest—ensued between the justices and the men of the area or their lord. In 1168 the considerable number of areas that were assessed per capita—while it seems unlikely that any areas in the recent past had been so taxed—suggests either that the proffered aids in common appeared inadequate to the justices, or that the latter had been instructed to levy the aid per capita on areas that had not been tallaged in this comprehensive fashion before. The same justices would be satisfied with the levy in common on some areas and insist on the tallage per capita on others.[44] It is likely therefore that the royal officials visited various parts of the shire, though probably not every vill. Perhaps groups of men from adjoining manors or towns met them at a convenient spot for the assessment. In any case, the time required for the assessment exceeded that of earlier levies, partly because of the great number of aids per capita, for the work was spread over two years. After the assessment had been completed, the justices delivered a copy of the roll to the exchequer and the sheriff received a duplicate copy, for he was the collector. In the case of the aid paid in common his role was simple. The men of the area (manor or town) had promised a certain sum; they allocated the shares among the property holders and collected it; then they paid it to the sheriff, who delivered it to the exchequer. If the whole sum was paid, the sheriff and the area were acquitted. The sheriff had no roll of the assessment or collection, merely a statement of the amount due from the

43. *Dialogus de scaccario*, p. 145.
44. *Pipe roll 14 Henry II*, pp. 103, 104, 129–131, 213.

aid. If however some taxpayers were delinquent, he was to make an inquiry into the default. If he found that the taxpayer had originally been unable to pay his assessment, then he was to compel the men of the area to allot his tax to others. If at the time of the assessment the debtor had been prosperous and then had met with such reverses that he was unable to meet his obligations to the government, the sheriff was to wait till he had recovered.[45] We should interpret this statement to mean that the sheriff expected to receive the whole sum with little delay, and the great bulk of the tallage usually was paid under Henry II by the Michaelmas exchequer of the year following the levy. However some places paid only part of their debt the first year; some seem to have paid nothing—at any rate the payment did not reach the exchequer.[46] Northampton promised £200 of aid and in 1170 still owed £6 13s. 4d.[47] The debt ran on till 1175 when the sheriff reported that this sum remained due from the land of the wife of Hugh Gubiun.[48] Two years later the debt was paid, but apparently without reallocation.[49] The government therefore sometimes allowed long delays in payment without apparently insisting on reassessment.

In the case of the aid per capita, the sheriff received a copy of the roll of assessment, probably collected the tax from the individual taxpayers, paid it in at the exchequer of receipt, and finally rendered the account at the upper exchequer. The exchequer officials were in doubt how to record such accounts so as to show the original assessment, the amounts paid, and the debts remaining against the individual taxpayers. They sometimes copied the roll of assessment of an area on the pipe roll, then stated the total amount paid, the number of tallies which the sheriff had presented from the lower exchequer, the total amount still due, and finally the amount still owed by each individual.[50] For example, the men of Axminster accounted for £16 6s. 8d. of the aid of 1168. The pipe roll clerk listed also the assessment of the fourteen persons taxed individually and the assessment on lesser people that were taxed as a group, the total amount paid (£11 10s.) and the amount still owed (£4 16s. 8d.), the amount each debtor still owed, the number of tallies (fifteen) cut for the sheriff in the lower exchequer which he presented as

45. *Dialogus de scaccario*, p. 145.
46. *Pipe roll 14 Henry II*, pp. 103–105, 129–132, 213.
47. *Pipe roll 15 Henry II*, p. 24.
48. *Pipe roll 21 Henry II*, p. 41.
49. *Pipe roll 23 Henry II*, p. 89.
50. *Pipe roll 14 Henry II*, pp. 103–104, 129–133, 147–148, 161–163.

vouchers, one for each person and one for the little special group, as if each had personally appeared at the exchequer.[51] With the expansion of the revenue in other lines, like amercements and the confiscation of the chattel of felons, the question was broached as to the extent to which the records of debtors should be written on the pipe roll as a means of supervising the collection of such debts.[52]

Such a procedure, it was found, would overload the roll with detail. The sheriff of Essex and Hertfordshire accounted for £77 19s. 11d. for the assarts of Essex, the waste of the forest, and amercements for forest offenses that had been combined in one sum, in accordance with the writ of Alan de Neville, because the items could not be contained in one roll.[53] Consequently in some cases the clerks explained that they had the detailed roll of assessment of a given area in the treasury but that it was too long to copy on the pipe roll; they stated the total sum paid into the treasury from that area with the number of tallies presented by the sheriff from the lower exchequer and the amount still due.[54] This made a much briefer account. In other cases the clerks wrote on the pipe roll the names of persons in an area who had paid part of their tax, with the amount that each was assessed, the amount each had paid and still owed, then the amount, if any, that a group of lesser men (*communa ville*) was assessed in common if they paid it only in part, the amount still due from each, and finally the sum charged against another group, "other men of the area," that had been completely paid, and the number of tallies (vouchers) presented for them at the upper exchequer.[55] In other cases however the clerks omitted such details of assessment and merely wrote down the amount assessed upon an area, the amount paid with the number of tallies, and the amount still due.[56] In some cases the farmer of the area rendered the account at the exchequer. Richard de Lucy accounted for the farm and the aid of Colchester; Robert Fitz Swein for Northampton; Ralph Blundus for Doncaster.[57] The number of tallies thus may correspond with the number of tallage payers from whom the sheriff had collected within an area assessed, or the number of groups that paid a sum in common as we have seen in Ax-

51. *Ibid.*, p. 129.
52. *Pipe roll 12 Henry II*, pp. 5–10, 33–34, 43–49. Hilary Jenkinson, "William Cade, a financier of the twelfth century," *English historical review*, XXVIII, 209.
53. *Pipe roll 15 Henry II*, p. 127.
54. *Pipe roll 14 Henry II*, pp. 76, 181, 190, 213.
55. *Ibid.*, pp. 40–41, 41–42, 47–48, 65–66.
56. *Ibid.*, pp. 217–218.
57. *Ibid.*, pp. 48, 53, 75–76.

minster, where fourteen persons accounted individually for their tallage, each receiving a tally, and a group of lesser men accounted for a sum of 2m. for which they received a tally as a group.[58] In form this was what happened; really the sheriff paid in these sums at the lower exchequer for each of fourteen individuals, receiving in return a tally for each and also one tally for the group of lesser men.[59]

In other areas some persons were entered by name as paying part of their tallage. For example, in Writtle, Joseph the clerk accounted for 1m. of the same aid. He paid ½m. and still owed ½m. Other men who were not named of that vill paid their whole tallage, and received seven tallies of receipt.[60] Sometimes the number of tallies represented the number of those who either paid in full or in part.[61] When the sheriff collected the tallage levied "in common" upon a whole area, or from a group of lesser men within a manor that paid him a lump sum, he paid the cash at the lower exchequer not for each person but for each area or group as a whole and received a single tally as evidence of the payment which he later presented at the upper exchequer. Thus a group of lesser men in Axminster paid 2m. de commune, and the lower exchequer issued a tally of receipt for this amount to the sheriff.[62] Similarly the sheriff accounted for the aid of Stanbridge, Eiton, and Weston to marry the king's daughter. He paid it into the treasury in three tallies (one for each manor) and was quit.[63]

The variety of entries employed in 1168 to enable the clerks to tabulate the debts of individual tallage payers in order to control the account, the debtors, and the sheriff too shows the novelty of the levy per capita upon the manors. Many individuals were represented as coming in person with their cash and accounts. Towns and rural areas seemed to have their own representatives. The sheriff was often omitted in the record of these transactions. Several considerations suggest however that he or the custodian ordinarily had collected the cash, paid it to the clerks of the lower exchequer, presenting either a tally for the individual taxpayer as a voucher or for the area as a whole.

First, in several instances, the rolls state that the sheriff or cus-

58. *Ibid.*, p. 129.
59. *Ibid.*, pp. 23, 40, 104, 127, 130, 132, 161–163.
60. *Ibid.*, p. 41.
61. *Ibid.*, pp. 40–42, 101–163, 181–182, 199. *Pipe roll 15 Henry II*, pp. 37, 109.
62. *Pipe roll 14 Henry II*, pp. 129–130.
63. *Pipe roll 15 Henry II*, pp. 90, 131, 173.

TALLAGE IN THE REIGN OF HENRY II 257

todian was the collector. Thus the sheriff of Northumberland collected from four vills—Sadberga, Newburn, Rowebena, and Bamborough—and the sheriff of Hampshire for the city of Winchester.[64] Second, in cases where boroughs, vills, and persons were rendering the accounts of their aid at the exchequer often for small sums, the sheriff was at the same time accounting for the farms of some of the same vills at the exchequer.[65] It would seem probable that the official who accounted for the farm would account for the aid of the same year. Third, sometimes in one county the area tallaged rendered its own account at the exchequer, while in another county the sheriff rendered it for similar areas (boroughs, vills).[66] Fourth, the receipt roll of 1184 shows that the clerks of the pipe roll were concerned with listing the names of debtors and amounts paid by them rather than the machinery of collection. Thus in the cases where an exact comparison can be made the receipt roll shows that the sheriff had received the money from debtors and paid it into the exchequer, while the pipe roll represents the debtors as rendering their account in person at the exchequer. So in the pipe roll Richard of St. Philibert accounted for 20s. *pro defectu;* in thesauro 10s., and he owed 10s. In the receipt roll the entry runs: "Received from the same [sheriff] 10s. for *misercordia* of Richard de St. Philibert." [67] While these entries came much later than the aid of 1168, they seem to embody a conventional practice.

In one respect the account of 1168 was different from that of later tallages, viz., in the smaller number of justices employed. That was due to ignorance of the extent of the task, particularly in view of the greater employment of the assessment per capita.

From 1168 to the close of the reign the system employed in 1168 continued with various amendments evolved from experience. The effort to assess and collect a tax on the demesne by only two or three groups of justices who were also levying scutages, holding pleas, and bargaining about *conventiones* required so much time that the aid on the demesne could not be finished before the following year. With this delay in mind, when the next aid was called for in 1173 the council divided the kingdom into circuits. Thirty-one shires appear in the roll, and twenty-seven of them were divided into six circuits. Thus the force of justices was greatly increased, and the

64. *Ibid.,* p. 131. *Pipe roll 14 Henry II,* p. 181.
65. *Ibid.,* pp. 15, 16, 23–25, 36, 40, 42, 47.
66. *Ibid.,* pp. 40–42, 181–182, 190.
67. *Receipt roll of the exchequer for Michaelmas term 1185,* ed. under the direction of Hubert Hall (London, 1899), p. 10.

amount of labor diminished for each group. As a result the work of assessment and collection was completed in 1173.

With this levy a marked change appears in the records on the pipe roll of the succeeding levies. In nearly every case the account represented the sheriff as the collector who rendered the account at the exchequer from each county, area by area. Occasionally a representative of a town that had evidently assessed and collected the sum that it had promised the assessors supplanted him at the exchequer, as in the case of London.[68] There is no list of individual persons rendering their accounts and few notices of tallies.[69] While there are some cases of the levy per capita, until 1187 most of the aids were made by the individual areas "in common." [70] The account is briefer and more uniform. The assessment per capita was passed over, perhaps because the assessors had the information of 1168 as a guide. They did not consider a detailed assessment each time as requisite. Is this not an indication that no careful evaluation of property was made? The revolt of 1173 made fresh taxation necessary, and in 1174 a supplementary aid was taken that was recorded in eighteen counties. Speed was evidently a consideration, for in nearly every case the sheriff was in charge in his shire, assisted by one or more small landholders. With the aids of 1177 and 1187 the circuits were again introduced. In 1187 a marked change was introduced in that nearly all the areas were assessed per capita. It may have been the extraordinary need that dictated this revision, but ten years had passed since the last aid, and it was felt that a new assessment should be made. However, since both methods of assessment were employed, the increase in the number of areas assessed per capita must be due to special instructions from the council. That body therefore believed that more fruitful returns lay in the assessment per capita. Is it not fair to conclude that they also thought a levy of this kind would come closer to the capacity to pay? Thus the levy of tallage was regarded as one of the prime tasks of the council. The development of this levy was not left in the hands of local officials, but received the attention of the central administration, and was developed pari passu with the new judicial system. Finance and justice went hand in hand.

A simplified statement in the pipe roll was adopted. The sheriff nearly always rendered the account; in most cases the clerks enter

68. *Pipe roll 20 Henry II*, p. 105.
69. *Pipe roll 22 Henry II*, pp. 34, 83.
70. *Pipe roll 19 Henry II*, pp. 48, 94, 101.

TALLAGE IN THE REIGN OF HENRY II 259

him as doing so, though they also clung to the old custom of writing down the area as rendering its own account.[71] They abandoned the device of copying the roll of assessment per capita on the pipe roll and of entering payments within areas by individual persons and their debts. While the sheriff presented tallies certifying the payments that he had made at the lower exchequer, the pipe roll clerks only recorded them if they entered two or more areas in a paragraph, one tally for each area, if the areas had paid in full.[72]

Thus they presented a uniform record by which the exchequer would know which towns or manors had paid in part and in full. In levies per capita, they omitted the names of persons in arrears, but they could ascertain them by comparing the names on the roll of collection with the assessment roll. It would seem however that the sheriff must himself have issued tallies as vouchers to the towns and rural areas, if they paid him a lump sum, and to persons from whom he collected individually. Upon him also would rest much of the responsibility for keeping an account of the details of the arrears.

By the close of Henry II's reign, the aids on the urban and rural demesne were taken from time to time on the occasion of some great need; the amount in each area was determined by negotiation between royal missi and the inhabitants or the lord of the area. While earlier called an aid, it could not be refused; though levied in general upon the royal demesne, the whole demesne as a unit was never consulted, the royal justices proceeding from area to area to arrange the assessment. The sheriffs, broadly speaking, collected it. The roll of areas, urban and rural, was drawn up for each shire and written on the pipe roll by shires, with the amounts paid, year by year, till the debt was discharged or dropped. The responsibility for collecting the tax and arrears from individual taxpayers was laid upon the sheriff, who alone of the local officials had any account of it.

Let us now turn to the period prior to 1168 and examine our levy. We shall find that the main adjustments were introduced in 1168. The number of towns taxed was smaller in the earlier period and there were almost no entries of aid on the rural demesne. The aids that show widespread returns were six in number with scattering entries in five other years. One comes from 1130, and two ad-

71. *Pipe roll 20 Henry II*, p. 105. *Pipe roll 23 Henry II*, p. 174. *Pipe roll 33 Henry II*, pp. 66, 133, 191–192.
72. *Pipe roll 23 Henry II*, pp. 56, 62, 78, 98, 207.

ditional doubtful levies appear in the roll of that year; the other five fall in the period from 1156 to 1165. Although a generation separated the aid of 1130 from the next recorded levy, the two taxes were essentially the same. The difference in the total amount charged, £678 3s. in 1156 as against £553 1s. in 1130, may be explained by the double levy of the aid on Lincoln for a total of £126 13s. 4d. in 1156 instead of £60 in 1130, and by the tax of £66 13s. 4d. on Milton in 1156, untaxed in 1130, and a few similar variations. About a third of the towns paid exactly the same amount both years.

The occasion for each levy in this series of aids was the same as later, a special need of the king for money. In the case of the first aid we are unable to state definitely the necessity, for the pipe roll of 1130 does not specify for what purposes it was raised. We can only suggest a reason. The year 1128 was one of heavy outlay. Henry I married his daughter Matilda to Geoffrey of Anjou; she would need a dowry. The same year he led an expedition into France. The Master of the Templars in Jerusalem, Hugh de Payens, visited France, England, and Scotland in 1128 seeking aid for the Holy Land. Henry received him with great honor, and gave him presents in gold and silver. In England many others gave him treasure.[73] Probably out of these events came not merely the aid of 1130 but also the request for aids in 1128 and 1129, which are noted in the pipe roll. No contemporary source however connects the taxes with any of these happenings. The early aids in Henry II's reign were specifically connected with war; in nearly every case they were correlated with a scutage.[74]

The method of assessment and collection of the early aids was essentially the same as in 1168. Special justices were appointed though not so elaborately organized; they were not so numerous as later and the number of circuits was not so large. The early pipe rolls contain no statement that the justices assessed the aid, but they were sent out to try cases and make new agreements with local people who desired some advantage from the king. The *nova placita et novae conventiones*, those of the current year, formed a regular section of the pipe rolls; the placita were amercements, the conventiones were agreements between the justices and those who de-

---

73. Henry of Huntingdon, pp. 237, 250. William Farrer, *An outline itinerary of King Henry I* (Oxford, 1920), pp. 123–124. *The Anglo-Saxon chronicle*, ed. and trans. by Benjamin Thorpe (Rolls series), II, 225.

74. James Fosdick Baldwin, *Scutage and knight service*, chap. ii. Stephenson, *Borough and town*, pp. 160–164, 222–223.

sired a favorable decision giving them an inheritance, a dowry, the postponement or the acceleration of a trial, or any such advantage.[75] The aids on the towns appeared in the roll under the heading of nova placita et novae conventiones, along with danegeld and aids of the county, and hence were probably assessed by the justices, who always performed a mixture of administrative and judicial tasks. Thus in the roll of 1130 Walter Espec and Eustace Fitz John had held new pleas in Yorkshire; Geoffrey de Clinton in Essex; Richard Basset and Aubrey de Vere in Sussex, Leicestershire, Norfolk, and Suffolk; Richard Basset and William de Albini in Lincolnshire.[76] In the roll of 1156 pleas were recorded that year or the year before, held by the constable Henry of Essex through most of the south, Thomas Becket acting with him in Kent and Essex; Gregory, bishop of Chichester, and Ralph Picot held pleas in Bucks and Bedfordshire, Surrey, and Middlesex; Richard de Lucy, later justiciar, also in Bucks and Bedfordshire; the archbishop of York held them in Yorkshire, and the bishop of Lincoln in Lincolnshire.[77]

In the succeeding pipe rolls (1157–65), only occasional references mention the justices who held pleas and no sections appear devoted to new pleas. If the sheriffs acted in this capacity, as Stubbs suggests, they could only do so as justices by virtue of a special command from the king. Usually the sheriff collected the aid and paid it to the exchequer, though the farmer of the town occasionally officiated.[78]

In these respects, the occasion for levying the aid and the method of assessment and collection, no difference in principle is discernible between the aids in the earlier and later parts of the reign. Nevertheless a gap separates the aids of 1168 and later from the earlier levies in administration, both in local and central machinery. How did this come about? The cause of the change was the great aid of 1168, when a concerted effort was made to raise an extraordinary sum on the occasion of one of the feudal aids, the marriage of Henry II's daughter. For example, in addition to the towns, the justices were instructed to lay under contribution certain lands in the king's hand and themselves to levy the tax as far as possible upon the individuals within the new areas that were to contribute. Here

---

75. *Dialogus de scaccario*, p. 142. Benedict of Peterborough, II, pp. lxiii–lxiv.
76. *Pipe roll 31 Henry I*, pp. 33, 34, 59, 70, 71, 88, 94, 114, 116, 117, 120.
77. *Pipe roll 2 Henry II, passim*.
78. *Pipe roll 31 Henry I*, pp. 138, 139. *Pipe roll 5 Henry II*, pp. 20, 68.

began an emphasis upon the assessment per capita. The council did not realize the additional work that the new instructions would entail, for evidently the number of justices appointed was not materially increased. Consequently the work of assessment and collection covered two years [79] and the problem of the accounts on the pipe roll presented new difficulties as we have seen. Hence arose in the later levies the increase in the number of justices, and a revised method of accounting built around the sheriff who ordinarily remained the collector. We have already described the two methods of assessing the tallage, in common, or by head, per capita. That is, either the townsmen or the men of the manor or its lord agreed with the justices to pay a lump sum in common, or if they were unable to reach an agreement on an amount satisfactory to both parties, the justices themselves assessed the levy on the individual persons. Beginning with 1168 the pipe rolls supply abundant examples of both methods. Both however show that the responsibility for paying the levy rested not upon the inhabitants as a group because of the bargain but on the individual tallage payers. This is obvious in the case of the levy per capita, though not so clear in the case of the levy in common.

The author of the *Dialogue* in his philosophical explanation of enforcing payment by the individual never thought of suggesting that the group as a whole was responsible for the levy although it had promised a certain sum. If a taxpayer did not pay, the sheriff was not empowered to seize city property or the property of the local assessors or of other citizens as an indication of the notion that they were responsible for the tax. He conducted an inquest to ascertain whether the local assessors had justly assessed this man, whether when the assessment was made he was able to pay or not. The inquest might show three possible conditions: first, that the debtor had property and revenue sufficient to pay his tallage; in that case, just as in the case of the levy per capita, the sheriff would seize his goods and lands, i.e., distrain him, until he had paid the debt. This is so obvious that the *Dialogue* does not mention it; but if the inquest showed that when the assessment was made the debtor had sufficient resources to pay his tallage but had lost them in the interim between the assessment and the collection, then the sheriff waited until the debtor had recovered his prosperity before he collected the debt; the third choice was that the inquest might show that this man who was now impoverished had no property or income

79. *Pipe rolls 14 and 15 Henry II.*

TALLAGE IN THE REIGN OF HENRY II 263

when the tallage was assessed, that is, an illegal assessment had been made. In such a case the amount of his tallage might be distributed among new tallage payers or the members of the original list. Thus the case illustrates the fact that the individual property holders were responsible for their tallage. By promising a lump sum they could apportion it among themselves as they desired. The inquest enabled the council to control the assessment in common to prevent evasions. The payment in common made possible to the townsmen a less heavy tax on the individual, if they succeeded in making a good bargain with the justices. Indeed the great men of the town might pay less by allotting larger shares of the tax to the less wealthy and influential than if it had been assessed by the skilled and powerful justices of the king, who might make the richer burgesses pay the most. In either case the final responsibility for the tax lay upon the individual, not on the group as a whole.

For example, the citizens of Winchester had paid all of their aid of £109 2s. levied in 1168 except £4 12s. 4d. by 1177. This amount was unpaid on account of the poverty of the taxpayers. It was not redistributed, but £4 4s. was pardoned by the king to Geoffrey Fitz Stigand (probably the original debtor) and the balance still remained charged against the sheriff.[80] Finally in 1182 this debt of 8s. 4d. was paid, we do not know by whom. Northampton promised £200 for the aid of 1168. By 1175 it had all been paid except £6 13s. 4d., which was charged against the wife of Hugh Gubiun, Hugh Gubiun probably being dead; the debt was paid two years later, probably by the wife.[81] The men of Malmesbury were assessed 10m. for this aid. They paid 81s. 8d. and owed 61s. 8d., assessed on Thomas Flemming. Then it appeared that Thomas had absconded and his whereabouts was unknown. The debt ran on for five years; the statement was repeated in the next two rolls and then dropped.[82] Thus the individual was responsible for his share of the aid. The rule of reapportionment was probably very difficult to enforce, because it went counter to custom.

Before 1168 there was no formal division into two methods of assessment. All the aids were lump sums, arranged by negotiation between the justices and the townsmen, even as early as 1130. The townspeople themselves adjusted the burden among their own mem-

80. *Pipe roll 23 Henry II*, p. 176. *Pipe roll 25 Henry II*, p. 104. *Pipe roll 28 Henry II*, p. 141.
81. *Pipe roll 21 Henry II*, p. 41. *Pipe roll 23 Henry II*, p. 89.
82. *Pipe roll 14 Henry II*, p. 162. *Pipe roll 19 Henry II*, p. 99. *Pipe roll 21 Henry II*, p. 101. *Pipe roll 22 Henry II*, p. 172.

264 TAXATION IN MEDIEVAL ENGLAND

bers. Sometimes they found that the total aid agreed upon was too heavy; on appeal to the king the town might be granted a pardon by writ of the king in whole or in part because of poverty (*pro paupertate*), as was done several times in 1130, or because of the waste caused by the civil war as in 1153 (*pro wasto*).[83] But many individuals also asked of the king a remission of some or all of their aid. If granted, a royal writ (*per breve regis*) instructed the collector to exempt each individual of a definite sum. The same procedure was followed in early levies of Henry II.[84] That the debt of the town really was incident permanently upon the individuals on whom it had been assessed is clear from the comments on the debts of two of the aids of London. In 1165 the city contracted to pay a donum of 500m. for the army of Wales (£333 6s. 8d.). That same year it was all paid or pardoned except £38 13s. 6d.[85] By 1171 the debt had been reduced to £18 13s. 6d.[86] This sum was definitely charged against the original debtors listed in the detailed account possessed by the sheriffs who declared that some of them were dead, others had no property, and the remainder had decamped.[87] No effort was made to reapportion the aid, a conclusion fortified by the later history of this and three other aids of London. The exchequer combined the outstanding debts of the four aids. The arrears amounted to £160 9s. 6d. Only one payment, 14s. 9d., was ever made, and the balance of £167 15s. 1d. remained in the roll year after year until 1201 when it was combined with other debts, but the new sum also remained unpaid.[88] If these aids were reapportioned, the measure had no effect. Thus although the aid was charged against the town the real obligation was incident upon individuals. Such a custom probably lay behind the device later adopted of the assessment per capita.

Beginning with the reign of Henry I there were various attempts to increase the returns from the aid on the demesne. The most obvious method from our viewpoint would be to increase the amount levied on each town, but we can say little about this at the beginning

83. *Pipe roll 31 Henry I*, pp. 6, 16, 63, 95, 138, 139. *Pipe roll 2 Henry II*, pp. 5, 14, 16, 20, 28, 37.
84. *Pipe roll 31 Henry I*, pp. 6, 23, 41, 52, 138, 149. *Pipe roll 2 Henry II*, pp. 4, 28. *Pipe roll 3 Henry II*, p. 94. *Pipe roll 5 Henry II*, pp. 35, 41, 46. *Pipe roll 7 Henry II*, p. 18.
85. *Pipe roll 11 Henry II*, p. 33.
86. *Pipe roll 19 Henry II*, p. 149.
87. *Ibid.*, p. 180. *Pipe roll 20 Henry II*, p. 50.
88. *Pipe roll 30 Henry II*, p. 138. *Pipe roll 33 Henry II*, p. 41. *Pipe roll 3 John*, p. 259.

in 1130. There are two cases which suggest that it was a fixed due: e.g., Wallingford, charged with £15 in three successive years (1128, 1129, and 1130), and Colchester, which seems to have been charged with £20 in 1129 and in 1130.[89] Furthermore ten of the towns in 1156 were charged with exactly the same amount as in 1130. The government of Henry II may have used old rolls as a guide in the assessment.

Another method of increasing the revenue from the aids was to make it into an annual due. In 1130 fifteen towns reported a sum due from a former aid, *de preterito auxilio*. The items are placed in the roll immediately before the nova placita, the pleas of the current year, and so it is likely that they were the arrears of one or two years immediately preceding. Three towns, Wallingford, Colchester, and Winchester, reported aids levied specifically in 1128, 1129, and 1130.[90] The attempt to levy the aid in successive years would explain the large number of towns (fifteen) that showed arrears of past aids, whereas only five were in arrears for the aid of 1130, partly because of the large amounts pardoned. Of the total sum levied in 1130, £553 1s., the towns paid in thesauro £358 11s. 1d., were pardoned £184 19s. 1d., and still owed £9 11s. 2d. That is, a third of the aid was written off. It would seem a fair inference that opposition had developed and that the cause could not be the high sums demanded but the repetition of the levy. The strength of the complaints is measured by the large percentage pardoned. The effort to expand the aid seems to have foundered.

In considering the development of the aid on the towns under Henry II let us recall that no statement has survived to show either the aims of the government or the reaction of the taxpayers. We have only the records of the amounts levied, paid, and pardoned, and very little information before 1173 of the methods of assessment and collection. We do not know whether the rolls contain a complete statement of the levies. Yet it seems fair to draw certain conclusions with some degree of assurance. Passing over Stephen's reign, we have five general levies before 1168, all resembling the aid of 1130. The number of towns taxed did not exceed 34. In 1130, 32 towns in 28 counties; in 1156, 30 towns in 24 counties; in 1161, 31 towns in 24 counties; in 1162, 25 towns in 20 shires, and in 1165, 30 towns in 17 counties. There was therefore no concerted effort over the period by the council to increase the number of areas taxed.

89. *Pipe roll 31 Henry I*, pp. 138, 139.
90. *Ibid.*, pp. 40, 138, 139.

We seem to be dealing with a conventional levy. The towns taxed also lay in all parts of the kingdom. We should recall that some towns paid aids also in other years, viz., 6 towns in 1158, 7 towns in 1160, and 3 towns in 1163. If conventional as to the number of taxable areas, considerable variation was exhibited in the number of times each area was taxed, and in the amounts placed on some towns from one levy to another. During this period York paid an aid seven times, ranging from £40 to £650 for a total of £1,634 13s. 4d.; London paid only three times, but it ranged from £120 at first through £666 13s. 4d. to £1,043. Norwich paid six times from £30 to £414 13s. 4d. By contrast fifteen towns, nearly half of the total number, show little or no increase over the amounts charged in 1130 or 1156.[91]

Fourteen towns paid five levies.[92] Eleven towns paid four times.[93] Eleven towns paid one, and nine (among them London, three times) paid two or three times. These variations indicate that this was not a purely automatic levy like the farm; it was taken at irregular times, depending on the need. A great expedition as in 1159, the French campaigns of 1160, 1161, and the campaign in Wales in 1165 would call for a widespread effort, as is reflected in the levies of 1159, 1161, and perhaps 1165. Possibly the other partial levies stem from local campaigns.

The variation in the sums levied on individual towns points both to the degree of need and to the fact that the amount was arranged by a bargain and not fixed at the will of the justices. But the king seems to have been endeavoring to increase the amount in individual cases and in frequency, in the direction consciously or unconsciously of an annual contribution. The year 1165 marks the abandonment of this effort toward an annual levy, for in the next twenty-three years only five aids on the towns were demanded. Does not this persistent struggle and partial yielding by the towns indicate that the king had some claim in custom to the aid rather than force? Does it not look like an attempt to develop a tax out of a customary levy, the aid on the demesne, to make a regular contribution out

---

91. Cambridge, Huntingdon, Hertford, Colchester, Winchester, Hereford, Canterbury, Ipswich, Thetford, Winchcomb, Guildford, Southwark, Wich, Rochester, Yarmouth.
92. Gloucester, Hereford, Canterbury, Rochester, Lincoln, Newcastle on Tyne, Northampton, Nottingham, Derby, Oxford, Shrewsbury, Stafford, Guildford, Southwark.
93. Bedford, Cambridge, Huntingdon, Exeter, Ilchester, Winchester, Ipswich, Thetford, Tamworth, Calne, Colchester.

of what had been an aid asked by the lord of the demesne on rare occasions in case of unusual necessity?

The expansion of the taxation of the towns and the rural demesne that were laid under contribution in 1168 offers a difficult problem. We may have to accept the explanation that Henry II or his ministers reflected on the expansion of the aid on the towns which they had effected and extended it by royal volition to about twenty hitherto untaxed areas, new towns, and to the rural demesne, including escheats and lands temporarily in hand, softening somewhat the exaction by calling it auxilium. By this theory a new tax on the demesne was created by royal command.[94] There is no doubt of the expansion and of the desire of the government for it and that such a general levy was unprecedented. But it was not wholly new. It was the expansion of an occasional levy which all feudal lords exacted. It has already been shown that the seignorial aid was well established in England in the thirteenth century, and that "it appears as a common aid taken by the feudal noble . . . from all his men. . . ." It is a great mistake to suppose that the baron's right of taxation was limited to his military tenants. The feudal aids were but one manifestation of a general authority exercised over all dependents.[95] While cases that illustrate its use are not numerous in the twelfth century, it seems to have been well established. Two religious houses granted lands in free tenure with the proviso that when they levied an aid from their free tenants, the recipient should participate.[96] From the turn of the eleventh century (1094–1113) comes an agreement between Walter, abbot of Burton, and a life tenant, Edwin. The latter was to hold for life lands held by his father for an annual payment of 20s. He was to entertain the abbot, and when he was in need and asked aid of his land and from his other men, Edwin was to aid him properly as his lord.[97] Thus three documents from three different shires early in the twelfth century refer to an occasional aid of the lord in time of need from his tenants which they ought to give in addition to the regular dues and services.

Let us now add to our statement further evidence that lords were accustomed from time to time to take aids from their nonmilitary

94. Stephenson, *Borough and town*, pp. 163, 164. Tait, *Mediaeval English borough*, p. 343.
95. Stephenson, "Seignorial tallage," pp. 465–466.
96. *Historia et cartularium monasterii Sancti Petri Gloucestriae*, ed. W. H. Hart (Rolls series), II, 220. *Cartularium monasterii de Rameseia*, I, 153.
97. Stephenson, "Seignorial tallage," p. 5.

tenants. Some fragmentary returns of the Inquest of Sheriffs of 1170 [98] have been preserved showing that lords were accustomed before 1170 to call upon the men of their demesnes for financial aid when there was great necessity—to pay the debts of the lord, to defray the expenses of a journey, or the like. Sometimes the aids were made *de bono animo, gratis, de bona voluntate*. They were made at irregular intervals; while in theory voluntary, the repetition of the grants suggests the existence of an element of compulsion. Thus the men of the soke of Dochinigia gave their lord 20m. "unjustly" after the king crossed the last time. The payment, which looks like one of these aids, was apparently unjust because in the time of King Henry (the First) they had given nothing except a just due.[99] The census was apparently the annual due; the special payment was the aid; apparently this soke had not been charged with an aid in the good old days of Henry I. But it is clear that there was an element of compulsion in the aid. On the manor of Snetesham the men of the demesne gave their lord, the earl of Arundel, 100s. after his campaign in the Marches of Wales; and at the same time Richard Fitz Atrac and his peers from a socage gave him 3m. gratis. Afterward the men of the earl's demesne gave 11m. to acquit his debts; Richard Fitz Atrac and his peers gave him 4m. to the same end and that freely (de bono voluntate). When the earl returned from France the men of the demesne again gave him 10m. and later another sum of 8½m.; while Richard Fitz Atrac and his peers gave him first 3½m. and again 3m. freely (de bono voluntate). These grants were apparently to discharge the earl's debts.[100]

The burgesses of Rising gave the earl of Arundel an aid to discharge his land of the debts owed the Jews and the roll of the levy has survived.[101] Lady Avelina, widow of Henry de Rye, took from Sumerton 10m. for knighting her son.[102] The men of Fekesham of the demesne of Robert Fitz Hugh freely gave him 13s. for the army of Wales and 20s. of aid to pay his debt to the Jews.[103] Reginald de Warenne, custodian of the heir of Henry de Rye, levied on Newton 5m. to marry Henry de Rye's daughter and again 5m. to stock this

98. J. H. Round, *The commune of London* (Westminster, 1899), p. 125. *Red book of the exchequer*, II, ccx, ccxi.
99. *Ibid.*, p. cclxxxi.
100. *Ibid.*, p. cclxvii.
101. *Ibid.*, p. cclxviii. For other cases see *ibid.*, pp. cclxix, cclxxii, cclxxiii, cclxxv, cclxxvi, cclxxvii, cclxxix, cclxxx, cclxxxi.
102. *Ibid.*, p. cclxxv.
103. *Ibid.*, p. cclxxvi.

TALLAGE IN THE REIGN OF HENRY II

manor.[104] That is, in time of great need the lord resorted to the tenants (nonmilitary) of his demesne for financial assistance and they gave it to him, even in successive years.[105] These aids clearly have nothing to do with the aids levied throughout the kingdom by the king. They represent the customary demands of the lord from the men of his demesne.

Turning now to a much later date we shall find the exchequer acting in the same way in escheated lands, evidently the continuation of a policy long pursued and unconnected with these special royal aids on the demesne. From 1185 exists a considerable list of aids levied either by the royal officials, by the custodians, or by the tenant on the men of his demesne. The levies are called aids and they seem to represent a custom of the lord. Round referred to them as aids exacted by the lords of manors.[106] He also connected them with the aids in the Inquests of 1170. Thus the sheriff took an aid of 10s. on an escheat while it was in the hand of a custodian.[107] William Basset was custodian of Berton and took from the men ½m. for their counsel and aid.[108] The land of Whitchurch was worth annually £20 "without aids and demesne and garden." [109] Hamo Fitz Hamo's land in Wolverton was worth annually £23 with demesne without pleas or tallages. Alice de Bidun had land in Morcote that was in the gift of the king. Besides the farm, she took from her land after the death of her husband 24s. of aid. The men of Alice de Beaufow gave her besides the farm 4s. and four summas of oats.[110] Herbert Blundus, ward of the king, had been put in the custody of the bishop of Ely; the heir received by the bishop's command 40s. of aid.[111] The men of two other manors belonging to Herbert gave him in aid 8m.[112]

Not only are there abundant notices that tenants levied aid on their demesnes from time to time when need was great, but the variety of needs indicates that the practice was old and well established. If an ordinary lay tenant exercised such a control over the free tenants on his demesne, we should expect that the king

---

104. *Ibid.*, p. cclxxiii.
105. *Ibid.*, p. cclxxxx.
106. *Rotuli de dominibus et pueris et puellis,* ed. J. H. Round (*Pipe Roll Society*), XXXV, p. xxx.
107. *Ibid.*, p. 10.
108. *Ibid.*, p. 21.
109. *Ibid.*, p. 34.
110. *Ibid.*, p. 45.
111. *Ibid.*, p. 63. For other cases see *ibid.*, pp. 46, 50.
112. *Ibid.*, p. 64.

would also enjoy the same rights on his demesnes, in addition to the ordinary dues. There is some indication of it in addition to his aids on the boroughs. In 1130 the burgesses of Grantham and the men holding of the soke owed £18 13s. 4d. of the donum of the king. Grantham was on the royal demesne.[113] This may be a donum on the royal demesne manors. The honor of Pembroke was in hand in 1130. Walter Fitz Witson, a tenant, owed 8m. of donum of the king, thus seemingly a donum levied by the king on an escheat.[114] The hundred of Milton in Kent in 1168 and afterward paid an aid or tallage. Now in 1156 the sheriff accounted for 100m. from the men of Milton.[115] The entry does not specify for what reason this sum was levied, but it follows two entries of aids on cities and an entry of the donum of the county and seems therefore to belong to this category of aids. The holding of Rusteshala, one fee, paid 10m. of aid in 1161; probably it was in hand.[116] A reference from the reign of Edward I (1275) which is recorded in an inquest declares that the men of King's Ripon of the ancient demesne of the king now (1275) were in the hands of the abbot of Ramsey. As a result of a dispute between the abbot and his tenants the inquest declared that the tenants owed certain rents and services and in addition, "of giving tallage whensoever the king tallaged his other manors and all their ancestors held these tenements by the said services till the Conquest of England and from the conquest till the time of King Henry, grandfather [sic!] of King John, grandfather of our present lord the king" (Edward I).[117]

Thus before 1168 certain boroughs and cities paid the assize, and undoubtedly the king, as other lords, took aids from his rural demesne and from escheats, or lands temporarily in hand. These rural areas that began to appear regularly in the pipe roll in 1168 as tallaged comprised only some of the ancient demesne and escheats or lands in the king's hand. Thus in Oxfordshire, apart from the city of Oxford, the following were tallaged in 1168:

Caveresham £20; Great Tew £8.

The men of Cudelinton and Weston were tallaged 40s.[118] Many

---

113. *Pipe roll 31 Henry I*, p. 114.
114. *Ibid.* p. 136.
115. *Pipe roll 2 Henry II*, p. 68. *Pipe roll 14 Henry II*, p. 213. *Pipe roll 19 Henry II*, p. 87.
116. *Pipe roll 7 Henry II*, p. 9. *Red book of the exchequer*, II, 483.
117. *Select pleas in manorial and other seignorial courts*, ed. F. W. Maitland (Selden Society) II, 100.
118. *Pipe roll 15 Henry II*, p. 83.

TALLAGE IN THE REIGN OF HENRY II 271

terrae datae were not enrolled as tallaged: Benton, Bensenton, Blockesham, and Hedendon, valued at £127 bl. and £77 8s. numero.[119] The omission of certain lands from the list of those taxed cannot be due to an imperfect report resulting from carelessness or ignorance of officials, for certain areas were regularly omitted. Nor can the omission be due to a stubborn opposition of the holder which could not be overcome; it would seem that some legal reason exempted certain manors from the tallage. Thus terrae datae were usually not tallaged. That is, the arrangements made between the council and the recipient of such areas seem to have exempted them from this levy. Many areas however that were farmed by the sheriff or other persons were tallaged. Many of the lands temporarily in hand were subject to this levy, yet often lands of this character were not subject. It would seem fair to conclude that the distinction was due to some arrangement made when the lands were delivered to the custodian. Thus Crendon, Wichendon, and Waddon belonging to the honor of Earl Giffard were tallaged in 1168–69, but Risenberga and Schiringeham, lands given to Richard de Humet, are not recorded as tallaged.[120] They were among the lands of that honor which were entered as terrae datae, and they do not appear this year or later under Henry II as tallaged.[121]

In Berkshire Richard de Lucy was granted Cookham and Bray as terrae datae. They were not tallaged in 1168 nor until 1187.[122] The cause of this change was probably the fact that the manors had been transferred from Richard de Lucy to Roger Fitz Renfrew.[123] That a shift in the holder might result in a change in financial arrangements is clear from the increased burden placed on Roger in connection with Bray. When Richard de Lucy was in possession he was charged with £60 bl. of farm, but he paid only 60s. blanched, the balance was pardoned by royal writ. Roger Fitz Renfrew however paid the full rent into the exchequer when he took over.[124]

Driffield was terra data allotted to the count of Aumale; it was

---

119. *Ibid.*, p. 82. Caversham was a demesne of the escheated honor of the Earls Giffard. *Pipe roll 19 Henry II*, p. 170. The land of Richard de Montaigu did not pay in 1168 but did in 1173. *Pipe roll 14 Henry II*, p. 140. *Pipe roll 19 Henry II*, p. 195.
120. *Pipe roll 14 Henry II*, p. 12. *Pipe roll 15 Henry II*, p. 90.
121. *Pipe roll 14 Henry II*, p. 12.
122. *Ibid.*, p. 200. *Pipe roll 23 Henry II*, p. 46. *Pipe roll 33 Henry II*, p. 191.
123. *Pipe roll 26 Henry II*, p. 38.
124. *Ibid.*, p. 42. *Pipe roll 14 Henry II*, p. 198.

not tallaged in 1168, 1173, or 1176. But in 1179 the sheriff began to account for the issues of this area, which the count of Aumale had held, and Driffield disappears from among terra data. In the next tallage (33 Henry II), Driffield was taxed for the first time, paying £25 19s. 4d.[125]

Lambourn, a rural area, was valued at £76. Part of it, valued at £66 bl., was terra data given to Hugh de Plugenoi, Henry Fitz Riulfi, and William de Lanvalay. The balance, Estbere, member of Lambourn, valued at £10 bl., was in the king's hand and paid tallage in 1168 and later.[126]

Fordham was terra data assigned to Leceline de Trailli, valued at £20 bl., and was not tallaged in 14 Henry II.[127] In 1173 it was tallaged £11 6s. 8d. and we find that the sheriff again accounts for it (no longer entirely in private hands as terra data). The next year this manor was assigned to Richard de Clare and Henry de Kemesech and valued at £20 bl., and no more tallage was levied on it under Henry II.[128] Manors that appear in the roll however for whose farms the sheriffs render the account were liable for tallage, that is, those manors whose custodians had not apparently made some special arrangement about tallage were subject to it, or the lands in 1168 that by custom paid it.[129]

Part of the great aid of 1159 was a donum of the sheriffs in fourteen shires amounting to 630m. This may have been a donum which they levied on the royal demesne.[130] A custom as well established as this seems to have been must have been the ground for the demand for an aid from the rural demesne of the king on an occasion as important as the marriage of his daughter, particularly when the military tenants were all paying an aid. What was new was the assessment and collection from all parts of the demesne at the same time for the same occasion. It revealed how great a source of revenue had been hitherto unexploited.

Henceforth the new method of levying the aid on part of the rural demesne throughout the realm became customary. In any case occasion, method of assessment, collection, and the entry on

125. *Pipe roll 25 Henry II*, p. 23. *Pipe roll 33 Henry II*, p. 91.
126. *Pipe roll 14 Henry II*, p. 200. *Pipe roll 15 Henry II*, p. 80.
127. *Pipe roll 14 Henry II*, pp. 100, 103.
128. *Pipe roll 19 Henry II*, pp. 159, 160. *Pipe roll 20 Henry II*, p. 63. *Pipe roll 23 Henry II*, p. 186. *Pipe roll 33 Henry II*, p. 81.
129. *Pipe roll 14 Henry II*, pp. 125, 129.
130. *Pipe roll 5 Henry II*, pp. 14, 17, 21, 25, 31, 37, 41, 46, 52, 59, 62.

TALLAGE IN THE REIGN OF HENRY II 273

the pipe roll of the aid on both the towns and the rural demesne were henceforth assimilated. The number of towns taxed rose from the neighborhood of thirty to between fifty and sixty.

The accompanying tables show that although the number of towns increased by about 60 per cent, the total amount charged against them did not materially increase over the levy of 1159, though the yield of the whole aid attained a higher level. The great addition was the charge against the rural demesne. Thus 1168 marked a transformation in taxation. Out of a casual contribution levied irregularly, an aid was developed, exacted on a given occasion, at first from all the towns and finally also from certain parts of the rural demesne. The initiative in effecting this change came from the royal government.

	Boroughs			Manors			Total		
	£	s.	d.	£	s.	d.	£	s.	d.
14 and 15 Henry II (34 shires)	2915	18	0	2346	9	4	5261	17	4
19 Henry II (31 shires)	2632	7	8	2020	17	11	4653	5	7
20 Henry II [131] (18 shires)	260	13	0	861	18	1	1122	11	1
23 Henry II (35 shires)	2505	13	4	2050	14	9	4556	9	0
33 Henry II (24 shires)	1577	11	1	2138	3	6	3715	14	7

The aid of 1159, levied exclusively on towns, amounted to £2723 6s. 8d.

If we compare the total of the aids on the towns in 1159 with that of 1168 and later, we observe that the levy of 1159 stands in second place, partly due to the great aid on London in the earlier year. The higher returns for 1168 over 1159 were clearly due to the thirty towns that paid the aid in the latter year. If we choose the towns taxed in 1159 and observe the total amount paid by them alone in the later aids of Henry II, the heaviest tallage was in 1159. If we omit London from this list, the heaviest levy was in 1168, with 1159 not far behind and 1161 appearing in third place. The tallage of 1187 was enrolled in only twenty-five shires; if we deduct from this list those towns omitted in 1187 the heaviest tax was still 1168, followed closely by 1159 and 1187 with 1161, 1173, and 1177 in order.[132] That is, omitting London, the burden of

131. This was evidently a supplementary levy. It covered eighteen shires that were taxed in 19 Henry II and three that were not.
132. Yield of the aid on the towns taxed in 1159 omitting London:

	£	s.	d.		£	s.	d.
1159	2723	6	8		1680	6	8
1161	1884	0	0		1218	6	8

tallage on individual towns was not steadily increased as we advance in the reign. Thus some check on the king's power in levying tallage existed. Broadly speaking, the levies were fairly completely paid, as will be seen from the accompanying table.

	Charged			Paid			Paid Later			Pardoned			Debita		
	£	s.	d.	£	s.	d.	£	s.	d.	£	s.	d.	£	s.	d.
1130	553	1	0	358	10	9	0	0	0	184	19	1	9	11	2
1156	678	3	0	562	9	6	0	0	0	115	9	4	0	0	0
1158	744	13	4	691	0	0	27	11	4	0	0	0	26	2	0
1159	2725	6	8	2538	14	1	157	17	11	28	6	10	0	13	4
1160	92	6	8	35	16	8	0	0	0	26	13	4	29	16	8
1161	1897	6	8	1701	12	0	87	3	4	60	4	8	48	6	8
1162	928	6	8	857	9	11	10	10	0	32	7	9	27	0	0
1163	56	13	4	56	13	4	0	0	0	0	0	0	0	0	0
1165	1237	0	8	1133	6	8	72	6	8	13	12	0	17	3	6
1168	5102	10	8	2216	9	9	2723	15	2	125	14	0	36	10	8
1173	4252	17	3	2373	4	6	1904	5	3	48	4	2	169	18	5
1174	891	0	7	726	4	4	57	9	8		?			?	
1177	4549	10	4	4249	8	3	70	16	2	116	3	8	113	2	3
1187	3706	17	1	1529	15	0	340	16	3	1483	17	3	337	1	0

The tallage of 1187 formed an exception to this rule. Only twenty-five counties appeared in the pipe roll of 1187 as assessed. Since in most cases this year the aid was assessed per capita, it is evident that despite the numerous justices, the work was not finished in time for the collection to be made and enrolled that year. Before the work was completed, the Saladin tithe was levied and probably it put a stop to the continuance of the assessment and collection of the tallage. Some sums were later paid, but in general

1168	2370	9	8	1753	12	0
1173	1789	2	8	1122	9	4
1177	1740	4	4	1073	11	0
1187	1020	9	9	1020	9	9

Yield of the aid on the towns taxed in 1159 omitting those not included in 1187:

	£	s.	d.
1159	1092	0	0
1161	884	0	0
1168	1304	18	8
1173	659	16	0
1177	592	17	8
1187	1020	9	9

Several towns were not taxed in 1173 and 1177 that appeared in 1187, but their totals were not great enough to affect the order.

TALLAGE IN THE REIGN OF HENRY II 275

the accounts were pardoned in the early years of Richard's reign because of the levy of the Saladin tithe.[133]

Probably the men on the demesne objected to paying the tallage when another aid of a new and startling kind was sought. Benedict of Peterborough states that Henry II himself met with groups of representatives at convenient times and places and arranged with them about the aid on movables of each town.[134] This special appeal by the king was perhaps motivated by criticism not alone of the newfangled aid but of its levy the year after the tallage had been exacted. Out of the opposition may have come the arrangement that the collection of this tallage should terminate, and perhaps too that sums already paid should be credited to the account of the Saladin tithe. No notice of this substitution has survived.

We must now turn to two allied questions—on what was the aid based and how was the amount assessed on an area or person determined? When the assessment was made either on an area as a whole or on a person, the justices followed a customary method employed in dues or offerings made at the same time. Scutage was levied at a rate per fee, but there was no similar uniform unit on which to calculate the tallage. An amercement might be a round sum, which would be allocated to various property holders, according to some bargain with the justices or the sheriff. For example, the honor of Blythe was amerced 40m. by the justices: they paid in thesauro £12 13s. 4d.; Ralph Taison was pardoned 8m.; Ralph Fitz William 40s.; the lesser men of Blythe 7m., and the honor still owed 40s.[135] Probably the capacity to pay played a part in determining the amount each owed; the lesser men (*minuti homines*) had 7m. alloted to them, and they in turn in some rough way divided the financial responsibility. Thus the apportionment of the aid probably resembled that employed in allotting murdrum or an amercement. The basis of the aid was the possession of land or goods. In 1169 the vill of Burton still owed 23s. of aid. William, a clerk, was pardoned by the king's writ 18s. because he had no lay fee and no merchandise.[136] Men paid the aid on assarts.[137] One hide of land paid 12s.[138] A carucate paid 10s.[139] In 1157 the char-

133. *Pipe roll 3 Richard I*, pp. 73–74, 83, 87–88, 95, 113. *Pipe roll 6 Richard I*, pp. 167–168, 173. *Pipe roll 2 John*, p. 93.
134. Benedict of Peterborough, II, 33.
135. *Pipe roll 31 Henry I*, p. 30.
136. *Pipe roll 15 Henry II*, p. 75.
137. *Pipe roll 19 Henry II*, p. 181.
138. *Pipe roll 23 Henry II*, p. 163.
139. *Pipe roll 15 Henry II*, p. 36.

ter of Lincoln stated that all men who dwelt within the four parts of the city and carried on trade would be subject to geld and customs and assizes of the city, as they had been liable in the times of Edward and William and Henry, kings of England.[140]

The amount of aid that was assessed on each person or area was not determined by an exact valuation of goods and land. The *Dialogue of the Exchequer* indicates that the sum agreed upon with the justices either for an individual or an area was arrived at by negotiation. Thus, "if it has been said by the citizens: 'We will give the king a thousand pounds' and this sum is judged worthy to be received, they themselves must provide that at the stated terms, the same is paid." This is not the way an experienced financial official would have described an assessment of property.[141]

The conclusion is confirmed by the evidence of the pipe rolls. Towns and manors were assessed in round numbers. The levies per capita may make the sums charged against areas uneven amounts, but the charges against individual persons were round sums. These are very different from actual assessments of movables as shown in the rolls of Henry III that present a picture of varying, irregular amounts. Consider also the differences in the valuations of movables in the case of fugitives that exhibit no such regularity.[142]

About 120 vills or manors appear as tallaged each time in 1168, 1173, 1177, and 1187. The sum assessed is remarkably uniform for the four years: 1168, £852 11s. 4d.; 1173, £813 19s. 6d.; 1174, £559 18s. 10d.; 1177, £790 2s. 4d.; 1187, £604 16s. 7d. The uniformity is deceptive and at the same time revealing. It does not mean that the individual areas were taxed at a uniform amount each time, for often the variation is very great. A manor may pay two or three times as much at one time as another. Nevertheless, these variations were within limits. A heavy assessment one year may be followed by a light assessment. These uniform totals indicate that there was no general trend upward, certainly the tallage did not keep pace with the increasing accumulation of movable property.

We have seen that despite the increased number of boroughs the total assessment on the boroughs did not increase, except in 1168, over the yield in connection with the great levy of 1159 for the ex-

---

140. Ballard, *Borough charters*, p. 108.
141. *Dialogus de scaccario*, p. 116.
142. *Pipe roll 23 Henry II*, p. 41.

TALLAGE IN THE REIGN OF HENRY II

pedition against Toulouse. Thus broadly speaking the levies allow one to compare the tallages on boroughs with the borough farms and the tallages on the rural areas with the farms on those areas. In a high proportion of cases the tallage on a borough was often as much or more than the farm, while the tallage on a rural area was generally less than the farm, usually varying from a third down even to a fifteenth part. How shall we account for this disparity?

One hesitates to draw an inference without more exact information about the internal finances of the manor. Were the justices able to exact more from the town because of the greater use of money among the townspeople? Was it because in rural districts services and payments in kind were more common and the use of money exceptional, or perhaps believed to be exceptional? As a matter of fact the manors were able to pay their tallages as quickly as the towns. Might they not have paid larger sums almost as readily? Was the landed magnate, the farmer of parts of the royal demesne, more influential in negotiation with the justices than the townsmen? Certainly some influence protected the rural area more effectively than the urban. Both towns and manors paid the aid promptly.

TABLE I
The Aids on the Urban Demesne

	1159	1168	1173	1174	1177	1187	Amount of Farms Henry II
	£ s. d.	£ s. d.	£ s. d.	£ s. d.	£ s. d.	£ s. d.	£ s. d.
Bedford	26 13 4	16 13 4	16 0 0	16 13 4	66 13 4		40 0 0
Buckingham		7 0 0	4 0 0	4 0 0	6 13 4		
Cambridge	6 13 4	33 6 8	40 0 0		20 0 0	73 10 0	60 0 0
Godmuncester			20 0 0				
Huntingdon	13 6 8	6 13 4	26 13 4			36 3 4	20 (1173–74) 80
Wallingford	10 0 0					10 0 0	40 0 0
Carlisle	13 6 8	33 6 8				40 0 0	
Helleston						38 19 8	
Exeter	263 13 4	133 6 8	40 0 0		66 13 4		12 19 (Rich. I)
Dorchester						15 11 8	
Ilchester	24 13 4	6 13 4	5 0 0	2 10 0	6 13 4	8 9 6	30 0 0
Warham						40 0 0	
York	133 6 8	333 6 8	76 2 8		133 6 8	226 6 4	100 (Rich. I) 34 0 0
Scarborough		40 0 0			13 6 8	34 0 0	20 0 0
Doncaster		33 6 8		66 13 4	26 13 4		
Hertford		18 10 0	6 13 4	20 7 0	13 6 8		24 (1154 and 1155)
Newport		6 6 8	20 0 12	20 0 0	13 6 8	12 3 4	

TAXATION IN MEDIEVAL ENGLAND

	1159			1168			1173			1174			1177			1187			Amount of Farms Henry II		
	£	s.	d.	£	s.	d.	£	s.	d.	£	s.	d.	£	s.	d.	£	s.	d.	£	s.	d.
Maldon				7	2	8				15	0	0	4	13	4	10	3	4			
Berchamsted				33	0	0	22	0	0				29	6	8						
Colchester	13	6	8	32	0	0	33	6	8				20	0	0	13	6	8	40	0	0
Winchcomb				2	3	4	1	6	8	1	0	0	2	13	4	1	6	8	50	0	0
Gloucester	66	13	4	77	13	4	66	13	4	33	6	8	66	13	4				55	0	0
Cirencester				15	6	8	3	6	8	8	13	4	13	6	8	13	6	8			
Winchester	133	3	4	109	2	0	53	6	8							93	11	7	142	0	0
																			300	0	0
Southampton				29	13	4							20	0	0	32	13	4	200	0	0
Hereford	33	6	8	20	0	0	10	0	0	6	13	4	26	13	4	10	0	0	40	0	0
Rochester	5	0	0	9	13	4							26	13	4	7	10	0			
Canterbury				72	13	4	46	13	4				66	13	4	20	0	0	49	0	0
																			500	0	0
London	1043	0	0	617	17	8	666	13	4*				666	13	4				22	0	0
Grimsby				14	0	0				52	19	4	13	6	8	45	15	0	111	0	0
Horncaster				29	3	4															
Lincoln	133	3	4	233	6	8	266	13	4				100	0	0	176	4	0	180	0	0
Loingeland				30	0	0	40	0	0				26	13	4	30	6	4			
Preston													16	10	0						
Dunwich				133	6	8							100	0	0	66	13	4	120	0	0†
Ipswich	5	0	0	53	6	8	46	13	4				13	6	8	16	0	0			
Thetford	6	13	4	26	13	4	23	6	8				13	6	8	3	3	0			
Norwich	414	13	4	200	0	0	133	6	8				66	13	4	93	16	8	108 (Rich. I)		
																			24	0	0
Oreford							13	6	8				10	0	0	20	16	8	40	0	0
Newcastle (Nld)	40	0	0	40	0	0							26	13	4	46	13	4			
Yarmouth				10	0	0	13	6	8				13	6	8	26	13	4	40 (1156)		
Len													53	6	8						
Colebrigge	6	13	4	46	13	4							20	16	8	29	3	8			
																			100	0	0
Northampton	133	6	8	133	6	8	200	0	0				200	0	0				120	0	0
Nottingham	13	6	8	20	0	0				31	1	8							52 (Rich. II)		
Derby	6	13	4	26	13	4				20	0	0	14	0	0				60 (Rich. I)		
Oxford	78	0	0	20	0	0	40	0	0	33	6	8	66	13	4				20	0	0
Shrewsbury	33	6	8	18	13	4				40	0	0	13	6	8	43	13	4	26	0	0
Bruges	6	13	4	4	10	0				10	0	0	13	6	8	10	0	0			
Stafford	10	0	0	32	0	0	10	0	0				13	6	8	13	0	0			
Newcastle (Staff)				4	6	8	23	6	8				3	6	8	15	4	8			
Tamworth	5	0	0	2	0	0							2	6	8	2	3	4			
Southwark	6	13	4	12	13	4							13	6	8	12	17	8			
Guildford	6	13	4	9	6	8	6	13	4				20	0	0	9	10	0			
Chichester	3	6	8	13	0	0							13	6	8	26	10	0	38 10 (Rich. I)		
Calne	1	6	8	3	0	0	2	0	0	2	0	0	3	0	0	8	17	4			
Malmesbury				6	13	4	3	6	8				13	6	8	9	13	4			
Wilton				10	6	8	5	0	0	5	0	0	13	6	8	25	6	6			
Salisbury				6	13	4	1	0	0	1	0	0	13	6	8	4	19	8			
Marlborough							26	13	4				26	13	4	40	0	0			
Worcester	40	0	0	26	13	4	26	13	4				26	13	4	20	0	0	24	0	0
Tamworth (W & L)				1	6	8							1	0	0						
Totals				2842	9	0	2029	3	0	389	24	8	2253	6	8	1534	3	3			

* A tallage of £666 13s. 4d. on London in 1171 and the same amount in 1173.
† Plus 24,000 herrings.

TALLAGE IN THE REIGN OF HENRY II 279

TABLE II

A Partial List of the Aids on the Rural Demesne.

	1168			1173			1174			1177			1187		
	£	s.	d.	£	s.	d.	£	s.	d.	£	s.	d.	£	s.	d.
Aylesbury	10	0	0	8	0	8	6	13	4	13	6	8			
Luton	20	0	0	23	6	8	20	0	0	26	13	4			
Wantage	6	13	4	6	13	4	5	0	0	16	13	4	9	14	8
Alconbury	2	0	0	6	13	4	0	0	0	6	13	4	10	6	8
Saham	6	13	4	6	13	4	0	0	0	8	0	0	29	3	4
Bottisham	20	0	0	17	10	4	0	0	0	8	0	0	5	13	4
Braunton	14	6	8	6	0	0	0	0	0	1	6	8	1	12	0
Congresbury	26	13	4	10	0	0	5	0	0	12	0	0	6	8	10
Waltham	10	3	4	17	13	4	26	13	4	26	13	4	14	2	8
Havering	4	13	4	10	2	4	20	0	0	10	0	0	11	3	4
Cheltenham	4	13	4	3	0	0	2	6	8	5	0	0	2	0	0
Andover	7	16	8	8	18	0	5	8	0	6	13	4	17	15	6
Aulton	10	16	8	10	8	0	5	6	8	11	13	4	12	2	8
Meon	10	0	0	13	6	8	0	0	0	49	6	8	28	12	8
Milton	132	13	4	66	13	4	0	0	0	40	0	0	38	13	4
Foulsham	20	0	0	26	13	4	0	0	0	16	13	4	15	0	0
Banham	3	6	8	6	13	4	0	0	0	6	13	4	1	13	4
Mansfield	13	6	8	12	0	22	16	15	4	4	0	0			
Caversham	13	6	8	10	0	0	6	13	4	10	0	0			
Worfield	1	6	8	0	0	0	8	13	4	10	0	0	3	2	6
Bromley	2	0	0	12	0	0	0	0	0	2	0	0	2	0	0
Tettenhall	1	3	4	4	13	4	0	0	0	0	13	4	3	3	8
Wolverhampton	2	13	4	2	0	0	0	0	0	1	6	8	1	14	0
Woking	2	16	8	4	0	0	0	0	0	13	6	8	3	8	8
Bramley	0	0	0	55	6	8	0	0	0	13	6	8	13	7	8
Bosham	6	17	8	18	18	0	0	0	0	13	6	8	6	16	8
Feckenham	2	0	0	0	0	0	3	6	6	3	6	8	2	3	0
Melksham	9	6	8	6	4	0	6	16	8	8	0	0	8	8	4
Bedwin	4	0	0	3	6	8	2	0	0	?	13	4	7	9	6

TABLE III

Tallages and Farms

	Farms of Manors 14 and 15 Henry II.			Tallages 14 and 15 Henry II.		
	£	s.	d.	£	s.	d.
Eiton	20	0	0			
Stanbrigge	8	0	0		100	
Weston	15	0	0			

	Farms of Manors 14 and 15 Henry II.			Tallages 14 and 15 Henry II.		
	£	s.	d.	£	s.	d.
Wycombe	72	0	0	8	13	4
Edulfberge	14	7	0		40	
Ravenston	7	13	4			
Estbena	10	0	0		13	4
Ferendum	145	0	0	6	13	4
Ketelestam	24	0	0	1	6	8
Lefton	15	0	0	3	6	8
Kenton	34	0	0	10	0	0
Fenotri	4	4	8		13	4
Ailricheston	3	0	0	2	0	0
Wichton	30	0	0	24	13	4
Wartre	30	0	0	13	0	0
Usebrunna	8	6	8	1	6	8
Sumburn	36	6	0	4	3	4
Ulferton	10	0	0	1	6	8
Osprimga	50	0	0	8	6	8
Newton	12	8	0	2	0	0
Buccheshal	5	0	0	1	0	0
Wihton	40	18	10	13	6	8
Meleburn	23	4	4	4	0	0
Bulewella	5	0	0		13	4
Hecham	120	0	0	10	0	0
Torp	15	0	0	13	6	8
Bosham	100	0	0	8	17	8
Bedingham	10	0	0	2	0	0
Henley	12	0	0	1	6	8
Bisselega	6	10	0		13	4
Efre	40	0	0			
Eiton	24	4	0	11	6	8
Chalgrave	33	19	6			

We must now ask who paid the tallage in the later years of the twelfth century among the inhabitants of the cities and boroughs, of the royal manors, and of demesne lands temporarily in the king's possession. Was it everyone or only certain specified persons? Were they the freemen or the serfs? Was it a list of the well to do that had become established by custom?

In boroughs and cities in the early history of the auxilium, freemen of all grades paid it, if we may judge from the exemptions that appear in the pipe roll of 1130. We see earls, bishops, clerks,

TALLAGE IN THE REIGN OF HENRY II

tenants in chief, alongside of freemen in the humble ranks of life. Thus in Winchester there was William Mauduit (Maledoctus), who was a landholder in both England and Normandy; the count of Meulan, Michael the usher, apparently of the exchequer or the chamber; the earls of Leicester and Gloucester; Earl Warenne; Adam the Chamberlain, an officer of the king's household; Anselm the sheriff; the abbess of Winchester; the bishop of Winchester; the bishop of Salisbury; the Chancellor; Nigel the nephew of the bishop of Salisbury; William de Pont de l'Arche, sheriff of Hants; Thurston the clerk, and others who have no such distinctive descriptions and so were probably burgesses of the city.[143] There were Sareto the sergeant, the men holding of the soke of Grantham, the thegns, drengs, and inferior tenants between the Tyne and the Tweed, the monks of Northampton, Erald the mason, the demesne carucates of the king of the land of Eudo the steward, a weaver of London, Conan the mason, Aluric the fat, Herman Boselin, Nicholas the mercer, the cobbler of the queen, Roger the usher, Manasser Biset and Henry Fitz Gerald in Rochester, and Roger the usher of the treasury.[144] These examples of exemptions could be multiplied from this pipe roll. Sometimes the aid was called the aid of the burgesses, an indication of the character of the taxpayers.[145]

Under Henry II in cities and boroughs it was paid by the citizens and burgesses, moneyers, and any others who dwelt within the walls and carried on business, or merely dwelt in a borough, whether or not they formed part of the body of burgesses.[146]

One great change is obvious as we advance into the reign of Henry II: the absence of the long lists of men who were exempted from the aid or donum, characteristic of the entries under Henry I. Such exemptions practically disappeared in the fifth year of Henry II. Many of those exempted had been men of high rank in church and state, great feudal lords and churchmen. What has happened? Do such great men no longer pay the tallage, no longer even appear as charged with it?

On the rural demesne, both free and unfree paid the aid. In the account of 1168 many names of persons appear in the pipe roll

143. *Pipe roll 31 Henry I*, p. 41.
144. *Ibid.*, pp. 47, 114, 132, 136, 138, 190. *Pipe roll 2 Henry II*, p. 5. *Pipe roll 5 Henry II*, pp. 53, 59. *Pipe roll 6 Henry II*, p. 45.
145. *Ibid.*, pp. 9, 12.
146. *Pipe roll 14 Henry II*, pp. 129, 131. *Pipe roll 15 Henry II*, p. 36. *Pipe roll 33 Henry II*, p. 200. Ballard, *Borough charters*, p. 108.

copied from the rolls of assessment or collection, but such entries tell nothing about their status except when they are qualified as *presbytu* (a freeman), or *prepositus*, sometimes, perhaps always, a villein, or a sokeman who might be free or villein.[147] Many cases appear where "homines" render the account of the aid and that noun might mean either free or serf. Once in 1177 the clerks of the pipe roll record that the sheriff of Gloucestershire accounted for 3*m*. of aid from the men of Badgworth and Ederlega and also 3*m*. from the freemen of the same vill.[148] Thus it is evident that *homo* may mean "unfree man" and that both free and unfree were subject to the aid. Two other terms used interchangeably seem to have the same significance, the unfree, viz., minuti homines, those not completely free. Thus in Caistor six men were listed each with the amount of aid assessed, the least sum being for ½*m*. "Other" (*ceteri*) men (49 in all) accounted for £21 of that aid, an average of less than 10*s*. each, then, minuti homines accounted for 53*s*. 4*d*.[149] In Grimsby six men were listed separately with their assessment, each either 20*s*. or 2*m*. The minuti homines were lumped at 2*m*. The "other" men of the vill (fifteen) were lumped at £6 6*s*. 8*d*., an average of less than 1*m*. each. In both these vills the sheriff accounted for all the aid payers individually but for the minuti homines as a group.

In neither case do we know the number of the minuti homines. But there must be some characteristic that divides them from the other men. In Oxford the line that separated them was between burgesses and nonburgesses.[150] An entry concerning Bedford suggests that the expression *de communi ville* refers to the minuti homines. The sheriff accounted thirty men who are named in his assessment roll of Bedford for the aid for so much and for 5*m*. of the commune of that vill (borough).[151]

It seems fair therefore to conclude that the aid was levied on both free and unfree. If it is true that the royal tallage included both these classes on the king's demesne, it is the continuation of the original custom of the lord's aid on his demesne, maintained by the growing use of money by both servile and free tenants. It was not a new development. The villeins and freemen on the royal manors that paid an annual tallage, as did serfs and freemen on the

147. *Pipe roll 15 Henry II*, p. 44. *Pipe roll 23 Henry II*, p. 133.
148. *Pipe roll 23 Henry II*, p. 46.
149. *Pipe roll 14 Henry II*, p. 66.
150. *Pipe roll 15 Henry II*, p. 85.
151. *Pipe roll 14 Henry II*, pp. 145–146.

TALLAGE IN THE REIGN OF HENRY II 283

manors of other lords, probably would not pay the special occasional aid to the king. If the aid began, as we have suggested, in an occasional aid to the king in time of great need, we should expect overlapping of the classes. The assessment rolls of rural and to a less degree of urban areas give some notion of the amount assessed on individual taxpayers. The sums range in general from ½m. to 3m., though some rise as high as 10m. (£6 13s. 4d.) or even more.[152] The minuti homines must have individually paid much less, for the sum total charged against them in most places was small.[153]

Some vills were charged with 1m. or 20s., or 2m.[154] Thus while some of the taxpayers fell into the group of petty property holders some of whom were unfree (villeins), the majority were men of substance. Recall that the aid of 1168 on knights' fees was at the rate of 1m. per fee. Many subject to the aid in borough and manor paid as much or more than the holders of one or more knights' fees.

Thus in the course of the twelfth century, the aids on the towns, on the ancient rural demesne of the king, and on some of the lands that came into the king's possession by the operation of feudal law developed into one of the most important sources of the occasional royal revenue. From our earliest references it was authorized on areas in all parts of the kingdom, assessed by justices specially appointed by the council, and collected by the sheriff or other royal official by special command. Hence it was accounted for at the exchequer and entered on the pipe roll.

The appearance of the account of this levy in the pipe roll has led to the conclusion that the king arbitrarily assessed it as a new tax. Thus in 1168 appeared for the first time this general aid on the rural demesne and it might be assumed the earlier general levies on towns that appear in the pipe roll of 1130 were similarly authorized by the arbitrary action of the council and king. But we have seen much evidence that lords on occasion of great need sought and obtained aids from the men on their demesnes or on lands in hand. The king was the greatest lord and he too could levy such aids. There is also some indication that he obtained such aids. It is likely therefore that the change recorded in the pipe rolls was the systematic levy of aid by the council on the royal demesne as a whole, for an occasion that affected the king as lord of all England instead of a local need; consequently he ordered it to be assessed

152. *Ibid.*, pp. 103–104, 129–134, 147–148.
153. *Ibid.*, pp. 40, 41, 104, 105, 130, 131, 132, 147–148, 195.
154. *Ibid.*, pp. 23, 24, 103, 129.

and collected by royal officials and accounted for in the national exchequer. The aid on the individual manors and towns of the demesne therefore was transformed into a general levy determined by a kingdomwide regulation out of a series of local levies each determined by customary rules of each area.

The aid on the demesne retained the original character of the manorial aid taken by the lord in the method of assessment. For the amount was always determined by negotiation between the royal officials and the lord or the men of individual areas, urban or rural. In this process, the justices undoubtedly emphasized the capacity of the latter to pay, but there is no evidence that the levy was based upon a valuation of revenues or movables, made under the direction of royal officials. It is true that in the case of London later the citizens raised a fine for the king and perhaps took a tallage by such an assessment. But this was a regulation within their competence. The royal officials had nothing to do with it. This tallage never evolved into a tax of this kind any more than the scutage evolved into a general tax on land. The inability of the council to introduce a change so advantageous to the royal government suggests that the aid itself must have developed out of an existing levy.

VI

TALLAGE UNDER RICHARD I AND JOHN

THE experiments made by the government with tallage were coincident with efforts to augment the revenue by taxes on property, scutage, feudal and customary dues and fines, and the revenues from the royal demesne, escheats, and other lands for the time being in the king's possession by action of the law, and by taxes on property. It does not seem altogether fair to say that the king's need of a money revenue under Richard and John was greater than under Henry II; although perhaps the increasing use of money in the commutation of services and payments in kind, the rise in prices, and the increasing expense of war may have been dimly perceived. Certainly the huge returns from the Saladin tithe and the aids for Richard's ransom must have impressed the government with the monetary wealth of the kingdom. In the light of such conditions, certain changes in tallage betoken at first an unconscious trend in the character of the levy and then a deliberate intention of changing it from an occasional to a much more frequent exaction. This is the period when the assisa, or donum, or auxilium on the royal demesne changed its name to tallagium, a term occasionally employed under Henry II in the pipe roll and in charters, till with the last aid on the demesne levied in the reign of Henry II, a sudden increase in the use of tallagium occurred.[1] In ten counties the title of the aid on the demesne was "Of the tallage of the demesnes of the king and of the lands that were then in his hand." Moreover several other cases of the use of the term occur, though not nearly so many as of the older forms descriptive of the levy, donum, auxilium, or assisa. It is however impossible to detect the slightest difference between the thing called tallagium and that designated by the other terms. Indeed while the title of the levy was tallagium in the pipe roll, the items under it were usually donum, auxilium, or assisa.

For Richard's ransom the levy of a fourth of revenues and mov-

[1] *Pipe roll 21 Henry II*, pp. 5, 8, 9. *Pipe roll 23 Henry II*, pp. 96, 134, 154. Adolphus Ballard, *Borough charters*, pp. 108, 185.

ables was paid also by property holders on the demesne. After the king's return in 1194 additional cash was necessary to complete the ransom, and consequently a tallage on the demesne was levied. In this connection Hubert Walter personally visited some of the great towns and secured from them promises of sums which were enrolled as auxilia, as though they were voluntary grants, whereas all the rest of the demesne paid tallagia. Here there were two levies on the demesne, one voluntary, the other obligatory; the one based upon an assessment of movable property and revenue, the other a conventional levy arranged by a bargain between assessors and taxpayers. Thus the feeling probably arose among the council of the need of a term to designate the obligatory due, tallagium, lest it take on the nature of a voluntary grant, the new auxilium. Hence the remarkable expansion on the pipe roll of tallagium as the proper term to apply to the ancient obligatory assisa, donum, or auxilium of the demesne. If this levy had really been a voluntary grant, no problem would have arisen at this time if it had continued to be designated by the old terms. However, as often happens, while the term tallagium predominated, the clerks continued to write occasionally donum and auxilium as synonymous with tallagium and for a long time no difficulty resulted. Yet the distinction remained clear in the minds of the council. In 1204 the men of Odiham promised 20m. as a fine in aid of the king's passage to France. The king declined to accept the fine for fear that he might lose the right to tallage the manor.[2] The issue was not the amount of the donation, for only once and that afterward, did the tallage of Odiham reach 20m.

The occasions on which tallage was levied from 1189 to 1216 were increased. In addition to war and the feudal aid (to ransom the king), was added debt and the payment promised to the English churchmen for the waste caused by the occupation of their lands during the interdict. A more significant change was the interpretation of the degree of financial necessity which would justify the levy of a tallage. In twenty-nine years five tallages had been levied by the king.[3] As against this record, nine tallages were taken during the period from 1194 through 1206, a run of five in five successive years from 1194 through 1199 and a run of four from 1202 through 1206. This development in the direction of a tallage every year may have resulted from the fact that the officials

2. *Pipe roll 6 John*, p. 129.
3. From 1165 to 1194 there were tallages in 1168, 1173, 1174, 1177, 1187.

TALLAGE UNDER RICHARD I AND JOHN

of the exchequer had noted that in the early pipe rolls of Henry II the aid on the towns was levied six times in ten years [4] and considered that it was permissible in time of great need to levy it year after year. Whatever the explanation, the financial necessity seemed great enough to justify a marked increase in frequency.

Certainly the king's necessities led him to increase the frequency with which tallage was taken. Although a campaign had been waged against the Welsh in 1190 for which a scutage was taken, no special levy was taken on the demesne till 1193, when in the tremendous effort to raise the king's ransom the fourth of revenues and movables was exacted from the royal demesne. While not a tallage, it was certainly a tax. The following year further levies were necessary to complete the payments for the ransom, and one of these levies was a tallage the assessment of which began in September, 1194.[5]

The renewal of the war against France in 1194 led to a scutage for "the second army of Normandy" recorded in the pipe roll of 1195.[6] As scutage was often accompanied by a tallage, the tallage of 1196 may have been taken to procure additional money for this campaign.[7] Another scutage, for the third army of Normandy after the king's return from Germany, was levied in 1196, and the tallage which appears in the roll of 1197, but which was taken in 1196 and 1197, may have been taken to help defray the expenses of that expedition.[8] The tallage of 1198 was also taken for the war in France.[9] Thus the aid on the demesne in 1193 and the four successive tallages of Richard were linked with the ransom and the campaigns in France, which followed on the king's return. They seem to represent a deliberate plan to expand the taxation of the demesne. During the first eight years of John's reign (1199–1206) war with France was almost continually waged or threatened, and except in the year 1200, a scutage was raised every year. During this period tallage was levied five times.[10] Thus in 1206 tallage seemed on the verge of becoming an annual due. As Richard I was absent in France after May, 1194, the initiative for these repeated levies on the demesne probably originated with the small

4. In 1156, 1158, 1159, 1161, 1162, 1165.
5. *Pipe roll 7 Richard I*, pp. xxiv, 91, 146, 249.
6. *Ibid.*, pp. 25, 216, 241, 242.
7. *Pipe roll 8 Richard I*, p. xxi.
8. *Ibid.*, p. 11 and *passim*. *Pipe roll 9 Richard I*, pp. xii, xiv.
9. *Pipe roll 3 John*, p. 218. *Pipe roll 10 Richard I*, pp. 25, 64, 76, 94–95.
10. Sydney Knox Mitchell, *Studies in taxation*, chap. iii.

council in England, perhaps with Hubert Walter, who in 1194 was entrusted with securing contributions from certain of the great towns and who in 1198 personally assessed some of the levies on the towns to supply money to pay sergeants in the army in France.[11] But a further change occurred. In 1207 came the thirteenth on personal property, and the interdict, which threw church property into royal control with a great increase of revenue, coincident with the cessation of the French war. Although four scutages were levied after 1206 (1209, 1210, 1211, 1214) only one, that of Ireland in 1210, was accompanied by a tallage. Thereafter one more was levied, the tallage of the interdict in 1214, to raise money to reimburse churchmen for the waste of their lands during the struggle with Innocent III.[12] Although the number of tallages increased, a puzzling problem is presented by the fact that the number of shires reported in the pipe roll as tallaged in any one of the levies markedly declined. From 1168 to the close of Henry II's reign the number of shires tallaged in any levy ranged from thirty-one to thirty-five, except in two cases: in 1174 when only twenty appeared in the pipe roll and in 1187 when only twenty-five were recorded. It has been suggested that the decline in 1174 was due to the fact that as a tallage had just been levied the preceding year, the taxpayers were opposed to another tax so soon. In 1187 I believe that the levy of the Saladin tithe in 1188 ended the assessment and the collection of the tallage.

Under Richard and John the number of shires reported tallaged ranged from fourteen in 1195 to thirty-three in 1214, only three exceeding thirty in number (thirty-one in 1199, thirty-three or more in 1210, and thirty-three in 1214). It is noteworthy that the number of shires that reported tallages declined. It may be that the cause was opposition to repeated levies, as seems to have been true in 1174 and certainly was true in 1187–88 with the Saladin tithe. If we recall that the demesne paid the fourth in 1193 we find that it was taxed in six successive years, if we add the tallage of 1199. The tallage of 1194 was levied on the demesne in only fourteen counties.[13] Perhaps the sheriffs of the missing counties rendered the accounts of the tallage at the "exchequer of the ransom," and thus no account appeared in the pipe roll. Or it may be that

11. *Pipe roll 10 Richard I*, pp. 25, 94–95.
12. Pipe roll 3 Henry III, m. 7. Pipe roll 4 Henry III, m. 7. Memoranda roll 3 Henry III, m. 8. Pipe roll 6 Henry III, m. 13d. Public Record Office.
13. *Pipe roll 6 Richard I*, p. 182.

TALLAGE UNDER RICHARD I AND JOHN   289

since the royal demesne had in 1193 paid the fourth for the ransom, opposition developed in 1194 to the tallage. In 1198 a cause of the limited number of shires that contributed (twenty-six in number) may have been the "great carucage." To that levy contributed all the escheats in the king's possession, and it may be that in some shires the demesne paid the carucage instead of the tallage, and so the demesne that paid the new levy may have been exempt from tallage, as in 1187–88.[14] It is possible that not all the tallages were accounted for by the sheriffs at the exchequer but were paid into the chamber or retained by the sheriff and disbursed on the receipt of orders from the council. In 1210 the returns for fines, aids, and tallages of the Irish expedition assembled in Yorkshire were not made at the exchequer, but by the king's command were paid at Nottingham before Brian de L'Isle.[15] Yet the formal statement on the pipe roll indicates that if a tallage from any shire were to be paid into the chamber or elsewhere, the clerks of the pipe roll would thus record it. Though it is confusing to us, it was not uncommon for the account of tallage to be rendered at the exchequer in a different year from that in which the assessment was begun or for two or more tallages in a shire to be enrolled for the first time in the same pipe roll. When a new levy was made in successive years it is sometimes difficult to distinguish the two or more levies.[16] A new tallage was levied in both 1195 and 1196; the first appearance of both these in Lincolnshire and Northumberland was in the roll of 1196;[17] in other shires the record of each levy appears in either 1195 or 1196.[18] Two new tallages appeared in the roll of Northampton in 1206, one belonging to that year, the other to 1204.[19] Three new tallages appeared in the pipe roll of 9 John in Oxfordshire; from the names of their assessors they seem to belong respectively to the levies of 1204, 1205, and 1206.[20] These vagaries in the records however need not mean that the officials of the exchequer had been remiss in their summonses to the sheriffs. It would not be fair to conclude from any of these citations that shires have been omitted through ignorance or carelessness on a

14. Roger of Howden, IV, 46. Sometimes a demesne paid both. *Memoranda roll 1 John*, p. 40. *Pipe roll 1 John*, p. 31.
15. Pipe roll 12 John, m. 10d, m. 19d. Public Record Office.
16. For example the tallage of 1194 was enrolled for the first time in various shires in 1194, 1195, and 1196. *Pipe roll 9 Richard I*, p. xiv.
17. *Pipe roll 8 Richard I*, p. xxi.
18. *Pipe roll 9 Richard I*, p. xiv.
19. *Pipe roll 8 John*, pp. 177, 178.
20. *Pipe roll 9 John*, pp. 46–47.

great scale. Indeed the general picture presented in the pipe rolls, particularly under Richard and John, is one of great expansion of the royal income from the royal demesne that was continually enlarged by a varying revenue from lands temporarily in hand, escheats, the lands of minors, the profits of justice, and the like. We should expect that tallage which by custom was entered in the pipe roll should continue to be recorded there whenever levied. The conclusion that seems inescapable is that a reduced number of the shires could be compelled to contribute year after year and that opposition of the tallage payers caused the decline in numbers of shires that paid in any given year.

The method of authorization is never entered in the pipe rolls. It was determined by the king in his small council. Thus in 1194 justices were sent out on a great administrative and judicial iter. All the items of business which they were ordered to carry out were such as would be authorized in the small council, and one of these was the levy of a tallage.[21] The authorization of tallage by the king is also illustrated by the case of Odiham. The men of this area had paid 100m. to hold the manor of the king as a fee farm for £50 per annum. This same year, 1204, they had promised the king 20m. as a fine in aid of passage. The king refused to accept this aid because he desired to retain his right to tallage them, and for the fine of 100m. the aid of 20m. was canceled.[22] The issue involved was not the amount but the character of the contribution, for only once under Richard and John did the tallage of Odiham amount to as much as 20m. This example draws the distinction between the aid, a free grant, and the tallage which was a due and so controlled by the king and his small council.

The references to tallage in the Articles of the Barons and Magna Carta lead to the same conclusion. The former document states that no scutage or aid was to be laid in the kingdom, other than the three regular aids, save by the common counsel of the realm, and the three regular aids were to be reasonable. "In the same way," continues the article, "let it be done with the tallages and aids of the city of London and of other cities that have liberties of this kind." That is, in the case of the three regular aids, tallages and aids should be levied by the king's will, but in reasonable amounts. On other occasions they should pay only by their own consent. In Magna Carta the statement applying to "other cities"

21. William Stubbs, *Select charters,* pp. 259–263.
22. *Pipe roll 6 John,* p. 129; *Rot. chart.,* p. 130b.

than London was dropped, the article reading, "In a similar way let it be done concerning the aids of the city of London." The reference to the other cities was omitted probably because it was recognized that such a regulation went counter to custom. Thus, according to this article, although London might be subject only to voluntary aids, other than in the three special cases, no doubt remains that both rural and urban levies on the rest of the royal demesne remained under the control of the king. Since both Articles XII and XIV were dropped in the reissues of the charter, it is certain that the king continued to enjoy his customary right to tallage with the possible exception of London.

Broadly speaking, the method of assessment employed at the close of Henry II's reign continued. If justices were sent out on a general eyre, they were instructed to include the assessment of the tallage among their duties. Such was the case in 1194, in the final tallage of Richard in 1198, and in 1202–3.[23] Justices were also sent out on special eyres, and they too might include the assessment of tallage among their duties. The bishop-elect of Durham and Hugh Bardolf assessed a tallage in 1196 in seven shires, in some at least of which they also held court.[24] In 1197 Robert Fitz Roger, Osbert Fitz Hervey, William de Glanvill, Michael Belet, and Master Roger of St. Edmunds tried cases in Norfolk and Suffolk and also levied tallage.[25] The abbot of Tewkesbury, Simon de Pattishall, John of Guestling, and Richard Fleming were itinerant justices in a circuit composed mainly of western shires;[26] the abbot and Simon and Henry, archdeacon of Stafford, who was not one of this group of justices, assessed the tallage in Herefordshire, Worcestershire, Berkshire, and Oxfordshire.[27]

In 1204 Simon de Pattishall, Eustace de Fauconberg, Richard Malebisse, Henry of Northampton, and Alexander de Pointon were justices itinerant in Lincolnshire, Warwickshire and Leicestershire, Northamptonshire, and Bedfordshire.[28] They tallaged Northamptonshire.[29] Simon de Pattishall with associates tallaged

23. Stubbs, *Select charters*, pp. 259–263. Doris Stenton in introduction to pipe rolls. *Pipe roll 7 Richard I*, pp. xix–xxii, xxiv. *Pipe roll 8 Richard I*, pp. xxi. *Pipe roll 10 Richard I*, pp. xxiv–xxvii. *Pipe roll 4 John*, pp. xvii, xviii. *Pipe roll 5 John*, pp. xiii–xv.
24. *Pipe roll 8 Richard I*, p. xxii. *Pipe roll 9 Richard I*, pp. xiii–xv.
25. *Pipe roll 9 Richard I*, p. 240.
26. *Pipe roll 1 John*, p. xvii.
27. *Ibid.*
28. *Pipe roll 4 John*, p. xviii.
29. *Pipe roll 5 John*, pp. 183–184.

various other counties: with William de Cantilupe and Henry of Northampton, part of the demesne in Gloucestershire; with William de Cantilupe, Herefordshire and Worcestershire; "with associates," Oxfordshire; with William de Cantilupe "and associates," Shropshire.[30]

James de Potterne was on a judicial circuit in 1205.[31] With associates he assessed the tallage in Cornwall, Devon, the honor of Gloucester, Hampshire, Dorsetshire and Somersetshire, Wiltshire, Norfolk and Suffolk, and Bucks and Bedfordshire.[32] In Devon and Cornwall, Dorsetshire and Somersetshire, Jocelyn de Welles is mentioned as one of his associates; in Hampshire, Eustace de Fauconberg; and in Norfolk and Suffolk, John, bishop of Norwich. These four justices with others probably assessed tallage in addition to the work of a judicial iter.

Henry, archdeacon of Stafford, Hugh de Chaucumbe, and associates assessed the tallage and levied amercements in Warwickshire and Leicestershire, Staffordshire, and Herefordshire, thus acting as justices and assessors.[33] Justices might be empowered to assess tallage when they were not on eyre. Richard Barre, archdeacon of Ely, an experienced justice, accompanied by Thomas, a clerk, assessed the tallage in Cambridgeshire and Huntingdonshire in 1197.[34] Geoffrey Fitz Peter, Theobald Walter, and their associates assessed the tallage on Colchester in 1197.[35] Richard Malebisse, long a justice, with Thomas de Amundeville assessed the tallage in four shires in 1199.[36] Eustace de Fauconberg, a justice, and Alexander de Pointon, who became a justice in 1202, were appointed to assess the tallage on the honor of Brittany or Richmond.[37] Hubert de Burgh and William Brewer assessed the tallage in Dorsetshire and Somersetshire.[38] In 1204 Simon de Pattishall, who does not seem to have been on eyre this year, assessed, with associates, a tallage in Herefordshire, Berkshire, Worcestershire, Gloucestershire, Cambridgeshire and Huntingdonshire, and Oxfordshire.[39] Geoffrey Fitz Peter, William Brewer, and

30. *Ibid.*, pp. 56–57, 63, 69, 193.
31. *Curia regis rolls*, IV, 19.
32. *Pipe roll 7 John*, pp. 7, 24, 92, 132, 142, 167, 252. *Pipe roll 8 John*, p. 40.
33. *Pipe roll 7 John*, pp. 36, 158, 276.
34. *Pipe roll 9 Richard I*, p. 82.
35. *Ibid.*, p. 73.
36. *Pipe roll 1 John*, p. 121.
37. *Ibid.*, p. 212. *Pipe roll 2 John*, pp. 34, 117.
38. *Pipe roll 5 John*, p. 157.
39. *Pipe roll 6 John*, pp. 19, 60, 61, 92, 151.

Peter des Roches assessed the tallage in Nottinghamshire and Derbyshire, and Yorkshire.[40]

Other important administrators, sheriffs, and wardens of great honors were drawn into the ranks of the assessors of tallage. In 1197 Simon de Beauchamp, a great magnate and sheriff of Bucks and Bedfordshire (1194–97) was the chief assessor in his sheriffdom with Ralph Hareng, a deputy escheator in the midlands, and associates.[41] Other men of importance in the royal administration were drawn into the ranks of assessors. In 1199 and 1200 Geoffrey de Norwich headed the group that assessed the tallage in Northamptonshire, Buckinghamshire and Bedfordshire, Warwickshire, Leicestershire, and Lincolnshire.[42] He was a clerk of the exchequer, of some ability, for in 1200 he was made one of the four bailiffs of the Jews for all England—the barons of the Exchequer of the Jews or as they were called the justices of the Jews.[43] In 1199 William de Falaise was with Henry, archdeacon of Stafford, and others, assessor of the tallage in Bristol outside the walls, in Shropshire, and Staffordshire.[44] He was not only a justice, but also, with Master Suenus, custodian of the great honor of Gloucester.[45] Hugh de Chaucumbe, who held six fees of the bishopric of Lincoln and one fee of the king, was a bailiff of Hugh Bardolf in Staffordshire, and then became sheriff of that shire for five years and tallaged Northamptonshire with the bishop of Coventry and others.[46] He was also assessor in Worcestershire with Hugh de Neville.[47] Hugh de Neville, a very active administrator, had been custodian of Marlborough, sheriff of Oxfordshire, a forest justice, and later sheriff of Essex and Hertfordshire.[48] In 1205 and 1206 Hugh de Chaucumbe was again employed as assessor and as justice in several shires.[49]

Sometimes men of no prominence officiated in the assessment. In 1196 in several shires the assessors consisted of local landholders,

40. *Ibid.*, pp. 173, 206.
41. *Pipe roll 9 Richard I*, p. 205.
42. *Pipe roll 1 John*, pp. 17, 117, 253. *Pipe roll 2 John*, p. 89.
43. *Rot. chart.*, p. 61a. *Rot. liberate*, p. 38.
44. *Pipe roll 1 John*, pp. 31, 77, 166.
45. *Ibid.*, pp. 34, 35–38.
46. *Pipe roll 4 John*, pp. 39, 279. *Pipe roll 4 Richard I*, p. 254. *Pipe roll 9 Richard I*, p. 91.
47. *Ibid.*, p. 192.
48. *Pipe roll 8 Richard I*, p. 33. *Pipe roll 9 Richard I*, p. 33. *Pipe roll 10 Richard I*, pp. 16, 63. Under John Hugh became chief justice of the forests.
49. *Pipe roll 7 John*, pp. 36, 91, 276.

in most cases none of great importance, but many of them had been royal officials and in most shires either the sheriff or his deputy formed one of the board. The most striking example of undistinguished members of the board of assessors was perhaps the case of Odo de Dammartin and Roger de Albini, who with associates were the assessors in 1197 in Surrey.[50] Twice, in 1194 and 1198, the council dispatched Hubert Walter alone to secure an aid from some of the great towns that would perhaps be larger than a tallage. They were following the trail made by Henry II who appealed personally to towns for the Saladin tithe by sending out this distinguished ecclesiastic and administrator. In 1194 he secured from London 1,500$m.$ of donum in return for the good will of Richard, for a guarantee of the liberties of the city, and as an auxilium for the ransom.[51] In Yorkshire he was promised 300$m.$ by York, 100$m.$ by Scarborough, and 50$m.$ by Doncaster; in Hampshire 100$m.$ from Winchester and 40$m.$ from Southampton; from Northampton 300$m.$; and from Oxford £100.[52] In 1198 the archbishop tallaged Southampton at 50$m.$ to pay the expenses of sergeants in France, Norwich at 300$m.$ and 100$m.$ extra for sergeants; he and Geoffrey Fitz Peter tallaged Northampton at £100 and all the areas in Worcestershire specifically for providing five hundred sergeants overseas.[53] Officials in charge of honors in hand might be designated as assessors in those areas. Gilbert Fitz Renfrew and Richard Brewer, the wardens of the bishopric of Durham, also assessed the tallage and aids on that honor.[54] Alexander de Pointon, custodian of the lands of the honor of Brittany, was with Eustace de Fauconberg the assessor of the tallage.[55]

In general therefore the assessors were men high in the administration who were concerned primarily with finance and justice, loyal to the central government, and able to bear responsibility, as is illustrated by the free hand they were allowed in interpreting their orders. Hence it seems likely that the exchequer would keep close watch over the records of the assessors and that pipe rolls would contain careful accounts of each assessment, with the pos-

50. *Pipe roll 9 Richard I*, p. 218. I am not so sure of the insignificance of these two men. The Dammartin family were holders of 11 fees of the Earl Clare in Surrey. Roger de Albini may well have been a little-known brother of the Earl of Arundel. (Editor.)
51. *Pipe roll 6 Richard I*, p. 182.
52. *Pipe roll 7 Richard I*, pp. 91, 105, 146, 211.
53. *Pipe roll 10 Richard I*, pp. xxvii, 25, 76, 94, 106.
54. *Pipe roll 8 Richard I*, pp. 255-257.
55. *Pipe roll 2 John*, pp. 87-91.

sible exception of the levy of 1194–95 which may have been reported in part at the exchequer of the ransom. This plan of assessment had one principle that united all the members: the royal order authorizing the commissioners to assess the tallage in one or more areas. They performed this task not as sheriff or justice or clerk but because of the special command of the king expressed in the writ. We have no copy of the writ, but from the reports in the pipe rolls we can reconstruct its contents, at least in part. Usually in each shire to which the assessors were sent they were to assess the tallage on the royal demesne and lands in hand.[56] The writ probably stated that the levy must be based upon the capacity to pay, for different persons or areas paid different amounts.[57] The commissioners were to assess it by negotiation in a lump sum upon the men of an area in common, or individually upon each taxpayer, per capita. The choice between the two methods was left to the justices, for both methods were used in the same levy, or sometimes both methods employed in the same shire.[58]

The assessors drew up a roll in duplicate.[59] In 1204 the roll of assessment made by the justices in Nottinghamshire and Derbyshire had not arrived at the exchequer when the sheriff rendered his account of the collection, but by the king's command the account was entered in the pipe roll according to the rolls of assessment produced by the sheriff.[60] In another case the exchequer noted that Thomas, a clerk, was to respond for various rolls, among them a roll of assessment of the tallage made by Reginald de Cornhill and his associates.[61] A similar case is the roll of the assessment of the tallage per capita on the city of Lincoln entered in the roll of 1204.[62] It amounted to £486 6s. 8d. and was perhaps a supplementary levy to the tallage of £79 20d. on Lincoln made by the assessors who assessed all of the king's demesne in Lincolnshire. I have however put it in 1203, since no tallage appears in Lincolnshire that year, but there is really no way of deciding this question. The assessors of this heavy tallage are not named. According to the pipe roll, it was assessed by the king's writ that contained the summonses of this tallage, or as the clerks of the exchequer phrased it

56. *Pipe roll 7 Richard I*, pp. 12, 257. *Pipe roll 8 Richard I*, p. 138. *Pipe roll 9 Richard I*, p. 181.
57. *Pipe roll 10 Richard I*, pp. 205–209. *Pipe roll 6 John*, p. 55.
58. *Pipe roll 1 John*, pp. 148, 218. *Pipe roll 2 John*, p. 117.
59. *Pipe roll 9 Richard I*, p. 61.
60. *Pipe roll 6 John*, p. 173.
61. *Memoranda roll 1 John*, p. 16.
62. *Pipe roll 6 John*, pp. 55–56.

"the tallage on the men whose names were listed in the writ which was sent from the *curia regis*."[63] This document contained the names of the tallage payers and the amount for which each was assessed. The levy was collected by the citizens and paid at the exchequer by William de Tilebroc, their representative. By whom was it assessed? Possibly the clerks of the exchequer drew it up, since it was sent down by the council, using as a basis the previous tallages and other information regarding the wealth of Lincoln citizens at their disposal.[64] A comparison of the tallage of 1202 shows such variations in the charges of the two years that it seems unlikely that the new list could have been properly made up except by taxers on the ground.[65]

The contents of the roll of assessment depended upon whether the tallage had been levied in common or per capita; if the former, it contained the names of the areas and the amounts due from each, as appears in the account of the tallage in Shropshire, or the account rendered by the sheriff of Northumberland "of the tallage of the vills whose names and debts appear in the roll which the aforesaid (assessors) delivered to the exchequer."[66]

If the tallage were levied per capita, the roll would contain the names of each individual person taxed, and the amount with which he was charged. In 1196 the tallage in Yorkshire was levied in each vill per capita and the justices delivered to the exchequer a copy of the roll containing the amount due from each person who was charged.[67] Sometimes the roll of assessment contained tallages intermingled with amercements by the justices.[68] In Kent the roll per capita was copied on the pipe roll when the sheriff rendered his account.[69] After the assessment came the collection. With his roll of assessment as a guide, the collector, usually the sheriff, collected the cash and paid it in at the lower exchequer. Then with the tallies of receipt and his rolls of assessment and of collection he passed to the upper exchequer where he rendered the account of the tallage.[70]

63. *Ibid.*, p. 55.
64. *Ibid.*, p. xlii.
65. *Pipe roll 4 John*, pp. 241–242.
66. *Pipe roll 8 Richard I*, p. 44. *Pipe roll 10 Richard I*, p. 147. *Pipe roll 1 John*, p. 74.
67. *Pipe roll 8 Richard I*, pp. 173–174, 251. *Pipe roll 9 Richard I*, p. 59. *Pipe roll 2 John*, p. 91.
68. *Pipe roll 4 John*, pp. 10–11. *Pipe roll 5 John*, p. 94.
69. *Pipe roll 10 Richard I*, pp. 205–209.
70. *Pipe roll 7 Richard I*, p. 257. *Pipe roll 8 Richard I*, pp. 8, 46, 67. *Pipe roll 9 Richard I*, pp. 82, 91, 150, 151.

TALLAGE UNDER RICHARD I AND JOHN

This division of labor arose from the fact that the sheriff was in charge of the local administrative organization, and hence could most readily collect the tax. As we have noted above, the pipe roll contains many entries of a different form. A person or an area accounted for a certain amount of tallage, as if the individual person or area rendered his own account at the exchequer.[71] In some cases this form of entry represented what actually took place. Usually the form was employed because it enabled the pipe roll clerks to record on the roll the names of persons or areas that still owed part of their tallage, so that writs could be issued to the sheriff the following year to summon them to pay the amount still due. For example, in 1202 the sheriff of Lincolnshire accounted for 102m. 5s. 10d. of the tallage of men and vills whose names were given in the roll of assessment which the justices had delivered into the exchequer. He paid in full the amount owed in seventy-three tallies and was quit. Then the roll continued: Peter Fitz Bering accounts for 100s. of the same tallage. In the treasury 50s. and he owes 50s. A list of persons and areas follows comprising about thirty names, each paying only part of the debt.[72] There seems to be no reason for changing the form of entry except the desire to make a record for future use of the debtors and their obligations.[73] Another plan was sometimes employed that described exactly what occurred. Thus the city of Canterbury, the sheriff on its behalf, accounts for 300m. of tallage.[74] Other evidence shows how conventional it was for all tallages to be collected and the account presented for audit by the sheriff unless some other royal official acted as collector. The pipe roll states that Feckenham accounted for 100s. of tallage. It paid £4 12s. and owed still 8s.[75] The memoranda roll records specifically this transaction. The sheriff paid £4 12s. of the tax. He placed 8s. upon a certain piece of land belonging to Hugh de Neville.[76]

The case of Milton in Kent that in form accounted for its tallage shows clearly that the sheriff had collected the money from a representative of the manor and rendered its account at the exchequer.[77] Notice the case of Henry de Beleauwe who was charged with 80m.

---

71. *Pipe roll 7 Richard I*, pp. 98, 249. *Pipe roll 10 Richard I*, pp. 205–209.
72. *Pipe roll 4 John*, pp. 236–238.
73. *Pipe roll 7 Richard I*, pp. 182, 215.
74. Pipe roll 16 John, m. 3, Public Record Office.
75. *Pipe roll 1 John*, p. 82.
76. *Memoranda roll 1 John*, p. 48.
77. *Pipe roll 2 John*, p. 214.

of tallage.⁷⁸ This item appeared in the rolls till 1203, when the debt was canceled with the comment that he should be quit because of the record of the archbishop of Canterbury and the king's writ.⁷⁹ There is no mention of the sheriff, but let us look at the memoranda roll, where in 1199 the sheriff had been called to account for his failure to collect this tallage. He immediately produced the letter which King Richard had written to the archbishop stating that the king had pardoned the debt. But the exchequer barons would not cross off the charge because the letter had not been written to them. Later the archbishop seems to have sent them a copy. But the collection of the tax was clearly made by the sheriff, and the later entries were cast in this form till the levy was all paid; yet here too the sheriff collected the money from the city and paid it to the exchequer where he also suffered the audit.⁸⁰ In 1210 the clerks of the pipe roll incidently reveal the part played by the sheriff as collector when they explain that he will not respond at Westminster for other fines, tallages, or aids because, by the king's orders, he will pay at Nottingham to Brian de L'Isle.⁸¹ Occasionally the custodian of an honor assessed and collected the tallage, as in the bishopric of Durham in 1196.⁸² But there are cases in which an area responded for its tallage. So it was in 1204 with the tallage of 1,000$m.$ on London. From the close roll we learn that the pipe roll entry stating that the citizens of London rendered their own account at the exchequer corresponds with the fact. The citizens paid 900$m.$ of silver by weight into the chamber at Stokes by the hand of Peter, the son of the mayor, and three others, "of the promise which they made of aid for our crossing." ⁸³ Similarly the burghers of Oxford promised to pay 100$m.$ of an old tallage on a certain date.⁸⁴ Hugh de Neville, custodian of Marlborough, was summoned for the tallage of that manor.⁸⁵ We should expect that boroughs would seek to render their tallage by their own hand for their charters provided that the farm "be rendered at the exchequer by their reeve." ⁸⁶

Even when the sheriff responded for a due at the exchequer there

78. *Pipe roll 10 Richard I*, p. 205.
79. *Pipe roll 5 John*, p. 24.
80. *Pipe roll 1 John*, pp. 218, 219. *Memoranda roll 1 John*, pp. 23, 51.
81. Pipe roll 12 John, m. 19d, Public Record Office.
82. *Pipe roll 8 Richard I*, pp. 255–257.
83. *Pipe roll 10 John*, p. 167. *Rot. claus.*, *I*, 35b.
84. *Memoranda roll 1 John*, p. 14.
85. *Ibid.*, p. 63.
86. *Rot. chart.*, pp. 20b, 39, 51b, 56b, 65b, 87.

is evidence that the holders of manors collected it themselves and delivered it to him, and thus sought to keep him off their lands. The council permitted the men of a manor to hold that area at farm and to collect the money and deliver it to the sheriff at fixed periods for payment at the exchequer.[87] The king promised by charter that no sheriff or bailiff should enter the lands of Boston and its soke of the honor of Richmond in Holland, but the men of that area themselves might appoint a bailiff to respond to the royal exchequer just as they used to respond to the earl of Richmond when in his hand.[88] Hugh, archdeacon of Wells, received by charter the manors of Cheddar and Axbridge with the hundreds of Winterstoke and of Cheddar at fee farm. The document provided that any money owed to the king from these areas should be collected by the hands of the bailiff of the manors and hundreds and paid to the sheriff of Somerset and by him delivered to the exchequer.[89]

The sheriff continued to play an important role. Without the assessment roll however he took no action. For example, the assessment roll in Warwickshire and Leicestershire that appears in the pipe roll was the copy of the roll sent to the exchequer by the justices, Geoffrey de Norwich and his associates. It consisted of a list of the manors and the amounts of tallage opposite the name of each manor, without any statement that these sums were owed, or that the sheriff had presented the list.[90] A mutilated comment on the memoranda roll explains this curious entry. When the sheriff was rendering his account of the county at the exchequer, he was asked about the tallage levied in his shire by Geoffrey de Norwich and replied that he had no roll of the assessment and hence, it would seem, he could not collect it. Then he was ordered to destrain the *villatas* to pay it, apparently according to this roll which the exchequer had received. The following year he collected and paid the sums charged in the roll of 1 John.[91] The existence of duplicate rolls of assessment is evident from the returns for Northamptonshire in 1197. King's Cliff was not on the copy delivered at the exchequer, but the sheriff collected £9 6s. 8d. from that village, for that was the sum for which the vill was assessed in his copy.[92]

Thus the assessment was for the most part made by experienced

87. *Ibid.*, pp. 85b, 87, 101b, 103b.
88. *Ibid.*, p. 118.
89. *Ibid.*, p. 129b.
90. *Pipe roll 1 John*, pp. 253–254.
91. *Pipe roll 2 John*, p. 180. *Memoranda roll 1 John*, p. 53.
92. *Pipe roll 9 Richard I*, p. 91.

and important officials of the central government. The sheriff collected the tax except in the case of those areas that by special arrangement were allowed to collect and pay it either to the sheriff or to the exchequer. Even in this case the sheriff played an important part and was jealously watched by local authorities. The great proportion of areas that paid tallage in a lump sum indicates that ordinarily the sheriff no longer entered the manor or borough unless the tallage was levied per capita. Thus the administration of tallage under Richard and John developed along the lines established under Henry II. During the period from 1194 to 1207, efforts were made to increase the revenue from this source by taking it more frequently and by employing a more searching method of assessment, the levy per capita, familiar to all. Coincident with these innovations were certain other devices, also of ancient origin, to expand the revenue from the demesne. Concerned also with the exploitation of boroughs and manors but arising out of conditions under which they were held of the king was the expansion of the revenue connected with farms.

Under Henry II the methods of administering the demesne and the lands that continually came into the king's possession by the operation of feudal and manorial law were already fixed by custom. Individual areas might be allotted to a salaried official, a *custos*, who collected the revenues and paid the expenses. Thus the king received all the profits or suffered the losses of management.[93] An area, urban or rural, might be allotted at farm to a person or a group, for a fixed annual sum, while the farmer bore certain expenses of management and received certain revenues, with the attendant profit or loss.[94] The farmer might also have to pay an additional sum, a fine, for the privilege of farming the land.[95] Both methods of administration were noted in manorial experience.[96] Lands that the king was continually acquiring by escheat, or otherwise, might be exploited by either of these methods.[97] The fine that was paid by the recipient of lands might amount to a large sum in

93. James Tait, *Mediaeval English borough*, p. 151. J. H. Round, *Geoffrey de Mandeville*, p. 297.

94. Ballard, *Borough charters*, p. lxxv. Tait, *Mediaeval English borough*, p. 123. Carl Stephenson, *Borough and town*, p. 154. Paul Vinogradoff, *English Society in the eleventh century*, pp. 374–381.

95. Ballard, *Borough charters*, pp. lxxvi, lxxvii.

96. Paul Vinogradoff, *Villainage in England*, pp. 301–307. N. Neilson, "Customary rents," pp. 7, 18.

97. *Pipe roll 23 Henry II*, pp. 63, 164, 165. *Pipe roll 24 Henry II*, pp. 73–74. *Pipe roll 33 Henry II*, pp. 26, 29.

the case of a barony or honor.⁹⁸ In addition to these sources of revenue from the demesne, the king from time to time exacted the tallage. It is evident that a surplus revenue existed on the manor that the king did not receive and that was enjoyed by the tenants of various degrees. From this surplus was drawn the salary of the custos, the profits of the farmers, the fines of those to whom the lands were allotted, and the tallages. The administration of the demesne thus yielded financial advantage to the royal treasury, but also to the domanial administrators.

The latter enjoyed other advantages. The amount they were to pay was definite; they had control of the administration of the area in question; and if it was well managed they might also enjoy a profit. This would be true whether the farmers were the burgesses of the town, the men of a manor, or some person, a magnate, one or two townsmen, a baron, or royal official. That the desire of the entrepreneurs, or speculators, to obtain these areas at farm was great is shown by the fact that they sometimes agreed to pay a farm larger than proved possible, and that even early in the twelfth century they sought to secure the desired area at fee farm or perpetual lease. Even the fine had its advantages. It was such a definite charge that it bestowed on the tenant the desired area. In contrast at first sight the tallage seemed to benefit only the king, yet if it were levied "in common" it was assessed and collected by the lord or the chief men of the manor, or the authorities of the borough. The receipts might well exceed the amount agreed upon with the royal justices. If so they would accrue to the lord or remain in the treasury of the town, or be retained by the chief tenants on the manor. Both parties to these transactions endeavored to augment their advantages and the gain was not all on the side of the powerful Norman or Angevin rulers. The county farms were fixed at some date prior to the accession of Henry II and only with difficulty was the king able to increase them somewhat in certain shires.⁹⁹ Borough farms were augmented in the eleventh century, and in some cases further enlarged in the twelfth century.¹⁰⁰ Yet the reign of Henry II saw some borough farms reduced in amount

---

98. Fulk Paynel promised 1,000m. for the honor of Bampton. *Pipe roll 26 Henry II*, p. 94.

99. R. L. Poole, *Exchequer in the twelfth century*, pp. 135–136. Sidney Smith in introduction to *Pipe roll 5 John*, pp. xxv, xxvi. G. T. Turner, "The sheriff's farm," pp. 122–124.

100. Tait, *Mediaeval English borough*, p. 152. Stephenson, *Borough and town*, p. 154.

while some remained unchanged. Still others that were recorded for the first time early in Henry's reign were not later augmented. Henry II also derived income from the fines paid him by burgesses for the privilege of farming their town.[101] Manors on the royal demesne often recorded no change in the amount of their farm in the twelfth century. For example, nearly all the farms on manors that appear in the pipe roll of 1130 remained unmodified during the century, except in some cases.[102] The manor of Great Tew was farmed for £36 in 1130 and paid it that same year.[103] It does not appear in the pipe rolls of Henry II till 1165 when the farm was £8.[104] It was raised to £16 in the following year, to £30 in 1168, and thereafter it was fixed at £40 where it remained for a long time.[105]

In many cases such lack of change illustrates the power of custom, the difficulty of modifying the amount of the levy without the consent or cooperation of both parties. The farmer was the sheriff, though a local baron might be the farmer.[106] There were some cases in which the men of the area sought and were given the privilege of administering the farm themselves, a step in the development of self-government.[107] They agreed with the representatives of the king on the amount of the farm, assessed and collected it, and they responded for it either to the sheriff or the excheqeur.[108] To this extent they excluded the royal officials from their area. Such activity indicates initiative and capacity to safeguard their own interests in the presence of experienced royal officials. These desires were

101. Tait, *Mediaeval English borough*, pp. 174, 175. Ballard, *Borough charters*, p. lxxvii.

102.

Manor	Farm 31 Henry I	Later Farm
Bergholt	100s.	100s. (1 John)
Wallop	£40	£40 (1 John)
Graften	60s.	60s. (1 John)
Wirksworth	£80	£80 (1 John)
Clipston	100s.	£4 (1 John)
Chapmaneshall	20m.	20m. (1 John)
Silverstone	£6	£6 (1 John)
Wargrave	£80	£80 (8 Richard I)
Windsor	£26	£26 (1 John)

The farm of Clipston was reduced in 1179. *Pipe roll 25 Henry II*, p. 81.

103. *Pipe roll 31 Henry I*, p. 6.
104. *Pipe roll 11 Henry II*, p. 72.
105. *Pipe roll 12 Henry II*, p. 119. *Pipe roll 14 Henry II*, p. 205.
106. Tait, *Mediaeval English borough*, pp. 156, 169–170.
107. *Ibid.*, pp. 156–158, 162, 172–176.
108. *Ibid.*, pp. 156–158, 175.

not entirely the result of the development of city life, for manorial groups also farmed their manors. The king's men in Tew accounted for the farm of that manor.[109] Thus the reign of Henry II exhibited all the methods for exploiting the royal demesne, the custos, the farm and its increase held by sheriffs, magnates, townsmen, and villagers, the fine for the right of farming, or for holding a barony that was temporarily in hand, and the tallage. There was evident the pressure that the king could bring to bear to increase his revenue and the capacity of the local authorities to resist change. Against such a background was projected the period of Richard I and John with their extraordinary needs for cash. The council would naturally turn to the demesne and the lands temporarily in hand as one of the sources for an augmented revenue. Fines continued to be exacted as a condition for granting the town or manor at farm and the farm itself, in the case of manors, was more often increased than under Henry II. From 1194 to 1206 the number of tallages grew and the sum total of the yield from this levy expanded. Fines, farms, and tallages might all be incident upon the same areas, and all were equally based on custom. The speculators or entrepreneurs who had sought for lands at farm as sources of profit found their chances of gain diminished. They tried therefore to reduce the king's opportunities for levying a fine by securing more frequently the grant of the farm in perpetuity, the fee farm; they also secured the right to collect all the revenue connected with the farm and pay it to the sheriff or even pass beyond him and render their account directly to the exchequer. In a measure therefore they arrived at greater control over their holding.

The tallages required different treatment. It was levied at the will of the king, at no established intervals; the account must meet the desires of the royal justices and if no sum satisfactory to these officials was agreed upon, they could by ancient custom enter the area and levy it per capita. Now the king was demanding it in successive years. Thus a legal conflict was waged over this levy. In this struggle as in the case of the farms, custom was more on the side of the speculators. It proved impracticable to levy tallage year after year on many of the manors and particularly on the great towns. By the persuasive influence, probably of money, some of the manors secured total exemption from paying tallage. Even the employment of the tallage per capita often failed to increase the amount assessed. Finally after 1206 the effort to levy the tallage in suc-

109. *Pipe roll 31 Henry I,* p. 6.

304 TAXATION IN MEDIEVAL ENGLAND

cessive years and to assess it per capita was practically abandoned. Nevertheless it was not a complete victory for the towns and manors. The last two tallages of John, 1210 and 1214, taken, except in one instance, in common, were the highest ever assessed, a striking illustration of the control over his demesne exercised by the king.

Richard and John followed no uniform policy in administering the demesne. The plan adopted in any given case depended on circumstances. Instead of placing a manor at farm, they might choose to place it in the hands of a custos. For example, William de Sainte Mère Église accounts as custos for the manor of Bramley (Surrey) and the lands of the abbey of Glastonbury.[110] Inquests into the value of manors were held with the instruction that the valuation was to be made as high as possible, no doubt to insure that a true rather than a conventional estimate should be made as a guide to future arrangements.[111]

The archdeacon of Wells was assigned Lothingland *ad custodiendum et respondendum.* The sheriff was ordered to deliver the manor to him complete and to report to the council the amount of stock and its value, the amount of stock that could be there and, in that case, the value per annum. The archdeacon was to render account at the exchequer for the sum which the manor would be worth when fully stocked.[112] When a borough or manor was let at farm on various conditions, including the perpetual lease, the bargain might involve an increase in the farm and payment of a fine in addition for the grant. For example, in 1201 the burgesses of Andover were granted their borough at fee farm for the ancient farm of £80 plus two increments, one of £15 and the other of £10; afterward, in 1215, the increments were reduced to a single one of £20 numero.[113] The burgesses of Helston received their town at the ancient farm of £8 and an increment of £4, "as long as they serve us faithfully and pay this farm regularly." [114] In 1204 Walter "Senior" of Aura paid £20 and a palfrey to have for life the manor of Aura for a farm of £16 and an increment of £4.[115] Hugh Bardolf paid 50m. to have the manors of Bremesgrave and Norton at fee farm for the ancient farm (£43 bl.) and a new increment of

110. *Pipe roll 7 Richard I,* pp. 37, 48.
111. *Rot. claus.,* I, 4, 5, 5b, 7, 12b.
112. *Ibid.,* p. 12b.
113. *Rot. chart.,* pp. 93b, 195.
114. *Ibid.,* p. 93b. *Pipe roll 3 John,* pp. 187, 189.
115. *Pipe roll 6 John,* pp. 149–150. *Rot. chart.,* p. 121b.

TALLAGE UNDER RICHARD I AND JOHN 305

20m. per annum.[116] In 1200 the men of Kingston paid 60m. to have their town at fee farm, paying an increment of £12 in addition to an ancient farm of £28 10s.[117] In 1208 the farm was raised to £50 but it was to be paid at the exchequer by their own hand.[118] In 1200 Thomas de Neville, a clerk of the king, paid 5m. to have the manor of Writtle at fee farm for £120 per annum.[119] In 1205 he was to pay an increment of 100s., but the charter extended the grant to cover his life.[120] Peter of Brimenton paid £100 to have Whitenton at fee farm for £20 per annum (formerly £6 13s.) for all service; the farm originally had been £2, an increment of £4 was added, in 33 Henry II, the increment was £4 13s., so until 1200 the farm was £6 13s.[121] In 1201 William de Stutevill, sheriff of Yorkshire, was given Bardsey, Colingham, Compton, and Richton for an annual payment of £100 at fee farm.[122] King John had secured these vills early in 1201 from Peter de Bruce in exchange for the vill farmed at £12 8s. 8d., and the forest of Danby, for which Peter was to furnish forever one knight's service.[123] For the exchange Peter paid a £1,000.[124] In 1200 the citizens of Gloucester promised a farm of £55 and £10 increment for Gloucester at fee farm.[125] In 1194 the men of Ipswich paid 60m. to have the area at the old farm of £35 and an increment of 100s. and to have their liberties.[126] In 1200 they paid 100m. to hold their vill at the same farm and to have their charter.[127] The burgesses of Dunwich promised to pay 500m. within a year to have their farm of £120 13s. 4d. and 24,000 herrings reduced permanently to £40,[128] an illustration of the persuasive power of the fine. In 1201 the men of two boroughs and two manors in Northumberland were granted by charter the right to hold their districts and to pay an increased farm for each at the exchequer, as long as they served well and paid their farm

116. *Pipe roll 2 John*, p. 33. *Pipe roll 7 John*, p. 266.
117. *Rot. chart.*, pp. 52b, 182b.
118. *Ibid.*, p. 182.
119. *Pipe roll 2 John*, p. 50.
120. *Rot. chart.*, p. 141b.
121. *Ibid.*, p. 44b. *Pipe roll 2 John*, p. 19. *Pipe roll 14 Henry II*, p. 96. *Pipe roll 26 Henry II*, p. 137.
122. *Rot. chart.*, p. 89b. *Pipe roll 3 John*, pp. 143, 145.
123. *Pipe roll 1 John*, p. 50.
124. *Pipe roll 3 John*, pp. 145, 159. *Rot. oblatis*, pp. 109–110. *Rot. chart.*, pp. 86b, 101.
125. *Ibid.*, p. 56b. *Pipe roll 2 John*, p. 119. *Pipe roll 6 Richard I*, p. 232.
126. *Ibid.*, pp. 47, 63.
127. *Pipe roll 2 John*, p. 148. *Pipe roll 3 John*, p. 138. *Rot. chart.*, p. 65b.
128. *Ibid.*, p. 159b. *Pipe roll 7 John*, p. 237.

promptly. Each area paid a fine for this arrangement.[129] The council at once canceled the bargain and the sheriff resumed payment for each area of the former farm by the grant of the king.[130] Individual entrepreneurs, barons, ecclesiastics, and royal officials sought for manors at fee farm rather than towns; probably the townsmen were too wealthy as competitors. Godfrey, bishop of Winchester, paid £1,000 for the confirmation of a charter by which he had recovered from Richard I the manors of Meon and Wargrave, formerly in the possession of his cathedral church; in 1190 he had recovered them by a grant in perpetuity and had paid for this concession £3,000.[131] In 1200 Earl William Marshal was granted the manor of Bosham in Sussex for the customary farm of £42 quit of all other services and dues as Richard I had granted it to John Marshal.[132] John confirmed to Baldwin de Bethune, count of Aumale, the grant in fee farm, payable annually, of the manors of Norton for £16 10s. bl. (Norhants), of Luton (Beds) for £80, and of Wantage (Berks) for £50. These had been originally granted to him by Richard.[133] In 1203 William de Ferrers, earl of Derby, was granted at fee farm by charter the manors of Wirksworth and Ashbourne for £80 and £40 numero for all service. For this grant by charter he paid 500m.[134]

In letting land the council might make unusual terms that cut across conventional methods of landholding, combining in the same tenure alms and fee farm, or fee farm and military tenure. The solvent was money. Thus Ralph de Sumeri in 1204 paid 100m. to have the manors of Clent, King's Winford, and Were by the old rent of £21 19s. 4d., an increment of £5, and the service of one knight's fee.[135] Roger de Sumerville paid 60m. and two palfreys to have the manor of Alrewas at fee farm for the old rent of £16, an increment of 100s., and for the service of a fourth of a knight's fee.[136] Geoffrey Fitz Peter received the manor of Ailsbury at fee farm by charter by the ancient farm of £50, an increment of £10, and the service of one knight's fee.[137]

Another modification in tenure looking to an addition of revenue

129. *Rot. chart.*, p. 87. *Pipe roll 3 John*, p. 249.
130. *Ibid.*, pp. xvii, 145.
131. *Rot. chart.*, p. 32. *Pipe roll 2 Richard I*, p. 136. *Pipe roll 1 John*, p. 244.
132. *Rot. chart.*, p. 47b.
133. *Ibid.*, p. 62. *Pipe roll 1 John*, pp. 4, 105, 255. *Pipe roll 2 Richard I*, pp. 31, 138. *Pipe roll 3 Richard I*, p. 153.
134. *Rot. chart.*, p. 108b. *Pipe roll 5 John*, **p. 171.**
135. *Rot. chart.*, p. 136. *Pipe roll 6 John*, p. 211.
136. *Ibid.*
137. *Rot. chart.*, pp. 127–128.

to the king was the grant of land in frankalmoign at fee farm, free from all secular exactions. For example, the canons of Cirencester received the manor of Cirencester and seven hundreds for £30 annual farm, in free and perpetual alms, free from all secular exactions.[138]

Thus the line of division between tenures seems to be becoming blurred; the same piece of land held by the same lord and tenant has both military and nonmilitary services in which the emphasis may be on money payments; a money rent appears connected with a tenure called elemosinary. This emphasis on increase in the cash returns, particularly from the rural demesne but to some extent also from the towns, seems to grow as we advance into these two reigns. In such an age what will happen to an old due like tallage, so different in character from the revenues we have been discussing? The farm and the increment were annual dues paid for a specific advantage—the possession of land or trade or manufacture. The fine likewise secured the tenant possession of a manor or a townsman the opportunity to control the affairs of his borough while he practiced his trade free from arbitrary interruption by royal officials. The king and men of the demesne profited from the rent and the fine. The tallage belonged in a different category. To the tallage payer it was in the nature of an incalculable element in his economic life—not an auxilium that could be refused. The occasion of its levy was determined by the lord. The amount, it was true, was determined by negotiation between the great men of the administration and the local area acting as a group, but if the royal officials should not be satisfied with the lump sum offered, they could, it was known, assess the tallage on individual taxpayers within the area. One advantage tallage might have in the collection and payment by the authorities of the area was that the amount collected might exceed the amount to be paid the king and the profit would accrue to the local authorities.

Thus the council tried to expand the revenue on the same areas both from fines and farms and tallage by levying the latter frequently, expanding the assessment on individual areas, and particularly by the employment of the levy per capita. In the twenty years from 1168 to 1187 five tallages were taken with an assessment of about £19,000. From 1194 to 1206 (thirteen years), nine tallages appear in the pipe rolls, with a total charge of £26,000, a marked increase. There were notable disparities in the levies of the two periods. The justices of Henry II's reign normally tallaged the de-

138. *Ibid.*, p. 10.

mesne in over thirty shires. The record of the levies during the period 1194–1206 includes the demesne in from fifteen to thirty-one counties, and the largest amount assessed never equaled that of the larger levies of Henry II. When we examine the number of individual boroughs and manors that paid tallage we find that the levies usually omit many areas that had been taxed in the past and the tallage within a shire is sometimes composed of levies upon escheats and wardships temporarily in the king's possession. There were also occasions when one group of areas in a county was tallaged one year and another group the following year, while in other shires the old areas on the demesne and the new escheats are tallaged at the same time. An examination of the individual areas that paid tallage shows that only a few paid more than six times. One difficulty in making an exact statement on this point arises from the custom of the pipe roll clerks of enrolling the amount collected from all or part of the demesne in a shire without specifying the return from each town or village.

If we assume, as we must, that this sum will often include no one or all of the areas usually taxed, then the numbers of areas tallaged fall into this sort of table:

Areas tallaged nine times	5, all in Norhants.
Areas tallaged eight times	1, also in Norhants.
Areas tallaged seven times	13 in six shires.
Areas tallaged six times	43 in eighteen shires.
Areas tallaged five times	47 in nineteen shires.
Areas tallaged four times	42 in nineteen shires.
Areas tallaged three times	30 in seventeen shires.
Total	181

We cannot be sure how many of the areas usually tallaged are included in these sums, so the numbers are probably too large. If we should assume that none of the areas usually tallaged are included in the sum entered by the clerks without giving specific names or amounts, we get the following table:

Areas tallaged nine times	0
Areas tallaged eight times	5
Areas tallaged seven times	5
Areas tallaged six times	21
Areas tallaged five times	33
Areas tallaged four times	43
Areas tallaged three times	57
Total	164

TALLAGE UNDER RICHARD I AND JOHN 309

It is hardly likely that these large sums of "tallages" or "assessments and tallages" would not include some of the areas ordinarily tallaged, and accordingly the true number of areas that paid tallage three or more times probably falls between the amounts given in these tables. These returns are radically different from the late tallages of Henry II. From 1168 to the close of his reign five tallages were levied (1168, 1173, 1174, 1177, 1187). That of 1174 was taken in eighteen shires; that of 1187 in twenty-five shires. Thus in some areas a perfect record would be three, four, or five tallages. One hundred and thirty-nine areas paid four or five times; fifty-seven paid three times only. The five levies thus were as a rule paid by the towns and manors that formed the main part of the royal demesne and had not been exempted from paying tallage.

This astonishing variation raises the question whether the pipe roll records are complete; whether the collectors made their returns to a special exchequer or to another body such as the chamber. In the tallage of one year, 1194–95, there is some evidence that returns were made into the special exchequer of the ransom.[139] In 1210 the clerks of the pipe roll state that the account of the tallage of that year was made elsewhere.[140] In many other cases the returns were made at the exchequer not in the year the justices made the assessment but in the following year, a conventional practice. In several cases they were delayed for more than a year but ultimately were made at the exchequer. All this information comes from the pipe roll itself. It is possible therefore that in some cases the returns of a tallage in a shire might be omitted from the pipe roll, but it seems unlikely that many shires would be reported elsewhere and no allusion would have found its way into the pipe roll. It would seem probable that our rolls are fairly complete since the customary method had long been to pay the tallage into the exchequer. How then shall we account for the omissions? Some manors are omitted because they are exempted from tallage by the terms under which the manor was held. The bargain by which a manor was to be held at farm might involve also the payment of a fine and the recipient of the area might be exempt from tallage. Thus Fulburn in Cambridgeshire was assessed 43s. 2d. of tallage in 1206. The charge was deleted because the justices reported that it ought not to be exacted since the lord of that vill, Roger de Mowbray, had immu-

139. *Pipe roll 9 Richard I*, p. 142. *Pipe roll 10 Richard I*, p. 122. *Pipe roll 1 John*, pp. 74, 81, 164, 216.
140. Pipe roll 12 John, m. 10d., m. 19d, Public Record Office.

nity.[141] Under Henry II, from 1168 or 1179, the manors of Norton, Luton, Wantage, and Foulsham paid tallage. In 1190 Wantage (valued at £50 annual income) and Luton (£80) were given to the count of Aumale; in 1191 Norton (£16 10s. bl.) was given to him also, and in 1192 Foulsham (£44 16s. 3d. bl.) to Henry de Vere.[142] Thereafter none of these manors paid tallage. The manor of Renham (Kent) paid tallage under Henry II. Its farm amounted to £20 (terra data). In 1190 Robert de Crevecor paid a fine of 200m. to have it at the customary farm.[143] Thereafter Renham disappeared from the list of tallageable areas. It seems clear that these exemptions from tallage arose from the bargain between the council and the new holder. All these arrangements of various kinds indicate that a strong desire had developed among the lords of manors to escape from this levy. Thus when the justices came to assess a tallage upon a town or manor they often had to deal with important men familiar with law and procedure. The freemen and serfs upon whom the tallage would ultimately rest had by craft and stubbornness already succeeded in protecting themselves from the excessive demands of their superiors and were establishing the principle that their dues should be definite in amount and time.

Sometimes the arrangement definitely stated that the fine exempted the holder from tallage. Fulk Painel fined for the possession of the honor of Bampton in 1,000m. The farms of certain manors of the honor in 1199 were as follows: Bampton, £13; Uffculme, £13; they were both charged with tallage this year. But these charges were deleted because tallage had been granted to Fulk when he fined for the honor.[144] In 1204 Roger de Sumerville paid a fine of 60m. and two palfreys for having Alrewas at the old farm of £10, an increment of 100s., and for making the knight service due from a quarter of a fee.[145] The manor is not recorded as paying tallage to the king in 1205 or later in the reign. Thomas Basset fined for having the custody of the honor of the earl of Warwick. He was pardoned the tallage.[146] In 1204 Geoffrey Fitz Peter was given the manor of Ailesbury at fee farm by charter for the ancient farm of £50, an increment of £10, and the service of one knight's fee. He

141. *Pipe roll 8 John*, p. 167. *Pipe roll 9 John*, p. 107.
142. *Pipe roll 2 Richard I*, pp. 31, 138. *Pipe roll 3 Richard I*, p. 153. *Pipe roll 4 Richard I*, p. 179.
143. *Pipe roll 2 Richard I*, pp. 147, 150.
144. *Pipe roll 1 John*, pp. 191, 196, 197. *Pipe roll 2 John*, p. 231.
145. *Pipe roll 6 John*, p. 211.
146. *Pipe roll 7 John*, pp. 32, 36.

was exempted from many dues, among them tallage.[147] In 1202 William de Ferrers, earl of Derby, was granted the manors of Wirksworth and Ashbourne at fee farm (£80 bl. and £40 numero) for all service. Both manors had been tallaged in 1198 but no tallage is recorded against them under John.[148] High Wycombe (Bucks) was charged with 112s. 8d. of tallage in 1199 and paid most of it. It was farmed for £72. In 1203 it was granted to Alan Basset at a fee farm of £20, and one knight's service for all service.[149] In 1206 the justices assessed it at £30 8d. of tallage, but the levy was pardoned by the court of exchequer because Alan held that manor by knight's service.[150] Alan also received the manors of Woking and Mapledurwell, for the service of one knight for all service and no tallage was henceforth assessed on these areas.[151] William de Stutevill received the manor and borough of Knaresburg for the service of three knights.[152] Thus lords of manors succeeded in gaining exemption from tallage by the terms of a bargain with the council. Unless the land was granted for knight's service, the exemption had to be specifically mentioned in the grant. As to knight's service, the same rule seems to have been followed at first. Thus if lands were part of the demesne and granted for a farm and a certain amount of knight's service, the charter might specify exemption from tallage. Certainly the justices seem to have believed that a grant for a farm and military service did not necessarily exempt the holder from tallage, for cases appear in which such men were tallaged. Custom would determine that ancient dues should continue, unless specifically canceled by arrangement between lord and tenant. Furthermore in this particular case the demesne lands were subject to a due called auxilium, or donum, as well as tallagium. If the money payment in the shape of the farm continued when the land owed some military service, why should the tallage also not continue unless specifically dropped by the bargain? The justices would assess tallage and the cases must have been brought before the court of exchequer by the lord who held the farm by the new arrangement. The new bargain applied only to the relation between the king and the tenant or farmer. It did

147. *Rot. chart.*, pp. 127–128.
148. Carta antiqua, Public Record Office. *Pipe roll 5 John*, p. 171. *Pipe roll 10 Richard I*, p. 119.
149. *Pipe roll 1 John*, p. 117. *Pipe roll 2 John*, pp. 36, 264. *Rot. chart.*, p. 107.
150. *Pipe roll 8 John*, p. 40. *Pipe roll 9 John*, p. 155.
151. *Rot. chart.*, p. 37.
152. H. G. Richardson, "The morrow of the great charter," *Bulletin of the John Rylands library*, XXVIII (1944), 23–24.

312   TAXATION IN MEDIEVAL ENGLAND

not affect the dues which the tenant or farmer received from the men on the manor. The farmer thus stood to lose if he paid a farm. He was subject to the obligations entailed on him by military tenure and paid tallage also. The king would gain if he could levy tallage. Furthermore, the tenant sometimes secured it in the bargain. The question was—if the tallage was not exempted by name, should it be exigible? The answer rendered by the court of exchequer took the side of the tenants, that land for which military service was performed was exempt from tallage as between king and his tenant. The latter therefore probably collected the tallage and retained it when the king exacted this levy.

The cases involving military service have another point of interest. These grants that concern one knight's service and upward clearly were made on the initiative of the council with the aim of maintaining the royal revenue but also adding to the armed forces. The provisions about service were not made because of the monetary returns, scutage, relief, and so forth, for already by socage tenure the king as lord had adequate opportunity to add to his revenue. The provision of military service was introduced to add to the number of knights available. It reflects the continuing importance of the knight in war and the difficulty of enforcing the old servitium debitum in full; it also indicates the increased expense of warfare, when the king allowed the tenant a farm of £52 to supply him with a single knight. Thus the royal demesne was exploited in various ways, by the imposition of military service, by fines and farms, and by tallage. In the competition that arose between king and tenant over these dues the tallage on manors was, in various cases, abandoned because tenants opposed paying farms and tallages and performing military service as well. The council still regarded the demesne as a source of additional revenue that could be exploited in two ways, by levying it more frequently, and by the use of the tallage per capita.

The government could pursue this double goal because custom did not sharply oppose either method of increase. The king had always decided when tallage should be levied—when it should be necessary. The king through his justices had determined when it was justifiable to levy a tallage per capita. We have observed that while nine levies are registered in the pipe roll as taken in this period, the figure is exaggerated for the majority of cases. Nonetheless a considerable number of areas that conventionally were tallaged were assessed from three to six times. There was a prece-

TALLAGE UNDER RICHARD I AND JOHN

dent for this increase in frequency but it was one that had been abandoned in 1168 and had not thereafter been followed. The tallage per capita was clearly established. It sometimes though not always yielded enormous returns in this period.

If we compare the tallages of Richard and John with those of Henry II in both manors and towns, in individual areas that run through two periods, it is impossible to distinguish any principle of variation in amounts. Increases and reductions in assessment seem to depend upon the skill in bargaining displayed by the local tenants and the royal officials, except in 1187 when the levies per capita on manors seem always to register an increase. If however we consider the total amount of tallage assessed in each period in comparison with the relative lengths of the two periods, we find an astonishing increase under Richard and John.

Taking first the towns:

	1154–1188			No. of Levies	1194–1206			No. of Levies
	£	s.	d.		£	s.	d.	
Lincoln	1,436	10	8	9	1,272	7	8	6
Worcester	236	13	4	9	243	3	11	7
Newcastle on Tyne	153	6	8	8	359	6	8	5
Northampton	876	13	4	8	548	15	4	5
Norwich	1,272	6	8	8	631	16	8	5
Gloucester	409	6	8	8	530	13	4	6
Winchester	553	6	11	6	912	13	4	4
Southampton	82	6	8	3	196	13	4	5
Hereford	160	0	0	9	254	7	8	6
Nottingham	85	15	0	3	70	16	4	4
Derby	72	6	8	5	60	12	8	4
Oxford	351	6	8	8	385	14	4	6
York	2,403	15	8	11	1,093	13	4	5
Scarborough	100	13	4	4	583	16	8	5
Shrewsbury	209	0	0	9	213	6	8	6
Grimsby	125	1	0	4	223	14	0	7
Bristol	0	0	0	0	1,345	13	4	6
Bedford	189	6	0	8	122	12	4	5
Ilchester	71	9	6	9	83	11	2	5
Cirencester	54	0	0	5	87	7	0	5
Bridgnorth	55	16	8	7	64	0	8	5

Then the manors, where the increase is not so marked but is nevertheless definite in most instances:

314   TAXATION IN MEDIEVAL ENGLAND

	Henry II, 20 Years 1168–1187			No. of Levies	Richard and John, 13 Years 1194–1206			No. of Levies
	£	s.	d.		£	s.	d.	
Congresbury	60	2	2	5	13	0	0	5
Meleburn					14	13	2	6
Somerton	36	6	10	5	51	1	6	6
Gillingham	45	15	8	5	38	2	3	6
Bath					35	16	2	5
Menestrewerde	5	6	8	4 (not in 1174)	13	2	4	5
Cheltenham	17	0	0	5	22	8	0	4
Arera	6	7	0	4 (not in 1173)	11	11	0	4
Berton	16	6	8					
Ailesbury	38	0	0	4 (not in 1187)	52	15	8	
High Wycombe	35	6	4	2 (not in 1168, 1177)	44	12	8	4
Scriveham	44	4	8	5	56	0	0	4
Windsor	30	8	10	3 (not in 1168, 1173)	73	6	8	5
Maurdin	11	6	0	5	23	16	4	6
Lugwidin	6	6	8	5	12	7	8	5
Erlisham	70	3	4	3 (not in 1173, 1187)	21	2	4	4
King's Thorpe	41	6	8	3 (not in 1174, 1187)	54	3	4	7
Selveston	2	13	4	3 (not in 1174, 1187)	13	16	0	8
Corbi	7	0	0	3 (not in 1174, 1187)	18	7	10	8
Brichestoke	8	16	8	3 (not in 1174, 1187)	29	9	8	8
Nassinton	17	10	0	3 (not in 1174, 1177)	17	13	2	4
Clive	16	0	0	3 (not in 1174, 1187)	51	11	2	8
Oswardesbec	39	14	0	3 (not in 1174, 1187)	50	16	2	5
Mansfield	46	3	10	4 (not in 1187)	35	18	2	4

TALLAGE UNDER RICHARD I AND JOHN

	1168–1187			No. of Levies	1194–1206			No. of Levies
	£	s.	d.		£	s.	d.	
Ernhal	16	17	4	4	38	10	0	4
				(not in 1187)				
Snotinton	8	0	0	3	3	13	8	3
				(not in 1177, 1187)				
Werrefeld	23	2	6	4	39	13	4	6
				(not in 1173)				
Nordlega	7	0	0	4	13	0	0	6
				(not in 1173)				
Claverleg	10	0	0	4	12	10	0	6
				(not in 1173)				

Almost without exception the towns were taxed more frequently from 1194 to 1206 than in the whole reign of Henry in proportion to the number of years involved. The only exceptions are York and Norwich. If we take the tallages of York from 1163 to 1188, they were six in number and totaled £1,002 9s. In the same period of twenty-five years Norwich was tallaged six times to a total of £623 16s. 8d. In the case of the manors the number of levies under Henry II cannot exceed five, for although I believe that occasional aids were levied on them from time immemorial, there is no record of such levies prior to 1168 in the pipe roll. In the majority of cases the number of levies cited here and the amount yielded were greater in the second period than in the first. Thus it is clear that tallage was expanded from 1194 to 1206. We would like to know, however, the reaction of the men of areas that were tallaged frequently and tallaged per capita at the same time.

The question of the repetition of a tallage on a given area cannot be separated from the method of levy. The council aimed at two goals at the same time, viz., to increase the tallage by a liberal use of the per capita method and to increase the frequency of levy. A glance at a list of tallaged areas over a period of years shows that a horizontal increase proved impossible. In some way, the individual taxpayers within the manor or borough often succeeded in keeping their assessment low. So it seems to have been in King's Thorpe where they never reached the marks set in 1195 whether they taxed in common or per capita. Yet three of the first four tallages were taken per capita (1195–99) and exhibit marked variation in amount of the last three tallages, two were "in common," and both were larger than the final tallage of 1208 which was levied per capita. Geddington paid only one or possibly two tallages per capita (1205, 1206). In the first three tallages it paid £26 13s. 4d., the other five yielded £21 7s. 4d., a decline apparently due to repetition in successive years; and the final tallage per capita was one of the smallest levies in the series. Thus successive levies hampered the justices in assessing per capita. Silverton paid eight times. The first four yielded £7 19s. 8d. and the last four £4 17s. 4d. The first and last only were assessed per capita and were the largest levies, but something limited the total yield, apparently the repetition, since the sum of the last four was so far behind that of the first four. These variations indicated that the justices in all cases were able to secure a levy but that the amount depended in great part on the relative skill of the bargainers, for the amount per capita may or may not exceed the levy in common.

In a different shire with different assessors, with more omissions, amounts in common may exceed the levies per capita. Ailsbury was assessed £5 in 1197, £18 in 1198, £7 11s. 6d. (in per capita) in 1199, the high levy of the preceding year leading to a reduction; then no tallage till 1206, when a tallage of £22 4s. was charged. High Wycombe in the same shire was uniform for three years, paying £5 in 1197, £4 in 1198, £5 12s. 8d. (in per capita) in 1199; then nothing till 1206 when £30 8d. were assessed and later pardoned. Thus omissions may lead to a high assessment. A tallage per capita following two years' assessment may be unable to increase the assessment materially. A run of three or three out of four years may show striking variations, though not always whether the levy was per capita or not:

Northamp-tonshire	7 Richard			8 Richard			9 Richard			10 Richard			1, 2 John			4, 5 John			6 John			7 John			8 John		
	£	s.	d.	£	s.	d.	£	s.	d.	£	s.	d.	£	s.	d.	£	s.	d.	£	s.	d.	£	s.	d.	£	s.	d.
Northampton	200									100			60	18		120		6				48	5	8			
Geddington	10			6	13	4	10			2	13	4	3	3					5			6	6	8	4	3	4
King's Thorpe	18	16	4				3	12		6	13	4	1	8					8			10			5	13	8
Silverton	3	6	4	1	13	4	1	13	4	1	6	8		13	4					13	4	1	6	8	2	3	
Corbi	3	5	4	3	6	8	2	13	4	1	6	8	2	6						13	4	2			1	16	8
Brichestoke	4	6	8	3	6	8	3	6	8	2				13					5			6			4	17	8
Apetorp	5	5	8	6	13	4				4			5	10	8				4			4			3	19	2
Tindal	20	2	8	10						7 inden.			4	17								10			11	17	2
Fordwich	13	6	8	0			0			13	6	8	10			8											
Feckenham	1	6	8	0			7	1	4	5			5			4											
Succheleg	5	0	0	0			5	9	0	10			12			5											
Brumesgrave	5	0	0				7	12	2	3	6	8	3	3	4										10		
Worcester	53	6	8							20			26	13	4	26	13		43	3	11	26	13	4	46	13	4

Dorset and

Somerset	1196			1198			1199			1204			1205			1206		
	£	s.	d.	£	s.	d.	£	s.	d.	£	s.	d.	£	s.	d.	£	s.	d.
Somerton	3	13	6	20			13	6	8	3	18	8	5	1	8	5	2	
Melburn	1	10	2	5	6	8	2			2	11	8	2	5	8	1	5	
Bath	1	1	2	13	6	8	13	6	8	3	13		4	8	8			
Gillinghain	3	14	2	13	6	8	8			16			7	12		4	13	4
Ilchester				20			12			6	19	8	37	8		7	3	6

Except for Ilchester the later levies were decidedly lower.

Shropshire	1194			1198			1199			1203			1205			1206		
	£	s.	d.	£	s.	d.	£	s.	d.	£	s.	d.	£	s.	d.	£	s.	d.
Bridgnorth	5			6	13	4	8			6	13	4	10			17	14	
Shrewsbury	26	13	4	20			40			53	6	8	33	6	8	40		
Cunedour	3	6	8	2			4			2			4	13		4	6	8
Ford	3	6	8	3	6	8	6	13	4	4			15	8		12		
Werfeld	5			10			10			6	13	4	3			5		

We must not expect that this was a rule, but that the majority of levies were taken per capita. The amounts assessed "in common" will probably be higher than they otherwise would have been.

Wilts	1195	1197	1199	1203	1204	1205	1206
Marlborough	£20		20m.		£11 8d.	£32 9s.	
Rodes	1	½m.	1m.		8s.	7s.	13s.
Ludgarshall	1		2m.	2m.	5s.	55s. 8d.	
Melksham	10m.	50s.	£8	£10	65s.	73s. 4d.	9m. 8d.
Malmesbury			£5	10m.	53s. 4d.	£4 2s.	5m.
Wilton				194m. 40d.		£7 19s. 4d.	25m.

Yorkshire	1195	1196	1197	1200	1203	1204	1206
Sneed	10m.	£8		10m.		£35 14s. 8d.	
Esingwald	5m.		£34 5s. 8d.			6 8d.	103s.
Poclinton	6½m.	6	37s. 8d.	15m.		12 14s. 5d.	£13 16s. 4d.
Driffield	10m.						
York	£200		£87		500m.	£285 3s.	£100
Scarborough	£100		£49 3s. 4d.		300m.	£194 13s. 4d.	100m.
Doncaster	50m.		£27 5s.				

In Wiltshire, Marlborough was tallaged only four times in this period, the last two levies being per capita, and the last one by far the heaviest tax. By contrast Melksham paid seven levies. The last three in successive years were the only levies per capita and showed some increase but were less heavy than three of the four earlier tallages in common. All the areas show variations. In Yorkshire the final levy on Sneid (taken per capita) exceeded the totals of three earlier tallages, two being per capita, and later. Pocklington paid four times per capita, the last two being the heaviest. The largest levy on York was in common, on Scarborough per capita.

Broadly speaking the levy per capita probably prevented the tallage from becoming stereotyped and as such a device it must have been disliked. It proved impossible to maintain the levy on an area at the highest assessment. The variations cannot be reasonably explained as due to variations in the capacity to pay; they depend rather upon the skill in bargaining of the parties to the deal. Even so, the repetition as well as the increases reflected the king's power over his demesne. Perhaps the strongest indication of opposition to frequent tallages and levies per capita is the policy of the council after 1206. Thereafter no further attempts were made to levy it in successive years, and there are only two cases of the tallage per capita, that of Cambridge, and Milton in 1214.

No one would expect a tallage to be levied in 1207, the year of the thirteenth of revenues and movables. Furthermore the years following saw the royal income bolstered by the income from the church lands in hand as a reply to the interdict. No excuse moreover was made of the Scottish expedition in 1209 to levy tallage although a scutage was taken. Not till the great expedition to Ireland in 1210 was a tallage exacted in company with a scutage at the unprecedented rate of £2 per fee, with enormous fines. It was the heaviest tallage ever levied in the history of this tax and was taken in thirty-one shires. The increase in the yield was not due to the larger number of areas taxed but to the remarkable increase in the assessment of the towns, a reflection not only of John's power in 1210 but of his control over tallage when he exacted it in the way sanctioned by custom, that is, occasionally, in case of great need. No tallage was taken for the campaign of 1211 in Wales and none in 1214 for the expedition to France, although a scutage was levied each year. John had in mind another reason for the tallage of 1214, an insistent need—that of raising money to indemnify the church for its losses during the interdict.

The writs for the levy of tallage, which are wanting, were accompanied or followed by a personal letter from John of an extraordinary character. In his great financial necessity, he planned to obtain a loan from the demesne instead of a tallage. The letter was

320 TAXATION IN MEDIEVAL ENGLAND

addressed to the *probis hominibus* of Canterbury and to other cities and boroughs. It related the success in military operations which John had enjoyed and continues,

We have received . . . the letters of the Lord Pope concerning the form of the relaxation of the interdict on England, which we have forwarded to our venerable father, Peter, bishop of Winchester, our justiciar, and we beg you urgently [*attentius*] to grant [*impendatis*] us a generous subsidy as a loan in accordance with what the bishop will tell you toward relaxing that interdict so that we may justly applaud [*commendare*] your affection [*delictionem*] and favor. Know that the loan which you accord us for this purpose, we shall return to you in full with gratitude.[153]

The levy however appears in the pipe roll as a tallage. No record appears of an attempt at repayment. What John may have planned to do was forgotten in the civil war and the responsibilities that fell to the barons after the king's death.

Except for the levy of 1210, the total yield surpassed all other tallages. The reason lay in the heavy assessments on the towns, particularly on certain larger ones. For the first time since 1187 a large proportion remained unpaid. Such an unusual occurrence was due to the baronial uprising against John with the aftermath of civil war between Henry III and Prince Louis. On the conclusion of peace in the autumn of 1218, the levy of another tallage probably was a final bar to completing the collection of the levy of 1214. Yet some of the great towns paid it in full: London, 2,000m.; Canterbury, £200; Milton (a hundred) £105 16s.; Newcastle on Tyne, £200; Nottingham, 100m.; Derby, £40; Oxford, £200; Shrewsbury, 200m.; and Worcester, £99 out of £100.[154] These huge assessments in the last two tallages reflect the measure of John's control over the levy, particularly when he exercised his authority in accord with custom, on occasions of genuine insistent need. While the efforts to increase the returns by more frequent levies coupled with repeated assessments per capita had proved partially successful, so much opposition developed that the plan was dropped. Thus John's reign ended with tallage an occasional due, taken in common and yielding greater returns than ever before.

153. *Rot. pat.*, p. 111b.
154. Professor Mitchell's footnotes for the last part of this chapter cannot be found. The last note supplied by him is No. 138. While the editor has supplied the necessary references where he could, the annotation is obviously incomplete.

VII

TALLAGE IN THE REIGN OF HENRY III

THE reign of Henry III gives a more complete picture of tallage than we have been able to secure for the earlier period, because we have not merely the accounts in the pipe rolls but the references to it in patent and close rolls, which are fuller. In addition the memoranda rolls are available. This reign was marked by a struggle between the king and his barons over the question of taxation and by the development of taxation, of administrative organization, and of law and legal definition. Such was in part the environment within which this tax developed.

We have additional evidence that tallage was authorized by the king in his small council; that the great council felt no concern about it; that its levy was a matter for the king alone. For example, in 1217 a scutage on all fees was levied and also a tallage, both to raise money to pay 10,000m. promised to Prince Louis of France when he made peace and withdrew. The writs for levy of the scutage state precisely that it was levied by the common counsel of the kingdom, that is, by the common counsel of the earls and barons.[1] The writs for the levy of tallage, both those addressed to the assessors and those notifying the sheriff or the men of the demesne of the impending tax, say only that certain persons have been appointed to go to tallage the royal demesne.[2] The determination to levy tallage was taken in the small council, the group of professional administrators, where decisions on all questions of tallage were taken.[3]

The conventional expression for the authorization of the levy of tallage was that the king had caused it to be levied.[4] Thus the writs say, "as often as we and our heirs tallage our boroughs and our demesne"; and again, "because the king tallages his demesne"; or "of his last tallage assessed by the king's command on his demesne,

---

1. *Rot. claus.*, I, 371. *Patent rolls, 1216–1225*, pp. 125, 171.
2. *Ibid.*, pp. 170, 171, 403.
3. *Rot. claus.*, II, 171b. A. B. White, *Making of the English constitution* (New York, 1908), pp. 102–103. George Burton Adams, *Council and courts*, p. 285.
4. *Close rolls, 1259–1261*, p. 404. *Ibid., 1268–1272*, p. 64.

the king pardoned £100 to the men of Norwich"; or "because we have tallaged the cities, boroughs, and our demesne generally throughout our realm of England"; or "It has been provided by our council that we shall levy a completely adequate aid on all our boroughs and demesnes." [5]

Thus it seems evident that tallage was not granted by the great council, the great curia regis. It is true that the Articles of the Barons in 1215 declare that no scutage or aid shall be laid in the kingdom except by the common council of the kingdom, save for the three regular feudal aids; and adds "in a similar way let it be done concerning the tallages and aids of the city of London and other cities which have liberties about this." [6] But this demand apparently went beyond the law and custom of 1215, for in Magna Carta itself no reference appears to any town except London. Article XII repeats almost verbatim the clause of the articles on this topic till it comes to the question of tallage. Then it merely says, "In a similar way let it be done with the aids of the city of London." After John's death the regency felt that the whole article was open to doubtful interpretation and substituted an article about scutage alone: "Scutage shall be taken henceforth as it used to be taken in the time of King Henry, our grandfather." [7]

As these articles were not replaced in the charter under Henry III and as the orders for assessment never indicate any authority for the levy other than the command of the king, while the writs for the levy of aids constantly cite the fact that they had been granted by a great council, it would seem as though tallage remained a levy entirely in the control of the king.[8] This conclusion is in harmony with that reached by George Burton Adams in his discussion of the levy of tallage as given in the *Dialogue of the Exchequer*.[9] When the tallage had been authorized, the amount to be paid by each area was determined by negotiation between the assessors and the authorities of the area in question; while this action did not amount to the right to refuse, as we should today interpret consent, it must be noted that in practice hardly any contribution which a lord might ask of a tenant could really be refused.

So the line of demarcation between a levy which was a due and

---

5. *Close rolls, 1227–1231*, pp. 309, 463. *Ibid., 1234–1237*, p. 215. *Rot. claus.*, II, 171.
6. William Stubbs, *Select charters*, p. 293.
7. *Ibid.*, pp. 342, 347.
8. *Ibid.*, pp. 360–361, 364.
9. George Burton Adams, *Origin of the English constitution*, p. 361.

occasionally paid and one that was a free gift, a donum, was one that must have been clear to the men of the time yet may seem a wavering one to us. As we have seen above, the king in the thirteenth century was clearly drawing the line in the writs between the manner of authorization of an auxilium and a tallage. Nevertheless when the commissioners came to a town to assess the tallage, they were unable to determine of their own free will the amount; they had to negotiate to arrive at the amount of the tallage. Often the power and prestige of the royal commissioners overbore the men of the local area, and a sum was assigned that led to a protest before the council and to a reduction in the amount charged. This was particularly true in the tallage of 1226, when a long list of areas appears in the close roll with tallage reduced by the council.[10] Very likely this unprecedented reduction by the council was due to the fact that the preceding year the demesne had paid the fifteenth.

The influence of an assessor is illustrated by the story related by the Barnwell chronicler concerning the tallage of 1258. The assessor was William of Horton, the prior of Wymondham. He tallaged the vill of Chesterton at 15m. though this vill which was the holding of the priory of Barnwell was exempt by royal charter. The prior showed William the charter, but he refused to believe in its authenticity; he was then offered a gift of 40s. which he refused to accept, but he finally suggested that he be given a palfrey worth 5m. In the end the prior of Barnwell escaped paying anything. But it is clear from the tale that knowledge of one's legal rights and native stubbornness both were necessary to protect one from the exactions of royal officials.

The limitations on the power of the inhabitants of an area in dealing with royal officials are further illustrated by two incidents concerned with tallage in the financial history of London. In 1226 the royal government issued orders for the levy of a tallage on the king's demesne, including boroughs and cities.[11] In the case of London the government sought an unusually large sum, according to Roger of Wendover 5,000m., alleging that the Londoners had given Prince Louis that amount in 1218.[12] According to the chronicles the Londoners were forced by the advice of quibblers to assent to the demand.[13]

10. *Rot. claus.*, II, 184.
11. *Ibid.*, pp. 188b, 208b.
12. Roger of Wendover, II, 317–318.
13. Matthew Paris, *Chronica maiora*, III, 121.

324   TAXATION IN MEDIEVAL ENGLAND

The official records confirm the main point of the chroniclers' statement—that London had to agree to an aid of unprecedented amount, since never before had the citizens paid over 2,000m. It was particularly burdensome since they had paid the fifteenth in 1225.[14] But the chancery rolls show in detail the pressure that the council was able to exert on London. The great city had never before paid a tallage per capita; for the first time the government enforced this form of the levy against London and the total sum charged was over 4,700m. It must have been done against the opposition of the inhabitants, for the king issued letters patent declaring that the citizens had granted this aid freely and liberally and that this method of aid should not form a precedent for future demands.[15] The council, six months later, issued a sharply worded writ to the mayor, sheriffs, and aldermen of London for the immediate payment of the first half of this tallage. If this were not done, the king would take severe measure against them.[16] Nevertheless, the total amount paid in the years 1227 and 1228 amounted to only 4,120m. Thus London was forced into an assessment per capita but was also able to extract as a condition a guarantee against repeated tallages of this character.

Another dispute arose in 1255 between the government and the city over tallage, the outcome of which shows beyond cavil that tallage was a due levied at the king's desire, not an aid in the strict technical sense. This incident has been the subject of controversy as to the meaning of tallage—whether it was an aid requiring the assent of the tallage payers or a due. Adams concludes that London claimed it stood in its relation to the king as a feudal vassal, that is, as a commune, and hence owed aid only. Petit-Dutaillis declares that in 1255 the government desired only a certain sum of money and was indifferent to the legal aspects of the dispute—as to whether the contribution was called tallagium or auxilium.[17] This legal struggle should be interpreted in the light of the age, for it illustrates the important part played at this time by law and custom. It reflects the inability of the government to create a new levy arbitrarily, and the far-reaching effects of the refusal of the barons, beginning with 1242, to grant aids to the king.

14. Roger of Wendover, II, 317.
15. *Patent rolls, 1225–1232*, p. 104.
16. *Ibid.*, p. 132.
17. Adams, *Origin of the English constitution*, pp. 359 *et seq.*; Charles Petit-Dutaillis, *Studies and notes supplementary to Stubbs' constitutional history* (Manchester, 1908), pp. 91–106.

Let us then examine anew this incident, first reviewing the main facts as preserved in the close and memoranda rolls. In January, 1255, Henry III returned from Gascony heavily in debt and at once sought to raise money from his barons and from churchmen.[18] His great financial need, therefore, led him to levy a tallage.[19] The representatives of London came to the exchequer and a tallage of 3,000m. was demanded of them; they replied by offering an aid of 2,000 m., and declared that they could and would not give more. Next day they came again to the exchequer, but no agreement was reached. Then a committee of the council went to London to levy the tallage per capita, thus following the procedure described in the *Dialogue of the Exchequer*. But the opposition to the tax was so bitter that none of the Londoners would cooperate by swearing to the value of their goods. So this effort to resolve the dispute failed. Then the mayor and others of the Londoners returned to the exchequer and a long debate seemingly ensued. Finally the issue seems to have been raised whether the Londoners owed auxilium or tallagium. The officials of the exchequer searched the rolls, both pipe and chancellor's, and produced six cases in which London had paid tallagium.[20] In the face of this evidence the citizens yielded and agreed that they were liable to tallage and promised to pay 3,000m. of tallage. In order to prevent further difficulty on this point, the council had the history of this case recorded in detail on the rolls.

All discussion of this struggle must be prefaced by the observation that both accounts in the close and memoranda rolls relate the government's side of the dispute. We have none of the evidence introduced by the Londoners in support of their contention that they owed auxilium and not tallagium. Hence let us not be surprised if we encounter no mention of Article XII of Magna Carta issued by King John, and its references to the aids of the city of London. Such a reference would not strengthen the case for the king. The narrative further implies that the significant point of difference at the commencement of the dispute was whether London owed tallagium or auxilium, each in the strict technical sense, the former being an obligatory payment and the latter a freewill grant. But such an interpretation passes over unjustifiably due consideration

18. Paris, *Chronica maiora*, V, 484, 493, 520. *Annals of Dunstaple*, p. 195. *Annals of Burton*, p. 336.
19. *Close rolls, 1254–1256*, pp. 159, 161.
20. *Ibid.*, p. 160. Exchequer to K. R., 39 Henry III, m. 9d, Public Record Office.

of the sum demanded and offered. The king being in great want asked for a tallage. The citizens offered 2,000*m.*; the royal officers refused to accept it and demanded 3,000*m.* Now the offer of the citizens was their ordinary grant; only once had they paid more and on occasions they had paid less. In 1226 they had paid tallage per capita and had received letters patent that this levy was not to constitute a precedent. Of course, 2,000*m.* could not have been proportionate to the capacity of the city to pay. The king did not accept the offer, probably because of his great financial necessity, for this was the time when he was pressing both laity and clergy for additional revenue.

When the city refused to agree to the 3,000*m.*, the administration resorted to the tallage per capita. In form this was a legal procedure. In this case, however, it was of doubtful propriety. In 1226 London had paid an aid, or tallage, per capita, and at that time Henry III had issued letters patent declaring: "As we are unwilling that any prejudice or injury should be created to the barons themselves [of London] or their heirs, or that this method of aid should be drawn into pattern or precedent, we affirm by these present letters of ours that the aforesaid method of aid has been granted out of the liberality of our aforesaid faithful."

The only time that London had paid a tallage per capita therefore it had been accompanied by a solemn statement that it had been done out of the liberality of the Londoners. To take a tallage per capita then would seem to violate an established custom fortified and recognized by royal letters patent. Hence, it may be suggested, arose the spirit of united opposition to the action of the government and the readiness with which the council abandoned the attempt to levy it per capita. Further discussion followed between the Londoners and the council at Westminster on Sunday, February 7.[21] The words of the record indicate that it was only at this time, when an agreement seemed out of the question, that the point was either raised, or became of vital importance, whether the payment was an auxilium or tallagium. Thus it says, "And since there had been controversy (dispute) whether this ought to be called *tallagium vel auxilium*, the king ordered his rolls to be examined whether they had given anything to the king or to his ancestors by the name of *tallagium.*"

Had issue been joined on this point earlier, the council would probably have followed the custom of settling the legal point raised

---

21. *Close rolls, 1254–1256*, p. 160.

TALLAGE IN THE REIGN OF HENRY III

before attempting to appeal to force. Nothing is more common than to have an individual claim exemption from some due and then when it is brought to court, the process of distraint is checked and an inquest is held to discover the truth. The time therefore of this present inquiry would seem to have been after the Londoners had forced the question; after they had failed to reach an agreement, compulsion had proved to be impracticable, and yet the council insisted that they had the right to levy 3,000m. on the citizens. Then apparently the latter asserted that they did not owe 3,000m. because they only owed auxilium, and the king could not fix the amount of that.

This claim excited the council to a high degree. How otherwise shall we explain the elaborate search, taking in both pipe and chancellor's rolls, for precedents of the payment of tallage by London and reaching back forty years to the reign of John? Why otherwise should the council order the exchequer barons to cause their triumphant list of cases to be enrolled *de verbo in verbum* lest contention of this kind arise again? [22] Unquestionably the council felt that here was a crucial case. Might it not also be true that London had adduced as argument something more than its mere belief or theory that it owed auxilium and not tallagium? But of this there is no statement directly in the record enrolled in 1255.

Let us look for a moment at the cases adduced by the council; from the omissions we may infer perhaps something of the legal argument of the Londoners. The earliest case cited was that of the levy of 1214, 16 John. The officials intended, it is clear, to construct an impregnable case in law by going a long way back. But why, it may be asked, did they stop with 1214? The answer of course is that London's contributions were not called tallagium earlier. In 1210 it paid 2,000m. *de dono;* in 1204, £1,000 *pro fine passagii;* in 1194, 1,500m. *de dono . . . et de auxilio suo* for the ransom of the king. Earlier tallages under Henry II were called auxilium or donum, or assisa.

The tallage of 1217 was omitted, perhaps because London did not appear charged with it in the pipe roll.[23] In 1223 the city paid tallage as has been noted. The tallage of 1226 is not cited although the pipe roll heads it *tallagium civitatis.* But the council probably did not wish to cite it, perhaps because of the letters patent concerning the levy per capita. In 1230 another tallage was taken to

22. *Ibid.*
23. Sydney Knox Mitchell, *Studies in taxation,* p. 129.

which London contributed, but the payment was called auxilium and it was omitted in this citation. In 1236 London gave 1,000m. de auxilio toward the dowry of the sister of Henry III in her marriage to Frederick II; and in 1253 in response to the king's general appeal to his demesne to grant him an aid (auxilium), London paid him 500m. *de subsidio.*

Thus it is clear in citing six cases in which London had paid what they could technically call tallagium, the council cited all that the rolls named tallagium, with the exception of that of 1226 which, though called tallagium, looked like a special grant by the citizens. Those letters patent imply that the king had no right in 1255 to a tallage per capita. The thoroughness of the search reveals the trouble of the council. This list also shows the cases which London may have brought up of times when it had paid auxilium. It should also be noted that the tallage of 1226 was called auxilium in the patent and close rolls, and the tallage of 1214 was also called auxilium. Thus there was a long list of cases in which London paid auxilium. Something like this list must have been produced by the citizens to stir up the council to such activity.

Despite the dispute of 1255, it is difficult to find any distinction earlier in the thirteenth century between the aid and the tallage. In 1210 London paid 2,000m. *de dono;* in 1214, 2,000m. de tallagio. No change in the legal status of London that has been recorded occurred between 1210 and 1214. Nor do we know of any between 1223 when the citizens paid tallagium and 1230 when they paid auxilium. The levy of 1223 was for a military expedition, that of 1230 for the same. The auxilium of 1236 was to marry the king's sister and the tallage of 1245 to marry his daughter, each being one of the regular feudal aids. Neither occasion nor amount shows any distinction. Can we find a better explanation that the terms tallagium and auxilium were interchangeable; that the clerks wrote down now one, now the other as descriptive of the same grant, or that one sheriff called it an aid and the other a tallage.

If this is true, then how can we account for the excitement of the council? Not because the question of London as a commune was being raised, or because the king was merely trying to get the grant of 3,000m. in 1255, but because behind the question of the name of the levy lay an important point. Why did the council insist on the term tallagium in 1255 when they had been quite indifferent to its use in 1236? It may be suggested that the great council had been giving a new meaning to the term auxilium since 1237. The auxilium was a freewill grant; and might be refused. Thus in 1217 the bishop of Winchester was excused from paying the aid on knights' fees of that year because he had never assented to it. In 1232 the count of Aumale and others refused to allow the fortieth to be collected on their lands although the great council had granted it. Not till 1236 was it collected from the lands of Richard de Percy who "then prevented it, but now has granted that it all shall be collected." [24] Even so, the fact remains that to all practical ends and purposes the auxilium was, in general, paid when the king desired it. It might take some negotiating and pressure, yet as the vassal ought to come to the aid of his lord in a pinch, it was hard for him in general to refuse to aid him on occasion and certainly no one ever saw so many grants of aids to the king as lord as took place from 1188 to 1237.

Thus aid began to seem like a new custom. So it was said by the clergy in 1244 when Henry asked for another grant on movables. How many times constitute a new custom? And they answered two times. Hence arose in part the opposition of the barons to the aids, and beginning in 1242 they refused to make any grant to the king. Thus the term auxilium took on a new connotation; it was a freewill grant to the lord, but at the same time it could easily be refused and if refused, the king would be unable to collect it. The corporate feeling developed by the baronage made this action possible. When the king attempted to collect it without the assent of the baronage he was unsuccessful.

Therefore, in 1255, when the Londoners raised the question whether their payment to the king was an auxilium or a tallagium, they were saying, "We do not owe this money; we will grant you a certain sum, but since this is auxilium, we can, if we like, refuse it." That was exactly the position of the barons; they might grant auxilium to the king, but they had on many occasions refused the grant, and the king had been unable to collect it. The attitude and the claims of the Londoners foreshadowed the possibility of a refusal of the aid. The treasury was threatened with the loss of an old, well-established due. Hence arose the excitement of the small council, their careful and exhaustive search for precedents of payment of tallage by London, and finally their formal and categorical enrollment that the great city was tallageable.

24. *Ibid.*, p. 386 *et seq.*

The dispute thus was settled in favor of the king. The Londoners came and acknowledged that they owed tallage.[25] They did more, according to the record of the close roll. They paid the 3,000m. The statement is true that they paid their tallage, but not on that Monday. In the memoranda roll of three years later, as also on the pipe roll, London stands charged with a debt of 3,000m. of tallage.[26] But it was all recorded as paid in the next year.[27] Accordingly, the Londoners not only acknowledged that they owed tallage but they also paid it, and they paid the amount which satisfied the royal officials. It forms an excellent example of the procedure described in the *Dialogue of the Exchequer* of the methods of levying tallage, of the importance of custom in taxation, and of the influence of political movements in the thirteenth century on old custom.

It seems clear, therefore, that tallage was not an aid, that it was levied at the will of the king, but the amount was paid by negotiation between royal officials, assessors, and the inhabitants of the area or its lord or custodian.

There was no marked increase in the frequency with which tallage was taken. It was levied nine times under Henry II, four times under Richard, seven times under John, and fourteen times under Henry III. The occasion for tallage did not change, but there was more emphasis upon levies for a special great financial need of the king. There was less connection with scutage than under Henry II.

We have seen that under Richard I one scutage (1191) was unaccompanied by tallage, that under John four scutages (1201, 1209 Scotland, 1211 Wales, and Poitou 1214) were unaccompanied by tallage, that under Henry II one tallage (1177) was levied when no scutage was taken, and under John one was taken for the relaxation of the interdict in 1214.

Year	Occasion
1217	To pay the 10,000m. to Prince Louis; accompanied by an aid on knights' fees
1223	A campaign in Wales; scutage of Montgomery
1226–27	To raise cash for campaign in France—no great campaign and no scutage

25. *Close rolls, 1254–1256*, p. 160.
26. Pipe roll 41 Henry III, m. 14d. Exchequer K. R., Memoranda roll 41–42 Henry III, m. 28d, Public Record Office.
27. Exchequer L. T. R., Memoranda roll 55–56 Henry III, m. 7d, Public Record Office.

Year	Occasion
1230	Campaign in Brittany; scutage of Brittany
1234	Campaign in Wales; scutage of Elveyn
1235	Marriage of king's sister; feudal aid; aid on knights' fees
1237	King's debts
1241–42	Campaign in Wales; perhaps should be for the campaign in Gascony; 1242, scutage of Gascony
1246	Aid to marry the king's daughter
1249	The king's debts
1251	Aid to marry the king's daughter
1255	The king's debts
1260	King's expenses; no special cause
1268	King's expenses; no special cause

Six scutages were levied unaccompanied by tallage. Eight tallages were taken to raise money for military purposes or to discharge debts of the king. Two were taken in connection with a feudal aid: marriage of the king's sister, and the king's daughter (1235 and 1245), and four as correlative to scutage. Thus tallage was losing its character of a tax on the demesne when the king taxed his fees held by military service, and it was becoming a tax to raise cash for the extraordinary needs of the king; to pay the king's debts. It was assuming the character of the taxes on personal property.

The levy coincided so often with the efforts to liquidate the king's debts that it tended to become a tax which could be levied at frequent intervals to raise cash for any insistent governmental need. The king's right to demand tallage thus was greatly expanded under Henry III. Hence the question was bound to arise how frequently should tallage be levied. In 1251 a tallage was levied to marry the king's daughter to the king of Scotland. In 1253 the king led an expedition to Gascony, but did not levy a tallage. Instead, he requested an aid from the demesne. Earlier in the reign occurs a statement that tallage should not be levied more often than every three years.[28] And again the king ordered the postponement of an assessment of tallage on Colchester because not more than two years had elapsed since it was assessed.[29]

The government was moving toward stabilization along another line. That is, that tallage should be levied on a manor only when the king took a general levy. This is the meaning in writs which

28. *Close rolls, 1237–1242*, p. 339.
29. *Ibid.*, p. 302.

granted a holder of land which had been of the ancient demesne the right to levy a tallage, for such writs begin, "because the king is tallaging his demesnes in England," [30] as justification for the grant to the present holder. Yet the indication is that tallage was to be a general and uniform levy. Henry of Hastings and his wife were granted by the king the manor of Mansfield temporarily for part of the inheritance of the earl of Chester.[31] He tallaged it annually at 10m. An inquest by John Gubaud and his companions later showed that it had not been accustomed to be tallaged earlier except when the king tallaged his demesne. "Nor is it fair or consonant with reason," says the writ, "that tallage should be levied otherwise than is it has been wont to be taken." [32]

While tallage was thus becoming stabilized as to frequency, it changed in other respects. The amount of rural demesne which paid this levy to the king diminished in the pipe roll, though the boroughs slightly increased in number. A partial explanation may be that the rolls do not contain a complete account, but it is more likely that the cause was the grant by the barons and the king of royal manors to holders in fee farm or other ways, and that the new holders received the tallage instead of the king. The close rolls contain many more grants of tallage under Henry III than under John.

Thus the bulk of the tallage paid to the king as reported in the rolls fell more and more upon the boroughs, supplemented by levies upon lands which continually fell into the king's hands. But ancient demesne and old escheats continually diminished. The revenue from them came from fee farms and from services. Taking individual groups and leaving to one side the question as to whether rolls are incomplete, the tallage on urban demesnes as shown by the accompanying table does not show any marked increase under Henry III as compared with earlier periods. Even leaving to one side the remarkably high levies of 1210 this remains true; nor do we find that the towns uniformly paid heavier tallages in the last half of the reign of Henry III than in the first half. Thus the amounts paid by the towns seem to be limited. We may infer that such a condition was due to the influence of custom and to the ability of townspeople to protect their rights.

When we turn to the rural demesne, it is a different matter. In

30. *Close rolls, 1242–1247*, p. 87.
31. *Calendar of patent rolls, 1232–1247*, p. 224.
32. *Close rolls, 1242–1247*, p. 505.

general the levies were heavier during the second half of the reign than in the first half, and heavier, though not always, than in the levies of the period of Henry II, Richard I, and John. Tallage was levied on the same areas, both rural and urban as before, unless an area had been granted with the right of tallage to some tenant.

In addition to ancient demesne and lands that had been long escheated to the king lands newly come into royal possession also paid tallage on their demesnes to the king. Thus the bishopric of Exeter, which was in hand, paid tallage on its manors and scutage on its fees.[33] The accounts of tallage in the pipe rolls however contain but few notices of tallage on similar lands under late John and all through Henry III. We may conclude that the council arranged with the custodians at first and then with the escheators as to the payments to be made during the vacancy.

The method of assessment during this long reign exhibits considerable variation due to experiment and political experience. The assessors must combine administrative experience, knowledge of local conditions, and fidelity to the king's interests in order to assure an equitable apportionment of the tax among the taxpayers, and a payment proportionate to the wealth of each area tallaged. In discussing the personnel of the assessors, the first topic of importance is the principle which guided the choice of these important officials. Undoubtedly one factor was custom. This is seen in the dispatch of a group of assessors (tallagers) to a single county or a pair of counties served by the same sheriff as in 1217, 1223, 1227, and 1230; a group also might cover a circuit of four or more shires.[34]

In the first levy of 1217 there was need to raise a large sum of money with as little delay as possible and consequently the groups of assessors do not seem to have been chosen according to any settled principle; the council sent out any experienced men that they could find. Thus to Gloucestershire went Earl William Marshal, Ralph Musard, the sheriff, William de Cantilupe, an important official under John, and Henry Fitz Gerald, three of whom were important officials. To Kent went Robert de Dean, seemingly a reliable royal official, though without special distinction, under John and Henry III, with Robert de Rokele and Roger Tancre,

33. Pipe roll 9 Henry III, m. 3d, Public Record Office.
34. *Patent rolls, 1216–1225*, pp. 171, 172, 403. *Rot. claus.*, II, 208b. *Close rolls, 1227–1231*, p. 294. *Pipe roll 14 Henry III*, pp. 87, 291.

both knights in Kent of whom we have no record of any official experience; to Surrey went Robert de Dean and Gilbert de Abingwerth, a royal justice, and Richard de Dole, apparently a clerk of the exchequer, for he was made one of the custodians of the Jews in 1218.[35] Thus in three adjacent counties, three different kinds of assessors were appointed—differences which reflect the varieties of officials that had acted as tallagers in the past.

When the second and third tallages of the reign were levied (in 1223 and 1227), the government had long been functioning in orderly fashion and had well considered the insistent problems of finance that faced it. In these tallages a more uniform system of assessors was adopted. The sheriffs had earlier been employed as tallagers, but had now assumed a leading role. If we recall that the sheriff was the collector of the tallage we see how this influence increased when he was also made one of the assessors. In 1223 Falkes de Bréauté, who was sheriff of six shires, was a member of the group of three who assessed the tallage in those counties.[36] In the lists of assessors of the tallage of this year given in the patent roll a sheriff or undersheriff appears in four out of the six lists, but he was still very important. Godfrey de Craucumb was an assessor in four counties besides Oxfordshire. In 1234 and 1235 the proportion is lower. Two sheriffs were assessors out of seven sheriffdoms in 1234, and three out of eight sheriffdoms in 1235.

From 1227 to 1241 (comprising six tallages: 1227, 1230, 1234, 1235, 1237, 1241) the record of lists of assessors which I have (though incomplete) indicates that the sheriff of the year was not uniformly employed as an assessor. Sheriffs of other counties were used and men who had formerly been sheriffs. Other officials employed as tallagers were those that developed out of the members of the small professional council. We had the itinerant justices as tallagers, then justices of assize—men appointed to try a single case. Thus William de L'Isle, who was a tallager in 1230 in Hampshire, had been a justice to deliver the gaol at Northampton in 1227 and one of the justices to try a case of *novel disseizin* in 1228, and later to try a case of *mort d'ancestor*.[37]

There are many cases like this. The employment of these men, like that of itinerant justices, grew logically out of the custom of sending royal justices to a locality to apply the law of the king's

---

35. *Rot. claus.*, I, 196b, 321b, 359. *Patent rolls, 1216–1225*, pp. 154, 208.
36. *Ibid.*, p. 403.
37. *Pipe roll 14 Henry III*, pp. 159, 197, 280, 365.

court. Another official of the same type was the escheator, who was very familiar with men and property on the royal demesne. These officials were naturally appointed as tallagers. Roger de Cusering, a tallager in Berkshire in 1235, was keeper of the escheats in that county in 1232; Nicholas Seculareus and Pauncevot were two of the assessors in Herefordshire in 1235, and also were keepers of escheats in the same shire in 1232.[38]

The same man might fill several of these offices. William Basset, who was a tallager in Nottinghamshire and Derbyshire in 1233–34, was a keeper of escheats in Leicestershire in 1232, a collector of the fortieth in the same shire in 1232, an itinerant justice in the same year, and a justice to deliver the gaols at Kenilworth and Roele (Rothley) in 1232, one of the justices to try a case under the assize *utrum* in 1231 at Leicester and in 1230 a case of novel disseizin also at Leicester.[39] Not every tallager can be shown to have had wide experience, indeed of some we have no further word. Thomas de Chelnerston, an assessor in Bucks and Bedfordshire, cannot be found in any other official record. But most tallagers had a wide experience—a reflection of the deliberate care taken by the council to insure a proper return of the tax. In 1241–42 John Gubaud was the chief assessor in eleven counties, sometimes acting alone. He was an official of long and varied experience, having been constable of the Peak, a collector of the aid of 1235, a marshal of the king's household, a county commissioner to assess the thirtieth of 1237, a justice to inquire into the riots at Oxford in 1236, an itinerant justice in Hants in 1240, a warden of the coast, a justice of assize in 1225, and in 1241–42 sheriff of Bucks and Bedfordshire.[40] To place one official in charge of tallaging eleven counties was an experiment which was not without result.

Thus the system of assessment which had developed in 1241 was to allocate to this task a small group of available administrators or justices, sometimes though not always familiar with the shire to which they were sent. They negotiated with local representatives so that the amount of tallage was fixed by the joint labors of representatives of the central government and local interests.

Now in 1241 there seems to begin a deliberate effort to combine in the assessing commissioners both administrative experience and

38. *Close rolls, 1231–1234*, pp. 130, 131.
39. *Ibid.*, pp. 130, 131, 136, 158. *Patent rolls, 1225–1232*, pp. 366, 445, 512.
40. *Ibid.*, p. 72. *Close rolls, 1227–1231*, p. 367. *Ibid., 1234–1237*, pp. 269, 343, 345, 552.

knowledge of local economic conditions, which resulted in an entirely new assessing organization; and then just as this had been accomplished, tallage, except for three cases levied over a period of nearly three fourths of a century, disappeared. The levy of 1241 again systematically emphasizes the employment of the sheriff as one of the assessors.[41] The others were taken as before from the reservoir of experienced officials.

While the tallage of 1245 seems to return to previous custom, that of 1248 continued to expand the effort to establish a more uniform system of assessment. Most of the kingdom was divided into circuits; one or two commissioners were sent out to each circuit, who with the sheriff formed a committee of assessment for each county.[42]

Thus the sheriff again became a vital part of the system of assessment. His associate seems sometimes to have been the leading member of the committee. Henry de Wengham was escheator in six counties, and was sent out as tallager to ten counties (an echo perhaps of the experiment with John Gubaud). Thomas de Stanford and William de Axemuth were commissioners to six counties and the archbishopric of York. Thomas was, in January, appointed escheator of the shires north of the Trent, and William seems in the liberate roll to be already an important financial official. In any case the representative of the central government had a great advantage when he had only one member of his local committee to deal with. Anyhow, a uniform system which combined a representative of the central government and a local representative was employed. In 1252 a further step in organization was taken, which carried out the principle of the combination of central supervision with local administrative information. All the shires were grouped in three circuits: to the first was sent Richard le Rus and Richard de Sherburne, two clerks of the wardrobe; to the second William de Axemuth, and James de Fresel; to the third Thomas de Stanford.[43] All five were officials of wide and varied important experience. Richard le Rus and Richard de Sherburne were very active in finance. William de Axemuth was a chief assessor in 1249, and his associate, James de Fresel, who had not been mentioned hitherto in the rolls, must have been a clerk of parts, for in 1253 he was made co-escheator of the counties south of the Trent.

41. *Calendar of patent rolls, 1232–1247,* p. 263.
42. *Close rolls, 1247–1251,* p. 216. *Calendar of patent rolls, 1247–1258,* p. 45.
43. *Close rolls, 1251–1253,* pp. 212–213.

London was not included in these circuits—its assessors were John Mansel, William Haverhill, the treasurer, and Edward de Westminster, all high permanent officials of the council.[44] In each county in their circuit these chief assessors collaborated with the sheriff and two knights of the shire who were named in the writ. Thus the council formed a committee of assessment for each shire, comprising central and local representatives, uniform, centralized, and composed of experienced and dependable personnel.[45]

Three years later in 1255 came another tallage in which the government modified the elaborate organization of 1252. The kingdom was divided into seven circuits, in four of which a sheriff of one of the counties in the circuit was an assessor.[46] All of the groups of assessors consisted of two officials, except in the North to which three commissioners were sent, Robert de Mameby, a royal clerk, Thomas de Stanford, and Robert de Crepping, who had been escheators north of the Trent in all the counties of this circuit.[47] In four other circuits the assessor associated with a sheriff was a royal justice, chosen from one of several justices who at this time were on an iter. As itinerant justices they did not assess in the counties in which they fulfilled their judicial duties.[48]

In the remaining two circuits, two royal justices, Roger de Whitcester and William Trussel, were the commissioners in one, and John de Wivill, a justice, and Thomas Espurun, an important clerk in the exchequer and late chamberlain of London, were commissioners in the other.[49] London was assessed by itself by important justices, Henry of Bath, Roger of Thurkelby, Philip Lovell, the treasurer of the exchequer, Peter de Rivaux, Edward de Westminster, and John Francigenae.[50] While the sheriff was not formally a part of the board of assessors in deciding disputed questions, practically he had great influence. He was instructed to bring together representatives of tallageable areas to meet the justices, and to be a constant aid to them.[51]

In 1260 there were again seven circuits, London again standing by itself and being assessed by the baronial justices. The character-

44. *Calendar of patent rolls, 1247–1258*, p. 142.
45. *Close rolls, 1251–1253*, pp. 212–213.
46. *Close rolls, 1254–1256*, pp. 161–162.
47. *Calendar of patent rolls, 1247–1258*, pp. 6, 359.
48. *Ibid.*, p. 436.
49. *Ibid.*, pp. 117, 436, 438, 490, 505. *Close rolls, 1254–1256*, p. 162.
50. *Ibid.*, p. 157.
51. *Ibid.*, p. 162.

istic personnel of the assessors remained constant except that no sheriff of the year forms part of the group of assessors in his county; the influence of this officer could be exerted when he co-operated with the justices in their work.[52]

In the final tallage of the reign came the generalization of a method long employed in Kent—the use of escheators—illustrating the expansion of that branch of the administration. The prior of Wymondham, escheator south, and John de Keygate, escheator north of the Trent (with Walter de Stokes), were each in his own area to assess the tallage.[53] The county co-escheators and the sheriffs probably assisted the chief escheators in their task, but the rolls are silent on the subject.

Thus the experiment and development of administration led the government gradually to the assessment of tallage by the officials who should have been familiar with the financial condition of men on the demesnes, the escheators, and an organization which would keep closely in touch with it. This brief survey shows also the value of close connection between the central and local governments.

When the assessors or tallagers entered their taxing circuit, of one or more counties, how did they get in touch with the tallage payers? Though we possess no writs authorizing a tallage before the reign of Henry III, there seem to have been two customary methods. One was for the assessors to visit the area to be taxed and negotiate with the borough or manor. The other, of which we have only a single record, seems to have been for the men of an area to come to a designated place to treat with the assessors. The men of Radeclive in Somerset were summoned to send twenty-four representatives to the exchequer to show cause why they were not tallaged when the rest of the demesne was tallaged. They had escaped assessment because when they had been summoned by the sheriff to send representatives to meet the assessors at some place in the shire they had failed to do so, and their absence made possible their evasion.[54]

The sources for the early part of the reign of Henry III indicate that the assessors were familiar with the method of levying tallage. For example, in 1223 and 1227 the writs state that the men of the demesnes are to meet the assessors on a certain day at a certain

52. *Calendar of patent rolls, 1258–1266,* pp. 75–76.
53. *Ibid., 1266–1272,* pp. 226, 306, 307.
54. *Memoranda roll 1 John,* p. 10.

place; the men of Kent for instance, in 1217, at Canterbury; and in 1227 the assessors were to tallage the town of Lancaster and all the other boroughs and demesnes of the king in Lancashire at the vill of Lancaster.[55] Yet such a procedure would be possible only if each area sent some kind of a representative group to negotiate as to the amount of their tallage.

Another customary procedure was to levy the tallage by poll or in common. The only possible levy in 1217 was the tallage in common, for collection was to begin at once and returns were to be made weekly—such was the necessity of the government for cash to get Louis out of the country as soon as possible.[56] Under these conditions it would be impossible to levy a tallage per capita by negotiation between the assessors and a few representatives of the manor or borough. Nevertheless it is clear that tallage per capita was levied to some extent in 1227, as is shown by the unevenness of the amounts of tallage charged against certain areas. If so, the assessors must have visited various areas within each shire, as in the past. This was the year of the famous "great tallage" of London, which was levied per capita and amounted to over 4,000m.[57]

It is clear that in 1230 when the justices came into the county, they met with representatives from each unit area of the demesne, manor, or borough. Thus in Lincolnshire the sheriff was ordered to summon twelve men from each unit of the demesne to meet with the assessors and himself. The assessors and the sheriff by negotiation with the representatives from each manor or borough fixed the tallage for that area.[58] This entry of the royal officials into a city was, as we have seen, disliked. Whether in the twelfth century, described in the *Dialogue*, the procedure involved an oath as to the value of goods we cannot tell, but the assessors entered the area and taxed men individually. Though there was some taxing per capita in 1223 and 1226, the method met with strong opposition. London secured letters patent that this method was not to constitute a precedent. A minority of rural areas and boroughs also were taxed per capita, but a great proportion of the amounts charged were reduced.[59] The reduction cannot be due primarily to opposition to

55. *Patent rolls, 1216–1225*, pp. 170, 403. *Close rolls, 1224–1227*, p. 209.
56. *Patent rolls, 1216–1225*, p. 170.
57. *Rot. claus.*, II, 184. *Close rolls, 1227–1231*, pp. 1, 285. Pipe roll 12 Henry III, m. 6, Public Record Office.
58. *Close rolls, 1227–1231*, p. 280.
59. *Ibid.*, p. 1. *Rot. claus.*, II, 180b.

the levy per capita. Probably it arose from the fact that the demesne had just completed paying the unusual levy of the fifteenth in 1225.

Anyhow, after 1227 taxing per capita seems to disappear and instead we have the levy in common. We may fairly conclude this from the fact that the sums charged were in whole sums of pounds or marks, or if in shillings, in whole sums of shillings. The irregular amounts in shillings and pence, such as would arise from the addition of odd sums of pence and shillings, are missing. There is no notice as to the method employed by the county tallager of getting in touch with the tallage payers till we reach the levy of 1252. The writs of this year mention that the tallage was to be levied individually or in common.[60]

In 1255 the writs emphasized the possibility that the levy might be made per capita and that the commissioners would exercise a control over the assessments even when made by the inhabitants of an area. Thus they instructed the assessors to assess the tallage "individually," per capita, or in common as may have been more advantageous. This year the council sent a detailed account of the preceding tallage to the assessors in order that the new levy might be an increase without too great a burden on the poor. Moreover if an area fined in a lump sum for its tallage and the assessors attended the assessment themselves, they were instructed to remain until the repartition was completed, as it was common knowledge that the rich were often taxed lightly and the poor too heavily, and by this action on the part of the royal commissioners the rich would not be spared nor the poor unduly burdened. This expression should not be interpreted to mean that the commissioners generally voyaged through the shire, for the writ adds that the sheriffs shall summon before the assessors all those from the cities, boroughs, and aforesaid demesnes whom they may consider necessary for assessing the tallage, that is, representative groups from each area.[61]

Let us recall that beginning with 1248 a distinct effort seems to have been made to establish a more uniform system of assessors with careful supervision by central officials, and now we see that combined with them there is a representative group from each area in the demesne such as we saw in 1230. Very likely these local groups in 1255 are the continuation of a practice that was in

60. *Close rolls, 1251–1253*, p. 212.
61. *Ibid., 1254–1256*, pp. 161–162.

effect all through the reign. In 1268 we find the local groups combined with representatives of the central government.[62]

Thus by the close of the reign the conventional method of assessment was by circuits, by representatives of the central government conferring with the representatives of each taxable area at some central point in the county on the amount of the tallage.

The renewed emphasis on the alternative between the tallage per capita and in common continued—which appears to be a desire to increase the amount derived from this tax.[63] Moreover the assessors were to keep an eye on the assessments within areas that had fined in a lump sum (in common) for this tallage to insure an equitable assessment and one commensurate with the ability of the taxpayer to pay.[64]

With this distinct effort at improvement in organization to increase the yield from tallage, let us look at the rolls of assessment to see the results. They are striking. From 1227 to 1252 the rolls record hardly a clear case of tallage per capita. In 1252 examples began to occur again. About twenty areas, nearly all boroughs, seem to pay per capita—a large enough proportion to stimulate increased assessments. Yet in 1255 only one case (Norwich £17 10s.) may be a levy by poll, although the instructions to the assessors emphasize the levy by poll or in common. But in 1260 (thirty-five per capita) and 1269 (twenty-seven per capita) the numbers per capita indicate the effective introduction of this device to control assessment.

Another indication of the more effective organization of assessment to a certain extent is the relative height of the assessment between the earlier and later parts of the reign. If we choose 1245 as the beginning of the change we find that on the boroughs, of which we have a fair number of cases of tallage throughout the reign, out of forty cases about twenty-four seem to show a certain increase in assessment, taking 1245 as central point, and sixteen remain about the same; whereas in the rural areas, not incorporated towns, out of sixty-two areas forty-four increase beginning with 1245 and eighteen remain about the same.

How can we account for the inability of the government to increase the levy on all areas, rural and urban, as well as to increase

---

62. *Calendar of patent rolls, 1266–1272,* p. 226. M. Bateson, *Records of the borough of Leicester* (Cambridge, 1899), p. 47.
63. *Calendar of patent rolls, 1258–1266,* p. 75. *Ibid., 1266–1272,* p. 226.
64. *Ibid.*

its frequency, and why should the urban areas show a less percentage of increase than the rural areas? There must have been opposition to change. One factor was the emphasis on law and custom. Rules had been established which government and taxpayers recognized. Consider the constant appeal to law and custom. What protected borough and manor against the expansion of their payments for tallage seem to have been custom and law that determined in the minds of both administrative official and taxpayer the amounts that were undeniably due. The expression, *lex et consuetudo,* or an equivalent phrase, was a watchword that appears often in the rolls and to which constant appeal was made. Thus the king ordered the officials of the exchequer to collect the debts owed to someone already deceased according to the law and custom of the exchequer. At times they spoke only of the "custom" of the exchequer. Again manors were assigned to a widow for her dowry "according to the law and custom of our kingdom." The same expression was employed in connection with the Jews, "the law and custom of the Jewry." Men were distrained *secundum legem et consuetudinem scaccarii.* It might happen that sheriffs who rendered account at the exchequer might be arrested contrary to the ancient and due custom of the exchequer. Views were made according to the assizes of the exchequer. Men claimed to hold manors by old and approved custom. Indeed the expression became so common that the clerks finally abbreviated it, completing it with an et cetera. The phrase was not used this way in connection with tallage. This evidence is introduced merely to call attention to the emphasis that was constantly laid upon the importance of custom in relation to taxation.[65]

Thus tallage should be levied in accordance with custom. As an example, the manor of Mansfield had been paying 10*m.* per annum as a tallage for some years, although earlier it had never paid tallage except when the king tallaged his whole demesne. Hence the council ordered this annual levy of 10*m.* to cease, "since it is not fair or in accordance with reason that tallage should be taken other than it has been taken in the past."[66] It was necessary to go further and begin to state how often it would be legal to levy a tallage. The significance of the answer lies in the fact that it should seem necessary to pronounce such an *obiter dictum,* that tallage (not the

65. Professor Mitchell left blank the footnotes for this paragraph. The editor is unable to supply the references.
66. *Close rolls, 1242–1247,* p. 505.

general tallage, but tallage on a special area) should not be taken more frequently than every third year.[67] When royal officials speak this language something has happened to bring to their attention the criticism of excessive use of the royal right to tallage. We may refer to the tallage of London of 1226, or that of 1225, as illustrations of opposition. For pure principles of law need some body or group to defend them, since every legal principle has more than one possible interpretation. It is a principle that tallage should be taken when the king is in great need, and that rule might conceivably lead to an annual tallage. The barons expressed their concern in the Provisions of Oxford by protesting against excessive tallage when they spoke of the city of London and all the other cities of the king which had gone to shame and destruction by the tallages and other oppressions.[68] When they insist that tallage should be taken according to law they refer specifically to the tallages which escheators levied on areas that fell into the king's hands.[69]

In a writ of March, 1261, the king speaks of the reports spread abroad by his enemies that he was proposing to levy on the magnates and the community of the realm undue tallages and customs not owed—these reports being intended to stir up hostility to him. The truth of such reports he strictly denied.[70] Now tallagia may be used here in the general sense, but it should be observed that in June, 1260, writs were issued for the levy of a tallage on the demesne.[71] In October, 1260, a writ of a remarkable character was issued to the effect that the king knew for certain that very many of the cities, boroughs, and manors had been tallaged beyond their means, and hence the payment was deferred until the following January (1261).[72] The postponement of payment for such a strange reason suggests opposition to the measures of the government, among them the tallage. This was the time when Henry III was regaining control of the government. All I am concerned to point out is that tallage as it had been levied had become a constitutional question in which the barons were interested in the later years of Henry III's reign.

The roll of the tallage per capita was sent to the exchequer, but

67. *Ibid., 1237-1242*, pp. 302, 339.
68. Stubbs, *Select charters*, p. 392.
69. *Ibid.*, p. 391.
70. *Close rolls, 1259-1261*, pp. 461-462.
71. *Calendar of patent rolls, 1258-1266*, pp. 75-76.
72. *Close rolls, 1259-1261*, pp. 135, 357.

only the sum total appeared in the pipe rolls.[73] Collection and assessment apparently were combined in 1217 because of the need for haste. No change seems to have been made in the method of collection. The assessors drew up a roll in duplicate, one copy of which went to the exchequer, and the other was kept by the sheriff who was on the board of assessors and was also the collector of the levy. Thus in 1255 the writ states that a copy of the roll of assessment was to be delivered to the sheriff to collect the tallage.[74] The other copy went to the exchequer.[75] Sometimes the busy assessors were slow in delivering the copy of the roll to the exchequer. In 1232 the exchequer complained that the roll of assessment of Berkshire made in 1227 had not yet been received.[76] This roll was either "in commune," that is, the list of lump sums charged against the manors and boroughs in the shire, or a roll of the names of persons who had secured the right to be tallaged individually apart from the area in which they lived or who held a manor of the royal demesne which was tallaged.[77] The number of such persons who thus appear tallaged in the pipe rolls of Henry is not large and the total amount with which they are charged is not of importance. They represent either men who have secured the right to be tallaged independently or who hold areas that have become separated from some larger holding and have hitherto escaped taxation. They thus represent the effort of the administration to recover taxable areas. This form of levy was collected by the sheriff from most of the rural areas, unless the farmer or custodian had been authorized to respond by his own hand.[78] Thus the mayor of Northampton promised to pay at the exchequer the debt still owed on an old tallage.[79]

But boroughs did not always choose to go to the exchequer. They assessed the amount agreed upon with the royal commissioner and collected and paid it to the sheriff.[80] When the tallage was assessed per capita, the levy might be collected by the inhabitants themselves, and paid to the exchequer or to some official by royal com-

---

73. Pipe roll 55 Henry III, m. 6d. Lay subsidy roll, E. 179/180. Fine roll 13 Henry III, m. 11, Public Record Office.
74. *Close rolls, 1254–1256*, p. 161. *Calendar of patent rolls, 1258–1266*, pp. 76, 226.
75. *Close rolls, 1259–1261*, p. 198.
76. Exchequer K. R., 16 Henry III, m. 8d. Exchequer K. R., 20 Henry III, m. 11d, Public Record Office.
77. *Pipe roll 14 Henry III*, pp. 32–33, 197–198, 263.
78. Pipe roll 7 Henry III, m. 4, Public Record Office.
79. Exchequer K. R., 40–41 Henry III, m. 10, Public Record Office.
80. Exchequer to K. R., 38 Henry III, m. 12d, Public Record Office.

TALLAGE IN THE REIGN OF HENRY III

mand.[81] The form of entry in the pipe roll often conceals the fact as to who renders the account at the exchequer.[82] Most of the receipts were paid into the exchequer. Perhaps that was the norm, but there were variants. The money might go to the wardrobe.[83] The practice of assignment applied to tallage, but as recorded in the pipe rolls it was an occasional custom.[84]

How was the collection of the tallage enforced? No matter how well established any due was, it was necessary to be able to handle recalcitrants in an effective way. I do not refer here to men who claimed to be exempt and had a legal basis for the claim, but to those who legally were liable, even though they might claim exemption. Sometimes inhabitants removed all their chattels from the town or city in the hope of escaping taxation, for thus they felt that they had nothing which could be distrained.[85] This procedure illustrates the nature of redress and of the inability of the government at times to compel payment. Normally the officials distrained for the payment of the tallage. The sheriff of Norfolk had seized the cattle of the prior of Thetford for the tallage assessed on the demesnes of Earl Warenne.[86] The sheriff was ordered to distrain the villata of Windsor for 7m. and 10s. which still remained unpaid of a tallage of 30m.[87] If the debtors failed to pay after a reasonable time had elapsed a city might be taken into the king's hand with all its "liberties."[88] If the officials of a district solemnly promised that they would pay tallage on a certain date and failed to keep their word they might be imprisoned.[89]

Upon what was the tallage based? We have concluded that at Henry's accession tallage was based upon a rough estimate of a man's wealth, taking into consideration land, and goods, revenues, and houses; and there was some feeling, at least in London, that the levy was not properly assessed but bore too hardly upon the poor or those least able to pay. We must recall that with the turn

---

81. Thomas Madox, *History of the exchequer*, p. 509.
82. Pipe roll 49 Henry III, m. 7d. Pipe roll 52 Henry III, m. 8d, Public Record Office.
83. Pipe roll 11 Henry III, m. 3d, Public Record Office.
84. *Rot. claus.*, I, 588.
85. Exchequer K. R., Memoranda roll 37–38 Henry III, m. 19d, Public Record Office.
86. *Close rolls 1237–1242*, p. 405.
87. Exchequer K. R., Memoranda roll 41 Henry III, m. 13, Public Record Office.
88. *Close rolls, 1227–1231*, p. 383. Exchequer K. R., 10 Henry III, m. 9. Exchequer K. R., Memoranda roll 21 Henry III, m. 4d, Public Record Office.
89. Exchequer K. R., Memoranda roll 20 Henry III, m. 11, Public Record Office.

of the twelfth century two new levies appeared which imposed a tax upon certain property and made it proportionate to the amount and value of that property held by each person—the carucage and the tax on movables. No doubt these imposts affected the attitude of the government toward the tallage, not because of the question of unfairness to the taxpayer but because from these levies it was evident that the rich and prosperous in the towns were escaping adequate assessment.

The writs from Henry III's reign (the earliest that have survived) never explain in detail how the amount of the tallage, either from a person or an area, was to be calculated, how property was to be evaluated, and how the amount of tallage was to be determined. Evidently a customary method was followed, or several customary methods, for individual towns and manors may well have devised customary methods of their own. In the case of tallage, just as in the case of scutage, uniformity was probably the result rather than the origin of an evolution and due to the insistence of royal government. The earliest writs that have survived from Henry III's reign merely instruct the tallagers to levy the tax upon towns and manors "as seems to you most expeditious."

They were also to inquire into escheats, one piece of information that was desired being their annual value. There was need of haste to secure the money, because the government needed the funds to pay off Prince Louis and get him out of the country. Hence the tallagers were ordered to send in the receipts weekly.[90] If custom had decreed a uniform method of assessment, the writs would have been likely to mention it. Hence it would seem that in areas tallaged a similar inquiry would be made in order to estimate a proper amount of tallage. Yet as the entries of tallage in the pipe roll were in round sums, no very exact correlation between revenue and tallage could be made. Furthermore, what standard of value could any group of assessors set up after they had an estimate of annual revenue for a levy which was only occasional, without any definite instructions from the central government other than custom? Later the writs became more specific, apparently to try to insure that the assessors should not fail to graduate the tax to the capacities of the taxpayers; they state that the tallage was to be levied according to the wealth of the taxpayers.[91] Later writs go more into detail "you shall tallage it by head or in common, according

90. *Patent rolls, 1216–1225*, p. 171.
91. *Rot. claus.*, II, 208b.

TALLAGE IN THE REIGN OF HENRY III

to the capacities of the taxpayers, not sparing the rich and not overburdening the poor." [92] The writs therefore represent a certain evolution in instructions, yet they never go beyond this point.

Such descriptions do not indicate a uniform rate of taxation based upon an exact valuation of property or revenue or both. Then we have numerous rolls of scutage, carucage, hidage, or the taxes on movables, and they all include not only the amount of the tax but also the property upon which the tax was based, or its rate per unit. The old-fashioned donum and tallage give only the amount of the tax, because it would seem that they were unable to tell in any statistical fashion upon what basis the levy was calculated. In one case we know how the wealth was to be valued. In 1255, in London, with the proposed tallage per capita, each taxpayer was to swear to the value of his property.[93] In cases when representatives of areas met with the commissioners in the shire to levy the tax in common, we are not told how they arrived at their conclusion, but in these cases the tallage on an area was in round numbers.

As in general the variation in amount was limited it seems a fair conclusion that the amount of tallage was based on a rough estimate of the capacity to pay modified by examination of the older assessments. The amount was not a purely mathematical calculation, but depended upon the results of a negotiation between the local representatives and the county assessors. The influence of previous assessments is indicated by the dispatch to the assessors in 1255 of the rolls of assessment of the preceding year with the hope that the current levy might be increased.[94]

Many of the accounts of tallage levied upon individual persons have survived in the pipe rolls and we may compare them conveniently with the entries on the tallage rolls of Leicester from the end of Henry III's reign. They resemble amercements in their amounts. There is great variation in the amounts charged, due undoubtedly to the varying wealth of the taxpayers. Yet a certain regularity exists in the amount of the tax on each. They exhibit a great tendency to omit small, irregular sums of pence and halfpence. If one compares the roll of the fifteenth of 1225, for example, which we know was based upon an assessed value of certain movables, with the tallage roll of London of 1226, made per

92. *Calendar of patent rolls, 1266–1272*, p. 226.
93. *Close rolls, 1254–1256*, p. 160.
94. *Ibid.*, p. 161.

capita, one discovers remarkable disparities. The roll of the fifteenth contains every conceivable combination of shillings, pence, and halfpence. In the tallage roll those who paid less than 5m. paid almost without exception in multiples of 5s. The disparities would seem to be due to the fact that the fifteenth was based upon an actual assessment of property. And the tallage was based upon a rough estimate of ability to pay conventionalized with memories of a traditional assessment.

If this conclusion is valid, how then can one explain the repeated statements that men and women were tallaged "according to their merchandise"; or "for certain revenues and houses which they had," or "by reason of their revenues or tenements," or tallage on the annual revenue?[95] At first sight one might think from these extracts that they refer to an assessed valuation of property like the tax on movables. The impression is strengthened by descriptions like that of the prior of Barnwell. In his case the assessors levied a tallage because of the annual revenue (*annum reddituum*) which the prior received from his tenants. The meaning of these expressions is quite clear and is different.

We find every kind of property valued on which to base the tallage. Men and women were tallaged "according to their merchandise," for revenues and houses, on their revenues and tenements, on goods, on annual revenue from tenants, on forty-eight acres of land which appear in Yllenworth, on a mill.[96]

Thus both real and personal property were assessed in levying a tallage. The question we must ask is, what was the ratio of the tax to the value of the property? How did the assessors determine the amount of the tax after they had evaluated the property? We get no information from the rolls that enables us to answer this query definitely. The tallage roll of Ipswich of 1227 of a levy per capita contains the assessment sent to the exchequer, for there is no statement as to any payment.[97] It embraces about five hundred names with the amount charged against each all in round numbers; and the roll contains no statement of valuation of property.[98] It

95. Close rolls 45 Henry III, m. 19. Exchequer L. T. R., 53 Henry III, m. 6d, Public Record Office. *Liber memorandorum ecclesie de Bernewelle*, ed. J. W. Clark (Cambridge, 1907), p. 92.

96. *Ibid. Close rolls, 1259–1261*, p. 331. Exchequer L. T. R., 53 Henry III, m. 6d. Exchequer K. R., 37–38 Henry III, m. 15, m. 21. Pipe roll 53 Henry III, m. 3. Public Record Office.

97. Lay subsidy roll, E. 179/180, Public Record Office.

98. See also Lay subsidy roll, E. 179/237. Pipe roll 16 John, m. 7, Public Record Office. Bateson, *Records of the borough of Leicester*, p. 128.

may be, of course, that only rolls containing amounts of tallage have survived.

The difficulty of the question is seen when we examine the levies made on land. In 1252 the king granted to Agnes de Rouden and her kin certain lands in Melksham, for £7 10s. annually, and in addition tallage to the king whenever he tallages his demesnes, "according to the quantity of the land, and the advantages of its holders." Thus the way was left open to increase the tax. Tallage on lands in hand was to be adjusted "so that the poor should not be too greatly burdened by it." [99] That no uniform system was followed is indicated by the order to the sheriff of Lancashire to tallage certain tenants "in the way he ought and to which they were accustomed." [100] The same is indicated by the repeated command to levy a reasonable tallage, not sparing the rich and not overburdening the poor.

Similarly, the assessments on land indicate varying methods of calculating the tax. Here were two bovates of land rendering annually 6s. rent, but no one wishes to pay such a rent unless they shall be quit of tallage, and the sheriff says that they are unoccupied.[101] Two shillings of tallage were levied on a messuage and half a virgate and 4m. on twenty bovates.[102] Engelard de Cigony held Bensenton by royal grant and in 1227 was allowed to tallage it to his own use. He levied the tallage at the rate of 15s. a hide.[103]

The instructions issued in 1255 illustrate the point that the tallage was based on wealth in general but without any definite ratio of determining the relation between the tax and valuation of property. The king declared that he was in great need of money, never before equaled, and so he was sending to the tallagers "the particulars and the total amount of the tallage last assessed in the cities, boroughs, and royal demesnes, that the assessors may note his great necessity and take care that the present tallage should exceed the former without too great a burden on the poor." [104] Thus all kinds of property were taken into account in arriving at the amount of tallage owed by a group, like a city, or by persons.

99. Fine roll 13 Henry III, m. 7, Public Record Office.
100. *Ibid.*, m. 11.
101. Exchequer L. T. R., 11 Henry III, m. 6, Public Record Office.
102. Exchequer L. T. R., 53 Henry III, m. 5d. Exchequer K. R., Memoranda roll 15 Henry III (Professor Mitchell states that he did not note the membrane). Pipe roll 7 Henry III, m. 4, Public Record Office.
103. *Rot. claus.*, II, 192.
104. *Close rolls, 1254–1256*, p. 161.

Yet there was no uniformity in calculating the ratio of the tax to the valuation of the property.

We may approach the question of the basis of the tallage in another way—by the complaints of taxpayers that excessive amounts were charged against them for tallage. Thus a man in London protested that his tallage was too high. The mayor and the sheriffs of the city were ordered to reduce it reasonably so that he would feel it had been reduced.[105] John Fish in Shaftesbury was tallaged 15m. "for the payment of which he declared that his goods and chattels hardly sufficed." The case was brought before the exchequer which considered that such a situation was possible. If an inquest should show that John's complaint was true, then the court stated that his tallage should be declared "according to his property."[106] Robert Burr in Cambridge was tallaged at 20m. "when his peers and men wealthier than he were only tallaged at a hundred shillings"; the court again thought that such a situation was possible and ordered that if an investigation showed that Robert spoke the truth his tallage be modified so that he might not be burdened more than his peers and the tallage owed the king from the city should not be diminished.[107] Gilbert de Winterburne held one and one-fourth virgates of the manor of Bensenton paying the king annually 6s. 3d. and some service and a tallage of 2s. when the king tallaged his demesne.[108] These cases all suggest that tallage was a more or less stereotyped levy that had lost any direct and immediate relation, if it ever had any, with exact valuations of property.

That men arranged with the king to pay a fixed amount of tallage whenever it should be levied points in the same direction. In the case of Tirgenton (Staffordshire), it happened that when the royal demesne was tallaged a certain man was responsible for £6 6s. 8d. of the tallage of these demesnes, regardless of the amount of the tallage on them.[109] Philip Marmium was given for life the royal demesnes in Tamworth and Wigenton for the farm of £34 6s. 9d. per annum, paying £6 6s. 8d. of tallage whenever the king tallaged his demesne.[110]

105. *Ibid., 1227–1231*, p. 138.
106. This reference was left blank by Professor Mitchell and the editor has been unable to find it.
107. Madox, *History of the exchequer*, p. 511.
108. *Calendar of charter rolls*, I, 70.
109. Pipe roll 51 Henry III, m. 3, Public Record Office.
110. *Ibid.*

TALLAGE IN THE REIGN OF HENRY III

In the final tallage of Henry III's reign (1268) the rolls of payments within the borough of Leicester have been preserved. This town, belonging to the earldom of Leicester, had been given to Edmund, the king's son, and he had been allowed to tallage it since the king was tallaging his demesnes. The town fined with Edmund for 80m. as their tallage.[111] The king had issued the order for this tallage in May, 1268, but the accounts in the pipe rolls do not appear till 1269, and grants of permission to tenants to tallage lands received from the king "because the king is tallaging his demesnes" began at once.[112] Leicester had come into the king's possession at the death of Simon de Montfort, and in April, 1269, the king had given the honor of Leicester to his son Edmund. He also, according to this writ, granted Edmund the right to levy a tallage on his demesne, because the king was tallaging his demesne. Edmund was then provided with 80m. as a tallage by the town of Leicester, which thereupon took charge of the assessment and collection. The point raised by this entry is contained in the last statement that the tallage of 80m. was raised by the twentieth of 1269 granted to the king throughout the realm. There were two levies at the close of Henry III's reign: first, the tallage on the demesne, put in charge in May, 1268; second, the twentieth on movable property levied for the crusade, the first notices of which appear in August, 1269, when it appears that the twentieth was already authorized.[113] This statement from the tallage roll joins the two levies and suggests that the tallage was a twentieth of the movable property. That is, that the townspeople after agreeing on a fine of 80m. with Edmund, levied a twentieth out of which they paid Edmund his sum and kept the balance.

In the first place, let us observe that this statement is not contemporaneous. It was written at some time after the twentieth was levied, for the writer was able to state those who were exempt. This would date it sometime in 1270. He states that *clerici* were exempt, with Hospitalers, Templars, and Cistercians. Had he written the statement before April, 1270, he would have been led to have included bishops and the men of their demesne, for their grant was not made till about April 27, 1270, that is, till the question of the twentieth was well in the mind of everyone.[114] The most likely inter-

111. Bateson, *Records of the borough of Leicester*, p. 128.
112. *Calendar of patent rolls, 1266–1272*, p. 226. *Close rolls, 1264–1268*, pp. 463, 484.
113. Mitchell, *Studies in taxation*, p. 295.
114. *Historical papers and letters from the northern registers*, ed. James Raine (Rolls series), p. 23.

pretation of this passage is that the men of Leicester promised Edmund 80m. before 1269 (March 24) and assessed it accordingly by some conventional method, and then collected it. The roll of collection is given by Bateson. Later in 1270, when the burgesses of the town were assessed for the twentieth, a second roll different from the tallage roll was made by representatives of the town. Thus when the clerk drew up the heading of the tallage roll he confused the two levies.[115] Even supposing that the twentieth covered the tallage, it was the royal levy, authorized by the king and great council, according to his account. From this we may not conclude that tallage was conventionally levied as tax of a fractional amount on a valuation of personal property.

Thus there were various methods of assessing tallage after property of all kinds had been assessed, perhaps by the method of making each swear to his own and his neighbor's property. Tallage was an old obligation and customary methods were employed. Men were familiar with various devices of apportioning a payment, such as an amercement, among several contributors. In 1200 the charter to the earl of Leicester speaks of the sheriff's aid, whether it is taken by hides or carucates,[116] an expression which suggests paying a fixed rate per carucate or hide.

This is like the provision for alms that each plowland should pay two sheaves or 2d.[117] Property of all kinds was assessed but some conventional method was employed to fix the amount of the tax after valuation had been established. For comparison observe how a complaint about improper assessment in a tax on personal property reveals clearly that property was assessed. In 1237 Henry III complained that the receipts from the thirtieth on movables would be too low because the valuation of the goods was too low. The writ goes on to specify: "they [the assessors] assess an ox at five shillings ordinarily when it is worth ten shillings and even more and for a pig that is worth two or three shillings, they put down six pence," and so on.[118] In 1225 a letter from the chancery to the assessors of the fifteenth of that year declares that they are assessing the poor to such an extent that their "curses are rising to heaven against the king." The writer does not stop with generalities. He goes on: "poor women that have a little silver buckle

115. Bateson, *Records of the borough of Leicester*, p. 128.
116. *Ibid.*, p. 36.
117. William Farrer, *Early Yorkshire charters* (Edinburgh, 1914), I, 97.
118. *Close rolls, 1234–1237*, p. 569.

worth one, two or three pence, or a small piece of cloth are being made to pay a fifteenth of its value. Let such procedure cease." [119] Thus casually and easily does the fact emerge that these levies are based on an actual assessment of valuation of movables. In the countless references and complaints of tallage no such clear-cut indication of its definite basis on revenues and movables appears.

In calculating rents from land, the amounts take account of pence and halfpence.[120] Tallage thus seems to be a stereotyped levy, with some general attention to the wealth of the taxpayer. But no effective method was devised to link closely the amount of the tax with the wealth of the taxpayer. Tradition, law, custom were so strong against such a change that the government was unable to transform it into a flexible, expandable levy. So inflexible was the levy that when in 1269 a levy for the crusade was conceded to the king by the great council and a group of the council, much as the fifteenth and other taxes on movables had been in the early reign of Henry III, the king seems to have been unable to levy it on personal property in the towns. What happened was that the towns, in many cases at least, fined for the twentieth, that is, in effect they paid a tallage which they called a twentieth. Now the tax yielded in the counties more than any scutage would have done, but these "twentieths" in the towns were just about the same in amount as previous tallages had been. Nothing could show more forcibly the fixed, unyielding nature of this levy as it had developed by the end of the reign of Henry III.

The commissioners to a shire and those who cooperated with them took an oath to perform their duties faithfully and work to the advantage of the king.[121] We now have notices of special payments to the assessors of tallage not as a salary but as expenses. Peter de Tarry, who received £10 per annum at the exchequer, was given 5m. for his expenses in tallaging the king's demesnes in four counties.[122] The liberate rolls are filled with the emoluments of various administrative officials in money. The feudal state was vanishing. Careful financial administration was essential if the king's expenses were to be met.

What proportion of the tallage was actually paid? We have seen

119. *Patent rolls, 1216–1225*, p. 572.
120. *Calendar of charter rolls*, I, 73.
121. *Rot. claus.*, II, 204.
122. *Calendar of liberate rolls, 1226–1240*, pp. 43, 161, 163, 171. Exchequer K. R., 37–38 Henry III, m. 11d. Exchequer K. R., 40–41 Henry III, m. 4d. Pipe roll 45 Henry III, m. 14d. Pipe roll 56 Henry III, m. 15d, Public Record Office.

that down to the close of John's reign a very high percentage of the amounts of tallage registered in the pipe rolls was paid, except for the tallage of 1214, which was launched contemporaneously with the upset caused by the baronial struggle. It is impossible to give as complete and categorical an answer to the question for the reign of Henry III without examining carefully all the pipe and memoranda rolls, particularly the former, only two of which are in print—a task which the writer has not performed. The lists in the pipe rolls may be incomplete, and only an examination of all the chancery rolls will show this. Yet it is possible to form some conclusions which may be of value.

The efforts to expand tallage and increase the revenue derived from it were partially successful under Henry III. An examination of the tables on tallages on boroughs of the period from 1154 to 1216, considering the general level rather than merely a single levy such as that of Ireland in 1210, shows that there was a slight horizontal increase in the reign of this incompetent ruler. If we examine the tables on rural areas (vills, manors, aggregations of population without charters), we find that although the early part of Henry III's reign shows a decline, the last half of the reign (1245-72) shows an increase not only over the years 1216-42 but also in comparison with the earlier period as well (1154-1216). Yet when one recalls an example, the liberate rolls of 1226-51 with their abundant evidence of the growth of a money economy in England, it would seem fair to conclude that the increase in tallage by no means kept pace with the liquid capital of the kingdom. Laying this last consideration to one side, however, let us examine the evidence which indicates that tallage was becoming stabilized.

There was unquestionably under Henry III a decline in the number of areas that paid tallage regularly, not the boroughs but the rural areas. This happened because of the continuous process by which the king granted out manors to men to hold in fee farm or sometimes by other service. It may be that the revenue which the king derived from these farms more than made up for the loss which might have accrued from tallage, but anyhow tallage ceased to develop into a greatly expanding source of revenue.

Who paid the tallage? With that question the royal government does not seem to have been greatly concerned. The problems that came up before the exchequer or council on this point had for settlement not the custom of England or the law of the realm, not at least in the thirteenth century, but the custom of the manor or borough, except in some minor points that had perhaps great significance, for they were decided apparently by the central authority. Thus widows, particularly poor widows, were to be exempt because "according to the custom hitherto in effect in our land widows ought to be freed from tallages," says one recorder; because the lord king wishes them to be entirely exempt, says another. Crusaders were also exempt, at least during the early part of the reign.[123] In neither case was the exemption based upon law or custom but by special command of the king.

A different sort of exemption was that which excused land held in frankalmoign or by military service.[124] In the former cases the property holders were exempt by special grant of the king. The assessors should assess them. In tenure by military service the assessors should not have assessed them, for they by their tenure were exempt. In some cases a line was drawn between free and serf. Tallage was levied on the abbey of Burton in 1260, apparently only on the customary tenants, and the same was true for the abbey of Shrewsbury in 44 Henry III.[125]

Nicholas de Hanpeltun and Picot de Flexburg, king's men in Marlborough, declare that they are freemen, that they hold by charter, and that neither they nor their ancestors paid tallage. Each proved that he had a royal charter, the first rendering four capons a year, and the second one a pair of golden spurs for all services and customs, and so they were confirmed in their lands and paid no tallage.[126] These are manors. In boroughs any dweller in the borough (Derby) of whatever fee he may be shall pay tallage with the burgesses.[127] Another town, Norwich, states, "whoever may wish to trade (*merchandizare*) in Norwich with the citizens of Norwich shall contribute with them in tallages and other aids." [128]

Thus in boroughs seemingly those who trade are tallaged. In manors held by private persons the tallage which they levy other than for the king is, at the close of Henry III's reign, upon customary tenants—the freemen are exempt. But on the royal demesne

123. *Rot. claus.*, I, 176. *Close rolls, 1234–1237*, p. 63.
124. *Ibid.*, p. 62. *Close rolls, 1237–1242*, p. 9. Exchequer K. R., 21 Henry III, m. 24, Public Record Office.
125. Pipe roll 46 Henry III, m. 21d. Pipe roll 45 Henry III, m. 22, Public Record Office.
126. Exchequer K. R., 39 Henry III, m. 14d, Public Record Office.
127. *Calendar of charter rolls*, I, 96.
128. Madox, *History of the exchequer*, p. 500.

when the king levies a royal tallage, he levies it upon those who have not been exempted by charter or prescription and who paid tallage in the past, whether free or customary tenants. Thus tallage was levied on the men of Havering regardless of their status.[129]

Repeatedly the king delivered over manors at fee farm or to a tenant to hold as custodian or manager, collecting all rents and dues and paying them to the king. In the first case, either with or without special assignment, the farmer (fee farmer) had the right of levying and collecting tallage whenever the king had tallaged his demesnes.[130] Thus the manor of Ormeby in Norfolk was held in 1227 by fee farm of £16 by charter, quit of tallages to the king.[131] In 1236 the king allowed the holder (Geoffrey Fitz John) to take a reasonable tallage because the king was tallaging his demesnes.[132] Thus part of the ancient demesne, and other lands granted out— like the manors given to Richard, earl of Cornwall, the king's brother as endowment had passed out of the king's hand, and along with them the tallage which went to the new holders whenever the king tallaged his demesnes.[133]

Roger de Sumeri holds land in Were at fee farm. In 1249 he was granted a reasonable tallage from his tenants in the manor.[134] Writtle and Hadfield (Essex) were once royal demesne; they were granted to Isabella de Bruce in exchange for other lands in 1241. In 1249 she was granted a reasonable tallage.[135] Sometimes tallage or reasonable aid was granted to the holder of a manor to sustain himself in the king's service.[136]

Thus tallage diminished. It was stereotyped; no area paid it unless it had paid it in the past. New areas were not added or were added only with difficulty. When we say it diminished, we mean that the areas paying it to the king decreased; his tenants continued to receive it. Nor did new boroughs join the list.

What then prevented its expansion at a time when the amount of liquid capital in England was increasing? The grants to relatives were a factor, though apart from Richard and one or two relatives of the queen, this does not seem to have been important.

129. Exchequer K. R., 39 Henry III, m. 14, Public Record Office.
130. *Close rolls, 1237–1242*, p. 403.
131. *Calendar of charter rolls*, I, 52.
132. *Close rolls, 1234–1237*, p. 240.
133. *Ibid., 1237–1242*, p. 404.
134. *Calendar of charter rolls*, I, 97. *Close rolls 1247–1251*, p. 172.
135. *Ibid.*, p. 147. *Calendar of charter rolls*, I, 262.
136. *Rot. claus.*, II, 188b. *Close rolls, 1237–1242*, p. 314. *Ibid., 1242–1247*, pp. 264, 448.

Grants to officials like Hubert de Burgh were of more importance. Certainly a significant factor was the system of revenue building by fee farms and the like by which the farmer or custodian retained in his own hands the right to tallage.

Yet there was no indication that the government would abandon it; the organization of its assessment and collection was better articulated with the central government than ever; the control of the central government over local officials was good, and the government had shown its interest in maintaining an effective and yet a fair assessment, a reasonable auxilium or tallagium, so that the poor were not overburdened. No indication appears that the central government established a limit of property beneath which tallage should not be levied. It was to be rationable tallagium, not sparing the rich and not overburdening the poor. Such was the note at the close of the reign of Henry III.

VIII

THE END OF ROYAL TALLAGE

THE close of Henry III's reign practically marked the end of tallage as a regular part of the royal revenue. Henry had levied fourteen tallages during thirty-six years; seven of them between 1216 and 1240. In addition he had taken three taxes on movables (1225, 1232, 1237), two aids on knights' fees (1217, 1235), and two carucages (1220, and 1224, the last only on the lands of the prelates). In 1217 there had been a partial carucage. In the second half of the reign, 1240–72, there were seven tallages, two aids on knights' fees (1245, 1253), and one tax on movables (1269–70). It is true that during this second period the clergy were heavily taxed by the assistance of the pope for the benefit of the royal exchequer.[1] But as far as the laity were concerned, the rapid development of taxation based on movable property between the years 1188 and 1240 ceased. With the accession of Edward I came a great change. Only two tallages (1304, 1312) were levied during his reign and that of his son, a period of fifty-five years (1272–1327). The tallage proposed under Edward III in 1332 was countermanded and never again was this levy taken. Instead taxes on movables were imposed following their resumption in 1269 for the crusade.[2]

Thus the factors that reduced the frequency of tallage after the accession of Edward I were the increase in the frequency of the taxes on movables and the subjection of towns and rural demesne to this levy. The change was not due to widespread discontent throughout the demesne with the tallage. There had indeed been efforts to secure exemption from it and opposition to its excessive frequency. There were claims that the king was exacting it il-

1. William Edward Lunt, *Valuation of Norwich*, pp. 52–95. William Edward Lunt, *Financial relations of the papacy with England*, pp. 255–311.
2. Sir James H. Ramsay, *A history of the revenues of the kings of England* (Oxford, 1925), I, 90. James Field Willard, *Parliamentary taxes*, pp. 9–10.

THE END OF ROYAL TALLAGE

legally, but such complaints arose in cases in which at some previous date an area had gained exemption from tallage and later the assessors had tried to exact it. All of these were individual examples of legal disputes over alleged violations of custom. No general movement had arisen or common claim been made that denied the king's right to tallage or criticized his methods of authorization, assessment, or collection. The initiative in the substitution of the aid on movables for the tallage had been taken by the king and his council; the change was made probably because it was believed that the aid would be more fruitful than the tallage. For example, in 1188 practically all the unpaid tallages of 1187 were pardoned, and the aid on movables and revenues substituted. In 1237 the demesne preferred to be tallaged rather than pay the thirtieth. Under Edward I it was found that the aid could be levied almost as frequently as the tallage although the consent of the men of each rural and urban area had to be secured. The inference that the tallage lost favor with the council because its yield was smaller than that of the aid is strengthened when we recall that it was somewhat stereotyped in amount and that, particularly in the rural demesne, a considerable proportion of areas had bought exemption. Furthermore, the council attempted a change in the basis of tallage, beginning incidentally in 1304, to make it a levy similar to the taxes on movables, basing it upon a valuation of revenues as well as of movables and demanding a fixed fractional amount of each, greater in the case of revenues than of movables. It was this attempt that ultimately created such opposition that the new kind of tallage was formally abandoned. The substitute was the tax on movables with the proviso that it was not a due that it could be taken only by the consent of each group expressed in parliament.

In 1275, when a fifteenth was levied, there is no mention of tallage and probably the fifteenth was paid by the demesne. In 1282, when there was great need of cash for the campaign in Wales, the council seems to have decided against tallage, perhaps because of the unsatisfactory yield. Instead they sent out John de Kirkby, a clerk of the exchequer, to secure a grant from towns, prelates, and "all others" of each shire. There is no mention of tallage but of subsidy or loan; London promised 6,000m., Newcastle 1,750m., York 1,040m., Lincoln 1,016m., Yarmouth 1,000m., Norwich £500.[3] These sums would have been unprecedented in tallage. But

---

3. John E. Morris, *Welsh wars of Edward I*, p. 186.

the total returns were inadequate and the council turned to an aid on the demesne, granted by representatives.[4]

The annals of Osney state that in 1288 at the end of a three years' stay in Gascony, King Edward through the bishop of Ely, the treasurer, sought from "the earls and barons, indeed also generally from all the inhabitants of the realm" a subsidy to discharge the expense of his stay in France. But the lay magnates, placing their reply in the mouth of the earl of Gloucester, declared precisely that they would give nothing unless first they should see the face of the king in England again. Then the treasurer, seeing that he would gain nothing by this demand, "began to tallage the cities and boroughs and royal demesne throughout the whole kingdom, assessing upon them an intolerable amount of money, to be paid at a set time." [5] No record of such a tallage is noted in any of the printed calendars of the patent, close, or fine rolls of the time, and it is likely that this order was countermanded. However that may be, it is clear that the chronicler, the treasurer, and the barons distinguished clearly between the tax on movables and the tallage. The former needed the assent of the great barons and the latter was exigible as a due.

In 1290 the clergy granted a tenth of movables and the laity a fifteenth, after Edward I had returned from Gascony. This levy probably superseded the tallage. Although the latter was a due, yet the king preferred to secure a tax on personal property. The reason is not far to seek. The tax on personal property levied upon all the laity yielded far more than any tallage, or than any possible annual combination of dues. If the king had levied the tallage on the demesne, it would be more difficult for him to secure in the near future the grant of movables from the towns. Hence the treasurer in 1288 turned from a tax on movables to a tallage, but reconsidered his decision, and the next year with the king on the ground the grant was secured from all the laity. Edward I had another reason for preferring the tax on personal property. Although he had to secure the consent of the taxpayers to levy it, he was able to obtain that consent whenever he asked for it with one exception (1304). He secured nine taxes on personal property in thirty-five years. His father from 1237 till 1272, the same length of time and

---

4. D. Pasquet, *Essay on the origins of the House of Commons* (Cambridge, 1925), pp. 83–85, 87.

5. *Annals monasterii de Oseneia*, ed. H. R. Luard, in "Annales monastici," IV, 316.

THE END OF ROYAL TALLAGE

a period during which he was granted only one tax on movables, secured only eight levies of the exigible due—tallage. Thus the astute Edward was able to obtain this much more abundant levy more frequently than his less capable father took his feudal due, tallage, even though the tax on movables was not in theory obligatory.

In 1297 several significant notices of tallage occurred in connection with the king's efforts to raise money and supplies for his campaigns of that year. The term tallage, as we know, might mean the specific due levied by the king on his demesne or on escheats, but also it was a general term for tax or exaction. It was in this latter sense that the word was used in that critical year. In chronicle and record much is said about the taxes on wool, of the prices of supplies, of tallages, and of aids, terms that were all to appear in the "De tallagio non concedendo" and the Confirmation of the Charters. The king ordered wool to be brought to the seaports; any merchant possessing five or more sacks was to surrender them to the royal officials and would receive tallies in payment which he would present at the exchequer for the cash; those with less wool could retain it on payment of a tax of 40$s.$ instead of $\frac{1}{2}m$. The feelings of these taxpayers are indicated by the name they applied to the tax, a "maltolte," and the action of the council was called an "extortion." [6] The earls and their associate magnates who had opposed the war refused to allow the officials to collect the wool, or hides, or other goods from those who were unwilling to pay. They also forbade the collectors to enter their lands on pain of loss of life or member.[7]

Another statement reflects the bitterness against this tax: "The whole community felt aggrieved by the tax on wool as too oppressive, a charge of forty shillings per sack and for dressed wool seven marks a sack"; they added: "The wool of England equals half the value of the total yield of the land and the tax paid on it to a fifth of the value of all other agricultural products." [8] These comments come from a statement of the grievances of the magnates, so probably there is some exaggeration, but undoubtedly the king had touched on a sensitive subject that aroused the magnates as well as the merchants. Nevertheless, Edward I insisted that the prise of

---

6. Walter de Hemingburgh, *Chronicon*, ed. H. C. Hamilton (English Historical Society), II, 119–120.
7. *Ibid.*, p. 122.
8. *Ibid.*, pp. 125–126. *Willelmi Rishanger et quorundam anonymorum chronica et annales,* ed. H. T. Riley (Rolls series), p. 176.

wool should be taken but that letters patent should be issued that no precedent for future levies would be created.[9] The king promised to pay for all the wool he seized.[10]

No one has offered a satisfactory explanation of the source of the customs that were adopted in 1275. Very likely they began with payments in kind that were commuted into money levied by local lords and by the royal officials in many individual cases; from this foundation they proceeded to the establishment of the customs of 1275 on wool, hides, and leather; thus the king found justification for his levies on wool in practices of the past. The prises of supplies in 1297 seem to be the application on a large scale of purveyance for the needs of the king's household and his castles. Edward I had great armies to equip and support against Scots, Welsh, and French. Hence the need of the supplies described by Walter of Hemingburgh: "two thousand quarters of wheat to be levied by the sheriff of each shire and transported to the ports; the same quantity of oats; a certain amount being allocated as a contribution on each man; those who had no grain were to supply a certain amount of beef or pork"; in the phrase of the chronicler, men were "tallaged at a certain number of quarters." [11] The chancery records show that the amount of commodities levied in the counties was however not uniform.[12] According to Morris the king paid for the provisions at "cost price or even low cost price"; "then the supplies were retailed to the leaders of the retinues or of the infantry." [13] The systematic method employed in 1297 reflects the experience gained in equipping armies by Edward I during his reign. These exactions created a hostile feeling toward the king's policy.

Both chronicle and record have several references to the tallages that aroused opposition. In every case this term was used in the general sense of exaction or tax, not to the levy on the royal demesne that we have been studying. We must examine these cases because against this background arose the celebrated document, "De tallagio non concedendo," which still is cited as evidence that the magnates sought to wrest from the king his ancient right to levy tallage upon his demesne. The author of the *Flowers of History*,

9. "Extracts from the memoranda rolls of the exchequer," *Transactions of the royal historical society* (new series), III (1886), 289.
10. *Ibid.*
11. Hemingburgh, II, 119–120.
12. Thomas Madox, *History of the exchequer*, p. 260.
13. Morris, *Welsh wars of Edward I*, pp. 83–84, 197.

THE END OF ROYAL TALLAGE

after relating the refusal of the earls and other magnates to perform military service in Flanders, states that they demanded in addition "first and foremost on the plea of the desolate state of the community, that in the future the king would take no tallages throughout England." [14] The only levies that could give rise to such a demand were the taxes on movables (three successive years—1294, 1295, 1296), the taxes on wool, and the levies of food for the army that have been described. Such must have been the tallagia that the magnates had in mind.

Walter of Hemingburgh reports that the earl marshal and the constable after their dismissal by the king still negotiated with him by intermediaries. One thing they said was that they and the whole community of the land were aggrieved beyond measure by the unjust hardships, tallages, and prises, and especially because they were not governed according to the liberties of Magna Carta.[15] The same grievances and the same use of the term tallagium in the same sense appear in the petition of the summer of 1297 attributed to the archbishops, bishops, abbots, and priors, the earls and barons, and all the community of the land. After raising the vexed issue of military service in Flanders, the document states,

And although it may be true that they ought to serve in Flanders as elsewhere, nevertheless, they have not the resources to do so, because they had been so afflicted by diverse tallages, aids, and prises, on grain, oats, malt, wool, hides, oxen, cows, and salt meat for which they never were paid a penny. And now they are unable to make an aid because of their poverty arising from the tallages and prises aforesaid.

These tallages levied upon the earls, barons, and prelates were clearly not the due owed by the men on the royal demesne, but taxes or aids levied upon the property of the lands of tenants in chief of the king.[16]

When the host assembled at London in July the magnates asked for a more effective enforcement of the charters but met with no favorable response. In displeasure the earls of Hereford and Norfolk, with other nobles, then withdrew and did not attend the great reconciliation scene at Westminster Hall. Perhaps their withdrawal led Edward I to order the Confirmation of the Charters and then to demand from those present that he should be granted an

14. *Flores historiarum,* ed. H. R. Luard (Rolls series), III, 102, 195–196.
15. Hemingburgh, II, 123.
16. *Ibid.,* pp. 124–125. Rishanger, p. 175.

eighth of movables in the shires and a fifth in the towns—a request that was acceded to at once by those present.[17]

When at the end of August the king left London to embark for Flanders, the earls and other magnates who had opposed unusual taxation earlier in the year and had not been present when the grant of the eighth and the fifth had been made, went to Westminster and forbade the barons of the exchequer to cause the sheriffs to levy the eighth of movables. "It had not been granted," they said, "with the knowledge of the people of England, and without them no tallage ought to be exacted or imposed."[18]

We have on the memoranda roll the letter written by the barons of the exchequer to Edward I describing this scene:

Sire, this same Thursday (22 August 1297) . . . there came to your exchequer at the bar the Earl Marshal and the earl of Hereford . . . and many others, bannerets and bachelors. And the earl of Hereford said that he was charged to speak on behalf of the Earl Marshal and the others who were present there, and on behalf of all the commonalty of the realm, clerks as well as laymen, who felt themselves aggrieved by two things: in the one respect by divers grievances, the articles whereof they had exhibited to you as to their liege lord, and in the other as to what they heard had been done by us of the exchequer without your knowledge, as in right of the eighth, to levy it and take wool; and said that in the writs which are issued for levying the eighth, etc., is contained how that the earls, barons, knights, and the commonalty of the realm have granted the eighth, in manner as by them and their ancestors used to be done in the past; whereas the said eighth by them nor by the said commonalty was never at all granted; and said further that nothing sooner puts men in bondage than to redeem their own and to be tallaged arbitrarily, and that if the eighth was here levied that would turn to the disinheritance of them and of their heirs; and said openly, and all the others after him, that such tallage and prise of wool were never to be suffered, and they would by no means suffer them; and they prayed us that these things should be redressed, and thereupon they departed without awaiting any answer.[19]

It is clear that in this case tallagium means a tax of an eighth and a fifth of movables, just as in 1296 the twelfth on the shires

17. *Flores historiarum*, III, 102, 295–296. *Parliamentary writs*, I, 53–55.
18. *Flores historiarum*, III, 102–103.
19. "Extracts from the memoranda rolls," p. 285.

and the eighth on towns granted by parliament was called a novum tallagium.[20]

The most celebrated of all the statements about tallage this year was that contained in Article I of the document preserved by the chroniclers, called "De tallagio non concedendo," which has been associated in the minds of people since early in the seventeenth century with the growth of the control of parliament over taxation in opposition to the king. Article I of this document runs: "No tallage or aid shall be imposed by us [Edward I] or our heirs henceforth without the common assent of the prelates, earls, barons, knights, burgesses, and other freemen of the realm." [21] No record survives of any contemporary discussion of the relationship between it and the statute, the "Confirmation of the Charters," issued by the same parliament. The Confirmation does not mention the word tallagium. The "De tallagio non concedendo" was not included in any contemporary list of statutes. Not till 1532 was it introduced in an unofficial collection of statutes by the king's printer, Berthelet, without comment, and thereafter it is usually found in the longer lists. Its constitutional importance commenced with its citation in the Petition of Right (1628) as the sole evidence that in the time of Edward I this statute had been enacted that no tallage or aid should be levied by the king or his heirs in this realm without the assent of the prelates, earls, barons, knights, burgesses, and other freemen of the commonalty of the realm. No doubt the authors of the Petition chose this statement rather than the one from the Confirmation of the Charters because of the terse sweeping prohibition of the king's right to tax, instead of the apparently limited restriction in the Confirmation. The latter runs: "We have granted for us and our heirs that we shall never draw such aids, mises, or prises into a custom for anything that hath been done heretofore, or that may be found by roll, or in any other manner." [22] In Article VI the king promises further that "we shall never levy *such* manner of aids, mises, or prises from our realm but by the common assent of all the realm and for the common profit thereof." [23]

In John Hampden's trial for ship money the lawyers for the defense, especially Oliver St. John in his brilliant plea, implemented

20. *Flores historiarum,* III, 98.
21. Charles Bémont, *Chartes des libertés anglaises,* "Collection des textes pour servir à l'étude et a l'enseignement de l'histoire" (Paris, 1892), p. 88.
22. Stubbs, *Select charters,* p. 495.
23. *Ibid.*

the argument about tallage with the first historical explanation of the relationship between the "De tallagio" and the Confirmation and the king's right to tallage his demesne. He pointed out that in early times the king tallaged his demesne (including the towns) without the consent of parliament (that is, of the great council). In 1297, continued St. John, the grievance of the people was that the aids, tasks, and prises levied for the war might become customary dues, and Edward I granted that he would not take them in the future except by "common consent in the parliament of the realm and for the common profit, saving the ancient aids and prises due and accustomed." Further, St. John continues, to resolve all doubts as to the meaning of this provision, the "statute, De tallagio, was made afterwards for that purpose, and is an absolute and general promise that no tallage [on the demesne] or aid shall be taken by the king except by parliamentary consent." [24] Some of the lawyers for the crown argued that the "De tallagio" was merely an abstract of the Confirmation, but all yielded the point because the king in the Petition had agreed to the parliamentary claim that the "De tallagio" was a statute that had established in the thirteenth century parliamentary control of taxation.[25]

So too tallage in the "De tallagio non concedendo" was interpreted to mean tallage on the demesne. In the eighteenth century Blackstone agreed that, because parliament and the courts had so decided, the "De tallagio" was legally a statute, but maintained that in the thirteenth century it was an abstract of the Confirmation made by some contemporary monastic scribe.[26]

Hallam agrees that it was an imperfect copy of the statute and the tallage was the ancient levy on the demesne that henceforth could not be levied by the king except with the consent of parliament.[27]

So we come to Stubbs, whose work marks an epoch in the study of English constitutional history. He follows Blackstone and Hallam in concluding that the "De tallagio" was a summary "unauthoritative and imperfect of the regent's act of confirmation and

24. *Complete collection of state trials*, ed. W. Cobbett, T. B. Howell, and T. J. Howell (London, 1809–28), III, 871–873, 896.
25. Bémont, *Chartes des libertés*, pp. l–lii.
26. William Blackstone, *The great charter and the charter of the forest* (Oxford, 1759), pp. lxvi–lxvii.
27. Henry Hallam, *A view of the state of Europe during the middle ages* (London, 1869), pp. 243, 252.

the pardon of the two earls." [28] He believed that it represents a movement among the magnates to change the law about tallage on the demesne, although he concedes that the formal statement of the law is to be found in the Confirmation. Thus he says, "The right of tallaging his demesne was not formally taken from the king by the act of October 10, 1297 [The Confirmation] although it was contrary to the interpretation of that act in the 'De tallagio non concedendo.' " [29] Again in his summary of the whole matter in the *Constitutional History*, he declares, "The right of the king to tallage his demesnes, cities, boroughs, or rural townships was not abolished by the 'confirmatio cartarum' " in terms so distinct as to leave no room for evasion; in a note on the same paragraph he says, "Unconstitutional the exaction [tallage after 1297] certainly was, but not contrary to the letter of the law." [30] Hence arose the inference that the Confirmation evaded the issue presented in Article I of the "De tallagio" by ignoring tallagium, as though it were too difficult and dangerous a topic; yet that the council must have discussed it with the magnates and objected to its inclusion as too forthright an attack on the king's rights which might result in Edward I's refusal to agree to the Confirmation. At the same time they hesitated to declare formally the king's right to levy tallage; instead they appended a general statement, saying to the king, "the ancient aids and prises, due and accustomed." In this way, by a subtle and technical device, tallage on the demesne remained a royal due. So Lefebre with the implied approval of Petit-Dutaillis follows Stubbs, saying, "The so-called statute 'De tallagio' was never admitted by him [Edward I]; . . . he thus evaded the demands of the barons." [31] It is clear that there is a school that believes the tallage in "De tallagio" referred to the levy on the royal demesne with all that such a theory implies.

In 1884 a young German scholar, Ludwig Riess, wrote a short history of English electoral law in the Middle Ages. Incidentally he touched on the question of the "De tallagio" and concluded for the first time that this document did not give the men of the demesne the right of granting the tallage on the demesne with the concurrent right of refusal.[32] Four years later the author advanced the theory

28. Stubbs, *Select charters*, p. 497.
29. *Ibid.*
30. Stubbs, *Constitutional history*, II, 565 and n. 1.
31. Charles Petit-Dutaillis, *Studies and notes*, p. 14.
32. Ludwig Riess, *The history of the English electoral law in the middle ages*, trans. by Miss K. L. Wood-Legh, Cambridge, 1940), p. 14.

that the "De tallagio" contained the demands of the barons which they presented at the September-October parliament (1297).[33] That is, the "De tallagio" was not a statute but a petition.

In 1886 were printed in the *Transactions of the Royal Historical Society* some extracts from the memoranda rolls of the exchequer (with a translation) of the correspondence between Edward I and the barons of the exchequer toward the end of August concerning the financial crisis preceding the Confirmation of the Charters. The unnamed translator and editor of these documents concludes that the negotiations that preceded the confirmation were directed by the king himself rather than by the provisional government, that "he was responsible for the management of the entire transaction and that the Regent did little else than carry out his father's instructions." [34] In 1892 M. Charles Bémont, following the suggestion of Riess and using these documents from the memoranda roll, decided that the barons formulated their demands as a petition when they answered the summons to the parliament of September, 1297, and this petition had the written approval of the king beforehand. This petition was the famous statute "De tallagio non concedendo." [35]

If we interpret tallagium in the "De tallagio" as the ancient due of tallage on the royal demesne that we have been studying, and if the document is a statute, the king surrendered his ancient right to this due and could henceforth levy it only by the consent of the men of the royal manors and boroughs, individually or by representatives. That is, tallage was transformed from a due into a gracious aid.

But if the "De tallagio" was a petition of the barons that the king's small council had refused to grant, its significance was only slightly less than if it had been a statute, for it means that the powerful group of magnates and knights (for the men of the demesne played no part in the October parliament of 1297) that had forced the king to accede to their demands and to confirm the charters had the additional aim of bringing tallage under the control either of the men of the demesne directly or of their representatives in parliament. That the regent and council refused to grant this petition does not alter the significance of the movement. We know

33. Ludwig Riess, "Der Ursprung des englischen Unterhandes," *Historische Zeitschrift*, LX (1888), 12–13.
34. "Extracts from the memoranda rolls," pp. 281–291.
35. Bémont, *Chartes des libertés*, pp. xxxvi–xliii.

that tallage on the demesne was only levied twice (1304, 1312) thereafter, that the orders to assess it in 1332 were revoked as a result of a petition in parliament presented by the magnates and delegates of the shires and it was never levied again. Thus according to this theory it was abandoned because of a definite movement on the part of the magnates for its abolition as a due that began in 1297 with the "De tallagio." If this theory is true, then here we have one of the ancillary roots of the rise of parliamentary control over taxation. One difficulty about this theory is the fact that the Confirmation of Charters, the authentic statute by which the struggle of 1297 between king and magnates was settled, makes no mention of tallage on the demesne. Yet the barons had placed the term tallagium at the beginning of the first article in their petition—an indication of their intense feeling on this subject. Most authorities follow Bémont in adopting the view that "De tallagio" was a petition, or a document presenting the demands of the barons when they met in the October parliament of 1297.[36]

It may be asked why in 1297 there was such a strong feeling among the magnates against the king's right to levy tallage on the demesne. They had never before manifested any interest in opposing it. Furthermore, tallage had not been taken since 1268, nearly thirty years before; it had been abandoned by the decision of the small council itself in favor of the tax on movables on the whole realm, including the royal demesne, apparently a more fruitful levy.

It had not been employed by the government even during the period from 1294 to 1297, the time of unusually heavy taxation. These facts suggest that the term tallagium in this document means tax, subsidy, aid as in the chronicles of these years and in the record of the protests by the earls related in the memoranda rolls with no reference at all to the tallage on the demesne.

Some modern scholars believe that tallage in this document does not refer to the ancient levy on the royal demesne. So Pasquet says, "It is doubtful if the word tallage is here used in the technical sense." [37] George B. Adams thinks that the word tallagium was used by the barons in this document carelessly since they all knew what tallage on the demesne meant and that consent was not re-

---

36. Hilda Johnstone in *The Cambridge medieval history*, VII, 410, n. 1. T. F. Tout, *History of England, 1216-1377* (London, 1920), pp. 208-209. K. H. Vickers, *England in the later middle ages* (London, 1913), p. 71.
37. Pasquet, *Origins of the House of Commons*, p. 109.

quired for its levy.[38] Jolliffe carefully distinguishes between tallage in the general sense of taxation and tallage as a levy on the royal demesne, placing the tallage of the "De tallagio" in the former class.[39]

By this interpretation, tallagium meant taxation or exaction. The conclusion is confirmed in various ways. In 1304 a tallage was levied on the royal demesne with no objection. The heading of this levy in Kent in the pipe roll indicates that the clerks of the exchequer believed that no tallage of the demesne had yet been levied by Edward I since his accession. The entry runs: "The first tallage of the time of King Edward, the son of King Henry, assessed in the county of Kent in the thirty-second year by . . . as is contained in the roll of originalia of the said thirty-second year."[40] Moreover in 1299 when a dispute arose between the king and his magnates and the latter insisted on a further formal confirmation of the charters in 1300 with additional articles, none of these articles alluded to tallage.[41] There was no complaint raised when tallage was levied in 1304. Thus it seems clear that tallage was not an issue at all in the reign of Edward I.

We have concluded that the allusions to tallagium in the account of the events of 1297 before the formation of the two great documents seem to interpret it as tax. Three contemporary chroniclers discuss in detail the gestation of these documents. Two authors include the "De tallagio" verbatim, giving the term tallagium; one gives only the "De tallagio" verbatim. But all give paraphrases in their own words of the term tallagium and none of them suggests that it has any meaning beyond the general one of tax.

Thus Walter of Hemingburgh summarizes the contents of both documents before inserting the articles themselves. He describes the negotiation between the council and parliament and the dissatisfied barons. At length, after much deliberation and discussion of the proposals through mediation of Robert of Winchelsea, archbishop of Canterbury, of blessed memory, it was found that the barons would consent to nothing else but the grant and confirmation of the Great Charter with certain articles annexed and the Charter of the Forest; that the king should ask and require no aid or exaction

38. George Burton Adams, *Constitutional history of England,* revised by Robert L. Schuyler (New York, 1934), pp. 189–190.
39. J. E. A. Jolliffe, *The constitutional history of medieval England* (London, 1937), p. 397 and n. 1.
40. Madox, *History of the exchequer,* p. 509.
41. Bémont, *Chartes des libertés,* pp. xlviii, 99–108.

from clergy or people without the will or assent of the magnates; he should also pardon the earls, their associates, and followers against whom he was deeply irritated because of their opposition to his policy.[42] Then follow in order the Confirmation and the "De tallagio." Trivet gives only the articles of the "De tallagio" preceded by a short general statement:

Thus, the council persuaded the king's son to summon the earl of Hereford and the earl marshal to induce them in any way possible to make peace. When they came, they would agree to the following terms and to no other: firstly, that the king should grant and confirm the great charter with certain annexed articles and the charter of the forest; secondly, that he should exact no aid or exaction from clergy or people in the future without their counsel or assent; thirdly, that he should renounce all feeling of hostility toward the earls and their associates.

Then follow the articles of the "De tallagio." [43] Both contemporaries were familiar with the documents and in their summaries of the articles on taxation they speak of *exactio vel auxilium* rather than tallagium as though they understood tallagium in the general sense of taxation. We conclude therefore that tallagium, as used in Article I of "De tallagio," should be translated tax or exaction because such a meaning fits better with the causes of the grievances of the period.

The constitutional difficulty to be solved was the danger that the king was acquiring a right to arbitrary taxation. This the barons feared and the king himself was aware of their apprehension. So he tried to persuade the magnates that his aims in taxation were not unconstitutional by giving his promise to issue letters patent to all who desired them that the eighth and fifth which he asked for in 1297 should not constitute a precedent. Unfortunately this was the fourth levy in four successive years.[44] The king's insistence on the levy of the eighth and fifth despite the barons' opposition led the latter to conclude that to him their consent was only a form.

The real danger was more subtle, that the king should always ask for taxes on movables at a time of danger to the kingdom, a crisis that might endure over many years, and the necessity would obligate the commonalty always to grant it years after. That is,

42. Hemingburgh, II, 148.
43. Nicholas Trivet, *Annales sex regum Angliae,* ed. T. Hog (English Historical Society), p. 366.
44. Willard, *Parliamentary taxes,* p. 16. J. A. C. Vincent, *Lancashire lay subsidies,* pp. 213-214.

out of the ancient gracious aid on movables might arise a new due.

The problem had arisen before under Henry III in a modified form, as we have already seen. At that time the magnates had believed an auxilium was necessary only rarely in cases of some extraordinary need and the safeguard against abuses lay in the provision that it could be taken only by the consent of the great curia regis. Although the provisions of the Great Charter of 1215 that covered this point (Arts. XII and XIV) had been dropped in later issues of the charter, the custom of summoning the magnates to consult on the grant of aids was systematically followed. The unusual need recurred at frequent intervals, six aids in twenty years (an aid on knights' fees in 1218; a carucage in 1220; a fifteenth on movables in 1225; a fortieth on movables in 1232; an aid on knights' fees in 1235; and a thirtieth on movables in 1237).

This frequent repetition of aids was, it was believed, creating a new due and when Henry III asked for a thirtieth in 1237, two demands were at once made by the magnates: first, that the king should confirm Magna Carta; and second, that he should promise never again to ask for an aid. Henry III immediately acceded to these requests. The barons' expectation of checking the king's demand for aids by this procedure failed to be realized. When in 1242 he repeated his demand, all they could do was to refuse the grant. He was unable to secure the tax, but by loans and other sources of revenue he was enabled to carry out his invasion of France, the reason for his demand of an aid. The refusals were repeated eight times from 1242 to 1258, and the barons succeeded in preventing any levy on movables during this period. Then came the baronial revolution and attempted reforms, followed by the civil war, the final triumph of the king, and his restoration to power in 1265. Let us remark that in this period the original individual consent to taxation by the magnates assumed traits of corporate consent and demonstrated for a time that it meant the right to refuse a tax.

The dispute of 1297 arose in a new climate of opinion. Since 1269 the magnates had accepted the necessity of a tax on movables every six or eight years, but beginning with 1294 such grants were totally inadequate to the king's needs; four taxes on movables in four successive years seemed to presage the establishment of a new annual due. That is, out of the gracious aid that could only be taken by consent of the magnates originally, and then by them and the deputies of the shires and towns, was threatening the establishment of a tax which could not be refused when the king declared that it was indispensable.

If the term tallagium in the "De tallagio" does not refer to the arbitrary levy of a tax upon the royal demesne, then we must explain the fear voiced in the Confirmation of the Charters and the "De tallagio" that the king was developing an arbitrary right of taxation, seeing that aids, the most comprehensive levies mentioned, could only be taken by consent. It should be observed that the aids on movables covered the property on lands held by lay tenure by tenants in chief of the king and the royal demesne as well. Notice, for example, the ninth granted after the Confirmation of the Charters by the parliament of October, 1297.[45]

Who were the people that feared such a contingency? They were the lay and ecclesiastical magnates supported by shire deputies and the men of manor and town on the demesne. Thus, the Confirmation of the Charters describes them as those who had granted the aids, mises, and prises recently for the king's wars. These men were listed as the archbishops, bishops, abbots, priors, and other folk of the Holy Church, and the earls, barons, and all the community of the land.

In the "De tallagio," Article I lists in addition "knights, burgesses, and other free men" who were to grant every tallage, or aid. In Article II the prises of grain, wool, hides, or any other movable goods could only be taken by the assent of the owner; in Article III, no maltolte was to be levied, i.e., the 40s. tax on wool, by the king's authority alone. From these two documents those who feared the danger of arbitrary taxation were not the property holders as such or those whose names appeared on the assessment rolls but those who normally would give consent to the tax.

If we examine the taxes levied under Edward I we shall see why these categories were included in these documents. The great levies of the reign were the taxes on movables. They were granted by the prelates and lay magnates, whose action was supplemented by a grant made by the knights of the shire. These grants covered movables on the lands held of the king by the tenants in chief, not those on the royal demesne. To secure an aid from the latter either a grant was made by the men of each manor or town to royal commissioners, or deputies were summoned (as in 1283, 1290, 1294, 1295, 1296) who consented to a grant on movables of the towns and rural demesne. This is the source of the provisions in Article

---

45. *Ibid.* Willard, *Parliamentary taxes,* p. 16.

I of the "De tallagio" and of the general statement in Article VI of the Confirmation concerning "all the community of the land" in addition to the magnates (*a toute la communauté de la terre*). Similarly the provisions against the maltolte in both the Confirmation and the "De tallagio" go back to the grant of the custom on wool, hides, and leather made by the magnates and the shire deputies at the petition of the merchants in the parliament of 1275. The prises of supplies of grain, and other food were included in the same category of levies only by consent, and fair prices were to be given, but the consent was individual, not by a group or by parliament, as was implied in the "De tallagio" and also the Confirmation. While smaller men as well as magnates in theory were considered to be in fear of arbitrary taxation by the king, the opposition of the great men was the decisive element in the crisis of 1297. Accordingly the petition presented to the king in the summer on the part of the earls came primarily from the magnates. "These are the grievances which the archbishops, bishops, abbots and priors, earls and barons and all the community of the land exhibit to our lord the king" and beg him to amend them.[46] The protest made at the exchequer against the eighth and fifth, the tallage, and the prise of wool was made by the earls and their supporters.[47]

Walter of Hemingburgh summarized the Confirmation and the "De tallagio" on taxation as follows: the king "should seek no aid or exaction from clergy or people in the future without the will and assent of the magnates";[48] Bartholomew Cotton more specifically declared that "prises should not be taken, nor mises, nor aids levied except by the consent of the archbishops, bishops, prelates, earls and barons, unless they were owed of ancient custom."[49] We should expect that the lead against the king would be taken by the magnates who thus were the leaders that were apprehensive lest the king was on the point of establishing an arbitrary right of taxation. The narratives of the October parliament show that the adoption of the Confirmation of the Charters was made by the insistence of the magnates. Thus Walter of Hemingburgh declares: "The magnates would not agree to any other form of statement"; Trivet states: "When those arrived that had been summoned to parlia-

46. Rishanger, p. 175. Hemingburgh, II, 174–175.
47. "Extracts from the memoranda rolls," p. 285.
48. Hemingburgh, II, 148.
49. Bartholomew Cotton, *Historia Anglicana*, ed. H. R. Luard (Rolls series), p. 337.

ment [that is, the magnates and shire knights], they would agree to no other form of settlement than the following." [50]

The issue was not raised over dues for the ancient aids and prises due and accustomed were specially excepted. Curiously enough therefore the fear had arisen about levies that the king had always taken only with the consent of the magnates, the shire deputies, and the men of the demesne. The exception was the case of the eighth and fifth of 1297 on which the king stubbornly insisted and to which a considerable group of magnates had assented. The difficulty was that a powerful body opposed the eighth and this objection proved insuperable.

A further problem was how to retain the aid as a freewill grant, have it conceded regularly at short intervals (not annual), and yet not turn it into a custom. The solution that was found may be felt inadequate; they merely drafted additional articles on taxation, incorporated them in the Great Charter, and confirmed it as modified. In this way that venerable document which was a symbol of the common law and the rights of freemen was given a new statement of the law on taxation that was also based on custom. Thus these articles implied that general taxes like the aids on movables and customs on wool, woolfells, and leather should be part of the financial resources of the king. Such had been customary all through Edward's reign. They were to be the law of the land and to be recognized as such by Magna Carta. In addition Magna Carta now also recognized the danger that repetition of aids threatened to make such levies a custom and that the magnates understood the peril. Hence the council and the king had to provide safeguards against such a contingency. This is the meaning of the repetitious statements of Articles V, VI, and VII of the Confirmation, viz., to prevent the aids, mises, and prises granted by the realm of their good will, howsoever they were made, from becoming a bondage to them and to their heirs; hence the king granted for himself and his heirs (just like a grant of land, as completely as possible) that he would never draw such aids, mises, or prises into a custom for anything that had been done heretofore or that might be found by roll or in any other manner. This vague confused statement reflects the difficulty of the authors with the phraseology. What they mean to say is that if the king's ministers appeal to rolls of assessment and collection, or to the rolls containing former writs ordering levies,

50. Hemingburgh, II, 148. Trivet, p. 366.

or rolls that contain earlier cases of enforcing payment of these taxes, as evidence that such levies were owed as a custom, or to any other similar kind of evidence, this article will stand as the law to show that any such interpretation is illegal. Article VI supplemented the statement by declaring that the king had granted for himself and his heirs to all lay and clerical magnates and to all smaller folk who grant taxes (the shire knights and the men of the royal demesne), that is, all the community of the land, that he will never take such kinds of aids, mises, or prises from the realm but by the common assent of all the realm and for the common profit thereof. Thus no tax of this sort could be levied on the ground that it has been levied in the past; moreover each tax must be authorized in the customary way. Consent was to apply only to those levies for which it had always been necessary; ancient aids and prises that were due and accustomed without consent continued to be levied as before. Another levy, the customs tax on wool, hides, and leather was not covered by the other articles because they were granted for a single occasion; the customs ran on year after year; they had been granted in 1275 and later the rate had been increased twice by the king's authority alone to an insufferable degree.

While the king undoubtedly gained in the new statement of the law, he was also checked by the emphatic declarations now enshrined in Magna Carta that aids, mises, and prises, including the customs taxes, could only be levied by the customary consent of the commonalty.

How shall we explain the settlement of the struggle between the magnates and the king in the absence of the latter? Why did the magnates and the royal council venture to go so far in the Confirmation of the Charters?

Both chronicle and record reveal the apprehension of the growth of the king's power in taxation in 1297; the fear was well known to Edward I before he departed for Flanders. For example, the grievances formulated by the magnates in July mention, among other points of criticism, taxation which, it was alleged, had reduced some to poverty, with particular reference to the taxes on wool; moreover, the failure to enforce Magna Carta and the Charter of the Forest had greatly damaged the commonalty.[51]

In the royal proclamation issued in August, 1297, before his departure for Flanders, after rehearsing his conflict with the earls that had resulted in the appointment of a new constable and a new

51. Bemont, *Chartes des libertés*, pp. 77–78.

marshal, the king alluded to certain articles for the common profit of the people and the realm which, it was alleged, the earls had shown him and which he had refused to adopt—a statement, he declared, that was false, for they had shown no document of this character. Rumor had however, he said, brought to his knowledge certain grievances which he discussed in this proclamation. First was the frequent levy of aids. He could not deny the truth of this report, but he defended the taxes. They were caused by his wars of defense in Gascony, Wales, Scotland, and elsewhere; he needed the help of his good people to insure their safety. Second, he noted that they demanded the confirmation of the Great Charter and the Charter of the Forest. This he would gladly concede if they would grant him a general aid which was now indispensable.[52]

The August letters between Edward I and the clerks of the exchequer disclose the aroused state of baronial feeling over their grievances, not merely their opposition but also their fear of the establishment of arbitrary levies, their determination to make an issue of the eighth and the prise of wool. The intensity of the emotion of the magnates emerges through the conventional expressions employed by the clerks who no doubt have toned down the language of the protestants: "And they prayed us that these things should be reformed and thereupon they departed without awaiting any answer." [53]

The actual conflict out of which immediately arose this Confirmation of the Charters was introduced by the impending departure of Edward I for Flanders. Possibly, as Stubbs infers, the confederate magnates and their associates believing him gone seized the opportunity to stop the levy of the tax on movables and the prise of wool. They appeared at the exchequer and forbade the levy which they claimed the clerks of the exchequer had put in charge without the king's knowledge; anyhow, since the clerks knew that the king had not yet sailed, they probably informed the magnates of that fact.

The major part of the magnates' protest dealt with the grievances that lay behind their drastic action concerning the taxes, as reported by the barons of the exchequer. These were that the eighth had never been granted by the earls, barons, knights, and the commonalty of the realm as had been customary in the past, although the writs of assessment asserted that the eighth had been conceded

52. *Ibid.*, pp. 82–84.
53. "Extracts from the memoranda rolls," p. 285.

in that way; nothing, they said, puts men in bondage sooner than the *rachat du sang* and to be tallaged at will; the levy of this eighth would lead to the disinheritance of themselves and their heirs. Such imposts they could never tolerate; such grievances must be redressed.[54]

The knowledge of this challenging action of the barons faced Edward I with the necessity of a new decision: should he continue with the invasion or return to quell a threatened uprising? Without much hesitation he decided to go on. (The letter of the barons of the exchequer was written on August 22 and given to the usher for delivery to the king at 3 P.M. of that day; the King's answer is dated "Winchelsea, 23 August" and it is followed by another letter from him, dated "at sea, off Dover, 24 August," enclosing a communication to the Prince Regent of the same date. On the morrow of St. Bartholomew (August 25) the regent addressed a letter to the barons, enclosing a further letter from the king which is dated, "Winchelsea, August 24." [55] It would thus appear that Edward had hurried back to Winchelsea, either in view of the crisis in London or to review his preparations. But before he left he must advise his son and the council how to deal with this new action of the magnates.

There was nothing new in the statement of principles made by the magnates. What was new was their acts prohibiting the levy of the eighth and the prise of wool. The combination warned Edward I that the magnates were prepared to go further in their opposition. He was in doubt how far to go in concessions; perhaps he did not sense the seriousness of the crisis, possibly because he was conscious that he had no intention of establishing arbitrary taxation. Probably his successes in dealing with the great council, the parliament, and the church blinded him to the fact that he must walk more warily. He aimed to conciliate but also to force concessions from the magnates. Thus he refused to withdraw the orders to levy the eighth of movables on the magnates and counties and the fifth on the urban and rural demesne. He insisted the eighth should be assessed and collected and emphasized his belief that no precedent for arbitrary taxation would thereby be established. The chancellor was to issue letters patent to the effect that the eighth would establish no precedent, and these were to be given to anyone who might fear such a result; the levy on wool should also be taken and

54. *Ibid.*
55. *Ibid.*, p. 283.

THE END OF ROYAL TALLAGE

the same assurance given that its levy would not constitute a precedent. The purchase price should be paid for the wool by the king's agents.[56]

No mention was made in these letters of the fifth on the movables of the royal demesne because this discussion was carried on between the exchequer barons and the magnates who were concerned only with the eighth. Thus the king and his council were well informed about the grievances of the magnates and people. The king was willing to negotiate. He was ready to confirm the charters under certain conditions; he declared and probably believed that his policy was not contrary to the advantage of the realm; he professed no aim to levy taxes contrary to custom, that is, without the consent of the people.

Thus the foundation was laid for the "De tallagio" and the Confirmation of the Charters. Both documents are appendices to the Great Charter and the Charter of the Forest of 1225. Both are cast in the form of statutes. Since the "De tallagio" in Article V declares the pardon of the earls and their supporters for opposition to the king, and since letters patent, sealed by the regent, were issued on October 10 pardoning them, the date of the Confirmation of the Charters, it would seem evident that the "De tallagio" was drawn up [57] before this date and probably before the earls came to the parliament. Thus the "De tallagio" must be a statement of the demands of the earls. Three weeks after Edward had sailed for Flanders the boy regent, by the advice of his council, summoned a parliament of magnates and deputies of the shires to meet at Westminster on October 6.[58]

The members of this assembly were to receive charters confirming the Great Charter and the Charter of the Forest, as well as letters patent that the grant of an eighth should not establish a precedent, and were to transact such other business as might be ordained by the regent and his council. The council decided to secure the cooperation of the earls of Norfolk and Hereford and their associates. They came with fifteen hundred knights and a great body of footmen.[59]

The earls refused to cooperate except upon certain conditions set

56. *Ibid.*, pp. 286–291. Vincent, *Lancashire lay subsidies*, p. 206. Thomas Rymer, *Foedera* (Record Commission, London, 1816), I, 877.
57. *Parliamentary writs*, I, 61–62. Vincent, *Lancashire lay subsidies*, p. 212.
58. *Parliamentary writs*, I, 56. Bémont, *Chartes des libertés*, p. xlii. Cotton, p. 337.
59. Rymer, *Foedera*, I, 877. Vincent, *Lancashire lay subsidies*, pp. 206–207. *Calendar of close rolls, 1296–1302*, p. 129. Trivet, pp. 366–367. Hemingburgh, II, 147–148.

forth in the "De tallagio non concedendo." As summarized by the chroniclers, the conditions were that the king should grant and confirm Magna Carta with certain additional articles and the Charter of the Forest; second, that he should exact no aid or impost from clergy or people henceforth without their counsel and assent; third, that he should dismiss his anger against the earls and their associates. Then in Trivet's chronicle follows the "De tallagio." [60] Walter of Hemingburgh's summary was almost exactly the same, but he adds: "The document to this effect was conceived and formulated in the following words"; he then introduced the Confirmation of the Charters in French, following it by the "De tallagio" in Latin.[61] On October 10 the Confirmation was agreed to by the regent and the council and with the charters forwarded to the king with the urgent request that if he wished to preserve his honor, his status, and his kingdom he would confirm the charters and the additional articles. On November 3 the king approved the Confirmation and the pardon of the malcontents. The contents of the Confirmation grew directly and in specific detail out of the grievances and fears aroused during the preceding three years. The chroniclers declare that the earls and their followers were in a position to dictate their terms and the documents substantiate the statement.[62]

Although Edward I had already ordered the charters to be confirmed, the magnates wanted more; they desired some interpretation and some additional articles that would show how the king understood the charters. A mere confirmation or letters patent to individuals promising that a tax would not constitute a precedent would no longer suffice. Yet there were good reasons for the king's not refusing to yield to the opposition and for his council in his absence agreeing to the compromise.

It is not hard to see why the council yielded to the demands of the barons for reasons other than the argument of force which the malcontents possessed. For Edward had continued to negotiate with the recalcitrants till his departure for Flanders, and no question of principle separated the two parties. He had declared that he was willing to confirm the charters if they would grant him the aid that was so necessary.[63] The two parties could not agree about the eighth and the fifth of movables, but the king declared that this

60. Trivet, pp. 366–367.
61. Hemingburgh, II, 148–154.
62. *Ibid.*, p. 148. Trivet, p. 366. Cotton, p. 338.
63. Bémont, *Chartes des libertés,* pp. 83–84.

levy would not turn to the prejudice or disinheritance of them or their heirs, that he would acquit everyone who doubted this by his letters patent "in such manner that the taxing nor the levying of this eighth shall turn to the prejudice nor the bondage of any nor be drawn nor used in time to come." [64] He was as good as his word and issued letters patent to all that desired them.[65]

Except for the eighth he had never levied an aid on movables save with the consent of the magnates, the shire knights, and the men of the demesne. In the October parliament of 1297 a ninth of movables was granted, a concession which could be interpreted as fulfilling the king's desire for an aid if he confirmed the charters. Then logically the eighth and the fifth were revoked.[66] This ninth was granted by a parliament composed of the magnates and the knights of the shire with the express provision that it was not to extend to the royal demesne.[67] On October 14 London granted a ninth; no record has come to my attention showing that other areas granted the ninth which was however certainly levied on the rest of the royal demesne.[68] But in 1294, 1295, and 1296 towns and manors of the demesne had made grants either individually or by representatives.

Shall we then conclude that the ninth on the demesne was only granted by London and not conceded at all by other areas, particularly in a year when the necessity of consent to a tax on movables had been emphasized? I prefer to suggest that the taxers were to secure the assent of the urban and rural groups at the time when they assessed and collected the ninth just as they did in 1290 and 1294. There was nothing in Edward's background that would lead him to refuse to agree to the provisions of the Confirmation, or for that matter to the principles that at the close of the thirteenth century underlay them.[69]

The pardons issued to the malcontents are not astonishing when we recall that negotiations were carried on between the king and the earls after the break, and that Edward had yielded on the question of military service.[70] We must notice the emotional appeal to Edward by his council—if he desired to preserve and maintain his

64. "Extracts from the memoranda rolls," p. 287.
65. Vincent, *Lancashire lay subsidies*, pp. 206–207, 212. *Calendar of close rolls, 1296–1302*, p. 129.
66. Vincent, *Lancashire lay subsidies*, p. 198.
67. *Ibid.*, p. 212.
68. *Ibid.*, p. 214. *Parliamentary writs*, I, 64.
69. *Ibid.*, pp. 61–64. Vincent, *Lancashire lay subsidies*, pp. 212–214.
70. Cotton, p. 327.

honor, his status, and his kingdom he should return the documents sealed and attested, without modification.

It had a profound influence upon him. No doubt he felt hampered in his freedom of decision, but after hesitating for three days, on November 5 he agreed to all the barons' demands and granted everything just as it was proposed to him.[71]

It has been remarked that the critical year of 1297 made a great impression on both Edward I and his subjects.[72] No tax on movables was granted after the ninth of 1297 till 1300 and this was not collected. In 1301 the king was granted a fifteenth and thereafter none till 1306. Thus the period of annual levies was succeeded by occasional levies of about the same frequency as in the earlier part of the reign. In 1302 the king collected an aid of 40s. per fee to marry his eldest daughter, an aid that had been decided on in 1290, one of the regular aids but never yet collected. Probably the king refrained from collecting it in the decade of the nineties lest it interfere with taxes on movables. In 1303 he asked the representatives of forty-two towns who met in assembly if they would increase the custom on wool, wine, and other merchandise, but they unanimously refused. In 1304, for the first time in his reign, the king resorted to a tallage. The levy of the tallage at this time was natural for a king who was in need of money and who had never yet resorted to this tax. If we accept the theory that no regulation had been made forbidding tallage, why should he be criticized for resorting to a due? The writs of assessment followed well-established precedent. A group of commissioners was sent out to a circuit of counties—two of the group were competent to act as a quorum. The sheriff of each county was to cooperate with the justices. On notice from the latter he would summon to meet them those men of the various cities, boroughs, and demesne manors whom he might think competent to aid in the assessment. The assessment was based on the wealth of the people within the aforesaid areas. The assessors should levy it per capita or in common as they thought best; they should not spare the rich and not overburden the poor. They were to deliver copies of the assessment to such persons as they thought proper to collect and report the assessment to the exchequer.[73]

71. Hemingburgh, II, 154–155. Trivet, p. 368. Bémont, *Chartes des libertés*, p. 96. Vincent, *Lancashire lay subsidies*, p. 220.

72. Hilda Johnstone in *Cambridge medieval history*, VII, 410. Tout, *History of England, 1216–1377*, pp. 208–209.

73. Stubbs, *Select charters*, pp. 501–502. *Calendar of patent rolls, 1301–1307*, pp. 201–202. *Rotuli parliamentorum*, I, 266.

When once the writs for the levy of this tallage—a tax not taken for at least thirty-six years—had been issued the problem arose as to how these valuations were to be made. We have no document surviving that contains the complete instructions for making the valuations of property or arriving at the amount of tallage on any given area. Some assessors employed the old method. They made a bargain for a lump sum with the town as had been done in tallage and sometimes in taxes on movables. Thus Cambridge was assessed £80; Lincoln, £100; Winchester, 200m., Gloucester, £100; Shrewsbury, £180; Ipswich, £60; Bristol, £200; Norwich, £400.[74]

Such was not always the method employed. Walter of Hemingburgh states that the king "exacted from his cities and boroughs the sixth penny, according to the valuation of their goods." [75] The annals of London are still more specific. They relate that Roger of Heyham, knight, and John Sendal, a venerable clerk of London, raised a certain tallage on the citizens of London by command of the king; it consisted of a fifteenth of movable goods and a tenth of revenues.[76]

According to these contemporary accounts, therefore, the tallage in some cases was a tax on both movables and revenues. From official documents, the rolls of assessment or collection, comes corroboration. In Canterbury the tallage was levied per capita and according to the roll was based on movables and revenues.[77] Such was also the case in London. In a roll of the Foreign Accounts of the exchequer the tallage on London was given by wards, separated into the amounts received respectively from movables and from revenues.[78] Now there is no indication in the writ of instructions to the assessors that the assessment should be made in this way. Yet the assessors of the tallage in Kent, London, and York employed this method.[79] How shall we explain the calculation of tallage as a percentage of the valuation of movables and also of revenues without orders to that effect in the writs of assessment? The mention by one chronicler of the tallage as a sixth of movables and by another in London as a fifteenth of movables and a tenth of revenues, and the fact that sundry towns compounded in lump sums, suggests that

---

74. Vincent, *Lancashire lay subsidies,* p. 250. *Calendar of patent rolls, 1301–1307,* p. 202.
75. Hemingburgh, II, 233.
76. *Annales Londonienses,* ed. William Stubbs, in "Chronicles of the reigns of Edward I and Edward II," I (Rolls series), 132.
77. Madox, *History of the exchequer,* p. 509.
78. Vincent, *Lancashire lay subsidies,* pp. 252–253.
79. Lay subsidy rolls, E 179/217/1, Public Record Office.

no uniform rate of assessment was authorized but that different assessors used their discretion in the method and the rate which they employed. They were empowered by the writs to use their judgment in the regulations about basing the levy upon wealth, levying it per capita or in common, not sparing the rich and so on, and to designate competent collectors. May they not also have been authorized orally to base the levy upon a percentage of the valuations? Some of these assessors were men high in financial administration. A group of ten of special rank was designated, one of whom was always to be consulted by the assessors of each circuit.[80] Six of them were barons of the exchequer, the other four were important justices, or royal clerks, an indication of their high position not merely because of their responsibility but because they were equated with barons of the exchequer.[81]

Yet what is the source of the new custom by which the council ordered the assessors to evaluate the revenues and movables and then fixed the percentage of each kind of property which should be taken as the tax and the sum of the two fractional valuations constituting the tax of each person? The practice must have taken its inception from some method familiar to both tallage payers and officials, or objection would have been raised that it was against custom. Now it is true that if they had examined the rolls of Henry III's time they would have found that in the tallages of that date revenues and movables both might be taxed. Further, they were habituated to the taxes on movables, taking a certain percentage of the valuation of certain movables. Then, too, since no tallage had been levied by the king since 1268 men had perhaps forgotten the actual method of assessment and hence were unable to observe that the scheme employed this year was not customary.

While the king had levied no tallage between 1268 and 1304, towns and lords had levied tallages for their own use. The new custom could not have been an outgrowth from these local tallages. Says Frances Page, "The repetition of these local levies had a tendency to become stereotyped in amount." [82] Possibly the notion took its rise from the papal taxes on revenues and the lay taxes on movables.[83] Anyhow a new kind of tallage began to evolve, a

80. *Calendar of patent rolls, 1301–1307*, p. 202.
81. *Calendar of close rolls, 1302–1307*, pp. 194, 266, 272, 461.
82. F. M. Page, *The estates of Crowland abbey* (Cambridge, 1934), pp. 105–106, 309–312.
83. Lunt, *Financial relations of the papacy with England*, pp. 240 et seq.

THE END OF ROYAL TALLAGE

fractional part of an assessed valuation of revenues and a different fractional valuation of movables. Since this levy was a tallage in the strict sense, would not existing exemptions apply? There was some confusion, for over a generation had elapsed since a tallage had been levied. The sheriff would know the dwellers on the royal demesne but not whether a given person was liable for tallage. Hence disputes arose.

The first order to assess the tallage was issued on January 20, 1304. It was to tallage the city of York. On February 6, 1304, the patent rolls record the appointment of tallagers throughout the rest of the realm.[84] The assessment apparently led to disputes as to who was liable to tallage. There could hardly be an official who had any actual experience with it. And the chancery did not issue any specific instructions but merely copied the old writs. It was moreover an age of definition in which there was greater reliance than ever before on written records. People claimed that they had never paid tallage and had been granted exemption from it by charter. Foremost among the opponents were the clergy. The opposition was so widespread that the matter was discussed by the council of the king and about April, 1304, the king ordered that religious orders and others who claimed to be quit of tallage in their lands by charter of the king's progenitors and of the king himself or in any other way (prescription) should have respite till three weeks after the following Holy Trinity.[85]

This order shows the opposition to the method of assessment and the resultant distraints which may have included many more taxpayers than before.[86] Though this order was only a stay of assessment, often it must have been really only the first step in legal procedure which finally resulted in exemption. One method of exemption was by a charter issued by King Edward I himself.[87] Thus arrangements previously made by the king interfered with the spread of this newly revived levy.

Generally the exemption dated from a previous reign. As all charters had been confirmed by the present ruler, such charters contained a clause freeing their recipient from tallage in one of those catchall clauses. The administration had to admit the validity

84. *Calendar of patent rolls, 1301–1307*, pp. 201–202. *Rotuli parliamentorum*, I, 266.
85. *Calendar of patent rolls, 1301–1307*, pp. 206–207.
86. *Calendar of close rolls, 1302–1307*, p. 135.
87. *Ibid.*, p. 137.

of those documents. A charter issued by Richard I and confirmed by Henry III was held good after inspection.[88] Not merely were old charters appealed to but new privileges were granted by Edward I himself under the pressure of a great man. Thus at the instance of the king's brother Edmund the earl of Leicester, John de Leutur, citizen of London, received letters patent that he should be quit for life of all tallages levied by the king or his heirs.[89] Sometimes the charter did not specifically mention tallagium but exempted the holder in general from exactions, for example, to be "quit of all gelds and tributes," and that was held a legal exemption.[90] Land held in frankalmoign was to be exempt as in the past, that is, in all these decisions the old custom was followed.[91]

We might expect that Edward I would insist on evidence by charter if the debtor sought exemption and such was often the case. But men who thought themselves illegally tallaged brought other proofs to show that they should not be subject to this tax. They aimed to demonstrate that the character of their tenure exempted them from the levy—men who held by other than by free alms. Joan, the widow of Robert de Gray, held in dower certain lands in Oxfordshire which her deceased husband had received as son and heir of his father, Walter, who in turn had received them by charter from Henry III by the service of one-twentieth part of a knight's fee for all service, custom, and demand.[92] Alan de Plunket, a king's yeoman, claimed to be quit of tallage because the land which he held in Somersetshire had been received by his father in exchange for the office of steward in the New Forest and for another manor in Hants, neither of which presumably were subject to tallage.[93] Robert Pugeys in Oxfordshire received a respite because he claimed that his manor of Brampton was held by homage and service and by rendering yearly a sword worth 18*d*. for all service.[94]

In some of these cases therefore the government could not insist on charter evidence to prove exemption but had to accept instead other legal proof that tallage was not owed. In addition it accepted the conventional proof as of old that if one had been quit of tallage

88. *Ibid.*, pp. 135, 145, 163, 175, 200, 201.
89. *Ibid.*, p. 135.
90. *Ibid.*, p. 201.
91. *Ibid.*, pp. 145, 201.
92. *Ibid.*, p. 203.
93. *Ibid.*
94. *Ibid.*, p. 202.

in the past he did not owe it now. The bishop of Hereford claimed that the tenants of the chapter in the city of Hereford were acquitted of tallage by the charters of the king's progenitors; and Edward I ordered the treasurer and the barons of the exchequer to search the rolls of the exchequer of Henry III and if they found that the tenants were acquitted of tallage under Henry III to acquit them now.[95] Joan de Byddik claimed that she would not pay tallage in London because her grandfather, whose heir she was, had charters of exemption from tallage.[96]

While the tallage thus was a tax on personal property and revenue, it retained characteristics of a conventional due payable only by certain inhabitants of boroughs, cities, and manors of the royal demesne. The law granted exemption to such as could prove satisfactorily by charter, or in some other way, that they or their ancestors holding this land had been exempt. Another characteristic of the earlier tallage was not at first recalled, but as time went on and the levy went into effect old practices were recollected. In former times when the king took a tallage from the men of his demesne his tenants were allowed to tallage the men of their demesnes if their land had belonged to the ancient demesne of the king. In November, 1304, nine months after the writs of tallage had been issued, the king granted Queen Margaret, his consort, the tallages from all the lands which she held.[97]

Before March, 1305, the bishop of Salisbury (of course with the approval of the king) had endeavored without success to tallage his episcopal city in accordance with the terms of a charter of Henry III that he should tallage the city of Salisbury whenever the king tallaged his demesne, and Edward I proceeded to enforce the law.[98] A little later in March, 1305, the king issued orders on behalf of a great number of his tenants to tallage their lands "if they were at any time the demesnes of the king and if they have been wont to be tallaged."[99]

In this regulation too, therefore, the customary rules of tallage were followed. Edward I has been reproached for permitting his tenants to tallage their men as a means of quieting their complaints because he had tallaged his demesne. So Stubbs refers to "the last

---

95. *Ibid.*, p. 145.
96. *Ibid.*, p. 202.
97. *Ibid.*, p. 267.
98. *Ibid.*, p. 242. *Calendar of patent rolls, 1301–1307*, p. 353.
99. *Calendar of close rolls, 1302–1307*, pp. 250–252, 305. *Rotuli parliamentorum*, I, 161.

and meanest, the almost forgotten tallage on the demesne."[100] If we can for a moment leave out of account our knowledge of the conflict between king and parliament in the seventeenth century and our natural sympathies with parliament, we shall see that the repeated grant of aids by parliament did not limit the power of the king at that time but enhanced it. From the point of view of contemporaries, the sovereign had acquired a new way to increase his power and income. Some day that grant, through the body called parliament, would limit the king's power but not in the reign of Edward I. As nearly as we can judge the tallage represented merely a dying, almost an extinct due, because of the greater advantage to the king of the taxes on movables. The grant to his tenants by Edward I of the power to tallage their men was something that the king was obliged to make if he was to pay due respect to the law of the land.

The primary significance of the tallage of 1304 lies in the method of levy, the initiation of a new method of assessment by which the council determined the percentages of the valuation of revenues and also of movables throughout the realm on the royal demesne, the sum of these percentages on each person or area determining the tallage of the year. Nothing like this method is encountered in the levy of tallage before 1304. By taxing both revenues and movables in this way, tallage had the possibility of being transformed into a far heavier levy than the tax on movables on those areas that were subject to both levies on different occasions, yet it was taken as always without the consent of the local property holders and rulers. It was undoubtedly introduced on the initiative of officials experienced in taxation who considered it an improved method of assessment. No opposition is recorded in this first experiment. That a change of this sort was made without attracting the attention of anyone is due to the fact that tallage had not been levied in a long time, as a matter of fact not in thirty-six years. It attracted the notice of the clerks of the exchequer.[101] But a levy of this kind made the aid and the tallage more alike. Both might still be a composition in a lump sum; or a certain percentage of the valuation, the aid of movables, the tallage of revenues and movables, even a different percentage of each kind of property; the assessment of both taxes was made by royal commissioners who might be assisted by local jurors. The name aid or tallage might be applied to both.

100. Stubbs, *Select charters*, p. 428.
101. Madox, *History of the exchequer*, p. 509.

Nevertheless, although tallage and aid seem to be becoming more and more alike, a fundamental difference remained between them in the method of authorization. For example, the people on the same areas, manors, and towns in the year 1294 were subject to an aid on movables that could be legally levied only by the consent of the men of the area, a freewill grant. The writ authorized the commissioner appointed to a group of shires to go to each manor and city of the royal demesne in company with the sheriff and require and persuade the men of each area to grant and supply to the king the sixth part of movables, as London had already granted. Then the commissioner was to report to the king, the treasurer, or the barons of the exchequer the results of his work; the assessment and collection were in charge of the assessors and collectors of the tenth that had been granted in each shire by the magnates and shire knights.[102]

In 1304 these same manors and cities were subject to a tallage levied solely by the command of the king. It was taken per capita or in common, as seemed best to the royal assessors according to the wealth of the tenants in the cities, boroughs, and demesnes of the king; the rich were not to be spared, nor the poor overburdened—provisions that were of ancient vintage. Yet in some cases the assessors secured from the men of the area a sixth of movables, in another (at least one) a fifteenth of movables and a tenth of revenues. Though such an arrangement was not commanded by the writ, it was not forbidden. It may have been suggested to the assessors by the barons of the exchequer or the council. Yet it would seem that a way had been found to transform tallage into a tax on revenues and movables, yet retain its original character as a due.

At the accession of Edward II in 1307 aids of a fifteenth and a tenth of movables were granted; in 1309, a twenty-fifth. Then followed the dispute with the barons and the establishment of the Lords Ordainers. In such a situation no grant of an extraordinary levy was made. When peace was restored after the death of Gaveston, orders were issued in December, 1312, for the levy of a tallage.

It was the first time such a levy had been made since 1304 and we have no evidence to show why the government chose this levy rather than a tax on movables. While peace had been restored, the hard feelings that still existed may have made it seem wiser not to ask for a contribution from the counties where the great lords were powerful, and so instead of asking the towns for a voluntary con-

102. Vincent, *Lancashire lay subsidies*, pp. 183, 185–186.

tribution the government had recourse to a tax that was a due. However that may be, the tallage was called for and the demand was of special importance. The orders for the collection follow the well-established precedents in all respects except one; the assessors were to assess the tallage per capita or in common on the cities, boroughs, and demesnes of the king according to the wealth of the tenants; the rich were not to be spared and the poor not overburdened. In all this they were employing ancient phrases. Then they added a provision which shows that the conception of tallage had radically changed in the minds of the exchequer officials. The assessors were in addition definitely instructed how they were to determine the amount of tallage owed by each individual or group that came before them—whether the tax was to be levied in common or per capita. They were to assess the tallage, taking a fifteenth of their movables and a tenth of their revenues. After the assessment was concluded, the assessors were to deliver their copies of the roll to the sheriff to collect the tax, a regulation that returned to the custom of Henry III.[103]

Tallage thus had ceased to be a due levied in some conventional fashion and had become a due based on movables and revenues according to assessed valuation. But just as towns fined for the tax on movables and also for tallage of the old sort, so they continued to compound. Following further the ancient custom, those tenants who had been granted some of the ancient demesne were authorized by royal writ to collect tallage from the men on those manors.[104]

Various manors in Hampshire, among them Ringwood, declared that they were not ancient demesne, had never paid tallage, and so did not now owe it, but that they had always shared with the commonalty of that county in general contributions and other burdens touching the whole community. It was found that Ringwood appeared in *Domesday* as part of the royal demesne and so it had to pay tallage while the other manors were exempted.[105] If, moreover, the charter of the debtor who claimed to be exempted from tallage made no mention of exemption, the town had to pay tallage.[106]

In 1304 there is no record of opposition to the new method of levying tallage. But in 1312 London vigorously resisted the levy. London, we know, had opposed tallage before. In 1215 the citizens

103. *Rotuli parliamentorum*, I, 449.
104. *Calendar of close rolls, 1307–1313*, pp. 519–520.
105. Thomas Madox, *Firma burgi* (London, 1726), pp. 58–61.
106. *Ibid.*, p. 248.

THE END OF ROYAL TALLAGE

secured a notice concerning their aids in the Great Charter; in 1226 they received special letters patent fixing the manner in which their tallage was to be taken, that is, in common and not per capita; in 1255 they waged a bitter but losing battle in which they vainly sought to prove that they owed auxilium and not tallage. Now again nearly sixty years later they declared that they did not owe tallage and based their argument on the same reasons as before.

The mayor, aldermen, and sheriffs of London were summoned before the king's council and informed that the king was to tallage his demesnes, cities, and boroughs throughout the realm by virtue of the rights of his crown; they were asked whether they preferred to fine for their tallage or be assessed per capita (or in common) both on their revenues and movables. The city officials replied that they must consult with the commonalty of London. Accordingly permission was granted them and they withdrew.[107] On their return they declared that although the king might be able to tallage at will his demesnes, cities, and boroughs, nevertheless they knew that the citizens of London were not tallageable.

They advanced various reasons for this conclusion. They and their ancestors had been free and by charter exempt from tallage since at least the days of Henry I; and in addition Magna Carta declared that the city of London had all its ancient liberties and free customs as they formerly had, and they had never been accustomed to be tallaged in the aforesaid manner, hence they begged not to be tallaged now.

Further, magnates and citizens had revenues and *tenementa* in London that could not be tallaged without their counsel, for that would be to disinherit and oppress them too heavily. Moreover, the citizens held the city by royal grant of a fixed fee farm of £300 per annum for all services and hence it would seem that they ought not to be tallaged. They begged that the levy should be postponed till the next parliament so that they might confer then with the magnates who had property in London as to what should justly be done.

Finally, they proposed to make a loan to the king, at first of £1,000, to secure a postponement; and in this connection the king agreed that if he later levied an aid on them or a tallage, this loan should be counted as part of the tax. In 1314 they granted a further loan of £400 and secured an additional postponement under similar conditions.[108] In 1318 the citizens were pardoned this tallage of

---

107. *Parliamentary writs*, II, 84.
108. *Ibid.*, pp. 84–85.

Edward II in consideration of their having released to the king divers sums which they had advanced to him as loans in connection with the tallage which ought to have been levied on rents and chattels in the city for the king's use in the sixth year of his reign and had been hitherto postponed because they asserted that they ought not to be tallaged.[109] These loans may therefore be regarded as a composition for tallage in whole or in part. Thus the citizens failed to establish their legal claim that they were not subject to tallage, but it is interesting to note that they made no appeal to the Confirmation of the Charters or the "De tallagio," nor did they question whether this was the conventional basis for tallage. In a measure however they were successful, for the council did not insist on their real aim, that is, to enforce a tax of a tenth of revenues and a fifteenth of movables despite the precedent established in 1304, when they collected those fractional sums from the great city.

This tallage could not be collected in Bristol till 1315, because of a local dispute on other grounds between the town and the royal custodian of the castle, Bartholomew de Badlesmere. The assessment was finally made on both revenues and movables to a total of £289 7s. 8d.; about £211 16s. 7d. were on movables and the balance on revenues.[110] In 1315 the pipe roll records that £277 78s. 4d. were paid.[111] The only case of frank opposition to tallage therefore was that of London and this dispute did not concern the basis of the tax.

No other tallage was levied in the reign of Edward II, but this fact must not be overemphasized any more than the infrequency of tallages in the reign of Edward I. For aids on personal property were regularly granted, taxes that yielded far more than any tallage. At this time they were recognized more than ever as part of the financial resources of the royal administration. In June, 1332, Edward III issued orders for the levy of a tallage. He followed the precedent established in 1312; it was to be taken in common or by head as the assessors might decide; the rich were not to be spared and the poor not overburdened; it was to be based on wealth; it was to be assessed by groups of commissioners, each group in a circuit of counties; they were to draw up a roll in duplicate to be sent to the exchequer as quickly as possible so that the collection

---

109. *Calendar of patent rolls, 1317–1321*, p. 110.
110. E. A. Fuller, "The tallage of 6 Edward II," *Bristol and Gloucestershire archaeological society transactions*, XIX (1894–95), 180, 200.
111. *Ibid.*, p. 187.

THE END OF ROYAL TALLAGE

might be made without delay; the assessment was to be based on the wealth of the property holders who were to pay a fourteenth of movables and a ninth of revenues in the cities, boroughs, and rural demesnes of the king.[112]

When the parliament of the following September assembled, the prelates, the earls and barons, the knights of the shire and the deputies of the towns as usual met in groups by themselves to discuss the matters laid before them by the king and to consider petitions that men rushed to present.[113] The deputies of the towns are not mentioned as present in this description of the parliament, but they were summoned, two citizens from each city and two burgesses from each borough, with the power to act and to consent for themselves and the communities of the cities and boroughs.[114] The writs of expenses were issued by the council for both knights and citizens and burgesses on September 12, so both groups were present at the same time and remained for the same period, and on the patent roll the writs of assessment state that the citizens and burgesses granted the tenth of all their movable goods in the present parliament of September. It is likely therefore that they participated in all the acts of this parliament.[115]

In sharp contrast to the unnoticeable reaction against tallage in 1312 (apart from London), this new levy aroused a formidable opposition. Very likely it began to develop during the summer, for as soon as parliament met in September hostility to tallage was displayed. On the second day of the session a fifteenth of movables on the shires and a tenth on the towns were granted for war against the Scots in response to an appeal from the king. Evidently this action was taken only after the king had agreed to revoke the order for the June tallage.[116]

Curiously enough the petition for the revocation of the tallage was made by the magnates and shire deputies, although it was probably initiated by the town representatives since tallage was of greater interest to them than to members of the other groups. It is likely that the town deputies had persuaded the magnates to take the lead in presenting the petition; the townsmen feared that they

---

112. Rymer, *Foedera*, II, 840. *Rotuli parliamentorum*, II, 446.
113. *Ibid.*, II, 66.
114. *Calendar of close rolls, 1330–1333*, p. 580.
115. Rymer, *Foedera*, II, 845. William Prynne, *A brief register, kalendar, and survey of the several kinds of all parliamentary writs* (London, 1659–64), IV, 115, 117.
116. *Rotuli parliamentorum*, II, 66.

would have difficulty in persuading the council to withdraw the tallage, for two tallages of this kind had been levied in the past (1304, 1312) on the towns, the slight protest proving ineffectual.

The strategy, if such it was, was successful. What is unusual was the collaboration of the three groups against the king and council. Clearly this action reflects the evolution of parliament, whose members had learned the political value of cooperation. If this completed the tale of opposition in 1332, the session would be significant enough. But there is more. The parliamentary groups were not satisfied with the mere recall of the tallage of 1332. This we can certainly deduce from the king's answer to the petition the words of which are still unknown. He declared that for the future he would not assess such a tallage except in the form in which it had been taken in the time of his "other" ancestors and as he ought reasonably to do.[117] Undoubtedly here is reference to tallages taken by certain of the king's ancestors to which objection is now made, but there were tallages levied by other ancestors of Edward III which aroused no complaint.

What then was the difference between the two forms of tallage that rendered one kind satisfactory to the men of the royal demesne and to the other groups in the parliament of September and the other kind so objectionable that all groups united in a petition that henceforth tallage should be radically modified or abandoned? It seems fair to draw this conclusion about the attitude of parliament, for the three bodies had united to request the revocation of the June tallage. That was in comparison a minor request, for it could be justified on the ground that it was an excessive burden of taxation for the king to levy a tallage on the demesne in June and in addition a tax on movables of a tenth in September of the same year. It made no alteration in the character of the levy. The additional request radically modified the nature of tallage, as it had become in 1332, to the disadvantage of the king. Its results would be profound. Hence it would be necessary to bring far more influence to bear upon the sovereign and his council and arguments of compelling weight to secure their assent to such a change. It seems clear that for this demand too the three groups in parliament would feel an impulse toward union. At any rate, the king's reply, as reported by the clerk, shows that the arguments that convinced the groups in parliament to combine also were strong enough to induce the king and his council to agree to modify the character of

117. *Ibid.*

tallage and restore it to its ancient constitution. The key word in this key clause of the king's declaration (*les autres auncestres*) is "autres," "our other ancestors." [118] If we omit it in our rendering of the passage the significance of the statement is wholly changed. Thus Stubbs states: "The king, in accepting a grant of a fifteenth and a tenth, recalled the commissions for the tallage, promising that henceforth he would levy such tallages only as had been done in the time of his ancestors and as he had a right to do." [119] The implication in this rendering is that in June, 1332, Edward III had introduced a fundamental change in the character of the tallage when he issued the writ ordering the assessors to take a fourteenth of movables and a ninth of revenues as a tallage. We know that he introduced no change at all; he followed the policy employed by his father in 1312, who ordered a fifteenth of movables and a tenth of revenues to be assessed. The same form appeared in several instances in 1304, though the writs of assessment contain no directions to levy it in this way; it is likely oral instructions were given by the members of the king's council to the assessors. No such precepts were ever issued in earlier writs, and no such methods of assessment of tallage have been recorded in earlier levies. This is the great change that was introduced in the tallage in the fourteenth century. There is no distinction in the method of authorization; both the earlier and the later tallages were authorized by the king and his small council. Neither was a voluntary grant by the men of the demesne.[120] Pasquet remarks: "The principle of a tallage might be different, but the procedure was exactly that used in the case of a granted aid. The difference between an aid like that of 1294 and a tallage like that of 1304 is more apparent than real." But he thinks that the tallage of 1304 was a sixth of movables.[121] That is partly correct. Some towns did pay a sixth. London paid a tenth of revenues and a fifteenth of movables. But as we have shown, this is the beginning of a change to make tallage into a tax on revenues and movables. It is not characteristic of tallages before 1304. Let us compare the writs of tallage of 1304 which are similar to earlier writs with the writ for the aid of 1294: we shall find the aid emphasizes the fact that the tax is a grant; the writ to assess the tallage has no such clause because it is a due.[122]

118. *Ibid.*
119. Stubbs, *Constitutional history*, II, 545.
120. Rymer, *Foedera*, II, 840, 845.
121. Pasquet, *Origins of the House of Commons*, pp. 119, 194.
122. Vincent, *Lancashire lay subsidies*, p. 183. *Rotuli parliamentorum*, I, 266.

Both levies were based on property. The writs for both state that the levy should be based on wealth. This might indicate both personal and real property. The assessors should not spare the rich or overburden the poor; they should levy it per capita or in common as they should decide—all ancient phrases that fitted the stereotyped levy that tallage was becoming during Henry III's reign. The assessors were often assisted by a local jury.

The only distinction was that the tallages of 1312 and 1332 made a notable addition to the older writs of authorization in the phrase, "taking a certain percentage of revenues and a certain percentage of movables," e.g., in 1312 a tenth of revenues and a fifteenth of movables, in 1332 a ninth of revenues and a fourteenth of movables. These ratios were fixed by the council that in this way determined the amount of tallage on each area in a way never before employed. After the commissioners had determined the valuation of each kind of property revenues and movables, the ratios assigned by the council were at once applied. By the old method, after consideration of the value of the property the amount of tallage was determined by a bargain between the commissioners and the local political lord. Hence the new method gave a sharper edge to the assessment, placing more control in the hands of the council.

Which of these two levies was the one the king promised to abandon at the petition of the parliament? It can only be the one which had aroused such opposition in 1332; the one which had led the magnates and deputies of the shires to join in support of the opposition of the towns; the one which the towns opposed because it was heavier than the aids on movables which from time to time they granted; [123] the one that they had experienced as a grievance; the one that the king had the right to levy without consulting them, without their consent, yet one that in essence was the same kind of a tax, only heavier than the tax on movables, a levy that could only be assessed with the consent of the towns. Unlike the protesting Londoners in 1312, the townsmen in 1332 must have presented evidence that the tallages of 1312 as well as 1332, though levied by the king's sole authority, were not merely of the same character as the taxes on movables but represented a new kind of tallage that began to appear in 1304 by the will of the king alone. We do not know what their arguments were, but they were strong enough to convince not merely the groups of magnates and shire deputies but also the king and his council that this kind of tallage could be dis-

123. Fuller, "The tallage of 6 Edward II," pp. 180, 198–199, 200, 203, 278.

tinguished from the aid on movables only by the fact that it was based on revenues as well as movables and required no consent from the local authorities. We know that it convinced the council because the king abandoned it. Clearly the writs differed and if examples of assessment rolls were at hand lists of the property of both sorts of all taxable individuals would show that both revenues and movables were definitely taxed. Why should the magnates be interested in the subject to such an extent as to petition the king to revoke the tallage of 1332 and later to oppose this kind of tallage? If the king was able to transform the tallage on his demesnes, his cities and boroughs by issuing a writ, might he not attempt it on the other areas that had paid aids on movables by grant of the magnates and others? Is this not really an illustration of what the barons feared might take place as depicted in Articles V and VI of the Confirmation of the Charters? It is said that because the king had the right to take a tallage without consent he could take a tax on movables without consent, and so the summoning of deputies to parliament was unnecessary for this purpose. The evolution of the tallage from 1304 through 1332 shows that the council was adopting that interpretation. But there is no indication that such was the interpretation earlier. It is true however that it was not necessary to summon deputies from the towns to grant an aid; commissioners could be sent out to the towns for this purpose. This method by which a tallage like that of 1332 was made illegal, that is, by a petition to the king, which he granted, saying that he would never levy such a tallage again but only such tallages as were levied under Henry III, illustrates the fact that tallage was a due and that the men of the demesne could not refuse it; it was not an aid. Otherwise they would have been content with the king's promise that he would never levy such a tallage again except by the consent of the men of the demesne. This promise they would not dream of asking since consent was never part of the authorization of tallage.

The document of 1332 that contains the king's statement of the compromise between him and parliament deserves a place as one of the important steps in the development of taxation and stands in the same line as the Confirmation of the Charters. Tallage in its ancient form remained, but the council had lost its power to continue the evolution of tallage as a tax on personal property and revenue by the king's sole authority. Such levies henceforth must be taken by consultation and consent of groups.

We can only speculate why the prelates, lay magnates, and

knights of the shire supported the men of the demesne. Perhaps because the bodies that composed parliament had met so often together that a corporate feeling of unity had begun to draw them together; perhaps because of the fear that a breach of customary law by the king against one group in parliament might pave the way for an attack upon the privilege of other groups. It certainly could not be because the king's action was held to be counter to the Confirmation of the Charters. Otherwise a reference would appear to that document. From the document in the rolls of parliament, the case against Edward III was based upon a breach of the domanial law.[124] The king's grant that he would not levy tallage any more except as it had been taken in the time of his other ancestors is a further indication that the Confirmation of the Charters did not apply to tallage of the demesne.

The aid of 1332 and the vigorous military policy of Edward III opened an era of frequent taxation. In 1334 came another levy on movables, a fifteenth and a tenth; in 1336 and 1337 three grants of a fifteenth and a tenth, in 1337 and 1338 the enormous loans in connection with wool; in 1340 the earls, barons, and all the commons of the realm granted the ninth lamb, fleece, and sheaf for two years, and the cities and boroughs the ninth part of all their goods and chattels; foreign merchants and others who did not live by tillage or store of sheep should pay a fifteenth of the value of their goods. In return for this grant, the king

conceded for himself and his heirs to the prelates, earls, barons and commons, the citizens, burgesses and merchants that this grant which was so heavy should not be drawn into a precedent or fall to their prejudice in the future, nor should they from henceforth be charged with any common aid or sustain any charge, except by the common assent of the prelates, earls, barons, and other great men and commons [communes] of the kingdom of England and that in parliament.[125]

This is the document celebrated by Stubbs as the "real act *de tallagio non concedendo* and the surrender of the privilege of taxing demesne lands which Edward I had retained as not expressly forbidden by the act of 1297." [126] With this statement Manning agrees: "By this Edward gave up the right of tallaging the de-

124. *Rotuli parliamentorum*, II, 66.
125. *The statutes of the realm* (Record Commission), I, 289–290.
126. Stubbs, *Constitutional history*, II, 400.

THE END OF ROYAL TALLAGE

mesne." [127] We have seen that tallage of the royal demesne was not concerned in the crisis of 1297 at all. It is clear that beginning in 1304 the council began to change the tallage into a tax on revenues and movables by arbitrary action. No record has survived of opposition to the change until 1332 when Edward III promised to levy tallage in the ancient manner and renounced the alteration in the tax. At the same time the rural and urban demesne granted him a tenth of movables while the magnates and the knights of the shire granted him a fifteenth. Thus the question of the tallage as modified since 1304 had been settled. The fear that haunted the parliamentary groups in 1340 was not concerned with tallage at all; it was the same fear that had haunted the magnates under Henry III and under Edward I in the late nineties, that repeated grants of taxes on movables would change the aid into a custom, that consent would become purely formal. Hence the statutory recognition by the astute Edward III that these grants should not form a precedent, that in the future no common aid or grant should be levied except by the consent of the magnates and the commons. A new note was added that the consent must be given in parliament. Now there is a reference to tallage here, that is, to the tallage on revenues and movables that had been renounced in 1332. But the old tallage, the ancient due, still remained owed to the king whenever he chose to levy it.

127. Bernard L. Manning in *Cambridge medieval history,* VII, 440.

INDEX

ABINGDON, ABBOT OF, 115, 131, 178, 183
Abingdon, Peter de, 85
Abingwerth, Gilbert de, 334
Adams, George Burton, 322, 324, 369; *Constitutional history of England,* 370 n.; *Council and courts,* 164 n.; *Origin of the English constitution,* 247 n.
Aid, 158–166, 179–180, 190–191, 193–194, 202, 205, 220, 231–233; of 1130, on urban demesne, 259, 265; of 1146 in France, for crusade of Louis VII, 114, 117; of 1156 on urban demesne, 265; of 1166, for the relief of the Holy Land, 2, 10, 114–116, 168–169; of 1168, 5, 22, 113, 153, 165–168; of 1183 in Palestine, 117–118; of 1184, 10, 24, 64, 67, 118, 169; of 1188, the Saladin tithe, 2–3, 6, 10, 12–14, 24, 52, 64, 67, 83, 87–88, 90, 96, 119–122, 124, 144, 169–170, 179, 190, 197, 207, 228, 285; of 1194, for the ransom of Richard I, 2–3, 14, 24–29, 52, 65, 67–68, 91, 97, 108, 112, 122–127, 151, 154, 171–175, 179, 285; of 1201, for the Holy Land, 16, 55, 64, 84, 131–133; of 1203, 16–17, 53, 65, 133, 177, 180; of 1207, 3, 9, 17, 30–33, 52, 54–55, 65–67, 69–74, 84–85, 91, 105, 109, 134, 177–179, 190, 202; of 1217, 19, 22, 42, 109, 135–136, 153, 192, 194–196, 202, 321; of 1222, to assist John de Brienne, 19, 35–36, 67, 138; of 1225, 20, 37–40, 52–53, 57, 65, 67, 74–78, 85, 88, 92, 105, 139–143, 151, 195, 347; of 1232, 20, 40–42, 53, 58, 61, 65, 67, 78, 83, 92, 105, 139, 143–145, 151–152, 195, 200–201, 204; of 1235, 9, 21, 42, 53, 58, 65, 67, 79, 100, 107, 153, 195, 201, 204; of 1237, 21, 42–46, 53–54, 65, 67, 79–81, 94, 100, 105, 109, 139, 145–147, 152, 194–195, 201, 204–205; of 1242, 21–22, 81, 153, 208; of 1245, 22, 81, 209–210; of 1253, 22, 81, 229; of 1269, 2, 22, 47–52, 66–67, 81–82, 84, 86, 93, 95, 102, 104–105, 109, 139, 149–150, 218–220, 229, 351–352; of 1275, 62, 224, 229, 359; of 1283, 62, 152, 225–226, 230; of 1290, 95, 227, 230; of 1294, 227–228, 230

Aids on movables, 1–3, 6–10, 23, 53, 55, 67, 88, 111, 113–115, 119, 123, 135, 139, 154, 162, 164, 168–169, 178, 193–195, 202, 221–222, 224, 231–235, 237, 239, 241–242, 285–286, 329, 358–361, 363, 368, 371, 375, 389, 397; assessment of, 7, 8, 10, 13, 63–65, 67, 88, 90–96, 108–109, 113–114, 120–122, 130–131, 150–151; collection of, 7, 10, 13, 96–102, 104–106; exemptions from, 116, 118–119, 134, 139, 148; refusal of by barons, 2, 9, 60, 89, 102, 161, 163, 208–210, 213, 218, 220–221, 372; yield of, 21, 31, 40, 48, 119. See also Aid, of 1146, 1166, 1183, 1184, 1188, 1194, 1201, 1203, 1207, 1225, 1232, 1237, 1269, 1275, 1283, 1290, 1294
Ailsbury, manor of, 306, 310, 316
Albini, Roger de, 294
Albini, William I de, Brito, 261
Aldermaston, 137
Alrewas, manor of, 306, 310
Amauri, Robert, 85
Amercements, 35, 157, 160, 243, 255, 260, 275
Amundeville, Thomas de, 292
Andover, 304
Anglo-Saxon chronicle, 260 n.
Anjou, count of, Geoffrey, 260
Annales Cambriae, 178 n.
Annals of Burton, 153 n.
Annals of Dunstaple, 48 n.
Annals of London, 383 and n.
Annals of Osney, 360 and n.
Annals of Tewkesbury, 205 n.
Annals of Waverley, 88 n.
Annals of Winchester, 223 n.
Arcy, Hervey de, 73
Arcy, Norman de, 79–80
Articles of the Barons, 291, 322
Arundel, earl of, William II de Albini, 268
Arundel, earl of, William III de Albini, 25
Ashbourne, manor of, 306, 311
Askeby, Thomas de, 80
Assize of arms, 83, 90
Assize of Clarendon, 66

Athies, Gerard de, 71
Aton, Gilbert de, 76
Audenarde, Giles de, 22, 47–52, 62, 86
Augustinian order, 208
Aumale, count of, Baldwin de Bethune, 16, 306, 310
Aumale, count of, William de Fortibus, 201, 329
Aumale, count of, William le Gros, 271–272
Aura, Walter de, 69, 71, 304
Austin monks. *See* Augustinian order
Avranches, William de, 82
Axbridge, manor of, 299
Axemuth, William de, 336
Axminster, 254, 256

Badgworth, 282
Badlesmere, Bartholomew de, 392
Baldwin, James Fosdick, *Scutage and knight service*, 168 n.
Ballard, Adolphus, *Borough charters*, 239 n.
Bamborough, 257
Bampton, honor of, 310
Bardney, abbot of, 80
Bardolf, Hugh, 291, 293, 304
Bardsey, 305
Barnwell, prior of, 323, 348
Barri, Gerald of, 87, 122. *See also* Giraldus Cambrensis
Basset, Alan, 311
Basset, Richard, 261
Basset, Thomas, 310
Basset, William (12th century), 83, 247–248, 250, 269
Basset, William (13th century), 385
Bat, Gerard, 35
Bateson, M., 352; *Records of the borough of Leicester*, 341 n.
Bath, bishop of, Jocelyn de Welles, 20, 36–39, 48, 53, 57, 61
Bath, bishop of, Savaric, 33, 182
Bath, Henry of, 337
Bayeux, William de, 77, 79
Baynard, Fulk, 83
Beauchamp, Simon de, 293
Beauchamp, William de, 82
Beaufow, Alice de, 269
Bec, Walter, 78
Beckerings, Peter de, 70
Becket, Thomas, 261
Bedford, castle of, 76
Bedford, siege of, 20, 137

Bedwin, 126
Belet, Michael, 291
Bémont, Charles, 368; *Chartes des libertés*, 365 n.
Benedictine order, 208
Beningworth, William de, 80, 81
Bensenton (Benson), 271, 349
Benton, 271
Berkeley, barony of, 69
Berkeley, Maurice de, 149
Berkeley, Robert de, 69–71, 84
Berton, William de, 17
Bertram, Roger, 79, 82
Bethune, Baldwin de, 41
Beverley, burgesses of, 30
Birkin, John de, 73
Black book of Peterborough, 157
Blackburn, hundred of, 152
Black monks. *See* Benedictine order
Blackstone, William, 366; *The great charter and the charter of the forest*, 366 n.
Blockesham (Bloxham), 271
Bloiho, Ralph de, 83
Blundel, William, 83
Blundus, Herbert, 269
Blundus, Ralph, 255
Blythe, honor of, 275. *See also* Tickhill, honor of
Bobi, Osbert de, 75
Bodrigan, Henry de, 46
Bohun, Margaret de, 122
Book of fees, 19 n., 78, 91, 129, 136
Bosham, chapel of, 15; manor of, 306
Bractoft, John de, 78–79, 81
Bradenstoke, prior of, 48, 52
Braibroc, Henry de, 77, 82
Braibroc, Robert de, 18
Brakelond, Jocelin de, *Chronica*, 176 n.
Bramley, manor of, 304
Brand, Robert, 87
Braose, John de, 76
Braose, Reginald de, 76
Bray, manor of, 245, 271
Bréauté, Falkes de, 334
Bremesgrave (Bromsgrove), manor of, 304
Breton, Hugh le, 78
Brewer, Richard, 294
Brewer, William, 292
Bridgewater, manor of, 205
Bridport, John of, 27–28, 69
Brimenton, Peter of, 305
Bristol, 14, 44, 46, 225, 383, 392; castle of, 21, 43

INDEX 403

Brito, Ely, 75
Brittany, count of, Peter of Dreux, 80
Broc, Robert de, 24
Bruce, Isabella de, 356
Bruce, Peter de, 76, 305
Bryan, Richard, 48, 50
Buckingham, Master William of, 27–28
Burgh, Hubert de, 35, 57, 68, 76, 80, 109, 208, 292, 357
Burgh, Walter de, 80
Burnell, Robert, 48, 50
Burton, 269, 275
Burton, abbot of, Walter, 267
Bury St. Edmunds, abbey of, 127
Buscel, William, 76
Bytham, castle of, 34, 137

CAISTOR, 282
Calne, 126
Cambridge, 319, 383
Canterbury, 150, 252, 297, 320, 339, 383
Canterbury, archbishop of, Anselm, 158–161
Canterbury, archbishop of, Boniface of Savoy, 214
Canterbury, archbishop of, Edmund Rich, 201
Canterbury, archbishop of, Hubert Walter, 16, 25, 27, 53, 57, 109, 172, 175–176, 184, 187, 286, 288, 294, 298
Canterbury, archbishop of, Robert of Winchelsea, 370
Canterbury, archbishop of, Stephen Langton, 138, 189–190, 196, 198–200
Canterbury, Gervase of, 24, 114, 117, 119, 122, 125, 171, 174; *Gesta regum,* 24 n.
Cantilupe, Fulk de, 71
Cantilupe, William de, 292, 333
Cartellieri, Alexander, *Philipp II August,* 114 n.
Cartularium monasterii de Rameseia, 48 n.
Carucage, 1–2, 11–12, 23, 67, 88, 111–113, 135, 154, 164, 178, 202, 237–238; of 1198, 14–15, 29, 53, 65, 67, 83, 85, 87, 91, 97–98, 108, 128–130, 177, 179; of 1200, 15–16, 29, 53, 65, 67, 83, 108, 177, 179; of 1217, 19, 67, 84, 92, 109; of 1220, 19, 33–35, 65, 67, 72–74, 83–84, 105, 136, 195–196, 202; of 1224, 20, 53, 92, 100, 137, 196, 220
Castille, king of, 214, 218
Chamber, 4, 18–19, 23, 31, 33, 110, 289, 298

Chamberlains, of the exchequer, 13–14, 20, 32, 40–41, 56, 58
Charter of Liberties, of Henry I, 243
Charter of Liberties, of Stephen, 243
Chastel, William de, 37–39
Chaucumbe, Hugh de, 292–293
Cheddar, manor of, 299
Chelnerston, Thomas de, 335
Chester, earl of, Ranulf, 152, 200
Chesterton, 323
Chichester, bishop of, Gregory, 261
Chichester, castle of, 71
Chronica de Melsa, 127 n.
Chronicon de Abingdon, 115 n., 164
Chronicon Petroburgense, 115 and n., 117
Chronicon Thomae Wykes, 104 n.
Cigony, Engelard de, 349
Cirencester, canons of, 307; manor of, 307
Cistercian order, 125, 128, 143, 146, 173, 204, 208, 351
Clare, Richard de, 272
Clent, manor of, 306
Clergy, lower, representatives of, 213–218, 225
Clergy, taxation of, 196–199, 358
Clinton, Geoffrey de, 261
Coggeshall, abbot of, 204
Coggeshall, Ralph de, 121, 125; *Chronicon Anglicanum,* 83 n.
Colchester, 252, 255, 265, 331
Coldingham, Geoffrey of, 121
Coleman, John, 74, 77–78
Colemerand, John de, 78
Collingham, 305
Commissioners to assess and collect taxes, 63–87, 91–93, 96–97, 99, 102–103, 144, 147, 247–253, 284, 291–294, 323, 333–338, 340, 396; appointment of, 84, 85; pay of, 85–87, 353. *See also Missi*
Compton, 305
Confirmation of the Charters, 3, 241–242, 361, 363–364, 366–369, 371, 373–377, 379, 392, 397–398
Cookham, manor of, 245, 271
Cormailles, John de, 86
Cornhill, Gervase de, 250
Cornhill, Reginald de, 17, 30, 295
Cornhill, William de, 32, 69, 71
Cornwall, earl of, Richard, 41, 212, 214, 217–218, 356
Cotton, Bartholomew, 374; *Historia Anglicana,* 374 n.
Council, the Great, 2–4, 8–10, 12, 20, 74, 89, 120, 151–152, 156, 160–162, 164, 169–

Council, the Great (*cont.*)
171, 173, 175, 177–180, 185, 190, 193–195, 197, 199, 202, 204–207, 209–212, 214, 218–228, 230–235, 238, 322, 329, 366, 372, 378
Council, the Small, 5, 7–10, 20–21, 23, 35, 42, 46, 52–53, 55–56, 60, 74, 84, 87, 90–91, 97–99, 106–108, 110, 113, 119, 124, 133–134, 136, 140, 144, 146, 153, 173–174, 176–177, 196, 198, 216–217, 219–220, 222, 226, 231–232, 237–241, 258, 287–290, 294, 296, 306, 319, 321, 325–327, 333, 360, 368, 380, 394
Coventry, bishop of, Hugh de Nonant, 182, 293
Coventry, Walter of, *Memoriale*, 138 n.
Craucumb, Godfrey de, 198, 334
Crendon, 271
Crepping, Robert de, 337
Crevecor, Robert de, 310
Cricklade, 126
Cumin, John, 248
Cunstable, William de, 76
Curia regis. See Council, Great, and Council, Small
Curia regis rolls, 70 n.
Cusering, Roger de, 335
Customs duties, 6, 222, 362
Cybecay, Martin de, 78

D ALHAM, RICHARD DE, 26
Dammartin, Odo de, 294
Danby, 305
Danegeld, 3–4, 6, 11, 112, 123, 129, 154, 157, 160, 164–165, 173, 178, 243, 261
Dean, Robert de, 333–334
Demesne, royal, 3–5, 8, 10, 121, 128, 133, 142, 156, 162, 164, 173, 178, 205, 213, 219, 224, 228–229, 233–234, 236, 238–240, 242, 251, 257, 286, 291, 295, 323, 355; exploitation of, 300–307, 312
Derby, 320, 355
Derby, earl of, William II de Ferrers, 89, 306, 311
"De tallagio non concedendo," 237, 361–362, 365–371, 373, 379–380, 392, 398
Devizes, 37; castle of, 44, 107
Dewias, Robert, 184
Dialogus de scaccario, 13 and n., 25, 37, 121, 181, 185, 238, 246, 252, 262, 276, 322, 325, 330, 339
Diceto, Ralph de, 115, 117, 121, 125–126, 174; *Opera historica*, 87 n.
Diva, Guido de, 28

Diva, Ralph de, 75
Docking, soke of, 268
Dodu, G., *Histoire des institutions monarchiques dans le royaume latin de Jérusalem*, 118 n.
Dole, Richard de, 334
Domesday Book, 63, 127, 237, 390
Domesday survey, 67, 90, 102
Dona, 7, 109, 111, 160, 164, 168, 180, 211
Doncaster, 255, 294
Dowell, *A Suffolk hundred in 1283*, 11 n.
Driby, Robert de, 78
Driby, Simon de, 70–71, 82
Driffield, 271–272
Duket, Richard, 77, 80–81
Dunwich, 305
Duredent, William de, 28
Durham, archdeacon of, Aymer, 18, 32–33
Durham, bishop of, Hugh de Puiset, 125, 174
Durham, bishop of, Philip of Poitiers, 291
Durham, bishop of, Richard Marsh, 9, 76, 195–196

E ADMER, *Historium novorum in Anglia*, 158 n.
Earl Marshal. See Pembroke, earl of; Norfolk, earl of
Eaton, 256
Eboraco, William de, 79–80
Economic conditions, 3
Ely, archdeacon of, Richard Barre, 292
Ely, bishop of, Hugh of Northwold, 145
Ely, bishop of, John de Kirkby, 360. See also Kirkby, John de
Ely, bishop of, William de Longchamp, 25, 172
Emperor, Holy Roman, Frederick II, 21, 42, 328
Emperor, Holy Roman, Henry V, 164
Emperor, Holy Roman, Henry VI, 172
Engayne, Warner, 78–80
England, king of, Edward the Confessor, 276
England, king of, Edward I, 1–2, 9–10, 93, 105, 161–164, 222, 226–228, 231, 233–235, 237, 240–243, 270, 358–367, 370, 373, 376–381, 385–388, 398–399. See also England, prince of
England, king of, Edward II, 237, 241–242, 358, 389, 392. See also England, prince of

England, king of, Edward III, 237, 358, 392, 294-399
England, king of, Henry I, 45, 112, 160, 164-165, 244, 260, 264, 268, 276
England, king of, Henry II, 1, 5, 24, 52, 66-67, 88, 90, 108, 112, 114-120, 122, 127, 160, 165, 168-171, 183, 185-186, 190, 193, 238-239, 244-246, 251, 254, 259-260, 264-265, 267, 271, 273, 275, 281, 285, 291, 294, 301-303, 307-310, 313, 315, 330
England, king of, Henry III, 1-3, 6-7, 9-10, 12, 19, 21, 43, 50, 52-56, 58-60, 63, 65, 68, 72, 75, 80, 88-89, 105-106, 109-111, 113, 135, 139, 144-145, 148, 151-152, 154, 161-164, 180, 192-199, 203-222, 226-227, 229, 232, 234-235, 237, 239, 240, 276, 320-322, 325-326, 328-331, 333, 338, 343, 346-347, 351-352, 354-355, 357-358, 372, 384, 386-387, 390, 396-397, 399
England, king of, John, 9, 11, 17-19, 33, 52, 66, 68-69, 73-75, 84, 108-109, 123, 131, 133-134, 178-180, 184, 186-187, 189-192, 194, 197, 235, 270, 285, 288, 290, 300, 303-305, 311, 313, 319-320, 322, 325, 327, 330, 333, 354. *See also* Mortain, count of
England, king of, Richard I, 2-3, 6, 9, 24-26, 52-53, 65-68, 70-71, 109, 120, 123-128, 130, 171-172, 174-177, 181, 184, 189-190, 197, 235, 285, 287-288, 290, 294, 298, 300, 303-304, 306, 313, 330, 333
England, king of, Stephen, 112, 165, 243-244, 265
England, king of, William I, 183, 244, 276
England, king of, William II, 4, 158-159, 161, 164, 244
England, prince of, Edmund, second son of Henry III, 2, 48, 60, 194, 212, 351, 352. *See also* Leicester, earl of
England, prince of, Edward, eldest son of Henry III, 2, 48, 50, 60, 194, 213. *See also* England, king of, Edward I
England, prince of, Edward, son of Edward I, 378. *See also* England, king of, Edward II
England, prince of, Richard, second son of King John. *See* Cornwall, earl of, Richard
England, princess of, Isabella, daughter of King John, 21, 42, 528

England, princess of, Joan, daughter of Henry II, 245
England, princess of, Joan, daughter of King John. *See* Scotland, queen of
England, princess of, Margaret, daughter of Henry III, 210
England, princess of, Matilda, daughter of Henry I, 164, 260
England, princess of, Matilda, daughter of Henry II, 165
England, queen of, Eleanor of Aquitaine, 25, 127, 172
England, queen of, Eleanor of Provence, 214, 356
England, queen of, Margaret of France, 387
Epistolae Cantuarienses, 170 n.
Escheats, 238, 244, 267, 269, 280, 295, 333
Espec, Walter, 261
Espurun, Thomas, 337
Esseby, Jordan de, 75, 78
Essex, earl of, Geoffrey Fitz Peter, 15-16, 32, 53, 57, 132, 306, 310. *See also* Fitz Peter, Geoffrey
Essex, Henry of, 261
Exchequer, 1, 4, 11, 13, 18, 20-23, 26, 31-34, 37-38, 42-54, 60, 62, 66, 94, 110, 119, 136, 166, 243, 255, 269, 284, 295, 298, 325, 344, 348; barons of, 5, 40, 46, 50-51, 55, 247, 254, 364, 378, 387; of account, 4, 5, 23, 26, 28, 40, 46, 56; of receipt, 4, 13, 23, 56, 58; special, 1, 6, 12-17, 19-20, 22-39, 41-56, 60, 62; terms of, 11
Exerpta ex rotulis finium, 201 n.
Exeter, bishop of, Henry Marshal, 15, 131
"Extracts from the memoranda rolls," 362 n.
Eye, honor of, 166

F*abric rolls of York minster,* 108 n.
Falaise, William de, 69, 71, 293
Farley, prior of, 86, 125
Farms, of manors, 243, 279-280, 300-301; of shires, 3-4, 105, 156-157, 243-244, 301; of towns, 3-4, 156, 243-244, 301
Farrer, William, *Early Yorkshire charters,* 352 n.; *Honors and knights' fees,* 69 n.; *Itinerary of Henry I,* 260 n.
Fauconberg, Eustace de, 291-292, 294
Feckenham, 268, 297

Fifteenth on merchants, 17, 29–30, 65, 67, 84, 91, 96, 98, 134; custodians of, 17, 29–30
Fines, 3, 243
Fitz Alan, Brian, 76
Fitz Alan, Roald, 88
Fitz Alan, William, 187
Fitz Atrac, Richard, 268
Fitz Benedict, William, 19, 33
Fitz Ernest, William, 27
Fitz Everard, Roger, 65, 68
Fitz Geoffrey, John, 89
Fitz Gerald, Henry, 247, 281
Fitz Gerald, Henry, son of above, 333
Fitz Hamo, Hamo, 269
Fitz Hervey, Osbert, 291
Fitz Hugh, John, 18, 33
Fitz Hugh, Robert, 268
Fitz John, Eustace, 261
Fitz Neal, Richard, 249. See also London, bishop of
Fitz Nicholas, Ralph, 76
Fitz Nigel, Adam, 69
Fitz Osbern, Richard, 87
Fitz Otto, Hugh, 47, 49
Fitz Peter, Geoffrey, 124, 292, 294. See also Essex, earl of
Fitz Ralph, Hugh, 80
Fitz Reginald, Ralph, 75
Fitz Renfrew, Gilbert, 294
Fitz Renfrew, Roger, 271
Fitz Robert, John, 76
Fitz Robert, Ranulf, 76
Fitz Robert, William, 78
Fitz Roger, Robert, 291
Fitz Simon, Thurstan, 250
Fitz Stephen, Ralph, 69, 97
Fitz Swein, Robert, 255
Fitz Warin, William, 82
Fitz William, Ralph, 275
Fitz William, Robert, 46
Fleming, Richard, 291
Flores historiarum, 363 n.
Fordham, 272
Fornell, William de, 17, 30
Foulsham, 310
Fowler, R. C., "An early Essex subsidy," 46 n.
France, king of, Louis VII, 114, 168, 170
France, king of, Louis IX, 207, 211–212
France, king of, Philip Augustus, 53, 118, 132, 175, 186, 189
France, prince of, Louis, 89, 135, 192, 320–321, 323, 339, 346
Francigenae, John, 337

Frazier, Ralph, 24
Fresel, James de, 336
Fulburn, 309
Fuller, E. A., "The tallage of 6 Edward II," 392 n.

G ASCONY, CAMPAIGN IN, 40, 58, 89
Gaveston, Peter, 389
Geddington, 120, 170, 316
Gerebut, Robert, 68, 125
Ghent, Maurice de, 77
Giffard, honor of, 271
Giffard, Hugh, 35
Giffard, Walter, 68
Gilbertines, order of, 128, 146. See also Sempringham, order of
Gild, Robert, 65, 68
Giraldus Cambrensis, *Opera,* 87 n. See also Barri, Gerald of
Gisors, 170
Glanvill, Ranulf de, 159; *De legibus,* 159 n.
Glanvill, William de, 291
Glastonbury, abbey of, 304
Gloucester, 14, 107, 305, 383; castle of, 70; honor of, 71, 246
Gloucester, earl of, Robert, 244, 281
Gloucester, Master Robert of, 69
Gloucester and Hertford, earl of, Gilbert I de Clare, 76
Gloucester and Hertford, earl of, Gilbert II de Clare, 360
Grantcourt, William de, 84
Grantham, 270
Gras, N. S. B., *The early English customs system,* 134 n.
Gray, Joan de, 386
Gray, Robert de, 386
Gray, Walter de, 386
Great Charter. See Magna Carta
Great Tew, 24, 302–303
Grenvill, Adam de, 69
Grimbald, Peter, 43
Grimsby, 282
Gubaud, John, 75, 76, 80, 332, 335–336
Gubiun, Hugh, 254, 263
Guernsey, island of, 133
Guestling, John of, 291
Gynet, Robert, 68

H ADFIELD, 356
Hallam, Henry, 366; *View of the state*

INDEX

of Europe during the middle ages, 366 n.
Halliwell, William de, 19
Hampden, John, 365
Hareng, Ralph, 293
Harington, Hugh de, 79–80
Harington, Richard de, 82, 84
Hastings, Henry of, 332
Hautein, Theobald de, 78
Haverhill, William de, 45, 337
Havering, 356
Hay, William, 86
Headington, 271
Helston, 304
Hemingburgh, Walter of, 362–363, 370, 374, 380, 383; *Chronicon,* 361 n.
Hereford, bishop of, Hugh Foliot, 145
Hereford, earl of, Humphrey II de Bohun, 363–364, 371, 379
Heyham, Roger of, 383
High Wycombe, 311, 316
Historiae Dunelmensis scriptores tres, 121 n.
Historia et cartularium monasterii Sancti Petri Gloucestriae, 267 n.
Historical papers and letters from the northern registers, 351 n.
Holegate, William de, 219
Holy Land, 16, 19, 64, 114–115, 117, 120, 122, 132, 169, 213–214, 260
Honorius, III, pope, 197–199
Horncastle, 252
Hospital, knights of, 12, 22, 35–36, 43, 45, 47, 49, 53, 56, 60, 64, 136, 146, 351
Howden Roger of, 14, 97, 120, 124–126, 129, 170–171; *Chronica,* 15 n.
Humby, Hugo de, 78
Humet, Richard de, 271
Huntingdon, Henry of, 244; *Historia Anglorum,* 165 n.
Huwell, Gerard de, 78, 80

Ilchester, Richard of, 247, 252, 318
Innocent III, pope, 131, 320
Innocent IV, pope, 206, 212, 214
Ipswich, 305, 348, 383

Jenkinson, Hilary, "William Cade," 255 n.
Jersey, island of, 133
Jerusalem, king of, John de Brienne, 19, 88
Jews, 18, 44

Jolliffe, J. E. A., 370; *The constitutional history of medieval England,* 370 n.
Juries, of assessment, 1, 6–7, 63, 65, 90, 93, 96, 98, 129, 131
Justices itinerant. *See* Commissioners; *Missi*

Kemesech, Henry de, 272
Kenilworth, castle of, 72
Keygate, John de, 338
King's Cliff, 299
King's Lynn, 40
King's Ripon, 270
King's Thorpe, 315
King's Winford, manor of, 306
Kingston, 305
Kirkby, John de, 225, 230, 359. *See also* Ely, bishop of
Knaresborough, manor of, 311
Knight service, inquest of 1166, 112–113, 167; quotas for, 183–184, 188–190
Kyme, Simon de, 69, 71, 75

Lacy, John de, constable of Chester, 76. *See also* Lincoln, earl of
La Marche, count of, Hugh de Lusignan, 207
Lambourn, 272
Land, William de, 78
Landon, Lionel, *Itinerary of King Richard I,* 25 n.
Langton, Henry de, 72, 73, 99
Lanvalay, William de, 272
Leadenham, Eustace de, 70
Le Gras, Stephen, 35
Leicester, borough of, 347, 351–352
Leicester, earl of, Edmund, 351–352, 386. *See also* England, prince of
Leicester, earl of, Robert II, 281
Leicester, earl of, Robert IV, 352
Leicester, honor of, 72
Le Mans, 114
Le Rus, Richard, 336
Lexington, John de, 43
Lexington, Robert de, 76–77
Liebermann, F., *Der Gesetze der Angelsachsen,* 164 n.
Liber de antiquis legibus, 219 n.
Liber memorandorum ecclesie de Bernewelle, 348 n.
Lincoln, 219, 225, 252, 276, 295, 359, 383
Lincoln, bishop of, Hugh of Avalon, 176, 208

Lincoln, bishop of, Richard Gravesend, 47
Lincoln, bishop of, Robert de Chesney, 261
Lincoln, earl of, John de Lacy, 80, 201. *See also* Lacy, John de
Lincoln, Alured de, 82
L'Isle, Brian de, 18, 76, 289, 298
L'Isle, William de, 77, 334
London, 14, 19, 44, 46, 48, 171, 174, 210, 212, 220, 223, 225, 229–230, 240, 258, 264, 273, 284, 290–291, 294, 298, 320, 322–330, 337, 343, 345, 347, 359, 363, 381, 383, 390–391, 395; citizens of, 108, 121, 219; exchange of, 18; New Temple in, 16, 19, 20, 34–35, 37, 44, 47, 49, 52, 57, 98–99, 106–107
London, bishop of, Richard Fitz Neal, 25. *See also* Fitz Neal, Richard
London, mayor of, Andrew Bukerel, 35
London, mayor of, Henry Fitz Alwyn, 25
London, mayor of, Richard Renger, 43
London, Tower of, 21, 41, 43, 46, 56, 61
London, William de, 76–77
Longbridge, 65
Longchamp, Nicholas de, 201
Longchamp, William de, 16
Lords Ordainers, 389
Lothingland, 304
Lovell, Philip, 337
Lucca, bankers of, 62
Luchaire, Achille, *Histoire des institutions monarchiques de la France*, 114 n.; *Manuel des institutions françaises*, 114 n.
Lucy, Richard de, 245, 249–250, 255, 261, 271
Lucy, Richard de, of Egremont, 75
Lucy, Stephen de, 198
Ludlow, 47
Lunt, William Edward, 118, 197; "Consent of lower clergy," 114 n.; *Financial relations of the papacy with England*, 47 n.; "Text of the ordinance of 1184," 118 n.; *Valuation of Norwich*, 93 n.
Luton, manor of, 306, 310
Lyons, Peter de, 73

M<small>ADOX</small>, T<small>HOMAS</small>, 97, 247; *Firma burgi*, 390 n.; *History of the exchequer*, 22 n.
Magna Carta, 72, 88–89, 139, 154, 178–179, 184, 191–194, 202, 206, 209, 213, 215, 218, 229, 235, 243, 290–291, 322, 325, 363, 372, 375–376, 380, 391

Magni rotuli scaccarii Normanniae, 171 n.
Maitland, Frederic William, 126–127
Malebisse, Richard, 291–292
Malmesbury, abbot of, 97, 125
Malmesbury, castle of, 69; manor of, 263
Mameby, Robert de, 337
Manning, Bernard L., 398
Mansel, John, 44, 53, 337
Mansfield, manor of, 332, 342
Mantel, Robert, 250
Marc, Philip, 33
Marlborough, honor of, 145, 293, 298
Marmion, Philip, 350
Marshal, John, brother of William Marshal, earl of Pembroke, 97, 306
Marshal, John, nephew of William Marshal, earl of Pembroke, 75
Mauduit, Thomas, 82
Mauduit, William, 281
Meaux, abbot of, 127
Medley, D. J., *Original illustrations*, 226 n.
Melksham, 126, 318, 349
Memoranda roll 1 John, 11 n.
Memorials of St. Edmund's abbey, 127 n.
Meon, manor of, 306
Meriet, Nicholas de, 68–69
Merlay, Roger de, 82
Meulan, count of, 281
Middleton, Thomas de, 74
Middleton, William de, 48–49
Milton, hundred of, 252, 270, 297, 320
Miserden, castle of, 76
Missi, 1, 4, 6–8, 66–67, 82, 131, 235
Mitchell, Sydney Knox, *Studies in taxation*, 40 n.
Moine, Henry le, 78–79, 81
Montfort, Simon de, 212, 218, 221, 351
Morcote, 269
Morris, John E., 362; *Welsh wars of Edward I*, 225 n.
Morris, W. A., *The constitutional history of England to 1216*, 165 n.; *The mediaeval English sheriff*, 66 n.
Mortain, count of, John, 97. *See also* England, king of
Mortimer, Roger, 48, 50
Moslems, 117
Mowbray, Roger de, 309
Mucegros, Richard de, 69–71
Muchelney, abbey of, 43
Muleton, Thomas de, 32, 73–77
Munimenta gildhallae Londoniensis, 64 n.

Musard, Ralph, 77, 82, 333
Munsorel, Robert, 85

N_{EILSON}, N., "Customary rents," 132 n.
Nevill, Jollan de, 70–71, 79
Neville, Alan de, 255
Neville, Hugh de, 293, 297–298
Neville, Thomas de, 305
Newburgh, William de, 122, 124, 126, 171, 174; *Historia rerum Anglicanum*, 87 n.
Newburn, 257
Newcastle on Tyne, 47, 225, 320, 359
Newgate, prison, 82
Newmarket, Adam de, 75, 79
Newton, 268
Nicholas Seculareus, 335
Niemeyer, N., "Assessment of the fortieth of 1232," 103 n.
Norfolk, earl of, Roger Bigod III, 363–364, 371, 379
Norgate, Kate, *England under the Angevin kings*, 186 n.; *John Lackland*, 185 n.
Normandy, duke of, Robert, 158, 160, 164, 244
Normanville, Ralph de, 73, 75
Northampton, 107, 170, 225–226, 230, 254–255, 263, 294, 344
Northampton, Henry of, 291–292
Norton, manor of, 304, 306, 310
Norwich, 223, 230, 266, 294, 315, 322, 341, 355, 359, 383
Norwich, bishop of, John de Gray, 15, 69 n., 292
Norwich, Geoffrey de, 293, 299
Nottingham, 44–46, 107, 173, 181, 289, 298, 320; castle of, 21, 43

O_{DIHAM}, 286, 290
Oiri, Fulk de, 70
Oiri, John de, 81
Ormesby, 356
Otto, legate, 56, 58
Oxford, 14, 107, 174–175, 177, 282, 294, 298, 320, 335
Oxford, earl of, Aubrey II de Vere, 71

P_{AGE}, F_{RANCES}, 384; *The estates of Crowland abbey*, 384 n.
Painel, Fulk, 310
Palestine. *See* Holy Land

Pandulph, legate, 137
Pantulf, William, 82
Paris, Matthew, 195, 201, 209–212; *Chronica maiora*, 57 n.
Parliament, 156, 212, 222–224, 230–231, 242, 366, 368–369, 374, 378, 388, 393–394, 396
Parliamentary writs, 226 n.
Pasquet, D., *Origins of the House of Commons*, 360 n.
Pattishall, Hugh de, 43
Pattishall, Martin de, 76
Pattishall, Simon de, 71, 291–292
Paunton, Baldwin de, 78
Payens, Hugh de, 260
Peche, Gilbert, barony of, 73
Pembroke, earl of, William Marshal, 16, 19, 187, 306, 333
Pembroke, honor of, 270
Percy, Richard de, 9, 89, 201, 329
Percy, Robert de, 69, 71
Peretot, William de, 43
Peterborough, abbey of, 18–19
Peterborough, abbot of, 125, 182
Peterborough, Benedict of, 64, 119–121, 229, 275; *Gesta regis Henrici secundi*, 83 n.
Petit-Dutaillis, Charles, 324, 367; *Studies and notes*, 324 n.
Petition of Right, 365–366
Peverel, William, 166
Picot, Ralph, 261
Pikot, John, 82
Pincebec, Walter de, 16, 70
Pipe roll 31 Henry I, 160 n.
Pipe roll 2 Henry II, 160 n.
Pipe roll 3 Henry II, 264 n.
Pipe roll 1 Richard I, 13 n.
Pipe roll 14 Henry III, 145 n.
Pipe roll 26 Henry III, 22 n.
Plessey, John de, 44
Plugenoi, Hugh de, 272
Plunket, Alan de, 386
Pocklington, 319
Poer, John le, 68
Pointon, Alexander de, 70–75, 78, 99, 291–292, 294
Poll tax, 135, 138. *See also* Aid, of 1222
Pollock, Sir Frederick, and Maitland, Frederic William, *History of English law*, 236 n.
Pont de l'Arche, William de, 281
Poole, Reginald Lane, *Exchequer in the twelfth century*, 13 n.
Port, Adam de, 83

Potterne, James de, 292
Premonstratensians, order of, 128, 146, 208
Property, valuation of for taxation, 112, 121, 135–137, 140–152, 155
Provisions of Oxford, 60, 343
Prynne, William, *A brief register of writs*, 393 n.
Pugeys, Robert, 386

RALEGH, WILLIAM DE, 74, 77
Ralph, brother, 45
Ramsay, Sir James H., *History of the revenues of the kings of England*, 358 n.
Ramsey, abbey of, 18, 270
Reading, abbot of, 203
Receipt roll of the exchequer for Michaelmas term 1185, 257 n.
Red book of the exchequer, 74 and n., 78
Redcliff, 338
Reepham, Alexander de, 73
Relief, 243
Renham, manor of, 310
Revenues, valuation of for taxation, 132
Richardson, H. G., "The morrow of the great charter," 311 n.
Richmond, castle of, 88; honor of, 71, 73, 76, 299
Riess, Ludwig, 367–368; "Der Ursprung des englischen Unterhandes," 368 n.; *History of the English electoral law in the middle ages*, 367 n.
Rigton, 305
Ringwood, 390
Ripariis, William de, 84
Risborough, 271
Rishanger, William, *Chronica et annales*, 361 n.
Rising, burgesses of, 268
Rivaux, Peter de, 35, 337
Roches, Peter de, 109, 293. *See also* Winchester, bishop of
Rokele, Robert de, 333
Roppeley, Robert de, 70–71
Roppeley, Simon de, 74–75, 78–80
Ros, Robert de, 79–80
Rot. chart., 70 n.
Rot. claus., 17 n.
Rot. liberate, 16 n.
Rot. oblatis, 15 n.
Rot. pat., 16 n.
Rotuli curiae regis, 87 n.

Rotuli de dominibus et pueris et puellis, 269 n.
Rotuli parliamentorum, 237 n.
Rouen, archbishop of, Walter de Coutance, 25, 172
Round, John Horace, 269; *Commune of London*, 268 n.; *Feudal England*, 128 n.; *Geoffrey de Mandeville*, 239 n.
Rowell, William de, 79–80
Rufus, William, 250
Rushall, 270
Rye, Avelina de, 268
Rye, Henry de, 268
Rymer, Thomas, *Foedera*, 379 n.

SADBERGE, 257
St. Albans, 25, 107
St. Albans, abbot of, Warin, 15, 108, 127, 174
St. Edmunds, Master Roger of, 291
St. Edwards, abbess of, 97
St. John, Oliver, 365
St. Martin, Geoffrey of, 125
St. Mary of Leicester, abbey of, 120
St. Paul's, Cathedral of, 25
St. Paul's, Cathedral of, dean of. *See* Swereford, Alexander
St. Philibert, Richard of, 257
Sainte Mère Église, William de, 172, 304
Saladin, 169
Saladin tithe. *See* Aid, of 1188
Salisbury, 13–14, 24, 119
Salisbury, bishop of, Herbert Poore, 97, 176, 208
Salisbury, bishop of, Richard Poore, 20, 37–39, 48, 53, 57, 61, 199
Salisbury, bishop of, Simon of Ghent, 387
Salisbury, earl of, William, 76
Salisbury, treasurer of, 47
Saxony, duke of, Henry the Lion, 165
Sawbridgeworth, Alexander de, 19, 33–34
Scalariis, William de, 187
Scarborough, 294, 319
Scotland, king of, Alexander II, 331
Scotland, queen of, Joan, daughter of King John, 43
Scudmore, Peter de, 86
Scutage, 4–6, 53, 88, 102, 111–112, 114, 123, 127, 135, 153–154, 157, 164–166, 178–191, 202, 220, 238, 241, 275, 285, 322, 330–331; of 1156, 186; of 1159, 186; of 1165, 186; of Ireland in 1172,

180, 182; of Galloway in 1187, 182, 246; of Wales in 1190, 182; of 1195, 186; of 1196, 186; of 1199, 186; of 1201, 187, 189; of 1204, 185; of 1205, 185, 187, 189; of 1206, 187; of Scotland in 1209, 181, 188; of Ireland in 1210, 188, 190; of Wales in 1211, 181, 188; of Poitou in 1214, 181, 188, 190. *See also,* Aid, of 1168, 1217, 1235, 1242, 1245, 1253
Sée, Henri, *Les classes rurales et le régime domanial en France au moyen age,* 115 n.
Segrave, Stephen de, 77
Selby, abbot of, 88
Select pleas in manorial courts, 270 n.
Sempringham, order of, 125. *See also,* Gilbertines, order of
Sendal, John, 383
Servitium debitum, 112, 135, 153, 183–184
Sherborne, 107
Sherburne, Richard de, 336
Sheriff, office of, 1, 4, 7, 10, 12, 14, 18, 36, 41–42, 66, 84, 93, 98–102, 106–107, 166, 251, 253–259, 296–300, 334, 336, 344
Sheriffs, inquest of, in 1170, 248, 268–269
Sherringham, 271
Shires, representatives of, 2, 8, 162, 164, 194, 213–216, 221–232, 234–235, 240, 242, 369, 381, 393, 396, 398
Shirley, W. W., *Royal letters,* 47 n.
Shrewsbury, 320, 383
Sicily, 212
Sicily, king of, William, 245
Silverton, 316
Sleaford, Alexander de, 79
Sneid, 319
Southampton, 14, 252, 294
Southwark, 107
Stafford, archdeacon of, Henry of London, 27, 71, 291–293
Stanford, Roger of, 99
Stanford, Thomas de, 336–337
Stannaries, 33
State trials, 366 n.
Statutes of the realm, 398 n.
Stenton, Doris, 14, 167
Stenton, F. M., 165; *English feudalism,* 112 n.
Stephenson, Carl, 3; *Borough and town,* 236 n.; "Seignorial tallage," 236 n.
Stikeswald, Roger de, 70
Stocton, Hugh de, 44
Stokes, Walter de, 338
Stubbs, William, 19, 125, 366–367, 377, 387, 395; *Constitutional history,* 223 n.; *Select charters,* 39 n.
Stutevill, William de, 305, 311
Sumeri, Ralph de, 306
Sumeri, Roger de, 356
Sumerville, Roger de, 306, 310
Swereford, Alexander, 35

Taison, Ralph, 275
Tait, James, 3; *Mediaeval English boroughs,* 244 n.
Tallage, 3–7, 10, 66, 88, 96, 102, 113, 121, 128, 135, 156–157, 162, 168, 170, 173, 207, 228–229, 231, 233–234, 236–242, 244–245, 286–287, 290, 303, 307–312, 319, 321–322, 358; of 1168, 253, 256, 262–263, 267, 270, 282–283; of 1173, 245, 248, 257–258; of 1174, 245, 249; of 1177, 245, 250, 258; of 1187, 121, 246, 251, 258, 274; of 1194, 286–288, 291; of 1195, 287; of 1196, 287, 296; of 1197, 68, 287; of 1198, 287, 289, 291; of 1199, 288; of 1204, 289; of 1205, 289; of 1206, 289; of 1210, 288, 319–320; of 1214, 288, 319–320, 327; of 1217, 321, 327, 339; of 1223, 327, 338; of 1226, 323, 326, 327, 338–339, 347; of 1230, 327, 339; of 1241, 336; of 1245, 328, 336, 341; of 1249, 336; of 1251, 331, 336, 340; of 1255, 324, 325, 337, 340, 344, 347; of 1260, 337, 343; of 1268, 351; of 1304, 369–370, 382–388; of 1312, 369, 389–390; assessment of, 246–253, 260, 275–277, 291–295, 333–341, 347–352, 382–384, 388; assessment of in common, 236, 252–253, 262, 295–296, 304, 339–341, 389–390; assessment of *per capita,* 236, 252–253, 258, 262, 295–296, 312, 315–316, 319, 324–326, 339–341, 343, 383, 389; attempt to levy in 1332, 392–397; collection of, 254–260, 262–264, 296–300, 332, 334, 344–345, 390; on rural demesne, 244, 259, 267, 273, 279–280, 283, 291, 313–315, 332–333, 342, 354, 381; on urban demesne, 244, 259, 265, 266, 273, 277–278, 280, 283, 291, 313, 315, 323, 332–333, 342, 354, 381; opposition to, 325–330, 358–359, 390–391, 393–396, 399; seignorial, 236–237, 267–270, 283–284; used as a general term for taxes, 361–364, 368–370, 374; yield of, 239, 260, 265, 273–274, 307, 320, 354, 359, 392. *See also* Aid, of 1130, 1156

Tameton, William de, 76
Tamworth, 350
Tancre, Roger, 333
Tateshall, Robert de, 80
Temple, knights of, 12, 16, 22, 35–36, 43–45, 47, 49, 53, 56, 60, 64, 143, 146, 351
Terrae datae, 271–272, 309–312, 354, 356–357
Tewksbury, abbot of, 291
Thetford, prior of, 345
Three rolls of the king's court, 28 n.
Thurkelby, Roger of, 337
Tickhill, honor of, 24. *See also* Blythe, honor of
Tilebroc, William de, 296
Tirgenton, 350
Tithe, 115–116
Torigny, Robert de, *Chronica*, 114 n.
Toulouse, campaign of, 160, 183, 277
Tout, Thomas F., *Chapters in administrative history*, 43 n.; *History of England, 1216–1377*, 369 n.
Towns, representatives of, 10, 162, 164, 171, 184, 221–223, 225–226, 231, 233–235, 240, 242, 381, 393, 396
Tracy, Henry de, 83
Trailli, Leceline de, 272
Treasurer, 13–14, 20, 40–41, 50, 56, 58
Trihampton, Ralph de, 51, 78
Trihampton, Ralph de, the younger, 51
Trihampton, Roger de, 82
Trivet, Nicholas, 374, 380; *Annales*, 371 n.
Trubleville, Ralph de, 134
Trussel, William, 337
Turner, G. T., "The sheriff's farm," 244 n.
Tyre, archbishop of, William, *A history of deeds done beyond the sea*, 117 n.

U LECOT, PHILIP DE, 18, 33, 75

V ALLIBUS, OLIVER DE, 82
Vere, Aubrey de, 261
Vere, Henry de, 310
Vetus registrum Sarisberiense, 143 n.
Viard, P., *Histoire de la dime ecclesiastique dans la royaume de France aux XII et XIII siècles*, 115 n.
Vickers, K. H., *England in the later middle ages*, 369 n.
Vieuxpont, Robert de, 76

Vincent, J. A. C., *Lancashire lay subsidies*, 48 n.
Vinogradoff, Paul, *English society in the eleventh century*, 128 n.; *Villainage in England*, 236 n.
Vita S. Hugonis, 176 n.

W AC, BALDWIN, 134
Waddon, 271
Wake, Guy, 79
Wallingford, 265
Walsingham, Thomas, *Gesta abbatum monasterii Sancti Albani*, 108 n.
Walter, Theobald, 292
Waltham, abbot of, 84
Waltham, dean of, Guy, 247–248, 252
Waltham, J. de, 15–16
Wantage, 306, 310
Wardrobe, 20–23, 56, 62, 110
Warenne, earl, Hamelin, 25
Warenne, earl, William II, 281
Warenne, earl, William IV, 33, 60, 89, 196
Warenne, Reginald de, 247–248, 268
Wargrave, manor of, 306
Wartre, barony of, 166
Waterford, Eustace de, 86
Welles, Jocelyn de, 292. *See also* Bath, bishop of
Welles, William de, 73–75, 78–80
Wells, archdeacon of, Hugh de Welles, 299, 304
Wells, dean of, Alexander, 69
Wendover, Roger of, 16–17, 24, 187, 229, 323; *Flores historiarum*, 16 n.
Wengham, Henry de, 336
Were, manor of, 306, 356
Westminster, 11, 16, 20–21, 23, 26, 31, 36
Westminster, statute of, 222
Westminster, Edward de, 337
Whitby, abbot of, 76
Whitcester, Roger de, 337
Whitchurch, 269
White, A. B., *Making of the English constitution*, 321 n.
Whittington, 305
Wickendon, 271
Wilkins, D., *Concilia*, 66 n.
Willard, James Field, *Parliamentary taxes*, 227 n.
Willoughby, William de, 73–74
Wilton, abbess of, 125

Wilton, burgesses of, 97
Winchester, 13–14, 19, 32, 37, 106–107, 208, 263, 265, 294, 383
Winchester, bishop of, Godfrey de Lucy, 306
Winchester, bishop of, Peter des Roches, 196, 320, 329. *See also* Roches, Peter des
Winchester, bishop-elect of, Aymer de Valence, 214
Winchester, Peter of, 47
Winterborne, 137
Winterstoke, hundred of, 299
Wirksworth, manor of, 306, 311
Witing, John de, 70
Witton, Andrew de, 70
Wivill, John de, 337
Woking, manor of, 311
Wolverton, 269
Woodbine, George E., "County court rolls and county court records," 66 n.
Worcester, 219, 320
Worcester, bishop of, William of Blois, 145
Worcester, Florence of, *Chronicon,* 164 n.
Worcester, Ralph of, 24
Writtle, 256, 305, 356
Wrotham, William de, 15–17, 30, 32–33, 53, 71
Wybetoft, Alexander de, 81
Wykes, Thomas, 104, 149, 171
Wymondham, prior of, William of Horton, 323, 338

Y ARMOUTH, BURGESSES OF, 219, 225, 359
York, 121, 171, 225, 230, 266, 294, 315, 359, 385
York, archbishop of, Geoffrey Plantagenet, 9, 125, 175, 177–178
York, archbishop of, Roger, 167
York, archbishop of, Walter Giffard, 48, 50
York Minster, 108, 127, 174